Thule Esq.
Maj. Provinces
... Plantation en
... of the same.
... is humbly
... Jelby
... Price

BOSTON in New England in America

the great Trade of this place. New England (of whic
World, the Winter being non-Moderate and pleasan
the Air is Exceeding Clear and pleasant. Perfectly
often go thither to Recover their Health: it abound
Fish of all Sorts, Either from Salt or fresh Water, Cat
and Expends great Quantitys of the Wollen and other

Battery 8 Gals ship yard, 9 Governor's house, 10 south meeting house, built 1669, 11 French meeting, built 1716.
... is Hollans, 18 yard, 19 Greenleaf yard, 20 old meeting house, built 1670, 21 M.r Phillips house, 22 2 asher.

The Diary of Samuel Sewall

Samuel Sewall

THE DIARY OF
Samuel Sewall

1674–1729 · NEWLY EDITED

FROM THE MANUSCRIPT

AT THE MASSACHUSETTS

HISTORICAL SOCIETY BY

M. HALSEY THOMAS

VOLUME I · *1674–1708*

FARRAR, STRAUS AND GIROUX, New York

Copyright © 1973 by Farrar, Straus and Giroux, Inc.

All rights reserved

First printing, 1973

Library of Congress catalog card number: 73–81968

ISBN 0–374–13952–0

Printed in the United States of America

Published simultaneously in Canada by Doubleday Canada Ltd., Toronto

The seal on the cover is that of the Superior Court

of Judicature of the Province of Massachusetts-Bay

in New England; it was used from 1692

until the adoption of the State Constitution in 1780.

The heraldic device is the portcullis

of the house of Beaufort, adopted by Henry VII.

Preface

Samuel Sewall, recent graduate and teaching fellow of Harvard College, began to keep a diary towards the end of 1673. His last entries were made fifty-six years later, three months before his death. Diary-keeping was common among the Puritans, and hundreds of these records have survived. Most of them are bare and factual, or documents of spiritual self-analysis, but Sewall set down the fullest existing record of how life was lived in his time, and it can be read for pleasure after three centuries because he wrote of so much that interests us today. Nearly all the Puritan diaries were honest: under the eye of an all-seeing and all-knowing God it was useless to try to cheat. The idea of creating a favorable image of himself probably never occurred to Sewall; diaries of that sort came with more sophisticated times. Neither is it likely that Sewall ever envisioned publication, since no diary was printed until John Evelyn's appeared in 1818. Sewall undoubtedly kept his diary locked up, along with his business records, but its existence was no secret. Because of his devotion to record-keeping, more details and facts of his life are preserved than for most of his contemporaries, and we have nearly everything, even his weight. In fact, Sewall revealed himself so fully that those who have undertaken biographies have usually disclosed more about themselves than about him.

Sewall's diary meets the test of a good diary or book of memoirs of any period: he knew and had continuing and far from casual contacts with all the notable people of his place and time. For several decades Sewall was an important figure in Massachusetts-Bay, a man entrusted with numerous public offices, a man of wealth, and a member of the *in*-group. Though he lived in a small town and was conversant with all of its goings-on, lawful and otherwise, both as a recipient of gossip and officially in his capacity as magistrate, Sewall was by no means a small-town person. Throughout the diary there are constant references to the happenings of the great world. Every time a ship came into port Sewall eagerly received the corantos and gazettes with the news of the home and foreign countries, and lost no opportunities to question the captains and passengers. When a newspaper was finally established in Boston in 1704, he preserved his copies, annotated them, made rough indexes, and had them bound.

Boston was in its thirtieth year when Sewall landed there as a boy, and it was certainly the most learned and cultivated frontier town in history. He was raised in Newbury, however, and did not become a resident until his marriage in 1676. Exact figures on population are not available, and the estimates vary, but at no point in Sewall's lifetime did Boston exceed the present population of Plymouth, Massachusetts, or the borough of Princeton, New Jersey: some 13,000.

It is impossible not to be impressed with the many-sidedness of Samuel Sewall. He was a man of learning, full of the scholastic-cum-Renaissance lore discussed at length by Professor Morison in *Harvard College in the Seventeenth Century*. He was a linguist, retaining his mastery of Latin, Greek, and Hebrew throughout his life, and he wrote English with the exactitude of those trained in these languages. He never lost his interest in theology from college days, he liked nothing better than a good discussion with learned clerical friends, and he kept abreast of the subject as new books came out. When he was public printer in Boston he went so far as to learn to set type himself. As a merchant and private banker and landowner, the evidence is that he was efficient and businesslike, and in the tradition of Boston men of wealth and trustees, he held on to his money. Like businessmen from that day to this, he endeavored to get along with everyone, even if it meant appeasing Increase Mather on one occasion with a haunch of venison. As to his service as Councillor, it is only necessary to point out that he was re-elected annually thirty-three times without interruption. In a day when lawyers were forbidden or regarded with suspicion, and the requisite qualifications for judges were integrity, biblical knowledge, familiarity with the *Laws and Liberties* and subsequent statutes, plus *Coke upon Littleton* and books of procedure, Sewall was respected and well-informed and seems to have given entire satisfaction as justice and later chief justice of the Superior Court of Judicature. On the basis of the few surviving records, Emory Washburn felt that Sewall must have been altogether better read in the principles of the common law than any other judge upon the bench. Of his conscientiousness as a rider of the circuit, there can be no question; whatever the weather or conditions of travel, Sewall almost never missed one of his stated journeys. He enjoyed such music as was available to him, he served many years as precentor at the South Church, and when his failings obliged him to give up the office, he did so with regret. Concerning Sewall's literary efforts, his Latin and English poetry, his books and his tracts, this editor, lacking the recondite qualifications, offers no opinion.

Modern commentators have written of the monotony of Boston life in Sewall's time. That life might seem dull to those accustomed to the rat-race of the present day, but it is wrong to project the feeling. Sewall and his contemporaries were all busy people, and the Boston peninsula was a beehive of activity six days of the week. Sewall held so many jobs and had so many interests that he could hardly have spent a day of boredom in his adult life. Cotton Mather could not have found life monotonous when he was writing 468 books and pamphlets, battling Satan every day, preaching four hours every Sabbath, and sending off communications to the Royal Society; his time was so occupied that he had to put up, where his callers could see it, probably the earliest office sign on record: BE BRIEF. Craftsmen led infinitely less monotonous lives than their counterparts today, since they began with raw materials and wrought them through all the stages to completion, whether the result was a pair of shoes, a house still standing and sound after three centuries, or a silver tankard or a chest of drawers highly treasured today. Life was anything but monotonous for the female population, who were given definite household duties as soon as they could amble about the kitchen, and had few dull moments after marriage, when they were producing and raising a dozen children and managing a household.

Sewall's diary entries relate to the days stated, although they may have been written up later; he was never without an interleaved almanac for immediate memoranda, particularly on his frequent journeys. He often skipped a day, sometimes months, in his record, and many times he failed to mention events of importance upon which we could reasonably expect his comment. Some of Sewall's omissions were inadvertent; this busy man just did not get around to making entries. Some omissions were unquestionably things he did not care to write about: if he had written as fully and frankly about the witchcraft trials as he did about other matters, it would be a record of the highest importance. We cannot avoid the feeling that he was dubious about the whole sorry business at the time, and he was the only one who publicly recanted his part in it, but then, there are the harsh words about his college-mate, George Burroughs. Because the happenings of his time and place were so fully recorded by others it has not been difficult to amplify Sewall's accounts.

The provenance of the diary and other manuscripts is not recorded. Evidently they were passed down in the line of Joseph, for the last family owner was his great-grandson, Rev. Samuel Sewall (Harvard 1804). Mr. Sewall spent a long and blameless life as minister of the orthodox Congregational church in Burlington, Middlesex County, Massachusetts (pop. 200), and was the author of the standard *History of Woburn*, which was going through the press at the time of his death, 18 February 1868. He had been interested in historical and antiquarian pursuits for many years and was a close student of his ancestor's diary, from which he supplied much information to James Savage (Harvard 1803) for his *Genealogical Dictionary of New England*, and to others. Mr. Sewall was elected to membership in the Massachusetts Historical Society 28 January 1836, but resigned 29 August 1837. In 1848 he was elected a corresponding member of the New-York Historical Society; subsequently he sent extracts relating to New York history from the diary which were published in the *Proceedings* of that society for March 1849. Some quotations had appeared in the 1840 edition of Josiah Quincy's *History of Harvard University*, but the New York publication was the first time any portion of the diary appeared separately in print.

The particulars of the acquisition and publication of the Sewall papers can be followed in the *Proceedings* of the Massachusetts Historical Society. At the July 1868 meeting, the Rev. Dr. George Edward Ellis spoke of the diary and of his understanding that the family wished to dispose of it; a committee was appointed to confer with the owners. He was able to report at the January 1869 meeting that the terms offered to the family had been accepted, and that funds for the purchase had been subscribed by certain of the members. A committee was then appointed "as to the time and manner of publishing the Sewall Diary." In 1870 a prospectus for publication was circulated; the copying and editing of the volumes was reported in June 1871 to be in progress, entrusted to William H. Whitmore. In the *Proceedings* for February 1873 Dr. Ellis printed twenty-six pages of selections from Sewall's letter-book. Nevertheless, he was obliged to report at the meeting of September 1874 that the subscriptions for publication had been inadequate, whereupon it was voted to print the volumes as part of the Society's *Collections*, on funds currently available.

Not until the meeting of November 1878 was Volume I on the table for distribution to the members. Dr. Ellis's name appeared as chairman of the committee of publication, and he had been tireless in forwarding the work, but he insisted on giving full credit to his colleagues. William Henry Whitmore, Hon.A.M. (Harvard and Williams), an erudite and testy antiquarian of the old school, whose career is recorded in the *Dictionary of American Biography*, supervised the transcription and printing, compiled the genealogies, wrote a large number of the footnotes, and made the index. Henry Warren Torrey, LL.D., McLean Professor of Ancient and Modern History at Harvard, a man of immense learning, identified quotations, contemporaneous European historical events and most of the authors and works alluded to by Sewall, no small feat when the indispensable reference works of the present day did not exist. James Russell Lowell, the fourth member of the committee, was unable to give much help because of his absence, but he read the galley proofs while U.S. minister at Madrid and London, and insisted on printing exactly what Sewall wrote, preserving especially all the archaisms of language.

At the time the Diary was first published there were no professional journals of history in this country. Long anonymous reviews appeared in *The Nation,* and two articles were required for each volume. The reviews of Vol. I (xxvii, 273–274, 286–287) are attributed to Whitmore, a frequent contributor, who did not mind ending up with flattering remarks on his own editing. Subsequent *Nation* reviews (xxx, 157–158, 177–179; xxxv, 77, 97–98) were by Charles Francis Adams Jr., who was outraged by the inadequacy of the index, which he called "an exasperating sham." Henry Cabot Lodge wrote a review for the *Magazine of American History* (ii, 641–642) which he expanded greatly as "A Puritan Pepys" in his *Studies in History* (1884). John Ward Dean printed two reluctant short notices in the *New England Historical and Genealogical Register* (xxxiii, 120–121; xxxiv, 222).

The present edition is based on the M.H.S. printing of 1878–1882, which was read with photocopies of the manuscript, and compared with the original in all cases of difficulty. Hundreds of corrections were made. The earlier editors took no liberties with the text, and their changes were mainly expansions of abbreviations which would have been spelled out by typesetters of Sewall's time: y^e, y^t, y^m, s^d, w^{ch}, thô, Chh, L^d, and the ampersand. Sewall did not usually capitalize *mr* and he omitted the apostrophe in contractions such as *usd* and *amazd.* He often used the $\bar{m}$ or $\bar{n}$ of the ancient scribes to repeat the consonant; his Dummer relatives almost always appear as Du$\bar{m}$er. Sewall's handwriting is generally large and bold, and though it is cursive, every letter is carefully formed. Evidently he took pains in making his ink, for it is uniformly dark and has not faded. His spelling has been reproduced exactly, and it must be said that his variations add interest and charm to the text. Some of Sewall's casualness in spelling has rubbed off on the present editor, and he does not wish to be held strictly accountable in his annotations for the spelling of such

names as Ann, Katharine, Mehitable, or Rebecca, which Sewall continually varied.

Sewall made use of marginal keys or notes throughout his diary.
Most of these were simply added to facilitate reference: *Dr. Cutler
Physician Dies, Swallows, Mr. Pemberton Wigg, Snow, Mr. Green
m.e. [mortuus est]*. Since most of these notes added no information,
the M.H.S. editors omitted them, and we have not restored them,
but all marginal notes which give further information have been
added to the text and labeled as such. Some of these were later additions, notably *Dolefull! Witchcraft*.

The M.H.S. editors recorded no explanation of their editorial
methods, and this omission of apparatus strengthens the feeling that
the first printing of the diary was essentially a private printing for a
small circle who knew all about the history of the manuscript and
the editorial methods employed. The annotations were certainly
tailored for this Boston group of gentleman-scholars, barristers, anti-
quarians, and genealogists. We have omitted or abridged a large
number of them, and written our notes for those interested in the
life of Sewall's time but with no vital concern for the politics,
theology, or real estate of that day. Our footnotes appear in the place
demanded by logic and a decent regard for the reader: at the foot
of the page.

The entire existing text of the diary has been printed in these
volumes, and any omissions which may be noticed are the author's,
not the editor's. Certain peripheral documents and letters received
which Sewall transcribed into the diary for convenience have been
paraphrased or omitted; these items are noted. Two passages which
the original editors, in the middle of Queen Victoria's reign, deemed
unsuitable for publication, have been restored: Sewall's remarks on
his wife's nipples, 7 and 9 April 1677, and his embarrassment about
the chamber-pot, 27 March 1706.

The original manuscript of Sewall's diary prior to 11 February
1684/5 has long been missing. The text of the early years of the diary
as first published was derived from a manuscript volume at the
M.H.S. entitled "Journal of the Honble Samuel Sewall Esqr 1672–
1677"; it contains two pages of accounts for 1672. The diary text
begins at 3 December 1673 and ends 11 July 1677. The volume is
prefaced by the following unsigned statement: "Transcribed from a
copy of the Original belonging to Mr. (Nathaniel G?) Snelling [*sic*]
of Boston. The original itself is now lost, having been consumed accidentally by a fire a few years since in the Office of James Savage
Esqr of Boston . . ." In an appended note the writer states that on

11 December 1857, "At an interview with Hon. J. Savage in Boston, he told me himself that the Original Manuscript Diary here referred to, was never in his possession." What was regrettably destroyed in a fire in Savage's office was the second manuscript volume of John Winthrop's Journal, which he was editing.

Nathaniel Greenwood Snelling was librarian of the M.H.S. from 1818 to 1821. A second copy of the early years of the diary at the Society is labeled "Judge Sewall's Journal No. I Dup." and inscribed "Note by C[*harles*] D[*eane*]. Handwriting of W. J. Snelling. Given about 1837." Why William Joseph Snelling, a crusading and battling Boston journalist and satirist (memorialized in the *Dictionary of American Biography*), should have undertaken to make this copy does not appear; he was not immediately related to N. G. Snelling, and we suspect that Deane got his Snellings confused.

The surviving volumes of Sewall's diary in his own handwriting at the M.H.S. are in good condition, in their original bindings, and in slipcases. The text runs as follows: 11 February 1684/5 to 8 October 1703 (square octavo, 514 pages); 26 November 1703 to 22 July 1712 (quarto, 133 pages); 25 July 1712 to 13 October 1729 (square octavo, 412 pages); "Judge Sewall's Journal of Voyage to England, 1688, 1689" (labeled in the handwriting of Rev. Samuel Sewall; narrow pocket-size volume, 8 x 3 inches, 68 pages).

We have not provided a glossary for our readers, but various archaic words have been explained in footnotes. Certain general remarks are necessary: Sewall uses the word COUSIN as we would use kinsman. His parents, uncles and aunts, siblings, and children were called by our terms, but all other relatives, near and remote, connected by blood or marriage, were cousins. Our footnotes show how remote some of these relationships were. Sewall often uses MANE, classical Latin for *in the morning*, especially *early in the morning*. The terms GOLDSMITH and SILVERSMITH were interchangeable in Sewall's time, but modern dictionaries make no mention of this, even the O.E.D. Webster began with the old usage in 1828, but by 1890, workers in the two metals were separately specialized. The epithet REVEREND was not much used by the Puritans as a title for their ministers, who were called Parson, or Master (pronounced mister) probably with reference to their academic degree. Sewall does not get around to calling any ecclesiastic Reverend until 1709. We have used the term throughout our notes in accordance with modern custom, in order that ministers might be quickly identified. Doctors were of the medical or surgical variety, though in Sewall's time, as in present-day England, few of them possessed a degree of M.D. Increase Mather was made Doctor of Theology at Harvard, when he was president, in 1692, but Sewall took some time before he called him doctor. Sewall's dubious reception of Jeremy Dummer's Utrecht Ph.D. is one of the more amusing passages in the diary. The title MISTRESS was used for both married and unmarried females of social standing, regardless of age. At first Sewall abbreviated it as Mis. or M^{ris}; later Mrs. appears consistently. Madam was used for women of higher rank, just below those with the title of Lady. At this time, in England, Miss was the term for a kept mistress. Goodman or Goodwife (usually Goody) Blank belonged to the lowest order; Sewall rarely uses the term. A servant would be called John. John Blank was somewhat higher. Mr. John Blank was an educated, established, or propertied person, and this was the normal title for ministers. In this rank were those with the better military titles, never omitted; sheriffs, magistrates, and deacons in the church. The appendage Esquire was a still higher designation, though it had lost the technical meaning it had in England. The title Honorable was bestowed sparingly. Because of his eminence and out of respect, the diarist was usually addressed as Hon. Samuel Sewall, Esq. In the very highest rank were the Governor, the President (of the college), the General, and the few local knights, baronets, and peers—and their ladies.

Throughout Sewall's life, England employed the Julian calendar. The year began on Lady Day, 25 March. March was the first month; the months of September through December were the seventh through the tenth, and their Latin names were then correctly applied. Sewall often abbreviated them as 7^r, 8^r, 9^r, but he usually wrote Decr or x^r. England did not adopt the Gregorian calendar until 1752, but it was in use in various European countries many years prior to that time, and the English who wished to be exact used the double-year from 1 January to 24 March; Sewall was careful to use it. Because of the universal familiarity of the Gregorian calendar at present, we have divided Sewall's text into Gregorian years. For some reason, Sewall occasionally dropped into the use of the Roman ecclesiastical calendar for the days between Monday and Friday, i.e., *feria secunda, feria tertia*, etc.

The idea of an edition of Sewall's Diary for modern readers originated with the late Ray C. Dovell. Great credit is due to the firm of Farrar, Straus & Giroux for their efforts to produce the sort of book originally planned. The exemplary patience of Roger Straus and Robert Giroux with a work that has been under contract since 1956 deserves something more than a footnote in publishing history. Our work with John Peck, editor, has been a satisfaction and a pleasure.

Without the cooperation of the Massachusetts Historical Society this book could not have existed. Even before this editor had been elected to membership, the Council voted permission for his editing and printing of one of the Society's choicest manuscript possessions. Stephen Thomas Riley, the director, and his staff have been continually helpful.

So many have given assistance on this book at one time or another that a complete list of personal indebtednesses would be practically a roster of the editor's learned friends. Clifford Kenyon Shipton, good friend of four decades and more, has constantly given encouragement and help, freely shared his vast knowledge of Colonial America, and has taken the time to read and improve our footnotes. The late Professor Moses Hadas of Columbia, the late Professor George Melville Bolling (Ph.D. Johns Hopkins 1896), and Richard Glenn Thurston (Princeton 1968) buttressed enormously this editor's weakened acquaintance with the Latin language.

Work on this book was begun at Columbia and completed at Princeton, and the writer is grateful to both institutions for grants made for research, free time, and travel. These volumes constitute Project 323 of the Columbia University Council for Research in the Social Sciences.

Our appendices were designed to increase the usefulness of this edition. Sewall's published writings have been listed to date, but we have not undertaken to record the many reprintings of diary extracts. The list of Sewall's imprints is the first to appear. We print again Sewall's famous tract, *The Selling of Joseph,* the first American antislavery appeal to be published. Sewall's narrative of his journey to Arrowsick Island in the Kennebec turned up too late for insertion in its chronological place.

M. HALSEY THOMAS

PRINCETON UNIVERSITY
  18 April 1973

Contents

of Volume I

The Diary of Samuel Sewall

1674

1675

1676

1677

1694

1695

1696

1697

1698

1699

Illustrations

of Volume I

FRONT ENDPAPER. Detail from A South East View of yᵉ Great Town
of Boston in New England in America; artist, William Burgis;
engraver, John Harris; publisher, William Price [1723]. *British
Museum*

FRONTISPIECE. Samuel Sewall, painted by John Smibert in June
1729; the artist was paid 20*l* (*The Notebook of John Smibert,*
with essays by Sir David Evans, John Kerslake, and Andrew Oliver
. . . M.H.S. 1969), 21, 88, 105; Henry Wilder Foote, *John
Smibert, Painter* . . . (1950), 189–190. *Museum of Fine Arts,
Boston*

Chronology of Samuel Sewall[1]

English ruler: Oliver Cromwell

1652 *March 28*	Born at Bishop Stoke, Hampshire, England; baptised 4 May at Stoke Church by the Rev. Thomas Rashley.

Charles II, 29 May 1660

1661 *July 6*	Arrived in Boston on the *Prudent Mary* with his mother, sisters, and brothers; joined there shortly by his father, who brought the family to Newbury.
1661-1667	At school under the Rev. Thomas Parker at Newbury.
1667 *August*	Admitted to Harvard College, where he was in residence until 1674.
1669 *October 4*	The Corporation made Sewall Scholar of the House.
1671 *August 8*	B.A. Harvard.
1673 *November 5*	Chosen Fellow of the College, and installed before the Overseers on the 26th; he is also listed as Tutor, 1673-1674.
1673/4 *March 1*	Made "Keeper of the Colledg Library"; succeeded 11 December 1674 by Daniel Gookin.
1674 *August 11*	M.A. Harvard.
1674 *August 14*	Returned to his father's home at Newbury.
1675/6 *February 28*	Married by Simon Bradstreet to Hannah Hull, daughter of John Hull, mint-master

---

[1] This section has been compiled from the Diary and the *Letter-Books*, from William H. Whitmore's *Massachusetts Civil List*, from Sibley's article in *Harvard Graduates* (II, 345-364), where he unaccountably places Sewall's birth at "Horton, four miles from Basingstoke, in Hampshire," and from public records.

of Massachusetts-Bay; took up residence in Hull's house on what is now Washington Street, Boston, his home for the remainder of his life. From this period Sewall "followed Merchandize."

1675/6	Major of a regiment.
1677 *March* 30	Admitted to membership in the Third Church of Boston (now the Old South Church).
1678 *May*	Freeman of Massachusetts-Bay Colony.
1679	Member of the Ancient and Honorable Artillery Company.
1681 *October* 12	Appointed by the General Court to manage the printing press in Boston; resigned 10 September 1684.
1683	Ensign, Ancient and Honorable Artillery Company.
1683 *October* 1	Death of John Hull, Sewall's father-in-law.
1683 *November* 7	Deputy (non-resident) from Westfield, Hampshire County, to the General Court.
1683 *December* 5	Captain of the late Captain John Hull's Company.
1684 *May* 7	Elected a member of the Court of Assistants, a post carrying judicial responsibilities as magistrate, and membership on the Board of Overseers of Harvard College (reelected 27 May 1685 and 12 May 1686).

James II, 6 February 1684/5

1685	Captain of the South Company of Militia in Boston.
1686 *November* 11	Resigned commission as Captain of the South Company, on account of an order to put the cross in the colors.
1688 *November* 22	Sailed for England on the *America*; landed at Dover, 13 January 1688/9.

William and Mary, 13 February 1688/9

1689 May 22	Following the surrender of Andros, representatives of fifty-four towns met in Boston, and Governor Bradstreet and the Assistants chosen in 1686 resumed office provisionally; this government lasted until the new charter arrived (1692). Sewall resumed his post upon his return from England.
1689 October 10	Sailed from Plymouth, Devon, on the *America*; landed at Great Island, Piscataqua, 29 November; returned to Boston, 2 December.
1690 April–May	Commissioner from Massachusetts at an intercolonial conference in New York City called by Governor Leisler to concert measures for the public safety against the Indians and French.
1691 October 7	Named member of the Council in the new Province Charter, dated 7 October 3 William and Mary, which arrived at Boston 14 May 1692; annually elected until June 1725, when he declined further service.
1692 May 25	Appointed by the Governor and Council Commissioner of Oyer and Terminer (with William Stoughton, John Richards, Nathaniel Saltonstall, Wait Winthrop, Bartholomew Gedney, John Hathorne, Jonathan Corwin, and Peter Sergeant—or any five of them) "to enquire of, hear and determine all manner of crimes and offenses perpetrated within the counties of Suffolk, Essex, and Middlesex, or of either of them" (*viz.*, the Salem witchcraft court).
1692 December 6	Made one of the Justices of the Superior Court of Judicature at the first appointment under the Province Charter; served until 1728.
c.1694	Præcentor of the South Church—to 1717/18.

1694	*August 6-31*	Overland trip to Albany as commissioner from Massachusetts-Bay to make a treaty with the Five Nations.

William III, 28 December 1694

1695	*June 21*	Death of Judith (Quincy) Hull, Sewall's mother-in-law; the Hull estate then passed into the possession of Samuel and Hannah Sewall and their children.
1695		Donated five hundred acres of land from the Pettaquamscutt Purchase in the Narragansett country for the support of a schoolmaster at Kingston, R.I.
1696	*July 6*	Donated five hundred acres of Pettaquamscutt land to Harvard College.
1697	*January 14*	On the Fast-day set by the General Court to expiate the Salem witchcraft tragedy, Sewall stood in his pew in the South Church while the pastor, Samuel Willard, read his petition confessing his guilt and asking pardon of God and men for his role in the affair.
1697	*November 9*	Published his first book: *Phænomena quædam Apocalyptica ad Aspectum Novi Orbis configurata. Or, some few Lines towards a description of the New Heaven as it makes to those who stand upon the New Earth.*
1698	*December 22*	Appointed by the Governor and Council Commissioner of Oyer and Terminer (with Thomas Danforth, Wait Winthrop, and Elisha Cooke) for the trial of Jacob Smith.
1699	*October 14*	Commissioner of the Company for the Propagation of the Gospel in New England and Parts Adjacent—till his death (also secretary and treasurer—resigned April 1724).
1700	*June 24*	Published "The Selling of Joseph, A Memorial."

1701	June 2	Captain, Ancient and Honorable Artillery Company.

Anne, 8 March 1701/2

1707	December 6	Became Overseer of Harvard College (as provincial magistrate) when the college charter of 1650 was restored by the Governor and Council (Resolve of 6 December 1707).
1713	August	Published *Proposals Touching the Accomplishment of Prophecies.*
1713	September 16	Ordination of his son Joseph as colleague-pastor of South Church.

George I, 1 August 1714

1715	December 9	Judge of Probate for Suffolk County (resigned in 1728 on account of age).
1717	October 19	Hannah Hull Sewall, his wife, died in Boston.
1718	April 16	Chief Justice of the Superior Court of Judicature; took the oath 25 April (resigned in 1728 on account of age).
1719	October 29	Married to Mrs. Abigail (Melyen) Woodmansey Tilley by his son, the Rev. Joseph Sewall.
1720	May 26	Sudden death of Abigail Sewall, his second wife.
1722	March 29	Married to Mrs. Mary (Shrimpton) Gibbs by his son-in-law, the Rev. William Cooper.
1725	June 4	Declined reelection to the Council after thirty-three elections under the Province Charter.

George II, 11 June 1727

1727	November	Second edition of *Phænomena quædam Apocalyptica* published.
1728	July 29	Resigned as Chief Justice of the Superior Court of Judicature (succeeded 12 Decem-

ber by Benjamin Lynde) and Judge of
Probate for Suffolk County (succeeded 19
December by Josiah Willard).

1729/30 *January 1*   Died at his home in Boston in the 78th
year of his age; buried in the Hull-Sewall
family tomb in Granary Burying-Ground, 7
January.

Sewall's Autobiographical Letter

to his son Samuel Junior[1]

Boston, April 21, 1720

Dear Son, You have often desired that I would give you some Account of the family of which you are. And although I am much less able to doe any thing of this nature now when I have been left of my dear Parents very near Twenty years; yet considering the longer I stay, the more unfit I shall be, take what I have to say as follows:

Mr. Henry Sewall, my great Grandfather, was a Linen Draper in the City of Coventry in Great Britain. He acquired a great Estate, was a prudent Man, and was more than once chosen Mayor of the City.

Mr. Henry Sewall, my Grandfather, was his eldest Son, who out of dislike to the English Hierarchy sent over his only Son, my Father, Mr. Henry Sewall, to New England in the year 1634, with Net [*neat*] Cattel and Provisions sutable for a new Plantation. Mr. [*John*] Cotton would have had my Father settle at Boston; but in regard of his Cattel he chose to goe to Newbury, whither my Grandfather soon followed him.[2] Where also my Grandfather Mr. Stephen Dummer, and Alice his wife likewise dwelled under the Ministry of the Reverend Mr. Thomas Parker and Mr. James Noyes.

On the 25th March, 1646, Richard Saltonstall, Esq. Grandfather of Gurdon Saltonstall, Esq. now Governour of Connecticut, joined together in Marriage my father Mr. Henry Sewall and my Mother

---

[1] This letter was first printed in the *New England Historical and Genealogical Register*, April 1847, I, 111-113; the Massachusetts Historical Society editors printed it in the 1878-1882 edition of the Diary after collation with a transcript made by the recipient. Our text is derived from a photostat at the M.H.S. of the original manuscript in possession of the Sewall family of Bath, Maine. The family genealogy is set forth more fully in an appendix to the present edition.

[2] Samuel Sewall Jr. later added the following postscript: "*June 30th* 1729. Rec^d the following acc° of my Hon^d Father: viz. my Great Grandfather Sewall lived at Newbury at Old Town Green, where the first Meeting House stood: and upon the Removal of the Meeting House where it now stands (being Mr. Tappin's [*Christopher Toppan's*] Meeting House), He sold his House and Ground and moved to Rowley where he died and was Buried."

Mrs. Jane Dummer, eldest Child of Mr. Stephen Dummer aforesaid
and Alice his wife. My Father being then about 32, and my Mother
about 19 years of Age.

But the Climat being not agreeable to my Grandfather and Grandmother Dummer, (whose Maiden name was Archer) they returned to
England the Winter following, and my Father and Mother with
them, and dwelt awhile at Warwick, and afterwards removed to
Hampshire. My Sister Hannah Tappan, their eldest Child, was born
at Tunworth May 10th, 1649. Baptised by Mr. Haskins.

I was born at Bishop Stoke, March 28, 1652; so that the Light of the
Lord's Day was the first light that my Eyes saw, being born a little
before Day-break. I was baptised by Mr. Rashly, (sometime Member
of the Old Church in Boston)[3] in Stoke Church May 4th 1652. Mr.
Rashly first preached a Sermon, and then baptised me. After which
an entertainment was made for him and many more.

Some months after, My Father removed to Badesly, where my
Brother John Sewall was born Octobr 10. 1654, and was baptised in
my Father's House Novembr 22 by Mr. Henry Cox [*Coxe*], Minister
of Bishop Stoke.

My Brother Stephen Sewall was born at Badesly Augt 19th, 1657,
Baptised in my Father's house Septembr 24, by the said Mr. Cox.

My Father had made one Voyage to New-England to visit my
Grandfather Mr. Henry Sewall. And in the year 1659 he went thither
again; his rents at Newbury coming to very little when Remitted
to England. In my Father's absence, Octobr 25, 1659, my Sister Jane
Gerrish was born at Badesly and was baptised by Mr. Cox at Bishop
Stoke in the house of Mr. Boys.

At this Badesly, by the merciful goodness of GOD, I was taught to
read English. And afterwards was educated in the Grammar School
at Rumsey of which Mr. Figes was Master.

My Father sent for my Mother to come to him to New-England.
I remember being at Bishop Stoke and Badesly, April 23, 1661, the
day of the Coronation of K. Charles the 2d, the Thunder and Lightening of it. Quickly after my Mother went to Winchester with 5 small
Children, Hannah, Samuel, John, Stephen and Jane; and John Nash
and Mary Hobs her Servants; there to be in a readiness for the Pool

[3] Thomas Rashley, M.A., sometime fellow of Trinity College, Cambridge, came to
New England about 1639 and was admitted to the First Church of Boston 8
March 1639/40 as "a studyent"; he was chaplain at Cape Anne and minister of
Exeter, N.H., but returned to England by 1648 and was minister of Barford St.
Martin, Wilts, Bishop Stoke, Hants, and preacher at Salisbury Cathedral. He was
ejected in 1662. Morison, *F.H.C.*, 397; A. G. Matthews, *Calamy Revised*.

Waggons. At this place her near Relations, especially my very worthy and pious Uncle Mr. Stephen Dummer took Leave with Tears. Capt. Dummer of Swathling treated us with Raisins and Almonds. My Mother lodged in Pump-yard, London, waiting for the going of the Ship, the *Prudent Mary*, Capt. Isaac Woodgreen, Commander, went by water to Graves-End where the Ship lay. Took in Sheep at Dover. Passengers in the Ship at the same time were Major Brown, a young brisk Merchant and a considerable Freighter; Mr. [*Thomas*] Gilbert and his wife, He was Minister at Topsfield; Madam Bradstreet (then Gardener)[4]; Mrs. Martha, Mr. Pitkins Sister[5], who died lately at Windsor, and many others. We were about Eight Weeks at Sea, where we had nothing to see but Water and the Sky; so that I began to fear I should never get to Shoar again; only I thought the Capt. and Mariners would not have ventured themselves if they had not hopes of getting to Land again. Capt. Woodgreen arrived here on Satterday. I was overjoyed to see Land again, especially being so near it as in the Narrows. 'Twas so late by that time we got to the Castle, that our men held a discourse with them whether they should Fire or no, and reckoned 't was agreed not to doe it. But presently after the Castle Fired; which much displeased the Ship's Company; and then they Fired. On the Lord's day my Mother kept aboard; but I went ashoar, the Boat grounded, and I was carried out in arms July 6, 1661. My Mother lodg'd at Mr. Richard Collucott's. This Week there was a publick Thanksgiving. My Father hastened to Boston and carried his Family to Newbury by Water in Mr. Lewis.[6] Brother Tappan has told me our arrival there was upon Lecture-day which was Wednesday. Mr. Ordway carryed me ashore in his Canoe. We sojourned at Mr. Titcomb's. My Father presently sent me to school to the Reverend and Excellent Mr. Thomas Parker, with whom I continued six years till my entrance into the College; being admitted by the very learned and pious Mr. Charles Chauncey.

    Sept[r] 3, 1662, Mother was brought to bed of Sister Anne, Mr.

[4] Anne, daughter of Emanuel Downing of Salem, married first Captain Joseph Gardner, who was killed at the Narragansett Swamp Fight in 1675. The following year she became the second wife of Governor Simon Bradstreet, whose first wife had been Anne (Dudley) Bradstreet, the poetess. Madam Bradstreet appears frequently in the Diary; she died in 1713 in Salem. *Savage*.

[5] Martha, sister of William Pitkin of Hartford, married Simon Wolcott of Windsor, Conn., and became the mother of Governor Roger Wolcott; she died in 1719 as the widow of the Hon. Daniel Clark. *Savage*.

[6] Sewall frequently economizes words by using this expression; it should be read here as "in Mr. Lewis's vessel."

Joshua Moodey the Minister's Mother being her Midwife. Baptised by Mr. Parker.

May, 8, 1665, Sister Mehetabel was born: Baptised by Mr. Parker. She became wife to the midwife's Grandson, Mr. William Moodey. Dorothy Sewall (now Northend) was born October 29, 1668. Baptised by Mr. Parker.

At this time the Commencement was in August. In the year 1667 my father brought me to be admitted, by which means I heard Mr. Richard Mather of Dorchester preach Mr. Wilson's Funeral Sermon.[7] *Your Fathers where are they?* I was admitted by the very Learned and pious Mr. Charles Chauncey, who gave me my first Degree in the year 1671. There were no Masters that year. These Bachelours were the last Mr. Chauncey gave a degree to. For he died the February following.

In July 1672, Dr. [*Leonard*] Hoar came over with his Lady and sojourned with your Grandfather Hull. (He [*Dr. Hoar*] was my Aunt Quincey's Brother) and preached, as an Assistant, to the Rev. Mr. Thomas Thacher at the South Church. The College quickly called him to be President. He was installed in the College Hall in Decemb[r] 1672. Gov. Bellingham lay dead in his House, and Dep. Gov. Leverett was the Chief Civil Magistrat present at that Solemnity. The March following Mrs. Bridget Hoar, now Cotton, was born in Cambridge.[8] In 1674 I took my 2[d] Degree and Mrs. Hannah Hull, my dear Wife, your honoured Mother, was invited by the Dr. and his Lady to be with them a while at Cambridge. She saw me when I took my Degree and set her Affection on me, though I knew nothing of it till after our Marriage, which was February 28th. 1675/6. Gov[r] Bradstreet married us in that we now call the Old Hall; 't was then all in one, a very large Room. As I remember, Madam Thacher and Madam Paige[9] with whom Gov. Bradstreet boarded visited us the next day.

On the 2[d] of April, 1677, it pleased GOD to favour us with the birth of your Brother John Sewall, our First-born. In June 1678 you were born. Your brother lived till the September following, and then

---

[7] John Wilson, M.A. (Cambridge), first minister of Boston, died 7 August 1667. Richard Mather, progenitor of all the Mathers here, did not print the sermon.

[8] Bridget Hoar became the wife of the Rev. Thomas Cotton of London; in the years 1724-26 the Cottons gave £500 to Harvard College.

[9] Anna (Keayne) Lane Paige. Her father had married Sarah Dudley, sister of Anne, the first Mrs. Simon Bradstreet. We will encounter the gay and worldly Madam Paige later in the Diary.

died. So that by the undeserved Goodness of GOD your Mother and I never were without a child after the 2ᵈ of April 1677.

In the Fall 1678, I was seized with the Small Pocks and brought very near to death; so near that I was reported to be dead. But it pleased GOD of his Mercy to Recover me. Multitudes died, two of my special Friends viz. Mr. John Noyes, and Ensign Benjamin Thirston, who both died while I lay sick: and Mr. William Dummer, Son of Jeremiah Dummer Esq. aged about 19 years. Presently after my Recovery, in December, Col. Townsend, Mr. Stoddard, and I were Bearers to Mr. Joseph Tappin one of the most noted Shop-keepers in Boston.

And now what shall I render to the Lord for all his benefits? The good Lord help me to walk humbly and Thankfully with Him all my days; and profit by Mercies and by Afflictions; that through Faith and Patience I may also in due time fully inherit the Promises. Let us incessantly pray for each other, that it may be so!

Samuel Sewall

Augt. 26. 1720.

Abbreviations

used in the footnotes

A.A.S. Proc.	*Proceedings of the American Antiquarian Society,* New series (Worcester, 1882-).
Appleton	*Appletons' Cyclopædia of American Biography,* edited by James Grant Wilson and John Fiske (New York, 1886ff).
C.S.M.	*Publications of the Colonial Society of Massachusetts* (Boston, 1895-).
Calamy	*Calamy Revised: Being a Revision of Edmund Calamy's Account of the Ministers and Others Ejected or Silenced, 1660-2,* by A. G. Matthews (Oxford, 1934).
D.A.	A *Dictionary of Americanisms on Historical Principles,* edited by Mitford M. Mathews (Chicago, 1951).
D.A.B.	*Dictionary of American Biography* (New York, 1928-).
D.N.B.	*Dictionary of National Biography* (London, 1885-).
Dexter	*Biographical Sketches of the Graduates of Yale College . . .* by Franklin Bowditch Dexter (New York and New Haven, 1885-1912).
Evans	*American Bibliography . . .* by Charles Evans [*et al.*] (Chicago and Worcester, 1903-).
Holmes	*Cotton Mather: A Bibliography of his Works,* by Thomas James Holmes (Cambridge, Mass., 1940) and *Increase Mather: A Bibliography of his Works,* by Thomas James Holmes (Cleveland, 1931).

Hutchinson	*The History of the Colony and Province of Massachusetts-Bay* by Thomas Hutchinson, edited . . . by Lawrence Shaw Mayo (Cambridge, 1936).
L.B.	*Letter-Book of Samuel Sewall* (1686-1729). Collections of the Massachusetts Historical Society, Sixth series, I, II (Boston, 1886-1888).
Mass.Bay.Rec.	*Records of the Governor and Company of the Massachusetts Bay in New England* . . . edited by Nathaniel Bradstreet Shurtleff (Boston, 1853-1854).
M.H.S.Colls.	*Collections of the Massachusetts Historical Society* (Boston, 1792-). Series indicated by prefixed numeral.
M.H.S.EDS.	This abbreviation has been appended to footnotes taken over verbatim or with slight changes from the 1878-1882 edition of the Diary.
M.H.S.Proc.	*Proceedings of the Massachusetts Historical Society* (Boston, 1859-). Series indicated by prefixed numeral.
Morison, *F.H.C.*	*The Founding of Harvard College*, by Samuel Eliot Morison (Cambridge, 1935).
Morison, *H.C.S.C.*	*Harvard College in the Seventeenth Century*, by Samuel Eliot Morison (Cambridge, 1936).
N.E.H.G.R.	*New England Historical and Genealogical Register* (Boston, 1847-).
N.E.Q.	*The New England Quarterly* (1928-).
O.E.D.	*The Oxford English Dictionary: a new English Dictionary on Historical Principles* (Oxford, 1888-).
Palfrey	*History of New England*, by John Gorham Palfrey (Boston, 1858-1889).
Sabin	*Bibliotheca Americana. A Dictionary of Books relating to America from its Discovery to the Present Time*, by Joseph Sabin [*et al.*] (New York, 1868-1936).

Savage

A Genealogical Dictionary of the First Settlers of New England, showing three generations of those who came before May, 1692 . . . by James Savage (Boston, 1860-1862).

Sibley

Biographical Sketches of the Graduates of Harvard University . . . by John Langdon Sibley (Cambridge, 1873-1885); continued as *Sibley's Harvard Graduates . . . Biographical Sketches of those who attended Harvard College . . .* by Clifford Kenyon Shipton (Cambridge and Boston, 1933-).

Weis

The Colonial Clergy and the Colonial Churches of New England, by Frederick Lewis Weis (Lancaster, Mass., 1936).

Whitmore

The Massachusetts Civil List for the Colonial and Provincial Periods, 1630-1774 . . . by William Henry Whitmore (Albany, 1870).

The Diary of Samuel Sewall

1674

TEACHING NATURAL PHILOSOPHY AT HARVARD / CAMBRIDGE TOWN
MEETING / BESTIALITY AT ROXBURY / BLASPHEMY OF THOMAS
SARGEANT / RAISING OF THE NEW COLLEGE / GRADUATION AS M.A.
AND RETURN TO NEWBURY / HARVARD'S DECLINE / PASTORATE
OFFERED AT WOODBRIDGE, EAST JERSEY

Dec. 3, 1673. I read to the Junior Sophisters, the 14th Chapter of
Heerboords Physick,[1] i.e. part of it, which beginnes thus, Sensus Communes &c. I went to the end, and then red it over from the beginning,
which I ended the 24th of March, 1673/4.

Feb. 20, 1673/4. Brother Stephen admitted. My Father brought
down my Brother Stephen to be admitted, which was done the 23d of
that month.[2]

March 9, 1673/4. I sent my Brother Stephen's cloaths to be washed
by Mrs. Clark.

Mar. 23. I had my hair cut by G[*oodman*] Barret.

Mar. 24. My Father came down; Harry Summerby attending him;
brought my Sister Jane to the Dr.'s. My Sister Anne was brought to
Mr. Butler's to live by my B[*rother*] John, March 20, 1673/4. In the
Evening the Townsmen of Cambridge had a meeting and Mr.
Gookin and I being sent for went to them. They treated us very
civilly and agreed that the School boyes should sit no longer in the
Students hinder seat. It was also consented to by us that some sober
youths for the present might be seated there. *Hæc hactenus.*

March 25, 1674. My Father went away and Henry Somerby with

---

[1] There is a copy 'of Adrian Heereboord's *Philosophia Naturalis* [Leyden, 1663?]
at the Massachusetts Historical Society which passed through various hands at the
college. Caput. XIV, Thesis. I, begins: "Sensus communis officia sunt varia." The
title-page is missing, but the names of several owners remain (*C.S.M.* xxviii,
408). Thomas Brattle (Harvard 1676) paid 18[d] for it 15 August 1673. It is also
inscribed "Samuel Sewall His Book 1675." A generation later the book belonged
to Samuel Moody (Harvard 1697), the fighting parson of York, Maine, who
married Sewall's niece.

[2] Stephen Sewall did not remain in college long. After commencement he returned to Newbury, and following a trial period, he was apprenticed 30 November 1674 to Edmund Batter of Salem, malter.

him intending for Salem. It rained hard in the afternoon. Madam How brought to bed of a daughter in the afternoon.

April 2. Benjamin Gourd of Roxbury (being about 17 years of age) was executed for committing Bestiality with a Mare, which was first knocked in the head under the Gallows in his sight. N.B. He committed that filthines at noon day in an open yard. He after confessed that he had lived in that sin a year. The causes he alledged were, idlenes, not obeying parents, &c.

April 6. Mr. Ganson, M^r of a Catch set sail for Liverpoll, in which Mr. Higginson went.

April 7. The D., Mr. Gookin and myself were invited and went to dinner with the Magistrates in the Court Chamber. Mr. Sherman and Mr. Willard came with me to my chamber.

April 8. Mr. Gookin and I gave Mr. Nehemiah Hobart a visit, 6^d to the P^ts man.

April 9. Mr. Gookin and I went down to Boston. I went to visit my Couzen Dummer and his wife my Couzen, who lay in of Mary Dummer, born the 14th of March 1673/4. To the Nurse 2^d, for a pair of sizers 4^d.

April 10. 3^d milk, 6^d for spice &c.

April 15, 1674. 4^d Beer. News of Peace in Lecture time. 3^s for Wine, 6^d to Onesiphorus. Tobacco Pipes 3^d. At night I lay with Sir Adams at Mr. Oakes's. *Memen.* it thundered and lightened and rained very much.

Friday, April 17. My Brother went to Boston and brought me an Hour-glasse and penknife 1. 1. 3^d. One shilling to my Brother. A pair of Glovs from Goodman Fissenden, 2^s. Laurence and Hannah Oakes were at my chamber in the evening. Received my Quarter pay;[3] borrowed money subducted, 2^1 12^s 9^d Mr. Henry Short married the 30th March '74. Mr. [*Samuel*] Treat to Mr. [*John*] Maihos [*Mayo's*] Granchild [*Elizabeth*] the 16th of April, '74.

June 5, 1674. Mr. Oakes gave me to understand that though he respected and loved me as formerly, yet he desired that I would refrain coming to his house, and that he did it *se defendendo*, least he should be mistrusted to discourage and dissettle me.[4]

[3] The Harvard Corporation had ordered on 15 April that "m^r Gookin and Sr Sewall fellowes of the Colledg have half a years salary of their proportion forthwith paid them of the Piscataway-gift now in the treasurers hands. According as the hon^rd overseers have directed the same to be proportioned. Also fifty shillings apeece due in ffeb^r¹¹ last by m^r Glovers gift." *C.S.M.* xv, 58.

[4] Urian Oakes, minister of the Cambridge church, had been passed by when the overseers chose a new president for the college in 1672. Leonard Hoar, M.D., took office late that year with great plans and high hopes, but resigned frustrated and

Monday, June 15, 1674. Mr. [*Peter*] Thatcher, Fellow. The Corporation met and chose Sir Thatcher Fellow, Mr. [*Marmaduke*] Johnson, Printer. N.B. There were this day two boyes killed at Watertown with the tumbling of a load of brush on them, on which they road: the one was about the age of 12 years, and the other 9.

Thomas Sargeant[5] was examined by the Corporation: finally, the advice of Mr. Danforth, Mr. Stoughton, Mr. Thatcher, Mr. Mather (then present) was taken. This was his sentence.

That being convicted of speaking blasphemous words concerning the H[*oly*] G[*host*] he should be therefore publickly whipped before all the Scholars. 2. That he should be suspended as to taking his degree of Bachelour (this sentence read before him twice at the P[rts] before the committee, and in the library 1 up before execution.) 3. Sit alone by himself in the Hall uncovered at meals, during the pleasure of the President and Fellows, and be in all things obedient, doing what exercise was appointed him by the President, or else be finally expelled the Colledge. The first was presently put in execution in the Library (Mr. Danforth, Jr. being present) before the Scholars. He kneeled down and the instrument Goodman Hely[6] attended the President's word as to the performance of his part in the work. Prayer was had before and after by the President. *July 1, 1674.* Sir Thacher Commonplaced, Justification was his head. He had a solid good piece: stood above an hour, and yet brake of before he came to any use. By reason that there was no warning given, none (after the undergraduates) were present, save Mr. Dan Gookin, Sr. the President and myself. *July 3, 1674.* N. B. Mr. Gookin, Jr. was gone a fishing with his brothers.

Had my hair cut by Goodman Barret, *July 6. 1674.*

July the 8th being Cambridge lecture day, Mr. Wallie set sail, with whom went Mr. Chauncy and Mr. Epps.

July 10. I Commonplaced.[7] Nobody save the 6 plm. [*placemen*] was present.

---

defeated in less than three years. Oakes was elected as his successor. Sewall's entry is one of the few contemporary records that suggest intrigue behind the disaffection and student rebellion which caused Dr. Hoar's downfall. The story of Harvard's troubles at that period is given in Morison, *H.C.S.C.* II, 401-408.

[5] Sargeant, a senior, was given his B.A. 21 December 1674 and the following week he went to sea; Sibley was unable to find any further record of him.

[6] William Healy was the local prison-keeper. In 1682 he was removed from office for gross misconduct, severely whipped, and confined to his own prison. L. R. Paige, *Hist. of Cambridge* (1877), 580.

[7] In the college lingo of the time this meant the delivery of a brief practice exercise or thesis on some set theme. *O.E.D.*

July 17. Sir Weld commonplaced. His subject was Man as created in God's Image.

July 21. Sir Bowles Commonplaced. His subject was the Creation of the Soul.[8]

August 7, 1674. New Colledge raised. John Francis helping about raising of the new Colledge had his right legg (both bones) broke a little above his anckle, and his left thigh about 4 inches below the joint, by a peece that fell on him, and had like to killed several others and yet hurt none.[9]

At the Harvard commencement on the 11th of August, Sewall was listed on the program to respond in the affirmative to the quaestion: An Peccatum Originale sit & Peccatum & Poena? He was then admitted to the M.A. degree by President Hoar.

Friday, August 14. I with my two Brothers went home to Newbury.

Tuesday, August 18. Visited Mr. Parker, Mr. Woodbridge and Mr. Richardson.

Aug. 19. Tim. Woodbridge visited me.

Thorsday, Sept. 3. Mis. Martha Noyes dyed.

Sept. 4. Buried. Her death suddain, the 5th day after her Travail.

Monday, Sept. 7. First Frost. *Sept. 8th* Generall Training. My Brother John went down and had discourse with my Sister Hannah, (that now is). Brought up my Sister Jane, *Sept.* 11. About the 18th of this month my Father went down, carried my Sister Jane, and brought up the Publishment.

Monday, Sept. 28th. My little Neece [*Jane Toppan*] Born.

Sept. 29. Broth. John went to Boston, and B[*rother*] Stephen to Mr. Batters, upon Tryal.

Tuesday, Oct. 6. My Father went to Cambridge. *Oct. 8.* My Father was at Boston, on which day he spake concerning my Buisines to a Gentleman there.

1674. Tuesday, Oct. 13. I went to Cambridge, being summoned to wait on the Court the next day.

[8] Sir Weld and Sir Bowles were classmates of Sewall. Undergraduates were called by their surname, bachelors of arts were called Sir (used as a rendering of the Latin *Dominus*), and masters of arts were called Master, abbreviated "Mr." and by this time usually pronounced "mister." *O.E.D.*

[9] This building, a brick structure containing a large hall, library, and twenty chambers for students (two in a chamber) was occupied in 1677 and destroyed by fire 24 January 1764. Called New College at first, it received the name of Harvard College following demolition of the original college in 1679. Francis, a Cambridge brickmaker, was granted a hundred acres of land by the colony in 1679 in consequence of his injury. *C.S.M.* xv, lxxxvi-lxxxvii.

QUÆSTIONES
Pro modulo Discutiendæ
Sub LEONARDO HOAR. M. D.

COL: HARVARDINI *CANTAB*: in *NOV--ANGLIA*

PRÆSIDE

Per Inceptores in *Artibus* in Comitiis

Tertio Ìdus Sextiles

M.DC.LXXIV.

N Peccatum Originale sit & Peccatum & Pœna?

Affirmat Respondens *Samuel Sewall.*

II. *An* Necessitas Decreti tollat libertatem & Contingentiam Creaturæ?

Negat Respondens *Petrus Thacherus.*

III. An Cœlum Stellatum sit Igneum?

Affirmat Respondens *Thomas Weld.*

IV. An Detur Theologia Naturalis ad Salutem Sufficiens?

Negat Respondens *Johannes Bowles.*

Oct. 16. by Mr. Richardson's means I was called to speak. The sum of my Speech was that the causes of the lownes of the Colledge were external as well as internal.[10]

The first day of my coming to Boston at night, I lay with my Couzen Dummer. The Thorsday Oct. 15 I rode first to Charlestown Ferry, thinking to have my horse over, and so accompany Mr. Gookin, but could not, and so was fain to ride round in the night.

Oct. 17. Nicol. Fissenden came with me home.

Tuesday, Oct. 20. My Father went down to see how things were after my information. Nic urged to have my Brother [*who?*] has gone too. My Mother and I withstood it. Father (as it was thought he would) set the match forward, her friends earnest.

Oct. 23. Brother Stephen came to visit us.

Oct. 26. Brothers John and St[*ephen*], with Father Lummacks, went down the next day. *Tuesday, Oct. 27.* Brother [*John*] was married by Mr. Danforth [*to Hannah Fessenden of Cambridge*].

Oct. 29. They came home, it being a rainy day.

Saturday [31*st*] They returned. Goodman Cheyny, Nic. Fissenden, and Thomas Cheyny. Stephen my Brother to Salem.

Nov. 3. Mr. Adams married. Mr. William Adams and Miss Mary Manning, his wife, coming from Salisbury came to visit me. *Memen.* They were married by Mr. Danforth on Wenseday, the 21 of Sept.[11]

Thorsday, Nov. 5, Mr. Edward Taylor, of Westfield is married (as he gave out.)[12]

[10] The decline of the college continued this year until only three students remained in residence. Dr. Hoar resigned the following March, and died, a broken man, in Boston, 28 November 1675. John Richardson of Newbury (Harvard 1666) was one of the Fellows who had resigned, leaving the Corporation without a constitutional majority, without a quorum to act, and the president without support. *Sibley.*

[11] William Adams, minister of Dedham, was a classmate of Sewall; he was married to Mary Manning, a Cambridge girl, Wednesday 21 October 1674. *Sibley.*

[12] Edward Taylor, another classmate of Sewall's, was married to Elizabeth, daughter of the Rev. James Fitch of Norwich, Connecticut, 5 September 1674. Taylor arrived in Boston from England 5 July 1668 at the age of twenty-three with letters of introduction to the Mathers and John Hull, and was matriculated at Harvard later in that month. Sewall wrote in 1729: "He and I were Chamber fellows and Bed-fellows in Harvard-College Two years: He being admitted into the College, drew me thither" [from lodgings with the Fessendens] (*Letter-Book,* II, 274). Taylor had a long, quiet, and useful career as minister and physician at Westfield, where he died in 1729; in due season he received commemoration in Sibley and in Sprague's *Annals of the American Pulpit* and joined the large company of estimable and forgotten New England parsons. For over sixty years, however, he had been an inveterate writer of poetry, and his manuscripts descended to his grandson President Ezra Stiles and later came into the possession of Yale Uni-

Copys of Letters in Almanack, 1672.

Memento, that about Novem. 12 I wrote four Letters to England. Imp. one to my Aunt Rider. It. one to my Aunt Mehetabel Holt. It. one to my Cousin Thomas Dummer. It. one to my Landlord Marice. In that of my Aunt Holts were also enclosed one of my Mothers to my Unckle, St[*ephen*] Dummer, one of my Brother John's to be sent to my Aunt Sarah Holt. The Copies of mine are in the Almanack for the year '72. My Bro. went to Salem Nov. 13, intending for Boston Saturday, Nov. 14 to give these Letters to Mr. Hull by him to be sent for England.

Thorsday, Nov. 19, My Mother and Self went to see Goodman Moody, whom we found extream ill of the yellow jaundice. We visited Goodman and Goodwife Little also.

Tuesday, Nov. 24. My Father received a letter from Capt. Pike, of Woodbridge[13] by which he sollicited my Father for my coming thether to be their Minister. Letters date, Sept. 10. '74.

Monday, Nov. 30th. My Father and self went to Salem. The next day my Brother Stephen was bound Apprentice to Mr. Edmund Batter, Merch. His time expires on the 29th of Sept. 1679 (unless Mr. Batter dye before). At the time specified he is to receive ten £ in good and currant pay.

Tuesday, Dec. 22, 1674. Lieutenant Way, Mr. Weaver, Tho. Norman came to our house. The Lieuten[t] related distinctly several things about Mr. Nicolets Church gathering at Lin.[14]

Wednesday, Dec. 23. I was at an Arbitration between Tho[s]. N. and John W. Weaver was cast 300 and odde £ in W debdt. The Arb. were Mr. Den, C[pl]. Saltonstall, Mr. Pike, C[pl]. Gerrish, and Mr. Doel. The last set not his hand at all, Mr. Pike but to part.

Friday, Dec. 25. Sam. Guile of Havarel [*Haverhill*], ravished Goodwife Nash of Amesbury, about G. Bailyes Pasture at the white Bottoms.

---

versity. Upon the publication of *The Poetical Works of Edward Taylor* by Dr. Thomas H. Johnson of Lawrenceville in 1939 Taylor took his place overnight as one of the choice figures of American colonial literature.

[13] The town of Woodbridge in East Jersey was largely settled by families from Newbury, Massachusetts, who named the place for their former pastor, John Woodbridge. Capt. John Pike was one of the settlers from Newbury; later he was a member of Governor Carteret's council. W. A. Whitehead, *Perth Amboy* (1856), 360-363.

[14] Unsuccessful attempts had been made at Salem and at Lynn to settle the Rev. Charles Nicholet, a preacher from Virginia. The details are given in 2 *M.H.S. Proc.* XVI, 513.

1675

FAST AT SAMUEL MOODY'S / SEWALL PREACHES FOR MASTER PARKER / DREAM OF CLIMBING TO HEAVEN / PRODIGIES IN THE SKIES / KING PHILIP'S WAR

Mond. Jan. 25, 1674/5. Mr. Smith came to visit us, and brought with him one Mr. Bradly, who is allso a Southton[1] man, and told me that he went to old Mr. Goldwire's to school at Broadling, with 34 more. He allso told me that Thos. Warren was Apprentice to an Orange Merchant at Billingsgate, and Sam. to a Coal-seller at Cheapside.

Thurs. Feb. 13. There was a Fast held at Sam. Moody's, principally upon the occasion of his sicknes: whereat were present, Mr. Woodbridge, Mr. Philips, Mr. Moody, Mr. Reinor, Mr. Richardson. The 3 first mentioned seemed to be very sensible of the state of things and of the plots of papists, Atheists &c. Mr. Phillips spake how the Ministers in England, when they had their liberty, look after their own houses, quarrelled, &c. I carried my Mother to the Fast, and there we with many more, had (I hope) a feast day.[2]

A Scotchman and Frenchman kill their Master, knocking him in the head as he was taking Tobacko. They are taken by Hew and Cry, and condemned: Hanged.

Nicolas Feaver, born in the Ile of Jersey, Robert Driver, born in the Ile of Orknye in Scotland, Executed, Mar. 18, 1674/5.

Monday, March 15, 1674/5. I visited Mr. Parker.[3] He told me what

[1] By Southton man, Sewall meant a Southamptonshire (or Hampshire) man. Broadling is probably Broadlands, not far from Baddesley, where Sewall first went to school.

[2] The clergy present on this occasion were John Woodbridge, Samuel Phillips of Rowley, Joshua Moody of Portsmouth, John Reyner Jr. of Dover, and John Richardson.

[3] Thomas Parker was the son of the Rev. Robert Parker, eminent nonconformist divine of Stanton St. Bernard, Wilts, and was educated at Dublin, Oxford, Leyden, and Franeker, where he took the degree of M.PHIL. and stirred up a violent controversy among the theologians. After teaching and preaching in Newbury, Wilts, for some years, he emigrated to New England with several relatives, and in 1635 was one of the founders of the town and church of Newbury, where he and his cousin James Noyes became ministers. There he caused some dissension

one Mr. Stockman related to Mr. Parker his father, at the table of the
Earl of Pembrook. This Stockman went into Spain with the Embassa-
dour, and there hearing of one that could foretell things went to
him to enquire concerning England. He showed in a glass for K.
Henry 3 time, the Cross leaning, and stooping: for K. Edward the
Wizard showed a Child, a cloud drawn over his head. Q. Mary, *Ferro
et Flammis:* Q. Elizabeth, *Excellentissima:* K. James, one coming over
a river with the crown on his head, *Infelix pacis amator.*

April 3. 1675. About one of the clock at night, Sam. Moody dyed
quietly, having lyen sick of the jaundice by the space of half-an-year.
He was buried on Monday. There was a great funeral.

April 4, Sab. day. Preach for Master. I holp my Master [*Thomas
Parker*], in the afternoon. Being afraid to look on the glass, ignorantly
and unwittingly I stood two hours and a half.[4]

April 29 Brother John and Sister Hannah Sewall begin to keep
house at the Falls.[5]

My Father having found things out of order at the Little Farm, viz,
Fences down, ground Eaten and rooted up by Cattle and hogs, and
wanting a good Tenant, the Season of the year now spending, resolves and goes to live there, notwithstanding the littleness and un-
pretines of the house. See the Alman[ack] Moonday May 3.

Saturday, May 15. Brothers house was raised, at the raising of
which I was. Two Pins lower Summer.[6]

Wednesday May 19, 1675. that place of the 1 Sam. 15. 26. came
to my mind (as I came down from my Brother,) which gave me great
comfort, especially for that presently after reading Mr. Caryl in
course, I found it there parenthetically paraphrased. *Thursday, May*
20. relieved by reading what he saith on the same verse, about limit-
ing God in works of Spiritual Mercy, p. 257.

Friday, May 21. Goodman Adams (coming to visit his Mother

---

by favoring Presbyterian government, but retained the affection of his congregation. He became blind in later life and conducted a free school to prepare boys
for Harvard. Sewall was one of his pupils and was devoted to his Master Parker;
he wrote a very touching tribute at his death, 24 April 1677. D.A.B., Morison,
F.H.C., 393 and *C.S.M.* xxviii, 261-267.

[4] This is the only recorded instance of preaching by Sewall.

[5] In 1635 an allotment of 500 acres of land at "the Falls" on the Parker River,
now Byfield Parish, had been made to Henry Sewall Sr., grandfather of John and
Samuel. J. J. Currier, *Hist. of Newbury* (1902), 64.

[6] Throughout the Diary Sewall records driving nails or wooden pins in buildings
under construction. This gesture of good will and voluntary association with the
enterprise is traced by H. W. Haynes to Roman and Old Testament sources in
2 *M.H.S. Proc.* iv, 101-102, 219-221.

Woodman) was invited by and came over and lodged with me.

N. B. Tuesday, May 4 C^{pt} Scarlet, Mr. Smith, Mr. Freak killed by a blow of powder on Ship board. Mr. Freak killed outright.[7]

July 31, at midnight, Tho. Wood, Carpenter of Rowly, had his house and goods burnt, and, *væ malum*, a daughter of about 10 years of age, who directed her brother so that he got out, was herself consumed to ashes.

This said Saturday night, in a dream, I fancyed myself to have Mis. Richardson's child in my arms, and herself following me up a pair of stairs going to heaven, all sorrowfull and weeping. I went up innumerable steps and still saw nothing, so that I was discouraged, doubting with myself whether there was such a place as *sedes beatorum*. Yet I strengthened myself as well as I could, considering how apt things only heard of are to be doubted (if difficultly obtained and not of a long time) though they be never so true. Thus thinking, I went on; at last I came to a fair chamber with goodly lodgings. When I saw that was all, I earnestly prayed that God would help us, or else we should never get to our journey's end. Amazed I was, not being able to conceive how furniture should be brought up those stairs so high. Afterward it was a chamber in the N[ew] Building, [at the College], after, part of an old [house] (Goff, as I take it) that joined to it, of the same height. A schollar told me that those things were drawn up by a pully, and so took in at a window which was all ranshacled like that in Goff Colledge over the Fellows' chamber, and all things began to seem more vile. Herabout I waked, being much troubled at the former part, and much wondring at the latter of my dream. 'Desinit in piscem mulier formosa superne.' Deus det, deus misericors et benignus, me, et comites meos, non tantum et de somnis, sed vere tandem divinis gradibus ad cœlum usque ascendere.

Novem. 10, 1675. Lecture day. Remember the courteous speech and behaviour of Tho. and Will Noyse. Ingenious men. Will came to me (speaking with Tim. Woodbridge) and excused his not coming to see me, &c.

Nov. 11. Morning proper fair, the wether exceedingly benign, but (to me) metaphoric, dismal, dark and portentous, some prodigie appearing in every corner of the skies. Father went to Attach Ben Goodridge, at which (as all) so especially Mother, troubled and disswaded him. Nothing moves, at which Mother was exceedingly troubled, and, e. h. w. o. L. w. h. [*every hour wishes our Lord would help?*]

N. B. Tuesday, Dec. 21, 1675, about the time of the Eclips Sister

[7] This explosion occurred in Boston Harbor. Captain Samuel Scarlet and Thomas Freak were substantial Boston citizens. *Savage.*

Sewall was delivered in my chamber of a daughter, Goodwife Brown being Midwife.

Sept. 18. Saturday, was that lamentable fight, when Capt. Latrop with sixty-four killed.[8]

Decem. 19. Sabbath day, that formidable engagement at Narraganset, 34 Engl[ish] put in one pit, 3 after Joseph Plummer, 26 gon already, 75 more pressed; advance towards Ipswich.[9]

Note: Wednesday Decemb. 29. '75 Mr. Reyner came hether in the even. Lodged with me. Upon enquiry he told me that one might not resolve to forsake such and such sins by reason of a jealousy that one should fall into the same again. He himself had experienced this, feared that he was not willing, because not resolved, till he saw it was through a foresight of the effects of his corrupt nature and infirmity.

[8] The frontier settlement of Deerfield had been attacked twice by Indians earlier in the month, and Captain Thomas Lathrop was evacuating the inhabitants. At the spot since called Bloody Brook, the company was ambushed by the Indians with the outcome that Sewall records.

[9] Sewall refers to the Great Swamp Fight in the Narragansett country at what is now South Kingston, R.I. Governor Josiah Winslow of New Plymouth, commander-in-chief of the forces of the United Colonies, had marched over 1000 soldiers and about 150 Indian allies from Smith's Garrison House (now Wickford, R.I.) on Saturday to Bull's Garrison at Pettaquamscutt near Tower Hill. Camping that night in the open, they resumed their march through deep snow at daybreak to the Indian fortification on an upland in the Great Swamp some fifteen miles west. An attack was made at the one vulnerable spot in the palisade, but was turned back with great losses. On the second attempt the English penetrated the fort and amid desperate fighting set fire to the wigwams. The English lost six captains among two hundred casualties, and the enemy losses were heavy; the power of the Narragansetts, routed and homeless, was broken forever.

King Philip's War, which lasted from June 1675 until Philip was killed in August 1676, was a series of Indian raids with retaliatory expeditions by the English. Sixteen towns in Massachusetts and four in Rhode Island were destroyed. Total war was resorted to by both sides, not sparing women and children in the alternating massacres. In proportion to the population, the war inflicted greater casualties than any other war in our history. See Douglas Edward Leach's modern study, Flintlock and Tomahawk (Macmillan, 1958).

1676

MARRIAGE TO HANNAH HULL / THE INDIAN WAR / TIM DWIGHT'S
SWOUN / DISSECTION OF THE BODY OF AN INDIAN / FAMILY ILLNESS
/ TRIP TO SANDWICH / GREAT FIRE IN BOSTON / BEGINNING OF
PRIVATE PRAYER-MEETINGS / SHAGGED DOGG STORY / DEATH OF
JOHN REYNER JR.

Lecture day Jan. 5. [1675/6] Hints of discourse.[1] One (speaking of
twelve +ide) said it may be we knew not 11 from 12. I said it was
best if (in that sense) we did not. In defence of Mr. Graves I said that
the Application of Xt's merits was a greater wonder than the sending
of Xt. into the world. That no person could be said to be mankind:
that such an one was not, which was thought very ridiculous. Jan. 3,
cold wether hindred writing till now.

Jan. 10, 1675/6. Felled the oak at the E. end of the house. *Matre et
Sorore valde plangentibus.*[2]

*Sewall made no diary entries of his courtship or his marriage. At the
age of sixty-eight, in his autobiographical letter, he told his son that his
"honoured Mother" had been invited by her uncle, Dr. Leonard Hoar,
the President of Harvard, and his lady, to be with them a while at Cambridge. At the commencement of 1674 Sewall came up for his M.A. "She
saw me when I took my Degree and set her affection on me, though I
knew nothing of it till after our Marriage."*

*On the 28th of February 1675/6 Sewall was married by Simon Brad-
street, Assistant, and later Governor of Massachusetts-Bay, to Hannah
Hull, only surviving child of John and Judith (Quincy) Hull. The wed-*

[1] The reader should be reminded that Sewall's manuscript of this portion of his
Diary is no longer in existence and that we are dependent upon fairly unsatis-
factory early copies. The text of this entry is certainly obscure. It appears that
Sewall attended the Thursday lecture in Boston and that the preacher was Thomas
Graves (Harvard 1656) of Charlestown, who was the tutor of Sewall's class at
college.
[2] In the centuries when America was being cleared and settled, trees were man's
enemies. It is interesting at this early date to find Sewall's mother and sister
beating their breasts in sorrow at the loss of this oak. Sewall wrote in a letter, 5
August 1712: "I cânt endure Trees of so great Bulk, near a house." *L.B.* II, 5.

ding was at John Hull's house on the east side of the main street of Boston (now Washington Street) between Summer and Pond (now Bedford) Streets, "in that we [now] call the Old Hall; 't was then all in one, a very large Room."

Hawthorne's story of the Sewall-Hull wedding in Grandfather's Chair must be regarded as a pleasant fiction. There is no evidence that Hannah was "round and plump as a pudding." Hawthorne pictures John Hull as ordering a great pair of scales brought in, placing Hannah in one pan and having servants fill up the other with pine-tree shillings till they balanced, then giving the shillings to Sewall as the daughter's portion with the remark that not every wife is worth her weight in silver. This is an agreeable picture, but one which cannot be justified by any direct authority. The editors of The Diaries of John Hull, published by the American Antiquarian Society in 1857, unearthed Sewall's own record in his ledger:

1675.	Dr.	1675.		Cr.
My Father-in-law, Mr.		Feb.11, By money received .		£30.0.0
John Hull, to his		Mar.13, " " "		35.0.0
Free Promise	£500.0.0	By balance when new Stated		
		Accts		435.0.0

Hannah's dowry was £500 (Hutchinson [Hist., 1, 152n] makes it 30,000l). Part of it was received seventeen days before the wedding, and another part a fortnight after the event; the balance was passed to a new account. The A.A.S. editors nevertheless point out that £500 would be ten thousand shillings, or fifteen hundred ounces of silver, and that this was one hundred and twenty-five pounds troy weight, "which is, perhaps, about the average weight of young ladies of her age."

April 5, Wednesday, Governour Winthrop dyes. Interred old Burying place Monday following.[3]

Nota bene. Friday about 3 in the afternoon, April 21, 1676, Capt. Wadsworth and Capt. Brocklebank fall. Almost an hundred, since, I hear, about fifty men, slain 3 miles off Sudbury: the said Town burned, Garrison houses except.[4]

[3] John Winthrop Jr., F.R.S., Governor of Connecticut, had come to Boston to attend a meeting of the Commissioners of the United Colonies. He was buried in his father's tomb in the first burial ground established in Boston, the area north of the present King's Chapel.
[4] Captain Samuel Wadsworth of Milton, with seventy men, were guarding the frontier at Marlborough. Learning that the enemy had appeared at Sudbury, they made an overnight march and engaged a force of about five hundred savages the next day. Only twenty Englishmen escaped death. Wadsworth and his lieutenant,

Sabbath day, evening, 23 April, considerable thunder shower. *Monday 24,* about 6 afternoon, a Woman taken, and a Man knocked in the head, at Menocticot, Braintrey.

April 25 Tuesday, Major Willard dyes at Charleston, buryed 27th. *April 26.* Mr. Lidget dyes: interred the 28th 1676.

Monday, May 8. Considerable Thunder and rain in the night. Mrs. Wharton Dyes: Buried Wednesday afternoon.

Tuesday, Fast, Magistrates, Deputies. Sisters sail toward Newbury.

Friday, May 5. 16 Indians killed: no English hurt: near Mendham. 19 May. Capt. Turner, 200 Indians. 22 May, about 12 Indians killed by Troop.[5]

Monday, May 9. Cold encreases mightily, all night burning Fever: next night rested indifferently.

Sabbath, May 14, 1676. 2 or 3 in the morning, Mr. Usher[6] dyes. At night Mr. Russel dyes, being drowned in flegm. Mr. Tho. Shepard buried Tuesd. 5, afternoon. Wednes: aftern. Mr. Usher buried. *Tuesd. 16.* Mr. Atwater dyes: buried Thursday following, after Lecture. Three such Funerals, one after another, imediately, I never before saw. Mr. Atwater was at meeting in the forenoon and afternoon the Sabbath before. N.B. As we came from the Funeral, we saw an huddle of persons, who were bringing Jabez Eaton that died just then in the street.

May 23, 1676. Fast at Mr. Gibbs for Mr. Thacher. *24,* he grows better, having taken reasonable [*medicine for*] health. N. B. Being distressed with melancholy and troubled concerning my State—I was relieved by Mr. Willards Sermon, especially at two places quoted, Ps.

John Sharp of Brookline, were slain on the field; five or six others were tortured to death. Captain Samuel Brocklebank was from Rowley. *Palfrey* III, 192-193, and *Savage.*

[5] Captain William Turner of Boston, in command of the English force in the upper towns on the Connecticut River, learned that a large party of Indians were planting and fishing around the upper falls of that river (now Turner's Falls). Making an overnight march with a hundred and eighty men, they killed about three hundred with the loss of only one man. On their return they were pressed by a large hostile force alerted by the tumult, and some forty men were lost on the way to Hatfield. Captain Turner was killed in Greenfield meadow. Captain Samuel Holyoke heroically protected the rear, but his strength was broken and he died a few months later. *Palfrey* III, 193-195, and *Savage.*

[6] Hezekiah Usher was a merchant and bookseller in Cambridge and after 1645 in Boston. He was agent for the Society for Propagating the Gospel among the Indians, and went to London in 1657-1658 to procure the types and paper with which Samuel Green of Cambridge printed John Eliot's Indian Bible in 1660-1663. *N.E.H.G.R.* XLVI, 434; G. P. Winship, *The Cambridge Press* (1945), *passim.*

16. ULT quoted for the latter part, which I (having a Bible) turned to and saw the beginning: I will shew thee the path of life. Jude 5. 24. Comfort against falling away.

Wednesday, May, 24, about 10 M., Capt. Davis dies, fever, he had been delirious severall times between while before his death.

Mr. Willard preaches the Lecture.

Mr. Woodrop, Hobart Ger[*shom and*] Nehem[*iah*], Phips, Weld, Taylor, came after lecture and sat with me. God grant we may sit together in heaven. *May 25.* Mr. Adams had a very pithy and pertinent discourse from Nahum 2. 2. Old Church.[7]

Monday, June 5. Mr. Hutchison chosen Capt., Mr. Turin, Lieut., Mr. Bendal, Ensign of the Artillery.

Tuesd. 6, late in the Afternoon, a violent wind, and thunder shower arose. Mr. Bendal, Mis. Bendal, Mr. James Edmunds, and a Quaker female were drowned: their Boat (in which coming from Nodle's Iland) being overset, and sinking by reason of ballast. Mr. Charles Lidget hardly escaped by the help of an oar.

Wednesday, June 7., 5 Afternoon Mr. Bendal, Mis, carried one after another, and laid by one another in the same grave. Eight young children. *Tuesday, June 6,* Hatfield fight, 5 English killed, about 14 Indians. *Wednesday, June 7,* Ninety Indians killed and taken by Connecticot ferry: 30 and odd by C[*apt. Daniel*] Henchman.[8]

June 10th, Received a Letter from Unckle St[*ephen*] Dummer, dated March 24, 1675 [-6] i. e. last March, for it was in answer to one wrote, Oct. 29. '75. Aunt Sarah died about a year and ½ before. Peace and plenty. Nothing of Father's buisiness.

---

[7] Cotton Mather lists William Woodrop of Lancaster in the *Magnalia* as a nonconformist driven from England, but he does not appear in A. G. Matthews' *Calamy Revised.* Sewall records his departure for England 12 July 1687. The Hobarts, classmates in 1667, were two of the five sons of the Rev. Peter Hobart of Hingham who were graduated from Harvard. The other gentlemen mentioned were classmates of Sewall in 1671. The Old Church was the First Church of Boston.

[8] Indians attacked Hatfield with a force of six or seven hundred on 30 May and burned several buildings. The flames were seen at Hadley, and twenty-five men were dispatched to relieve the place; on their way they encountered a detachment of a hundred and fifty savages, killed twenty-five of them and routed the rest with a loss of only five killed. After the affair at Turner's Falls, Major John Talcott of Hartford was sent there with two hundred and fifty English and two hundred Mohegans to form a junction at Brookfield with Captain Henchman, who was leading a force from Boston. On their way, both had successful engagements with the enemy, Talcott killing and capturing more than fifty in what is now Dudley, and Henchman killing six and taking twenty-nine prisoners near Lancaster. *Palfrey* III, 196-197.

June 16, 1676. Went with my Father to Mr. Smith's, there to see the manner of the Merchants.[9]

June 22. Two Indians, Capt. Tom and another, executed after Lecture.

Note, at the Execution I delivered 2 Letters, one to Unckle Steph, another enclosed to unckle Nath, unto John Pike, to be by him conveyed. Last week two killed by Taunton Scouts, as they were in the river, fishing.

Note. This week Troopers, a party, killed two men, and took an Indian Boy alive. Just between the Thanksgiving, June 29, and Sab. day, July, 2, Capt. Bradfords expedition 20 killed and taken, almost an 100 came in: Squaw Sachem. July 1., 9 Indians sold for 30£. Capt. Hincksman took a little before. The night after, James the Printer[10] and other Indians came into Cambridge. Father Sewall came Tuesday June 27. Went home Friday last of June.

Saturday, July 1, 1676. Mr. Hezekiah Willet slain by Naragansets, a little more than Gun-shot off from his house, his head taken off, body stript. Jethro, his Niger, was then taken: retaken by Capt. Bradford the Thorsday following. He saw the English and ran to them. He related Philip to be sound and well, about a 1000 Indians (all sorts) with him, but sickly: three died while he was there. Related that the Mount Hope Indians that knew Mr. Willet, were sorry for his death, mourned, kombed his head, and hung peag in his hair.

Saturday, July 8, 9 Indians, 2 English sallied out, slew 5 and took two alive. These Indians were killed not many miles from Dedham.

July 9, 10, &c. This week Indians come in at Plymouth to prove themselves faithful, fetch in others by force: among those discovered are some that murdered Mr. Clark's family: viz, two Indians: they accuse one of them that surrendered to the English. All three put to death.

Saturday, July 15. Quaker marcht through the town, crying, "Repent, &c." After, heard of an hundred twenty one Indians killed and taken. *Note.* One Englishman lost in the woods taken and tortured to

---

[9] By this time Sewall had given up the idea of entering the ministry, and was being introduced by John Hull to the business world, in which he soon became active.

[10] James Printer was a native Indian, son of a deacon of the church of "Praying Indians" at Grafton. He had been educated at the Indian School in Cambridge, and was an apprentice to Samuel Green, helping in the printing of Eliot's Bible. He ran off to join his own people in their assaults on the settlements of the English, but availed himself of a declaration of amnesty, returned, and was allowed to resume his trade. His name, with that of Green, is on the title-page, as printer of the Indian Psalter (1709). M.H.S.EDS.

death. Several Indians (now about) come in at Plymouth, behave themselves very well in discovering and taking others. Medfield men with volunteers, English and Indians, kill and take Canonicus with his son and 50 more.

July 27. Sagamore John comes in, brings Mattoonus and his sonne prisoner. Mattoonus shot to death the same day by John's men.

Friday, July 28. Mr. Chickery dyes, about 5, afternoon. Commencement day: Mr. Phips married.

Saturday Even. Aug. 12, 1676,[11] just as prayer ended Tim. Dwight sank down in a Swoun, and for a good space was as if he perceived not what was done to him: after, kicked and sprawled, knocking his hands and feet upon the floor like a distracted man. Was carried pickpack to bed by John Alcock, there his cloaths pulled off. In the night it seems he talked of ships, his master, father, and unckle Eliot. The Sabbath following Father went to him, spake to him to know what ailed him, asked if he would be prayed for, and for what he would desire his friends to pray. He answered, for more sight of sin, and God's healing grace. I asked him, being alone with him, whether his troubles were from some outward cause or spiritual. He answered, spiritual. I asked him why then he could not tell it his master, as well as any other, since it is the honour of any man to see sin and be sorry for it. He gave no answer, as I remember. Asked him if he would goe to meeting. He said, 'twas in vain for him; his day was out. I asked, what day: he answered, of Grace. I told him 'twas sin for any one to conclude themsclves Reprobate, that this was all one. He said he would speak more, but could not, &c. Notwithstanding all this semblance (and much more than is written) of compunction for Sin, 'tis to be feared that his trouble arose from a maid whom he passionately loved: for that when Mr. Dwight and his master had agreed to let him goe to her, he eftsoons grew well.[12]

Friday, Aug. 25. I spake to Tim of this, asked him whether his convictions were off. He answered, no. I told him how dangerous it was

---

[11] On this date Sewall wrote in his interleaved almanac, "Philipus exit." King Philip had been shot by an Indian in the English service at Mount Hope (Bristol, R.I.). As a traitor to the king, he was beheaded, drawn, and quartered, and his head was exhibited on a pole at Plymouth for many years. *D.A.B.*

[12] Timothy Dwight (1654-1691/2) was a son of Captain Timothy Dwight of Dedham by the second of his six wives. He was an apprentice to John Hull, learning the trade of goldsmith (i.e. silversmith), which he later practised in Boston. He left no descendants. *Savage.* John Alcock (1657-1690) was another apprentice residing in the Hull home, a son of Dr. John Alcock (Harvard 1646). Sewall had to speak to him about "his ill courses" 1 January 1687. Unckle Eliot was Deacon Jacob Eliot (1632-1693) of the South Church.

to make the convictions wrought by God's spirit a stalking horse to any other thing. Broke off, he being called away by Sam.

Sabbath day, Aug. 20, we heard the amazing newes of sixty persons killed at Quinebeck, by barbarous Indians, of which were Capt. Lake, Mr. Collicot, Mr. Padashell. *Dilati sunt in futurum.*

Aug. 27. We hear of Major Talcots coming on Indians travailing towards Albany, to dwell on this side Connect. river. He slew some, took others with most of the plunder.

Aug. 31. Cousin Annah Quinsey is taken ill of the flux, accompanied, as it is fear'd, with a Fever. *Note*, Aunt Quinsey is providentially here. My dear Mother, Mrs. Judith Hull grows sick the same night and is extreamly distrested.

Sept. 1. Her Face very much swelled. Night following, Mother's pains something abated: humours dissipated.

Sept. 3. Anna Quinsey Died about ten of the Clock, A. M.[13] Buried Monday Sept. 4. N. B. Cousin Anna's Water was carried to Dr. Snelling on Sab. morn. He affirmed her not to be dangerously ill. My Father-in-Law from the first feared her death, from her trembling pulse, restlessness, Wormes coming away without amendment, and the well-looking of her Water, when she was manifestly very ill.

Relations at the Funeral: Unckle and Aunt Quinsey, Parents, Epr. Savage, Ruth Quinsey, germans,[14] Experience, whom my Father led, Sam. and Hannah Sewall, Cousin Henchman, Pounden. Bearers, Henry Philips, Tim. Dwight, Joseph Tappin, John Alcock. *Note*. This is the first person (that I know of) buried out of an house where I was then dwelling.[15] The Lord in his mercy Sanctify it to me, and overcome death for me by Jesus Christ.

---

[13] Anna Quincy, a girl of thirteen, had been residing with the Hulls. She was the daughter of Edmund and Joanna (Hoar) Quincy and niece of Sewall's mother-in-law, Judith (Quincy) Hull. Our diarist used the appellatives of relationship very freely, never making any distinction between connections by blood and those by marriage.

[14] "Having the same parents" *O.E.D.*

[15] Although there is ample evidence in the Diary that Sewall and his wife resided with the Hulls from the time of their marriage in the house whose site is now covered by the Jordan Marsh store, the M.H.S. editors allowed themselves to be misled, and placed their residence on Cotton Hill in the present Pemberton Square area. The General Court on 15 October 1684 granted Sewall permission to build "a smale porch of wood" on "his house of wood in Boston, at the hill where the Reverend Mr. John Cotton formerly dwelt." This was a rental property, but the M.H.S. editors deposited the Sewalls there and resolutely ignored all data revealing a Washington Street domicile, such as the above entry and others to which we shall draw attention. See also 2 *M.H.S. Proc.* 1. 312-316.

Sept. 13. The after part of the day very rainy. Note, there were eight Indians shot to death on the Common, upon Wind-mill hill. This day a Souldier, Thom. Fisk, leaves part of a Libel here by accident. His debent. was signed to Muddy River, when it should have been to Cambridge, which he came to have altered. The paper he wrapt them in was wet, wherefore I profered him dry, that so his writings might not be spoyled. He accepted it and left his old wet paper, which, coming after into the room, I read.

Sept. 14, at night my Mother Hull, praised be God, had comfortable Rest.

Sept. 15. Friday, received Letters by Mr. Clark from my Unckle St[*ephen*] Dummer, to Father and Mother Sewall, where in he informs, "We do through some difficulty hear Mr. Cox[16] most Lords dayes." Letter to Mother of May 29, '76. In that to my Father of same dates, "Mr. Quinsey is copying out your Writings. He shall also take my Account. I am at a weak Hand. Something hangs about me like a consumption. You must imploy some other man in your Buisiness, for I think I shall not be able to doe it. You may see that the Leases (in that of June 20, mentions onely Stoak Lease) of your Bargains are almost run out. You must take some course to new Let your Land, or come and live in it, or else it will lye to the wide world, and nothing will be made of it &c." *Paulo ante.* "The Bill of £20 you ordered me to pay Tho. Papil. of London, I have paid, also Dr. Oakes, Jno. Saunders' Bills. Mis. Hatten's Bill is not yet paid. I am out of purse already, and if I pay hers I must borrow money, the which I think to doe this time, but hope that you or some other of my Cousins will come over, or get some other to doe your business here. I have done it a long time, and am unwilling to meddle of paying or receiving any more. I desire you would send me in your next what Goods and money you have received of mine. Before finishing my Letter in comes Mr. Quinsey, &c." [17]

My Aunt Mehetabel writes to Mother, May 26, '76. Informs that she hath four children living, viz: Thomas, Robert, Jane and Mehetabel. Cousin Thomas, enclosed "We have been in many fears for you, because your enemies are many, both at home and abroad. But I hope the Lord will deliver you out of all their Hands, in his due time."

Unckles of May 29, saith "before I finished my Letter, in comes

---

[16] Henry Coxe, minister of Bishop-Stoke.
[17] We omit here the text of a letter from Stephen Dummer to the elder Sewall, listing receipts of rents at Lee and Stoke covering fifteen years to Lady-day, 1676, £495.10.0, and disbursements of £525.14.2.

Mr. Quinsey. Mr. Quinsey's to me from London, is dated May 27, so that Mr. Quinsey made very little stay at Bishop Stoke: *ex consequentia.*

Sept. 16, '76. Mother Hull rested not so well on Friday night, as before. Mrs. Brown was buried, who died on Thursday night before, about 10 o'clock. *Note.* I holp'd carry her part of the way to the Grave. Put in a wooden Chest.

Sept. 18. Mr. Broughton and his son George being here, said Mr. George agreed to deliver up his Writings of the Mills, and give up the management of it to Father Hull. *Mement.* sent Letters to Newbury by Mr. G. B. *Imprimis,* a little packet 6 Letters, Stoke Lease, Unckles Account, one letter, which had enclosed two from England to my Father, Unckle Riders, Mary Gouldings: one to Mrs. Noyes, the last to Richard Smith.

Mr. Reyner, of Sept. 25, saith that their Indian Messengers returned the night before, and informed they saw two Indians dead, their Scalps taken off; one of them was Canonicus his Captain. 'Tis judged that Canonicus himself is also killed or taken by the same Hand, viz, of the Mohawks.

This day, viz, Sept. 18. Goodman Duee, meets with a Lively Spring, the Well 23 foot deep.

Sept. 19. Mane, Eliza Alcock informs that Mother had a good night, though she Rested ill on Sabbath day night. *Laus Deo qui orationem non vult non exaudire.*

Sept. 20. Judith Hull slept better last night than at all since her sickness. *Note,* mark Kerseyes, &c.

Sept. 21, '76. Stephen Goble of Concord, was executed for murder of Indians: three Indians for firing Eames his house, and murder.[18] The wether was cloudy and rawly cold, though little or no rain. Mr. Mighil prayed: four others sate on the Gallows, two men and two impudent Women, one of which, at least, Laughed on the Gallows, as several testified. Mothers last nights rest was inferiour to the former. Dr. Brackenbury called in here. *Note.* Mr. Joseph Gillam comes in from St. Michaels, five weeks pasage, Loading, Wheat, Wine.

Sept. 22, Spent the day from 9 in the M. with Mr. [Dr.] Brakenbury, Mr. Thomson, Butler, Hooper, Cragg, Pemberton, dissecting the middlemost of the Indian executed the day before. [*Hooper*] who,

---

[18] Stephen and Daniel Goble had killed three friendly Indians. Daniel was executed the 26th. On 1 February 1675/6 Indians had burned the house of Thomas Eames at Sherborn, killed his wife and some of his children, and captured others. *Savage.* Thomas Mighill (Harvard 1663) was then preaching in Milton.

taking the [*heart*] in his hand, affirmed it to be the stomack. I spent 18s., 6d, in Ale, 6d in Madera Wine, and 6d I gave to the maid.[19]

Sept. 23. Looked into Mr. Russels Accompts. Mother rests indifferent well now a-nights. Father ill of a pain caused in his shoulder, and then on his left side, by reason of taking cold.

Mr. Reynor, in a Letter dated at Salisbury, Sept. 21, '76., hath these passages: "God still is at work for us. One-ey'd John, with about 45 of your Southern Indians, have been apprehended since the Souldiers went Eastward. They we judge them All of our Southern Indians. And nothing yet lately heard of damage in the Eastern parts. A Sagamore of Quapaug is one of the Indians taken and sent. Canonicus we believe was killed by the Mohawks, when his Captain was slain. *N.B.* We have in our Business here great discoveries of our shameful Natures. Pray that the Sanctification and Reconciliation by Xt. may prevail to his honour."

Sept. 26, *Tuesday*, Dr. Hawkins takes away from my Mother Hull about 4 ounces of blood. Sagamore Sam goes, and Daniel Goble is drawn in a Cart upon bed cloaths to Execution. *I. Mat. Temp. pomor.* One ey'd John, Maliompe, Sagamore of Quapaug, General at Lancaster, &c, Jethro (the Father) walk to the Gallows. *Note.* One ey'd John accuses Sag. John to have fired the first at Quapaug, and killed Capt. Hutchison. Mothers two last nights were very restless.

Sep. 27, Brother John Sewall came to visit me. Told me of my friends Wellfare, and of the death of Goodman Titcomb last Sabbath day, after about a fortnight sickness of the Fever and Ague. One week or thereabout lay regardless of any person, and in great pain.

Sept. 28. Brought my Brother John going so far as the little Locust tree, beyond, the Caus[*ewa*]y, on the Neck.

Sept. 30. This morn. about the dawning of the day, H. Sewall is called up by the Flux, which it seems troubled her Friday in the afternoon, though unknown to me.

[19] Dr. Samuel Brackenbury (Harvard 1664) makes several appearances in the Diary at this time. He compiled an *Almanack* for 1667, joined the Second Church of Boston, preached for about two years at Rowley, and married Mercy, daughter of the Rev. Michael Wigglesworth. John Hull recorded his death 11 January 1677/8 from smallpox. This dissection, which was not an autopsy, but obviously performed from curiosity and for instruction, was a very early one here, preceded, it may be, only by Giles Firmin's "anatomy" in 1647. We feel that its significance escaped Albert Matthews (Early Autopsies and Anatomical Lectures, *C.S.M.* xix, 273-290). Of the participants, we venture to identify only three: Benjamin Tompson (Harvard 1662), schoolmaster, physician, and versewriter (see *D.A.B.*); Richard Hooper of Watertown, physician and surgeon; and Dr. Thomas Pemberton of Boston, later a surgeon in the Phips expedition, who died in the fleet-fever epidemic 26 July 1693 (*q.v.*). *Savage*.

Oct. 1, Sabbath day. The last night H. Sewall rose twice. Had sundry Stools this day. Mother recovers more and more. *Oct. 2.* H. S. had a very ill night and day. *Oct. 3.* Last night I watched. Han. S. had an extream restless night. 8 or 10 Stools. Dr. Brackenbury advises to Diacodium to move Rest, and approves Peppar boyled in Milk and Water, alike of each. Diacod. 6 ounces. Mother hath scarce any Rest. *Oct. 4.* Mis. Herlakendine Simonds watches: two stools. Considerable sleep. 6 ounces Diacod. I lodge in the Chamber over the Kitchen. Mother hath a very ill night: concerned for her daughter. I should have noted before that Dr. Brackenbury said such malignity in the lower bowels was most times accompanied with an extream binding in the upper, and therefore things tending to solubility most proper, though he was loath to give an absolute purge unless necessity required. Monday, first visit in the even. Tuesday two visits, to-day one.

Oct. 5. Wednesday. I lodge with my wife. Nurse Hurd watches. But one Stool, that in the morn., tho. slept not all night, yet rested indifferently. *Note.* Mother had very little or no sleep. Chirur. Hawkins Breaths two veins in her Foot, takes away about 7 or 8 ounces of blood. Drs. Brakenbury and Avery present. Dr. Avery saith the Diacodion would render persons faint. News of Canonicus Squaw and Sonne taken at Salmon Falls Mill, being seen as they went over the Boom. Information of Canonicus being killed by Mohawks (according with the first Story) and that they had not seen a fire of some weeks eastward. Wife rose in Lecture time.

Oct. 6. One Stool. I rose about 10., went not to bed again. Betty is taken ill. Mother rests finerly, had not Betty been ill. My wife sits up almost all day, without faintness: so that I mistrust Diacodion. *Oct. 7.* last night, H. and S. S. sleep together (small intervals except) till break of day, then I rise. She hath one Stool. Mother hath little or no sleep: Betty no good night. Cousin Mary Savage dies about noon. *Oct. 8.* Last night no Stool: all 3 sick persons had a very good night, praised be God. *Note.* this Even. Mr. Brak [*Dr. Brakenbury*] visits Mother, Wife; Dr. Alcock, Betty: both together at our chamber. *Oct. 9.* Sabbath night a good night of all hands. An hard Frost, *Teste Isabele Pierce Nutrice.*

Oct. 9. Cousin Mary Savage buried in the afternoon. Father and I at the Funeral.

Bro. Stephen visits me in the evening and tells me of a sad accident at Salem last Friday. A youth, when fowling, saw one by a pond with black hair, and was thereat frighted, supposing the person to be an Indian, and so shot and killed him: came home flying with the

fright for fear of more Indians. The next day found to be an Englishman shot dead. The Actour in prison.

Mr. Dwight tells that the Minister, Mr. Woodward, dyed ravingly
distracted. *Dei Semitæ investigabit*.[20]

Oct. 10. Last night, H. S. somewhat feverish, slept not so well as
formerly, yet indifferently; cheerly notwithstanding, this day. Violent
rain and cold. *Oct. 11.* Had a comfortable night, tho. rose once. *Oct.
12.* Had a comfortable night. Betty extream ill of the bloody Flux,
which almost casts Mother down.

Note, went not to Lecture. Two Indians executed.

Oct. 13. Mother and wife had a good night. Betty indifferent. *Mement.* Made an Hen Coop. Mr. Clark came and stood by me. He,
Capt. Henchman, C. Green, Mrs. Flint, Mrs. Plaisted, dined with
me.

Gave Mrs. Williams Letter and my own to Mr. Broughton to be
given Mr. Hill for conveyance.

Oct. 14. Last night very comfortable to wife and Mother. *Oct. 15,*
a good night. This day we have intelligence that the Garrison at
Blackpoint is surrendered to the Indians. *Note,* Capt. Scottow at
home, here at Boston.

16. Good night. Mr. Brackenbury, the 17*th*. Best night that mother
has yet had, slept without so much as dreaming. 18, 19, 20, all Good
nights. Mother conversant in the Kitchen and our chamber. My
Wife every day since the Sabbath goes to Mothers chamber without
hurt. 21. Good night, all Hands. Cousin Reynor comes to Town: in
the night passes to Braintrey, because of 's wife there.

A Copy of the first Letter I ever wrote to my Cousin, Mr. Edward
Hull:

Mʀ Edward H. ᴀɴᴅ Loving Cousin, Although I never saw you, yet
your Name, Affinity to me, and what I have heard concerning you, make
me desirous of your acquaintance and Correspondence. Your Remembrance to me in my Father's I take very kindly. And I, with your Cousin,
my Wife, do by these, heartily re-salute you. My Wife hath been dangerously ill, yet is now finely recovered and getting strength. It hath been
generally a sick summer with us. The Autumn promiseth better. As to our
enemies, God hath, in a great measure, given us to see our desire on them.

---

[20] Probably Hezekiah Woodward (1590-1675), schoolmaster, independent vicar
of Bray, Berkshire, B.A. of Balliol College, Oxford, and a prolific writer. His
daughter Sarah had married Daniel Henchman, schoolmaster of Boston. *D.N.B.,*
A. G. Matthews, *Calamy Revised;* H. F. G. Waters, *Genealogical Gleanings in
England* (1901), II, 1029-1030.

Most Ring leaders in the late Massacre have themselves had blood to drink, ending their lives by Bullets and Halters. Yet there is some trouble and bloodshed still in the more remote Eastern parts. What is past hath been so far from ushering in a Famine, that all sorts of Grain are very plenty and cheap. Sir, my Father in Law hath consigned to yourself two hh of Peltry, to be for his and my joint Account, as you will see by the Letter and Invoice. I shall not need to entreat your utmost care for the best Disposal of them according to what is prescribed you: which shall oblige the writer of these Lines, your loving friend and Kinsman,

SAMUEL SEWALL.

BOSTON, Oct. 23, 1676

Now dies Capt. Tho. Russel, well the preceding Sabbath, and intended for England in Mr. Anderson. *Homo prop. Deus disp. Omnia.* *Oct.* 22. Mother slept not so well as formerly, yet went to Church in the Afternoon.

Oct. 22. Musing at Noon and troubled at my untowardness in worship, God, he holp me to pray, Come, Lord Jesus, come quickly to put me into a better frame, taking possession of me. Troubled that I could love Xt. no more, it came into my mind that Xt. had exhibited himself to be seen in the Sacrament, the Lords Supper, and I conceived that my want of Love was, that I could see Xt. no more clearly. *Vid.* Mr. Thacher Dec. 10. 2^d Answer to the objection under the 2^d Reason. *Vid.* Mr. Shepard, Dec. 15. Use 3. *Vid.* Mr. Thacher, Decr 17. Direction 9. which I am sure was spoken to me. The Lord set it home efficaciously by his Spirit, that I may have the perfect Love which casts out fear.

Oct. 23. Went from Boston about five T. P. [*tempore post-meridiano*] to Milton, there accidentally meeting with Moses Collier, Mr. Senderlen and I went on to Hingham, to John Jacobs. *Oct.* 24, Tuesday, went from thence to Plymouth, about noon; refreshed there. *Note,* James Percival met us there, and so we went cheerfully together from thence about 2. T. P.; got to Sandwich about a quarter of an hour by sun: lodged at Percivals with Mr. Senderlen. *Oct.* 25, Wednesday, Breakfasted at Stephen Skiphs. He, Percival and I rode out about 12 miles, within sight of Marthah's Vinyard, to look Horses: at last happily came on 11, whereof five my Fathers, viz, three chessnut coloured Mares, and 2 Colts: put them in Mr. Bourns sheeppen all night.[21] *Note.* Supper at Mr. Smiths, good Supper. *Oct.* 26,

21 John Hull owned a herd of horses which roamed at large "in the wilderness called Wequoiett" [Waquoit] on Cape Cod. Later he bred horses on his Narragansett lands. S. E. Morison, *Builders of the Bay Colony* (1930), 179-180. Mr.

Thursday, Took up the young four yeer old Mare, slit the two near ears of the Colts, their colour was a chesnut Sorrel, whiteish Manes and Tails. The Bigger had all his Hoofs white: the Lesser all Black. Both Stone-Colts. The Hair of the Tails cut square with a knife. After this Mr. Smith rode with me and shewed me the place which some had thought to cut, for to make a passage from the South Sea to the North: said 'twas about a mile and a half between the utmost flowing of the two Seas in Herring River and Scusset, the land very low and level, Herrin River exceeding Pleasant by reason that it runs pretty broad, shallow, of an equal depth, and upon white sand. Showed me also the 3 Hills on the which 4 towns kept Warders, before which was such an Isthmus of about 3 miles and barren plain, that scarce any thing might pass unseen. Moniment Harbour said to be very good. *Note.* Had a very good Supper at Mr. Dexter's. Being in trouble how to bring along my Mare, in came one Downing and Benjamin his son, who, being asked, to my gladness promised Assistance. *Oct.* 27, Got very well to Plymouth, Tailing my Mare, and Ben strapping her on, though we were fain to come over the Clifts the upper way because of the flowing Tide. There saw Acorns upon bushes about a foot high, which they call running Oak; it is content with that Stature. From Plimouth Ben and 's father mounted a Trifle before me, I waved my Hat and Hankerchief to them, but they left me to toil with my tired jade: was fain at last to untail and so drive them before me, at last ride and lead the Mare with great difficulty. When came to Jones his Bridge, (supposing the house had been just by) put the bridle on the Horses neck, drove him on the Bridge, holding the Halter in my Hand. When I came on the other side, could not catch my Horse, but tired myself leading my tired Mare sometimes on the left Hand into the Marsh, sometimes on the right Hand: at last left him, went to the Bridge to ensure myself of the path, so led her to Tracies about ½ mile. He not at Home, could scarce get them to entertain me, though 'twas night. At length his son John put up my Mare, then took up his own Horse, and so helped me to look for mine, but could not find him: after his Father and he went on foot, and met him almost at the House, Saddle Cover lost, which John found in the Morn. *Oct. 28*, Saturday, Goodman Tracy directed and set me in the way, so I went all alone to the end, almost, of rocky plain, then, by God's good providence, Mr. Senderlen overtook me, so we came along cheerfully together, called at my Aunt's [*in Brain-*

Senderlen is probably John Sunderland, formerly a parchment-maker in Boston, who had removed to Eastham. Stephen Skiff of Sandwich was at various times selectman, constable, and representative. *Savage.*

tree], refreshed, left my tired jade there, set out to Boston–ward about half an hour by Sun, and got well home before shutting in, Praised be God. *Note.* Seeing the wonderfull works of God in the journeye, I was thereby more perswaded of his justice, and inhability to do any wrong: put in mind likewise of Mr. Thachers Sermon, Oct. 22.

> The Humble Springs of stately Sandwich Beach
> To all Inferiours may observance teach,
> They (without Complement) do all concur,
> Praying the Sea, Accept our Duty, Sir,
> He mild severe, I've (now) no need: and when–
> As you are come: go back and come agen.[22]

Novem. 6. Very Cold blustering wether. *Note,* I and John went on board of Mr. Downe, to see Father's Horse and my Mare Shipped. 7, clear wether. *Wednesday,* cloudy. In the night great deal of rain fell. *Thurs.* Thanksgiving day, cloudy, soultry, wind, S. E. *Friday, Nov.* 10 clears up, westerly, wind roars. Mr. Downe sets sail.

Nov. 11. Brave, mild, clear whether, and fresh Gale of Wind.

Novem. 27, 1676, about 5 M. Boston's greatest Fire[23] brake forth at Mr. Moors, through the default of a Taylour Boy, who rising alone and early to work, fell asleep and let his Light fire the House, which gave fire to the next, so that about fifty Landlords were despoyled of their Housing. *N. B.* The House of the Man of God, Mr. Mather, and Gods House were burnt with fire. Yet God mingled mercy, and sent a considerable rain, which gave check in great measure to the (otherwise) masterless flames: lasted all the time of the fire, though fair before and after. Mr. Mather saved his Books and other Goods.

Dec. 12, Mr. Ben. Davis came from on Board Boon at Marthah's Vinyard to Boston on foot.

Dec. 13, Cousin Savage, my wife and self, visited Mr. Hezekiah Usher and his wife (*Note,* that she spake for Jane) where saw Mr. Davis. This day at even went to a private meeting held at Mr. Nath.

---

22 Sewall rewrote this verse, substituted Plimouth for Sandwich, and published it in the *Boston News-Letter,* 28 March 1723, with the title: "Upon the Springs issuing out from the foot of Plimouth Beach, and running out into the Ocean." 23 This was the second great fire in Boston, the first being in 1653. About five houses were blown up to prevent the spreading of the fire, yet when it was over, a large part of the north end of Boston was in ruins, including the Second Church in Clarke's Square. Increase Mather lost less than "a Hundred books from above a Thousand" his son Cotton reported in *Parentator* (1724), and "Of these also he had an immediate Recruit, by a Generous Offer which the Honourable Mrs. Bridget [Lisle] Hoar made him, to take what he Pleased from the Library of her Deceased Husband [President Leonard Hoar]." M.H.S.EDS.

Williams's. Emans, Smith spake well to Script. Philip 2. 3. latter part.[24] Smith spake more to my satisfaction than before. *Note,* The first Conference meeting that ever I was at, was at our House, Aug. 30, '76 at which Anna Quinsey was standing against the Closet door next the Entry. Mr. Smith spake to Ps. 119. 9. The next was Oct. 18, at Mis. Olivers: Capt. Henchman spake well to Heb. 6. 18. The Wednesday following [*Oct.* 25] I was at Sandwich. The 3ᵈ at Mr. Hill's. Goodm. Needam and my Father spake to Heb. 3. 12. Nov. 1. The 4ᵗʰ, Nov. 15, at Mr. Wings where Mr. Willard spake well to that proper place, Malach, 3, 16. The 5ᵗʰ, at Mrs. Tappins, where Mr. Sanford and Mr. Noyes spake to 1 Peter, 5. 7. Nov. 22. Mr. Fox prayed after. 6ᵗʰ, Nov. 29, at Mrs. Aldens, where Mr. Williams and Wing spake to Heb. 5. 7. Dec. 6. no meeting because of the ensuing Fast. The 7ᵗʰ. at Mr. Williams's mentioned first.

Dec. 14, 1676, Seth Shove was brought to our House to dwell, i.e. Father Hull's.[25] *N. B.* In the evening, seeing a shagged dogg in the Kitchin, I spake to John Alcock, *I am afraid we shall be troubled with that ugly dogg:* whereupon John asked which way he went. I said out at the Street door. He presently went that way, and meeting Seth (who went out a little before) took him for the dogg, and smote him so hard upon the bare head with a pipe staff, or something like it, that it grieved me that he had strook the dogg so hard. There arose a considerable wheal in the childs head, but it seems the weapon smote him plain, for the Rising was almost from the forehead to the Crown, grew well quickly, wearing a Cap that night. 'Twas God's mercy the stick and manner of the blow was not such as to have spilled his Brains on the Ground. The Devil, (I think) seemed to be angry at the childs coming to dwell here. Written, Dec. 18, '76.

Dec. 18, Mr. Rowlandson and Mr. Willard came and visited my Father. While they were here, Mr. Shepard also came in[26] and dis-

---

[24] This was the beginning of a series of private prayer-meetings conducted by Hull, Sewall, and their neighbors, which went on for several years.

[25] Seth Shove, a lad of nine, was the son of the Rev. George Shove of Taunton, who had recently brought a second wife into the parsonage. *Savage.* Sewall sent him to Harvard, where he was graduated in 1687, and paid his expenses to come and get his M.A. in 1690. Shove taught school at Newbury, and was minister at Danbury, Connecticut, for thirty-nine years. *Sibley.* Readers are invited to observe Clue No. 2 to Sewall's residence in the first sentence of the entry.

[26] The clergymen who visited Hull were Thomas Shepard of Charlestown (Harvard 1653); Samuel Willard (Harvard 1659), who had been driven from his pastorate in Groton in March by Indian raids and was shortly to become colleague-pastor of the South Church; and Joseph Rowlandson (Harvard 1652), who had gone through worse horrors in February when seventeen of his family or connections were killed or taken prisoners by the Indians at Lancaster. *Sibley.* Mrs.

coursed of Reformation, especially the disorderly Meetings of Quakers and Anabaptists: thought if all did agree, i.e. Magistrates and Ministers, the former might easily be suprest, and that then, The Magistrates would see reason to Handle the latter. As to what it might injure the country in respect of England, trust God with it. Wished, (speaking of Mr. Dean's) that all the children in the country were baptised, that religion without it come to nothing. Before Mr. Shepards coming in, one might gather by Mr. Willards speech that there was some Animosity in him toward Mr. Mather: for that he said he chose the Afternoon that so he might have a copious auditory: and that when the Town House was offered him to preach to his Church distinct, said he would not preach in a corner.

Dec. 20, Went to the Meeting at Capt. Scottows, where Edward Allin and John Hayward spoke to Prov. 3. 11. How get such a Frame as neither to Faint nor Despise. (8) meeting. Mis. Usher lyes very sick of an Inflammation in the Throat, which began on Monday. Called at her House coming home, to tell Mr. Fosterling's Receipt, i.e. A Swallows Nest (the inside) stamped and applied to the throat outwardly.

Væ malum. Dec. 21, being Thorsday, Worthy Mr. Reyner fell asleep: was taken with a violent vomiting the Friday before, Lightheaded by Saturday, Lay speechless 24 hours, and then died on Thorsday even. We heard not that he was sick till Friday about 9 at night: on the Sabbath morn. comes William Furbur and brings the newes of Death. After last Exercise Father dispatches Tim to Braintry. Monday morn. Uncle and Tim come back. Uncle concludes from the Winter, his own infirmity and my Cousins indisposedness, to dispatch away Wm. Furbur with Letters onely. O how earnestly did I expect his coming hether, and say with myself, what makes him stay so long? I might have seen him as I went to Sandwich, but God had appointed I should see him no more. The Lord that lives forever, grant us a comfortable joyous meeting at Christ's appearance. *Note.* None of us saw Mr. Reyner Oct. 21, for he posted to Braintrey in the night, and he went back when I was at Sandwich.[27]

Rowlandson (Mary White) wrote an exceptionally able *Narrative* of her captivity and restoration, published first at Cambridge in 1682, which quickly became an American classic.

[27] John Reyner Jr. (Harvard 1663), minister of Dover, New Hampshire, was the son of John Reyner (B.A. Cambridge 1625/6), second minister of Plymouth and later minister of Dover. The son married Judith Quincy, cousin to Mrs. Sewall, and daughter of Edmund and Joanna Quincy of Braintree, at whose home he died. *Sibley.*

I suppose the last time that I saw and discoursed him was [*blank*].
He was here with Mr. Broughton earnestly urging to make sure Lands
of Mr. Broughton at Dover to my Father, and so take him Paymaster
for the annuity laid on it. Mr. Broughton withstood, and Mr. Reyner
feared it was because he would not let it go out of his hands, though
he pretended other things and seemed to reflect on Mr. Reyner. *Note.*
Mr. Reyner and I discoursed of it in the orchard, and he professed
his integrity in it, and that he thought Father would never have it
sure, if not that way. Advised me not to keep over much within, but
goe among men, and that thereby I should advantage myself.[28]

Decem. 27. Ninth Meeting that I have been at. Which was at
Edward Allin's. Script. Jer. 10. 24. *N. B.* Mr. Moody got me to supply his room: Capt. Scottow concluded.

Dec. 28. Mr. Willard preaches. *N. B.* I got but just to hear the
text. This day pleasant and smiling were it not the day of Mr.
Reyner's Funeral.

Dec. 30, *Saturday.* Capt. Henchman and I witnessed Mr. Dudlyes
Commission for collecting the Customs.

[28] George Broughton of Dover had married Abigail Reyner, sister of John Jr.

Vita fine literis eft Mortis Imago ; At
Vita fine Chrifto eft Morte pejor.

Si *CHRISTUM* difcis, nibil eft fi cætera nefcis.
Si *CHRISTUM* nefcis, nibil eft fi cætera difcis.

SAMUELIS SEWALL

Liber.

Anno Domini.

1677

BEGINNING OF BUSINESS CAREER / JOHN HULL LOSES HIS TEMPER /
JOINS THE SOUTH CHURCH / BIRTH OF HIS FIRST CHILD / QUAKER
DISTURBANCE AT SOUTH MEETING

*January 3, 1676/7. Mr. Nath. Oliver et Elizabetha Brattle, a
Simon Bradstreet, equit. connubio junguntur. Note.* This day we
have intelligence of Boon's being at Road Iland.

Jan. 6. Note. Mr. Dean came hether this morning, and spent a
considerable time in discoursing my Father. Advised me to Acquaint
myself with Merchants, and Invited me (courteously) to their Ca-
balls.[1] A great deal of rain last night and former part of this day.

Jan. 8. Bro. Stephen came to see us in the even: I walked out after
Supper and discoursed with him.

Jan. 9. Tuesday, at noon stepped out and visited Mr. Nath. and
Eliza. Oliver. Snowy day.

Jan. 10. Cloudy, Cold, noren wind. *Note,* went on foot to Mr.
Flints at Dorchester, there to be in the company of Ministers: but
none came save Mr. Torry. Mr. Fisk was gone to his sick Father:
Mr. Hubbard and Adams hindred (as conjectured) by the wether. So
that there was Mr. Flint, Mr. Torry, Elder Humphreys, John Hoar,
Mrs. Stoughton, Mis. Flint, Senior, Junior, Mis. Pool and her daughter Bethesda, with a Nurse named Clap. Notwithstanding the few-
ness of persons, the day (thro. Gods grace) was spent to good purpose.
Mr. Flint prayed, then preached singularly well from that place, Cant.
1. 6. But my own Vineyard have I not kept; which he handled well,

---

[1] Savage calls Thomas Dean "a merchant of extensive business." Sewall's business life began at this time, but any further details he may have recorded are
lacking because of the loss of eight years of the diary record. From 1685, when
the surviving record is resumed, he wrote almost nothing of his commercial activities, but his *Letter-Books* reveal him as an extensive exporter of mackerel and
codfish, whale oil, pork, shingles, beaver skins, cranberries, etc., and importer of
cotton-wool, sugar, rum, various fabrics from calicoes to broadcloth, tobacco-pipes,
books, oranges, and a great variety of manufactured articles. His trade was with
London, Bristol, Bilbao, Bermuda, and the Caribbean islands. Sewall also acted
as a trustee and private banker, and some of his letters read as if they had been
dictated in State Street or Wall Street last week.

Pressing every particular person to look to their own Souls. Elder H. prayed. After some pause (because the day much spent and I to goe home) Mr. Torrey prayed onely: which he did divinely, that we might not think strange of fiery Tryal, might be sure not to deceive ourselves as to our union with Christ. Indeed, the exercise was such, preaching and praying, as if God did intend it for me. I prayed earnestly before I went that God would shew me favour at the meeting, and I hope he will set home those things that were by him Carved for me. Mr. Flint sent his Man after the Exercise, so when I had well supped, comfortably rode home. Chief design (it seems) in Meeting to pray for Mr. Stoughton.[2]

Jan. 13, 1676/7. Giving my chickens meat, it came to my mind that I gave them nothing save Indian corn and water, and yet they eat it and thrived very well, and that that food was necessary for them, how mean soever, which much affected me and convinced what need I stood in of spiritual food, and that I should not nauseat daily duties of Prayer, &c.

Jan. 17. Wrote a letter to my Uncle St[*ephen*] Dummer, to desire him to pay Mr. Papil[*lon's*] Bill, and at present (at least) take care of my Fathers Lands, espec. Lee, writing down all his Receipts and payments, &c. Sent it in Father H's Packet to Cousin Hull.

Jan. 17. Went to the Meeting at Mis. Macharta's, which is the 10th I have been at. The Script. spoken to was Hoseah 6. 3. Then shall we have knowledge and cndcavour ourselves to know the Lord (as in the Translation I have by me). Capt. Henchman handled it.

Jan. 19. Father and self went to visit Mr. Sanford, who was very short-winded. He said he had been a careless Xn. And when I mentioned Mr. Dod's words, he said that was his very case, *viz:* he feared all he had done for God was out of hypocrisy. If so gracious and sober a man say so, what condition may it be expected many will be in on a Death-bed.

Monday, 2 of the Clock, P. M. *Jan,* 22. 1676/7. went to Mr. Thacher's, and spake to him about joyning to his Church.[3]

Jan. 22. Went to Mr. Thachers, found him at home, mentioned my desire of communion with his Church, rehearsed to him some of my discouragements, as, continuance in Sin, wandering in prayer. He said 'twas thought that was the Sin Paul speaks of, Rom. VII. At my coming away said he thought I ought to be encouraged.

2 The Rev. Josiah Flynt (Harvard 1664) was host for this prayer-meeting. Samuel Torrey was minister of Weymouth.
3 The Rev. Thomas Thacher had been minister of the South Church since its organization in 1669.

Wednesday, Jan. 24. Went to the 11ᵗʰ Meeting at Mr. Haywards, in the Chamber over Mr. Brattles Room, where G. James Hill and Joseph Davis spake to Job, 22. 21. Acquaint thyself with him, &c. *Note.* Mr. Brattle and his Son-in-law Mr. Oliver were there. See the Copy of the Letter wherein the Houses of some were threatened to be burnt. Jan. 23. 76/7.

Thorsday, Jan. 25, Mr. Numan was here, to whome and to Mr. Serjeant (who staid here near an hour) I showed the Copy of the Letter cast into the Governours the Tuesday before.

Jan. 26. Went to Charlestown Lecture, was ½ an hour too soon, so went in to Sir Allin, whether came also the Governour, his Lady, Mr., Mis. Dudley, Mr. Hubard, &c.

Jan. 30. Sent a letter to Cousin Quinsey, which enclosed a piece of Gold that cost me 23ˢ. Gave the Letter to Mr. Jesson. In it ordered to buy 2 pair of Silk Stockings, pink colored, black, 1 pair Tabby Bodyes, cloath-coloured, ½ wide and long wastied: also Turkish Alcoran, 2ᵈ Hand, Map of London. Sent him a copy of verses made on Mr. Reynor. *Jan. ult.,* sent a letter to Mr. Thacher, by the Bagg, in which Salutations, and some newes. *Wednesday, 31* Brother John Sewall brought down Sister Jane to live with Mrs. Usher, but the next morn I went to her and she gave me to understand that she thought Jane would not come, and so had supplyed herself. Father Hull kindly invited her to stay here till she should change her condition if she so liked. *Note.* Just now wanted a Maid very much, courted Goodwife Fellows Daughter: she could not come till spring: hard to find a good one. So that Jane came in a critical time.[4]

Feb. 2. Brother journeys homeward. Had him in to Dr. Brakenburyes as he went along, who judgeth he may cure him.

Feb. 8. John Holyday stands in the Pillory for Counterfieting a Lease, making false Bargains, &c. This morn. I visited Mr. Sanford, who desired me to remember his Christian (he hoped) Love to my Father Sewall, and mind him of Discourse had between them at Belchers, Cambridge, which he professed pleased him as much or more than any he had heard from any person before.

Feb. 10. Mr. Sanford dyes about 9 in the morning. Buried Sabbath day after Sun-set.

Feb. 7. Went to the 12ᵗʰ meeting at Mr. Morse his House, where

---

[4] Jane Sewall was then seventeen. In September she returned to Newbury and was married to Moses Gerrish. Sewall wrote to Madam Bridget (Hoar) Cotton in London, 12 April 1726: "When Madam Usher [Mrs. Cotton's mother] dwelt at Cambridge (where you were born) my sister Jane was her Maid; and now two or three of her Grandchildren are my Servants."

Mr. Gershom Hobart spake well to James 1. 19. *Feb. 14*, 13th Meeting at Goodman [*Joseph*] Davis's, where G[*oodman Joseph*] Tappin and Cousin [*Ephraim*] Savage spake to 1 Peter 1. 6. By which words I seriously considered that no godly man hath any more afflictions than what he hath need of: *qua meditatione mihi quidem die sequente usus fuit: nam socer (jam pene fervidus propter avenas sibi in consulto oblatas) de stipite æquo grandiore quem in ignem intempestive (ut aiebat) conjeci mihi iratus fuit, et si ita insipiens forem dixit se mihi fidem non habiturum, et ventosam mentem meam fore causativam. Deus det me sibi soli confidere, et creato nulli.* Psal 37. 3. 4. 5, *principium hujus psal. canebat conscius, quam propter ea quæ dicta sunt mœstus petivi.*[5]

Feb. 15. Having been often in my mind discouraged from joining to the Church by reason of the weakness, or some such undesirableness in many of its members: I was much relieved by the consideration of 1 Cor. 1. 26, 27. which came to my mind as I was at prayer. What is spoken there was set home on me, to take away my pride and be content with God's wisdom: thought it might seem to uncovenanted reason foolishness.

Having often been apt to break out against God himself as if he had made me a person that might be a fit subject of calamity, and that he led me into difficulties and perplexing miseries; I had my

---

[5] This passage, in Sewall's something-less-than-Ciceronian Latin, transmitted in an imperfect copy, was the subject of considerable study by the Rev. Samuel Sewall of Burlington (Harvard 1804), the last descendant to own the Diary, and his interpretation was published in *The Diaries of John Hull* (1857), 253-254:

"The general meaning of the passage . . . with the aid of a little conjecture, seems to be plainly this: Mr. Hull, being *much chafed* (pene fervidus, almost glowing with passion) at some one's bringing oats to him, as Treasurer of the Colony, in payment of taxes, instead of *money*, 'inconsulto,' without having previously consulted him, was angry with his son-in-law, Sewall, for throwing upon the fire, unseasonably, as he said, a larger billet of wood than was necessary or meet; and declared, that, if he would be so foolish, he should have no confidence in him: for that his mind would be as unstable as if it were akin to the wind.

"Now, all that Mr. Hull here said was doubtless said in a moment of irritation, which had been kindled by another occurrence, and soon subsided. But Mr. Sewall, always sensitive to every thing that looked like contempt or reproach, laid these words of his father-in-law much to heart; and, feeling that the severity of the reprimand was unprovoked and unmerited, he had recourse, for instruction or admonition, to the doctrine of the text discussed at 'the meeting' the preceding evening; and for consolation to the 37th Psalm, which, in his sorrow, he turned to for the sake of things said therein (or on account of the things which had been said to him), and the beginning of which, conscious of his not deserving the censure passed on him, he sang."

spirit calmed by considering what an absurd thing it was to say to God—"Why hast thou made me thus?," and startled at the daring height of such wickedness. These thoughts had reference to Isaiah XLV. 9, 10. This was at prayer time, *Feb. 19. Mane.* Death never looked so pleasingly on me as Feb. 18 upon the hearing of Mr. Thachers 3 Arguments. Methought it was rather a privilege to dye, and therein be conformed to Christ, than, remaining alive at his coming, to be changed.

In the thorsday even [*February 15*] Mr. Smith of Hingham speaks to me to solicit that his Son, and my former Bedfellow, Henry Smith, might obtain Mr. Sanfords House and authority therein to teach School. Sister Jane brought us in Beer. *Friday morn Feb. 16,* I go to Mrs. Sanford and (by her hint) to Mr. Frary, one of the overseers, who gave me some encouragement, and said that within a day or two, I should have an Answer.

Feb. 17. Wrote a Letter to Mr. Smith that Frary had given an encouraging answer, and that I thought no Delay was to be made least the Scholars should be lodged elsewhere. *Feb. 18.* The seats full of Scholars brought in by a Stranger who took Mr. Sanfords place: this I knew not of before.

Friday, Feb. 16. Brewed my Wives Groaning Beer.[6]

Feb. 21. Went to the 13th Meeting at Cousin Savage's; where my Father-in-Law and Goodman Needham spake to Psal. 6. 1.

Feb. 23, 1676/7. Mr. Torrey [*Rev. Samuel of Weymouth*] spake with my Father at Mrs. Norton's, told him that he would fain have me preach, and not leave off my studies to follow Merchandize. *Note.* The evening before, Feb. 22, I resolved (if I could get an opportunity) to speak with Mr. Torrey, and ask his Counsel as to coming into Church, about my estate, and the temptations that made me to fear. But he went home when I was at the Warehouse about Wood that Tho. Elkins brought.

Mar. 1. Was somewhat relieved by what John read occasionally out of Antipologia,[7] concerning the unwarrantable excuse that some make for not coming to the Sacrament: viz. unworthiness.

Satterday, Mar. 3, 1676/7 went to Mr. Norton to discourse with him about coming into the Church. He told me that he waited to

---

[6] The *O.E.D.* defines groaning-beer as a drink provided for attendants and visitors at a lying-in, and cites this entry of Sewall's.

[7] Thomas Goodwin and other Independents published *An Apologeticall Narration* (London, 1643); it was answered by Thomas Edwards with a volume called *Antapologia: Or, A Full Answer to the Apologeticall Narration of Mr. Goodwin* [*et al.*] (London, 1644).

see whether his faith were of the operation of God's spirit, and yet often said that he had very good hope of his good Estate, and that one might be of the Church (i. e. Mystical) though not joined to a particular Congregation. I objected that of Ames, he said *vere quærentibus*, the meaning was that such sought not God's kingdom in every thing. I said it was meant of not at all. He said, was unsettled, had thoughts of going out of the country: that in coming into Church there was a covenanting to watch over one another which carried with it a strict obligation. And at last, that he was for that way which was purely Independent. I urged what that was. He said that all of the Church were a royal Priesthood, all of them Prophets, and taught of God's Spirit, and that a few words from the heart were worth a great deal: intimating the Benefit of Brethrens prophesying: for this he cited Mr. Dell. I could not get any more. Dr. Mason (whom I have often seen with him) came in, after him Mr. Alden, so our Discourse was broken off.[8]

March 6,   O great Menasseh, were it not for thee,
             In hopes of Pardon, I could hardly be.

March 7. A pretty deal of Thunder this day. Went to the 14th Meeting at B. Needham's, where Mr. Noyes and Mr. Alden spake to 1 Sam. 15. 22. To obey better than Sacrifice, &c.

March 9, 1676/7, Cold and Clear. N. B. The corner House in the Street called Conney's, next the Harbour, toward the North end of the Town, was set on fire about four in the Morn, as is rationally conjectured: for the middle of the roof onely was fired, and upon a Roof of a Leanto that came under that there were several drops of Tallow. It was discovered by an ancient Woman rising early, and so prevented, praised be God. .

March 11. Thanks were returned by the Selectmen in behalf of the Town, for its preservation.

March 12. Went to the first Town Meeting that ever I was at in Boston. Capt. Brattle, Capt. Oliver, Mr. Joyliff, Mr. Lake, Mr. Turell, Mr. Allen, Deacon, Mr. Eliot, Deacon: the last pleaded hard, but could not get off. Severall Constables, Fin'd, as Mr. Hez. Usher, Mr. Jonath. Corwin.[9]

[8] John Norton shortly became minister of Hingham. The works of William Ames, English Puritan who taught at the University of Franeker, were held in high esteem by New Englanders at this time. William Dell, another Puritan writer, had been master of Gonville and Caius College, Cambridge. (Both are discussed in Morison, *H.C.S.C.*) Dr. Mason was probably Daniel Mason (Harvard 1666), who went as surgeon of a vessel from Charlestown and was captured by Barbary pirates. John Alden Jr. will come into these pages frequently.
[9] The Town Records show that John Joyliffe, Lt. Daniel Turine [Turrell], Capt.

March 13. Capt. Lake, the Remainder of his Corps, was honourably buried: Captains and Commissioners carried: no Magistrate save Major Clark there, because of the Court. I was not present because it was Tuesday.[10]

March 14. Visited Mr. Willard, and so forgot to goe to the Meeting at Mr. Smith's.

March 15. Mane, oravit Socer (indefinitè) ne simus oneri tentationi crucis locis quibus posuit nos providentia.

Mar. 15, even. Was holp affectionately to argue in prayer the promise of being heard because asking in Christ's name.

March 16. Dr. Alcock dyes about midnight. *Note,* Mrs. Williams told us presently after Dutyes how dangerously ill he was, and to get John to go for his Grandmother. I was glad of that Information, and resolved to goe and pray earnestly for him; but going into the Kitchin, fell into discourse with Tim about Mettals, and so took up the time. The Lord forgive me and help me not to be so slack for time to come, and so easy to disregard and let dye so good a Resolution. Dr. Alcock was 39 yeers old.[11]

March 19, 1676/7 Dr. Alcock was buried, at whoes Funeral I was. After it, went to Mr. Thachers. He not within, so walkt with Capt. Scottow on the Change till about 5, then went again, yet he not come. At last came Elder Rainsford, after, Mr. Thacher, who took us up into his Chamber; went to prayer, then told me I had liberty to tell what God had done for my soul. After I had spoken, prayed again. Before I came away told him my Temptations to him alone, and bad him acquaint me if he knew any thing by me that might hinder justly my coming into Church. He said he thought I ought to be encouraged, and that my stirring up to it was of God.

March 19, 1676/7 Accidentally going to look about the woman of

---

Thomas Brattle, Mr. John Lake, Capt. James Oliver, Deacon Henry Allen and Deacon Jacob Eliot were chosen selectmen. Mr. Jonathan Corwin and Mr. Hezekiah Usher were chosen constables, but refused to serve and paid 10*l* each. *Boston Record Commrs. Report* VII, 107.

[10] Captain Thomas Lake was, with several others, surprised and killed by the Indians, on 14 August 1676, near a fort on Arowsick Island, Maine, during the continuance of the war at the eastward. He had escaped to another island, and his fate was not known, nor his mangled body recovered, till many months afterward. His monument may be seen on Copp's Hill. M.H.S.EDS.

[11] Dr. Samuel Alcock (Harvard 1659) was the son of Dr. George Alcock of Roxbury; his tuition at college was paid in considerable part by his father's patients, who are credited on the college books with barley malte, wheatt, a small weather [sheep], 3 small lambes, a turkey, 3 checkenes, etc. *Sibley,* and *C.S.M.* XXXI, 204.

Cana, Mr. Chauncye's Sermons on her, I at first dash turned to that
Sermon of the 7th and 14 March.

March 21, 1676/7. Father and self rode to Dorchester to the Fast,
which is the first time that ever I was in that [*new*] Meeting-House.
So was absent from the private Meetings.

March 21. *Mane.* God holp me affectionately to pray for a communication of his Spirit in attending on him at Dorchester, and the
night before I read the 9th and 10th of Nehemiah, out of which Mr.
Mather happened to take his Text, which he handled to good purpose, and more taking it was with me because I had perused those
chapters for my fitting to attend on that exercise. Mr. Flint prayed
admirably in the morn, & pressed much our inability to keep Covenant with God, and therefore begged God's Spirit. Mr. Thacher began the afternoon: then Mr. Flint preached and so concluded.

Note.[12] I have been of a long time loth to enter into strict
Bonds with God, the sinfullness and hypochrisy of which God hath
showed me by reading of a Sermon that Mr. [*Cornelius*] Burgess
preached before the House of Commons, Nov. 17, 1640, and by the
forementioned Sermons and prayers. *Omnia in bonum mihi vertas,
O Deus.* I found the Sermon accidentally in Mr. Norton's Study.

Remember, since I had thoughts of joining to the Church, I have
been exceedingly tormented in my mind, sometimes lest the Third
church [*the South*] should not be in God's way in breaking off from
the old. (I resolved to speak with Mr. Torrey about that, but he passed
home when I was called to buisiness at the Warehouse. Another time
I got Mr. Japheth Hobart to promise me a Meeting at our House
after Lecture,—but she that is now his wife, being in town, prevented him.) Sometimes with my own unfitness and want of Grace:
yet through importunity of friends, and hope that God might communicate himself to me in the ordinance, and because of my child
(then hoped for) its being baptised, I offered myself, and was not
refused. Besides what I had written, when I was speaking [*about admission to the church*] I resolved to confess what a great Sinner I
had been, but going on in the method of the Paper, it came not to
my mind. And now that Scruple of the Church vanished, and I began
to be more afraid of myself. And on Saturday Goodman Walker[13]

---

12 This note was dated March 1678/9 by the M.H.S. editors. In the manuscript
it is without date and follows the entry of 21 March 1676/7.
13 Robert Walker, linen-webster, was one of the founders of the South Church
in 1669; he made an affidavit in 1679 that he had known Sewall's father and
grandfather in England. *N.E.H.G.R.* vii, 46.

came in, who used to be very familiar with me. But he said nothing of my coming into the Church, nor wished God to show me grace therein, at which I was almost overwhelmed, as thinking that he deemed me unfit for it. And I could hardly sit down to the Lord's Table. But I feared that if I went away I might be less fit next time, and thought that it would be strange for me who was just then joined to the Church, to withdraw, wherefore I stayed. But I never experienced more unbelief. I feared at least that I did not believe there was such an one as Jesus Xt., and yet was afraid that because I came to the ordinance without belief, that for the abuse of Xt. I should be stricken dead; yet I had some earnest desires that Xt. would, before the ordinance were done, though it were when he was just going away, give me some glimpse of himself; but I perceived none. Yet I seemed then to desire the coming of the next Sacrament day, that I might do better, and was stirred up hereby dreadfully to seek God who many times before had touched my heart by Mr. Thacher's praying and preaching more than now. The Lord pardon my former grieving of his Spirit, and circumcise my heart to love him with all my heart and soul.

March 22. 23. Plenty of Rain after a great deal of dry and pleasant wether. In the afternoon of the 23ᵈ, Seth and I gather what herbs we could get, as Yarrow, Garglio, &c.

March 26, 1677. Mr. Philips arrives from Scotland, brings the Newes of the Messengers Arrival about the beginning of December. They send Letters of the latter end of January. Brought likewise the lamentable newes of Mr. Samuel Danforth's Death, of the Small Pox.[14]

March 30, 1677. I, together with Gilbert Cole, was admitted into Mr. Thacher's Church, making a Solemn covenant to take the L. Jehovah for our God, and to walk in Brotherly Love and watchfulness to Edification. Goodm. Cole first spake, then I, then the Relations of the Women were read: as we spake so were we admitted; then alltogether covenanted. Prayed before, and after.[15]

---

[14] This was the first death to occur among Sewall's classmates. Sewall outlived them all.

[15] Our diarist was a devoted member of the South Church for the rest of his life, and had the satisfaction of seeing his son Joseph become pastor. The extensive extracts from the Diary in the *Historical Catalogue* (1883) and the *History of the Old South Church* by Hamilton Andrews Hill (1890) testify to Sewall's great interest in the organization and in the lives of its members. The Relations mentioned were the statements of religious experience of the candidates; the men gave them orally and those of the women were read from accounts previously recorded by the pastor.

Mar. 31. Old Mr. Oakes[16] came hether, so I wrote a Letter to his Son, after this tenour:

Sir, I have been, and am, under great exercise of mind with regard to my Spiritual Estate. Wherefore I do earnestly desire that you would bear me on your heart tomorrow in Prayer, that God would give me a true Godly Sorrow for Sin, as such: Love to himself and Christ, that I may admire his goodness, grace, kindness in that way of saving man, which I greatly want. I think I shall sit down tomorrow to the Lords Table, and I fear I shall be an unworthy partaker. Those words, *If your own hearts condemn you, God is greater, and knoweth all things,* have often affrighted me.

Samuel Sewall

April 1, 1677. About Two of the Clock at night I waked and perceived my wife ill: asked her to call Mother. She said I should goe to prayer, then she would tell me. Then I rose, lighted a Candle at Father's fire, that had been raked up from Saturday night, kindled a Fire in the chamber, and after 5 when our folks up, went and gave Mother warning. She came and bad me call the Midwife, Goodwife Weeden, which I did. But my Wives pains went away in a great measure after she was up; toward night came on again, and about a quarter of an hour after ten at night, April 2, Father and I sitting in the great Hall, heard the child cry, whereas we were afraid 'twould have been 12 before she would have been brought to Bed. Went home with the Midwife about 2 o'clock, carrying her Stool, whoes parts were included in a Bagg. Met with the Watch at Mr. Rocks Brew house, who bad us stand, enquired what we were. I told the Woman's occupation, so they bad God bless our labours, and let us pass. The first Woman the Child sucked was Bridget Davenport.

April 3. Cousin Flint came to us. She said we ought to lay scarlet on the Child's head for that it had received some harm. Nurse Hurd watches. *April* 4. Clear cold weather. Goodwife Ellis watches. *April* 7, Saturday, first laboured to cause the child suck his mother, which he scarce did at all. In the afternoon my Wife set up, and he sucked the right Breast bravely, that had the best nipple.

April 8, 1677. Sabbath day, rainy and stormy in the morning, but in the afternoon fair and sunshine, though a blustering Wind; so Eliz. Weeden, the Midwife, brought the Infant to the third Church when Sermon was about half done in the afternoon, Mr. Thacher

[16] Edward Oakes of Cambridge, lieutenant in King Philip's war, selectman and representative, was the father of President Urian Oakes of Harvard. *Savage.*

preaching. After Sermon and Prayer, Mr. Thacher prayed for Capt. Scottow's Cousin and it, then I named him John, and Mr. Thacher baptized him into the name of the Father, Son, and H. Ghost. The Lord give the Father and Son may be convinced of and washed from Sin in the blood of Christ.

April 9, morn. hot and gloomy with scattered Clouds: about 11 clock there fell a considerable Storm of Hail, after that it thundered a pretty while. [*Note*] The Child sucked his Mothers left Brest well as she laid in the Bed, notwithstanding the shortness of the Nipple.

April 4th was at the 15th Meeting, kept at our house in the little Hall, because of my wives weakness. Mr. Scottow spoke to Is. 27. 9. *prin.*

April 11 Stormy, blustering fore part, left raining a little before night. Went to the 16th Meeting at B. Easts, where Br. Edward Allen and John Hayward spake to John 6. 57, which was very Suitable for me, and I hope God did me some good at that meeting as to my Love to Christ. We heard after of the Slaughter of some persons at York by the Indians, among whom was Isaac Smith, who went thether about boards. This is Isaac Smith of Winnesimmet.

April 9, 1677. Seth Shove began to goe to School to Mr. Smith.

April 18. My Father-in-Law and I went on foot to Dorchester, so were not at the Meeting. 'Twas a cold blustering day, as the last of March, and almost all this month has been very cold. Mr. Adams at Supper told of his wife being brought to bed of a Son about three weeks before, whom he named Eliphelet.

April 25. *even.* Mr. Gershom and Nehemiah Hobart gave me a visit.

April 27, *Friday.* Hannah Henchman and Susannah Everenden with two Eastern women taken into Church. Warm fair wether these two dayes. *April* 28. Considerable Claps of Thunder.

April 28, 1677. Mr. Moody was here, he told me that Mr. Parker dyed last Tuesday, and was buried on Thorsday. Mr. Hubbard preached his funeral Sermon. The Lord give me grace to follow my dear Master as he followed Christ, that I may at last get to heaven whether he has already gone.

April 30. Went to Mr. Oakes, carried him 50s, discoursed largely with him concerning my temptations: he exhorted me to study the Doctrine of Xt. well, to read Dr. Goodwin. Spake to him of the Doctor's death: he told me that he died of a Cough and Cold which he caught standing in the cold after being hot in going from the Ferry. Told me 'twas not safe to conceive a resemblance of Xt. in ones mind any more than to picture him. Read to me occasionally part of his Sermon yesterday, wherein he amply proved the confirmation and gathering together in a head the elect Angels in Xt. Heb. 12. 22, 33: *cum multis aliis.*[17]

Note. [*May Training, no date*] I went out this morning without private prayer and riding on the Common, thinking to escape the Souldiers (because of my fearfull Horse); notwithstanding there was a Company at a great distance which my Horse was so transported at that I could no way govern him, but was fain to let him go full speed, and hold my Hat under my Arm. The wind was Norwest, so that I suppose I took great cold in my ear thereby, and also by wearing a great thick Coat of my Fathers part of the day, because it rained, and then leaving it off. However it was, I felt my throat ill, the danger of which I thought had been now over with the winter, and so neglected it too much, relapsed, and grew very sick of it from Friday to Monday following, which was the worst day: after that it mended. Mr. Mather visited me and prayed on that day.

May 5, Saturday: Mr. Gillam arrived from the Streights. *May 9*, Mr. Tanner arrived from London, wherein came Mr. Thacher who brought news of the death of Mr. George Alcock, he dyed of the Pocks:[18] also *May 11* Mr. Thacher and his Sister Davenport were here.

May 15. Mr. Anderson's Vessel Arrived; as for himself, he dyed yesterday about 4 of the clock. *T. pomer.* [*i.e., tempore post-meridiano.*]

May 16, went to the 17th Meeting at B. Hills, where B. Tapin and Cousin Savage spake to Heb. 10. 24.

May 30, went to the 18th Meeting at Mr. Wings, where Mr. Thacher spake to the 4 last verses of 92 Psal.

June 4. Went to Plimouth. *June 6.* Returned.

June 13. Went to the 19th Meeting at B. Williams, where G. Needham and my Father spake to Ps. 119. 11.

June 17. Sabbath day about 7 m, John Sewall had a Convulsion Fit. He was asleep in the Cradle, and suddenly started, trembled, his

[17] This was a visit to President Oakes. Thomas Goodwin was president of Magdalen College, Oxford, in Cromwell's time and a prolific author. The doctor whose death is referred to was Samuel Alcock.

[18] George Alcock (Harvard 1673) was the son and grandson of physicians, and went to London, probably intending to follow their profession, but died of the smallpox, unmarried, in March 1676/7 at the age of twenty-one. A diploma, testifying to his attainment of the B.A. degree, dated 19 April 1676, is the earliest Harvard degree diploma that has survived. It was handed down in the family to A. Bronson Alcott of Concord and is now in the Harvard Archives. See C.S.M. xxviii, 350.

fingers contracted, his eyes starting and being distorted. I went to Mr. Brackenbury, and thence to Charlestown, and set him to the child.

June the nineteenth he had another about noon.

June 21, 1677. Just at the end of the Sermon (it made Mr. Allen break off the more abruptly) one Torrey, of Roxbury, gave a suddain and amazing cry which disturbed the whole Assembly. It seems he had the falling sickness. Tis to be feared the Quaker disturbance and this are ominous.

July 8, 1677. New Meeting House [*the third, or South*] Mane: In Sermon time there came in a female Quaker, in a Canvas Frock, her hair disshevelled and loose like a Periwigg, her face as black as ink, led by two other Quakers, and two other followed. It occasioned the greatest and most amazing uproar that I ever saw. Isaiah I. 12, 14.

July 11th *1677* Cousin Daniel Quinsey Came Home to our House, sayling by night from the Lands in Mr. Hammonds Boat, otherwise he had not been suffered to come on shore for that some of the ship (Genners) dyed of the Pocks and one is still sick.

1677-1684

The Sewall papers which were acquired by the Massachusetts Historical Society in 1869 did not include any diary record for the period from July 1677 to February 1684/5. References in the surviving papers indicate that Sewall continued his diary as usual during those years, but this manuscript has not turned up since. The editors of the 1878 edition of the Diary gathered up numerous items from Sewall's commonplace books, interleaved almanacs, and other sources in their endeavor to bridge this gap; some of them are jottings which Sewall undoubtedly expanded later into full diary entries, now lost. To these we have added a number of items from other sources, to present the recoverable record of Sewall's life in that period. The material in text-type is from Sewall's pen.

1677. *Sept. 12, 4 [Wednesday]. Legg appulit [Capt. Samuel Legg arrived]. 16, 1 [Sunday]. Eliezer Danford arrives. 19, 4 [Wednesday]. Hatfield. 23, 1 [Sunday]. Sam Bridgham. 24, M.G.J.S.*

1677. *Oct. 20, 7 [Saturday]. Capt. S. Mosely.*

1677. *Oct. 31, 4 [Wednesday]. Dorchester.*

De Autophonia. 1677, *Nov. 16. Friday,* day after publick Thanksgiving, Jn° Tomlin hanged himself in his Garret in the day time, fastening his Rope to a pin that held the Rafters at the pot.

Nov. 18 [1677]. Sabbathday one Williams, an old man, the Winnisimet Ferry man cut his own throat. *Vid. Diar.*

1677. *Dec. 14, 6 [Friday]. T. Smith.*

1677. *Dec. 21. Shephard.*

1677/8. *Jan'y 17, 4 [Wednesday]. Brackenbury.*

1677/8. *Jan'y 22, 3 [Tuesday]. Dorchester.*

1678, *Apr. 5th.* Mr. Josiah Allen, a young Merchant of a very good estate and Account, was slain on board of Benj. Gillam's ship by the accidental firing of a fowling piece, out of a Boat of Joss. Gillam, as they were going from the jolly Ship. *vid. Diar.*

1678. *May session of the General Court. "Mr. Sam: Seawall" was made a freeman of Massachusetts-Bay Colony. Mass. Bay Rec. v,538.*

1678. *May 3, Frid.* Welcome arrived from London.

1678. *May 23.* Johnson and Knott arrived.

June 11, 1678. Samuel Sewall, second son of S. and Han. S. was

Born. Baptized *per* Mr. Thomas Thacher June 16. I held him up.

1678. Aug. 23, 6 [*Friday*]. Watch begins to be warned out of my precincts.

[*1678. September*]. John Sewall, the Son of Samuel and Hannah S. was Born Apr. 2, 1677. . . . Dyed Sept. 11, 1678, and lyeth buried in the New burying place, on the South side of the grave of his great Grandfather, Mr. Robert Hull.

In the Fall 1678, I was seized with the Small Pocks and brought very near to death; so near that I was reported to be dead. But it pleased GOD of his Mercy to Recover me. (*From Sewall's autobiographical letter to his son.*) 1678. *Oct. 29, son Sewall taken sick of the same disease* [*small-pox*]. (*Diary of John Hull, p. 163*)

1678. Dec. 15, 1 [*Sunday*]. Returned to my own bed after my sickness of the Small Pox.

1678. Nov. 9, 7 [*Saturday*]. Mr. Jno. Noyes dies. 10. Buried. E. Thurston dies. Teste Sarah Noyes.

1678/9. Jan. 18, 7 [*Saturday*] and Feb. 15, 7. Visit Public Houses.

1678/9. *March 10. The Boston selectmen made the following choice Perambulators for Muddy Riuer wth Roxbury & Cambridge, Deas Jacob Eliott, John White, Junr Thomas Gardner Junr Mr John Vsher, Mr Benjn Dauis, Mr Sam^{ll} Seywall, who vpon the 15th day of Aprill next, are to meete with those sent from Cambridge at Symon Gates his house at nine of the clock in ye forenoone And with those of Roxberrie at two of the clocke, in ye afternoone at ye bounds corner where Bostone, Roxbury & Cambridge meete. (Boston Record Commrs. Report* VII, 127)

1678/9, March 16, 1 [*Sunday*]. Governour [*John*] Leverett dieth. 25, 3. Is buried.

167[8-]9. Mch. 18, 3 [*Tuesday*]. Const. Collation deferred.

1679. April 15, 3 [*Tuesday*]. Perambulation.

1679. April 30. Hannah Hitte.

1679. June 13, 5 [*Thursday*]. Laurenc Oakes dyes at night of the Small Pocks.

1679. June 24, 3 [*Tuesday*]. Miss Mary Adams dyed.

1679. June 25, 4 [*Wednesday*]. Mr. Samll Haugh dyed. S.S.C.

1679. July 10, Balston ar[*rived*].

1679/80. Feb. 3, 3 [*Tuesday*]. Hannah Sewall was Born, just after a great snow. Baptized Feb. 8 in the New-Meeting-House, *per* Mr. Samuel Willard. I held her up. Mr. Thatcher dyed in the Autumn, 1678.

May 21, 1680. I carry Sam. to Newbury, where his Grandmother nurses him till May [16]81, to see if change of air would help him against Convulsions; which hope it did, for hath had none there, nor since his coming home.

June 3, 1680. Mr. [*Samuel*] Torrey hath another sore Fit in Lectur-time, old Mr. [*John*] Eliot Preaching.

July 8 [1680], two Indians Kill'd and severall carried away by the Mohauks from Spy-Pond at Cambridge; it was done about 1 in the Morn. In the afternoon a Whirlwind ariseth (at first in a small Body) near Sam¹ Stones. Passeth on to Mat. Bridge. Passeth by Mat. Bridges (taking part of Stones Barn with it) Kills John Robbins who was at Hoe, breaking his Arm and jaw-bone. It hurled stones and brake off and transported Trees in an unusual manner.

1680. Aug. 24, 3 [*Tuesday*]. His Excellency, Thomas, Lord Cul-peper, Baron of Thorsway, Gov. of Virginia, came to Boston.

1680. Sept. 16. Sergt. Wait.

1680. Sept. 19. Marthah Clark, widow, 85 years old.

1680. Sept. 23, 5 [*Thursday*]. Dorch. Elder Bowld *occiditur a curru.* [*Elder John Bowles of Roxbury was killed by a cartwheel run-ning over him. Savage.*]

Nov. 7, 1680. A Negro Man and Woman Murdered themselves.

A certain dweller in the Town of Cambridge made away with him-self. In his bosom was a Writing to this effect that God did show mercy on great, grievous and desparat Sinners; and therefore he said that he hoped of mercy though he hanged himself.

Dec. 8, 1680. Mr. Edmund Quinsey married Mrs. Eliza. Eliot before Thos. Danforth, Esq.

Decʳ 18, 1680. Josiah Winslow, Esq. Govʳ of Plymouth, dyeth after sore Pain with the Gout and Griping. His flesh was opened to the bone on's leggs before he dyed. Thorsday Xr. 23, buried.

Wednesday Xr. 22, '80. John Russell, the Anabaptist minister is buried, scarce having time to read his Print in favour of that Sect; come over in the last ships, Jener or Foy.

1680/1 Jan. 10. Charles River frozen over, so to Nod[*dles*] Island.

1680/1. Jan. 11. D. Lawson.

Friday, January 14, 1680-1. Benjamin Thwing, Carpenter, one of the South-Church, was goeing from Mount-Hope to Rhode-Island in a Canoo with an Indian, was overset by the wind and Ice, drowned. The Indian escaped.

January 25, 1680-1. Tuesday. Thoˢ Eams drops down dead in the Morning at Mr. Pain's stable, as he and others saw Hay thrown before their Horses. He was come to Court about Sherborn Contro-versy with respect to their Meeting House, its Situation.

Feb. 1 [1680-1]. Schollars get sooner out of School than ordinary by reason of the Bell's being rung for fire; which was quenched at the House where it begun.

Last night one Dyer of Braintrey shot an Indian to death as he was breaking his window and attempting to get into his House against his will, Saying he would shoot him a Dogg, bec. would not let him come in to light his Pipe. Man was abed. Indian's gun found charg'd, cock[t] and prim'd in his Hand.

Tuesday night Febr. 1. Pet. Codnar an honest Fisherman goeing to come over the Draw-Bridge, (as is supposed), missed it and was Drowned: For Feb. 2, his dark Lantern was taken up out of the Crick by the wharf at Low-water. His is supposed to have fallen in about 7. the Tuesday night. Hath left a wife and Children.

Feb. 3 [1680-1]. Lectr. Newes is brought of Mr. Deans son Robinson, his Killing a Lion with his Axe at Andover. Not many weekes agoe a young man at New-Cambridge was Kill'd by a Tree himself Felled.

Friday Feb. 18. [1680-1]. Mr. Sam[l] Legg cast away, was bound for Barbados.

Tuesday, Feb. 22. [1680-1]. Eclips of the Moon. N[ote]. Mr. Samuel Worster, Deputy from Bradford, coming down to the Gen. Court, when he was within ¼ Mile of the first Houses of Lin, dyed: Mr. Gidney coming down from Salem saw him dead in the way, went to the next House where were two Men that first saw him; so gave a Warrant for a Jury and his Burial. [*Another entry for this day reads:*] Mr. Samuel Worster, Deputy for Bradford, coming to the Court on Foot, dyes on the Rode about ¼ mile short of the House at the end of the Town next Ipswich. Vid. P.78. Newes comes this day of nine men being found dead at Pigeon-Iland near Shelter Iland: 'tis feared it may be Jeremiah Jackson.

[22 *February* 1680-1] Sylvanus Davis went out on Saturday to carry Corn and other necessaryes to the Fort at Casco, is driven on the Sand, essaying to put in again in the Sabbath day storm. So the Corn lost and Souldiers disappointed. Men saved.

Thorsday, Feb. 24, 1680-1. This morn, the Wife of Mr. Elias Row is found dead in her bed; much blood about her, so some think she was choak'd with it. A Jury was impanelled and 6 grave matrons and a Chirurg[eon], to view the Corps to see if any Violence had been offered her: found none; she and her Husband seldom lay together; she was given to Drink and quarrelling. Her death puts in mind of the Proverb wherein we say such an one hath drunk more than he hath bled today.

1680/1 *Feb. 28.* Coragious South wind breaks the ice between Boston and Dorch* Neck. Hath been a very severe winter for snow and a constant continuance of cold weather; such as most affirm hath not been for many yeers.

Tuesday, March 8, 1680-1. Mr. Edward Mitchelson, Marshall-General is buried.

1680/1 *16 March. Sewall was added (as a reviser) to a committee chosen at a town meeting on the 8th to draw up a petition to the General Court "that some concideration might be had of the inconveniencie and damage this town sustaines for want of a proportionable nomber of Deputies in the Generall Court to our nomber of freemen." (Boston Record Commrs. Report VII, 142, 143)*

Sabbath-day, March 20, 1680-1. Thomas Woodbridge is so burnt in his own Fire, that he Dyeth of the insupportable Torment in about 12 Houres time. Newbury.

Not long agoe an Irish woman living by my Father Hull's Pasture, was found dead, without dore, having her forehead on her hands, as she lay on the ground. Great Rumours and Fears of trouble with the Indians. Persons to Carry a competent number of Arms to Meeting.

[*April 1681*] Major William Hathorn dyes April—.

1 Ap. '81. Note. At Connecticot the Noise of a Drumme in the air, Vollies of Shot, Report of Cannons have been Heard by divers; as pr. Letters rec'd this week.

[*April 1681*] Mr. Philip Nelson [*Harvard 1654*] of Rowley wanders away and is lost from Ap. 5, to Satterday Ap. 9. Rowley and Newbury seeking him; on Satterday is found, having walked out of his place to take the air; it was between two Rocks on Crane-Neck. See Bro. Longfellow's Letter.

Goodwife Everit, Winthrop, and Capt. Richard Woode dye suddainly, *vid. Diar.* P.102.

Sabbath-day, May the first, 1681. Mr. Angier of Cambridg, his Tenant dyes very suddainly and unexpectedly, having been at meeting and riding home with his Neighbor, Agur &c. Look in and smil'd on his wife through the Window, but sunk down before he got in at the doore, and his wife hearing a noise came out; but her Husband scarce spoke ten words before he utterly ceased to speak. The Newes of it came to us yesterday as we were at Dinner. About 3 weeks agoe a little Boy of Braintrey playing with a bean, in 's mouth, got it into his wind-Pipe, of which in six or seven dayes he dyed.

Monday, May 2. [*1681*]. Mr. Richard Hubbard of Ipswich Farms, dyeth suddainly in the afternoon, goeing to ly on's Bed after dinner was there found dead by his daughter accidentally goeing in thether. *teste* Guil. Gerrish, sen^r.

May 2 [1681]. Had discourse about putting the cross into colors. Captain Hall opposed, and said he would not till the Major [Denison] had it in his. Some spoke with the Major, it seems, that afternoon, and Mr. Mather was with him, who judged it not convenient to be done at this time. So is a stop put to it at present. (Quoted by Palfrey, III, 348n.)

Satterday, May 7th [1681], there was a Hurrican at Newbury, which blew down Rich. Bartlett's Barn, uncover'd Capt. Pierce's new house at the upper end of Chandler's Lane, blew down the chimneys.

July 11 [1681], Captain Walley, instead of having no cross at all, as I supposed, had it unveiled. . . . Captain Henchman's company and Townsend hindered Captain Walley's lodging their colors, stopping them at the bridge. (Quoted by Palfrey, III, 348n.)

[1681. 24 July]. The Reverend Mr. Urian Oakes dyeth July 24, 1681, Sabbath-day night, suddainly, as to most, who are startled at the newes, being just before the Commencement and he so Learned, Godly, Orthodox a Man and so Discerning of the Times. [*Another entry reads:*] The Reverend Mr. Urian Oakes, President of the College, and Pastour of Cambridge Church Died; scarce any Knowing of his Sickness till his Death was sadly told up and down the street, Monday July 25. *vid.* Diar. p. 109.

1681. July 28. Barrett arrives.

1681. Sept. 9, 6 [*Friday*]. *Autor* John Foster *obit.*[1]

1681. 12 October. "*Att a Gennerall Court, held at Boston . . . Mr Samuel Seawall, at the instance of some friends, wth respect to the accommodation of the publicke, being prevajled with to vndertake the management of the printing press in Boston, late vnder the improovement of Mr John Foster, deceased, liberty is accordingly granted to him for the same by this Court, and none may presume to sett vp any other presse wthout the like liberty first granted*" (*Massachusetts Bay Colony Records*, v, 323-324)

---

[1] John Foster (Harvard 1667) was the earliest wood-engraver of English America. In 1675 he bought the printing plant of Marmaduke Johnson, who had just died, and became the pioneer printer of Boston. The earliest portrait engraved in the colonies, a wood-cut of Rev. Richard Mather, was done by Foster, and it is generally conceded that he engraved the first map, the "White Hills" Map of New England (1677). He compiled several almanacs and wrote two papers on comets before his death at thirty-three. *D.A.B., Sibley*; S. A. Green, *John Foster* (1909); *Princeton Univ. Lib. Chronicle*, XIV, 177-182.

The Soveraign Efficacy of Divine Providence;

Over ruling and Omnipotently Difposing and Ordering all Humane Counfels and Affairs, Afferted, Demonftrated and Improved, in a *DISCOURSE* Evincing,

That (not any *Arm of Flefh*, but) the right Hand of the Moft high is it, that Swayeth the *Univerfal Scepter* of this Lower World's Government.

Oft Wheeling about the Prudenteft Management of the Profoundeft Plotts, of the Greateft on Earth; unto fuch, Iffues and Events, as are Amazingly contrary to all Humane Prbab'lities, and crofs to the Confident Expectation of Lookers on.

As Delivered in a

SERMON

Preached in *Cambridge*, on *Sept.* 10. 1677. Being the Day of *ARTILLERY ELECTION* there.

By Mr. *URIAN OAKES*, the late (and ftill to be Lamented) Reverend Paftor of the Church of Chrift in *Cambridge* : And Learned Prefident of *Harvard Colledge.*

Pfal. 29. 10. *The Lord fitteth upon the flood: yea the Lord fitteth King for ever.*
Ifai. 41. 14, 15. *Fear not thou worm of Jacob. I will help thee, faith the Lord, and thy Redeemer. Thou fhalt threfh the Mountains.*
Rom. 11. 36. *For of him, and through him, and to him, are all things: to whom be glory for ever. Amen.*

BOSTON In *NEW-ENGLAND*:
Printed for *Samuel Sewall.* 1682.

A check-list of Sewall's imprints is given in our Appendix.

Thorsday, Xr. 1, 1681. The well-accomplish'd merch^t and Accomptant, Mr. Paul Dudley dyed, being a little above 30 yeers old.

Xr. 13, '81. Jonathan Jackson's wife hangs herself in the lower room of her dwelling House near my Father's ware-House.

Xr. 17 [1681]. Foye arrives, in whom Mr. [*Edward*] Randolph and his new wife and family.

Xr. 25. They sit in Mr. Joyliff's Pue; and Mrs. Randolph is observed to make a curtesy at Mr. Willard's naming *Jesus*, even in Prayer time. Since dwells in Hez. Usher's House, where Ministers used to meet.

1681. 26 December. Samuel Sewall was surety on the town's book for Samuel Green, printer, and his family, that they should not be chargeable to the town. (Boston Rec. Commrs. Report x, 71)

1681. Thorsday, December 29th, Elizabeth Daughter of Sam^{ll} and Hannah Sewall is Born. Two of the chief Gentlewomen in Town dyed next Friday night, viz. Mrs. Mary Davis and Mrs. Eliza. Sargent.

Sabbath-day, January 1, 1681[-2]. Elizabeth is Baptized *per* Mr. Samuel Willard, I holding her up. Elizabeth Weeden was Midwife to my Wife bringing forth the four mentioned children [*John, Samuel, Hannah, and Elizabeth*].

Satterday, Feb. 11 [1681-2]. Is a bloody-colour'd Eclipse of the Moon, onely middle of the upper part of a duskish dark.

1681/2. Feb. 14, 3 [Tuesday]. Major Savage dyes, Rox[*bury*].

Feb. 15 [1681-2], Wednesday. 2 Houses and Barns burnt at Cambridge. Dep^t Govr [*Thomas Danforth*] hardly escaped. Sometime in the Court's sitting, there is a child born near the north Meeting-House, which hath no Tongue at all; or the Tongue grown fast to the roof of the Mouth; one finger too much on one Hand, and one too little on the other: And the Heels right opposite one to another, the Toes standing to the Right and left outward.

Feb. 15. [1681-2]. Tuesday, 14, past midnight, or Wednesday morn; —the Day the General Court was to sit upon adjournment;—Major Tho. Savage dyeth suddenly, very suddenly, having been well at the Wedding on Tuesday, and sup'd well at home afterward, and slept well till midnight or past.

Mar. 24, '81-2. Goodw. Fox dyes suddenly. The Town was sadly alarm'd the Tuesday night before at the Fire at Mr. Wing's, which, had the Wind promoted, a great part of the Town had been consumed, it being near or in the Center.

1682. July 12, 4 [Wednesday]. Wm. Taylour, Merc. *exit.*

1682. July 22, 7 [Saturday]. Col. Robert Richbell.

1682. Aug. 17, 5 [*Thursday*]. Blazing St[*ar*]. [Aug.] 23, 4 [*Wednesday*]. Seen in evening, plain.[2]

1682. [Aug.] 21, 2 [*Monday*]. The Rev. Mr. Isaac Foster buried.[3]

Thorsday, Novemb. 9, 1682. Cous. Dan¹ Quinsey Marries Mrs. Anne Shepard Before John Hull, esq. Sam¹ Nowell, esq. and many Persons present, almost Capt. [*Thomas*] Brattle's great Hall full; Capt. B and Mrs. Brattle there for two. Mr. Willard begun with Prayer. Mr. Tho. Shepard concluded; as he was Praying, Cous. Savage, Mother Hull, wife and self came in. A good space after, when we had eaten Cake and drunk Wine and Beer plentifully, we were called into the Hall again to Sing. In Singing Time Mrs. Brattle goes out being ill; Most of the Compª goe away, thinking it a qualm or some Fit; But she grows worse, speaks not a word, and so dyes away in her chair, I holding her feet (for she had slipt down). At length out of the Kitching we carry the chair and Her in it, into the Wedding Hall; and after a while lay the Corps of the dead Aunt in the Bride-Bed: So that now the strangeness and horror of the thing filled the (just now) joyous House with Ejulation: The Bridegroom and Bride lye at Mr. Airs, son in law to the deceased, going away like Persons put to flight in Battel.

*Satterday night, Nov*ʳ 11. [1682]. Twelve Jurors come before my Father [*Hull*], to give Oath as to the Cause and Manner of one Johnson, a Turnour, his immature death; which was by letting a Barrel of Cider into a Trap-dore Cellar (*Marginal note:* Just by Cous. Quinsey's); the Board he stood on gave away, he fell in, and the end of the Barrel upon his Jaw and Kill'd him outright. Jury came to swear about eight a clock.

One Blood of Concord about 7 days since or less was found dead in the woods, leaning his Brest on a Logg: Had been seeking some Creatures. Oh! what strange work is the Lord about to bring to Pass.

The Wednesday fortnight before Mrs. Brattles Death, Mr. Gardener of Salem, who lives p. the Meeting-House, going into his Shop after Lecture to open it, as he was hanging up a net of Cotton-wool, fell down dead over his Threshold: which made a great Hubbub.

*Nov*ʳ 12 [1682], at night or even, Capt. Benj. Gillam's Mate is drowned off the outward wharf.

[2] This was Halley's Comet. Increase Mather preached a sermon on it (The Latter Sign) at the Boston Lecture, 31 August 1682. The sermon was published in his *Heaven's Alarm to the World* (Printed for Samuel Sewall, 1682) and in his *Kometographia* (Printed by Samuel Green for Samuel Sewall, 1683). See T. J. Holmes, *Increase Mather . . . Bibliography*, Nos. 62-B and 67-A.

[3] Mr. Foster was minister of the Hartford church; his death was the second to occur among Sewall's classmates.

Wednesday, Novr 15, 1682. Mr. *[John]* Sherman Ordains Mr. Nath. Gookin Pastor of Cambridge-Church: Mr. Eliot gives the Right hand of Fellowship, first reading the Scripture that warrants it. Mr. Sherman, Eliot and Mather laid on Hands. Then Mr. Gookin ordain'd Deacon Stone and Mr. Clark Ruling Elders. The Presence of God seem'd to be with his People. Mr. Jonathan Danforth, the Dep^t Governours onely Son, lay by the Wall, having departed on Monday Morn, of a Consumption. Tis a comfortable day and much People at the Ordination. I go and come on foot in Comp^a of Mr. *[Stephen]* Zadori, the Hungarian, whom I find to be an Arminian.

Friday, Novr 17 [1682] one Smith is drowned, coming up from Mr. Edwards, sailing for Lond[on]. Not many weeks before, a Man fell into the Dock, up by my Father's Ware-House, and was drowned: and Josiah Belcher, Senr was drowned at Weymouth.

Sabbath-day, Novr 19. [1682]. Mr. Edw. Winslow, Ship M^r, died suddenly: He took Physick the Friday before and John Alcock discours'd with him, he seeming to him no iller than Men ordinarily are when taking Physick. A Woman dyed suddenly at the North end of the Town.

Tuesday, Novr 28, '82. One Horton coming from Nevis, makes the Land this day, and stands in; but the Rain and Snow take him so that in the night drives him over Rocks and Sholes, cast Anchor; but all Cables break. So about 3 a clock at night, that violent Storm strands the Ship on Nahant Beach, about ¼ mile to the Northward of Pulling Point Gut; the Ship about 100 Tun. Persons on Board 13, 3 whereof drowned; 4 perished in the Cold, not being able to grope out the way to Mr. Winthrops: and 6 onely escaped: 3 of the above if not all four, lay frozen like sticks, in a heap. One of the six was so frozen that will hardly escape. Very little goods saved. About 200 £ in P 8/8 lost.

1682. Dec. 5, 3 [Tuesday]. Gov. Cranfield.[4]

1682. [December] 20, 4 [Wednesday] Fast at Mr. Mather's.

1682. Dec. 30. Mr. Joseph Pynchon dyes.

1682/3 Jan'y 12, 6 [Friday]. Landlady, Jane Fissenden dyes. Buried 16, 3.[5]

[4] Edward Cranfield's three oppressive and stormy years as Governor of New Hampshire (1682-1685) are detailed in *Palfrey*, iii, 407-419.

[5] Jane was the wife of John Fessenden, glover and selectman of Cambridge, who settled there as early as 1638, and died in December 1666. His house was on the westerly side of Eliot Street. (L. R. Paige, *Hist. of Cambridge*, 542). It is this editor's opinion that Sewall resided at the Widow Fessenden's during his first year at college. Sewall's brother John married Hannah Fessenden, probably a niece of John, but there was evidently an earlier relationship between the families

1682/3 *Jan'y* 17, 4 [*Wednesday*]. Mr. T. Weld, Roxb[*ury*] dyes. Buried 19th, 6.

1682/3 [*January*] 25. Fast, O[*ld*] Meet[*ing*] House. Flocks of Pigeons are seen this month at Newbury.

1682/3 *Feb.* 2, 6 [*Friday*]. Edw. Dudley F.

1682/3 *Feb.* 6, 3 [*Tuesday*]. Calf Braintrey.

Febr. 9. 1682-3. A considerable deal of Snow being on the Ground, there falls such plenty of warm Rain as that the Waters swell so as to do much damage. Ipswich Dam and Bridge is carried away by the Flood and Ice violently coming down; so that they now go over in a Boat, Horse and Men. Rowly Mill Dam also spoyled, and generally much harm done in Dams and Bridges; so that 'tis judged many Thousands will scarce repair the Loss. Woburn hath suffered much. Roxbury Bridge carried away just as persons on it; so that a woman was near drowning.

1682/3 13 March. Sewall, with John Saffin, Anthony Checkley and the selectmen were appointed by the town to draw up instructions for the Deputies to the General Court. These instructions were recorded 15 March; they ask that the "whole body of lawes be revized"; that "Candles made up for sale shall be under the cognisance of the Clarkes of ye market & be liable to be weighed & forfeited for want of being full weight as butter & bread is"; that "butter made up for sale whether in pounds or larger p'cells be liable to be weighed per ye Clarkes of the Markett in any part of Boston within the fortification"; that 'a note set vp vnder the Towne house vpon one of ye pillars, concerning the price of wheat shall be suffitient notice to ye Bakers to size their bread by, accordinge to Law" and that "upon the first Monday of every moneth the men y^t set the price of wheate shall set up such a note . . ." (Boston Rec. Commrs. Report VII, 160)

1683. Aug. 14, 3 [*Tuesday*]. My father [*in-law John Hull*] watched his last.

1683. 31 August. At a town meeting Sewall was chosen one of seven Commissioners for the ensuing year to assess rates. (Boston Rec. Commrs. Report, VII, 163)

1683. 1 October. John Hull died at Boston.

1683. 7 November. Sewall's name appears on the roll of the General Court as a Deputy from Westfield, a town in Hampshire County which John Hull represented in 1674.

Satterday, March 22, 1683-4, there was an extraordinary high Tide,

---

in England, or Sewall was stretching kinship rather far, for he recorded 18 January 1688/9: "Arrived at Canterbury, visited Aunt Fissenden . . ."

which did much hurt at Boston and Charlestown, coming into Houses and Ware-Houses that stood low. All that I hear of at Cambridge, Charl. and here, say 'tis higher than ever any was known before.

1684. *Mch. 27, 5 [Thursday]*. Jack, Negro.

1684. *May 6, 3 [Tuesday]*. Commissioners Court.

1684. *June 10, 3 [Tuesday]*. Henry Pease. [*See note to the entry of 22 July 1684*].

1684. *June 21, 7 [Saturday]*. Thos. Powes drowned.

1684. The President [*John Rogers of Harvard*] dies July 2d just as the sun gets from being eclipsed. *Sepultus est* July 3d.

1684. *July 8, 3 [Tuesday]*. Hull Sewall *natus*.

1684. *July 22, 3 [Tuesday]*. Special Court of Assistants.[6]

1684. *July 30, 4 [Wednesday]*. Mr. Nath. Gookin.

1684. 10 *September.* "By the Gou^r & Company of the Massachusetts Bay in New England, at a speciall Generall Court, called by the Gouerno^r, to be held and sett in Boston . . . Whereas, at a sessions of the Generall Court in October, 1681, this Court was pleased to intrust Mr Samuel Sewall wth the mannagem^t of the printing press in Boston, lately vnder the improvement of Mr John Foster, deceased, and whereas, by the prouidence of God, Mr Seawall is rendered vnable to attend the same, he judging it reasonable to acquaint this honoured Court therewith, desiring that he may be freed from any obligation vnto duty respecting that affaire, wth thankfull acknouledgm^{t}s of the liberty then granted,—The Court grants the request aboue mentioned.". (Massachusetts Bay Colony Records, v, 452)

1684. *Oct. 2, 5 [Thursday]*. Mr. Philip Jones buried.

1684. *Oct. 8, 4 [Wednesday]*. Clark arrives.

1684. *Oct. 18, 7 [Saturday]*. Gardener arrives.

1684. *Oct. 20, 2 [Monday]*. Foy arrives.

Wednesday, Octr 29 [1684], a Maid's Brains shot out, her head broke all to pieces, at Salem.

1684. *Nov. 8, 7 [Saturday]*. *Dom* Wade *Sepult. est.*

1684. *Nov. 15, 7 [Saturday]*. Jolls Belcher.

1684. *Nov. 18, 3 [Tuesday]*. Mehetabel.

1684. *Nov. 19, 4 [Wednesday]*. Capt. Johnson *obit.*

1684. *Nov. 25, Tues.* A very high tide, begun to run into our Cellar. Filled C. Hills.

---

[6] Sewall's name is not listed among those present. The court was called to try Vines Ellacot for the murder of Henry Pease by knocking him down with a violently ridden horse; Ellacot was acquitted and discharged after paying the Widow Gurtrude Pease 10l. *Records of the Court of Assistants*, i, 251-252.

Friday Nov 28, 1684. Wm Allen, a Plummer, receives a blow by a piece that was used for a Scaffold falling on's head, of which he dyes at night. Boston. About a fortnight agoe, one at Sparks, the Ordinary at Ipswich near the Meetinghouse, falls down stairs or the like, and dies. About that time Jn° Poor of Newbury perrisheth in the Snow, near the Fresh-Meadows, about a Mile from my Father's Farm.

1684. *Dec. 4, 5* [*Thursday*]. Capt. Berry sails.

1685

*The surviving text of the Diary is resumed at this point in a new
volume. From this date to the final entry in 1729 our published text is
derived from the three original volumes in Sewall's handwriting.*

Wednesday Febr. 11, 1684/5. Joshua Moodey and self set out for
Ipswich. I lodge at Sparkes's. Next day, *Feb.* 12, goe to lecture which
Mr. Moodey preaches, then I dine with Mr. Cobbet, and so ride to
Newbury; visit Mr. Richardson sick of the dry Belly ake. *Monday,
Febr.* 16, Get Mr. Phillips and Payson to Town and so keep a Fast-
day, Mr. Moodey Preaching Forenoon, Mr. Phillips Afternoon, Mr.
Woodbridge and Payson assisting in Prayer; was a pretty full Assembly, Mr. Moodey having given notice the Sabbath-day, on which
he preached all day. At Wenham and Ipswich, as we went, we were
told of the Earthquake in those parts and at Salem (Feb. 8) the
Sabbath before about the time of ending Afternoon Exercise; That
which most was sensible of was a startling doleful Sound; but many
felt the Shaking also, Peter and Jane Toppan. Mr. Phillips had not
finished his Sermon, and was much surprised at the Sound, expecting
when the House would have Crackt. In several places Exercise was
over.

Tuesday Febr. 17, I and Brother, sister Stephen Sewall Ride to
Sparkes's by the Ferry, great part in the Snow; Dined with Ipswich
Select-Men. 18*th* I Lodged there; the Morn was serene; came to Salem,
seeing Mrs. Hale by the way; staid Lecture, came to Boston, found
all well. *Laus Deo.*

Tuesday March 10th. 1684/5. Deputies for Boston are Mr. Isaac
Addington votes 90 and odd, Mr. John Saffin 70 and odd, Mr.

Timothy Prout 50 and odd, Mr. Anthony Stoddard passed by, who hath been annually chosen about these twenty years: Mr. John Fayer-wether left out. Are chosen for the year. Mr. Addington chosen a Commissioner also to seal up the Votes and carry them. In the After-noon I carried my Wife to see Mrs. Flint; wayes extream bad.

Thorsday, March 12, 1684/5. Mr. John Bayly preached from Amos 4. 12, and Mr. Willard from 2 Cor. 4. 16-18; both Sermons and Prayers Excellent. In the even 2 first Staves of the 46 Ps. sung. Watched with Isaac Goose and Sam Clark, had a pleasant Night, Gave each Watch 12d. to drink. *Satterday March 14th.* went to Mr. Goddard of Watertown to buy Hay, Dined as I went with Thomas Danforth, Esq. and Lady; visited Mr. Sherman as I came back. *Wednesday March 25th, 1685.* went to Cambridge with Capt. Elisha Hutchinson, there meet with Lieut. Johnson; at Mr. Cotton's Chamber the Deputy Governor tells how Major Bordman dyed that morning; he had been College–Cook a long time. Dined with the Commissioners of Middlesex at the Ordinary, then proceeded in our Errand to Mr. Sherman from the Council to enquire when Easter Day was, and consequently our Election,[1] because by the Rule in the Prayer Book it should be a Week sooner. Mr. Sherman was pleasant and took it for granted 'twas as the Almanack had set it, *i.e.* an Eng-lish Almanack, which I shewed him. Deputy Governour told the Commissioners this was the last time they were like to convene for such a purpose.

Thorsday March 26th. 1685. Went to the Gathering of the Church at Sherborn and ordaining Mr. Daniel Gookin their Pastor. But six Brethren and three of the names Mors. Mr. Wilson, Mr. Adams and Mr. Nathaniel Gookin of Cambridge managed the Work; Mr. Nath¹ Gookin the younger introduced the Elder, a happy Type of the Call-ing the Jews. Mr. Torrey, Brinsmead, Fisk, Estabrooks, Man, Moodey, Hubbard (Neh.), Sherman, Woodrop, Rawson (Grindal), Wilson junʳ there, and Fellows of the Colledge: Only Major General and self of Magistrates. No Relations were made, but I hope God was with them. I put up a Note to pray for the Indians that Light might be com-municated to them by the Candlestick, but my Note was with the latest, and so not professedly prayed for at all.

Tuesday, March the last [31], went to Weymouth, heard Mr. Brins-

---

1 John Sherman, the Cambridge-trained minister of Watertown, Fellow and lecturer at Harvard, was the local authority on astronomy (Morison, *FHC*, 400). By the Charter, the annual election was to be held on "the last Wednesday in Easter terme yearely." This plan made the day vary each year, the extremes being 2 May 1638 and 2 June 1641. In 1685, the day observed was 27 May. M.H.S.EDS.

mead preach from Prov. 10. 29; see my Book of Records. After Lecture I took the Acknowledgment of many Deeds. In the even Angel Torrey brings word that little Hull was seized with Convulsions; His first Fit was when I was at Watertown, 25th March. Lodged with Mr. Brinsmead.

Wednesday morn April 1. Speaking to Mr. Brinsmead to pray for drying up the River Euphrates,[2] he told me he had prayed that God would reveal to some or other as to Daniel of old, the Understanding of the Prophesies of this time, that so might know whereabouts we are. Went home: Mr. Torrey accompanyed me to Monotocot Bridge; found things pretty calm at home and the Child sleeping.—*Friday April 3rd,* Mr. Joseph Eliot and I Graft some Walnut Trees. *Apr. 14th 1685.* A Ship arrives from New Castle and brings News of the death of Charles the 2nd, and Proclamation of James the 2nd, King. Brought a couple of printed Proclamations relating to that affair. News came to us as we were busy opening the Nomination, just before Dinner; it much startled the Governour and all of us. In the morn before I went the Governour said that a Ship master had been with him from Nevis, who told him Gov[r] Stapleton should say, we should have a new Governour before he got to Boston. Master dined with Magistrates and Commissioners at Capt. Wing's. Carried my wife to George Bairsto's yesterday, April 13th.—*Thorsday, April 16th,* a Vessel arrives from London. Mr. Lord, commander, brings Orders to the several Colonies to proclaim the King. Mr. Blathwayt writes to Simon Bradstreet, Esq. superscribed For His Majestie's Service, advising that 't would be best for us early to doe it; and our Charter being vacated in Law and no Government setled here, was the reason we were not writt to: Copies and forms sent to us as to the other Colonies, but no mention of Governour and Company. Also another letter was writt to Simon Bradstreet, Wm. Stoughton, Jos. Dudley, Peter Bulkeley, Sam'l Shrimpton, Richard Wharton, Esquires, to proclaim the King. Suppose this was done lest the Government should have neglected to do it. The Council agreed to proclaim the King before they knew of the Letter. Major Richards counted the

[2] Sewall continued throughout his life to pursue those biblical and theological studies to which his attention had been drawn when he had in view the work of the ministry. He was especially interested in the enigmas of prophetical interpretation, and in solving the question of the Lost Tribes, the Peopling of America, the Two Witnesses, etc. The symbols represented by the river Euphrates, its drying up, etc. (Rev. XVI, 12), engaged his earnest thought, and were frequently the subjects of his correspondence with divines, as bearing upon the triumphs of the Gospel. Two editions were published of what he considered his magnum opus, *Phaenomena Quaedam Apocalyptica* . . . (Boston, 1697 and 1727). M.H.S.EDS.

Votes for Mr. Dudley, told them twice over, and still found them 666, and so 'twas entered and sent to the Towns. s.s.

Monday April 20th. The King is Proclaimed; 8 Companies, the Troop, and several Gentlemen on horseback assisting; three Volleys and then Canon fired. This day a child falls upon a Knife which runs through its cheek to the Throat, of which inward Wound it dies, and is buried on Wednesday. 'Tis one Gees child.—*Thorsday, April* 23, Mother Sewall comes by Water in Stephen Greenleaf to see us. —*Sabbath, April 26th,* I go to Meeting; staid at home last Sabbath and April 20th by reason of my Sore Throat, with which was taken the night before Mr. Lord came in.—*April 27.* Father Sweet buried —*Tuesday, April 28th* Began to wean little Hull to see if that might be a means to free him of Convulsions; he had one yesterday.— *Wednesday, April 29th,* The Vessel of which Matthew Soley died Master in London, arrives, and brings Gazettes to the 2d. of March. The King was buried 14th of Febr. in the even privately.

Friday, May the first, Mother Sewall goes to Salem; my Wife and I go with her to visit Mrs. Bellingham, and so to the Ferry Boat in which met with a Hampshire Man that had been well acquainted with Mr. Cox and such Hampshire People, several of them, as mother knew: rode to Capt. Marshal's and there took leave. White Oaks pretty much put forth: 'tis a forward very green Spring. An Apsoon[3] man arrives of about 5 weeks' passage, brings word that the King was to be Proclaim'd the 23rd of April, and the Parliament to sit the 4th of May. Mr. Tho. Smith from Barbados brings the Honourable Francis Bond, one of His Majestie's Council for that Iland, and of a great Estate, also one Mr. Middleton: Former comes to recover his health. Father Town[4] is buried at Cambridge this first of May. Sundry other vessels come from England, which I mention not. The like has hardly been known as to earliness.—*Sabbath May 3rd,* a letter read from the N[orth] Church wherein Mr. Willard and Messengers desired to be sent in order to ordain Mr. Cotton Mather, Pastor of that Church; signed, Increase Mather, at the desire and order of the Church. The Governour and self with the Deacons, nominated to goe.—*May 6th,* General Court Assembles; Magistrates vote an Address to be sent by the Ship now ready to sail, on which a Negative put. A Committee chosen to Revise the Laws,[5] at the earnest Suit of

[3] Probably from Bergen-op-Zoom, North Brabant, Netherlands.
[4] William Towne was tythingman of the Cambridge church. Sewall often used the title Father for old patriarchs.
[5] The report of this committee, dated 27 May 1685, is printed in *Mass. Bay Records* v, 476. At this date, also was passed a new law establishing a Court of

the Deputies, which they would have had them made a Report of next Tuesday, but agreed to be next Election Court. Took the word *"such"* out of the late Law printed Title *"Conveyancies"*; made some Freemen, it may be Twenty: Dissolved the Court on Friday May 8th, 1685.—*Thorsday, May 7th.* a youth was Cut for the Stone and a great one taken out as big as a Hen's Egg.—*Friday morn, May 8ᵗʰ 1685*, the Lad dies, at Neighbour Mason's, and now his Son will not be cut, seeing this stranger fare so ill. Mr. John Bayly preached the Lecture for Mr. Mather, from Ps. 37. 4. Delight thyself also in the Lord &c.

Friday May 8th—past 6, even, Walk with the honored Governour [*Bradstreet*] up Hoar's Lane, so to the Alms House; then down the length of the Common to Mr. Dean's Pasture, then through Cowel's Lane to the New Garden, then to our House, then to our Pasture by Engs's, then I waited on his Honour to his Gate and so home.[6] This day our old Red Cow is kill'd, and we have a new black one brought in the room, of about four years old and better, marked with a Crop and slit in the Left Ear, and a Crop off the right Ear, with a little hollowing in. As came with his Honour through Cowell's Lane, Sam. came running and call'd out a pretty way off and cried out the Cow was dead and by the Heels, meaning hang'd up by the Butcher. At which I was much startled, understanding him she had been dead upon a Hill or cast with her heels upward, and so had lost her; for I was then looking for her and 't was unexpected, Mother having partly bargained and the Butcher fetcht her away in the Night unknown. Had served this family above Ten years, above Nine since my dwelling in it.[7]

Satterday May 9th, Brother Stephen Sewall visits me.—*Monday,*

Chancery to exercise equity jurisdiction. This revision of the Colony laws, "especially those more lately made," was entered upon and very slowly, and grudgingly pursued, in compliance with the peremptory exceptions made to them by the Attorney and Solicitor General of England. Among the laws which were annulled was that which sentenced to death Quakers returning from banishment, and that passed in 1659 "against keeping Christmas." The *Records* add: "For greater expedition in the present revisall of the lawes, this Court doth order, that they shall be sent to the presse sheet by sheet, & that the Treasurer make payment to the printer for the same paper & worke, June 10ᵗʰ, 1685, and yᵗ Elisha Cook & Samuel Seawall, Esqrs., be desired to oversee yᵉ presse about that worke." (*Ib.* 479). M.H.S.EDS.
6 We omit W. H. Whitmore's footnote on this entry, discussing Boston streets and real estate, which runs to 149 lines in the M.H.S. edition.
7 The old Red Cow provides another clue to Sewall's residence: she had served the Hull family above nine years since he dwelt in it, i.e., since his marriage in February 1675/6.

May 11th, 1685, I accompanied Mr. Moodey to Mr. Eliot's [*the Apostle to the Indians*] to persuade Mr. Benjamin[8] to go to the Ordination of Mr. Cotton Mather, in which I hope we have prevailed; the mentioning of it drew Tears from the good Father so as to hinder his Speech. The Father was abroad and preached yesterday. Visited Mr. Dudley also. Deacon Parkes dyed last night, and Goodman Woodward of Dedham, father to the Minister, is dead within 's day or two. At Mr. Dudley's was Wm Hahaton and David Indian, who Acknowledged the Papers I offered him in Feb. Court, at Capt. Paige's, speaking English.—*Tuesday, May 12th*, I weary myself in walking from one end and side of the Town to t'other to seek our lost Cow.—*Wednesday, May 13, 1685*, Mr. Cotton Mather is ordained Pastor by his Father,[9] who said, My son Cotton Mather, and in 's sermon spake of Aaron's Garments being put on Eleazer, intimating he knew not but that God might now call him out of the World. Mr. Eliot gave the Right Hand of Fellowship, calling him a Lover of Jesus Christ. Mr. Benjamin Eliot was there who hath not been at Town these many years.—*Thorsday May 14th*, Mr. Torrey and Unkle Quinsey dined here. Have agreed to have a Fast here at our house next Friday. 'Twas first to be on Tuesday, but altered it. I invited all the Magistrates: to most writ the following words—"To Samuel Nowell, Esq "Sir—The Ministers of this Town are desired to Pray and Preach at my House next Friday, to begin about half an hour past Nine; which I acquaint you with that so yourself and Wife may have the opportunity of being present. Sam. Sewall. May 18. 1685."

Tuesday May 19th. 1685 went to Roxbury Lecture, invited Mr. Eliot and his Son to be with us on Friday next. When I come home I find Hullie extream ill having had two Convulsion Fits, one of them very long: the Child is much changed.—*Friday May 22d. 1685*, had a private Fast: the Magistrates of this town with their Wives here. Mr. Eliot prayed, Mr. Willard preached. I am afraid of Thy judgments—Text Mother gave. Mr. Allen prayed; cessation half an hour. Mr. Cotton Mather prayed; Mr. Mather preached Ps. 79, 9. Mr. Moodey prayed about an hour and half; Sung the 79th Psalm from the 8th to the End: distributed some Biskets, and Beer, Cider, Wine. The Lord hear in Heaven his dwelling place.—*Satterday May 23d*,

---

[8] Benjamin Eliot (Harvard 1665) was the youngest son of the Apostle Eliot. Sewall apparently took a special interest in him because of his affliction; see the entry of 25 August 1687.
[9] Cotton Mather had been assisting his father as colleague pastor of the Second Church for two years previous to his ordination; he was now twenty-two. Increase Mather was in his forty-sixth year.

morn, Thunder and Lightening. Satterday 5 p.m. Mr. Wharton and Saffin offered me an Address, which I saw not cause to sign. Governour had signed, J. Winthrop, Capt. Fones and some others interested in the Narraganset Lands. Mr. Lynde, Mr. Smith (Nar.) and Mr. Brindley were by at the same time. *Sabbath May 24th*, we read the ninety-seventh Psalm in Course: Mr. Francis Bond at our House. —*Tuesday May 26th*, 1685, Mary Kay comes hither to dwell in Hannah Hett's stead, who is upon Marriage.—*Wednesday, May 27, 1685*, Election day, being very fair Wether all day. Mr. William Adams preaches from Isa. 66, 2. Capt. Blackwell and Mr. Bond dine with us: Mr. Philips craves a Blessing and returns Thanks, in which mentions the Testimony of Jesus, that God would make us faithfull in it. Governour chosen without counting; Mr. Nowell (I think) came next. Mr. Danforth Deputy Governour clear. Assistants,

Esqrs.		*Esqrs.*	
D. Gookin	1312	P. Tilton	1234
J. Pynchon	1257	S. Appleton	1200
Wm. Stoughton	757	R. Pike	1168
J. Dudley	694	Elisha Cooke	1067
N. Saltonstall	1080	Wm. Johnson	932
H. Davie	1131	John Hathorn	1031
J. Richards	1267	Elisha Hutchinson	777
S. Nowell	1257	S. Sewall	1065
J. Russell	1263	Oliver Purchas	683

Commissioners United Colonies		Reserves
Mr. Stoughton	307	Mr. Danforth
Mr. Nowell	485	Mr. Dudley.

Persons left out this year, Mr. Bulkeley 667; Mr. Woodbridge 559: in last year—In the room now Mr. Dudley, Oliver Purchas. Mr. Brown had votes 398, Mr. Gidney 598, John Smith 608, Dan¹ Pierce 471. Major General and Treasurer, no telling; Mr. Addington had a great many Votes for Secretary. My dear child Hull had a Convulsion Fit in Lecture Time. Mr. Adams, prayed after the Election over. The Governour, Deputy Governour and about nine Assistants sworn, of which myself one: Court adjourned till Thorsday 8 of the clock.

Thorsday about noon, one Jonathan Gardner of Roxbury commits Bestiality with a mare; he is sent to Prison, but one Witness. Hull hath two Convulsion Fits which bring him extreme low; Mr. Philips prays with us.—*Friday, May 29th*. Mr. Nowell and I go to Mr.

Stoughton and Dudley to acquaint them with the Freeman's Choice of them, in the Court's Name, and to desire them to come and take their Oaths: I doubt Mr. Bulkeley's being left out will make them decline it. Mr. Eliot was ill and not at this Election, which knew nothing of till Mr. Philips told me the last night.

Monday June 1, 1685. Artillery Election day; Eliakim sets out to see his mother at N. Hampton, Connecticot. I Train not. Mr. John Phillips is chosen Captain. Capt. Hill Lieutenant, Mr. Benj. Alford Ensign, Henry Dering eldest Sergeant, Crick second, Seth Perry third, Sam. Chickly fourth, Roby, Clark. The 46th Psalm sung at Mr. Wing's, from the 6th verse to the end. About 3 of the clock in the Afternoon this day, Cousin Anne Quinsey is brought to bed of a daughter. *June 2, 1685.* In the Afternoon Mr. Stoughton and Dudley come and confer with the Council thanking them for their respect in acquainting them with their choice, and to say they were not of another mind as to the Substance than formerly, relating to the great Concerns of the Country, lest any might be deceived in desiring them to take their Oaths. Also that if things went otherwise than well in that great Trial [we] were like shortly to have, all the blame would be laid upon them. Said, supposed things would be so clear when the day came as that [there] would be a greater unanimity what to do than now was thought of. Deputy Governours Cloud and Pillar. Seemed, throw the importunity of friends, Ministers and others to incline to take the oath. Take leave. When gone Deputy Governour relates a saying of his Wife.—*June 3*, very seasonable Rain. *Wednesday June 3d, '85*, at night very considerable Thunder and Rain. *In somniis visum est mihi, me rediisse Novoburgo vel alio aliquo oppido; et me absente, uxorem mortuam esse Roxburiæ vel Dorcestriæ; quam narrationem ægerrime tuli Nomen sæpius exclamans. Dum percontarer ubi esset socer, dixerunt eum in Angliam profecturum; Filiâ scilicet mortuâ liberum esse ei ut iter faceret quo vellet. Hanc mortem partim ex incuria mea et Amoris indigentia accidisse, Elizabetha susurravit quod adhuc me gravius pressit. Excusso somno prae gaudio uxorem quasi nuper nuptam amplexus sum.*[10]

[10] It is another evidence of Sewall's delicacy of feeling that he put this passage into Latin. It may be translated as follows: I had dreamt that I returned to Newbury or some other town, and that during my absence my wife had died at Roxbury or Dorchester. I took the tidings very hard, and repeatedly called her name out. While I was inquiring where my father-in-law might be, they said that he had started for England: since his daughter had died he was free to travel as he wished. Elizabeth [Sewall's daughter, then in her fourth year] whispered that the death had occurred in part because of my neglect and want of love. When I shook off sleep, I embraced my wife for joy as if I had newly married her.

At this point Sewall has inserted four pages in the handwriting of a scribe, on which is copied the address of the Governor and Company of the Massachusetts Bay to King James II, dated 28 January 1684/5, regarding the vacating of their charter, and the covering letter from Edward Rawson, Secretary. These documents are printed in Mass. Bay Records v, 466-467, 468.

1685. *Thorsday, June 4th,* Mr. Mather preaches from Isa. 14. 32. Doct[*rine*] The Church of God shall stand and abide for ever. Probable that N. E. Church shall doe so. The 87th. Psalm sung. Mr. Stoughton and Dudley dine with us. Mr. Stoughton inclines to take his Oath; Mr. Mather, Capt. Scottow and Capt. Gidny dine with us likewise. This day the Chancery Bill is passed.

Monday, June 8th. 8 Companies Train: in the morn. between 7 and 8 o'clock. Asaph Eliot comes in and tells me a Rumor in the Town of the New Governour being come to New York, and the certain News, doleful news of Mr. Shepard of Charlestown, his being dead, of whoes illness I heard nothing at all. Saw him very well this day sennight; was much smitten with the News. Was taken on Friday night, yet being to preach and administer the Lord's Supper on Sabbath day, forbore Physick, at least at first. This day Mr. Stoughton and Dudley come in, and in their places at Court in the afternoon, take their Oaths. N[*ote*]. Charlestown was to have had a great bussle in Training on Tuesday with Horse and Foot, Capt. Hammond engaging some of Boston to be there; but now 'tis like to be turned into the Funeral of their Pastor: he dying full and corpulent. Mr. Bayly, Sen'r dined with us at Mr. Pain's. The reverend Mr. Tho. Shepard was ordained May 5, 1680 by Mr. Sherman, Mr. Oakes giving the Right Hand of Fellowship. Mr. Sh.'s Text Heb. 13. 20—That great Shepherd of the Sheep.

On the Sabbath June 7th '85, Cous. Quinsey had his Daughter Anne baptized.

Tuesday, June 9th The Reverend Mr. Thos Shepard buried: Governour, Deputy Governour and Magistrates there. Mr. Bulkely dined with us and was there. Bearers, Mr. Mather, Mr. Simmes, Mr. Willard, Mr. Hubbard of Cambridge, Mr. Nathaniel Gookin, Mr. Cotton Mather: the two last preached at Charlestown the last Sabbath day. It seems there were some Verses; but none pinned on the Herse. Scholars went before the Herse. A pretty number of Troopers there. Capt. Blackwell and Counsellor Bond there.[11]

[11] Rev. Thomas Shepard (Harvard 1676) was the third of the name and title; he had succeeded his father in the Charlestown ministry. His grandfather was the

Tuesday, June 9th 1685. Govr Edw. Cranfield sails away in his Sloop from Portsmouth. It is like is gone to Barbados. *Teste Petr. Weare.*

Thorsday Even, June 11th Brother Steven Sewall lodges here: hath been extream ill.

Satterday, June 13th Capt. Benjⁿ Gillam buried. Govr Bradstreet's Effigies hung up in his best Room this day.

Wednesday, June 17th a Quaker or two goe to the Governour and ask leave to enclose the Ground [*on the Common*] the Hanged Quakers are buried in under or near the Gallows, with Pales: Governour proposed it to the Council, who unanimously denyed it as very inconvenient for persons so dead and buried in the place to have any Monument.

Thorsday, June 18. A Quaker comes to the Governour and speaks of a Message he had which was to shew the great Calamities of Fire and Sword that would suddenly come on New-England. Would fain have spoken in the Meetinghouse, but was prevented. Eliakim comes home this day, brings word that Capt. Henchman is coming away from Worcester with his Family.

Noyes this day of a French Pirat on the Coast, of 36 Guns.

Satterday, June 20th 1685. The Court not agreeing about the Proviso in the end of the 2^d Section of the Law, title Courts, adjourns till Tuesday July 7th except Occasion be, and then the Governour is to call them sooner. Also the Dep^t Governour goes to keep Court at York next week with Mr. Nowel, and several other Magistrates will go out of Town. The final difference between the Magistrates and Deputies is: The Governour and several with him would Repeal the Proviso, letting the rest of the Law stand as it does; the Deputies have voted the Repeal of the Proviso; and withall that the Remainder of the Law have this alteration, viz: in stead of greater part of the Magistrates,—greater number of the Magistrates present—so to make the Law new as [*it*] might be construed contrary to the Charter: the Governour, Mr. Stoughton, Dudley and several others could not consent.

Voted. the 16th of July to be observed as a Fast.

Satterday, P. M. Carried my Wife to Dorchester to eat Cherries, Rasberries, chiefly to ride and take the Air: the Time my Wife and Mrs. Flint spent in the Orchard, I spent in Mr. Flint's Study, reading Calvin on the Psalms &c. 45. 68. 24.

Sabbath, June 21, 1685. Mr. Solomon Stoddard preaches in the

---

famous minister of Cambridge. "Mr. Hubbard of Cambridge" was Rev. Nehemiah Hobart of Newton, according to Sibley, II, 487.

Afternoon from Gal. 5. 17. shewing that there is a principle of ·Godliness in every true Believer; and how it differs from Moral Vertue, &c. Some little disturbance by a Quaker about the time of Baptism.

Wednesday, June 24, 1685. Carried my Wife to Cambridge-Lecture; Mr. Willard preached from those words, He that knows and does not his Master's will, shall be beaten with many Stripes. Dined with Mr. Nathaniel Gookin.

June 25. Mr. Russel of Hadley preacheth the Lecture from Zech. 7. 5. Did ye at all fast unto me, even to me?

June 25ᵗʰ A Ship comes in to Marble head, and brings news of the King's Coronation.

June 26. Mr. Jnᵒ Cotton, and Mr. Solomon Stoddard dine here.

Satterday, June 27ᵗʰ It pleaseth God to send Rain on the weary dusty Earth.

Wednesday, July 1, 1685. Commencement day; Peter Butler comes in from London, brings news of the King's Coronation, Sermon and Formalities, with a Letter from Mr. Humfryes, and a Copy of the Judgement entered up against us that [*is*] about 145 pages, cost 5ˡ 10ˢ. having Pengry's Recᵗ upon an outside Leafe. [*In margin:* Judgemᵗ Entred up against Charter.]

Cous. Nath. Dummer is brought by Cous. Jer. to our House this day, he came in Mr. Butler who came in Late Last Night; so came not ashoar till this morn. Goes to the Commencement with Eliakim. Besides Disputes, there are four orations, One Latin by Mr. Dudley; and two Greek, one Hebrew by Nath. Mather, and Mr. President after giving the Degrees made an Oration, in Praise of Academical Studies and Degrees, Hebrew Tongue: Mr. Collins, Shepard, &c. Dept. Governour and Mr. Nowell absent; not returned from keeping Court in the Province of Mayn. Governour there, whom I accompanied by Charlestown. After Diner the 3ᵈ part of the 103 Psalm was sung in the Hall.

Thorsday, July 2ᵈ 1685. Mr. Cotton Mather preaches from 2. Cor. 5. 5. In's Father's Turn, who keeps at Cambridge.

After the County Court is over, is a Conference at his Honours; present the Governour, Mr. Stoughton, Dudley, Richards, Sewall, Mr. Torrey, Brinsmead, Willard, Adams. Were unanimous as to what discoursed, relating to our Circumstances, the Charter being Condemned. Every one spake.

Satterday, July 4ᵗʰ 1685. Little Hull hath a Convulsion Fit: it took him sleeping in the Cradle after Dinner.

I was taken ill myself very feverish so as feared the Fever and Ague, took some Cardnus Drink at night, Sweat pretty well, and so it went off, blessed be God.

Satterday, about 4 *mane* Isaac Woode dyes pretty suddenly: for was abroad the day before tho' had been not well a 14 night.

Monday, July 6ᵗʰ. I am taken with a Feverish Fit; yet go to Court in the Afternoon, the County Court, where was read Major Pynchon's Letter to the Council; which is that 5 Men came to one of the Houses of Westfield (I think) about midnight 28ᵗʰ June, knockt at the door, the Man bid him come in, so in they came all Armed with drawn Swords, and threatened to run the man and his wife through if they stirred: so plundered that House, and another in like manner: told they had 60 Men in their Company and that if they stirred out of door, they would kill them; so stayd in a great part of Monday, then when thought the Coast was clear told the Neighbours and some were sent to Search after them; at last found them: one of the 5 snapt and missed fire, another shot, then one of ours shot so as to shoot one of theirs dead: another of the 5 fought one of ours with his sword, till another of ours knockt him down. One or two that were taken are brought to Boston, one at least is escaped. Major Pynchon writes 'twill cost near an hundred Pounds.

An Indian was branded in Court and had a piece of his Ear cut off for Burglary.

Tuesday, July 7ᵗʰ Brother Moody visits us. General Court sits in the Afternoon. Time is spent in ordering a Drum to beat up for Volunteers about 30. Samson Waters, Capt., to go with Mr. Patteshal's Brigenteen to fetch in two Privateers that this morn are said to be in the Bay, a Sloop and Shalop, in the Shalop, Graham.[12]

Wednesday I take a Vomit, after 12 Sweat much, when cold fit past. Mr. Stoughton and Dudley visit me and Mr. Secretary. Thorsday morn take Cortex Peruvianus in a glass of Wine. Marshal Genˡˡ comes to speak with me, being sent to call me to Court because all the Magistrates might be together to give their sence what to do when Col. Kirk comes, and how to receive him. Brother and Sister Gerrish lodged here last night. I had very little sleep. Brother and Sister Gerrish Lodged here.

Now about News comes to Town that Panama is taken by one

---

12 This fright was caused by the pirates Veale and Grayham. On 8 July the General Court issued its proclamation for volunteers. Finding that men were not enlisting readily, the Court then decreed that "free plunder be offered to such as shall voluntarily lyst themselves, or that a sufficient number of men be forthwith impressed to that service." *Mass. Bay Rec.* v, 489.

Banister an English Man; and that by the help of the Natives he intends to hold it.

Friday, July 10ᵗʰ. I take another dos of the Cortex: my Fit stayes away. Brother and Sister Gerrish go home. Between 2 and 3. P. M. as Mr. Fisk and Mr. Wyllys were talking with me, it grew darkish, thundered, and a very sudden, violent storm of Rain, Wind and Hail arose which beat so upon the Glass and partly broke it, as startled us. The Window of Mothers Bed-Chamber next the Street hath many Quarrels broken in it, all over, except the sidelong Pane next the Shop. We were speaking about Col. Kirk's coming over.[13]

Mr. Stoughton visits me and tells of the Court's Adjournment till next Tuesday Sennight and then the Elders to meet them and advise.[14] Mr. Dudley and Mr. Bullivant visit me at the same time. Mr. Stoughton also told me of George Car's Wife being with child by another Man, tells the Father, Major Pike sends her down to Prison. Is the Governour's Grandchild by his daughter Cotton.[15]

One Vicars drowned, the boat he was in being sunk in the Harbour by the Gust; our Washer's Son.

Jnᵒ Balston arrives; when was below, was some rumor that the Governour was come. July 10ᵗʰ '85, brings news the Parliament had sate, and were adjourned for a day or two. Dr. Oates has been whipt and set in the Pillory. Was set in the Pillory before the Exchange, May 19, the day of the Parliamentˢ Sitting: 'Tis for Perjury.[16]

Sabbath-day, July 5. Mr. Sherman the Father is taken delirious in Sudbury Pulpit; so fain to be born away; is now sick of the Fever and Ague.[17] Orders go out to Towns that have not sent, to send a Deputy or Deputies at their peril against the 21. Instant, and the Elder

[13] The infamous Colonel Percy Kirke had been designated by James II as Governor of the colony. Palfrey writes (III, 395), "that campaign in the West of England had not yet taken place, which had made the name of Kirk immortal; but fame enough had gone abroad of his brutal character to make his advent an anticipation of horror to those whom he was to govern." Massachusetts was spared the infliction.

[14] By formal vote, the General Court ordered the elders to convene 21 July. *Mass. Bay Rec.* v, 492.

[15] Ann Cotton, was the daughter of Rev. Seaborn Cotton (Harvard 1651) and his wife Dorothy, daughter of Governor Simon Bradstreet; Ann was born in 1661 and died in December 1702 of the smallpox at Boston. Her first husband was George Carr, her second a Johnson. *Savage* and *N.E.H.G.R.* I, 164.

[16] Titus Oates (1649-1705), originator of the Popish Plot, and one of the most unsavory characters in English history, was getting severe treatment under James II. Under William and Mary he was pardoned and given a pension. A biography of Oates by Jane Lane was published in London in 1949.

[17] He died 8 August 1685, *q.v.*

warned also to appear; I read the paper to Watertown. The Deputies that were present on Friday, are to warn the respective Elders.

Wednesday, P. M., July 15. Very dark, and great Thunder and Lightening.

One Humphry Tiffiny and Frances Low, Daughter of Antony Low, are slain with the Lightening and Thunder about a mile or half a mile beyond Billinges Farm,[18] the Horse also slain, that they rode on, and another Horse in Company slain, and his Rider who held the Garment on the Maid to steady it at the time of the Stroke, a coat or cloak, stounded, but not killed. Were coming to Boston. Antony Low being in Town the sad Bill was put up with [regard] of that Solemn judgment of God; Fast-day Forenoon. July 15, 1685. 2 Persons, 2 Horses.

July 17. Mr. Allin makes me an Issue in my left Arm.

July 19th By accident the Spear was not sent on Satterday, but this night; I not being very thoroughly recovered, Mr. Goose Watches accompanied by Sam. Clark, and Cous. Nath. Dummer. This Sabbath-day Mrs. Sarah Noyes's House broken up in time of Afternoon-Exercise; and Money Stolen; Ens. Pecker's the Sabbath before.

A Bristow-Man comes in this day, and fires five Guns at the Castle, which a little startles us.

Tuesday July 21. Cous. Nath. Dummer goes to Salem in order to pass to Newbury next day, Brother Stephen coming for him.

This day about 31 Ministers meet, Mr. Higginson Prayes excellently: Governour gives the Question. Dine all together at Monk's. After Dinner about 3 or 4 aclock, they give their Answere, i.e. Mr. Hubbard Speaks in behalf of the rest, that their Opinion was the Government ought not to give way to another till the Generall Court had seen and judged of the Commission; so should be called if not Sitting at the Arrival of a Commissioned Governour. But several expressed some Dissent: And after, shewed themselves extreamly dissatisfied, saying that Mr. Hubbard had greatly abused them and that he was not ordered by the Ministers that they knew to speak their minds, which six gave in under their Hands. The Meeting has been uncomfortable, and I doubt will breed great Animosities.[19]

Thorsday 23d July. Five Ministers gave under their Hands that Mr.

---

[18] They were on a journey from Swanzey (now Swansea, Bristol County) to Boston. *Savage.*

[19] Of the Rev. William Hubbard of Ipswich (Harvard 1642), Palfrey says (III, 153n), "Sometimes a person enjoys with his contemporaries a high reputation, which posterity is unable to account for." George Monk kept the Blue Anchor Tavern on what is now Washington Street.

Hubbard was appointed by the Ministers to deliver their mind, and that [he] had delivered it right. First five were, Mr. Jnº Higginson, Sam. Chiever, Joseph Estabrooks, Nicholas Noyes, Tho. Barnard.

The Governour goes from Lecture sick of a Cold, and dines not with us, nor comes to Court. Col. Pye dines with us, who comes hether by Land from Mary-Land.

Friday, July 24. Governour not abroad, very sharp debates about submission &c. upon a Governour's Arrival, occasioned by a vote from the Deputies to the purpose that the Court be Adjourned till 3ᵈ Wednesday in August except some demand of the Government from His Majestie be made before, then that effectual Order be taken for convening the Court by Governour, Dep. Governour or 3 Magistrates of Boston, and no Answer to be given till then. Magistrates past a Negative and another Vote for Adjournment till 2ᵈ Wednesday in October. Address is past but several did not vote, of which Self one. Mr. Stoughton and Dudley called as went home.[20]

Mr. Higginson gave in his Opinion for Submission this day in case a Commissioned Governour come over.

Satterday, July 25. Governour is prevailed with to sign the Address. Court is Adjourned by the Dept. Governour (for Governour at home) till the 2ᵈ Wednesday in August at one aclock: Several Freemen first made.

July 29ᵗʰ Cous. Dummer returns, and brings word of Mr. Batters Death this morn. He went from Court, as Mr. Addington the Speaker remembers, last Thorsday. Mr. Nath. Green arrives this day, comes from London June the 6. Jolls arrived in whom went the Letter concerning the Kings Proclamation.

Tho. Fayerwether a day or two before, by whom we hear of Argyle's Rising in Scotland, Landing there from Holland with the preparations against him. Act of Parliament for Settling the King's Revenue, as to the former King.

Thorsday, July 30. Actions (33) being heard, Court is Adjourned till Tuesday next, Jury not dismissed because of Several Criminals.

Friday, July ult. Condey arrives, hath had the Small Pocks of which Jnº Cutts, his own Son, a youth, and one more are dead; but 'tis said have been well a 14 night. When came a little above the Castle, took in the Colours and cast Anchor, and a Man coming from on Board would not tell what the matter was, so began to noise it that the new Governour was come, flocking to the waterside. Not considering that Condey came out before Green.

---

[20] The text of the address to the king is printed in *Mass. Bay Rec.* v, 495-496.

Satterday, Augt 1. An order from the Council is signed to cause the Ship to remove lower to Lovel's Iland, and there the Passengers, Ship, and Goods between Decks to be Aired: None to come to any Town till further Order. And None to entertain persons coming from the Ship. Yet Mr. Vaughan and Wyar gone homeward. Mr. Saml Epps dyed in London last April. It seems upon the 30th of July Mr. Eliot riding home his Horse stumbled and threw him, by which means his Collar-Bone is broken near his shoulder which puts him in great pain.

Wednesday, Augt. 5. rode to Dorchester Lecture with Cous. Nath. Dummer; was kindly entertained at Mr. Stoughton's after Lecture. Going thither I saw a few Feet of Ground enclosed with Boards, which is done by the Quakers out of respect to som one or more hanged and buried by the Gallows: though the Governour forbad them, when they asked Leave.

Augt 7th Eldridge Sails for London, wherein goes the Address to King James the 2^d. Hath been hindered from July 27. by running on a Rock, essaying to go out at Broad Sound.

Satterday 8. at night August 8. 1685. The Reverend Mr. Jno Sherman dyes: seemed to be cheerly in the morn and on Friday: the wether extream hot: Is buried on Monday August 10. 1685. Not many Ministers there, I suppose knew not of it. Dept. Governour, Major General Gookin, Mr. Stoughton, Dudley, Davie, Richards, Nowel, Russel, Hutchinson, Cook, Sewall, there: Governour not present. I saw one or two Coaches. He is much Lamented as a Godly, prudent, peacable Man. By Ed. Oaks I understand Mr. Adams is seised again with his Fever-Ague, so that said Oaks preach'd there all day on the Sabbath. When return from the Funeral, I find my little Hull extream ill.

Augt. 12. General Court meets: *Thorsday Augt. 13.* Adjourns till 3^d Wednesday in September, excepting Emergency. This Court ordered Court of Assistant Jurymen from Salem, and other Towns, not of late usual. The Treasurer refused to send out Warrants for Valuation, without a special order of Court, lest thereby he should seem to accept of that Office; so in his Bill he drew up, mentioned their providing a Treasurer against October. So the Secretary is ordered to give forth Warrants to the Towns to send in Votes for Treasurer to be presented to October Court. Is a Rumor that a Commission will be granted to some Gentlemen here, before the Governour come.

Augt. 14. I go to the Funeral of Robert Saunderson's young Son and Mr. Danl Allen's young Son. At night Mr. Willard, Eliot Jacob, Robt Walker, Frary, Nath. Oliver, Benj. Davis meet here to discourse.

Because the two last named desire to come into the Church without making any Relation at all; or having Mr. Willard report the Substance of what they said to him.

Tuesday, Augt. 18. The Posthumous Daughter of James Richards Esqr. is to be buried this day, died very suddenly.

Monday Morn. Augt. 17. The sad and unexpected Newes of Mr. Adams's Death came to Town.[21] Is to be buried on Wednesday. Relations of the young Nymph above, are also Relations to Mr. Adams.

Mr. Adams sate down to Supper with us on Thorsday even Augt. 6. in Company with Mr. Torrey. Mr. Torrey craving a Blessing, thanked God for the Interview. This day his Election Sermon came out, and Augt. the 7th Friday morn, he gave me the Errata, which was chiefly carried *away* in stead of carried with ambition. Supped with a new sort of Fish called Conners, my wife had bought, which occasioned Discourse on the Subject. Mr. Adams returned Thanks.

Wednesday, Augt. 19th 1685. I ride to the Funeral of the Reverend Mr. W[m] Adams from Roxbury, in the Company of Mr. Hutchinson, Sergeant and their wives. Magistrates there, Dept. Governour, Mr. Stoughton, Dudley Richards, Cook; Four of our Class, viz: Mr. Thacher, Bowls, Norton, Self. I took one Spell at carrying him. Is laid in Mr. Lusher's Tomb. Mr. Wilson prayed with the Company before they went to the Grave.[22] Dy'd a strong Death about Sun-Rise on Monday morn.

Augt. 20, 1685. Mr. Moodey preaches from Ps. 74. 9. There is no more any Prophet: With respect to four Ministers taken away in less than twice so many Moneths: Shewed that 'twas a peculiar Aggravation to all other Afflictions and Fears. Mr. Edw. Taylor lodges here this night, he hastened to Town against Lecture-day that so might see Mr. Adams among the Ministers after Lecture; but coming, found me gone to His Funeral.

Augt. 26. Mr. Condey the Shipmaster dyes about 9. last night. Hath been sick but a little while.

Aug. 27. Mr. Thomas Bayly preaches in Mr. Mather's Turn. After Lecture Capt. Condey buried. Gloves given to the Magistrates. Eight

[21] The Rev. William Adams of Dedham was one of Sewall's classmates. He left an interesting journal covering the years 1666 to 1683 which was printed in 4 *M.H.S.Colls.* I, 8-22.

[22] Sibley points out (II, 384n) that this is "Probably one of the earliest instances in New England of a prayer at a funeral. To avoid everything which would appear like idolatry and popery, the Puritans had no services, but the [relatives and] neighbors came together at the time appointed, and carried the body solemnly to the grave, standing by while it was buried."

Companies warned to Train next Monday. Capt. Eliot also warns the Troop.

Friday, Augt. 28, 1685. Mr. Foy arrives from London, about 8 weeks Passage, brings News of Argyle's being taken: and of Monmouth's being in Arms in England, with Rumors of a great Engagement and 30 or 40.000 slain, which Solomon Raynsford told us at Dinner. 'Tis said there are Black Boxes sent to Mr. Stoughton, Dudley, Bulkly, and Wharton. Many are clapt up in London, so that the Halls [*of the Companies, e.g., Fishmongers, &c.*] full.[23]

This day Augt. 28. is a Church Meeting at which 'tis consented that Persons may be taken in, the Church only being present, and not the Congregation: at the same time Mr. Benj. Davis, Mr. Nath. Oliver and Mr. Sam¹ Checkly were propounded.

Monday, Augt. 31. Eight Companies and the Troop Train. Dine with the South-Company, Capt. Blackwell, Mr. Brown of Barbados, Mr. Tho. Bayly, Capt. Gerrish, Capt. Jnᵒ Higginson, Cous. Dummer Trained. This morn Commissioners chosen, and by reason of the Training, persons came and delivering their Votes went away, and some came not at all, so that was but Nine Persons when they were proclaimed and but eleven at any time in telling. Most had 61 Votes, generally 50 odd. Mr. Nowell and my self present for 2.

After went to see my sick Ensign, and staid while Mr. Willard went to prayer with him, his Life is feared. A Ten-pound Horse was stab'd and killed with a Pike this day, Jnᵒ Bemis's: Company made a Gathering 16s. In the South-Company, Mr. Allen Prayed, 5-9 verses 149 Ps. sung.

[23] Soon after he came to the throne James II had two anti-Catholic revolts on his hands. Archibald Campbell, ninth Earl of Argyll, who had escaped to the Netherlands four years before under sentence for treason, landed in May in the west of Scotland where he was joined by twenty-five hundred men. They were hemmed in on all sides by superior numbers and quickly defeated. Argyll was taken to Edinburgh and executed 30 June. James Scott, natural son of Charles II, who had acknowledged him and made him Duke of Monmouth, had been residing in the Netherlands, treated with distinction by the Prince of Orange. He landed in June at Lyme Regis on the Dorset coast with a small force and issued a proclamation inviting patriotic Englishmen to join him in expelling James from the throne. Some two thousand men joined him and repelled a great force of royal troops under the Duke of Albemarle. At Taunton he proclaimed himself king and six thousand flocked to his standard, but James assembled an effective army, and at the Battle of Sedgemoor, 6 July, the insurgents were routed. Monmouth was captured, taken to London, and beheaded on Tower Hill 15 July. *Palfrey* III, 449-451 and *D.N.B.* By the first of October witnesses to both executions had reached Boston.

Thorsday, Septr 3^d My Ensign Mr. Asaph Eliot dyes about 3 *post Meridiem*, of a Fever. Is to be buried next Satterday about 2 of the Clock. Mr. Jno Bayly preached the Lecture. Several desirable persons are lately dead at Watertown in a week or two.

Friday, Septr 4, '85. about 6 aclock Mr. Asaph Eliot, Ensign of the South-Company was buried: 'twas rainy wether, but had 7 Files Pikes and 6 Musketeers. Mr. Eliot was about 34 years old.

Sabbath-day, Septr 6. in the time of Afternoon-Exercise, a considerable Gust of Thunder, Lightening, Rain.

Suppose this to be the day that a Barn was burnt by it at Roxbury.

Tuesday Sept. 8. A Porpus was pursued and taken within the inward Wharfs.

Wednesday, 7 [month]: 9th Dined at Mr. Dudley's in Company of Counsellor Bond, Mr. Stoughton, Blackwell, Davie, Torrey, Willard, Shrimpton, El^m Hutchinson, Paige, King, Allen, Mrs. Willard, Mrs. Paige. Mr. Hutchinson shewed me his Letter concerning his Mill at Piscataqua, wherein is sollicited to build a Fort, lest the Indians burn it. When came home heard of a Body of Indians near Chelmsford, 3 or 400. The Rumors and Fears concerning them do much increase.

The Indians are near Albany: Wonolanset brings the news to Chelmsford; and mistrust of theirs mischievous Designs.

Thorsday 7 [month]: 10th Mr. Jno Cotton preaches the Lecture. After Lecture Counsellor Bond dines with the Court, Thanks them all for their curtesy and kindness to him. Goes off in Mr. Smith.

Sabbath-day Septr 13, 1685. Mr. Benj. Davis, Nathl Oliver, Saml Checkly and his wife are received into the Church, which is a Sabbath or 2 sooner than I expected: The Lord's Supper not being to be administered till Octr 4th. Saml Checkly had most in 's Relation: two wear Perriwigs:[24] viz: Davis, Checkly.

Mr. Bond with us to day. Were first propounded Augt. 28.

Sept. 14, 1685. Go to Cambridge, and there hear Mr. Wigglesworth preach excellently from those words, Fight the good Fight of Faith, Lay hold on eternal Life. *vid.* Notes.[25] Capt. Hill chosen Capt. Mr.

---

[24] Sewall's intense dislike for wigs is one of the amusing threads that runs all through the Diary. Mr. Worthington Chauncey Ford has a disquisition on Sewall and wigs in *C.S.M.* xx, 109f.

[25] Several small manuscript volumes in which Sewall made full notes of sermons he heard are preserved at the Massachusetts Historical Society and the Boston Public Library. The sermons of that time followed a definite form which facilitated their recollection for later discussion or recording. We give Perry Miller's analysis: "The Puritan sermon quotes the·text and 'opens' it as briefly as possible, expounding circumstances and context, explaining its grammatical meanings, reducing its tropes and schemata to prose, and setting forth its logical implications;

Lynde Lieut. Mr. Williams of New-Cambridge [*Newton*] Ensign. Mr. Hill I think will not accept. Coming home, hear of Meadfield Mill being burnt, and their confusion at Malborough last Satterday night. A suspected Indian is put in Prison. It seems were in Arms last Sabbathday at Dedham, somway knowing of Meadfield Mill being burnt. People are much perplexed.

Tuesday, Septr 15. Take leav of Mr. Bond and give him Mr. Oakes's Artillery Sermon to read at Sea, stitched in Marble paper. Sails in Mr. Smith.

Tuesday, Septr 15, 1685. Mr. Barns tells me the Governour of Carolina is come to Town this day for his health: is so weak that stumbled at a pebble and fell down. Name, West.[26] Mr. Willard speaks to the 7th Commandment, condemns naked Brests[27]: and seems to be against the Marriage of First-Cousins.

Thorsday, Septr 17. News comes to Town of the rising of the Negros at Jamaica. Proves nothing answerable to the Rumor.

Generall Court having Voted that care be taken to see that all Persons are furnisht with Arms and Ammunition according to Law because of Indians, that Wonolanset have £10. given him to appease [*him*], because he alledges some of his carried away contrary to safe Conduct, and for his late Service; that the West end of the Town-House be secured with Lead at the Country's Charge, Court is adjourned to the 2^d Wednesday in October at one of the Clock. Tim^o Prout made surveyor general in Mr. Stoddard's Room, to look after stock of Powder &c.

Mr. Dudley, Saltonstall, Buckley, to say whether they will accept their Commissions as Majors.

Sabbath-day night, Septr. 20. 1685. Watch with Isaac Goose, and Cous. Nath. Dummer. Sam. Clark keeps on Board his Brother's Ship, intending a Voyage to Sea, having no work in the Shop.

Note, Sabbath-day, Septr 20. Mr. Jno Baily preaches with us all day: Mr. Willard at Watertown. In the Afternoon from those words of

---

the sermon then proclaims in a flat, indicative sentence the 'doctrine' contained in the text or logically deduced from it, and proceeds to the first reason or proof. Reason follows reason, with no other transition than a period or a number; after the last proof is stated there follow the uses or applications, also in numbered sequence, and the sermon ends when there is nothing more to be said." *The New England Mind: The Seventeenth Century* (1954), 332-333.

26 Joseph West was deputy for the Duke of Albemarle in the first permanent settlement made in Carolina in 1669 and had served as governor for several years. *D.A.B.*

27 It was the Indian maidens who went about this way in the summer, not the Puritans, but Willard was probably discussing *haute couture.*

Job, Till my Change come. Doct[*rine*] Death a very great Change.

Monday, 7ʳ [*September*] *21.* Shewed Mr. Tho. Chiever, School-master, in the Evening, what had received from Jamaica concerning Zadori [*a stranger from Hungary*].

Tuesday, 7ʳ 22. 1685. Jnᵒ Gardener came in late last night; this morning the News he brings runs throw the Town, viz. that James late D[*uke*] of Monmouth was beheaded on Tower-Hill on the 15ᵗʰ July last. Argyle drawn, hanged and quartered. Neighbor Fifield brought me the News, who had it from the Cryer of Fish.

Mr. Nowel and Moodey called here, having been to see sick father Porter, this morn 7ʳ 22.

7ʳ 22. This day Mr. Morgan, his Lady and Family arrive from Bar-bados intending to dwell here for some time.

By the same Ship word is brought of the death of Mr. Henry Hig-ginson of the Small Pocks.

7ʳ 22. In the Afternoon I visit Father Porter, and Mr. West late Governor of Carolina, who comes hether for cure of the Dry Gripes.

Wednesday 7ʳ 23. Cous. Nath. Dummer and I ride to Milton Lec-ture. Before Lecture, I went to Anthony Gulliver and got him to go with me to Penny-Ferry and shew me the Marsh [*he*] was to buy of Mr. Gardener. He owned that he hired the Marsh 6 Acres of my Father at fifty shillings and would see me paid; seemed to say he hired it for his Son. Dined at Mr. Thacher's.

Wednesday night, Septʳ 23. Mr. Clutterbuck Arrives from New-Castle and brings word that he saw Argile's head cut off June the last; and the certain Newes of the Death of Monmouth about the middle of July. Dissenters in the North released, and Scotland in quiet.

'Tis remarkable that Clutterbuck should from Ocular Testimony contradict diametrically the Rumors that were spread in Town Friday was Sennight and strongly propagated, said to come by Clutterbuck: which was a meer Lye.

Laurence Vandenbosk Fr[*ench*] Minister Marries [*Giles*] Sylves-ter and Widow Gillam; though had promis'd the Court to do no more such things: this about the beginning 7ʳ: is since gone to New York.[28]

---

[28] Laurence Vanden Bosch, a Huguenot minister, had violated the law by per-forming marriages, a privilege strictly limited to magistrates and other civil offi-cers, and also by failing to publish the intentions of marriage (or banns) two weeks ahead. Giles Sylvester was the son of Nathaniel, who owned Shelter Island, and Savage believed that the minister accompanied or followed the Sylvesters there. The bride was Hannah, daughter of Thomas Savage and widow

7ʳ 25. Brother and Sister Stev. Sewall visit us. His Honour visits the Carolina Governour.

7ʳ 26. Jnᵒ Turner arrives from Newfound-Land, brings above 20 Passengers, though his vessel so very small. 14ⁿᵗˢ Passage.

Monday, Septʳ 28, 1685. Meeting of Boston-Freemen to chuse a Treasurer for the Country. Mrs. Stanbury buried last night.

The last high Tide carried away the Bridge at Cambridge [*to what is now Brighton*], part of it; so that Cous. Fissenden now keeps a Ferry there. Seth tells me 'tis that part the Town was to maintain. Friday was Sennight, by a Raft of Boards.

Septʳ 29. Cous. Nath. Dummer goes to Salem in Capt. More to try to sell what remains of his Goods, for Fish there. Cous. Fissenden calls in, all were well lately at Newbury, he having visited them.

Thursday, Octʳ 1. 1685. Mr. Samson Stoddard arrives, who came from London the 25. July: brings the particulars of the Taking and Executing of the Late Duke of Monmouth whoes Head he saw struck off. Persons confined are now released.

Friday, Octʳ 2. go to Andrew Gardener's at Muddy River to gather Chestnuts in Company Mr. Dudley, Shrimpton, Lidget, Luscomb: 3 last I knew nothing of till came to Roxbury. Made us Eat there after came from Nutting.

Monday Octʳ 5. Cloudy Lowring day, yet the Artillery Company goes over to Charlestown: the 2 Companies Train: we divide into 2, and with Cambridge Artillery oppose them upon the Hill in prospect of the Harbour. Mr. Cotton Mather prayed with us in the morn, and at breaking up. Capt. Wade with his Troop there: the Major Generall with a small Guard. Major Richards, Mr. Treasurer, Mr. Nowel, Cook, dine with us at Jackson's. Mr. Cotton Mather Craves a Blessing and Returns Thanks. Got over about dark.

Wednesday, 8ʳ [October] 7ᵗʰ Meeting at our House, Mr. Zech. Walker speaks from Gen. 6. 8, 9. to very good purpose, shewing how may walk to be in a way of finding favour in God's Sight. Last Direct. was to carry it as inoffensively as might towards Men, that our own Rashness and indiscretion might not be the cause of our suffering.

Thorsday, Octʳ 8. Dolebery arrives being 7 weeks this day from London: brings little News that I hear of; only 'tis rumored, we are not like to have an alteration of the Government this year. A youth about

---

of Benjamin Gillam. It is known that Vanden Bosch later officiated at Rye, Staten Island, and Kingston, in New York province. *M.H.S.Proc.* LII, 122-124; *Savage; Andros Tracts* II, 36-37; E. T. Corwin, *Manual of the Reformed Church in America* (1879), 499-500.

nine years old, Son to Emmanuel Wishart, drowned this day. County Court dissolved.

Satterday, Octr 10, 1685. We read in course the defeat of Adonija; and the illustrious Coronation of King Solomon.

Sabbath-day, Octr 11. A day of Sore Rain almost all day Long: Rained very hard going to and from Meeting forenoon and all Meeting time till 2 aclock, and great part Afternoon, and now at dark Rains hard. Hath been cloudy, Rainy, dark Wether above this week: but this Day exceeds. Eliza. Foxcroft Baptised this Afternoon.

Monday, Octr 12. South-Company Trains, rest discouraged by the wet because thought could not perform their intended Exercise.

Tuesday, Octr 13. Is a rumor in Town of Jolls's being cast away on the Cape and all the Passengers Lost but five Persons; Mr. Randolph drowned: but suppose all groundless.

Friday, Octr 16. The Reverend Mr. Michael Wigglesworth is chosen by the Magistrates to Preach the next Election-Sermon.

Satterday, Octr 17. Yesterday Mr. Stoughton and Dudley were grossly abused on the Road by James Begelo [*Bigelow*] of Watertown, and others. Begelo lay in Gaol all night, and to day bound over to the County Court first Tuesday in November. Court adjourned till Tuesday Morning next; partly because of the designed Training. Before Adjournment the Deputies sent down a Smart Bill, alledging that they were no blameable cause of the Laws not being Printed.

Monday, Octr 19th Training of Six Companies. Exercise was Taking of the Fort and advancing White Colours with Red Cross, above the Red Colours: so it stood while went to Dinner. Then Retaken. Firings on the Common: Vollies to the Governour. About Nine aclock at night News comes to Town of Capt. Henchman's Death at Worcester last Thorsday; buried on Friday. Very few at his Funeral, his own Servants, a white and black, carried him to, and put him in his Grave. His Wife and children following and no more, or but one or two more.

Tuesday, Octr 20th Mr. Torrey here, prays with me and my Wife in the Morning. Great Rain and Storm.

Octr 21, 1685. Capt. Jn° Phillips finally refuses to be Treasurer; the Magistrates chuse Mr. Nowel: but the Deputies would have it done by the Freemen, that their Priviledges may not be clipt, as many of them have of late been. Mr. Walker speaks at Mrs Oliver's from Isa. 59, 19. When the Enemy shall come in like a Flood, &c., being the place propounded by said Oliver. Very rainy day. Din'd 5. times, as suppose.

Wednesday, Octr 21. '85. very high Tide, went into our Cellar over the Wharf: but did not fill it: filled several other Cellars.

Thorsday, Octr 22. Deputies reassume their Vote as to the Treasurer and consent with the Magistrates, provided it be not drawn into an Example: so after Lecture Mr. Nowel took his Oath as Treasurer, having first made a worthy Speech. The Bill is passed that Persons must be Arrested 14 days inclusive before the Court. Court Adjourned to the 3ᵈ Tuesday in November at one aclock: except there be some great Occasion to convene sooner. A Half Money-Rate and whole Rate in Country-pay passed. Mr. Mather preached from Ps. 73. 28. first part: 'Tis good for all to draw near to God. No Thanks-Giving this Session.

Octr 31. 1685. Mrs. Prout, the Mother, is buried; Rain part of the way, so but a few comparatively at the Grave; Rainbow seen. *Note,* Little Hull had a sore Convulsion Fit this day about Noon, so that I was sent for home from Court: had another near Sunset.

Satterday, Octr 31. in the even I read in course in the Family Mr. Norton's Sermon on Jnᵒ 8. 20. Lib^r 22. 8ᵗʰ 3ᵈ 1659. Doct. All Engagements of Spirit, and Advantages notwithstanding; the Changes that befall Men, they come neither before nor after, but in the appointed Hour, or the precise Time, foreappointed of God.[29] Sometime this Week a virulent Libel was fixed on Mr. Dudley's Fence, extreamly abusive, especially to Him.

Novr 3ᵈ Capt. Brown Dines with the Court. Giles Goddard is brought in Not guilty respecting Mr. Nowel's Trunks, lost in Time of the Fire. 1679.

Novr 3ᵈ James Begelo fined 10£ and Stebbin 5£ for their Abuses to Mr. Stoughton and Dudley. To find Bond for good Behaviour till next Court, then Appear; Fees of Court, standing Committed till performed.

Wednesday, Novr 4ᵗʰ The County Court was Adjourned to Thorsday come Sennight at 2 aclock.

Mr. Allin preached Novr 5. 1685—finished his Text 1 Jnᵒ 1. 9. mentioned not a word in Prayer or Preaching that I took notice of with respect to Gun-powder Treason.[30] Part of the 132ᵈ Ps. sung; viz. from

[29] Sewall wrote in the margin: "An Excellent Doctrine. Providence of God." John Norton of Ipswich (1606-1663), B.A. Cambridge 1623/4, was a fanatical persecutor of the Quakers. The only sermon he published in 1659 was called *The Heart of N-England Rent at the Blasphemies of the Present Generation,* and was a bitter attack on the Quakers, written by order of the General Court. *D.A.B.*

[30] James Allen, B.A. Oxford 1652, was minister of the First Church. Sewall writes as if it were customary on this date to refer to the unsuccessful Gunpowder

11th v. The Lord to David Sware—to the End. In the Even I met at
Serj^t Bull's with Capt. Frary, Serj^t Gardener, Pell, Raynsford, Corp^{ll}
Odlin, Quinsey, Paddy, Clerk Mason, Wheeler; Ten mentioned sate
down to Supper, Serj^t Bull and his Wife waited: After by the Fire
spake as to an Ensign, all said they were unanimous for Serj^t Gardener
upon Serj^t Bull's refusal, who alledged, as formerly, the loss of 's 4th
Finger of 's right Hand, and a Pain in the same Shoulder: and as to
me, is not of any Church, nor a Freeman, nor of Estate, besides the
former Objections. Although it rained hard, yet there was a Bonfire
made on the Common, about 50 attended it.

Friday night being fair about two hundred hallowed about a Fire
on the Common.

Friday, Novr 6. Mr. Willard calls in and tells me of a Thanks-
Giving intended by the Ministers through the Colony upon the 3^d
of the next Moneth: Go to the Governour to get his Approbation,
which He doth not presently grant; but will speak of it in Council
on Thorsday next; whether convenient for the Churches generally to
attend such a Day without an Order from Authority, as usual. The
difficulty of Printing an Order is, lest by putting in, or leaving out,
we offend England. Having occasion this day to go to Mr. Hayward
the Publick Notary's House, I speak to him about his cutting off his
Hair, and wearing a Perriwig of contrary Colour: mention the words
of our Saviour, Can ye not make one Hair white or black: and Mr.
Alsop's Sermon. He alleges, The Doctors advised him to it.

Sabbathday Novr 8. By Mr. Willard's Prayer in the Morn, I understood some Minister was dead: Enquiring at Noon was told by my
Wife, from Mr. Willard, that it was Mr. Nathaniel Chauncy of Hatfield. Was a Learned Godly Man.

In the Afternoon Mr. Willard Ordained our Brother Theophilus
Frary to the Office of a Deacon. Declared his Acceptance Jany 11th
first, and now again. Propounded it to the Congregation at Noon:

Plot of Guy Fawkes and others to blow up James I and the Lords and Commons
on 5 November 1605. The celebration of Guy Fawkes Day with bonfires went
on in England and the colonies for two centuries. (On this date, John Evelyn
wrote in his *Diary* in London, ". . . indisposed by a very great rheum, I did not
go to church, to my very great sorrow, it being the first Gunpowder Conspiracy
anniversary that had been kept now these eighty years under a prince of the
Roman religion.") In later years in Boston, in addition to the usual effigies of
Guy Fawkes, the Pope, and the Devil, those of other unpopular characters, such
as Governor Hutchinson and General Gage, were carried about the streets and
finally burned. For the history of the celebration in New England, see *C.S.M.*
xii, 289f.

Then in Even propounded if any of the Church or other had to object they might speak: Then took the Church's Vote, then called him up to the Pulpit, laid his Hand on 's Head, and said I ordain Thee &c., gave Him his Charge, then Prayed, and sung the 2ᵈ part of the 84ᵗʰ Ps. 4 Children Baptised before the Ordination. Thomas Eyre; William, Eliza, Joseph. So God in some measure is building our House when pulling down others.

Going to Mr. Willard's I understand Mr. Thomas Cobbet died last Thorsday Even, to be buried tomorrow Novʳ 9ᵗʰ; was abroad at some of his Neighbours the Monday before. Mr. Chauncey died on Tuesday last. So two Ministers dead this last week.

Monday Novʳ 9. Mr. Cobbet buried about 4. in the Afternoon. Flight of snow. This day about 6 or 7 at night a Male Infant pin'd up in a sorry Cloth is laid upon the Bulk [*stall*] of Shaw, the Tabacco-Man: Great Search made tonight and next day to find the Mother. So far as I can hear this is the first Child that ever was in such a manner exposed in Boston.

Thorsday, Novʳ 12. Mr. Moodey preaches from Isa. 57. 1. Mr. Cobbet's Funeral Sermon; said also of Mr. Chauncy that he was a Man of Singular Worth. Said but 2 of the First Generation left.

After, the Ministers of this Town Come to the Court and complain against a Dancing Master who seeks to set up here and hath mixt Dances, and his time of Meeting is Lecture-Day; and 'tis reported he should say that by one Play he could teach more Divinity than Mr. Willard or the Old Testament. Mr. Moodey said 'twas not a time for N. E. to dance. Mr. Mather struck at the Root, speaking against mixt Dances.[31]

An order is made to summon Mr. Shrimpton to Answere Mr. Sergeant by virtue of the new Law: about the Fathers Will, next Monday 14 night, which is the last of Novʳ Mr. Shrimpton and Sergeant differ about Will. Ecclips at night. County Court adjourned till this day 14 night. Governour's Hat blew off and fell flat on the Ground just as went to go in at 's Gate. Hath a new Border which began to wear Catechising day or Sabbath last, as I take it. Dept. Governour not in Town. New Almanack comes out this Day intituled New-England's Almanack, by Mr. Danforth.

The Ship Capt. Berry went out Master of to Jamaica, came in this day: He dyed in the Voyage, and was buried in the Sea.

[31] The unfortunate Francis Stepney, dancing master, had a very cool reception in Boston, and was in continual trouble with the authorities until he fled the town the following July.

Friday, Nov 13. Barington arrives, brings word of the beheading my Lady Lisle, Mrs. Hez. Usher's Mother, at Winchester.[32] 4 Executed at London, Mr. Jenkins's Son, Alderm Hayes Son, and 2 more, and whipping the Taunton Maids. Capt. Jolls dead in London. Is a Rumor that the Government will be Changed, this Fall or Winter, by some Person sent over, or a Commission to some here.

It seems there was a Thanksgiving kept at Deacon Allin's this Day, which knew not of till Satterday. Madam Usher there. Have a Gazette to the 24th of August which mentions the raising the Sieg of Grann, taking Newheusel, defeating the Turkish Army by the Imperialists.

This Friday night began to read the Revelation in Course, having begun Pareus just about the same time though not on purpose.

Sabbath-day, Nov 15, 1685. In the Afternoon Mary Smith, Widow, Mr. Wheelwright's Grandchild, was taken into Church; then Mr. Willard mentioned what the Elders had done as to a Thanks–giving, and propounded to the Church that we might have one on the First Thorsday in December: because had Fasted, and God had graciously answered our Prayers; so should meet Him in the same place to give Thanks for that, and any other Providence that hath passed before us. Silence gave Consent, no one speaking.[33]

Monday, Nov 16. Brother Stephen here, and gives an Account of what had done at Kittery, for which was glad, but sorely saddened by Hullie's being taken with Convulsion Fits that Even. Gave of Dr. Winthrop's Physick and Cordials.

Tuesday Even Mr. Moodey here, prays with us; then I go with him to see Madam Usher, expecting to have seen some Prints; but had

[32] Alice (Beckenshaw) Lisle was the wife of John Lisle (B.A. Oxford 1626), barrister and M.P. and legal adviser to the High Court of Justice which condemned Charles I to death. At the Restoration Lisle fled to Lausanne, where he was assassinated. Following the suppression of Monmouth's rebellion the incredibly brutal Lord Chief-Justice Jeffreys was turned loose on the survivors of the Battle of Sedgemoor in what became known as the Bloody Assizes. Over a thousand men were sent to the Barbadoes as slaves and three hundred were put to death and their carcases hung along the roadways. Alice Lisle had harbored two fugitives without knowing their identity. For this she was condemned to be burned alive, but James II commuted the sentence to execution by beheading. A fresco in the Commons Corridor of the Houses of Parliament depicts Dame Alice concealing the fugitives. Bridget Lisle, her daughter, was the wife of President Leonard Hoar of Harvard; after his death she married Hezekiah Usher Jr., merchant of Boston. *D.N.B.*; M.H.S.EDS.

[33] At this time, and for many years to come, Thanksgivings were not held as a matter of routine on a stated day, but were called at any season and always for a special reason which was emphatically stated.

only a Letter from a Sister which reached to the day of Condemnation [*of her mother*]. Mr. Moodey prayed there: took leave.

*Wednesday, Nov*ʳ *18.* Uncomfortable Court day by reason of the extream sharp words between the Deputy Governour and Mr. Stoughton, Dudley and Others. Some Essay to have put a Sanction upon the Appointment for a Thanksgiving; but it fell throw. I argued 'twas not fit upon meer Generals, as (the Mercies of the year) to Command a Thanksgiving and of Particulars we could not agree. Governour would have had one Article for the Peace of England, according to His Majesty's Proclamation.

Hollowells business heard, as to Land: about that grew the fiercness in discourse. Mr. G. Boroughs dined with us.[34] Major Generall not well. Mr. Shove comes to Town today; but I see him not.

*Thorsday, Nov*ʳ *19.* Mr. Mather Preaches from Numb. 25. 11. Shewed that Love was an ingredient to make one zealous: those that received good People, received Christ, Mat. 25. Said that if the Government of N. E. were zealous might yet save this People. 2ᵈ Part of 79ᵗʰ Ps. sung. Madam Usher, her Daughter and Husband in Mourning. Mr. Stoughton and Dudley called here. 'Tis reported that a Frigot is to come yet before Spring with a Commission for a Governor here, upon the place: Mr. Dudley is talked of and 'tis said Healths are drunk to the new Governour already, and were so Novʳ 17. the day the Ship came in. I presented a Bill for Serjᵗ Andrew Gardener to be Ensign of the South-Company, which past the Magistrates, the whole Court.

Mr. Tho. Weld is approved by about 11 Magistrates Novʳ 19ᵗʰ in his intended Work of Gathering a Church the 16ᵗʰ of December next, Wednesday.

*Friday Nov*ʳ *20*ᵗʰ a very rainy and dark day, and in the Afternoon turns to a storm of Snow: Court is adjourned to Tuesday, February 16ᵗʰ at One of the Clock, except some Frigot or Ships Arrival from England with His Majesty's Commands that may call for one sooner; then the Secretary, or if he sick or dead, the Treasurer, to send forthwith to the Members of the Court, and to such others as Freemen may chuse to convene two days after the Date of such Signification, to which time the Court is adjourned in such Case. No Freemen made, nor Prayer. Ground covered with Snow by that time Court done, which is een quite dark. Mr. Stoughton and Dudley not here today. 'Twas Essayed again to have had a Sanction put on the

---

[34] It fell to Sewall seven years later, as a member of the Salem court, to sit in judgment on his dinner guest and college-mate, Rev. George Burroughs (Harvard 1670), and condemn him to execution for witchcraft.

Thanksgiving: but 'twas again pleaded, to do it without mentioning particular causes would be to impose too much on those Commanded: So fell.[35]

Monday night Novr 23. 1685. I go the Rounds with Cous. Quinsey and Isaac Goose, a very severe night for Cold, yet 'twas fair and comfortable: came home at 5. *mane.*

Novr 25, Wednesday. Just before I went to the Meeting at Brother Hayward's, where I was to speak from Ps. 79. 8, Jn° Turner, Master of the Brigenteen, came in and told me that James Mudge, one of his seamen, having carried a Pass to the Castle, coming on Board again, fell between the Boat and Brigenteen into Water and was drowned. He several years since gave his Daughter to Capt. Chips Daughter at Charlestown. Thawing Wether.

Novr 26, Thorsday. Nurse Goose dyes about 2. or 3. aclock in the night; having lien sick about a Week: was here it seems Wednesday was Sennight. Was helpful to her self all along till this last sickness: washt her own Cloaths. She saw her great Grandchildren: was a good Woman.

Mary an Indian, James's Squaw, was Frozen to death upon the Neck near Roxbury Gate on Thorsday night Novr 27th 85, being fudled.

Novr 30. Nurse Goose buried. Was not well yesterday, Feverish and tossing most of the night; so not at the Court nor meeting of Magistrates, nor at the Funeral. Mr. Willard here, I returned Alsop of Scandal. Mr. Secretary here.

At night viewed the Eclips, which in the total obscuration was ruddy; but when began to receive some Light, the darkish ruddiness ceased. Horizon somewhat Hazy. Read in course the Eleventh of the Revelation.

30. Novr Cous. Nath. Dummer visits us.

Wednesday, Decr 2. Elias Parkman comes in, and hath a man drowned near the Castle, as E[*liaki*]m [*Mather*] tells me. See last Wednesday.

Friday, Decr 4th Being at Mr. Addington's upon Business, He tells me Mr. Shrimpton's Answer in writing last Monday was, that the Court proceeded upon a Law made since the vacating the Charter, and therefore he should not attend: so that this Monday we begin palpably to dye [*i. e., the Government by the Colony Charter*].

Sabbath-day, December 6. Hull hath a Convulsion Fit as he sits in

---

[35] The court was carefully non-committal on matters of English politics, to which a reference was proposed in the proclamation. M.H.S.EDS.

his Grandmother's Lap at Table, dining, with which we are much surprised.

Monday, Decemb^r 7th 1685. About One in the Night my Wife is brought to Bed of a Son, of which Mother Hull brings me the first News: Mrs. Weeden Midwife.

Wednesday Decr 9th 1685. Our Neighbor Gemaliel Wait eating his Breakfast well, went to do something in his Orchard, where Serj^t Pell dwells, there found him Self not well and went into Pell's his Tenant's House, and there dyed extream suddenly about Noon, and then was carried home in a Chair, and means used to fetch him again, but in vain: To the Children startled about him he said, here is a sudden Change, or there will be a great Change, to that purpose. Was about 87 years old, and yet strong and hearty: had lately several new Teeth. People in the Street much Startled at this good Man's sudden Death. Govr Hinkley[36] sent for me to Mr. Rawson's just as they were sending a great Chair to carry him home.

Satterday, Decr 12, '85. Father Wait buried: Magistrates and Ministers had Gloves. There heard of the Death of Capt. Hutchinson's Child by Convulsions, and so pass to the Funeral of little Samuel Hutchinson about Six weeks old, where also had a pair of Funeral Gloves.

Peter Butler comes in this day, Several have had the Small Pocks; buried a Negro. Several very green, hardly recovered; among whom Nathl Parkman is one. Snowy day.

Esther Kein at her Time, falls into Convulsion Fits, and dyes last Thorsday: No likelihood of the Child's being born.

Sabbath-day, Decemb^r 13th 1685. Mr. Willard baptizeth my Son lately born, whom I named Henry: David Stoddard, the son of Mr. Simeon Stoddard, was baptized next, and then Several other grown Children. Nurse Hill came in before the Psalm was Sung, and yet the Child was fine and quiet: Mr. Willard preached from John 15th 8. Herein is my Father glorified, that you bear much Fruit, so shall ye be my Disciples: which is the first Sermon my little Son hath been present at.

Monday, Dec. 14. County-Court meets about Mr. Sergeant's Business chiefly: Mr. Shrimpton's Letter is read: but 'tis not agreed on to proceed, and some Heat, the Vote being in a manner equal. Mr. Stoughton and Maj^r Richards not there. Mr. Shrimpton pleads that he has fullfilled his Father's Will dated July 17th One Thousand Six

36 Thomas Hinckley (c.1618-1706) was Governor of Plymouth Colony; he was the last to hold that office.

hundred Sixty and Six: and cannot submit to this arbitrary way, especially the Law being made since the Dissolution of the Charter of this Place. Govr seems somewhat resolute: the Court Adjourned till Thorsday. Something of Bushnell, the Barber's, relating to his Estate was now also done: He dyed in '67. just about the same Time Mr. Wilson did, as I remember.

This Monday a Jury is summond who sit on the Body of Joseph Johnson, and the verdict they find, a wound an inch or 2 above his Navel which they judge to be the cause of his Death, and that they were informed James Morgan did it with a Spit. So were Sworn in Court Decr 14. 1685., and James Morgan ordered to have Irons put on him. He committed the Fact last Thorsday night.

Wednesday, Dec. 16. A very pleasant Day for gathering the Church at Dunstable, and Ordaining Mr. Thomas Weld.

Thorsday, Decr 17th Mr. Mather preacheth from Mat. 16., former part of the 25th Verse. For whosoever will save his Life shall Lose it. At County-Court nothing done in Mr. Sergeant's Business: So he makes a Speech when the Court open, that if the Court did nothing they would give him a Record of it, that he might go elsewhere for he would not be kept out of 's Money; speaking warmly.

Mr. Francis Stepney, the Dancing Master, desired a Jury, so He and Mr. Shrimpton Bound in 50£ to Jan^r Court. Said Stepney is ordered not to keep a Dancing School; if he does will be taken in contempt and be proceeded with accordingly. Mr. Shrimpton muttered, saying he took it as a great favour that the Court would take his Bond for £50.

Sabbath, Decr 13. 1685. Jno Maryon, the Father, faints in the Old Meetinghouse, in time of Worship, which obstructs Mr. Allen, and makes considerable disturbance.

Decr 17. One Trescot, an ancient woman of Dorchester, riding over the Neck, Tide being high, her Horse drowned and she hardly saved: questioned whether she may live or no. This night Little Hull hath a Convulsion Fit, as he lay with me in Bed. Henry very restless.

Friday, Decemb^r 18, 1685. Father John Odlin, one of the very first Inhabitants of Boston, dies; know not of above one more besides the Governour [*Bradstreet*].[37]

Satterday, Decr 19th Father Jno Odlin buried in the first Burying place [*corner of Tremont and School Streets*] as father Wait the Satterday before.

---

[37] John Odlin was one of four survivors of the earliest settlers of Boston, and had testified before Sewall, 10 June 1684, as to the purchase of the peninsula of Boston from William Blaxton.

Friday Dec. 18. Begun in Course to read the New-Testament, having ended the Revelation the night before.

Satterday Dec. 19. Mr. Willard Prayes with my little Henry, being very ill.

Sabbath-day, Dec. 20. Send Notes to Mr. Willard and Mr. Moodey to pray for my Child Henry.

Monday, about four in the Morn the faint and moaning noise of my child forces me up to pray for it.

21. Monday even Mr. Moodey calls. I get him to go up and Pray with my extream sick Son.

Tuesday Morn, Dec. 22. Child makes no noise save by a kind of snoaring as it breathed, and as it were slept.

Read the 16ᵗʰ of the first Chron. in the family. Having read to my Wife and Nurse out of John: the fourteenth Chapter fell now in course, which I read and went to Prayer: By that time had done, could hear little Breathing, and so about Sun-rise, or little after, he fell asleep, I hope in Jesus, and that a Mansion was ready for him in the Father's House. Died in Nurse Hill's Lap. Nurse Hill washes and layes him out: because our private Meeting hath a day of Prayer tomorrow, Thorsday Mr. Willard's Lecture, and the Child dying after Sunrise (wether cloudy), have determined to bury on Thorsday after Lecture. The Lord sanctify his Dispensation, and prepare me and mine for the coming of our Lord, in whatsoever way it be. Mr. Tho. Oakes our Physician for this Child. Read the 16ᵗʰ Chap. of the First Chronicles in the Family.

Tuesday night read the 15ᵗʰ Jnᵒ in the Chamber, out of which Mr. Willard took his Text the day Henry was baptized: in the Family, the 3ᵈ of Matthew, both requiring Fruit.

Wednesday, Dec. 23. Go to the privat Fast at Brother Williams's. Capt. Scottow begins and is enlarged and fervent in praying for the Church and Christ's Witnesses: Made me conclude. Sung part 137. Ps. But if I Jerusalem, &c. Just before I went, Brother Longfellow[38] came in, which was some exercise to me, he being so ill conditioned and so outwardly shabby. The Lord humble me. As I remember, he came so before; either upon the funeral of my Father or Johnny.

Thorsday, Decʳ 24ᵗʰ 1685. We follow Little Henry to his Grave: Governour and Magistrates of the County here, 8 in all, beside my Self, Eight Ministers, and Several Persons of note. Mr. Phillips of Rowley here. I led Sam., then Cous. Savage led Mother, and Cousin Dummer led Cous. Quinsey's wife, he not well. Midwife Weeden and

---

[38] William Longfellow of Newbury was the husband of Sewall's sister Anne; see the entry of 21 November 1690.

Nurse Hill carried the Corps by turns, and so by Men in its Chesnut Coffin 'twas set into a Grave (The Tomb full of water) between 4 and 5. At Lecture the 21. Psalm was Sung from 8ᵗʰ to the end. The Lord humble me kindly in respect of all my Enmity against Him, and let his breaking my Image in my Son be a means of it. Considerable snow this night. At night little Hull had a sore Convulsion Fit.

Friday-morn Dec. 25. had another; Wave upon Wave. Mr. Phillips Prayes with Hullie. Receive Newes this 25ᵗʰ Dec. that Broʳ St[*ephen*] Sewall hath a Son.

Dec. 25. Friday. Carts come to Town and Shops open as is usual. Some somehow observe the day; but are vexed I believe that the Body of the People profane it, and blessed be God no Authority yet to compell them to keep it. A great Snow fell last night so this day and night very cold.

Satterday, Dec. 26. Dreamed last night of Mr. Chauncy, the President, and of Sam. Danforth.

Dec. 27. Dr. Oakes had like to have had his little Son killed with the Jack's falling almost on top of 's head. Upon which was hastily called out as the Psalm was Singing after the Lord's Supper.

Dec. 28. Cous. Fissenden here, Saith he came for Skins last Friday, and [*there*] was less Christmas-keeping than last year, fewer Shops Shut up.

Dec. 30ᵗʰ An Indian Man is found dead on the Neck with a Bottle of Rumm between his Legs. Fast at Charlestown this day. Mr. Cotton Mather Preaches forenoon, mentions the Notion Mede has about America's Peopling. Mr. Moodey preaches Afternoon excellently. Hull (as suppose) hath a sore fit in the night; but I asleep, and find it by the Effects.

Dec. 31. Mr. Allen preaches from 2 Tim. 2. 19. Saith should pray for the Natives that they may name Christ. Spoke against Observing the 25. Instant, called it Antichristian Heresie: Spoke against the Name. Canker began in the Tongue.

1686

DREAM OF JESUS CHRIST IN BOSTON / FRANCIS STEPNEY FINED FOR
BLASPHEMY / STRANGE BEAST REPORTED AT MIDDLETOWN / COCK-
SKAILING IN BOSTON / INCREASE MATHER DENOUNCES DANCING /
CONVICTION AND EXECUTION OF JAMES MORGAN / PANIC IN OLD
MEETING-HOUSE / THE CASE OF SAMUEL SHRIMPTON / VISIT TO
NEWBURY / ARRIVAL OF EDWARD RANDOLPH AND THE CHANGE OF
GOVERNMENT / DEATH OF HULL SEWALL / OBJECTIONS TO THE CROSS
IN THE FLAG / GOVERNOR ANDROS ARRIVES

Satterday, Jany 2^d [1685/6] Last night had a very unusual Dream;
viz. That our Saviour in the dayes of his Flesh when upon Earth,
came to Boston and abode here sometime, and moreover that He
Lodged in that time at Father Hull's; upon which in my Dream had
two Reflections, One was how much more Boston had to say than
Rome boasting of Peter's being there. The other a sense of great
Respect that I ought to have shewed Father Hull since Christ chose
when in Town, to take up His Quarters at his House. Admired the
goodness and Wisdom of Christ in coming hither and spending some
part of His short Life here.[1] The Chronological absurdity never came
into my mind, as I remember. Jany 1. 1685/6 finished reading the
Godly Learned ingenious Pareus on the Revelation.[2]

Satterday, Jany 2. discoursed with Ralf Carter about *Lignum Vitæ.*
He saith thinks 'tis found no where but in America, there a common
Wood at Antego and other places. Is physical [*medicinal*].[3]

January 5th The Infant exposed the beginning of the winter, is

[1] This sentence seems to us to reveal far better than pages of historical argument
the deep sincerity of Puritan belief in the Boston Zion.
[2] *A Commentary upon the Divine Revelation of the Apostle and Evangelist John,*
by David Pareus, Sometimes Professour of Divinity in the Universitie of Heidel-
berg . . . Translated out of the Latine into English, by Elias Arnold (Amsterdam, 1644).
[3] Lignum vitae (or guaiacum) trees are native to the West Indies and the warmer
parts of America; a drug prepared from their resin was used at this time against
the French disease. O.E.D.

buried this Day. Mr. Moodey and his wife visit us after the Catechising. He full of great pain.

Thorsday, Jan^r 7th Mr. Moodey preached excellently from those
words, Ye are my Friends if ye do what I command you: Exhorted
not to disown Christ when in adversity, i.e. his Members in a low
Condition. A very blustering, snowy day that hindered many from
going to Meeting, which took special notice of in Prayer; and God's
letting us stand another year in 's Vinyard. *Note.* His lecture this day
twelvemonth we had the newes of our Charter's being condemned,
just as going to Meeting. Some coming over the Neck to day, had
much ado to find the way.

Satterday, Jan^r 9th A very great Storm of Snow and Wind. Mr.
Tho. Oakes here, who tells me there is news come to Town of the
French King's Death.[4]

Sabbath-day Afternoon. My Wife goes to Meeting, which is the
first time since her Lying-in.

Tuesday, January 12. I dine at the Governour's: where Mr. [*Joseph*]
West, Governour of Carolina, Capt. Blackwell, his Wife and Daughter, Mr. Morgan, his Wife and Daughter, Mis. Brown, Mr. Eliakim
Hutchinson, and Wife, Mr. Peter Sergeant, and Wife, Mr. Secretary,
and S. S. Mis. Mercy sat not down, but came in after dinner well
dressed and saluted the two Daughters. Madam Bradstreet and Blackwell sat at the upper end together, Governor at the lower end. I sat
next Mis. Frances, Capt. Blackwell's Daughter. After Dinner Madam
Blackwell Swowned, or very ill, so was lead into the Chamber.

Wednesday, Jan^r 13th very cold day. Meeting at Brother Allen's:
I speak from Eph. 4. 3.

Thorsday exceeding cold: Mr. Jno Bayly preaches the Lecture for
Mr. Mather from Eccles. 9. 10. Whatsoever thy hand, &c. After Lec-
ture the Court sat, and adjourned till Tuesday 1. aclock, to hear Mr.
Shrimpton's Case, i. e. Mr. Sergeant's Complaint against him. Mr.
Shrimpton resolves to appeal to the Court of Assistants upon the
Pleas he hath made.[5] Mr. Stoughton, Dudley, and Mr. Thomas call'd

[4] The death of "Lewis the 14th" was hopefully reported again in August 1688
and in April 1695, but he did not oblige until 1 September 1715.
[5] The case of Samuel Shrimpton is referred to several times this year, but the
particulars of Peter Sergeant's complaint against him cannot be learned from
the existing records. Shrimpton was a leading man in the colony and a merchant
and large landowner in Boston. Because of his love of religious and civil liberty
he frequently came into collision with the authorities of the time. He and Sergeant were signers of the successful demand made upon Sir Edmund Andros 18
April 1689 to surrender the government. W. H. Sumner, *East Boston* (1858),
187-219. See also 2 *M.H.S. Proc.* xix, 38-51.

here; their Horses all broke away, and fain to run beyond Capt. Frary's before any had stopt, it being night and excessive cold.

Satterday, January 16. Notwithstanding the three very severe Nights last past and Snow in abundance lately fallen, yet, by reason of the Spring Tides, and wind 2 of the nights, the Harbour remains fairly open, and the Channel between the Castle and Dorchester Neck; though much loose Ice floating up and down. Isaiah Tay told me yesterday, that the 17th January last year he went on the Ice to the Castle, and Nine hundred were told by their Company going and coming on the Ice, and at the Iland.

Sabbathday, Jan^r 17th 1685/6. Rain and Thaw all day. This day Mr. Willard begins to preach upon the 11th of the Hebrews. Faith is the substance, &c.

Wednesday Jan^r 20th Went to Dorchester Lecture. Mr. Danforth preached from Rev. 22. 17. Said that Chapter treated of Heaven, that Christ dy'd for Mankind.

[*January* 21] On Tuesday last the Court sat, and as it fell out, I was not there. Agitation was about Mr. Shrimpton's Business. 2 *pro.* 2 *con.* of those that pretended to vote; Mr. Addington knew not what to enter. Governour, Mr. Stoughton and Dudley went away thinking the Court ended; 'tis said Mr. Davie gon also but called back, and he Mr. Cook and C. Hutchinson adjourned the Court to the Governour's that evening, and from thence 'twas adjourned to the Town-House on Thursday after Lecture, Jan^r 21. Was very hot discourse about the irregular pretended Adjournment of the Court. Mr. Stoughton and Dudley fell especially on Mr. Cook. After much hot Dispute nothing at last done as I know. Mr. Stoughton argued the new Law was not determinal and so worth nothing: and that the Ordinary could not act after an Award and mutual agreement as was produced in this case: must be relieved by some Superiour Court, as Chancery. Thus the symptoms of Death are on us.[6] This morn about 5, Hull had a Fit. Mr. Willard preached excellently from *Buy the Truth.* Must have a care of being cheated, our Natures encline to falshood. Must not take Great Men, Rulers, for our Rule, but the written Word of God. Must have no man's person in admiration. Mr. Stoughton and Dudley called here.

It seems Mr. Hubbard's Son of Long Iland, presented a Gun at his Sister and it went off and killed her. Cous. Fissenden tells me there is a Maid at Woburn who 'tis feared is Possessed by an evil Spirit. Mr. Eliot not at Lecture Jan^r 21. which I think is the 3^d day of his absence.

[6] The reference is to the demise of the chartered Colony of Massachusetts Bay.

Friday, Jan^r 22. Hull hath another Fit about 5 or 6 *mane*, and is extream ill after it. Mr. Willard prays with him in the Even, Capt. Scottow present.

Friday, January 22. Joseph Redknap of Lin buried, being about 110 years old: was a Wine-Cooper in London, was about 30 years old at the Great Frost. Ralph King *teste*.[7]

Sabbath, Jan^r 24. Friday night and Satterday were extream cold, so that the Harbour frozen up, and to the Castle. This day so cold that the Sacramental Bread is frozen pretty hard, and rattles sadly as broken into the Plates.

Monday, Jan^r 25. I call in Andrew Gardiner and deliver him his Commission for Ensign, he disabling himself, I tell him he must endeavour to get David's heart; and that with his stature will make a very good Ensign. Capt. Scottow present, to whom have lent my Gr. Testament, and Governor Pen. Mrs. Harris and Baker present their mutual offences against each other as to their seating [*in Cambridge Meeting-house*], before Mr. Willard and the Overseers.

Tuesday, Jan^r 26. Walked with Isaac Goose and Cous. Quinsey: though the Snow extream deep by reason of this day's snow and what was before, yet had a very comfortable night. Nehemiah Perce's Wife is brought to bed of a Daughter.

Wednesday, Jan^r 27. Peter Butler is Non-suited in suing for his 500 £ Legacy, at which I doubt Mr. Nowell and his wife grieved.[8] Is talk of a Ship below and some think it may be Jenner from London.

Thorsday, January 28. Mr. Jenner having lodged at Capt. Clap's last night, with Mr. Belcher and others, come near twenty together to Serj^t Bull's over the Ice and bring the News of the Rose Frigot ready to come and bring Mr. Randolph, who is to be Deputy Governour, and Mr. Dudley Governour. Sheriff Cornish executed [*in London*], and a woman burnt about the [*Popish*] Plot and such like Treason. The Town much filled with this discourse. Jenner came from Ile Wight the 13, of November. When Mr. Jenner came in the Magistrates went all off the Bench to hear his News in the Lobby. Mr. Addington also came in. Isa. 33. 17. was preached from, by Mr. Cotton Mather. Thine eyes shall see the King, &c. whoes Sermon was somewhat disgusted for some expressions; as, sweet–sented hands of Christ, Lord

[7] Savage discusses Redknap's age and concludes that 90 was a closer estimate. Sewall, he felt, "was very apt to believe what old persons told him, often when their habits or power of mind should rather have led to distrust their evidence."
[8] Sewall refers to Peter Butler Jr. of Boston. After his father's death, his mother, Mary Alford, married Hezekiah Usher Sr., and following his death, Samuel Nowell (Harvard 1653) of Charlestown, then Treasurer of the Colony, who died in London in 1688. *Sibley*.

High Treasurer of Æthiopia, Ribband of Humility—which was sorry for, because of the excellency and seasonableness of the subject, and otherwise well handled. Doct[rine] 'Tis a matchless priviledg to behold Christ in his Beauty. Mr. Eliot not at Lecture. Mr. Jenner rumors that the Oxford Frigot is to come in the Spring, and bring a Governour from England, and that one Vincent, Brother to the Minister, most talked of; which Mr. Dudley laughs at.

Friday, Jan^r 29th Isaac Goose proves his Mother's Will. Mr. Belcher dines with the Court. It seems there's a discourse that the K[ing] should motion to have all the Negroes at Jamaica baptized. Mr. Francis Stepney has his Jury to try his speaking Blasphemous Words; and Reviling the Government. 'Tis referred till next Tuesday.

Sabbath, Jan^r 31, 1685/6. 125th Psalm Sung by us in course in the family, They that trust in the Lord, &c. In publick *mane* the 56th from 8th verse, *ad finem*, of all my wanderings, &c. Mr. Willard speaking of Faith, instanced in things past before we had a being, and Things to be, as Destruction of the Man of Sin, seemed very much concerned for God's People. Madam Br. Usher taken into the first Church, and Mr. Royse taken in and baptized in the North Church. Gallant warm thawing weather.

Feb. 1. Nath. Man brings me a Letter wherein am told of my Brother St^n Child's Death last Friday about noon. Had from the Satterday before till then more than 200 Fits.

Feb. 1. In the Afternoon a great Cake of Ice comes from Cambridge-ward and jostles away the Body of Ice that lay between the outward Wharfs and Noddle's Iland: so now our Harbour open again.

Feb. 2. Several Ships Sail. This day Return Wait is by Sentence of Court turned out of his Marshal's Place, many complaints coming against him. The Persons injured left to their remedy in Law against him.

Wednesday, Feb. 3. Mr. Henry Phillips is buried with Arms, he having been an Ensign at Dedham, and in Boston several years of Capt. Oliver's Company. Capt. Hutchinson led the Souldiers, his and Capt. Townsend's Company springing of said Oliver's. Capt. Townsend and Capt. Hill each of them Trailed a Pike: were about 24 Files, 4 deep. Snow very deep; so in the New-burial Place [*Copp's Hill*], 3 Paths, 2 for the 2 Files of Souldiers, middlemost for the Relations. Edw. Cowel and Mr. Winchcomb go before the Governour. Return Wait is refused though I see he was there. About eight of the South-Company there attending. Bearers, Deacon Eliot, Saunderson, Allen, Bridgham, Frary, and Mr. Chiever.

Thorsday Feb. 4. Francis Stepney fined 100£. 10£ down, the rest respited till the last of March, that so might go away if he would. He appeals: Mr. Shrimpton and Luscombe his Sureties. Mr. Moodey preaches from Luke 12. 4. Especially this day from those words, My Friends. *Friday, Feb. 5.* Fast at Cous. Dummer's: I and Mother there.

Sabbath, Febr. 7ᵗʰ 1685/6. Went to the first Meeting House both parts of the day, sat down there at the Lord's Table. Mr. Moodey preached from Isa. 12. 1. beginning upon that Scripture this day— In that day thou shalt say, &c. Shewing that 'twas chiefly a Directory of Thanksgiving for the Conversion of the Jews; and that should get our Praises ready before hand. Very warm day, and so till Wednesday Feb. 10., when Mr. Willard Preaches at Maccartas from Rom. 8. 1. Seems very sensible of the Countries Danger as to Changes.

Febr. 12ᵗʰ Ice breaks up from Gill's Wharf.

Febr. 13ᵗʰ Satterday, pretty well clear our Dock of Ice by a Passage Cut open. Shut up about 7 weeks. Balston sails. An Indian Squaw died on the Neck last night. Mr. Eyre's little Son dyed, went well to Bed: dyed by them in the Bed. It seems there is no Symptom of Overlaying.

Sabbath-day, Febr. 14. Little Hull speaks *Apple* plainly in the hearing of his Grand-Mother and Eliza Lane; this the first word. At the Burial of Mr. Eyr's Child, Mr. Moodey discoursed of the grievous spreading of the Small Pocks in, and round about Portsmouth, at Exeter, &c.

Tuesday, Feb. 16. 1685/6. Generall Court meets. Dine 3 times. Is a discourse this day of a strange Beast killed at Middletown, or 4 miles off that place, last Dec., 10 foot long his Body, 10 foot his Tail, as tall as a two year and vantage Horse; Had a dead Horse and two Dear lay at 's Den, and Indians waiting for him, at last saw him coming with another in 's Mouth, as a Cat carries a Mouse almost. Indian shot him down. [*Sewall writes in the margin:* all untrue.] Great disorder in the Town by Cock-skailing: I grant 2 warrants. Tho. Barnard has one, and James Barns the other, whereby several Companies broke up: but for want of a Law and Agreement shall find much ado to supress it.

Mr. Eliot at Meeting on Lecture day.

The Arrow against Dancing comes out.[9]

[9] *An Arrow against Profane and Promiscuous Dancing. Drawn out of the Quiver of the Scriptures.* By the Ministers of Christ at Boston in New-England. (Boston, 1684). This pamphlet was occasioned by the activities of Francis Stepney, and was written by Increase Mather. The date on the title-page was a misprint. T. J. Holmes, *Increase Mather . . . Bibliography* I, 20-26.

Friday the Court adjourns to the 11th of May on the Conditions of former Adjournment. The Law about Wills is made in a new Edition.[10] Some Freemen made, and I think Sam. Chekly an Ensign. Order for a Fast to be on March 25, 1686. Great Heat about the Libel, and Mr. Clark's Fine the occasion of the Discourse at this time.

Satterday, Febr. 20. I send for Edw. Cowel and blame him for his ill carriage at Richd. White's Wedding, Dec. 10. He denys the fact, and saith he came not nigh her (i. e. the Bride) and stooped down only to take up his Hat taken off in the Crowd.

Wednesday, Feb. 24. Privat Meeting at our House: Mr. Willard preached excellently from Act. 1. 7. I had pray'd before, privatly, and he prayed at the Meeting in the very same words, that God would make our Houses Bethels. Question was, How shall we attend known Duty with cheerfullness and Constancy: though God impart not so much of his Counsel to us as we could desire? Which Mr. Willard propounded and opened excellently, shewing the reference to the foregoing and following verse, as was desired. Many People present.

Thorsday, Feb. 25. The Law about Wills and Administrations is published; and almost as soon as the Drumm had done beating, Mr. Serj^t comes with his Petition: and an order is made for a Hearing next Monday, 3 weeks, the 22^d of March: some would have had it sooner, and Mr. Nowel and Self thought it very indecent that it was so soon, especially considering, the Order made upon a Law scarce yet out of the Marshal's Mouth.

Mr. Jno Winchcombe is made Marshal of Suffolke, his Oath is given him; and the Marshal Generall declares it. Very rainy fore-noon, and dark most part of the day.

Sabbath-day, Feb. 28. A Jury is summoned to sit upon the Body of Sarah, the Daughter of Henry and Mary Flood, about 13 weeks old, for that said Mary was suspected of Murder. So now 3 in Prison for suspected Murder.

Tuesday, March 2. Brother St[*ephen*] and Wife visit us. Mr. Chickly is cast in his Attaint. Morgan, Indian and Flood put upon Tryal.[11]

Wednesday, March 3^d James Morgan is brought in guilty by the Jury, Saml Phips Fore-Man. Mr. Wyllys cast by Anna Haugh, as to Haugh's Farm. Mr. Stoughton calls at night and shews me the Names of the Persons in the Commission, telling me that a Copy of the

---

10 The text is printed in *Mass. Bay Rec.* v, 508-509.
11 Sewall was sitting on the Court of Assistants. The details of the cases of Anthony Checkley, James Morgan, Joseph Indian, Mary Flood, and others mentioned may be found in the published *Records of the Court of Assistants* i, 287f.

Commission is come to Town. Comes by Eldridge, who bore away to Montserrat. The Address sent to his present Majesty, is sent back to Mr. Dudley by Mr. Humphrys. Sabbath-day, or Monday, we hear of the Death of Abel Porter and above 60 more, going from Scotland to Pensilvania. Tuesday, March 2, hear of the Death of Jeremiah Green at Salt Tatoodas [*Tortugas*]; was a hopefull young Shipmaster, Mr. Nathaniel's Son.

Thorsday, March 4. Mr. Moodey preaches. After Lecture, James Morgan is condemned to dye: He said was murdered; but spake not of Appealing, which I expected he might.

Friday 5. Joseph Indian is acquitted. James Morgan is sent to, and acquainted that he must dye next Thorsday, and ordered that Mr. Mather be acquainted with it who is to preach the Lecture. *Note.* Mr. Stoughton and Dudley voted not in the Judgment, and went off the Bench when Sentence was to be passed. Major Richards slid off too. Judgment was voted at George Monk's before rose from Table, on Thorsday.

Friday, March 5. Capt. Clap's Son, a very desirable Man and Gunner of the Castle, though Mr. Baxter hath the name, at the Castle Iland hath one of his eyes shott out, and a piece of his Scull taken away by the accidental firing of a Gun as he was going a fowling.

Satterday, March 6. James Morgan sends a Petition by one Vaughan, signed with said Morgan's own hand, wherein he acknowledges his own sinfull Life, the justness of the Court's Sentence; and desires longer time to live, but 'tis not granted.

Sabbath-day, March 7th. P.M. Capt. Clap hath a Bill put up, wherein he desires Prayers that the untimely death of 's Son may be sanctifyed to him; dyed this day.

Monday, March 8th 1685/6. Anniversary Town-Meeting: Select-Men as last year; Mr. Cooke, Hutchinson, Joyliff, Prout, Frary, Allin, Fayerwether, Wyllys, Turell. Mr. Hutchinson had 86 Votes, which were the most: Capt. Frary 82. Constables; Wm Sumner 90. votes, the highest; Jabez Negus, Wm Rawson, Isaiah Tay, Tho. Adkins, Henry Emes, Joshua Windsor 51. Saml Marshall 37., being chosen after the refusal of Joseph Parson, Edw. Bromfield, Benj. Alford, Humphry Luscombe, which 4 last fined. Mr. Wyllys chosen Treasurer by the Town, and Mr. Joyliff Recorder. Meeting very comfortably held, being not so full as sometimes, and not such contention about Priviledges. Mr. Nowell begun with Prayer, and I, by mere accident being left, was fain to conclude. 7. Sworn by Major Richards same day, viz: all save Isaiah Tay. The Governour seems to mention it with some concernment that the 18, said to be of the Commission are publickly to be seen at the Notaries; so there is a Nomination before we put in votes.

Tuesday, March 9ᵗʰ 1685/6. Supply Clap, Gunner of the Castle, is buried at Dorchester by the Castle-Company about Noon; after the Vollies there, Several great Guns were fired at the Castle; both heard by the Town.

Mr. Tho. Kay our Maid's Father, dyes about 8. or 9. aclock. An Order is given for the Execution of Morgan next Thorsday; which the Marshal Generall acquaints him with.

Court sits, so the Votes for Nomination are put in, in the other Room. Dine 5 times.

Note. Wednesday Morn about 5. aclock, little Hull hath a Convulsion Fit in Bed. *March 10ᵗʰ* About 8. aclock this evening Father Abel Porter dyeth. Mr. Kay buried this day. Robert Orchard comes to town.

Thursday, March 11. Persons crowd much into the Old Meeting-House by reason of James Morgan;[12] and before I got thether a crazed woman cryed the Gallery or Meetinghouse broke, which made the People rush out with great Consternation, a great part of them, but were seated again. However, Mr. Eliot, the Father, speaks to me that I would go with him back to the Governour, and speak that the Meeting might be held in our Meeting-House [*the South*] for fear of the worst. Deputy Governour forwarded it, so Governour proceeded, met Mr. Mather, paused a little and then went to our House, the stream of People presently following and deserting the Old: first part of the 51. Ps. Sung. Mr. Mather's Text was from Num. 35. 16. And if he smite him with an Instrument of Iron, &c. Saw not Mr. Dudley at

---

[12] According to custom, a condemned culprit was brought to the meeting-house to be made the subject of discourse on the Sunday, or at the Thursday Lecture, preceding the execution. Morgan was compelled to listen to three sermons: one on Sunday morning by Cotton Mather, another on Sunday afternoon by Joshua Moodey (Harvard 1653), and this one on his day of execution by Increase Mather. John Dunton, the London publisher and bookseller, had arrived in Boston recently. Learning that this was to be the first execution there in nearly seven years, he was impressed with the bookselling possibilities of the event, and in connection with Joseph Brunning and Richard Pierce became responsible for the printing of all three sermons (T. J. Holmes, *Increase Mather . . . Bibliography* II, 480; idem, *Cotton Mather . . . Bibliography* I, 109; *Sibley* I, 379). In his *Letters written from New England, A.D. 1686* (Boston, 1867, 118-136), Dunton tells the story of Morgan's last days fully; however, all users of Dunton's book should consult the exposé of the work by Chester Noyes Greenough in *C.S.M.* XIV, 213-257.

Meeting, nor Court; suppose he might not be in Town. Mr. Stoughton here. Morgan was turn'd off about ½ an hour past five. The day very comfortable, but now 9. aclock rains and has done a good while.

Know not whether the mad woman said the House fell, or whether her beating women made them scream, and so those afar off, not knowing the cause, took it to be that; but the effect was as before; and I was told by several as I went along, that one Gallery in the old Meetinghouse was broken down. [*The mad woman was*] the Daughter of Goodm. Bishop, master of Morgan. She went in at the Southwest Dore, beat the women, they fled from her: they above supposed they fled from under the falling Gallery. Mr. Cotton Mather accompanied James Morgan to the place of Execution, and prayed with him there.

Friday, March 12. Father Porter laid in the Old Cemetery; is acknowledged by all to have been a great Man in Prayer. A very winterly day by which means many hindered from coming to the Funeral. I perceive there is a considerable disgust taken at the use of our House yesterday.

Sabbathday. Mr. Jn° Bolt, and Jn° Nichols are received into our Church. Mr. Bolt mentioned profan Courses he had been entangled in after Conviction. Relations of both well accepted, being such as gave good hope.

Monday, March 15ᵗʰ. Mr. Wigglesworth here, speaks about a Council respecting Mr. Thomas Chiever.

Tuesday, March 16. 1685/6. Went to Muddy-River and met with the Deputy Governour to adjust the matter of fencing: measured from a Stake by the Crick 16 Rods Marsh, then Upland 40, 40, 52. which reached a little above the Dam, then guess'd that might be 16 Rods to the beginning of the Ditch. Then measured from the Dam to about a Rod below an Elm growing to Boston-side of the Fence, which accounted the middle: Deputy Governour to fence thence upward above the Dam 16 Rod to the Ditch: Simon Gates to fence downwards to the Stake by the Crick where by consent we began. Had a good Dinner at Simon's; Capt. Scottow accompanied me. Deputy Governour expressed willingness for Simon and his Wife to go on foot to Cambridge Church directly throw his Ground.

When came home, found all well; but they told me the Small Pox was in Town, one that came in Peter Butler being sick of it at one Wolf's, whos House stands on some part of Capt. Oliver's Land, in the Town-House-Street.

Wednesday, March 17. 1685/6. Little Hull had a Sore Convulsion between 5. and 6. a little after his Mother and I gon to our privat Meeting. A cry of Fire this night but not one House burnt quite down; 'twas Bachelour White's that fell on fire thereabouts where Mr. Sanford dwell'd.[13]

Monday, March 22. 1685/6. Went to Braintrey, viewed Albies Farm, and treated with Jonathan Paddleford about Letting of it to him: Lodged in the Lower Room of Unkle Quinsey's new House.

Tuesday, March 23. Went and run the Line between us and Tho. Faxon: and between us and Jn° French, the Father; came home in Company Ephr. and Jn° Hunt; found all well; but hear of the sad consequences of yesterday's County-Court, Mr. Shrimpton's saying there was no Governour and Company. Heat between the Members of the Court. I can't yet understand that Mr. Nowell, Cook, or Hutchinson were there. Some are much offended that Mr. Shrimpton was not sent to Prison.

Fast-day, March 25, 1686. Mr. Willard exerciseth all day, Mr. Bayly being constrained to keep house by reason of the Gout. Tho. Hollinsworth, sick of the Small Pocks, prayed for.

Friday, March 26, 1686. Court of Assistants. Go to the Governour's and accompany him to Court; was slow to go out till knew the Court pretty full: Deputy Governour and about ½ Duzen went down, among whom Mr. Stoughton: Mr. Dudley went not. At the Town-House debated what was best to do respecting Mr. Shrimpton: Mr. Stoughton related matter of fact. Governour had adjourned the Court from Thorsday to Monday, beside the Appointment to hear Mr. Sergeant, which was done Feb. 25. The Court not being full as the Governour alledged, several malefactors were call'd and sentenced, before which ended, Mr. Stoughton and Dudley came in; a while after the Governour said to Mr. Sergeant, Will you have your case called now, Here is but a thin Court,—which was somewhat grievous to Mr. Stoughton; At length Mr. Sergeant and Shrimpton called, Mr. Shrimpton in a great fury, said he was no Thief, &c. though called among them; and he perceived he was to Answer Mr. Sergeant and not the Court, because of the Governour's speech above; told the Governour he had wronged him much, which some apply to his Arbitraitorship, some otherwise: said there was no Governour and Company, and the Governour had notice of it from Mr. Humphryes, and would not Answere: substance was what subscribed before in 's Paper given in more silently; but now spoken, in a great Croud with con-

---

13 We omit here the text of a resolution of the General Court, 16 February 1685, proclaiming a Fast Day on the 25th of March "that we may obtain Favor from God for the diverting of these Tokens of his anger [the smallpox epidemic and the severity of the winter], and his Smiles toward us in the Spring and Seed-Time approaching," which appears in *Mass. Bay Rec.* v, 509-510.

temptuous Pride and Rage. Govr, Stoughton, Dudley, Davie, Richards. Court cleared the Room, debated among themselves. None but
the Governour Spoke to send Mr. Shrimpton to Prison, one reason
was because he had given the Essence of it in writing long before,
and nothing had been done to him: But would have spoken to him
and the People, desiring the Governour to begin; Governour said he
despised it, or the like, speaking to Mr. Davie who propounded it in-
conveniently: So went away angry, and rest followed him; So is
extream Displeasure among the People, against Stoughton and Dudley chiefly: This 26th Shrimpton sent for, not coming, (was not at
home) Court and Council is Adjourned to the next Thorsday after
Lecture, and Marshal ordered to Summon him.[14]

Satterday, March 27th Capt. Eliot, Mr. Wyllys, Allin, Frary go to
the Governour's to comfort Him and strengthen his Hands, seeming
to be extreamly concerned. I vindicated Mr. Stoughton, being the
Senior Magistrate, all that ever I could; but I question whether it
takes much place or no. Mr. Addington entered nothing, and professed before the Council that was so surprized and 'twas such a sudden Gust, that scarce knew what he said: and all say 'twas extream
sudden and tumultuous: I perceiv Sundry Oaths are taking, what
avail they'll be of as to things done in Court, I know not.

Ship comes in from Dartmouth to Salem this week, about 8 weeks
passage, brings news of horrid progress of the Persecution in France;[15]
of severals relating to England, Parliament prorogued to May; Rose-
Frigat set out for Portsmouth, &c.

Natalis.[16] *March 28.* 133 Ps. sung in the morn in course: The Lord
give me a holy godly Life without End. Letter read from Maldon directed to the three Churches in Boston, desiring Council respecting
their Pastor Mr. Tho. Chiever, who is charg'd with scandalous immoralities, for which hath not given satisfaction. Mr. Eliot and my

---

[14] The official *Records of the Court of Assistants of the Massachusetts Bay*,
edited by John Noble, 1 (1901), 297f. should be read in connection with Sewall's
entries on the Shrimpton case. Apparently the case collapsed with the change of
government in May.

[15] The Edict of Nantes, issued by Henry IV of France 13 April 1598, secured a
legal existence and a degree of religious freedom and personal safety to the Protestants in that country. Louis XIV revoked the edict 17 October 1685, and the
bloody persecutions of old began again. About half a million Huguenots, including military leaders, men of letters, and the best part of the artificers of France,
fled to England, Germany, Holland, and America, greatly enriching these countries.

[16] Sewall usually made reference to his birthday on its recurrent anniversaries.

Self to accompany Mr. Willard thither next Wednesday come Sennight, 7ᵗʰ April.

March 29. I visit Mr. Mather, and Mr. Nowell confined by his Lameness. About 6 aclock P. M. Hull hath a very sore Convulsion Fit.

March the last [31] walked with Isaac Goose and Cous. Quinsey, had a very pleasant Moon-shiny night.

Thursday, April 1, 1686. Mr. Shrimpton comes before the Council, gives in a Paper shewing that March 22. he did say there was no Governour and Company in being in this place, which he still did averr, and was ready to prove if called to it. Council adjourned to April 15ᵗʰ and the Essex Magistrates writt to, to be here. Mr. Shrimpton said he never did disown a Government here, but honoured them. Mr. Secretary in writing the Letter writt *Henry,* in stead of *Samuel.* Am afraid little can or will be done, we shall only *sentire nos mori;* for Governour seemed to own before the People that the Charter was vacated in England, and insisted upon a Proclamation sent him: And the Deputy Governour said the Government must not be tumbled down till His Majesty call'd for it, or to that purpose: Such discourses and arguings before the People do but make us grow weaker and weaker. Said 'twas voided as much as London's; and they durst not since hold a Common–Council.[17]

April 2, 1686. Mr. Thomas Thacher dyes about 9 or 10 aclock. Hath had a pretty long Indisposition. Buried on the Sabbath Afternoon.

Monday, Apr. 5. Mr. Nehemiah Hobart chosen to preach the next Election-Sermon Artillery, hardly any other had Votes, though Mr. Cotton Mather is even almost Son in Law to the Capᵗⁿ and a worthy Man.

Apr. 7. 1686. Get up about 4 *mane* to go and accompany Mr. Willard to Maldon, went most by Water, some by Land. Those that went by Water were landed at Switzer's Point, then went about 2 miles on foot.

Apr. 8. Came home about 4 or 5 P. M. Visited Mr. Nowell. Mr. Tho. Bayly preached the Lecture. *Vide Locos Communes, quoad Concilij factum.*

Sewell refers here to his Commonplace Book, which has survived, and is among his papers in the Massachusetts Historical Society. We transcribe his record of the church trial in Malden which occasioned his

---

17 The judgment against the city of London on a *quo warranto* was pronounced by the Court of King's Bench in June 1683. M.H.S.EDS.

journey. Thomas Cheever (Harvard 1677), colleague minister of Malden since 1681, was the son of the great schoolmaster, Ezekiel Cheever.

At MALDEN, Wednesday, Apr. 7th. 1686.
A council of the 3 Ch^{hs} of Chr^t in Boston, met. Persons were Mr. James Allin, Joshua Moody, John Wiswall, Mr. Elisha Cook, Mr. Isaac Addington, Mr. Henry Allin, Mr. Increase Mather, Mr. Cotton Mather, Major John Richards, Mr. Adam Winthrop, Mr. Daniel Stone, Lt Richard Way, Mr. Saml Willard, Sam Sewall, Jacob Eliot. Met at the House of Father Green;[18] Mr. Allin went to Prayer, when discoursed whether should have 2 Moderators or one; Mr. Allin put it to vote, and carried for one, being but a small Company. Then voted for a Moderator by Papers. Mr. Increase Mather was chosen, had more than ten votes and but 15 Persons in all. Discoursed of our work, then went into the Publick. Mr. Moderator prayed. When had heard some Debates there, went to our Quarters, had the witnesses and Mr. Tho. Chiever face to face. Mr. Chiever, the Father, desired to be present, was admitted and bid wellcom, except when Council debated in private all alone (Mr. Sam. Parris present throughout, though not of the Council).

In the evening Mr. Chiever the Pastor was sent for, Mr. Moodey and others acquainted him how grievous his carriage had been and that day not so humble and in such a frame as ought; told him expected not an Answer, but that should sleep on't. Debated considerably what to do till about 10 at night Mr. Moderator pray'd, went to Bed. Mr. Moderator and his son to Mr. [*Michael*] Wigglesworth's, some to Mr. Chiever, Major Richards and self Kept the House. In the Morn, Thorsday, Ap. 8, Mr. Moderator went to prayer: read over what was drawn up, then discours'd about it. Sent for Mr. Chiever, to see what he had to say; then not finding satisfaction, all agreed on the following Declaration and Advice.

The Elders and Messingers assembled in Council at Maldon, April 7, 1686, at the Request of the Church there, after humble Invocation of the Name of God for his Guidance in the solemn Case propos'd unto them, do declare and advise as follows.

1. We find that Mr. Tho. Chiever, the present Pastor of the Church in Maldon, has been accused as Guilty of great Scandals, by more than 2 or 3 witnesses; and that since his being in Office-Relation Particularly, he is

---

[18] Cornet Henry Green of Malden (1638-1717) and his wife Esther Hasey were the hosts of the church council, as well as Sewall's hosts for the night; the editor of these volumes is one of their lineal descendants.

by two or three Witnesses charged with speaking such words as are scandalous breaches of the Third Commandment, as appears by the Testimony of Mrs. Eliza. Wade and Abigail Russell. He is moreover accused with Shamefull and abominable Violations of the Seventh Commandment. There are several who have testifyed that they heard him use light and obscene expressions (not fit to be named) in an Ordinary at Salem, as by the Testimony of Samuel Sprague, Jacob Parker, Isaac Hill: Also as he was travailing on the Rode, as per the Testimony of Thomas, Esther and Eliza. Newhall.

2. We find that although Mr. Chiever has been convicted of very scandalous Evils since his being a Preacher in Maldon, the Church there has declin'd all Testimonies against him as to Scandals committed before his Ordination; as also some other Testimonies respecting matters very criminal since that; because they judged the Witnesses on account of Prejudices and otherwise, incompetent; upon which Consideration we have also waved these Testimonies.

3. We find that in Augᵗ 9, 1685, Mr. Chiever made an Acknowledgement of some Evils to the Brethren of that Church, whereto he stands related; and that the most part of them were willing to take up with a slender satisfaction: But that on the next Lord's-day, he manifested before the Congregation so little sense and sorrow for his great sins, as that the generality of the Brethren were more dissatisfied than formerly.

We find by our own enquiries since we met together, that Mr. Chiever has absolutely deny'd some things, which are by sufficient Witnesses prov'd against him. Mr. Chiever's filthy words testifyed by Tho., Esther, and Elizabeth Newhal, he utterly deny'd to Lᵗ Samˡ Sprague, also to Cornet Green and his son, saying that Thomas Newhal was forsworn. Likewise he did to Capt. Sprague and Tho. Skinner utterly deny that ever he spake the words at Salem, so fully prov'd against him.

Also we find, that as to some particulars he pretends he does not remember them: Nor have we seen that humble penitential frame in him when before us, that would have become him: but have cause to fear that he has been too much accustomed to an evil course of Levity and Profaneness.

These things considered, we conceive it to be Duty and accordingly advise the Church of Maldon, to Suspend Mr. Tho. Chiever from the Exercise of his ministerial Function; and also to debar him from partaking with them at the Lord's Table, for the space of Six Weeks, untill which time the Council will adjourn themselves, to meet in Boston. And that in case he shall in the mean while manifest that Repentance which the Rule requires, they should confirm their Love to him, and (if possible) improve him again in the Lord's Work among them.

And this, our Advice, is grounded on these Scriptures and Reasons. (1). Among the Lord's People in the dayes of the O. Testament, no man might be permitted to execute the Priest's office that had a blemish: He might not come nigh to offer the offerings of the Lord. Levit. 21, 17, 21, which teaches that Men under moral blemishes, are unfit for holy ministrations, untill they be, in a way of Repentance, healed. (2) It is in the New Testament required, that an Elder should be sober and of good behaviour, and moreover he must have a good Report of them that are without, 1 Tim. 3, 2, 7. (3) Christ's Discipline ought to be exercised impartially, without respect to Persons. 1 Tim. 5, 21. Nor does Mr. Chiever's standing in a Sacred Office-Relation any way lessen, but greatly aggravate his sin. (4) There is no probability that Mr. Chiever's Ministry will be blessed for good to Souls, untill such time as his Conversation shall declare him to be a true penitent. Mat. 5, 13.

Finally, we exhort and advise our beloved Brethren of the Church of Maldon to set a day apart, solemnly to humble themselves by Fasting and Prayer before the Lord under this awfull dispensation, and for whatever failings have attended them, as to the management of their Differences, in this hour of Temptation which they have been subject unto. Particularly, for not observing the Rules of Christ, in endeavouring to prevent Evils by giving seasonable notice to Mr. Chiever of their Dissatisfactions. And for that want of Love, and for that bitterness of Spirit, which appears in sundry of them. So we pray the God of Love and Peace and Truth to dwell among you.

> INCREASE MATHER, Moderator,
> In the Name, and with the unanimous
> Consent of the whole Council.[19]

Thorsday, Ap. 8 the Bell was rung; went in publick. Mr. Moderator pray'd, read the Council's Report. Mr. Wigglesworth spake, thank'd him and the Council; said had cause to condemn themselves, as for other sins, so their sudden laying Hands on Mr. Chiever; and now God was whipping them with a Rod of their own making. Mr.

---

[19] Sewall added a note here: "Mr. Chiever was ordained July 27, 1681, Wednesday, Mr. [*Urian*] Oakes dying the Sabbath before." The Diary carries no entries for the adjourned meetings of the church council, held 20 and 27 May and 10 June in Boston. Cheever was dismissed from his pastorate, and lived in comparative retirement for nearly thirty years at Rumney Marsh (Chelsea), where he taught school. In 1715 a church was established there, and he was chosen to be the first minister. Sewall attended his installation on 19 October. Cheever served until his death in 1749; he was in his ninety-second year and the oldest living Harvard graduate. *Sibley; N.E.H.G.R.* xxxviii, 174-176; Mellen Chamberlain, *Documentary History of Chelsea* (1908), *passim.*

Chiever the Father, stood up and pathetically desir'd his son might speak, but Mr. Moderator and others judg'd it not convenient, he not having by what he said given the Council encouragement. Mr. Allin pray'd; went to Dinner; Council adjourned to that day 6 weeks. Came Home well.

Monday, Apr. 12. Mr. Lewis (in whom Mr. Wear goes for England to answer for Hampshire,) going out, runs on Shore upon a Rock a little below the Castle, at high-Water: so judg'd the Voyage may be much obstructed. High wind, and flurries of Hail.

Tuesday, Apr. 13, 1686. Have news by Madera that Col. Kirk was set sail in order to come hether.

Nomination.

S. Bradstreet Esq.	1144.	Rob. Pike	1113.
T. Danforth	1052.	E. Cooke	1121.
D. Gookin	1002.	W. Johnson	872.
J. Pynchon	1097.	J. Hathorn	983.
W. Stoughton	656.	E. Hutchinson	978.
J. Dudley	619.	S. Sewall	868.
P. Bulkly	475.	J. Smith	619.
N. Saltonstall	852.	I. Addington	510.
H. Davie	1127.	O. Purchis	507.
J. Richards	896.	D. Pierce	474.
S. Nowell	1203.	Jnº Blackwell	331.
Jam. Russell	1095.	*Left Out,*	
P. Tilton	1125.	Wᵐ Brown	99.
Bar. Gedny	387.	Jnº Woodbridge	325.
S. Appleton	1129.		

Persons that came next are—Capt. Phillips of Charlestown, 307—Lt. Thurston of Meadfild, 207—Samˡ Partrigge of Hadley, 176—Capt. Daniel Epps 146. Mr. Saffin had very few Votes. Mr. Stoughton not present. Mr. Dudley dined (as I think) at Mr. Shrimpton's, which will go near to give great offence. Commissioners dined at Wezendunk's,[20] Governour gave us his Company there, and Mr. Dudley came and abode with us some time; said remembered not 'twas the Day for opening the Nomination.

Thorsday, Apr. 15. After Lecture the Court meets, Mr. Shrimpton sent for, Evidences sworn. Considered how to hear him, as County Court, I voted for the County Court, and three more, or Assistants. When some were for Satterday, others for next Thorsday: first carried

[20] Werner Wesendunk was the proprietor of a Boston tavern.

it because of Major Appleton and Pike: so Juries to be summoned then to appear. Mr. Shrimpton would not take any blame to himself as to substance of what had said, and pleaded that might be heard by the County Court, else refused to give Bond to appear. The Deputy Governour said his Case was Capital, which Mr. Stoughton earnestly spake against. In the hurry Deputy Governour Adjourned the Court, bid the Marshal Generall look to Mr. Shrimpton; Marshal Generall required a Warrant which Secretary would not grant because the Court Adjourned: So Mr. Shrimpton under no obligation to appear. Boston to chuse Jury-Men for the County Court, Friday 3 aclock all under one [*ballot*] and read the Nomination-Bill. This Thursday 15. April, Capt. Ephraim Savage's Maid is known to have the Small Pocks, to the great saddening of the Town, besides all our other Deaths.

Warrants run for the Jury to appear 17th *Inst.* at 8 aclock *mane* to try a Case that concerns Limb, Life, or Banishment; and for a Grand jury. Doubt the terms of the Warrant extream inconvenient.

Thorsday, 15. April, pomerid. The Companies warned to Train. News is brought by Mary-Land that Mr. Randolph alone was come for N. England. Am told a Letter from Mr. Ive of Dec. 10. saith was then in the Downs waiting for a wind. So that the Report that the Devil Kirk was coming (as was said the Mariners called him) now abates.

Satterday, April 17, 1686. After much discourse an Indictment is drawn up, the Grand jury find the Bill *per* Pen Townsend, Foreman. Mr. Shrimpton appears not: so an Attachment ordered to goe out for him against next Thorsday, upon which the Marshal is to take Bond of him with Sureties of 1000. which if refuse to give, to carry him to prison. The Towns sent to as far as Weymouth sent their Jury Men very soon Satterday Morn; which was to me a very rare sight, seeing the warrants to arrive a Thorsday night. Mr. Stoughton and Dudley call'd here. Mr. Stoughton said would not come again till after the Election, [*if it*] should make me lose all my Votes.

Sabbath, Apr. 18. Capt. Ephr. Savage puts up a Bill to have God's hand sanctified in sending the Small Pocks into his Family.

Apr. 19. Mr. Seaborn Cotton dyes.[21]

Thorsday, Apr. 22. Court Assistants. Mr. Shrimpton gives no Bond,

21 Seaborn Cotton, son of the Rev. John and Sarah (Story) Cotton, was born on the *Griffin* while his parents were on their voyage to New England. He took his degree at Harvard in 1651 and was minister at Hampton, N.H., until his death. *Sibley.*

but is sent to Prison, Marshal did not light on him before. In the afternoon pleads against the illegality of the Indictment it having no Date: which suppose will be granted; is dismissed tonight on 's Parol to appear tomorrow. Acknowledged was ashamed of the manner of 's behaviour in the County Court, but stood to the Substance, that no Governour and Company.

Mr. Tho. Smith comes to Nantasket; was much feared to be lost. Cous. Nath. Dummer here. Mr. Cotton's Sermon printed off. Apr. 22, 1686.[22]

Satterday, Apr. 24. Court makes a Decree in the Admiralty Case. Mr. Shrimpton's Paper satisfies not; Court overrules his Plea as to the Indictments not having a Date; because alledge the giving in to Court makes it have a Date sufficient and determins 22ᵈ March last past, and order the Secretary to underwrite it when Received in open Court: near half the Magistrates could not vote for either. Court is adjourned to the 14ᵗʰ May, 8 aclock, Mr. Shrimpton promises then to appear, and Jury ordered to attend. Is a Rumor that the Frigot hath been long at Sea. Gave the Magistrates one of Mr. Cotton's Sermons on 2 Sam. 7. 10., each of them one, being now just come out. Ap. 24., 1686.

Monday, Apr. 26, 1686. I and my wife set out for Newbury with little Hull; Brother St[ephen] Sewall meets us at the Gate next the little Bridge near where Boston and Cambridge Rode join: yet Eliakim went on to Salem, whether we got well in good time. Was kindly entertained by Capt. Gedney, Mr. Hathorn, Epps; Visited by Mr. Noyes.

Tuesday, Ap. 27. Being in a strait for a Horse, Brother accidentally meets with Stephen Jaques, who had a Horse exceeding fit for our purpose, and was a Newbury Man; so got to Newbury very well in good time.

Wednesday, May 5, came home-ward, took Rowley-Lecture in the way. Text—Denying the Power, shewed that true Goodness was a powerfull Principle. Came to Salem, Gilbert Cole to our great Benefit overtaking and accompanying us, and bringing my wife from Salem, else must have Troubled Brother.

Thorsday, May 6, 1686. Got home about four aclock, found all

---

[22] This was John Cotton's farewell sermon, *God's Promise to his Plantation,* preached at Southampton early in 1630 to Governor John Winthrop and his associates before they sailed for America. It was printed in London in 1630 and 1634; the Boston reprint was by Samuel Green and was probably made at Sewall's instance. See the entry of 30 August 1686.

well, blessed be God. 'Twas Lecture-day at Lin too and is so once a Moneth, but we have miss'd both: And indeed my wives painfull Flux such, that had we known of Lin Lecture before past the Place, could not have took it. Mr. Wharton buried a Child since our going: and Mr. Cotton Mather married Mrs. Margaret [*i.e., Abigail*] Phillips before Major Richards (Mr. Russell and Capt. Hutchinson also present.) Tuesday May 4ᵗʰ 1686. 'Tis said was a great Wedding, But Eliakim not bidden.²³

Going to Newbury, at Ipswich Farms met with Richard Waldron, who told me what an Eastward Master reported about the coming out of the Rose-Frigot, shewing me a Letter written to the Capt. of the Rose at Boston in N. E. which causes great thoughts and expectation. Left Hull well at our coming away. God did graciously help us out and home this journey, and answer Prayer. Capt. Frary met us and bid us wellcom Home.

May 10ᵗʰ. Went to Charlestown and wished Mr. Cotton Mather Joy, was married last Tuesday.

Monday, 10ᵗʰ May, Night and Tuesday Morn, plenty of warm refreshing Rain which was extreamly wanted.

Tuesday Morn. Mr. Mather's Maid, a Member of [*blank*] Church is brought to Bed of a Child. Nothing suspected before that I hear of. 'Tis said He has turn'd her out of 's House.

May 12, 1686. Pleasant day. Governour ill of 's Gout, goes not to Meeting. Mr. Wigglesworth preaches from Rev. 2. 4 and part of 5ᵗʰ v. and do thy first works, end of the Text. Shew'd the want of Love, or abating in it, was ground enough of Controversy, whatsoever outward performances a people might have. In 's prayer said, That may know the things of our peace in this our day, and it may be the last of our days. Acknowledged God as to the Election, and bringing forth him as 'twere a dead Man,—had been reckoned among the dead,—to preach. Governour being at Home adjourned to his House, and there the Deputy Governour and Assistants took their Oaths, being much obstructed and confused by the Drums and Vollies from which the Souldiers would not be refrained.

²³ Eliakim Mather, born in 1668, son of the Rev. Eleazar Mather (Harvard 1656) of Northampton, who died the following year, appears many times in these pages between 1685 and 1691. Sewall nearly always calls him by his first name alone, indicating a rather humble walk of life. He is said to have resided in the family of his Uncle Increase (H. E. Mather, *Lineage of Rev. Richard Mather*, 1890, 57, 59), but the diary entries lead rather to the conclusion that he was Sewall's clerk and resided with him. Sewall's last mention of him (28 August 1691) implies that he may have been lost in the French war.

Gookin	1107.	Gedny	509.
Pynchon	1295.	Appleton	1272.
Stoughton	664.	Pike	1229.
Dudley	500.	Cook	1143.
Bulkly	436.	Johnson	987.
Saltonstall	1036.	Hathorn	1176.
Davie	1260.	Hutchinson	1066.
Richards	1160.	Sewall	957.
Nowell	1269.	Addington	903.
Russell	1273.	Smith	842.
Tilton	1178.		

Thorsday, May 13. Major Richards and I were sent by the Magistrates to wait on Mr. Stoughton to invite him to take his Oath; Called at Major Dudley's for Extract of his Letter.

The political events now taking place require explanation. In the half-century and more since the Puritans had established their Canaan in the Massachusetts wilderness, the experiment had not only succeeded, as other settlements had not, but prospered greatly, and they had had evidence from time to time that God had intervened directly to foster or save them. It was natural that the colonists came to construe their charter as giving them a degree of political independence unintended by the home government. Repeated attempts were made after the Restoration to procure the repeal of the charter. Edward Randolph, the royal emissary, who came over first in 1676, was received with scant courtesy, and met with quiet but effective resistance. He shuttled back and forth across the sea many times, making reports exciting the cupidity of the Stuarts and creating opinion unfavorable to the colonists. The result was the decree of the Court of Chancery, 21 June 1684, vacating the charter, which was made final 23 October 1684. News of the decree reached Massachusetts in September 1684.

Charles II died 6 February 1684/5 before any changes in the Massachusetts government had been arranged. James II at first simply confirmed the existing arrangements, and Bradstreet was reëlected Governor in May 1685. He was again elected 12 May 1686. Instead of God's usual intervention to enable the Puritans to continue administering the government as before, two days later the hated Randolph arrived with the exemplification of the judgment against the charter of the Governor and Company of the Massachusetts Bay. In the words of Palfrey (III, 394), "Massachusetts, as a body politic, was now no more. . . . It was on the charter

. . . of Massachusetts Bay that the structure of the cherished institutions of Massachusetts, religious and civil, had been reared. The abrogation of the charter swept the whole away. Massachusetts, in English law, was again what it had been before James the First made a grant of it to the Council for New England. It belonged to the king of England, by virtue of the discovery of the Cabots."

Randolph also brought with him the royal commission for instituting the new government, which extended over Massachusetts, New Hampshire, Maine, and the King's Province. It was to consist of a president, deputy-president, and sixteen counsellors. The new government was proclaimed 25 May 1686. Joseph Dudley (Harvard 1665) was made interim president and William Stoughton deputy-president. Sewall was not made a councillor, and held no office until 1689.

The story of these sad and stirring days is fully set forth in John Gorham Palfrey's History of New England and in Charles Deane's chapter, The Struggle to Maintain the Charter of King Charles the First, and its Final Loss in 1684, in the Memorial History of Boston I, 329-382. The details of the transition to Dudley's government and the records of his administration appear in a communication of Robert Noxon Toppan in 2 M.H.S.Proc. XIII, 222-286. Toppan and A. T. S. Goodrick have treated Edward Randolph exhaustively in the seven volumes edited for the Prince Society (1898-1909).

Friday, May 14. The Rose-Frigot arrives at Nantasket, Mr. Randolph up at Town about 8 *mane:* takes Coach for Roxbury: Major Pynchon and Mr. Stoughton are sent to the Magistrates to acquaint them with the King's Commands being come, and that Mr. Deputy, with whóm he pleased to take with him, might go to Capt. Paige's and see the Commission, Exemplification of the Judgment and Seals. Mr. Shrimpton in the morn was sent for and told, by reason of the Governour's absence, and other business, should not now proceed with his Tryal, and that the Court would be adjourned and he should be acquainted with the time. Had a small Admiralty Case. Jury dismissed after Dinner. Major Pynchon has not took his Oath, I saw him not till came in with Mr. Stoughton.

Elder Humphryes of Dorchester buried this day. Major Richards and Self saw his Grave digging when went to Mr. Stoughton's.

Satterday, May 15. Govr Hinkley, Major Richards, Mr. Russell and Self sent to by Major Dudley to come to Capt. Paige's, where we saw the Exemplification of the Judgment against the Charter, with the Broad Seal affixed: discoursed about their acceptance: had some thoughts of shewing their Seals to the Magistrates and Deputies, though not to them as a Court; but before we returned, the Magistrates were gone to the Governour's and from thence they adjourned till Monday one aclock. Major Generall came home and dined with me. Went to George Monk's and paid him in full, drank half a pint of Wine together.

Friday morn Capt. Townsend is chosen Deputy for Boston in his Brother Addington's room. Mr. Jnº Saffin is chosen Speaker the day before. Mr. Nicholas Noyes, the Minister, told me the first News of the Frigot.

Sabbath, May 16. The Lord's Supper administered with us: In the morn the 2ᵈ Ps. sung from the 6ᵗʰ v. to the end. In the family, sung the 139ᵗʰ in course. Mr. Randolph at Meeting, sate in Mr. Luscombe's Pue. Mr. Willard prayed not for the Governour or Government, as formerly; but spake so as implied it to be changed or changing. It seems Mr. Phillips at the Old Church, prayed for Governour and Deputy Governour. Govʳ Hinkly, Major Pynchon, Rawson and Self with Mr. Willy in the Fore-Seat at the Sacrament.

Monday, May 17ᵗʰ 1686. Generall Court Sits at One aclock, I goe thither, about 3. The Old Government draws to the North-side, Mr. Addington, Capt. Smith and I sit at the Table, there not being room: Major Dudley the Præsident, Major Pynchon, Capt. Gedney, Mr. Mason, Randolph, Capt. Winthrop, Mr. Wharton come in on the Left. Mr. Stoughton I left out: Came also Capt. [of] King's Frigot, Govʳ Hinkley, Govʳ West and satc on the Bench, and the Room pretty well filled with Spectators in an Instant. Major Dudley made a Speech, that was sorry could treat them no longer as Governour and Company; Produced the Exemplification of the Charter's Condemnation, the Commission under the Broad-Seal of England—both: Letter of the Lords, Commission of Admiralty, openly exhibiting them to the People; when had done, Deputy Governour said suppos'd they expected not the Court's Answer now; which the Præsident took up and said they could not acknowledge them as such, and could no way capitulate with them, to which I think no Reply. When gone, Major Generall, Major Richards, Mr. Russell and Self spake our minds. I chose to say after the Major Generall, adding that the foundations being destroyed what can the Righteous do; speaking against a Protest; which some spake for. Spake to call some Elders to pray tomorrow which some think inconvenient, because of what past, and the Commissioners having several times declared themselves to be the King's Council when in the Town-House.

Tuesday, May 18. Mr. Willard not seeing cause to go to the Town-House to pray, I who was to speak to him refrain also. Major Bulkley and Mr. Jonathan Tyng came to Town last night. Mr. Phillips had very close Discourse with the President, to persuade him not to accept: 'twas in Mr. Willard's Study Monday after noon just at night. Mr. Stoughton and Mather there too. Now are reading the beginning of the Psalms and the Acts.

Tuesday, May 18. A great Wedding from Milton, and are married by Mr. Randolph's Chaplain, at Mr. Shrimpton's, according to the Service-Book, a little after noon, when Prayer was had at the Town-House: Was another married at the same time. The former was Vosse's Son. Borrowed a Ring. 'Tis said they having asked Mr. Cook and Addington, and they declining it, went after to the President and he sent them to the Parson.[24] In the even Mr. Moodey, Allen, Willard, Addington, Frary visit me. It seems neither of the Mathers, nor Baylys, nor Major Richards were at the Fast.

Wednesday, May 19. Capt. Eliot tells me that he hears Salem Troop is to be here on Friday, Capt. Higginson is Mr. Wharton's Brother in Law, and Capt. Gedney is of Salem, commands one of the Companies. Mr. Higginson and Mr. Noyes steady for Submission; the former is the Captain's Father. My Son reads to me Isa. 22 in his course this morning. In the Afternoon Major Richards and Self sent for to Capt. Winthrop's, and desired to have our Companyes in Arms next Tuesday, Boston Troop to bring the President from Roxbury; what was thought of the former notion is now laid aside.

Friday, May 21, 1686. The Magistrates and Deputies goe to the Governour's. I was going to them about 11. aclock, supposing them to be at the Town-House, and seeing a head through the Governour's Room, and, Brisco in the Street, I asked if Magistrates there; so went in and they were discoursing about delivering the Keys of a Fort which had been asked, seemed to advise him not to do it till the Gentlemen Sworn. Mr. Nowell prayed that God would pardon each Magistrate and Deputies Sin. Thanked God for our hithertos of Mercy 56 years, in which time sad Calamities elsewhere, as Massacre Piedmont; thanked God for what we might expect from sundry of those now set over us. I moved to sing, so sang the 17. and 18. verses of Habbakkuk.

The Adjournment which had been agreed before, Second Wednes-

---

[24] This was the first marriage performed by an Anglican clergyman in New England: Lieutenant Henry Vose, son of Captain Thomas Vose of Milton was married to Elizabeth Badcock, daughter of Captain Robert Badcock of Milton (E. F. Vose, *Robert Vose and His Descendants*, 1932, 31-32). The parson was Robert Ratcliffe, M.A., and Fellow of Exeter College, Oxford. Sewall's references to the President have heretofore meant the President of Harvard College; in this entry he refers to President Joseph Dudley.

day in October next at 8 aclock in the Morning, was declared by the Weeping Marshal-Generall. Many Tears Shed in Prayer and at parting.

This day the Præsident goes on Board the Frigot a little below the Castle, so the Flagg is hung out at the Main Top. About 4. or 5. P. M. She comes up with a fair wind, Castle fires about 25 Guns; a very considerable time after the Frigot fires, then the Sconce and Ships, Noddles Iland, Charlestown Battery, Frigot again, Ships with their Ancients out, and Forts their Flaggs. Not very many Spectators on Fort Hill and there about, I was for one, coming from the Warehouse. I waited on the Præsident in the morn to speak with him, and so accompanied Him to Town. Wednesday, Major Richards and I were sent for to Capt. Winthrop's to speak with us about attending with our Companyes on Tuesday; this was near night. Were advised to consult our Officers; Major Richards objected the discontent of the Souldiers and may be it might prove inconvenient. On Thorsday, before Lecture, at Capt. Paige's, I told the President thought I could do nothing to the purpose: On Friday waited on him on purpose and propounded Lieut. Hayward: when came home, after Dinner went to speak with Lieut. Hayward, found him at George's. There he was speaking with his Capt., the Præsident having spoken to him; he was to return an Answer to the Præsident. I hear no more of it, so I suppose 'tis left with him. On Wednesday Major spake of warning by Corporals not Drum.

May 25, mane we read the seventeenth Psalm in Course, a precious seasonable Prayer for this Day.

Wednesday, May 26. Mr. Ratliff, the Minister, waits on the Council; Mr. Mason and Randolph propose that he may have one of the 3 Houses to preach in. That is deny'd, and he is granted the East-End of the Town-House, where the Deputies used to meet; untill those who desire his Ministry shall provide a fitter place.[25] No Body that I

---

[25] No record of this action appears in the minutes of the Council. The Town House was a wooden structure set on pillars, with an open street floor used as the public market place; the original building was erected with funds bequeathed by Captain Robert Keayne, whose will was probated in 1656. The councils, courts, and public assemblies were held in the rooms upstairs. This building was burned in the great fire of 2-3 October 1711, and the next year a brick town house was built on the same spot and for similar uses. On 9 December 1747 a fire destroyed all of this building except the walls; the rebuilt structure now survives as the Old State House. About 1742 the town and market activities were moved to the new Faneuil Hall, but provincial and state affairs were conducted in the old State House until the Bulfinch State House was occupied in 1798. J. H. Benton, *The Story of the Old Boston Town House 1658-1711* (1908) and M.H.S.EDS.

observed went to meet the President at his first coming to Town that I know of.

Thorsday, May 27. Lieut. Checkly and I wait on the President and Mr. Stoughton to Mr. Allin's. Mr. Whiting of Hartford preaches. Mr. Danforth sits in the Gallery, Major Gookin with me. Ministers generally dine with the President and Co.

Friday, May 28. I pay my Respects to Mr. Stoughton as Deputy-President, break fast with him, and ride part of the way to Town. Then I goe with Capt. Eliot and adjust the Line between him and me at Muddy-River. Visit Mr. Benj. Eliot as we come back. Yesterday a very refreshing Rain.

Sabbath, May 30ᵗʰ 1686. My Son reads to me in course the 26ᵗʰ of Isaiah—In that day shall this Song, &c. And we sing the 141. Psalm, both exceedingly suited to this day. Wherein there is to be Worship according to the Church of England as 'tis call'd, in the Town-House, by Countenance of Authority. 'Tis deferred 'till the 6ᵗʰ of June at what time the Pulpit is provided; The pulpit is movable, carried up and down stairs, as occasion serves; it seems many crouded thether, and the Ministers preached forenoon and Afternoon. Charles Lidget there.[26]

Satterday, June 5ᵗʰ. I rode to Newbury, to see my little Hull, and to keep out of the way of the Artillery Election, on which day eat Strawberries and Cream with Sister Longfellow at the Falls, visited Capt. Richard Dummer, rode to Salem, where lodged 2 nights for the sake of Mr. Noyes's Lecture, who preached excellently of Humility, from the woman's washing Christ's feet. Was invited by Mr. Higginson to Dinner, but could not stay, came alone to Capt. Marshal's, from thence with Mr. Davie, who gave me an account of B. Davis Capt., Tho. Savage Lieut. and Sam Ravenscroft Ensign, of the Artillery; Jnᵒ Wait was chosen but serv'd not. Mr. Hubbard preached from Eccles., There is no Discharge in that War.

Friday, June 11. Waited on the Council, took the Oath of Allegiance, and rec'd my new Commission for Capt. Was before at a privat Fast at Deacon Allen's: so Capt. Hutchinson and I went about 5. aclock, and all the rest were sworn, Capt. Hutchinson at present

[26] This is one of Sewall's delayed entries, written Sunday, 6 June, or later. On that date, in the library room at the east end of the Town House, Mr. Ratcliffe in his surplice read the liturgy from the Book of Common Prayer publicly for the first time in New England, and preached a sermon. On 15 June "the Church of England as by law established" was organized in Boston; this was the beginning of the religious society now known as King's Chapel. H. W. Foote, *Annals of King's Chapel* I, Ch. ii.

refuses. I read the Oath myself holding the book in my Left hand, and holding up my Right Hand to Heaven.[27]

Friday, June 18. My dear Son, Hull Sewall, dyes at Newbury about one aclock. Brother Toppan gets hither to acquaint us on Satterday morn between 5 and 6. We set out about 8. I got to Newbury a little after Sun-set, where found many persons waiting for the Funeral; so very quickly went; Mr. Woodbridge and Richardson there: Bearers Mr. Sam¹ Tompson, Jnº Moodey, Jnº Toppan, Johnny Richardson. Had Gloves. Gave no body else any because 'twas so late.

Sabbath-day Morn. [*June* 20] Goodman Pilsbury was buried just after the ringing of the second Bell. Grave dugg over night. Mr. Richardson Preached from 1 Cor. 3, 21.22, going something out of 's Order by reason of the occasion, and singling out those Words *Or Death.*

On *Monday* [*June* 21] I distributed some Gloves, and in the Afternoon about 6 aclock came with Deacon Coffin to Salem about 10. at night. From thence early in the Morn by reason of the flaming Heat, and got to Winnisimmet before the Ferry-men up, Got home about ¾ after seven, found all well. Hullie was taken ill on Friday Morn. Mr. Clark of Cambridge had a Son of 9 years old drownd the Tuesday before. Two women dy'd suddenly in Boston. James Mirick that lived just by my Father at Newbury, had his House suddenly burnt down to the Ground on Sabbath-day Even before this Friday.

The Lord sanctify this Third Bereavement.

Tuesday, June 22, 1686. Betty Lane's Father dyes suddenly.

Wednesday, Junij ult° [30] Went to a Fast at Dorchester, Mr. Danforth and Williams exercised, and no other. In the Evening supped with Major Gidney, Mr. Moodey, Allin, at Mr. Stoughton's.

Friday, July 2. Mis. Chancy, widow, dyes having been sick a day or two, of a Flux. Her Body is carried in the night to Roxbury there to be buried.[28]

July 9. Mr. Richard Collicot buried.

Monday, July 12. Mr. Thomas Kellond dyes, is to be buried on Thorsday between 4 and 5. Is the only son of Madame Kellond, and Mis Luscombe is now her only child. Conversed with Mr. Thomas

---

[27] Sewall took the oath in the New England fashion; the English custom was to hold the Bible or kiss it. The manner of taking oaths became the occasion of dispute in Andros's time, and Rev. Samuel Willard wrote *A Brief Discourse . . .* on the subject, published in London in 1689 and reprinted in the *Andros Tracts* 1, [179]-[191].

[28] Probably Thomasine, widow of Dr. Elnathan Chauncy (Harvard 1661).

when at Newbury in the beginning of June. He was so fat and corpulent that most thought he could not live.[29]

Wednesday, July 21. Went to Cambridge-Lecture and heard Mr. Morton. Considerable Rain this Day. Dined at Remington's.

Mr. Jn° Bayly preaches his farewell Sermon from 2 Cor. 13, 11. Goes to Watertown this week. *July 25, 1686.*

July 26, 1686. More Rain this day. Major Richards and most of the Captains gave in some Military Orders for the Council's Approbation and Passing: and before the Council agreed that this day fortnight be a Training-Day.

July 27, 1686. Mr. Stoughton prayes excellently, and makes a notable speech at the opening of the Court. The Foreman of the Grand-Jury, Capt. Hollbrook, swore laying his hand on the Bible, and one or two more. So Mr. Ballard, Foreman of the Petit Jury, and one or two more. Others swore lifting up their hands, as formerly. Attorneys are sworn and none must plead as Attorneys but they.

July 28. A considerable Troop from Watertown come and fetch Mr. Bayly, some of ours also accompany them. Francis Stepney the Dancing Master runs away for Debt. Several Attachments out after him.

Thorsday night, July 29, 1686. I goe the Grand Rounds with Isaac Goose and Matthias Smith: Comes eight dayes sooner than it ought because Capt. Lidget's Lieut. refuses, and so the rest of the Company.

Friday, July 30. Church Meeting, at which Richard Draper, Mrs. Clark, Sarah Chapin, and Eliza Lane admitted.

About the same time Wᵐ Johnson Esqʳ is sharply reproved by the Council for his carriage on the Fast-day, staying at home himself and having a Duzen Men at 's House. Told him must take the Oath of Allegiance; he desired an Hour's consideration, then said he could not take it; but when his *Mittimus* writing, or written, he consider'd again, and took it rather than goe to Prison. Objected against that clause of acknowledging it to be Lawfull Authority who administred; would see the Seals.[30]

Augᵗ 4. Mr. Moodey exercises at our House, being our Meeting-day. Mr. Shove in Town.

[29] Kellond was the son of a Boston merchant from England, a royalist, who had been commissioned in May 1661 to pursue the regicides Whalley and Goffe. *Savage.*

[30] Johnson was a prominent citizen of Woburn, the son of Captain Edward Johnson, author of *Wonder-Working Providence,* and noted for his zeal for the old charter. He had been dropped as an Assistant in the government just set up. Rev. Samuel Sewall (1785-1868) writes extensively of him in his *History of Woburn* (1868), 165f.

Augt 5. Wm Harrison, the Bodies-maker, is buried, which is the first that I know of buried with the Common-Prayer Book in Boston. He was formerly Mr. Randolph's Landlord. This day Capt. Paige hath a Judgment for Capt. Keyn's Farm: Mr. Cook Appeals. Mr. Morton preaches the Lecture. One Jn° Gold, Chief Commander of the Military Company at Topsfield, is sent to Prison for Treasonable Words spoken about the change of Government, is to be tryed this day fortnight. Council said he was not bailable.

Sabbath-day, Augt 8. 'Tis said the Sacrament of the Lord's Supper is administered at the Town-House. Cleverly there.

Augt 9. Pretty sharp Thunder and Lightening.

Augt 10. Ridd to Braintrey in Company of Mr. Pain, and Mr. Joseph Parson, and home agen. 'Tis said a Groton Man is killed by 's cart, Bowells crushed out; and a Boy killed by a Horse at Rowley; foot hung in the Stirrup and so was torn to pieces; both about a week ago.

Augt 10. at night. Two Brothers die in one Bed, the Mate and Purser of the Ship which brought the Frenchmen. Died of a Malignant Fever. *Aug^t* 11. Buried together. Mr. Parris spake at Mrs. Noyes's.

Augt. 18, 1686. Went and came on Foot to Cambridge-Lecture. Dined at Mr. Gookin's in Company of Mr. Hubbard, N. Cambr. [*New Cambridge, now Newton*] and others.

Augt. 21. mane Mr. Randolph and Bullivant were here, Mr. Randolph mentioned a Contribution toward building them a Church, and seemed to goe away displeased because I spake not up to it.

Friday, Augt. 20. Read the 143, 144 Psalms *mane*, and Sam Read the 10th of Jeremiah. I was and am in great exercise about the Cross to be put into the Colours, and afraid if I should have a hand in 't whether it may not hinder my Entrance into the Holy Land.

Sabbath-day, Augt. 22. In the Evening seriously discoursed with Capt. Eliot and Frary, signifying my inability to hold, and reading Mr. Cotton's Arguments to them about the Cross, and sayd that to introduce it in Boston at this time was much, seeing it had been kept out more than my Life-time, and now the Cross much set by in England and here; and it could scarce be put in but I must have a hand in it. I fetcht home the Silk Elizur Holyoke had of me, to make the Cross, last Friday morn; and went and discoursed Mr. Mather. He judged it Sin to have it put in, but the Captain not in fault; but I could hardly understand how the Command of others could wholly excuse them, at least me who had spoken so much against it in April 1681, and that Summer and forward, upon occasion of Capt. Walley's putting the Cross in his Colours.[31] *Augt.* 22. Balston arrives.

Monday, Augt. 23. At even I wait on the President and shew him that I cannot hold because of the Cross now to be introduc'd, and offer'd him my Commission, which he refus'd, said would not take it but in Council. Receiv'd me very candidly, and told me we might expect Sir Edmund Andros, our Governour, here within six weeks; for ought I know that might make him the more placid. Came over the Neck with Mr. Sherman. *Laus Deo.*

Balston arrives Augt. 22: came from Graves-End June 24, 1686. Had news there by several vessels that the Rose-Frigot was arrived here. Mr. Lee[32] and another Minister come over with many Passengers.

Augt. 29. *Lord's day.* Mr. Lee, the Minister, now come over, came to our Meeting in the Forenoon, and sate in my Pue.

Augt. 30. Eight Companyes Train, but I appear not save to take leave in the morning, getting Mr. Willard to goe to Prayer. Lieut. Holyoke led the Company which had Lt. Col[s] Colours: in the morn Lt. Way came to me and told me the likelihood of Mr. Lee's being my Tenant; so invited said Way to Dinner. Gave each Souldier a Sermon: God's Promise to his Plantations; and 20s. [*to the Company for a treat*].[33]

Augt. 31. Mr. Nowell, Moodey and Rawson visit me and comfort me.

Augt. 31. Mr. Lee views the House at Cotton-Hill in order to taking it.

---

[31] The English colors at that time bore St. George's cross; and the use thereof, as savoring of idolatry or Popery, aroused Puritan feelings at an early date. In 1634, Endicott and Davenport had altered the ensign used at Salem by removing one part of the red cross. Palfrey points out that this act placed the colonial government in a difficult position, since the act would be construed in England as a defiance, and yet at home it had the sympathy of the people. Finally, it was decided to leave out the cross on the colors of the military companies, but to keep it on the flag at Castle Island. Hutchinson writes (*History of Massachusetts Bay*, 1936 ed., I, 35n): "This scruple afterwards prevailed, and the cross was left out of the colors and generally condemned as unlawful." M.H.S.EDS.

[32] Rev. Samuel Lee, Puritan divine, sometime Fellow of All Souls and Dean of Wadham College, Oxford, became minister of Bristol (then in Massachusetts) in 1687. In 1691 he sailed for England with Captain John Foy; the ship was captured by the French and taken to St. Malo, where he died in December. His daughter Lydia, the widow of John George, was the third wife of Cotton Mather. *D.N.B.*; *C.S.M.* XIV, 142f.

[33] Sewall's brief speech to the South Company on this occasion is printed in 5 *M.H.S.Colls.* VI, 9*.

Septr 1. Went to Natick Lecture, Simon Gates shewing me the way; called as went at Noah Wiswall's; came home accompanied by Major Gookin and his Son Sam. till the way parted. Mr. Dan¹ Gookin preached; were about 40 or 50 Men at most, and a pretty many Women and Children [*at the Indian Meeting-House*]. Call'd at the President's as came home, who was very pleasant; Excus'd my giving himself and the Deputy President occasion to say what they did on Thorsday night. Met with there, Capt. Blackwell and Mr. Hubbard and his wife, with whom I came over the Neck.

Septr 3. The report about Sir Edmund Andros coming, is refreshed by Martin in his way to N. York.

Friday, Septr 3. Mr. Shrimpton, Capt. Lidget and others come in a Coach from Roxbury about 9. aclock or past, singing as they come, being inflamed with Drink: At Justice Morgan's they stop and drink Healths, curse, swear, talk profanely and baudily to the great disturbance of the Town and grief of good people. Such high-handed wickedness has hardly been heard of before in Boston.

Monday, Septr 6. Artillery Training. Not one old Captain there. Dartmouth Frigot arrives from Barmudas last night. Lieut. Holyoke's little Daughter buried today: died on Satterday.

Tuesday, Septr 7th The Dartmouth Frigot comes up. I goe with my wife, Cous. Ruth, Savages and Mis. Baker and their Children to Hog-Iland. We put off just as the Frigot and Ships and Town Salute each other mutually. Got home by 9. aclock.

I little thought of its being the day signed by the Almanack for the Court of Assistants, till coming home I accidentally spy'd. It has been a great day of feasting on Board Capt. Head. Mr. Lidget and Shrimpton there. I suppose they are little concerned for being bound over in the morn for their Friday night Revel.

Monday, Septr 13, 1686. Mr. Cotton Mather preaches the Election Sermon for the Artillery, at Charlestown, from Ps. 144. 1. made a very good Discourse. President and Deputy President there. As I went in the morn I had Sam. to the Latin School, which is the first time. Mr. Chiever received him gladly.³⁴ The Artillery Company had like to have broken up; the animosity so high between Charlestown

---

³⁴ Samuel Sewall Jr. was nine. Before long it must have been apparent to Ezekiel Cheever that Sam was not going to follow in his father's footsteps, for we find 14 May 1688 that he had been put to Eliezer Moody to learn to write. Sam's adolescence was a difficult period and the family prayed more than once for guidance as to his calling. He finally became a bookseller. In 1702 he married Rebecca, daughter of Governor Joseph Dudley, and later built a house at Muddy River (Brookline), where he engaged in farming.

and Cambridge Men about the Place of Training. Were fain at last to vote the old Officers to stand for next year, in general. Major Gookin, Richards and Self, by as Spectators. Major Gookin to order.

Wednesday, Septr 15. Mr. David Geffries marries Mrs Betty Usher before Mr. Ratcliff.[35]

Monday, Septr 20. The President, Deputy President, Capt. Blackwell, Councillour Usher, Mr. Moodey, Lee, Morton, Allen, Willard, Cotton Mather, and Self, goe and visit Mr. Baylye at Watertown, and there dine.

Septr 23. Lecture day. Govr Bradstreet is gone with his Lady to Salem. President and Deputy President call'd here.

Septr 24. Friday. Capt. Clapp leaves the Castle; about nine Guns fired at his going off. It seems Capt. Clap is not actually come away, but Capt. Winthrop, and Lieut. Thomas Savage did this day there receive their Commissions.

Satterday, Septr 25. The Queen's Birthday is celebrated by the Captains of the Frigots and sundry others at Noddles Iland. King and Council's Proclamation of Novr 6. last, was published by beat of Drum throw the Town to hinder their making Bonfires in the Town however. Went with their Boats to the Ships and Vessels and caused them to put out their Ancients. Many Guns fired. A kind of Tent set up at the Iland and a Flagg on the top on 't. Made a great Fire in the Evening, many Hussas.

Sabbath, Septr 26. Mr. Willard expresses great grief in 's Prayer for the Profanation of the Sabbath last night. Mr. Lee preaches with us in the Afternoon from Isa. 52. 7. Said that all America should be converted, Mexico overcome, England sent over to convert the Natives, look you do it. Read in course this day Cant. 6. vid. Bright'm fol. 121.[36]

Septr 27. Hannah clambring to the Cupboard's head upon a chair breaks her forhead grievously just above her left Eye: 'twas in the morn.

Septr 28. Mr. Edward Grove who kept the Salutation,[37] dyed this day of the bloody Flux. Yesterday's Training was hindred by the Rain. No Drumms beat.

---

[35] David Jeffries had emigrated from Wiltshire to Boston in 1677. His grandson David Jeffries was town treasurer, and his great-grandson was John Jeffries, Harvard 1763 and M.D. Aberdeen, who made a celebrated balloon voyage across the English channel in 1785. *N.E.H.G.R.* xv, 14-17; *D.A.B.*

[36] Thomas Brightman's *Commentary on the Canticles, or The Song of Solomon* (London, 1644).

[37] The Salutation was a tavern on the street leading to the Charlestown ferry.

Wednesday, Sept 29. Set forth toward Narraganset, went to Woodcock's.

Oct 2*ᵈ*. Mr. Joseph Eliot and I went from Joseph Stanton's to Stonnington and kept the Sabbath with Mr. Noyes.

Oct 6. Went with Mr. Byfield to Rode-Iland about the middle on't, go to Bristow, there lodged. *Oct* 7. Went to Newport and back again to Mr. Byfield's. *Oct* 8. Rode to Plat's Farm. *Oct* 9. *Satterday*. Mr. Eliot and I got home about one aclock, and found all well. *Soli Deo gloria.*

Sabbath-day, Oct 10. By reason of the Fires the Meeting-Houses are much filled with Smoke; so 'twas a Lecture-day, one might feel it in ones eyes. Mr. Willard preached in the afternoon from Ps. 43. *ult.*

Wednesday, Oct 6. Mr. Bayly is ordain'd at Watertown, but not as Congregational Men are.[38]

Thorsday, Oct 7. Deacon Bright carrying home chairs, &c. used at Mr. Baylys, is hurt by his Cart none seeing, so that he dyes *Oct* 9. Satterday. It seems he was the only Officer left in that Church. Several of his Ribs broken.

Oct 12. Mr. Shove dines with us.

Wednesday, Oct 13*ᵗʰ* Carry Mistress Bridget Hoar behind me to Cambridge-Lecture, where Mr. Lee preached. After Lecture was invited to Dinner by the late Deputy Governour;[39] at his Table sat down Deputy Governour and his Lady, Mr. Lee, Morton, Bayly, Hubbard of the Village, Russell, Sewall, Wyllie, Ballard, Leverett, Brattle, Williams, [*of*] Derefield. Mr. Lee craved a Blessing and returned Thanks. Came home in Company Mr. Hez. Usher and Lady, and from widow Clark's, with Capt. Eliot and his Sons Elizur Holyoke and Mr. Joseph: got home about 8. aclock at night. Went in Company of the same save Mr. Hez. Usher and Lady who were not ready.

Wednesday, Sept 29. Capt. Clap went to Dorchester-Lecture, so to Boston, where he dwells, having actually left the Castle this day 29ᵗʰ September. Gunner Baxter also is here, having laid down his place, and both aged.

Thorsday, Oct 14. Many Guns fired, and at night a Bonfire on Noddles Iland, in remembrance of the King's Birth-day; 'tis the more

---

[38] The ceremony was performed without the laying on of hands, "a circumstance which intimates that Mr. [John] Baily regarded his previous ordination in England as valid, and therefore did not think it necessary to have the token of consecration to the sacred office renewed." Convers Francis, quoted in W. B. Sprague, *Annals of the American Pulpit* I, 202.

[39] Thomas Danforth of Cambridge was deputy governor from 1679 to 1686 and again from 1689 to 1692 in the temporary government after Andros's departure. Whitmore.

remarkable because Wednesday Octr 13th was the day the Generall Court was adjourn'd to at 8 aclock. Upon Thorsday before Lecture the Guns fired; some marched throw the Streets with Viols and Drums, playing and beating by turns.

Satterday, Octr 16. Accompanied Judge Stoughton as far as Dorchester Burying place, at his return from the Eastward.

Monday, Octr 18. Pretty deal of Rain. *Sabbath, Octr 17.* Mr. Edw. Taylor preaches in the Forenoon.

Tuesday, Octr 19. Wait on Major Richards to Braintrey, where He joins in Marriage his Cousin John Hunt and Cousin Ruth Quinsey; present, Capt. Quinsey the Father, Mr. Fisk who pray'd before and after, his wife, Cap. Daniel Quinsey and Exper. Quinsey, wife, Capt. Savage and wife, Lieut. Tho. Hunt and wife, Hunt of Weymouth and wife, Mr. Sam Shepard. Came home after Dinner. Wedding was about one of the Clock. This day Mr. Smith and Butler come in from London. I receive Gazetts next morn to the 26th of August. 'Tis reported that the King-Fisher rides no longer Admiral in the Downs as being ready to sail and bring Sir Edmund Andros our Governour.

Satterday night, Octr 23, about 7 aclock the Frigot fires many Guns, Drums and Trumpets going. I heard the Guns.

Sabbath-day, Octr 24. A Man Swoons in our Meeting-House, and falls down, which makes much disturbance, yet Mr. Willard breaks not off preaching.

Tuesday, Octr 26. I set sweet-briar seeds at the Pasture by Mr. Saunderson's, next the Lane at the upper end. Little red Heifer is this day brought from Braintrey to be killed.

Octr 29. Mr. Saml Danforth preaches at the Meeting at Cousin Quinsey's, Luke 3. 8.

Friday, Novr 5. Mr. Morton is ordained the Pastor of the Church at Charlestown; Propounded to the Church and to all if any had to object; then the Churches Vote was had; Mr. Mather gave him his charge, Mr. Allen, Moodey, Willard pray'd. Mr. Morton's Text was out of Rom. 1. 16. Took occasion to speak of the 5th of November very pithily, and said the just contrary to that Epistle was taught and practised at Rome. Mr. Mather spoke in praise of the Congregational way, and said were [*he*] as Mr. Morton, he would have Hands laid on him. Mr. Moodey in 's prayer said, though that which would have been gratefull to many was omitted, or to that purpose. I dined about 3. or 4. aclock at Mr. Russel's.[40]

[40] Charles Morton was M.A. and Fellow of Wadham College, Oxford, and had been rector and schoolmaster in England. He emigrated in the expectation of becoming president of Harvard, but this was prevented by unsettled conditions,

Friday, Novr 5. One Mr. Clark [*of the English Church*] preaches at the Town-House. Speaks much against the Presbyterians in England and here.

Satterday, Novr 6. One Robison Esqr., that came from Antego, is buried; first was had to the Town-House and set before the Pulpit, where Mr. Buckley preached. The President and many others there. [*Book of*] Common-Prayer used.

Monday, Novr 8. Lewis arrives. I have a Gazett to the 6th of September, by which are inform'd of the taking of Buda [*by the Imperialists*], which heard of before by a vessel from Bilbao.

Novr 9. Mr. Shove at our house, went on to Roxbury, after had sat with me awhile. I am ill of a Cold I took on Friday, lies much in my head.

Novr 10, 1686. Second year of His Majesties Reign.

Thorsday, Novr 11. I deliver'd my Commission to the Council, desiring them to appoint a Captain for the South-Company; left it with them to put 'em in mind on't. As was coming home Capt. Hill invited me to his House where unexpectly I found a good Supper. Capt. Hutchinson, Townsend, Savage, Wing and sundry others to the number of 14 or 15, were there. After Supper sung the 46th Ps.

Friday, Novr 12. I go to the Meeting at the Schoolhouse.

Jn° Griffin is this week buried with the Common-Prayer: Which is the third funeral of this sort, as far as I can learn.

In the Preamble to the Order for the Thanksgiving, are these words —As also for that His Majesties Kingdoms, and other His Majesties Plantations, flourish in all happy peace and tranquillity. It is therefore ordered &c.

Tuesday, Novr 16. I goe to Roxbury Lecture, and hear Mr. Eliot, the father, pray and preach. Came home with Mr. Moodey. This day Gardener arrives and brings Gazetts to the 16th of September, in one of which is that on the 13th of September His Majestie accepted of Rode-Iland Surrender by their Address. At night Brother Longfellow lodges here.

Wednesday, Novr 17. At parting I give him 2 French crowns and 15^s English money, and writt to Stephen to furnish him with cloths to the value of £5., and charg'd him to be frugal.

---

and he became minister of Charlestown. The early ministers, beginning with John Wilson, though regularly ordained in England, considered a reordination, by the imposition of hands, requisite when they assumed another pastorate. Morton objected to it, as did John Bailey, and the resettlements of previously-ordained Congregationalist ministers were thereafter termed installations. D.A.B. and M.H.S.EDS.

Novr 18. Jn° Neponet, alias Nemasit, executed. Mr. Eliot hopes well of him.

This day sent for my Coat home from Capt. Gerrishes, where I suppose I left it the 25th May, and now the cold wether made me look after it.

Friday, Novr 19. Went to Capt. Gerrish and paid him 18d., which laid out for crying my Coat, from thence Eliakim calls me to Mr. Moodey, so we together viewed the Eclips. As to the time and digits the Cambridge Almanack rightest; had he not unhappily said 'twould not be visible. Clouds hindered between whiles that could not so well see how much the Moon eclipsed, but when near half darkened, and when emerging, had a good view.

This night Eliza Damon, servant to Nash the Currier, dyes about midnight of the small pocks, to our great startling, lest it should spread as in 1678. Had hop'd the Town was clear of it. But one that I know of dyed on't before, and that a great while since.

Satterday, Novr 20. Capt. Davis buries his Serjeant, Henry Messenger, in arms.

Tuesday night, Novr 23. Mr. James Whetcomb dyes.

Wednesday, 24. Robert Combs taken up drown'd.

Thorsday, 25. Public Thanksgiving.

Friday, Novr 26. Marshal arrives from England.

Monday, Novr 29. Mr. Whetcomb buried. Coffin was lin'd with Cloth on the outside, and below the Name and year a St. Andrew's Cross made, with what intent I can't tell. Bearers, Mr. Wharton, Joyliff, Hutchinson J^ms Paige, Sergeant, Nelson. Gave scarvs to the President, Mr. Bradstreet and the Ministers, and Mr. Oakes. Should have been buried on Friday, but the storm of rain hindred.

This day Wm Clendon the Barber and Perriwig-maker dies miserably, being almost eat up with Lice and stupified with Drink and cold. Sat in the watch-house and was there gaz'd on a good part of the day, having been taken up the night before.

Decr 8, 1686. Going to Cambridge-Lecture, a little beyond Daniel Champney's I saw a Rainbow to the North, being just about Noon: only Herl. Simons with me just then; but Capt. Eliot and Mr. Tho. Oliver saw it, with whom rid over the Causeys. Mr. Oliver said he had not before noted a Rainbow in the North. Cloud rose suddenly very black and hail'd afterward. Ministers pray together at Boston this day.

Sabbath, Decr 12. Clutterbuck arrives, brings news of Capt. Jenner's death,[41] Widow Winsley's Son: and that the Capt. of the Kings-

[41] Captain Thomas Jenner of Charlestown was a noted shipmaster.

fisher expected to sail in a day or two: this was Octr 13, and then in
the Downs. Mr. Cotton Mather preaches with us.

Decr 13. Mr. Mather, Willard, Mr. Cotton Mather, Mr. Moodey,
Allin visit me. Very pleasant wether.

Tuesday, Decr 14. Capt. Legg arrives, who brings 60 Beds for Soldiers, and a considerable quantity of Goods for the Governour. 120
Soldiers to come. This day Mrs. Crines, Mr. Dering's Daughter, dies
of the Small Pocks.

Sabbath, Decr 19, 1686. Day of the Fort-fight. As I was reading the
Exposition of Habakkuk 3^d, which this morn sung and read in the
family, I heard a great Gun or two, as I supposed, which made me
think Sir Edmund might be come; but none of the family speaking of
it, I held my peace. Going to Mr. Bradstreet's, Tho. Baker told me
Sir Edmund was below, which Winchcomb and Brisco confirmed;
said they saw the Frigot with the Flagg in the main Top, and sundry
gon down. President and Deputy come to Town; President comes and
hears Mr. Willard, whoes Text was Heb. 11. 12. Therefor sprang
there of one &c. 113. Psalm sung. Mr. Willard said he was fully persuaded and confident God would not forget the Faith of those who
came first to New England, but would remember their Posterity with
kindness. One Doct. Faith usually reaps the greatest Crops off the
barrenest Ground. Between Sermons, the President and several of the
Council goe down. Mr. Lee preaches with us in the Afternoon from
Zech. 3. 9, 10.

Mercy Lincorn and [*blank*] Dinsdale baptized. Jn° Eastman taken
into Church, Mis. Harris as to her owning the Covenant dismissed. A
youth, one Bradish, of about 10. years old, that was drowned, buried.
Fine, serene, moderate wether.

Mr. Secretary indispos'd, so I wait on Madam Bradstreet morn.
and even. Capt. Wing absent.

Monday, Decr 20. 1686. Governour Andros comes up in the Pinnace, touches at the Castle, Lands at Govr Leveret's wharf about 2
P.M. where the President, &c. meet him and so march up through
the Guards of the 8 Companyes to the Town House, where part of
the Commission read: He hath power to suspend Councillors and to
appoint others if the number be reduced to less than Seven. He and
Council to make Laws. Then took the Oath of Allegiance and as
Governour, then about eight of the Council sworn. Court clear'd.
Governour stood with his Hat on when Oaths given to Councillours.
It seems speaks to the Ministers in the Library about accommodation as to a Meeting-house [*for church services*], that might so con-

trive the time as one House might serve two Assemblies.[42]

Last Satterday, Mr. Cook not prosecuting his Appeal, Possession was given by Major Bulkly and Marshal Green, of the Farm to Capt. Paige and his wife. The Constables were ordered this day to come and take new Staves, little thinking the Government should have been before altered, or at this time. Mr. Nath. Oliver was the person first spyed the Frigot under sail about 7 *mane* Sabbath-day, knowing her by the Flagg; he went to Capt. Davis, Capt. Davis to the President. Governour was in a Scarlet Coat Laced; several others were in Scarlet. Mr. Bradstreet and Mr. Danforth there, to meet the Governour at the Wharf. At Dinner Mr. Mather crav'd a Blessing. The day was serene, but somewhat cold. Major Richards made the South-Company change their Colours for the 8th Colours. Andrew Gardner led them.

Tuesday, Decr 21. There is a Meeting at Mr. Allen's, of the Ministers and four of each Congregation, to consider what answer to give the Governour; and 'twas agreed that could not with a good conscience consent that our Meeting-Houses should be made use of for the Common-Prayer Worship.

Decr 22. Kings-fisher comes up but neither salutes the Castle nor the Town. In the evening Mr. Mather and Willard thorowly discoursed his Excellency about the Meeting-Houses in great plainness, shewing they could not consent. This was at his Lodging at Madam Taylor's. He seems to say will not impose.

Friday, Decr 24. About 60 Red-Coats are brought to Town, landed at Mr. Pool's Wharf, where drew up and so marched to Mr. Gibbs's house at Fort-hill.

Satterday, Decr 25. Governour goes to the Town-House to Service Forenoon and Afternoon, a Red-Coat going on his right hand and Capt. George on the left. Was not at Lecture on Thorsday. Shops open today generally and persons about their occasions. Some, but few, Carts at Town with wood, though the day exceeding fair and pleasant. Read in the morn the 46. and 47. of Isa., and at night Mr. Norton from Jnº 9. 3. Neither this Man nor his Parents.

Thorsday, Decr 30. The Council meets. Gentlemen from Plimouth and Rhode-Iland here and take their Oaths without any Ceremony,

---

[42] Sir Edmund Andros, as royal governor, took over the reins of office from Joseph Dudley, and was now in charge of the Dominion of New England, uniting under one government all of the colonies except Connecticut and Rhode Island, which came in shortly.

perhaps for sake of the Quakers, who have promised to deliver up their Charter. Mr. Lee preaches the Lecture from Isa. 4. 5, 6. But the Governour and most of the Councillours absent. Mr. Stoughton, Gov.ʳ Hinkley, Mr. Usher and some other at Lecture.

1687

Satterday, January 1, [1686/7]. Took Capt. Elisha Hutchinson with me and went to Jnᵒ Alcocke, talked throughly with him about his ill courses. Told him by reason of our fear of the Small Pocks must fetch his chest away; would have had him done it then, but he would not, yet promis'd to do it Monday next.

Monday. Jan. 3, 1686/7. Jnᵒ Alcocke not coming, Robert Saunderson carries home his Trunk and Chest with Cloaths, Books, Papers.

Wednesday, Jan. 5. Sam. is taken ill of a Fever and we fear the Small Pocks.

Jan. 6. I sup at Capt. Wing's with Capt. Hutchinson, Phillips, Townsend, Turell, Prout, Sugars, Hill. Major Wally came in afterward.

Friday, Jan. 7ᵗʰ I went to Capt. Winthrop's upon business, and the Governour happen'd to be there, Capt. Winthrop had me up to him, so I thankfully acknowledged the protection and peace we enjoyed under his Excellencie's Government. Capt. Wing waited on him at the same time about a Man slain at Worster yesterday by a Logs rolling upon and over him which he just before had cut off. Capt. Davis carries his wife out of Town for fear of the Small Pocks, she being with Child. This day Dame Walker is taken so ill that she sends home my Daughters, not being able to teach them.

Sabbath, Jan. 9. Goe to Mr. Mather's Church and there sit down with them at the Lord's Supper. Mr. Cotton Mather preach'd and administred. Text was the Words of Thomas, My Lord and my

God. 'Twas a comfortable day. Mr. Brown, the Scot, preached in the afternoon. Micah 4. 5. Scope was to shew that the Errors of the Times should incite them to more strict Godliness in their whole conversation.

Thorsday, January 13, 1686/7. Cous. Savage's wife buried in Major Savage's Tomb.[1] Capt. Hutchinson, Self, Townsend, Turell, Davis, James Hill, Bearers. Died yesterday morn about 4. aclock of the Small Pocks; came out upon her about a week ago, two or three dayes after her Travail. Suppose this to be the first Funeral Govr Andros has been at, Blew-Coats going before him. The Charter is demanded and the Duplicate, last Monday or Tuesday. Though some say 'tis not so.

Tuesday, January 18, 1686/7. Between two and three in the Afternoon, for near an hour together, was seen in a clear Skie such a Rainbow, Parelions and Circles as were on January 2. 1684/5. In the night following falls a snow, not much. I was at the North-end when I first saw it. People were gazing at it from one end of the Town to tother.

Wednesday is snowy storm, but not much falls. Mr. Stoughton and Dudley and Capt. Eliot and Self, go to Muddy-River to Andrew Gardener's, where 'tis agreed that 12£ only, in or as Money, be levyed on the people by a Rate towards maintaining a School to teach to write and read English. Andrew Gardener, Jn° White, Tho. Stedmand are chosen to manage their affairs. Boilston Clark, Capt. Eliot and I, formerly chosen with Stedmand, refuse.

Thorsday, January 20. Mr. Lee preaches the Lecture. Eccles 7. 13. From whence exhorted to quietness under God's hand: about middle of Sermon fire was cry'd, which made a great disturbance, by many rushing out. 'Twas only a chimney I think. Spake of the inverted Rainbow, God shooting at sombody. And that our Times better than the former, and expected better still, Turks going down, a sign on't: Jews call'd, and to inhabit Judea and old Jerusalem.

Satterday, 22. Governour and Mr. Dudley ride in a Sled. Zebit's Letters came to hand last Thorsday, January 20. brings Gazetts to the 4th Novr came out of the Downs 16th. In them is the Parliaments Prorogue to 15th February, and Taking of Napoli di Romania [*by the Venetians from the Turks*].

Sabbath, Jan. 23. Sun rises extreamly red so as I think I have not seen it before.

Tuesday, January 25. This day is kept for St. Paul, and the Bell was rung in the Morning to call persons to Service. The Governour (I am

---

[1] Sarah Haugh Walker, daughter of Rev. Samuel Haugh of Reading, was the second wife of Ephraim Savage.

told) was there. Court sits in the Afternoon; suppose through the extraordinary cold, snowy, blustering wether yesterday, Persons concern'd were not got together.

Thorsday, Jan. 27. At night between 10. and 11. was a grievous Alarm of Fire, by reason of Mistress Thacher's chimney greatly blazing out.

Friday, Jan. 28. Mr. Moodey and I goe to visit Mr. Morton at Charlestown, went on the Ice from Broughton's Warehouse. I came home upon a Streight Line from his House to Boston.

Satterday, Jan. 29. Hannah not well, vomits and hath Qualms.

Sabbath, January 30ᵗʰ 1686/7. About ¾ past eight at night my wife is delivered of a Son, Eliza. Weeden, Midwife. Was fine moderate wether though had been very severe for near a week together before. My wife sent not for the Midwife till near 7. at night. But one staid at home with her, though was not well most part of the day. The child large, so my wive's safe delivery is much to be heeded, considering our former fears. 'Twas much another had not intercepted the Midwife, to whom went from us.

Monday, January 31. There is a Meeting at the Town-house forenoon and afternoon, Bell rung for it, respecting the beheading Charles the First.² Governour there, very bad going by reason of the watery snow. Joseph Brisco's wife gives my son suck.

Feb. 1. Last night, or very early this morning, Mistress Luscomb dyes, so that now Mr. Kellond hath neither Child nor Grandchild left.

Thorsday, Feb. 3. Spring Tides shake the Ice and carries away part; near night it suddainly breaks away to the outward Wharfs more suddenly than hath usually been known.

Friday, Feb. 4. A woman found dead under the Ice within the Wharfs. A Souldier falls into the Ice and is drowned. Mrs. Luscomb buried.

Satterday, Feb. 5. I visit Mr. Stoughton.

Thorsday, Feb. 3. Mr. West comes to Town from New York.³

² The Anglicans were observing the Martyrdom of Charles I (30 January 1649).
³ John West, an English merchant residing in New York, was a tool of Andros, who made him secretary of the Province of New York in 1680. Governor Dongan, who succeeded Andros, sent him, and John Palmer, to Maine in August 1683 as commissioners. They proceeded to appropriate large tracts of land to themselves and compelled the inhabitants to buy, at exorbitant prices, new patents for their lands. West turned up in Boston soon after Andros. Edward Randolph had been commissioned secretary and registrar for the Dominion of New England in September 1685 and continued under Andros. On 3 May 1687 he leased his job to West, who resumed his extortions. Two years later, 7 June 1689, West was im-

Sabbath, Feb. 6. Between ½ hour after 11. and ½ hour after 12. at Noon, many Scores of great Guns fired at the Castle and Town, suppose upon account of the King's entring on the third year of his Reign.

Feb. 6, 1687/7. Between 3. and 4. P.M. Mr. Willard baptiseth my Son, whom I named Stephen. Day was Louring after the storm, but not freezing. Child shrunk at the water but cry'd not. His Brother Sam. shew'd the Midwife who carried him, the way to the Pew, I held him up. Thomas Bumsted was baptiz'd at the same time. This Day the Lord's Supper was administered at the middle and North Meeting-Houses; the ratling of the Guns during almost all the time, gave them great disturbance. 'Twas never so in Boston before.

Feb. 15, 1686/7. Jos. Maylem carries a Cock at his back, with a Bell in 's hand, in the Main Street; several follow him blindfold, and under pretence of striking him or 's cock, with great cart-whips strike passengers, and make great disturbance.[4]

Friday, Feb. 25. Last night Mr. Elijah Corlett, Schoolmaster of Cambridge, died.[5]

Satterday, Feb. 26. There begins to be a talk of the new Captains.

March 3. Mis. Abigail Moodey buried in the old place near Messenger's house. This week the new Officers of the Militia receive their Commissions; viz: Lieut. Col. Shrimpton, Major Charles Lidget, Capt. Humph. Luscomb. Capt. Antho. Haywood, Capt. Benj. Davis, Capt. Tho. Savage. Capt. Wm White, Capt. Saml Ravenscroft. 'Tis said Mr. Nelson and Foxcroft refus'd; else I suppose Savage and Davis had dropt. Left out Richards, Checkly, Dummer. Sewall had returned his Commission before the change of Government, as see in August. This week also, the Law for annual publick Charges is anew engross'd. Written Satterday, March 5, 1686/7.

Satterday, March 5, 1686/7. The Massachusetts Books and Papers

prisoned in the Castle when Andros was overthrown, and remained there until February 1690, when he, Andros, Dudley, Randolph, et al., were shipped off to England. *Palfrey* III, 523, 533; *Andros Tracts, passim.*

[4] This was mummery in observance of Shrove Tuesday, the day before the beginning of Lent, a day of celebration in Catholic countries, and in England "Pancake Tuesday." The M.H.S. editors remark that Sewall's keenness in noting, and his sensitiveness in observing, any token, however trivial, of the presence and manifestation for the first time in the old Puritan town of observances associated with the English church, are equally significant with his despondent view of the changes in civil affairs. For more on Maylem, see *C.S.M.* XXXII, 88-89.

[5] Elijah Corlet, B.A. (Oxon.) and M.A. (Cantab.), an "eminently serviceable and faithful man," was master of the Grammar School at Cambridge by 1642, and continued fitting English and Indian youths for the college until his death. Morison, *F.H.C.; C.S.M.* XVII, 131-142.

are fetcht away from Mr. Rawson's to the Town-House by Mr. Lynde and Bullivant.[6]

Thorsday, March 10, 1686/7. Mis. Margery Flint dyes at Braintrey, this morn. Mr. Mather preaches the Lecture. Speaks sharply against Health-drinking, Card-playing, Drunkenness, profane Swearing, Sabbath-breaking, &c. Text [*Jere. 2. 21*], Degenerat Plant. Mr. Stoughton treated the Governour and Council March 9th.

Satterday, March 12. Went to the burying of Mistress Flint, in Company Mr. Hez. Usher and Lady, Capt. Eliot, Cous. Quinsey carried Mrs. Bridget. Mr. Torrey and Thacher there, Mr. Torrey prayed. Was buried about Noon. This day several Orders published at Boston, Governour and Council standing in Mr. Usher's Balcony. Refer to Ministers, Moneys, Pirats, &c. as Eliakim tells me.

March 14, 1686/7. Anniversary Town-Meeting. Select-Men chosen —Mr. Elisha Cook, Mr. Elisha Hutchinson, Mr. Jn⁰ Joyliff, Mr. Tim⁰ Prout, Mr. Theoph. Frary, Mr. Jn⁰ Fayerwether, Mr. Henry Allin, Mr. Edw. Wyllys, Mr. Daniel Turell. Constables—Arthur Smith, Robert Cumby, Richard Kates, James Hawkins, Tho. Hunt Turner, Jn⁰ Nicholls, Benjᵃ Walker, Edmund Brown. Select-Men had, most of them, I think all, save Deacon Allen, above a hundred Votes apiece. Capt. Gerrish begun and ended with Prayer. Capt. Winthrop and Mr. Wharton of the Council present. Governour was busy.

This day Mrs. Willard removes to Roxbury with a great part of the family and Goods for fear of the Small Pocks, little Betty Willard lying sick of it.

Monday, March 14. Capt. Thaxter of Hingham sinks down and dyes as went to fodder his Cattel.

Tuesday, March 15. Mis. Ballard, Mr. Lee's Sister, dyes suddenly.

March 16. About 1. aclock Mr. Anthony Stoddard dyes, was the ancientest shop-keeper in Town.

March 17. Father East dyes. Both good men.

March 18. Dr. Wᵐ Avery dyes. I go to Charlestown-Lecture, and then with Capt. Hutchinson to see dying Major Gookin. He speaks to us.

March 19. Satterday, about 5. or 6. in the morn, Major Daniel Gookin dies, a right good Man.

Sabbath, March 20. Dr. Stone and Abraham Busby dye.[7]

---

[6] The thoughtfulness of the magistrates in caring for the archives at this troubled time deserves notice. The early records of the colony are still in existence and in the proper hands.

[7] All the prominent citizens who died that week are easily identified. John Thaxter was in command of the troop of cavalry. Anthony Stoddard, a linen-draper,

·*Monday, March 21.* Mr. Stoddard and Dr. Avery buried. Mr. Avery about 3, Stoddard between 5. and 6. aclock. Father East was buried on Satterday, On 's Rail 'twas said was 94 years old.

Tuesday, March 22, 1686/7. Major Gookin and Abraham Busby buried. This day his Excellency views the three Meetinghouses.

Wednesday, March 23. The Governour sends Mr. Randolph for the Keys of our Meetinghouse, that may say Prayers there. Mr. Eliot, Frary, Oliver, Savage, Davis and my Self wait on his Excellency, shew that the Land and House is ours, and that we can't consent to part with it to such use; exhibit an Extract of Mrs. Norton's Deed, and how 'twas built by particular persons, as Hull, Oliver, 100.£ apiece, &c.

March 22. a considerable Snow on the ground, that fell last night. Mrs. Eliot of Roxbury dyes. Now about Goodm. Francis an ancient and good Man indeed, of Cambridge, dies.

Friday, March 25, 1687. Mrs. Nowel, Samuel Nowell Esqr's, Mother, dies.

Satterday, 26. Eliza. Scot, a good ancient Virgin, is buried at Boston.

Friday, March 25, 1687. The Governour has service in the South Meetinghouse.[8] Goodm. Needham [*the Sexton*], though had resolved to the contrary, was prevailed upon to Ring the Bell and open the door at the Governour's Command, one Smith and Hill, Joiner and Shoemaker, being very busy about it. Mr. Jnº Usher was there, whether at the very beginning or no, I can't tell.

March 28. Went to Mrs. Eliot's Funeral, which was a very great one; no Scarfs.

---

had been an inhabitant of Boston since 1639 and a selectman and deputy to the General Court. Francis East, a carpenter, had lived to the great age of 94. William Avery of Dedham was a physician and apothecary. Daniel Gookin of Cambridge had been deputy, speaker, assistant, and superintendent of Indian affairs; he visited England twice and on his last return had the regicides Goffe and Whalley under his protection. Dr. Daniel Stone had been a chirurgeon in Cambridge and Boston. Busby was a linen-weaver. *Savage* and L. R. Paige, *Hist. of Cambridge.*

[8] In December, as soon as he had reached Boston, Sir Edmund spoke to the ministers about the part-time use of one of the three churches for Anglican services (as Mr. Ratcliffe had proposed the previous May) and he met with their polite but emphatic refusal. The governor did not press the matter until Lent was drawing to a close, then the above-narrated events occurred, and a Good Friday service was held. Palfrey probably overstates the sentiment when he says: "If the demand had been for the use of the building for a mass, or for a carriage-house for Juggernaut, it could scarcely have been to the generality of the people more offensive." (III, 521). During the remainder of Andros's administration the Episcopalians continued to have joint occupancy of the South Meeting-house. H. W. Foote, *Annals of King's Chapel* I, 43, 63f.

March 29. To Mrs. Nowell's [*funeral*], the widow of Mr. Increase Nowell a Patentee. Mr. Danforth, Davie, Richards, Russell, Cook, Sewall, Bearers. None else of the old Government were there but Mr. Secretary Rawson. I help'd to lift the Corps into Mr. Shepard's Tomb, and to place it there, carrying the head. Mr. Nowell went not in: 84 years old. *Note.* Last Sabbath-day, March 27, Governour and his retinue met in our Meetinghouse at Eleven: broke off past two because of the Sacrament and Mr. Clark's long Sermon; now we were appointed to come ½ hour past one, so 'twas a sad Sight to see how full the Street was with people gazing and moving to and fro because had not entrance into the House.

Satterday, April 2. Mr. Lee goes to Dedham in order to his going to Bristoll next week, to settle there if can compose their differences respecting Mr. Woodbridge.

Monday, Ap. 4. Great Storm of Rain, Thunders several times. No Artillery Training; and I think would have been none if it had not rain'd. Capt. Wm White appoints the Serjeants and Corporalls to meet him at Serjeant Bulls at 3. aclock Ap. 4. In the Even Mr. Willard, Eliot, Frary and Self have great debate about our meeting for the Lord's Supper [*on account of the seizure of their place of worship*].

April 7. 1687. Weare sails, in whom Mr. Clark, the Church of England Minister, goes, Mr. Sheaf, &c.[9]

April 8. I goe to Hog-Iland with Cous. [*Ephraim*] Savage, to view the place. Got Willow-Blooms.[10]

April 10. Mr. Moodey helps Mr. Willard in the Forenoon. Text Job 23. 10. Shewed that Afflictions were for Tryal, and where the Tryal met with sincerity, the issue would be glorious. Mr. Solomon Stoddard here.

April 9. One Wm Sargent of Almsbury is trapand into a Tipling house about 9 at night and robbed of Money, a Gold Ring and several papers. Affidavit taken before Mr. Bullivant.

April 12. Goe to Weymouth-Lecture accompanied by Capt. Eliot. Mistress Torrey very ill, Mr. Rawson there.

[9] Rev. Josias Clarke, B.A. (Cantab.) who had been chaplain of the fort at New York, 1684-1686, seems to have served briefly as assistant to Mr. Ratcliffe.

[10] In Sewall's Commonplace Book (1677-), now at the Massachusetts Historical Society, he copied part of Act I, Scene 2, of John Dryden's play, *The Indian Emperor, or the Conquest of Mexico*, adding: "An extract of the Dramatique Poem. Read it as went to Hog-Island Ap.9.1687. Accidentally met with the Book at Sam. Green's." A note in *American Literature*, May 1942, xiv, 157-158, states that this is perhaps the first positive evidence of an acquaintance with a work of Dryden on the part of a New Englander.

April 15. Grafted the Button-pear tree stock, which dies at the lower end of the Garden, and several Apple Trees.

Tuesday, Apr. 19. 1687. The Eight Companyes are warn'd to Train next Satterday, being the 23. Instant. Serjeant Bull warns the South-Company *now under the Command of Capt. Willm White*: those the words; and so, *Satterday next being the 23^d of April, at the 2^d Beat of Drumm.*

Thorsday, Apr. 21. Mr. Winchcomb is sworn Deputy to Mr. Sherlock, who is this week made high Sheriff of the Dominion.

Mr. Shove died on Thursday about 9. *mane;* was buried the Friday following. Mr. Fisk, Keith, Anger, Woodbridge there and Major Walley.

Friday, 22. Seth Shove comes to Town in the morn, and brings news of 's father's death yesterday, I let him have my Horse to ride to Taunton. Mr. George Shove was a principal Light in those parts, and the death of their Saint George at this time calls for special mourning.[11]

Thorsday, Apr. 21. Mr. West of New York, and his wife and family come to Town in the even. Mr. Cotton Mather preach'd the Lecture from Heb. 6. 20. Jesus being our Fore-runner.

Friday, 22. Two persons, one array'd in white, the other in red, goe through the Town with naked Swords advanced, with a Drum attending each of them and a Quarter Staff, and a great rout following as is usual. It seems 'tis a chaleng to be fought at Capt. Wing's next Thorsday.

Satterday, Ap. 23. Eight Companies Train: Many persons: some officers have red paper Crosses fastened to their Hats. The Governour rode by and among the Souldiers, accompanied by the President, Mr. Davie and others. Major Lidget the Chief Commander, Col. Shrimpton, he, and Luscomb on Horse-back. Gave a Volley or two on the Common, march'd out about one aclock to the Market place. The Rose fired and others. Companies gave three Vollyes, broke off about 3. in the afternoon. In the night a Bonfire or two were made on Fort-

---

11 George Shove was the son of Rev. Edward Shove, M.A. (Cantab.), who sailed from England to be assistant to Rev. Ezekiel Rogers at Rowley, but died on the voyage. Margery Shove, the widow, settled in Rowley; although she had a legacy of 40s to send George to college, she was unable to keep him there for more than two years (1650-1652). He was made minister of Taunton in 1665. Seth Shove was his son by his first wife, Hopestill, daughter of Rev. Samuel Newman of Rehoboth; after his mother's death Seth went to live with the Sewalls, and Sewall sent him to Harvard. He was then a senior. *Sibley;* G. B. Blodgette and A. E. Jewett, *Early Settlers of Rowley* (1933), 343; F. L. Weis, *Colonial Clergy of New England* (1936).

hill. After followed fire-works with Huzzas, ended about 11. or 12. His Excellency on Mr. Shrimpton's House to behold the works.

Monday, Apr. 25. Another Challenge goes with his naked Sword through the Street with Hitchborn Drummer, and a person carrying a Quarter-Staff.

On Sabbath-day Old Meeting and ours much disturbed in Sermon-Time the afternoon by a distracted Fr. [*French?*] Man. Mr. Willard fain to leave off for some time. The same afternoon the Governour's Meeting was broken up by the Fire of Capt. Paige's chimney: and rallyed not again.

Tuesday, 26. Court sits, President in the Governour's seat, Mr. Stoughton at his right hand, Col. Shrimpton next him; Mr. Lynde at his left hand, Major Lidget next him. One Haman, Clerk, Massy Cryer: Sheriff, Justices, Constables, waited on the Judges to Town with other Gentelmen.

Ap. 28. After the Stage-fight, in the even, the Souldier who wounded his Antagonist, went accompanyed with a Drumm and about 7. drawn Swords, Shouting through the streets in a kind of Tryumph.

Monday, May 2. I go to Hog-Iland. Mr. Moodey, Oakes, Capt. Townsend and Seth Perry in one Column; Capt. Hill, Mr. Parson and Mr. Addington in the other, witness my taking Livery and Seisin of the Iland by Turf and Twigg and the House.[12]

As we went met with Mr. Barns just come in. Hail'd the Brigenteen as sail'd along, and after spoke with them and drunk with them, lashing to their side. Came from Antego; they told us the Parliament was not to sit till the latter end of April, having had February Newes. Went first to Capt. Townsend's who hath a goodly situation; then to Hog-Iland. After Dinner take possession, and then I planted some

[12] Hog Island, in the northeast corner of Boston Harbor, was granted to the inhabitants of Boston in 1635. Later the town disposed of its interest, and the fee became vested in Major Thomas Savage, Elias Maverick, and John Newgate, in severalty. Sewall and his wife purchased the greater part of the island, by deed of Ephraim Savage, son of Major Thomas Savage, 21 April 1687. The property contained 498 acres, and the consideration was £2000 current money of New England. The deed was acknowledged before Wait Winthrop and recorded in Suffolk Deeds, 15:181. The personal property which went with the estate included: "Seven oxen and Steers. Eight cows. One hundred and sixty sheep. Thirteen swine, none under half a year old. Two horses and one mare. Four stocks of Bees. Three Turkey Hens and one Cock. Twelve Dunghill Fowles. One boat with mast, saile, oars and road." There is an exhaustive note on Hog Island in the *Letter-Book*, 1, 68-73. For the attempt of the Andros government to unsettle Sewall's title, see the Diary entries of 12 July 1688 and following.

Chesnuts for a Nursery. Mr. Moodey dropt several of them. Gave every of the witnesses one of Mr. Lee's Books apiece.[13] It was past 9. before we got home.

May 3. Sign'd the Leases. Mr. Addington, Robert Saunderson and Elisa. Lane, Witnesses.

May 4. I spend a pretty deal of time in the burying place to see to the Graver of the Tombstone: Push Catterpillars off the Apple-trees; goe to the Meeting at Mistress Averyes; read out of Dr. Sibs about submitting to God's Providence, Sing the 110. Psalm.

May 5. Mr. Mather preaches against Covetousness. Text, Thou Fool, &c. Speaks against neglecting Prayer, pressing the Instance of Daniel. It seems was no Prayer last County-Court. A paper is found by Haman, the Clerk, which, pasted up at the Townhouse, giving an account of an Election yesterday.

May 6. Brother Stephen visits us.

May 9. Hamilton, Capt. of the Kingsfisher dies. 'Tis said the North Bell was toll'd as he was dying.

Tuesday, May 10. Mr. Bullivant having been acquainted that May 15th was our Sacrament-day, he writt to Mr. Willard, that he had acquainted those principally concern'd, and 'twas judg'd very improper and inconvenient for the Governour and his to be at any other House, it being Whit-Sunday and they must have the Communion, and that 'twas expected should leave off by 12. and not return again till they rung the Bell, that might have time to dispose of the Elements. So remembering how long they were at Easter, we were afraid 'twould breed much confusion in the Afternoon, and so, on Wednesday, concluded not to have our Sacrament for saw 'twas in vain to urge their promise. And on the 8th of May were bid past One a pretty deal.

May 15. Goes out just ½ hour after one; so have our Afternoon Exercise in due season. But see they have the advantage to lengthen or shorten their Exercises so as may make for their purpose.

Monday, May 16. 1687. I go to Reading and visit Mr. Brock, and so to Salem; this day Capt. Walker, a very aged Planter, buried at Lin. Visit my Sister and little Cousin Margaret.[14]

---

13 *The Joy of Faith,* a 247-page volume by the Rev. Samuel Lee, was printed by Samuel Green in Boston in 1687.

14 John Brock (Harvard 1646) was minister of Reading; Sewall attended his funeral 19 June 1688. Captain Richard Walker was said to be ninety-five at his death. The sister whom Sewall visited was Margaret Mitchel Sewall, wife of his brother Stephen.

Tuesday, May 17. Brother and I ride to Newbury in the rainy Drisk;[15] this day Capt. Hamilton buried with Capt. Nicholson's Redcoats and the 8 Companies: Was a funeral-Sermon preach'd by the Fisher's Chaplain: Pulpit cover'd with black cloath upon which Scutcheons: Mr. Dudley, Stoughton and many others at the Common Prayer and Sermon. House very full, and yet the Souldiers went not in.

Wednesday, May 18. Mr. Cotton Mather preaches Newbury-Lecture, Ps. 39. I am a Stranger with Thee. This day Mr. Foye comes in and brings the Kings Declaration for Liberty of Conscience.

Thorsday, May 19. Goe to Salem in company with Capt. Phillips and Mr. Cotton Mather.

May 20. Went home and found all well, as found them at Newbury to our great comfort.

Monday, May 23. Am invited to the Funeral of Mrs. Bowls.[16]

May 24. Mr. Fisk, Thacher, Denison, Self and two others bore Mrs. Bowls to her Grandmother's Tomb.

May 25. A Fast is kept at Cambridge. This day Mr. Bayly marries Mary Kay.[17]

May 26. Marshal Green visits me, and tells that he is wholly left out of all publick employment. Sam¹ Gookin Sheriff for Middlesex. Said Green told me he knew not of it till today, and that he was undone for this world. It seems the May-pole at Charlestown was cut down last week, and now a bigger is set up, and a Garland upon it. A Souldier was buried last Wednesday and disturbance grew by reason of Joseph Phips standing with 's hat on as the Parson was reading Service. 'Tis said Mr. Sam¹ Phips bid or encouraged the Watch to cut down the May-pole, being a Select-Man. And what about his Brother and that, the Captain of the Fisher and he came to blows, and Phips is bound to answer next December, the Governour having sent for him before Him yesterday, May 26. 1687.

May 27. Went to Charlestown-Lecture and heard Mr. Morton

---

15 Drisk is defined by the O.E.D. as a drizzly mist (U.S.). The editors give two citations: Sewall's use of the word in his entry of 27 April 1717 (they missed the earlier use above which had been misprinted as Dusk in the M.H.S. edition) and Thoreau's use in *The Maine Woods* (Riverside ed., p.239), where he puts the word in quotation marks.

16 Sarah Bowles was the wife of John Bowles of Roxbury, Sewall's classmate. She was the daughter of Rev. John Eliot Jr. of Newton (Harvard 1656) and his wife Sarah Willet, daughter of Thomas Willet of Plymouth, first English mayor of New York City. *Savage* and *Sibley*.

17 Mary Kay had been a servant at the Sewalls' since 26 May 1685. Her predecessor was Hannah Hett, whose name was set down by Sewall 30 April 1679, probably the date she began work.

from those words—*Love is a fruit of the Spirit*. [*Gal.* 5, 22.] Mr. Danforth sat in the Deacon's Seat.

Friday, May 27, between 5. and 6. Father Walker is taken with a Lethargy as was shutting up his shop to goe to their privat Meeting: His left side was chiefly struck with a kind of Palsy: His speech came to him something between 6. and 7. He told me there was plenty of Lavander in the Town where he was Prentice. He overheard some discourse about the May-Pole, and told what the manner was in England to dance about it with Musick, and that 'twas to be feared such practices would be here. Told me he had been liable to be overtaken with Sleep for three-score years, and that 'twas his Burden which he something insisted on. Had a blistering plaister to his neck, Drops of Lavander in 's mouth and his neck chaf'd with Oyl of Amber.

May 28. Mr. Cook scrapes white Hellebore which he snuffs up, and sneizes 30. times and yet wakes not, nor opens his eyes. Hot wether.

May 29. Sabbath. Dame Walker desires me to pray with her Husband, which I do and write two notes, one for our House and one for the Old. Sam. carries the first. Between 12. and one Robert Walker dies, about a quarter after Twelve. He was a very good Man, and conversant among God's New-England People from the beginning.[18] About one, several great Guns were fired.

Tuesday, Maij ult. [31] Goodm. Walker is buried, Capt. Eliot, Frary, Hill, Deacon Allen, Mr. Blake, Pain, Bearers; Mr. Saunderson and Goodm. Serch lead the Widow, Gov' Bradstreet, Mr. Cook, Mr. Addington, with the chief Guests, were at our House. Burial over about four aclock. Mr. Torrey came to Town yesterday, and supp'd with us this night. Mis. Long of Charlestown buried to-day.

June 3. The widow of Gemaliel Wait buried, Thunder Shower took us at the Grave, the mourners went into the Schoolhouse; I to Mr. Chiever's. When broke up a Rainbow appeared: was great Thunder in the night. All my married Cousins were in Town yesterday.

Wednesday, June 1. A privat Fast of the South-Church was kept at our house, Mr. Willard pray'd and preach'd in the morn. Mr. Cotton Mather pray'd first in the afternoon, Mr. Moodey preach'd and pray'd. Mr. Willard dismiss'd with a Blessing. Mr. Willard's

---

[18] Robert Walker has been mentioned (p.39) as an acquaintance of Sewall's grandfather in Manchester, Lancs. He joined the old church in Boston in 1632. Dame Walker survived him until 21 December 1695. It was the custom at that period to put up a note on the church door requesting prayers for the afflicted; since Walker had belonged to the First Church as well as the South, Sewall had two notes posted.

Text, Deut. 32. 36. For the Lord shall judge his People, &c. Mr. Moodey's Text, Ps. 46. 10. Be still &c. Occasion of the Fast was the putting by the Sacrament the last Turn, and the difficult circumstances our Church in above others, regarding the Church of England's meeting in it.

Note. *Monday, June 6.* Ebenezer Holloway, a youth of about 11 or 12 years old, going to help Jnº Hounsel, another Boston boy, out of the water at Roxbury, was drown'd together with him. I follow'd them to the Grave; for were brought to Town in the night, and both carried to the burying place together, and laid near one another. Eben, as I take it, was the only Son of Mr. Holloway by his deceased wife, and was boarded at Roxbury with his Aunt Swan to goe to School, and be the better looked after.

June 8. Went to Dorchester-Lecture. Din'd at Mrs. Flint's, who tells me that her Son Henry is in a Consumption. This day the Quarter-Sessions is held at Boston, Col. Shrimpton Judge, Tho. Dudley Clerk, Hudson Leverett Cryer. Judge Shrimpton sat in the Governour's Seat. No Civil Action try'd today.

June 9. Mr. Willard preached from Prov. 29. 27. Shew'd there was a radicated Antipathy between the Wicked and Godly.

June 10. Carried my wife to M[*uddy*] River. This day Mrs. Willard and her family return from Roxbury.

Sabbath, June 12. Lord's Supper at the South-Church. But Church of England men go not to any other House: yet little hindrance to us save as to ringing the first Bell, and straitning the Deacons in removal of the Table.

Munday, June 20. Went to Muddy-River with Mr. Gore and Eliot to take a Plot of Brooklin.

Tuesday, 21. June. Is a great Training at Cambridge: His Excellency there.

Wednesday, June 22. Went to Muddy-River. Mr. Gore finishes compassing the Land with his plain Table; I do it chiefly that I may know my own, it lies in so many nooks and corners. Went to Cambridge-Lecture.

June 28, 1687. Went to Roxbury and heard Mr. Cotton Mather preach from Colos. 4. 5. Redeeming the Time. Shew'd that should improve Season for doing and receiving good whatsoever it cost us. His Excellency was on the Neck, as came by, call'd Him in and gave Him a glass of Beer and Claret and deliver'd a Petition respecting the Narraganset Lands.

July 1, 1687. Went to Hog-Iland; had Eliakim thither: went to see where to make a Causey to land handsomly: brought home a Basket of Cherries: As went, saw a Surveyor with two red-coats, and another measuring and surveying Noddles-Iland. Came home about ½ hour after four aclock. About 6. aclock Abigail Saunderson is buried, who died yesterday.

Wednesday, July 6. Waited on his Excellency to Cambridge. Eleven Bachelors and Seven Masters proceeded. Mr. Mather, President, Pray'd forenoon and afternoon. Mr. Ratcliff sat in the Pulpit by the Governour's direction. Mr. Mather crav'd a Blessing and return'd Thanks in the Hall.

July 8. Carried my wife to Cambridge to visit my little Cousin Margaret, they were going, so went to Mr. Leverett's Chamber, the Library, Hall, Sir Davenport and Mitchel's Chamber, and so home well, blessed be God. Little Stephen hath a Tooth cut two or three dayes agoe.[19]

Monday, July 11. I hire Emms's Coach in the Afternoon, wherein Mr. Hez. Usher and his wife, and Mis. Bridget her daughter, my Self and wife ride to Roxbury, visit Mr. Dudley, and Mr. Eliot, the Father, who blesses them. Go and sup together at the Grayhound-Tavern with boil'd Bacon and rost Fowls. Came home between 10. and 11. brave Moonshine, were hinder'd an hour or two by Mr. Usher, else had been in good season.

Tuesday, July 12. I go to Mr. Usher's about 5. *mane,* [*Harris*][20] having been here: about 7. or eight we goe on Board, the Ship being under Sail. Go with them to Alderton's Point, and with our Boats beyond, quite out of the Massachusets Bay, and there catch'd fresh Cod. Went to Nantasket, in which way lost my hat, and for fear of running the Boat on the Rocks, left it. From Nantasket, in less than an hour and half sail'd home between 7. and eight. Goe in the Ship Mr. Wharton, Sam. Newman, Mr. Charles Morton, Mr. Wooddrop, Mis. Bridget Usher, and her Daughter Mis. Bridget Hoar, and others. Had an extraordinary good wind. Mr. Usher wept at taking

---

[19] John Davenport and Jonathan Mitchel had received their degrees on the 6th. Mitchel was a brother of Mrs. Stephen Sewall. "Little Cousin Margaret," the diarist's niece, was born the 7th of May and he had visited her the 16th; she grew up to become the wife of John Higginson of Salem. "Little Stephen," Sewall's own child, died later in the month.

[20] Under this date in his almanac Sewall wrote "Harris sails" (*N.E.H.G.R.* VIII, 20), but the diary entry looks more like *Wan* or *Warr.* Point Allerton, the cape on the long spit guarding Boston Harbor on the south, was named by Pilgrim explorers for Isaac Allerton; for many years it was erroneously called Alderton's Point.

leave of 's Wife and Daughter. Before went from Mr. Usher's, Mr. Moodey went to Prayer in behalf of those going to sea, and those staying behind, in a very heavenly manner.[21]

Wednesday, July 13. Mis. Eyre, Mr. Jnᵒ Eyre's Mother dies; and Jnᵒ Davis, a hopefull young Man.

Thorsday, July 14. Much Rain. Mr. Allen preaches. None save Mistress Bayly, Self and Mr. Usher in his Pue.

July 15, Friday. Thunder-Shower in the Afternoon. Mis. Eyre buried: Bearers, Mr. Rawson, Joyliff, Cook, Addington, Wyllys, Oakes. Governour not there. This same day Andrew Bordman, Steward and Cook of Harvard Colledge, is buried.[22] Sore Tempest of Wind and Rain this day in the afternoon, blew down Trees and Barns.

Satterday, July 16. At night a great Uproar and Lewd rout in the Main Street by reason of drunken raving Gammar Flood, came from about Wheeler's pond, and so went by our House into Town.[23] Many were startled, thinking there had been fire, and went to their windows out of Bed between 9. and 10. to see what was the matter.

Monday, July 18. Was startled in the morn as was at prayer in the Kitchen, at a sudden unusual noise; which prov'd to be two Cows running into our little Porch; the like to which never fell out before, that I know of.

July 18. Mr. Mather had two Venice Glasses broken at our Meeting.

Massie is some weeks since made Prison-keeper, and Earl dismissed; viz: June 17. 1687.

July 20. One of the Fisher's Men is found dead, suppos'd to be murder'd. Two men are stab'd (not mortally) at Charlestown last night, viz: Capt. Hunting, and one Adams; occasion was their going into street upon a stone's being thrown into Adams' House, which endangered his child.[24]

21 At the close of this pleasant fishing party Mrs. Bridget (Lisle) Hoar Usher (see p.84n) sailed for England, where she had an ample estate, with her daughter Bridget Hoar. She never saw her husband, Hezekiah Usher Jr., again. Their marriage was an unhappy one, and Usher was probably shedding crocodile tears. He died in Lynn 11 July 1697 leaving a will abusing his wife savagely and cutting her off from all his property except "what the law doth allow" (Printed in part in L.B. I, 138-139n, and in full, with extensive notes, in *Historical Magazine* xiv, 120-126). Madam Usher was back in Boston by 1699. Sewall acted as agent for her and was one of the executors of her estate.

22 Three generations of Bordmans were stewards and cooks at Harvard from 1663 to 1747; there is an account of them in 1 *M.H.S.Proc.* v, 156-158.

23 Wheeler's Pond was back of Sewall's house and a short distance to the south on Pond, now Bedford, Street.

24 Nathaniel Adams and Samuel Hunting, sea-captain, were stabbed by Unton

July 25. Town-Meeting to choose a Commission. Mr. Addington chosen had 16 votes; Mr. Saffin 8; Col. Shrimpton 2; Col. Lidget 2; and I think Mr. Foxcroft, One. Town was generally dissatisfied, partly said were not all warn'd, and partly at the work it sett; so most of them that were there went away and voted not. Mr. West there and Voted. In the afternoon Mr. and Mrs. Willard visit us. He prays with little Stephen who is very sick.

Tuesday, July 26, 1687. About Nine aclock my dear Son Stephen Sewall expires, just after the Judges coming to Town; died in his Grandmother's Bed-Chamber in Nurse Hill's Arms. Had two Teeth cut, no Convulsions. Mr. Willard pray'd with him in the Morning; Mr. Moodey coming in when at Prayer.

Wednesday, July 27, 1687. Between 6. and 7. after Noon, The Body of my dear Son Stephen is carried to the Tomb by Jnº Davie, Samˡ Willard, Joseph Eliot and Samuel Moodey. Samuel Clark and Solomon Rainsford put him into Tomb. Sam. had the head; Solomon's foot, on a loose brick, slipt, and he slid down the steps and let go the Coffin; but the end rested upon Jonny's stone set there to show the Entrance, and Sam. held his part steadily; so was only a little knock. I led my wife, Brother Stephen led Mother Hull, Sam. led Hannah, Billy Dummer led Betty, Cous. Quinsey led his wife, Cous. Savage and Dummer went together. Got home between 7. and 8. Mr. Torrey visited us but could not stay the Funeral. Sam. and his sisters cryed much coming home and at home, so that could hardly quiet them. It seems they look'd into Tomb, and Sam said he saw a great Coffin there, his Grandfathers.

July 28. Mr. Cotton Mather, and Mr. Bayly visit me.

Monday, Augt. 1, 1687. Brother comes to Town and brings word that two Salem Catches are taken by the French, of which his Newbury Ketch is one, and the whole Fare due to him, so that his Livelihood is in a manner taken away. Here is wave upon wave. I writt to Mr. Nelson to see, if Brother might have his Ketch again. Mr. Lidget buried a Daughter yesterday in the even, with the Service-Book.

Tuesday, Augt. 2. Wᵐ Rawson's little Ebenezer dies; He was about a week old, baptiz'd the last Sabbath. This day Brother writes me

---

Dearing of the *Rose* frigate, man of war. When Adams and the rest of the Charlestown constables went to Governor Andros "to have his Advice how they should Act to keep the Kings peace in case there should be another fray or Ryott . . . Sir Edmund fell into a great Rage, and did curse them, and said they deserved to be sent to Goale and indited and called them ill names . . ." *Andros Tracts* 1, 153; T. B. Wyman, *Genealogies and Estates of Charlestown* (1879), 1, 9, 530; R. Frothingham, *Hist. of Charlestown* (1849), 220.

word that his Catch, the Margarett, is return'd, parting from the
Frigat in a Fogg and leaving the Master behind, and bringing a
Frenchman hether that was put on board of them. *Laus Deo.*

Wednesday, Augt. 3. Capt. Gerrish is carried in a Sedan to the
Wharf and so takes Boat for Salem, to see if there he may find amendment of his Distemper. It seems the French and the confederat Indians made war upon the Mohawks and theirs; and Mohawks have
killed about a Thousand of them. This about a month or three weeks
agoe. Govr Dungan is concern'd, it seems, to animat the Mohawks
and hinder the French from coming on this side the Lake, which
they give out they will doe.[25]

Tuesday, Augt. 9, 1687. Sam. Toppan comes to Town and brings
me a Letter signifying that Capt. Gerrish died this day about Noon,
so that Mr. Willard, if he sail'd yesterday, is gon to his Funeral.[26]

Thorsday, Augt. 11. I ride to Salem with Cous. Savage and Mr.
Dering to the Funeral of Capt. Gerrish. Major Gedney, Major Brown,
Mr. Hawthorn, Weld, Dering and Self, Bearers. Was laid in Capt.
Price's Tomb. Capt. Winthrop, Edw. Tyng, Mr. Willard were by
accident there. Mr. Higginson, Willard, Noyes had Scarfs and the
Bearers. Hardly above two of Newbury there, viz: Nath. Clark, James
Smith. Was late before done, so lodg'd there.

Augt. 12. Cous. Savage and I come home by Reading and visit Mr.
Brock. Come home just to the Funeral of Isaac Goose's Child which
dyed suddenly. Went to the Grave.

Augt. 15. Went into Water alone at Blackstone's Point.[27]

Tuesday night, Augt. 16, 1687. Elder Wiswall dies, having liv'd,
as is said, fourscore and six years.[28] This day goe to Charlestown to

[25] Thomas Dongan, afterward Earl of Limerick, was made Governor of New
York by its proprietor, James, Duke of York, in 1682. He was an energetic and
far-sighted governor, recognizing early the growing threat of French power to the
northward. He established a form of protectorate over the Iroquois Confedera-
tion, which was sanctioned after James came to the throne, and recognized many
years later in the Treaty of Utrecht. The Mohawks were the easterly division of
the Iroquois, and bore the brunt of the early conflict with the French; their alliance with the English continued through the American Revolution. *D.A.B.;*
Dict. Amer. Hist.
[26] William Gerrish had come from Bristol, England, and was the first captain of
the Newbury militia band and a representative; he had settled in Boston in 1678.
Savage.
[27] It was the opinion of the M.H.S. editors that Blackstone's Point was a little
projection on the line of Beacon Street beyond Charles Street.
[28] John Wiswall of Dorchester and later of Boston was an ironmonger and general trader and ruling elder of the First Church of Boston. *Savage.*

make an addition to Col. Lidget's Farm out of the waste Lands; or on Monday.

Augt. 19ᵗʰ Mr. Morton's Text, out of the Fruits of the Spirit, falls in course to be PEACE, indeed very seasonably, as to the Exercise that Town is under respecting the Common, part of which was laid out and bounded to particular persons. Just a little before Sunset Elder Wiswall is buried. Govʳ Bradstreet, Mr. Saltonstall the Father, Mr. Davie, Major Richards, Mr. Nowell, Mr. Cook, Capt. Hutchinson, Mr. Johnson, Mr. Addington and my Self, ten of the old Government, followed to the Grave. Wooburn Church is under much disquiet.

Tuesday, Augt. 23. Balston arrives and brings Gazetts to June 13, and a Privy Seal whereby Capt. Nicholson is added to the Council, being sworn.

Augt. 24, 1687. Bartholomew-day. Indulgence for Liberty of Conscience published here.[29]

Augt. 25. Mr. Mather preaches from the 5ᵗʰ verse of Jude, shewing that persons deliver'd, yet through Unbelief left to eminent Judgments. Praised God for the Liberty good People enjoy in England. Said, 'tis marvellous in our Eyes. Mr. Dudley tells me His Father and Mr. Stoughton are petitioning for Patents. After Lecture, I visit Mr. Benjamin Eliot, who is much touch'd as to his Understanding, and almost all the while I was there kept heaving up his Shoulders: would many times laugh, and would sing with me, which did; he read three or more staves of the Seventy first Psalm, 9 verses, his Father and Jnᵒ Eliot singing with us; Mr. Benjamin would in some notes be very extravagant. Would have sung again before I came away but 's Father prevail'd with him to the contrary, alledging the chil-

---

29 This was King James's first Declaration of Indulgence, issued 4 April 1687, in which penal laws against Nonconformists were suspended, Catholics and Dissenters were authorized to perform their worship publicly, molestation of all religious assemblies was forbidden, and religious tests for civil and military office were abrogated. Actually it was a tricky and illegal move in James's war against the Church of England, but the English Nonconformists relaxed and took advantage of it, and the news was agreeably received, for the most part, in Boston. When a second Declaration was issued 25 April 1688, the Archbishop of Canterbury and six bishops protested and refused to read it in the churches, whereupon James had them locked up in the Tower. The action outraged the English people and stirred up a vast protest from all ranks and parties and all Protestant sects. The trial of the clergymen in the Court of King's Bench was a tense moment in the nation's history, and the verdict of acquittal was received with joy by milling thousands. Macaulay, *History of England*, Chaps. vii and viii.

dren would say he was distracted. Came with me to the Gate when took horse.[30]

Monday, Augt. 29. Carried my wife to Braintrey, Cous. Savage and Quinsey in Company.

Augt. 30th. Carry her to Weymouth, Unkle Quinsey in Company. Ly at Mr. Torrey's: Preach'd from Ezek. 36. 37. Mr. Fisk is sent for to bury his Brother.

Augt. 31. Carry'd my Wife to Hingham, Unkle Quinsey and Cous. Hunt accompanying, visited Cous. Hubbard, saw their two little Daughters; saw the Meetinghouse and Mr. Norton and Mis. Came home with Unkle to Braintrey. He brought my wife on his horse.[31]

Sept[r] 1. Mr. Torrey comes thether to us early and accompanyes us to Boston. Find all well, and are so ourselves. Mr. Willard preaches from 1 Peter, 4. 4. wherein they count it strange, &c. Gov[r] Hinkly came in and lodged at Mr. Torrey's the same night as we did.

Thorsday, Sept. 1. This day we receive a Sloop Load of Boards from the Salmon-falls Saw-mill, and the same day, I think by the same Boat, I receive a Copy of a Writt of Ejection which Mr. Mason has caus'd to be serv'd on John Broughton respecting the said Mill.

Friday, Sept. 2. One Wakeam falls down in the Street and dies without speaking a word. I accompany Mr. Torrey to Roxbury, visit Mr. Benj. Eliot, and consult with Mr. Dudley, and then ride to Dorchester and consult with Mr. Stoughton about my Law-Suit.

Friday, Sept. 9th. Mr. Cook and I set out for Portsmouth. Dine with Brother Sewall at Salem, call on Mr. Phillips. Lodge at Brother Gerrishes.

Satterday, call on Major Pike at Mr. Wears, of Hampton, stay a good while. Our Horses well baited, in this time the Judges got before us, overtook them at the Ordinary at Dinner. Din'd with them at the Sheriff's cost. Went, But Mr. Cook and I cast behind by alighting to take off our Coats, so rode alone till overtook Mr. Hutchinson, who staid for us. Went into Town another way than they

[30] Benjamin Eliot (Harvard 1665) lived at home with his father, the Apostle Eliot, and had assisted him in the Roxbury pulpit, though he was never ordained. Benjamin died the 15th of October.

[31] Unkle Quinsey was Edmund Quincy, brother of Mrs. Sewall's mother, Judith (Quincy) Hull. The cousins mentioned were all members of his family: Ephraim Savage of Boston, husband of Mary Quincy; Daniel Quincy, goldsmith of Boston; John Hunt of Weymouth, husband of Ruth Quincy; and David Hobart (Cousin Hubbard) of Hingham, husband of Joanna Quincy. The parsons mentioned were Samuel Torrey of Weymouth, Moses Fiske of Braintree, and John Norton of Hingham.

did, so miss'd of the Invitation and lay at the Ordinary in the Porch of the great Chamber alone.

Sabbath. [*Sept.* 11] Mr. Loree preaches from James 5. 16.[32] Dine at Mr. Waldron's with Mr. Stoughton and there goe to Duties and Sup. Mr. Stoughton pray'd. Lodge this night at Mr. Vaughan's with Mr. Cook.

Monday, Sept. 12. The Court sits. Our case is deferr'd till March next. Was no Declaration filed, no Jury out of the Province of Main, and we had no time to provide. Court was kept at Partridge's and there we dine at Sheriff's cost again, unwittingly. Lodge at Mr. Vaughan's.

Tuesday, 13th. Breakfast at Mr. Grafford's. After, a Fellow plays Tricks. Cook, Hutchinson and Self ride to Bloody Point, so to Hilbon's point over the Ferry; visited Mr. Pike while Mr. Hutchinson and Broughton came over; Boat would not carry all. Mr. Pike not at home, but his wife and two Sons. Call'd at Major Waldron's, where Mr. Cook lodg'd, but Hutchinson and Self rode to the Salmon-falls, George Broughton being our Guide, who was accidentally at Otisses. Lodge at Wm Love's in a very good House and Bed.

Wednesday, See the Mill, get a Cut, visit Mrs. Rainer and her Daughter Broughton. Breakfast there. Ride into Swamp to see a Mast drawn of about 26 Inches or 28; about two and thirty yoke of Oxen before, and about four yoke by the side of the Mast, between the fore and hinder wheels. 'Twas a very notable sight. Rode then to York, through very bad way, Jn° Broughton Pilot. Saw Mr. Sawyer's singular Saw-mill. Lodg'd at Cous. Dummer's with Mr. Martin. Rode to Wells on Thorsday 15th, to view the Records. Din'd at the Ordinary, (call'd at Mr. Wheelrights in the way.) Then I rode with Jn° Broughton to the Salmon-falls, got thether about 8; Lodg'd at Love's.

Friday 16. See Hobs his Hole, Quamphegen.[33] Stay a little at George and Jn° Broughton's: by then at Capt. Wincoll's; by this time Mr. Cook come. Din'd at Wincoll's. Came to Hampton, by that time

[32] Gilbert Laurie of Crossrig, M.A. (Edinburgh 1673) was ordained by the Scots Presbytery of London in 1686 and came to Boston; he preached that year at Portsmouth in the absence of Joshua Moody. He returned to Scotland, and was minister of the parish of Hutton and Fishwick, Berwickshire, from 1693 until his death in 1727. Hew Scott, *Fasti Ecclesiæ Scoticanæ* ii (1917), 52.

[33] Quampegan is now part of South Berwick, Maine, on the Piscataqua; Salmon Falls is a mile and a half up the river. The M.H.S. editors tried unsuccessfully to relate Hobshole to the Hobbs family settled in that region. The name may be generic or descriptive, since it is found at Plymouth as early as 1623, and also in Delaware, but it has escaped the dictionary-makers. W. T. Davis has some reflections on its derivation in *Ancient Landmarks of Plymouth* (1883), 326-327.

'twas dark. Supped there, then to Newbury. Mr. Cook and I lodge at Brother Gerrishes.

Satterday, 17. Ride homeward. Dine at Mrs. Gedney's: whether sent for my Brother. Major sends a Letter by me to his Excellency: we ride round by Charlestown, and get home between 7. and 8. finding all well, blessed be God. *Note,* The Friday we set out, at night, a Shallop riding at anchor in the Sea was run over by a Brigantine, and two Men drown'd. This day the Justices get a Town-Meeting at Ipswich; but they adhere to the former votes. And as we come home find Jnº Appleton Clerk, Lt. Andrews Moderator, and another, in Custody at Mr. Gibbs House under the charge of Souldiers.[34]

Monday, Sept. 12. Mr. John Alden, the ancient Magistrate of Plimouth, died.[35]

Monday, Sept. 19. Capt. Ravenscroft with his Company level Fort Hill. *Tuesday,* Capt. White—*Wednesday,* Capt. Savage—*Thorsday,* Capt. Davis—*Friday,* Capt Haywood—*Satterday,* Major Luscomb.

Wednesday, Sept. 28. Col. Lidget. (Monday and Tuesday it rained.) This day went with Mr. Mather and visited Capt. Bradstreet, who was much distracted last night; but now pretty well; said had not slept in several nights, being confin'd at Fort-Hill. After,

---

[34] One of the ways in which Andros and his government immediately exasperated the citizens was the arbitrary imposition of taxes. From the earliest times, the towns had taxed themselves, and when the General Court had imposed a colony tax this was assessed locally in orderly fashion. Now taxes were imposed by the Governor in Council, the act requiring compulsory assessment of them by commissioners and selectmen. When the warrant came from the province treasurer for each town to choose a commissioner, several towns in Massachusetts, including every town but three in Essex County, refused to proceed with the election which was ordered. In Ipswich the leader of the resistance was Rev. John Wise (Harvard 1673); the town voted not to choose a commissioner and refused to allow the selectmen to lay the rates. Six of the principal resisters were put in prison in Boston: Wise, John Appleton, John Andrews, Robert Kinsman, William Goodhue, and Thomas French. At a trial before a special court 3 October they were fined from £15 to £50 each, plus costs, which brought the total expenses to £400. It was obviously fruitless to persevere, and the towns thereupon capitulated. Wise had been suspended from the ministry as well as being fined £50, but in November Andros reversed his judgment and allowed him to return to his church duties. *Palfrey* III, 525-529; G. A. Cook, *John Wise: Early American Democrat* (1952), Chap. iv; *D.A.B.*

[35] John Alden was the cooper hired at Southampton to look after the beer and water casks on board the *Mayflower.* Though free to return to England, he remained with the Pilgrims, married Priscilla Mullins, had a family of eleven children, and became a leading citizen, holding office in the New Plymouth government continuously from 1632 until 1686. He was the last surviving signer of the Mayflower Compact. We will encounter his son Captain John Alden during the witchcraft troubles. *D.A.B.*

I went and visited Major Appleton. Major Saltonstall is gon home this day, giving Bond to appear at Salem-Court.

Thursday, Sept. 29. Col. Shrimpton works, and the School-boys there, my little Sam. among the rest.

Friday, Sept. 30. Capt. Paige and his Troopers work. This day Mrs. Rawlins is buried. Fast at Mr. Allen's, where my mother, wife and self were: Mr. Nowell and Allen exercised.

Monday, Oct. 3. I and my wife ride to Sherborn, George Bairstow accompanying us. Husk Corn and trace [*braid ears of corn by the inner husks*].

Tuesday, Oct. 4. Take a view of the Meadow, ride to Joseph Morse's; set an H on a sear Pine, which said Morse shewed me that it was certainly our Bound-Tree, and another little green Pine with Stones at the Roots. It wet, and so rode home. This Night Horse breaks out.

Wednesday, Oct. 5. Ride near round the Farm, Goodm. Holbrook shewing me the Bounds in Company of Joseph Moss and Moses Adams.

Thursday, Oct. 6. Joseph Moss and Goodm. Whitney shew me the Stone-wall, what was wanting to finish it, that so the Meadow might be secured. About Noon my Unkle and Goodm. Brown come from Braintrey. On my Unkle's Horse after Dinner, I carry my wife to see the Farm, where we eat Apples and drank Cider. Shew'd her the Meeting-house. In the Even Capt. Prentice's Negro brings my Horse. In the Morn Oct. 7th Unkle and Goodm. Brown come our way home accompanying of us. Set out after nine, and got home before three. Call'd no where by the way. Going out, our Horse fell down at once upon the Neck, and both fain to scrabble off, yet neither receiv'd any hurt. *Laus Deo.*

Oct. 10. Between 9. and 10. at night, Seth Shove goes on Board Daniel Lunt at a Wharf over against Mr. Mumford's Shop at the North End: Should have gon away at noon, but the Master Let his Bark fall aground before he was aware.

Thorsday, Oct. 13. A Boy of about 5 years old is burnt to death by his Shirt catching fire.

Friday, Oct. 14. Eight Companyes in Arms, and great Guns fired. At night a Bonfire on Fort-Hill round a Mast; The upper works fired not, but the Mast weakened with the fire, bowed and fell. Strong wind at first and so blaz'd not upright. I went this day to Hog-Iland, and carried Plank to make a way.

Satterday, Oct. 15. Mr. Bowls brings word to Town of the death of Mr. Benjamin Eliot this morning. Mr. Saffin buries his only surviving Son this day, Oct. 15. Thomas died of the Small Pocks in London, the news of which came just about the Death of this.

Oct. 16*th*. After Exercise went to the Funeral of Mr. Benj. Eliot, met the Funeral. Many were there, some of which came at noon to hear Mr. Joseph Eliot preach. Had the Sacrament today at the North Church; Mr. Ratcliff also had the Sacrament, and sent to Mr. Willard yesterday to leave off sooner. To which Mr. Willard not consenting Governour sent for him in the night.

Oct. 17, 1687. Weare Arrives, in whom comes the Governour's Lady. Lands about eleven aclock at Fort-hill; Takes Coach in the narrow way that leads by Mr. Gillam's; Governour, his Lady and one more ride together. Many Guns fired. Mr. Stoughton here.

Oct. 18. Carried Mother Hull behind me to Roxbury-Lecture; Mr. Joseph Eliot preached. Mr. Stoughton, Moodey, Allen, Hobart, Brown and Self there. House not very full because of the rawness and uncertainty of the day. Got home about ½ hour after Three. Belcher arrives this day, who it's said is Deputy to Sir Wm Phipps, Provost Marshal. Mr. Eliot said the King was turn'd a Puritan, and he was ravish'd at it; suppose 'twas from something he had heard as to som Nonconformists, Aldermen and Lord Mayor. As came home from Roxbury, I met the Governour's Lady riding in her Coach hitherward. The same day the Governour's Lady arriv'd, word came that Capt. Phips was Knighted, so have two Ladies in Town.[36]

Friday, Oct. 21. I went to offer my Lady Phips my House by Mr. Moodey's, and to congratulate her preferment. As to the former, she had bought Sam. Wakefield's House and Ground last night for 350£. I gave her a Gazett that related her Husband's Knighthood, which she had not seen before; and wish'd this success might not hinder her passage to a greater and better Estate. Gave me a cup of good Beer, and thank'd me for my Visit. The Governour has a Gazett of the 22th of Augt, that relates great success of the Imperialists against the Turks in a Battel [Battle of Mohacs, in Hungary].

Wednesday, Oct. 26. His Excellency with sundry of the Council, Justices and other Gentlemen, four Blew-Coats, two Trumpeters, Sam. Bligh one, 15 or 20 Red-Coats with small Guns and short Lances in the Tops of them, set forth for Woodcocks,[37] in order to goe to Connecticut to assume the Government of that place.

[36] Captain William Phips was knighted at Windsor Castle 28 June 1687.
[37] John Woodcock was licensed in 1670 to keep an ordinary at the Ten-mile river "in the way from Rehoboth to the Bay"; this is now Attleborough. J. W. Barber, *Hist. Colls. of Massachusetts* (1840), 111.

Monday before Capt. Tho. Dudley comes with his Company to digg. Tuesday, 25ᵗʰ Andrew Gardener; Wednesday, Dorchester Company to shovel, and carry stockados; so the Lecture put by.

Oct. 27. Mr. Joseph Eliot preached the Lecture from 1 Cor. 2. 2. parallels the diseases of New England with Corinth; among others mentions itching ears, hearkening after false Teachers, and consequently sucking in false Principles, and despising, sitting loose from the true Teachers. Advis'd to fly into the Arms of a crucifi'd Christ, because probably might have no whether else to goe. This morn, Mr. Simms thanks me for my kindness to Goodm. Huchins.

Oct. 29. Mr. Taylor rides to Malborough in Company of Mr. Jonᵃ Russell.

Oct. 30. Have the Lord's Supper; got home rather before 12. both by my Clock and Dial. Mr. Oliver's James was baptized in the Afternoon.

Tuesday, Nov. 1. Mis. Elisa Saffin dies after about six years languishing, keeping her Bed a great part of the time. Dies about 5. *mane.* Joseph Cowell is sent away Post to Hartford to acquaint Col. Lidget and Counsellour Usher. They are there waiting on his Excellency. Mr. Willard preached Roxbury Lecture from Job. 1. 21. The Lord gave, and the Lord hath taken away, &c. Col. Shrimpton there, and sat by me. Mr. Moodey preaches this day at Reading. Connecticut Government changed.

Nov. 3. Mis. Anne Williams tells me that an English Maid was Executed last Thorsday at Bristow, for murdering her Indian Child.

Thorsday, Nov. 3. The Long House upon Fort-Hill is raised.³⁸

Satterday, Nov. 12. About 5 P.M. Mis. Elisa Saffin is intombed. Major Richards, Mr. Cook, Mr. Chiever, Mr. Joyliff, Mr. Addington and Sewall, Bearers: had Scarfs and Rings. Rings given at the House after coming from the Grave. The Lady Andros and Phips there. Mother not invited.

Wednesday, Nov. 16. The Governour comes to Town returning from taking the Government of Connecticut. In the Even sends for the Ministers and so Schools them that the Thanksgiving is put by which was to have been the 17ᵗʰ.

³⁸ Sewall has referred several times to construction activities on Fort Hill. Sir Edmund was building a fort. Soon after his return from Connecticut he wrote home to the Lords of the Committee, 28 November: "I have now effected a palisado fort of four bastions on Fort Hill, at the south end of this town, commanding the harbor, in which also a house is erected for lodging the garrison, much wanted and necessary for his Majesty's Service." Quoted by *Palfrey* III, 549n.

Tuesday, Nov. 15ᵗʰ Began to lay down the Wharf at Hog-Iland, went thether with Mr. Newgate; prosecuted the same business on Wednesday.

Friday, Nov. 18. I goe over with Cousin Savage, and are so late about the Wharf that I lodge there all night. 'Tis the first time that I have lodged at the Iland.

Satterday Afternoon, come to Town with Cous. Savage. We meet Major Gedney who tells me a Thanksgiving is appointed to be next Thorsday Fortnight.

Tuesday, Nov. 22. I goe to Hog-Island with James Mirick. Being late at work, and wind and Tide contrary, I lodge there all night, which is the second time of my Lodging there; on Wednesday come home and hear of Justice Lynde's death yesterday about noon.

Brother Stephen lodged here in my absence, and the next night with Unkle Quinsey.

Friday, Nov. 25. Mr. Willard hath an order for the Thanksgiving left with him.

Satterday, Nov. 26. Mr. Simon Lynde is buried. Bearers, Col. Shrimpton, Mr. Nowel, Justice Bullivant, Justice Hutchinson, Mr. Addington, Mr. Saffin. His Excellency there, went in a Scarlet Cloak. This last week the Companies of Boston work again to finish the Fort. Friday, Nov. 25, Capt. Dudley brings his Company.

Friday, Decʳ 2, 1687. About 10. at night Mr. Jnº Hayward dies, having been speechless 48 hours. This Friday Wild sets sail from Marblehead, in whom goes Capt. Hutchinson.

Sabbath, Decʳ 4. Mr. Willard baptiseth his little Margaret, born about 8. last night. In the Even Capt. Eliot, Frary, Williams and Self, Treat with Brother Wing about his Letting a Room in his House for a man to shew Tricks in.[39] He saith, seeing 'tis offensive, he will remedy it. It seems the Room is fitted with Seats. I read what Dr. Ames saith of Callings, and Spake as I could, from this Principle, That the Man's Practice was unlawfull, and therefore Capt. Wing could not lawfully give him an accommodation for it. Sung the 90ᵗʰ Ps. from the 12ᵗʰ v. to the end. Broke up.

Decʳ 7ᵗʰ 1687. Foye Sails, in whom goes Mr. Saltonstall and Mr. Nowell. 'Tis reported that Wilde sail'd but this morning.

Decʳ 9. Mr. Palmer at the Coffee-House said Connecticut had received Letters from their Agent by Prentice, gone in to New London, in which desires Money; and that they are troubled at their hasty Surrender.

[39] John Wing, member of the South Church, owned and ran the Castle Tavern on Hudson's Lane (now Elm Street) at Dock Square.

Monday, Decr 12. Col. Mason calls here with Mr. Hutchinson; I stick at his Reservation of Masts 24 Inches Diameter.

Decr 13. Carry my wife to Roxbury Lecture. Note, *Friday Decr 9th* Major Appleton is by a Mittimus committed to the Stone-Prison,[40] remov'd from Gibbs's House. Sabbath, *Dec^r* 11. Mr. Mather propounds his going to England, to his Church for their Consent.

Decr 15. Mr. Mather preaches the Lecture from Judges 8. 27.— which thing became a snare unto Gideon and to his house. Shewed that Good Men might fall into such scandalous Sins as might bring temporal Wrath and ruin upon themselves and upon their posterity. Mr. Stoughton and Dudley not at Lecture.

Sabbath, Decr 18. Is a very Rainy and dark day, a great Thaw. Sung at the Meeting in the Morning the 129th Psalm, Many a time, &c. Mr. Willard preach'd from Heb. 11. 36-37, to the word *tempted*, inclusively. Sung in the Family the 34th. In the night it thunder'd and lightend pretty much.

Tuesday, Decr 20. A cold blustering day; in the even Mr. Eliot and Frary visit me: we sing the 4th Psalm. President calls on Horsback but lights not, speaks about Mr. Mason, said Mr. Morton not to be called till next Term.[41] This day, or Monday, was buried one Mr. Lock in Capt. Hamilton's Tomb. It's thought he kill'd himself with Drink. Was in the Riot that Capt. Hunting was wounded in at Charlestown, as is said.

Friday goe to Charlestown Lecture.

Satterday, Decr 24th Very dark and much warm Rain. The sun appeared not all day that I saw, or yet hear of.

Sabbath, 25. Have the Lord's Supper at the South Church, break up about noon, at which time I hear that Mr. Mather was, on Satterday between 1. and 2. P.M. Arrested by Larkin, to answer for a Trespass on Mr. Randolp, 500.£. damage.[42] Major Richards and Capt.

[40] Major John Appleton was one of the Ipswich resisters. Colonel Robert Gibbs had built a £3000 mansion by the shore at the east end of the town; he died in 1673.

[41] Rev. Charles Morton had told his Charlestown congregation in September that "persecution . . . was come amongst us and settled amongst us" but he bid them to have courage; he hoped it would not last long. For these and other seditious expressions he was bound over for trial at the first session of the Superior Court. The trial was held in Suffolk County, not in Middlesex, where the alleged offence occurred, and Morton was acquitted. *Palfrey* III, 547.

[42] In 1683 Increase Mather had written some rather frank letters to friends abroad criticizing the royal attacks on the Massachusetts-Bay charter. On 16 July 1684 Mather wrote in his diary that he was "in some distress of spirit" because he heard that certain letters which he had sent to Holland had fallen into the hands of "y^m at Whitehall." Edward Randolph in Boston turned up with a copy

Turell bound. Just as Morn-Exercise ends Mr. Cotton Mather's child dies; yet he preaches at Charlestown in the afternoon.

---

of a letter dated 3 December 1683, signed I.M., containing matter "perilously near sedition," and used it to build up hostility to Mather. Mather declared this particular letter a forgery and no one has ever disproved his charge, but he made the mistake of asserting in a letter to Joseph Dudley that the forger was "Randolph himselfe." Randolph thereupon secured a warrant for Mather's arrest. The case came to trial 31 January 1688. Mather was acquitted and Randolph was ordered to pay the court costs. K. B. Murdock, *Increase Mather* (1925), 183-186; *Palfrey* III, 556-558.

1688

Wednesday, Jan. 4 [1687/8] Rode to Cambridge-Lecture, Mr. Jn°
Bayly preached from Ephes. 2. 1.[1]

Visited Aunt Mitchell and Cousin Fissenden, where I dined in
company of him, his wife and father Chany.[2] Very cold day, yet got
home comfortably.

Tuesday, Jan. 10th 1687/8. Carried Mother Hull on my Horse to
Roxbury-Lecture, where Mr. Moodey preached from Jn° 15. 6. shewing, that not abiding in, or apostatizing from Christ, is a ruinating
evil. Mr. Stoughton, the President, and Unkle Quinsey there. A very
pleasant comfortable day.

Monday, Jan. 9th Lieut. Alford arrested for not Watching.

Wednesday, Jan. 11th Sam. falls ill of the Measels: Joshua Gee,
come in Capt. Legg, visits me, and returns thanks for my kindness
to him when Captive in Algier.

Thorsday, Jan. 12. Eliakim falls ill of the Measels. Joshua Gee dines
with us. Mr. Allen preaches the Lecture.

Friday, Jan. 13. Betty Lane falls sick of the Measels. Get Mehetabel

---

[1] Our diarist neglected to record the fact that his wife Hannah Hull Sewall became a member of the South Church on January first 1687/8.

[2] Aunt Mitchell was Margaret Boradaile, who married first Rev. Thomas Shepard
(Emmanuel College, Cambridge, 1623/4), and after his death, married his successor in the Cambridge pulpit, Rev. Jonathan Mitchel (Harvard 1647). Her
daughter, Margaret Mitchel, was the wife of Sewall's brother Stephen. Cousin
Fissenden was Nicholas Fessenden, glover, of Cambridge, whose wife was Margaret Cheney, daughter of Thomas and Jane (Atkinson) Cheney. Paige, *Cambridge*, 509, 542, 653.

Thirston to help us. Sabbath only Mother and self at Meeting: Betty vomits up a long worm: Mehetabel goes home sick.

Friday, Jan. 13. Joshua Gee with Joseph Bridgham, Jn° Barnard and Dyar, come to agree with me what I must have for my Money disbursed in London: said Gee presents me with a pair of Jerusalem Garters which cost above 2 pieces 8/8 [*Spanish dollars*] in Algier; were made by a Jew.

13ᵗʰ Jan. Mr. Moodey hears that Martha, a Grandchild of 4. or 5. years old, is scalded to death at Barnstable. Speaks at Mrs. Sarah. [*Mrs. Sarah Noyes?*] Mother and I hear him.

Monday, Jan. 15 [16]. Mary Draper comes to help us.

Jan. 18. Capt. Ravenscroft having petition'd for a Farm at Blew Hills, Cranes who Rents it, is said, in stead of defending the Towns Interest, joins in petitioning: Complains that the Select Men slighted him and did not take care for his defence. Crane was Summoned the Thorsday before to this Council-day.

Friday, Jan. 20. Coming from Charlestown Lecture, I saw Mr. Wears Ship lying on her Larboard side, fell so on Wednesday by reason of Melasses between Decks, as she lay at Scarlet's Wharf. Are now by Boats and empty Buts trying to right her again. Is much damage to Sugar that was laden, the water coming into her: besides what damage the Ship may receive. Many people looking at this odd sight. This is the Ship my Lady [*Andros*] arriv'd in, Octᵣ 17ᵗʰ and in which Mr. Mather hath bespoke his passage for London.

Satterday, Jan. 21. My dear Daughter Hannah is put to bed, or rather kept in Bed, being sick of the Measles. Droop'd ever since Thorsday.

Sabbath, 22ᵈ Hannah's Measles appear very full in her face: had a restless night, read in course the 38ᵗʰ Psalm. My Lady Andros was prayed for in Publick; who has been dangerously ill ever since the last Sabbath. Today I hear that Mr. Brown of Salem, the Father, dyed on Friday last in the afternoon. One of a Dutch Church in London is admitted to the Lord's Supper with us. About the beginning of our afternoon Exercise, the Lady Andros expires.

Monday, Jan. 23. The Clarks take Lists of the Companies, take in the Deacons.

Monday, Jan. 23. The Measles come out pretty full on my dear Wife, which I discern before I rise. She was very ill in the night.

Tuesday, Jan. 24. Betty Sewall keeps her Bed; but is not so full as her Sister Hannah. Capt. Nicholson sat with me an hour or two on Monday night.

Tuesday, Jan. 24ᵗʰ About noon, the Physician tells me the Measles are come out in my face, and challenges me for his Patient.

Wednesday, Jan. 25. Harris arrives from London, brings a Gazett to the 5ᵗʰ of December wherein is the Address of the N. E. Ministers.³ I hear the notable firing as I lye abed.

Friday, Jan. 27. Mr. Willard having been at Mr. Brown's Funeral, acquaints me of Brother's being very ill of the Measles, and his family was taken rather before me. In the afternoon I arise to have my sweaty Bed made and dri'd.

Monday, Jan. 30. Near noon Mr. Bullivant gives a Warrant to the Constables, and causeth the Shops to be shut. [*Martyrdom of Charles I.*]

Jan. 31. Mr. Randolph, in his Action against Mr. Increase Mather, is cast. Mr. Hale being subpœna'd by Mr. Randolph, pleaded he might not lay his hand on the Bible; must Swear by his Creator, not Creature. 'Twas granted that he only lift up his Hand as customary in New England. Col. Shrimpton lent Mr. Mather his Coach to ride home: He abode there the time of the Tryal, to be at hand if need were.

Feb. 2. Mr. Cotton Mather visits me, and tells me that Col. Shrimpton and Mr. Brown are made of the Council.

Feb. 3. Unkle Quinsey visits us, and tells us that one Withrington, a lusty young man of Dorchester, is dead of the Measles. News comes by Mr. Harris of the Death of Mr. Jnᵒ Collins.

Satterday, Feb. 4. Mr. Stoughton visits us and tells that Mr. Shrimpton and Brown were sworn of the Council last Wednesday. Watertowns Trouble about a Town-Rate.

Sabbath, Feb. 5ᵗʰ I go to Meeting after the Measles; read in course at home the 39ᵗʰ Ps. I said I will look to my ways, &c. which was also sung in publick. Mr. Willard's Sermon about keeping a Conscience void of offence, in the afternoon when I was there. See Mr. Carre's Letter.

Monday, Feb. 6. Towards noon the Shops are again shut up by a Warrant from a Justice, 'tis said Col. Lidget.

Tuesday, Feb. 7. My Aunt Gerrish dies between 7. and 8. *mane:* Had the Measles lately, and now by Flux, vapours and others inconveniencies, expires before I had so much as heard of her being ill, that I know of. This day, my wife, Sam. and self purge after the Measles.

³ Increase Mather had suggested to the local ministers that an expression of gratitude for the Declaration of Indulgence be sent to the king, and ten churches complied. Drafts are printed in the Mather Papers, 4 *M.H.S.Colls.* viii, 697-698. See also K. B. Murdock, *Increase Mather,* 182-183.

Wednesday, Feb. 8. Obad. Gill, Jnᵒ Atwood, and Jos. Davis are fined by Judge West [*blank*] Marks⁴ apice, for refusing to lay their hands on the Bible in Swearing.

Friday, Feb. 10, 1687/8. Between 4. and 5. I went to the Funeral of the Lady Andros,⁵ having been invited by the Clark of the South Company. Between 7. and 8. (Lychni [*torches*] illuminating the cloudy air) The Corps was carried into the Herse drawn by Six Horses. The Souldiers making a Guard from the Governour's House down the Prison Lane to the South-Meetinghouse, there taken out and carried in at the western dore, and set in the Alley before the pulpit, with Six Mourning Women by it. House made light with Candles and Torches. Was a great noise and clamor to keep people out of the House, that might not rush in too soon. I went home, where about nine aclock I heard the Bells toll again for the Funeral. It seems Mr. Ratcliffs Text was, Cry, all flesh is Grass. The Ministers turn'd in to Mr. Willards. The Meeting-House full, among whom Mr. Dudley, Stoughton, Gedney, Bradstreet, &c. 'Twas warm thawing wether, and the wayes extream dirty. No volley at placing the Body in the Tomb. On Satterday Feb. 11, the mourning cloth of the Pulpit is taken off and given to Mr. Willard. My Brother Stephen was at the Funeral and lodged here.

Satterday, Feb. 11. Cary arrives from Jamaica, 5 weeks Passage: brings word that the Duke of Albemarle was there, and Sir William [*Phips*] upon the Wreck.⁶

---

⁴ A silver mark at that time was 13s 4d; Sewall's entry of 30 March reveals that the men were fined one mark apiece.

⁵ Lady Andros was Mary Craven, daughter of Sir Thomas Craven of Appletree-wick, co. York. On 7 April Sewall recorded the sailing of Madam Craven for England, undoubtedly one of Lady Andros's relatives.

⁶ Captain William Phips, who came from the humblest of origins on the Maine frontier, and was successively a ship-carpenter, ship-contractor, and ship-master in Boston, had heard from sea-rovers of the fabulous wealth in sunken Spanish ships and determined to search for one reported in the Bahamas. He succeeded in interesting Charles II, who equipped him with a vessel for his first quest in 1683. This venture failed, but a second, backed by the Duke of Albemarle and a company of gentleman adventurers, was successful in finding a vessel off Hispaniola from which some £300,000 was raised. For this achievement medals were struck and Phips acquired a knighthood and a coat of arms. *D.A.B.* Sewall was misinformed about the Duke; he was not on the expedition. Cotton Mather wrote the first life of Phips, *Pietas in Patriam* (London, 1697; reprinted in his *Magnalia*, Book II); see also V. F. Barnes, The Rise of William Phips, *New England Quarterly*, I, 271-294; C. H. Karraker, The Treasure Expedition of Captain William Phips to the Bahama Banks, *ibid.* v, 731-752; R. H. George, The Treasure Trove of William Phips, *ibid.* vi, 294-318.

Thorsday, Feb. 23. Sam. Toppan brings word of my sick Mother, and my being sent for to see her.

Friday, Feb. 24. I set out, get to Newbury by 9. at night, ways being very bad. Find Mother something better, so that speaks to me comfortably. Father and Brother Sewall were gone to Bed before I came in.

Satterday, 25ᵗʰ Brother St[*ephen*] goes home to Salem.

Sabbath, 26ᵗʰ. I sit down with the Church of Newbury at the Lord's Table. The Songs of the 5ᵗʰ of the Revelation were sung. I was ready to burst into tears at that word, *bought with thy blood.* Me thoughts 'twas strange that Christ should *cheapen* us; but that when the bargain came to be driven, he should consent rather to part with his *blood*, than goe without us; 'twas amazing. Before night Dr. Weld comes with Sam. Toppan, being sent by Brother to see if he could reliev Mother, so he and Mr. Doel consult.

Feb. 28. Dr. Weld and I came to Salem in good wether and ways much mended.

Feb. 29. Come home about 3. aclock and find all well through God's Grace.

Feb. 29. Mis. Foster is buried, and Mr. Giles Masters, the King's Attorney, dies. Yesterday Mr. West's only child buried.

Thorsday, March 1. Mr. Masters is buried.

Tuesday, March 6. Ride to Newbury in Company of Mr. Cook, Hutchinson, and Sam. Walker, Mariner.

Wednesday, went to Portsmouth.

Thorsday, March 8. Went up the River to Capt. Hammond who keeps Kittery Town–Book. Mr. Hutchinson to Nichewanook.

Friday, March 9. Goe to the Great Iland, saw the Mast-Ship sail.

Satterday, March 10. Rid to Sagamore's Crick. Several went to meet the Judges.

Sabbath, March 11. Heard Mr. Lorie preach from Psal. 45. 7. Going home at noon Mr. Stoughton fell off a Long [*sic*] into water with his right Legg and hand.

Monday, March 12. Mr. Mason discontinues his Actions against Mr. Cook and me, saying, That Mr. Masters being dead, the papers could not be come at.

Tuesday, March 13. Waited on the Judges to Ipswich, Mr. Cook and Hutchinson going up the river. I lodgd at Sparks's whether Mr. Stoughton and Capt. Appleton came to see me in the evening.

March 14. Came home, riding round by Roxbury, the wind being extream high. Got home between 3. and 4. Met with some Rain between Cambridge and the Town. Found all well. *Laus Deo.*

March 14, about 2. P.M. Mrs. Downs, Mr. Eliot's Sister, dies of Convulsions.

On Monday, March the 12. There was no anniversary Town-Meeting at Boston, to choose Select-Men and Constables, &c. as hath been formerly used. This day Capt. Wait Winthrop falls down his stairs and is grievously hurt.

March 15. Capt. Tho. Dudley is thrown by a Horse, on oxen, and is much endangered.

Satterday, March 16. The order is pass'd about Select-Men, to be of an even number, not exceed Eight any where; if any refuse, Justices to supply. To make Rates approv'd by Justices. To be chosen the 3^d Monday in May. Not to meet at any other time on any pretence whatsoever, i. e. the Town. Published March 19. On which day Salem Gentlemen come wilily to Town early in the morn and buy up a great quantity of Salt, they having advice that none to be had at Salt-Tartoodas [*Tortugas*].

Thorsday, March 22. Mr. Mather preaches his farewell Lecture, from Exod. 33. 15. If thy Presence goe not—mentioned the sound of going on the tops of the Mulberry Trees. Desired Prayers and Presence for Goers and Stayers.

Friday, March 23. Shaller's Still-House with English Hay in the Loft, fell on fire, and had not the wind carri'd the flame into the Commonward in all probability many Houses had been consumed and ours among the rest. 4 P.M.[7]

March 25, 1688. Mr. Increase Mather preaches at the South-Meeting from Ezek. 47. 11. But the mirie places, &c. See the Sermon Preacht in the morning.

March 27th 1688. Last night a cold, blustering N.W. wind. Three Indian Children being alone in a Wigwam at Muddy-River, the Wigwam fell on fire, and burnt them so that they all died, youngest bowells burnt out in the Wigwam. Eldest, 10. or 12. years old, got to an English House a little before day; but died quickly.

March 28, 1688. Capt. [*Benjamin*] Davis spake to me for Land to set a Church on. I told him could not, would not, put Mr. Cotton's Land to such an use, and besides, 'twas Entail'd. After, Mr. Randolph saw me, and had me to his House to see the Landscips of Oxford Colledges and Halls.[8] Left me with Mr. Ratcliff, who spake to me for

---

[7] Michael Shaller (Shailer) was made a freeman in 1690. He had property on Washington (then Newbury) Street near Frog Lane (Boylston Street) about two blocks south of Sewall's house. *Savage* and M.H.S.EDS.

[8] This was David Loggan's great work, *Oxonia Illustrata* (1675), which com-

Land at Cotton-Hill for a Church which were going to build: I told him I could not, first because I would not set up that which the People of N. E. came over to avoid: 2ˡʸ the Land was Entail'd. In after discourse I mentioned chiefly the Cross in Baptism, and Holy Dayes.

March 29, 1688. Mr. Moodey preaches from Isa. 9. 12, 13. for all this his anger, &c. This day my wife sitts with very good liking in the place I procured for her in Mis. Baker's Pue: several being dead that us'd to sit there.

March 30, 1688. Obadia Gill, John Atwood and Joseph Davis are by a Writt from the Sheriff imprisoned, because they paid not the 13ˢ 4ᵈ which each was fined, Feb. 8., for not laying their Hand on the Bible: Judgment run thus—refusing to take the Oath as by Law is required. Though they offer'd to take the same Oath, the oath the others did, that Ceremony set aside. They pay the Fine and charges and Ly not in Prison one night. Mr. Larkin sought after Mr. Mather this week to Arrest him. Mr. Mather on Tuesday was taking Physick and so was free, and since hath purposely avoided him.

Satterday, March 31. I, Daniel Maio and another hand plant Six Chestnut Trees at Hog Iland.

Ap. 2, 1688. Mr. Robert Sanderson rides with me to Neponset and gives me Livery and Seisin of his 8ᵗʰ of the powder-mill Stream, Dwelling-House and Land on each side the River, Mr. Jnᵒ Fayerwether, Desire Clap, and Walter Everenden, witnesses, having the Deed there and exhibiting it, when he gave me Turf, Twigg and Splinter. Mr. Thacher's Son, Tho., dies this morn. Lodge at Unkle Quinsey's with Cous. Danˡ Gookin, who has a Son born last Satterday.

Ap. 3. See the Orchard Jnᵒ Hayford has planted, help Mis. Flint, Sir Shepard and Newman in dividing their Goods. Come home in Company of Mr. Blake, Coroner, who has been at Hingham to view the body of father Beal, a good man of an hundred years old, who was found dead in 's yard the last Sabbath. *Note.* Mr. Fayerwether's House was near burning when he and I at Neponset: Bells rung, and Town alarm'd.

Wednesday, Apr. 4. At night Sam. Marion's wife hangs herself in the Chamber, fastening a Cord to the Rafter-Joice. Two or three swore she was distracted, and had been for some time, and so she was buried in the burying place.

Friday, Apr. 6. The Exposition of the Church of England Catechise

---

prised forty folio engravings. For an account of it, see Falconer Madan, *Oxford Books* III (1931), no.3035.

by the Bishop of Bath and Wells comes out printed by Richard Pierce, with the 39. Articles.[9] Foy and Wild are arriv'd as 'tis told on Change today. Sailed Dec. 7th 1687.

Satterday, Apr. 7th 1688. Capt. Arthur Tannar sails about 10 aclock, a shallop follows quickly after, which 'tis said is to prevent Mr. Mather's getting on Board: 'tis certain all the Town is full of discourse about Mr. Mather. Carie sails a little after. Many Guns fired at Madam Craven's going off.

Friday, March 30. I am told Mr. Mather left his House and the Town and went to Capt. Phillips's at Charlestown. Sabbath, Ap. 1. To Aaron Way's by Hogg-Island. Tuesday, Ap. 3. At night from Aaron Way's to the Boat near Mr. Newgate's Landing-place, so through Crooked-Lane and Pulling Point Gut to Mr. Ruck's fishing-Catch, thence to the President, Capt. Arthur Tannar's Ship, as above.[10]

Tuesday, Apr. 10. Went to Muddy-River to shew Mr. Gardener his Bond; to Andrew Gardener, Simon Gates, George Bairstow, Subael Seavers: home. After I came home a Redcoat was buried with Arms in the old burying place.

Apr. 13, 1688. Grafted a Stock next Jn⁰ Wait's, pretty high out of the Cows reach, with cions from Mr. Moodey's Orange Pear, and grafted Two Appletree Stocks with Mr. Gardener's Russetings; the Cow having eaten last year's Grafts all save one Twigg. Mr. Moodey, Willard, Cotton Mather, Capt. Townsend, Mr. Eyre were here last

---

[9] The book was by Thomas Ken, bishop and hymn-writer, *An Exposition on the Church-Catechism: Or the Practice of Divine Love.* It was printed in London in 1685, and now reprinted at Boston by Pierce.

[10] In March Increase Mather had announced his plans to go to England, and on the 22d he had preached his farewell lecture. Edward Randolph, who was defeated in his court action against Mather in January, had much to fear from Mather should he reach England and get the ear of the king. He therefore made an attempt to arrest him a second time, but the warrant was not served. Mather kept behind closed doors for several days. On the night of the 30th he put on a wig and a long white cloak, bade his family farewell, and emerged into the darkness. The sight of this figure was too much for Thurston, Randolph's creature, who was guarding the house and awaiting the chance to make an arrest, and Mather walked away in safety. In a short time he was under the hospitable roof of Captain John Phillips, Cotton's father-in-law, in Charlestown, and he remained there the next day while Randolph's emissaries were searching for him. At Pulling Point Mather's two sons, Cotton and Samuel, joined him; he gave his blessing to Cotton, and went aboard the ketch with Samuel, thirteen, a sophomore at Harvard. The ketch sailed for the Gurnet, off Plymouth, and was at anchor there for two days, until the seventh, when a shallop manned by friends came and put Mather and his son aboard the *President*, on which he had first shipped himself. K. B. Murdock, *Increase Mather*, 186-188.

night. It seems Mr. Watter and Elisha Odlin were fined last Wednesday, 13. 4ᵈ, apiece, for refusing to lay their hand on the Bible in Swearing.

Apr. 13, 1688. Elder Chipman visits me, and tells me that the Indian Meetinghouse at Sandwich is raised.[11]

Satterday, Apr. 14. Mr. West comes to Mr. Willard from the Governour to speak to him to begin at 8. in the morn, and says this shall be last time; they will build a house. We begin about ½ hour past 8. yet the people come pretty roundly together. 'Twas Easter-day, and the Lord's Supper with us too.

Tuesday, Apr. 17. First Training of the Eight Companies. I went to Dorchester Lecture, and visited Mis. Poole.

Apr. 18. Went to Hog-Island, set six Chesnut Trees, and took Livery and Seisin of Mr. Maverick's Marsh. This day about Sun-set, Jack, alias Jacob Negro, dies at my Unkle Quinsey's by the oversetting of the Cart, he (probably) sitting in it, the Rave[12] fell on 's neck and kill'd him. This day an Order is made that next Sabbath-day sennight be a Thanksgiving for the Queen's being with Child.

April 18. The news about Lima's Ruine comes abroad. Mr. Cotton Mather mentions it on the 19ᵗʰ at the Lecture. Above 60.000 persons perished, and now there is a Pool of Water where it stood, if the news be true.[13]

Apr. 19. Mr. Eᵐ Hutchinson, Fayerwether, Cornish and my self goe to Braintrey; have much adoe to get a Jury because of the Training at Weymouth, whether His Excellency went by Water. As came back we treat with Mr. Ryal about setting up a Fulling-Mill at Neponset.

April 20. Joshua Atwater's wife dies. It seems he carried her out of Town but last Monday. She was a worthy Gentlewoman.

Apr. 22, 1688. Mr. Willard having rec'd no Order mentions not the Thanksgiving: though it seems one was sent to him at noon to mention it, but left no Order with him.

Wednesday, Apr. 25, 1688. I went to Govʳ [Simon] Bradstreet, to

---

11 This was one of Sewall's benefactions. Captain Thomas Tupper had been preaching to the Indians at Sandwich, and Cotton Mather recorded in the *Magnalia* that he had 180 hearers. In a letter to Edward Milton, carpenter at Sandwich, 26 September 1687, Sewall engaged to pay for this meeting-house ("Thirty pounds, not above one Third in Money"), which was to be twenty-four feet in length and eighteen in width. John Chipman was ruling elder at Sandwich for many years. *L.B.* 1,62 and *Savage.*

12 The upper side-piece of timber on the body of a cart.

13 Lima and Callao have been almost completely destroyed by earthquakes and tidal-waves several times. Great disasters occurred in 1586, 1630, 1687, and 1713, but the worst was in 1746 when some 5000 were drowned.

enquire about the Custom of Swearing in New England: He told me That of lifting up the Hand had been the Ceremony from the beginning; that He and some others did so swear on board the Ship, 1630. And that He never Knew an Oath administred any other way after he came on Shoar.

Apr. 29. Mr. Willard received an Order about the Thanksgiving on Satterday night; yet read it not this day, but after the *Notes* said such an Occasion was by the Governour recommended to be given Thanks for. Mr. Allen sings the 6 first verses of the 21. Ps. and the first Part of the 72^d, which gives offense to some of his Church. Mr. Willard prays more particularly and largly for the King, but else alters not his course a jot.

Monday, Apr. 30th. Mr. Cotton Mather, my wife, Cous. Anna Quinsey and Self ride to Dorchester in Mr. Emms his Coach, to visit Mrs. Pool, then goe to Mr. Stoughton's, who sends a Basket of Apples to sick Mr. Nelson.

Wednesday, May 2. Went to Hog-Island with Mr. Newgate, where by appointment we meet with Cousin Savage trying to adjust the difference between them as said Newgate's claim of Marsh. Water the Chesnut Trees. The Bristow man who arriv'd Apr. 29th speaks of a Dispute was to be between the Roman Catholicks and Protestants.

Thorsday, May 3. Fast at the old Church and several other Churches for Rain. Great likelihood of Rain in the morn and considerable Thunder. Thunder at noon and beginning of the night to the Eastward: but no Rain to speak of. Mr. Willard began in the Forenoon with Prayer. Mr. Phillips of Rowly in the Afternoon. Mr. Allen and Moodey preached.

Friday, May 4th 1688. Last night there was a very refreshing Rain; this 4th May, a Print comes out shewing the Lawfullness of Swearing according to the English mode, Laying the hand on the Bible. Taken out of Mr. Baxter's Directory, printed by Richard Pierce May the 1. 1688; were publickly known May 4. Sent Mr. Noyes one May 7th.

Monday, May 7. Mr. West removes to dwell in the House of Mr. Hezekiah Usher upon the Common. About 7. P.M. begins a plenteous Rain. *Laus Deo.*

Tuesday, May 8. Discourse with Mrs. Woodmancy as to her pretended Marriage, which Mr. Willard, Eliot, Frary and self find to be nothing at all.

May 10. Mr. Dudley and his Son call here. I speak to him about the mode of swearing, if no remedy might be had, of which had no encouragement, but said Lifting up the Hand was the handsomest way.

May 11. Go to Charlestown Lecture. In the even Mrs. Woodmancy comes to me and says Mr. White and she took each other on the 2^d of June last, and her child last Monday was 8. weeks old.[14]

Sabbath, May 13. Lord's Supper at the South-Church. Near half an hour after twelve by that time I got home, by my Clock: and five by that time got home in the afternoon: Day cloudy. Mis. Nowel here, sits in our Pue, and dines with us. A fine Rain begins at 7. P.M. Mr. Lawson who came to Town to dwell last week, with us.[15]

Monday, May 14th 1688. Put Sam. to Eliezer Moodey to learn to write.

May 15. Mr. Stoughton calls here to discourse about Mis. Avery who is like to break. Mr. Farwell went to her last Thursday by Col. Lidget's appointment to demand 2 or 3 hundred Pounds Money, for which her House and Ground is mortgaged.

Thursday, May 17th 1688. Capt. Leach arrives from London, brings news of the 10th of March, or Later. Col. Dongan is to be Governour of Barbados, and New-York annexed to this Government.[16] Fears of War with Holland. Now is talk that no Parliament till October next.

Friday, May 18, 1688. Went to Hog-Island with Capt. Eliot and Frary. This day Cratey comes to Marblehead, brings a Packet for the Governour.

Sabbath, May 20. Mr. Willard preach'd in the morn from Heb. 12. 4. Have not yet resisted unto bloud, &c. In the Afternoon rain'd ex-

---

14 Elizabeth, one of the seventeen children of Elder Jonas Clark of Cambridge, was the second wife of John Woodmansey, merchant of Boston, who died before 4 June 1685 (*Mass. Bay Rec.* v, 485). She afterward married George Monck, vintner at the sign of the Blue Anchor, and Sewall records her death in his entry of 21 November 1717. She was apparently censured by the South Church at this time for her "pretended Marriage"; Sewall records her restoration to membership 5 February 1692/3, "having made a satisfactory Confession." H. A. Hill, *Hist. of the Old South Church*, I, 293; *Savage*; Paige, *Cambridge*, 510.

15 Rev. Deodat Lawson came to New England from Denton, Norfolk, and became a member of the South Church in 1680. He preached in Salem Village (now Danvers) from 1683 to 1688, and returned in the time of the witchcraft troubles. On 24 March 1691/2, during the examination of the suspected women, he preached a stirring and consoling Lecture Day sermon, *Christ's Fidelity the only Shield against Satan's Malignity*, which was printed in Boston and London. Lawson was settled as minister of South Scituate (Norwell) in 1694, but returned to England about two years later. *Savage*; *Hist. Cat. Old South Church* (1883), 269-270.

16 In the summer of 1688 New York and the Jersies were added to the Dominion of New England, which then extended from the St. Croix River to Delaware Bay. Governor Dongan was succeeded by Andros, with Captain Francis Nicholson as lieutenant-governor to act for him in New York (see 5 July 1688). Dongan did not go to Barbados; he remained at his Long Island home until 1691, when he returned to England. *D.A.B.*

ceeding hard, so that I doubt many staid to hear the Service who had not been wont.

Monday, May 21, 1688. Town-Meeting. Present, Capt. Wait Winthrop, Col. Sam¹ Shrimpton, Councillors; Major Luscomb, Mr. Eᵐ Hutchinson, Mr. Jnº Joyliff, Mr. Benjᵃ Bullivant, Justices; Mr. Bullivant said he protested against voting by Papers, and opposed it much, at last voted in the old way. Capt. Timº Prout 85—Capt. Turell 74—Mr. Fayerwether 55—Mr. Wyllys 50. Cook, Joyliff, Hutchinson, Frary, Allin, left out. New chosen—Capt. Penn Townsend 84—Capt. James Hill 80—Mr. Addington 44—Mr. Adam Winthrop 35. Came next, S. Sewall 31—Peter Serjeant 29—Robᵗ Howard 24. Of the old, Capt. Frary had 40—Mr. Cook 37—Mr. Joyliff 33—Deacon Allen 25. Mr. Elisha Cook chosen Commissioner. Constables—Jos. Townsend 70. Jarvis Ballard 63. Michael Shaller 59. Abraham Blush 57. Jnº Gooding 56. Ambrose Daws 52. Jonᵃ Bill 47. Jnº Conney junʳ 35. Hugh Flood for Rumney-Marsh. Came next, Isaac Griggs 32. James Halsey 27. Jnº Atwood 26. [*In margin:* Sam. Plummer.]

Nota. Jnº Conney and Isaac Griggs at first had 32 each; so voted again, and Jnº Conney had 35 votes. No Prayer.

About Six aclock went with my wife, being invited, to Mr. Willard's to eat Salmon, where sat down with Govʳ Bradstreet and 's Lady, Madam Leverett and her daughter Cook, Mr. Joyliff and 's wife, Mr. Willard and wife: came away about 9. at night.

May 23, Wednesday, 1688. Went to Hog-Island with Brother Stephen Sewall, Brother Toppan and Sam. Shepard: Upon the Hill we agreed that Sam. Toppan should be bound to Brother Stephen for five years from September next, to be bound to Brother only during his Life. Brother Toppan chose it rather than that he should be bound to a Trade as a Taylor, or the like; Hopes by going to Sea or the like after his Time is out, may get a livelihood.

Thorsday, May 24ᵗʰ. Bell is rung for a Meeting of the Church of England Men, being in their language Ascension day.

May 25. Brother and Sister Toppan goe home to-day, came 22ᵈ This day Mis. Elisa. Greenough, Elder Rainsford's daughter, is buried; a very desirable woman of about 40 years old.

May 25ᵗʰ 1688. Col. Peter Bulkley of Concord dies, having languished for a long time. Died this Friday about eleven aclock.

Sabbath, May 27ᵗʰ. Councillor and Judge Bulkly buried, because could not be kept: word of which was sent to Boston on the same day to prevent persons going in vain on Monday to the Funeral.

Monday, May 28. News comes of his Excellency lying at Newbury last night, so sundry Gentlemen ride out to meet Him coming home this day.

Tuesday, May 29. About 5. *mane*, all the 8. Companies are warn'd by Beat of Drum to be in Arms at the 2ᵈ Beat of the Drum. Mr. Joseph Eliot preaches at Roxbury, where I goe. There, Mr. Stoughton and Capt. Blackwell, Capt. Prentice, Townsend, Hill, &c. besides several Ministers.

Wednesday, May 30. Eliakim sets forth with his Brother Williams for Connecticut.[17] Mr. Joseph Eliot here, says the two days wherein he buried his Wife and Son, were the best that ever he had in the world.[18]

Friday, June 1, 1688. Went to Watertown Lecture in Company of Mr. Moodey and Capt. Townsend. Text 1. Cor. 11. 31. If we would judge, &c. Mr. Dudley, Blackwell, Mr. Danforth, Councillor Usher, Mr. Russel Graves, and many more there, Madam Phipps for one, who was ready to faint at word was brought in by the Coach-man of Sir William's being spoke with at Sea. By that time we got home, we heard that Sir William came in his Pinace from Portsmouth this day. Many of the Town gone to complement Him.

Satterday, June 2, 1688. I sought God in behalf of my wife and family and of the Country.

Sabbath, June 3. Neither Mr. Bradstreet, nor Mr. Rawson at Meeting, both the places empty. Mr. Bradstreet taken very ill last Satterday night. Sir William not abroad in the forenoon, in the Afternoon hears Mr. Mather; so the Whitsuntiders have not his company.

Monday, about 3. mane, June 4. My wife is taken very ill with pains like travailing pains, of which afterward has an abatement. *Laus Deo.*

Tuesday, June 5ᵗʰ Mr. Nathˡ Newgate marries Mr. Lynds Daughter before Mr. Ratcliff, with Church of England Ceremonies. Mr. Payson and Mr. Farwell his Bridemen, a great wedding.[19]

---

[17] Rev. John Williams (Harvard 1683) was returning to Deerfield on the Connecticut River, where he had been settled as minister since 1686; Sewall recorded his ordination there 17 October 1688. Mrs. Williams was Eunice Mather, sister of Eliakim, who lived with the Sewalls. The Williams family were carried off as prisoners by the Indians at the Deerfield Massacre of 29 February 1703/4. *Sibley.*

[18] Rev. Joseph Eliot of Guilford (Harvard 1658) was the son of the Apostle Eliot, and father of Jared Eliot (Yale 1706), the Connecticut minister, physician, and scientist. Joseph had lost his first wife, Sarah, daughter of Governor Brenton of Rhode Island, and a son in the winter of 1681/2. The remark quoted by Sewall should be read with the Puritan joy in the after-life of the chosen and sainted in mind.

[19] The young lady was Sarah, daughter of Simon Lynde. Newgate (or Newdigate) was her cousin. *Savage.*

Wednesday or Thorsday Mr. Graham comes to Town with his wife and family; dwells in Mr. Jn° Howard's brick House.[20]

Thorsday, June 7ᵗʰ Mr. Dudley and Stoughton call here. In comes Mr. West and hath one Mr. Newton, a newcomer, sworn an Attorney. Mr. Dudley ask'd for a Bible, I ask'd if it might not better be done without. He laugh'd and seeing a Bible by accident, rose up and took it.

Friday, June 8. Sir William at Charlestown Lecture. In the Even Capt. Hill and I discourse with Roger Judd and Mrs. Willy.

Satterday, June 9. Mr. Sheaf is set upon on the Common in the night by Hamilton and two more, sorely wounded and Robb'd.

Sabbath, June 10. Sacrament with us, finish so that I got home just about a quarter past 12. by the Dial. Governour angry that had done so late, and caused their Bell to be rung about a quarter past one; 'twas rather more before the Bell had done: So 'twas about a quarter past Three before our Afternoon Bell Rung about 1½ hour later than usual.

Monday, June 11. About 3. this Morn Major Luscomb dies of a Fever. He was abroad, I am told, on the 3ᵈ of June morning and evening and Receiv'd the Lord's Supper.

June 12. In the Afternoon I wait on Sir William Phipps.

June 13. Brother and Sister Moodey visit us. Goodw. Moss of Newbury dead and buried.

June 15, 1688. Major Humphrey Luscomb buried between 7. and 8. P.M. Six Companies attended, viz: all except Col. and Lt. Col. After the Vollyes several great Guns fired. None of our family were invited. A considerable deal of Thunder and Lightening with Rain this day. About the Funeral time pretty dry.

Tuesday, June 19. Went to the Funeral of Mr. Brock of Reding, a worthy good Minister, generally lamented. Was very Laborious in catechizing and instructing Youth. Mr. Danforth, Mr. Russel there, Mr. Morton, Wigglesworth, Fisk, Fox, Shepard, Lorie, Pierpont, Lawson, Carter &c.; buried between 2. and 3. Dined at Cousin Savage's. Got home about nine aclock.[21]

June 22. I goe to Hogg-Island with Mr. Newgate to see if could agree about his Marsh: Father Griggs and Samˡ Townsend there. When came back, went and bid Sir William welcom to Town, who

[20] James Graham was Andros's attorney-general and became one of the most bitterly hated of the whole tribe.
[21] John Brock (Harvard 1646) had been minister of Reading since 1662; previously he had preached at Rowley and at the Isles of Shoals. *Sibley.*

landed an hour or so before me, being come with his Frigot from Portsmouth. This day Mrs. Joyliff and Mrs. Grecian goe to his Excellency, and expostulat with Him about his Design of meeting first on Sabbath-days in our Meetinghouse.

Satterday, June 23. Capt. Frary and I goe to his Excellency at the Secretaries Office, and there desired that He would not alter his time of Meeting, and that Mr. Willard consented to no such thing, neither did he count that 'twas in his power so to do. Mr. West said he went not to ask Mr. Willard Leave. His Excellency asked who the House belong'd to; we told Him the Title to the House was on Record. His Excellency turned to Mr. Graham and said, Mr. Attorney we will have that look'd into. Governour said if Mr. Willard not the Parson, so great an Assembly must be considered. We said He was Master of the Assembly, but had no power to dispose of the House, neither had others, for the Deed expressed the Use 'twas to be put to. Governour complain'd of our long staying Sabbath-day sennight; said 'twas the Lord's Supper, and [*he*] had promised to go to some other House on such dayes; Mr. Randolph said he knew of no such promise, and the Governour seemed angry, and said He would not so break his word for all the Massachusetts Colony, and therefore, to avoid mistakes, must give in writing what we had to say; we answered, Mr. Randolph brought not any writing to those he spake to. Governour said we rent off from the old Church against the Government, and the Land the House stood on was bought clandestinely, and that one should say he would defend the work with his Company of Soldiers. Mention'd folks backwardness to give, and the unreasonableness; because if any stinking filthy thing were in the House we would give something to have it carried out, but would not give to build them an house: Said came from England to avoid such and such things, therefore could not give to set them up here: and the Bishops would have thought strange to have been ask'd to contribute towards setting up the New-England Churches. Governour said God willing they would begin at Eight in the Morning, and have done by Nine: we said 'twould hardly be so in the winter. Mr. Graham said if they had their Service by Candle-Light what was that to any: And that the Service appointed by the Church for morning could not be held after Noon.

Sabbath, June 24. We read and sing in course the 57th Psal. Altaschith. They [*the Church of England congregation*] have done before nine in the morn, and about a quarter after one in the afternoon; so we have very convenient time.

July 1. Governour takes his old time again after our coming out, and Sir William Phips's Chaplain preaches. We were a little hurried and disappointed in the morning, the Bell ringing about quarter before nine.

Monday, July 2. Mr. Joseph Bridgham goes to Newbury.

Thorsday, July 5th. Tells me of his being there with his Son, but refers me to another time for a full account. This day Foy arrives, brings a Commission for Capt. Nicolson to be Lieut. Governour: New-York to be annexed to this Government. Mr. Randolph, a new Commission to be Secretary of the whole Dominion.

Wednesday, July 4. Commencement managed wholly by Mr. Wm Hubbard; compared Sir William, in his Oration, to Jason fetching the Golden Fleece. Masters procceded, no Bachelours.[22] Several French came over in Foy, some, Men of Estates.

Friday, July 6. 'Tis said Sir William is this day sworn to officiat according to his Commission [*of High Sheriff*].

Sabbath, July 8. Wants above 5 Minutes of 12. when I get home.

Thorsday, July 12. Mr. Jn° Hubbard tells me there is a Writt out against me for Hog-Island, and against several others persons for Land, as being violent intruders into the Kings Possession.[23] George Keith [*a Quaker*] doth this day send a Challenge to the 4 Ministers of Boston, in an open letter by Edward Shippen, to dispute with them about the false Doctrine they delivered. Wild arrives, 9 weeks from the Downs; Mr. Bromfield comes in him.

Satterday, July 14th Jeremiah Belcher comes and brings me the Information Mr. Sherlock left with him on Thorsday last in the Afternoon, when he served on him a Writt of Intrusion. I try'd to goe to the Island yesterday but could not, wind and Tide being against me,

---

[22] William Hubbard was taking the place of President Increase Mather. Up to 1869 Harvard B.A.'s were entitled to receive the M.A. in course at the third commencement following their graduation, without examination or requirement of residence. In the seventeenth and eighteenth centuries it was customary for the master-candidates to participate in the exercises.

[23] When the Massachusetts Bay charter was vacated in 1684, the lands reverted to the crown, and the inhabitants were at the mercy of the officials. Sewall wrote to Increase Mather in London, 24 July 1688, telling of the serving of writs of intrusion on Colonel Samuel Shrimpton for Deer Island, on Joseph Lynde and James Russell for lands in Charlestown, etc. "Mr Lynde quickly made his peace with Mr Graham, the Attorney-General. Mr Russell follow'd not long after, prevailed with by Mr. [*William*] Stoughton's advice. I was urg'd by my friends two contrary wayes; but at last have this day petition'd for a Patent for Hogg-Island." (4 *M.H.S.Colls.* viii, 517). Sewall copied his petition into the Diary 24 July. Apparently he hit upon the proper course of action, for we find no further mention of the matter after the Council ordered a survey on the 26th. The text of Andros's warrant to survey the island, issued 27 July, is printed in *C.S.M.* xxi, 360-361.

and one Oar broke. Went from Winnisimmet to the Point, but none fetch'd me over. Wind is out [*from the east*], and so Sir William comes up and Capt. Belcher.

Satterday, July 14. Writt to Mr. Wharton, Mr. Mather, Capt. Hutchinson, inclosing the state of my case and craving their help to give Check; sent the Letters under covert to Cousin Hull, ordering him to pay them Fifty pounds if they call'd for it.

Monday, July 16. Sir William's Frigot, and the Swan set sail.

July 17. I discourse Mr. Stoughton, with whom I find Mr. Moodey and Mr. Russell. After Catechising I and my wife visit Mis. Man.

Thorsday, July 19th. Eight Companies in Arms, and Sir Edmund's Commission is published, extending his Authority from the remotest eastern parts so as to take in East and West Jersy.

To Sir Edmund Andros Knight, Capt. General and Governour in Chief of
    His Majesties Territory and Dominion of New-England in America,
    the humble Petition of Samuel Sewall of Boston, Sheweth.

That whereas your Petitioner stands seized and possessed of a certain Island or Islands, commonly called and known by the name of Hogg-Island, lying scituat near Boston aforesaid, in the present tenure and occupation of one Jer. Belcher, having been peacably and quietly possessed by your Petitioner and his Predecessors for the space of fourty years or upwards by past: And whereas the said Belcher hath been lately served with a Writt of Intrusion at His Majesties Suit, And your Petitioner not being willing to stand Suit, but being desirous of His Majesties Confirmation for the said Island or Islands:

He therefore humbly prays your Excellencies favour that he may obtain His Majesties Grant and Confirmation of the said Hogg-Island, with the members and Appurtenances thereof, unto your Petitioner his Heirs and Assigns forever under the Seal of this His Majesties Territory. To be holden of His Majesty, His Heirs and Successors, upon such moderat Quit-Rent as your Excellency shall please to order.

And your Petitioner shall ever pray.

SAM SEWALL.

Presented the above written Petition to the Governour with my own hand July 24th 1688.

July 26th 'Twas read in the Council, and an order made upon it for a Survey.

Sabbath, July 22^{d}. Read the Sixty first Psalm in course: July 29th, the 62. Truly my waiting Soul, &c.

Monday, July 30th. With many others I went to Dedham to accom-

pany his Excellency in his way to New-York and Jersy: who goes to
take the Government of those places.

July 31. Writt to Mr. Wharton inclos'd to Cous. Hull, to do what
he could to settle Proprieties. Towards which if it might be done, was
willing to give 50 or a hundred pounds. Writt by a small Bark of
which one Mr. Baily Master. If Mr. Wharton not there, give it to Mr.
Mather.

Augt. 3. Went to Neponset with Capt. Fayerwether and Mr.
Wyllys to see the Fulling-Mill lately set up, and to direct for the right
fitting and ordering of it. Placed a Stone in the Column of Sir Williams House next to Mr. Nowells.

Monday, Augt. 6, 1688. Mr. James Sherman Married Richard Fifield and Mary Thirston: Mehetabel Thirston, Giles Fifield and
Elisa his wife, Elisa Lane and my Self at the Wedding in our Bed-
Chamber, about 9. at night, being disappointed by Mr. Willard's
being out of Town, and desired Privacy all that might be.

Thorsday, Augt. 9th. Mr. Moodey, Willard, Mather, Capt. Townsend here, Mr. Thacher was here before. This day I goe for Mrs.
Weeden, my wife having been ill a week or more, and now ready to
conclude her time to Travail was come. Midwife staid and went to
Bed here; in the night was call'd away by another woman about 2.
mane. It seems the Monday the Governour went hence towards New-
York, Five Indians were killed at Spectacle Pond not far from Springfield, four taken Captive, two escaped. They that did the Murder are
some of our late Enemies who have since lived under the protection
of the French.

Tuesday, Augt. 7. Capt. Nicholson, Lieut. Governour, returns to
Town from New-London, as is said upon this report of the Indians
slain; where intended to have gone to New-York and resided there.

Satterday, Augt. 11. Jn° Marion buries a Son of about 11 Moneths
old. Sam. Clark and Eliakim Mather, Bearers and had Gloves.

Sabbath, Augt. 12. My wife stayes at home as last Sabbath, but
that Mother goes to Meeting and the Children only bear their
Mother Company: who hath much pain, yet holds up still.

Augt. 14, 1688. About ½ hour past Nine at Night Stephen Greenleaf comes in and brings my Mother Sewall; they set sail from Newbury about 10. in the morning, had a brisk Norwest Gale, turn'd up
from Dear-Island and lay aground a pretty while before they could
fleet in. Cous. Greenleaf sups with Mother. I give him the Catechise,
Day of Doom, &c. bound together in a good Cover, in part for Mother's passage.

Wednesday, Augt. 15th. About 4. *mane*, I rise to make a fire, and

to call the Midwife, Charlestowns Bell rung for 5. as came away
from Mrs. Weeden's House. Very cool day. My Wife is brought to
Bed of a Son between 8. 9. while the Service-Bell was ringing. Cous.
Anne Quinsey first tells me of it.

Thorsday, 16ᵗʰ Put up a Bill for Thanksgiving. About 9. in the
night news comes from Salem, by a Vessel from Holland, that the
Queen was deliver'd of a Prince,²⁴ June 10ᵗʰ So from 11. to 1. or 2. is
Drumming, Bonfire, Huzas, small and great Guns, Ringing of Bells,
at which many startled for fear of fire or an Alarm; because the thing
was so sudden, People knew not the occasion. Brother Needham was
called out of 's Bed to deliver the Keys, which at first he refus'd, they
not telling him the occasion.

Sabbath, Augt. 19ᵗʰ 1688. Town is full of the news of 5. English
persons killed at Northfield; So the Councillors sent for; and by that
means Mr. Stoughton at our House in the afternoon to hear Mr.
Willard, who after Sermon, baptized my young Son, whom I named
Joseph, in hopes of the accomplishment of the Prophecy, Ezek. 37ᵗʰ
and such like: and not out of respect to any Relation, or other person, except the first Joseph.²⁵ The Lieut. Governour goes this day to
Woburn to secure some Indians there, now busied in gathering Hops.
It seems were met together and praying when secured, or just before.

Augt. 20ᵗʰ. Went to Capt. Marshall's and discoursed with Brother
Stephen about Sister Dorothy.

Thorsday, Augt. 23. Fast at the old Church, respecting the Indians,
at which was my dear Mother Sewall, set in Mrs. Baker's Pue, went
not out at Noon because of the Rain. Mr. Willard begun with Prayer
in the morn. Mr. Mather in the Afternoon; Mr. Allen and Moodey
preached.

Friday, Augt. 24. I carried my Mother over Winnisimmet Ferry
to Salem, there met with Mr. Noyes. Left my Horse at Salem and
came home in Mr. Grafton's Sloop the *Lark.* Loosed from the Wharf

²⁴ The prince was James Francis Edward Stuart, born to James II and Mary of
Modena, and known in later life as the Old Pretender. Since it would have suited
James perfectly at this time to produce a Catholic heir to the throne, and since
there were dubious goings-on in connection with the *accouchement* (Mary's sudden removal from Whitehall to St. James's Palace, the appearance of the baby
before the scheduled time, and the absence of the proper attendants and witnesses
—Anne was at Bath taking the waters and the Archbishop of Canterbury had
been confined to the Tower a few hours before), the charge was generally believed
that the "Prince of Wales" was a suppositious child. When he was six months
old his parents fled the country, and he spent seventy-seven years of his life in
exile. Macaulay, *Hist. of England*, Chap. VIII and *D.N.B.*
²⁵ Joseph was a model son; he grew up, took his degree at Harvard in 1707, became pastor of the South Church in 1713, and lived to the age of eighty.

at Winter-Island about 4. P.M. and got into my own House at Boston about 11. at night. Wind was East if not somwhat Southerly, so, very bare till we got past Marblehead Neck. Had Moon-shine. The Widow Bordman, and Mr. Kitchin's daughter by Mary Bordman, came Passengers, Landed at Scarlet's Wharf. Got to Salem about noon. Left my Horse for Mother to goe to Newbury.

Wednesday, Augt. 29. Mr. Torrey comes to our House, Mr. Sherman there at the same time, who hath bespoke a passage for England in Mr. Gillam. When he was gon Mr. Torrey and I had pretty much Discourse together about England and going thether. I had been wishing to speak with him.[26]

Augt. 31, 1688. Mr. Kitchin and my Brother come to see me, and Inform me that the French King died July 4th. News came to Salem from Newfound Land.

Thorsday, Sept. 6th The Duke of Albemarl's Yott arrives, fires in Lecture time. In the even Mr. Cotton Mather comes and prayes with my little sick Joseph.

Sept. 7th Visit sick Tho. Gardener, the son, bespeak 3 Barrels of Apples of the Father and Andrew; goe to Simon Gates's, from thence to Cambridge to see my little cousin Margaret; visit Mr. Brattle, and then Mr. Leverett, Fellows of the Colledge. Come home and find my own Child somwhat better as is hop'd.

Sept. 10, 1688. There is a press in Boston, of 32 Men, four out of a Company, to goe to the Eastward, by reason of the fears and dispersions people there are under. It seems 10. or 11 English persons are taken away as hostages till those Indians sent to Boston, be return'd. Richard Cornish and his wife come to me about their Money in England.

Tuesday, Sept. 11th Two and thirty Men are press'd in Boston, and 6 from Charlestown and sent away to the Eastward, and a Post dispatcht to acquaint the Governour at Albany.

Sept. 12th Rid to Cambridge Lecture, being rainy in the afternoon, Madam Paige invited me, and I came home in her Coach, with Mr. Willard and his wife, and Mrs. Paige's Boy rid my Horse.

Sept. 11th I discours'd largely with my Wife, and 12th *mane* with my Mother, Betty being gone on foot to Cambridge Lecture.

Thorsday, Sept. 13th Major Saltonstall comes to visit me, saith his Daughter [*Elizabeth*] married about 2 moneths agoe to Mr. [*John*] Denison; is equal sharer with Mr. Hubbard in the Work of the Ministry. Mr. Gourdin [*Saltonstall*] like to settle at New-London; two

26 Samuel Torrey did not accompany Sewall to England; he was the parson at Weymouth.

youngest Sons at Ipswich School where Mr. Rogers's Son teaches.

Sept. 15, 1688. Corrected Sam. for breach of the 9th Commandment, saying he had been at the Writing School, when he had not.

Satterday, Sept. 15. at night one who came over a Souldier, and was diverted to a Tanner, being himself of that Trade, hangs himself.

Sabbath, Sept. 16th Mr. Willard preaches from Heb. 12. 11. afternoon from Eccles. 7. 29th I was too late in the Afternoon; Mr. Willard prayd for His Majesty morn and even, and said, whereas prayers and giving of Thanks commanded, they did so, and prayd that might be a Blessing. 126. Ps. sung morn. Afternoon, 19th from 9th v. to the end. Even, 84th from 9th to the end. Had done before Eleven by my Clock; the afternoon, quarter before four. About one, many great Guns fired just as first Bells for afternoon rung; vollies of small shot I think first. At night a Bonfire with the usual Huzzas between 7. and 8. Very cloudy and dark day. I want of Caryl [*on the Book of Job*] the 30th, 31, 32, 33, and 34th Chapters.

Sept. 17th I speak to Mr. Gillam for a passage in his Ship. This day Capt. Frary sees a 'Souldier with an Indian Squaw in the Common and open Sun.

Tuesday, Sept. 18. Several persons are Listed of the Governours Life-Guard. Mr. Maccartas Son, of about 10 years old, who was at School on Friday, was now buried Sept. 18, taken with a vehement Fever and Delirium at once. About noon Capt. Gillam falls down, fires Seven Guns, and the Fort answer with five. Capt. Townsend, Gilbert Cole and I look on.

Sept. 19th The rain hinders my going to Salem, and so to Newbury. Eldridge comes in, who sais the Amsterdam Gazett reported that Mr. Mather's Petition is granted, said Eldridge sais that one Ales was come out of the Downs, who brings Mr. Palmer of New-York, Chief Judge of the Territory of New England.[27]

Sept. 20. Mr. Lee preaches from Ezek. 47. 11. Shew'd that Edom was on the South side of Asphaltites, and probably they would not be converted. Jews understood it of Italy, called that Edom. This a

[27] John Palmer had been judge of the Court of Oyer and Terminer at New York and was one of the commissioners sent by Dongan to Maine (see note to 3 February 1687), where he "incurred odium by his arbitrary conduct in the matter of land titles," as the *D.N.B.* tactfully puts it. He went to England in 1687 and was now returning as councillor of the Dominion. Palmer was locked up by the Boston insurgents in 1689, and while imprisoned at the castle wrote *An Impartial Account of the State of New England,* a lumbering justification of Andros, which was circulated in manuscript there, printed in London in 1690, and reprinted in the *Andros Tracts* I, 21-62.

Prophesy of the great abundant enlargement of the Church not yet accomplished, 'twas now hastening; but then also, some wicked hardened Wretches. Had not heard of an Edomite converted; though that of the 10th Generation implied there might be such a thing. Mr. Mather's last Sermon was on the same Text. Pray'd for Bristow before and after Sermon.

Sept. 21, 1688. The Letters of Ayles come to hand, in whom comes Judge Palmer, about 8 weeks from the Downs. Alba Regalis [*Stuhl Weissenburg, in Hungary*] surrendered: Belgrade besiegd. This day I ride to Newbury with Mr. Lorie and Penhallow, to visit my friends, and ask them about my going for England; met with my fellow-Travailers at Mr. Moodey's by accident the night before. Brother Stephen there with whom I Lodge. Visit Mr. Woodbridge and Mrs. Noyes.

Monday, Sept. 24th Come to Brother Moodey's and dine with him, his wife, Mother and James Noyes; then Brother brings me going to Rowley-Mill; I call at Mr. Payson's; drive a Nail in Mr. Gerrishes Meetinghouse, gave 2ˢ. Visit Mr. Higginson.

Sept. 25th Visit Mr. Nath¹ Mather, sick at Salem at Mr. Swinnerton's. Come home in Company Major Gedny and Brown, a very fair wind over, went in and drunk at Brookins [*tavern*], came home and found all well, blessed be God.

A Press in Boston of 16 men to send Eastward; several being kill'd by the Indians, which news was at Newbury on Monday morn.

Thorsday, Sept. 27. Capt. Goodenough makes an Alarm at Sudbury in the night, which is taken at Concord, Malborough, Sherborn, as am told.

Sept. 28. I go to Charlestown-Lecture, Mr. Lee preaches from Mat. 25. 6. After Lecture din'd at Mr. Russell's. Then went on Board the Duke's Yott with Major Richards, Capt. Phillips, Mr. Cotton Mather, Madam Phipps, Richards, Shrimpton, Kelland; Had Sturgeon, Wine, Punch, Musick.[28]

Satterday, Sept. 29th. Lydia Moodey comes hether to dwell, helping my wife to nurse the Child Joseph.

Monday, Oct. 1. A Whipping Post is set up by the middle Watchhouse. Brother Stephen visits us.

Tuesday, Oct. 2. I goe with Mr. Newgate in the rain to Hogg-Island, having a canvas Tilt [*boat-awning*], and take Livery and Seisin

[28] The arrival of the Duke of Albemarle's yacht in Boston was noted by Sewall on the 6th. Christopher Monck, second Duke of Albemarle, was Governor General of Jamaica; he died there a few days later, 6 October 1688. *D.N.B.*; *Complete Peerage.*

of his Marsh, Joseph Lowle, Ambrose Honywell, John Sweeting and Elisabeth Warren being witnesses; only the first could write his name.

Wednesday, Oct. 3ᵈ Have a day of Prayer at our House: One principal reason as to particular, about my going for England. Mr. Willard pray'd and preach'd excellently from Ps. 143. 10:, pray'd. Intermission. Mr. Allen pray'd, then Mr. Moodey, both very well, then 3ᵈ–7ᵗʰ verses of the 86ᵗʰ Ps., sung Cambridge Short Tune, which I set. Then had Govʳ Bradstreet and his wife, Mr. Moodey and wife, Mr. Allin and Mr. Willard and wife, Cous. Dummer and wife, and Mrs. Clark her sister, Cousin Quinsey and wife and Mrs. Scottow, should have reckon'd formerly Mother Hull and Self. My wife was so lately very ill of the Ague in her face, she could not come down out of the Chamber. Fifteen sat down together. Mr. Addington, Mr. Eyre, Capt. Townsend and several others here beside the Meeting.

Thorsday, Oct. 4ᵗʰ. About 5. P.M. Mr. Willard married Mr. Samuel Danforth and Mrs. Hannah Allen. Mr. Morton began with prayer before Mr. Willard came. Mr. Willard just before married Jonathan Evans and a Daughter of Mr. Bronsdon's. I was at Mr. Danforth's Wedding, being invited by the Father.[29]

Friday, Oct. 5. Mis. Anger of Cambridge [*Ann Batt, second wife of Edmund Angier*] is buried: Was Sister to Mrs. [*Peter*] Toppan of Newbury. Went to Mis. Williams's Meeting where Mr. Moodey preached. About 9. night, Thomas, an Indian and very usefull Servant of Mr. Oliver, hang'd himself in the Brewhouse.

Satterday, Oct. 6. The Coroner sat on him, having a Jury, and ordered his burial by the highway with a Stake through his Grave.

Wednesday, Oct. 10ᵗʰ Went on Board the America, Mr. Isaac Addington one of the Owners, introducing me: took up the Starboard Cabbin, and when came back, met Capt. Clark and gave him Earnest 20ˢ; then went to Mr. Moodey's to a Meeting. At night read in course the Seventh of the Romans. Received a Letter from Mr. Taylor this day, and writt to him before I had received it. Both of us concluded alike from Joseph's Blessing, Deuteronomy.

Oct. 11ᵗʰ Writt to Mr. Solomon Stoddard to acquaint him with my design.

---

[29] Samuel Danforth Jr. (Harvard 1683) succeeded George Shove as minister of Taunton, where he labored for forty-four years. Hannah was the daughter of James Allen, minister of the First Church, who had invited Sewall to the wedding; the elder Danforth (Harvard 1653) had died in 1677. Evans married Mary, twin daughter of Robert Bronsdon, merchant of Boston. *Sibley* and *N.E.H.G.R.* xxxv, 362. Samuel Willard (Harvard 1659), who appears constantly in the Diary, became minister of the South Church in 1678.

Oct. 12ᵗʰ. Thomas Brown comes from Sherborn and acquaints me of the wellfare of our Cousins.

Satterday, Oct. 13ᵗʰ. Went to Watertown with Mr. Joyliff, Hutchinson, Serjᵗ Taylor, Sampˢ Stoddard. Din'd at Cambridge, there was trimmd by Barret [30] 12ᵈ, gave Goodm. Brown 12ᵈ; visited Sister, her child asleep, so saw it not, 'tis very ill. Visited Mr. Tho. Baily who is recovering. Came home without seeing the Governour, whom went to meet. When I come home here the sad news of a family of 8 persons being cut off by the Indians. Gillam, who sail'd on Thorsday, is put back by a Storm, and now stopt to wait the Governour's coming.

Sabbath-Even. Capt. Eliot and Frary visit me, Oct. 14. 1688.

Monday, Oct. 15. Speak to Gilbert Cole to Bottle me a Barrel of Beer for the Sea.

Tuesday, Oct. 16. Little Hannah going to School in the morn, being enter'd a little within the Schoolhouse Lane, is rid over by David Lopez, fell on her back, but I hope little hurt, save that her Teeth bled a Little, was much frighted; but went to School; one Stebbin took her in, who lives next Solomon Rainsford's Shop up the Lane, on the left hand as goe up. This day the Ground-Sills of the Church[31] are laid; the stone foundation being finished. Visit Cousin Dummer sick abed.

Wednesday, Oct. 17, 1688. Ride in the Hackney-Coach with Govʳ Bradstreet, his Lady, Mrs. Willard, Mrs. Mercy Bradstreet, Josiah Willard, to Roxbury, to the Ordination of Mr. Nehemiah Walter. Mr. Eliot, Allen, Willard, Danforth of Dorchester, laid on Hands. Mr. Eliot ordain'd. Mr. Allen gave the Right Hand of Fellowship, desir'd he might keep to Christ's Institutions in the Purity of them, for which God's people came over hether. Mr. Walter, giving the Blessing, said, Happy are they who are faithfull in the work Christ calls them unto, &c. The 132 Psal. sung from the 13ᵗʰ v. to the end. Din'd at Mr. Dudley's, Mr. Bradstreet and Mr. Eliot sat at the upper end of the Table. After Dinner sung Zech'ˢ song from 76ᵗʰ v. to the end, and the song of Simeon. At meeting, in the foreseat, sat Mr. Bradstreet, Danforth, Richards, Cook, Sewall, Wilson [of] Meadfield, Gookin [of] Cambridge. *Note*. In time of the first Prayer the Governour came by from his Progress. This day a great part of the [*Angli-*

30 William Barrett, the tailor, had trimmed Sewall's hair when he was in college; his house was on the west side of Dunster Street. He died the following March. Paige, *Cambridge*, 483.

31 This was the modest wooden structure the Anglicans were building on the corner where King's Chapel now stands; it cost £284 16s. Since Sewall and others refused to sell land for the church, the governor and council apparently appropriated the site from the old burying ground. Foote, *Annals*, I, 80-81.

can] Church is raised. Mr. Cotton Mather not there; he stays at Salem to close the eyes of his dying Brother Nathaniel; died this day about one aclock.

This day a Church is to be gathered, and Mr. [*John*] Williams ordained at Dearfield.

Friday, Oct. 19. Carried my wife on Horseback to Mr. Airs's to a Fast. Mr. Willard pray'd, preach'd from Ezek. 9. 4. pray'd. P.M., Mr. Phillips pray'd, Mr. Moodey preach'd from Psal. 57. 1. Pray'd, Sung the 125th Psal. Mr. Willard was call'd out to Isaac Walker who lay dying, was taken but last Sabbath-day. Very rainy day. I. Walker dies about 3 P.M.

Monday, Oct. 22. Mr. Isaac Walker is buried. Bearers, Mr. James Taylor, Mr. Francis Burroughs, Capt. Tho. Savage, Mr. Simeon Stoddard, Mr. George Elleston, Mr. Sam¹ Checkly; Deacon Eliot and I led the young widow, and had Scarfs and Gloves. The Lord fit me, that my Grave may be a Sweetening place for my Sin-polluted Body. Can't see that anything has been done towards raising the [*Anglican*] Church since Wednesday: Friday and Thorsday had so much rain. Rained as went to the Grave.

Tuesday, Oct. 23. Went to Mr. Wilkins and heard Mr. Bayly preach from Numb. 33. 8, 9. Sung the prayer of Jonah. Visited Cous. Dummer.

Wednesday, Oct. 24, 1688. Mr. Bayly and his wife, Mr. Moodey and his wife and Cous. Richard Dummer dined with us. In the afternoon coming out of Town, I met Mr. Ratcliff, who ask'd me if I were going for England; he ask'd when, I said in Capt. Clark. He pray'd God Almighty to bless me, and said must wait upon me.³² Capt. Clark tells me at the Coffee-House, that he will sail next week, or Monday come sennight at out-side.

Oct. 25. Presented my final account to his Excellency respecting the French-Contribution [*for redeeming captives*], as He landed at Mrs. Gillam's stairs, from seeing the Sloops set sail with Souldiers and Provisions for the Eastward. Mr. Eliot and I eat together after Lecture. Mr. Stoughton and Dudley call at the Gate as they goe home at night.

Satterday, Oct. 27. The Rose-Frigot comes up, and his Excellency goes off to Charlestown and so to Dunstable: At both which, firing.

Oct. 28. Lord's Supper at the South Church Mr. Willard preached from Heb. 9. 24. Mr. Cotton of Hampton preached in the afternoon, His Text, Quench not the Spirit. *Note.* It seems the Governour took

---

³² Although Sewall greatly resented the establishment of the Church of England in Boston, he seems to have been on friendly terms with the rector.

Mr. Ratcliff with him, so met not at all distinct in our House this day. Several of them with us in the afternoon. Col. Lidget, Mr. Sherlock, Farwell in one Pue: went to Contribution.

Monday, Oct. 29. Went to Hogg-Island, had Sam., Hannah and Betty thether, Mr. Oliver's two daughters, Mr. Johnson's daughter, Mr. Balston's daughter: Mr. Oliver himself went; Sam¹ Marshall and his boy carried us. Landed at the Point because the water was over the Marsh and Wharf, being the highest Tide that ever I saw there. Cous. Savage came and din'd with us on a Turkey and other Fowls: had a fair wind home, Landed at Gibbs his Wharf, got home about Sun-set. Visited Mr. Smith who lies very ill.

Oct. 30. We have the news of Herbert Wanton and Blagg being cast away on the Isle of Pines. Very high Tide to day, in so much I feared 'twould have carried away the Island-Dam, and sent on purpose to see: All was firm and sound, blessed be God.

Wednesday, Oct. 31. Went to the Funeral of Mrs. Gookin: Bearers, Mr. Danforth, Mr. Russell, Sewall and Hutchinson, Eliakim, Mr. James Taylor, and Mr. Edw. Bromfield. *Note.* The Tide was over the Cause[wa]y, and Mrs. Willard, whom Mr. Pain carried, fell into the water, so that she was fain to goe to Bed presently in stead of going to the Grave, the Horse verg'd to the right, till fell into the Ditch. Mr. Hutchinson's Coach-Horses also plung'd.

Joshua Gee Lanches to day, and his Ship is called the Prince. Bant sails. Capt. Clark treats his Owners and Passengers: I was invited but the Funeral took me up. I help'd to ease the Corps into the Grave. Mr. Torrey goes home. More mischief done at the Eastward by the Indians. Mr. Alden dispatch'd again with Souldiers.

Satterday, Nov. 3. Mr. Offly and Mr. Clark come and speak to me about laying in for the Cabbin. Yesterday was Cous. Quinsey's Meeting where Mr. Moodey preach'd.

Nov. 3, about two P.M. Capt. White comes and presses me in His Majesties Name to appear at the Townhouse compleat in Arms next Monday at 11. aclock.

Gunpowder-Treason-day [November 5] 1688. I had sent for Robert Grundy; but his wife being great with child, and Jonathan Wales offering to serve in my stead for five pounds, I agreed with him, and had him to the Market-place at the hour, where Capt. White listed him in my stead and dismiss'd me.

Nov. 7. Brother Stephen comes to Town and brings my Letter of Attorney and other writings. I go with him to the Governour's where the witnesses are sworn, and after that I ask his Excellency if He has any service for me to Hampshire or Coventry: He ask'd where; I said in England. He said none in particular; Ask'd whom I went in; said in Capt. Clark. He said 'twas very well, and passed away out of the Porch.

Nov. 8. Capt. Tho. Smith dies about 5. *mane*; buried Nov. 10. Where the Corps was set was the room where first my Father Hull had me to see the manner of the Merchants, I suppose now above 12 years agoe. Bearers, Capt. Prout, Fayerwether, Wm Clarke, Foye, Tanner, Legg; Mr. Serj^t and Benj. Brown led the widow, buried in the old burying-place. The Lord grant I may be ready when my turn shall come to be becken'd away. There is a considerable snow upon the ground which fell last Thorsday night and Friday, near half a foot deep.

Sabbath, Nov. 11. Mr. Moodey preached with us in the forenoon from Luke 12. 47, *knew:*—many got home just about a quarter after 11. Afternoon got home about half an hour by Sun.

Nov. 13. My Unkle Quinsey visits me, and Mr. Torrey, Willard, Mather. I see Mrs. Nowell, Hutchinson, Mathers. America comes to sail this day, and runs aground as turns up and down but gets off quickly. Governour went out of Town yesterday, or to day, towards the Eastward.

Wednesday, Nov. 14, 1688. Went to the Meeting at Mis. Averies, Brother Emons pray'd much about Death: I read out of Mr. Allen about the Good, bad Angels, Death, Means of Grace, being given in to the Covenant. Sung the 23^d Ps. I concluded with prayer. None but Brother Emons, Davis, Self, Mother Hull, Mis. Avery, Mis. Noyes of the Meeting there, so none to invite the Meeting next time.

Nov. 16. The Upholsterer tells me the Ship is loaden too much by the head and sails badly. About 11 M. The Widow Glover is drawn by to be hang'd.[33] Mr. Larkin seems to be Marshal. The Constables attend, and Justice Bullivant there.

Nov. 16. Went to Capt. Davis's to meeting: Mr. Willard preachd from Job 30. 23. At night read in course the first Chapter 2 Cor. the

[33] This is all that Sewall has to say about the only execution for witchcraft that occurred at Boston in his time. Goody Glover, the Irish washerwoman in the John Goodwin household, was hung for the charge of bewitching the four Goodwin children. Cotton Mather, learned in medicine among his many attainments, took the eldest child, Martha, 14, into his home to observe her case and try to cure her witchcraft and possession by prayer and faith. After months of patience with the girl's hysterical antics, Mather had the satisfaction of seeing her quite cured, and wrote up her case in *Memorable Providences, relating to Witchcrafts and Possessions* (Boston, 1689), reprinted in G. L. Burr, *Narratives of the Witchcraft Cases* (New York, 1914), 89-143. See also W. F. Poole, Witchcraft in Boston, in *Memorial History of Boston* (1882) II, 142-146.

9th verse, of which have often thought on of late. Sentence of death. Brother Stephen visits me this day. Mrs. Rainsford, the aged Mother, dies.

Satterday, Nov. 17. Brother Stephen and I with Mr. Pole and Capt. Clarke goe on Board the America. It rained before we got aboard, and all the way as we came from the Ship; had a glass of good Madera. Brother commends the Ship, dines with us and returns to Salem.

The journal of Sewall's visit to England is contained in a separate MS. volume, a copy of which here follows. We have combined with this in the same chronology the entries which Sewall made in an interleaved almanac (Thomas Trigg's, published at Oxford and London, for the year 1689); these entries were furnished to the M.H.S. editors by John Ward Dean of the New England Historic Genealogical Society. This accounts for occasional repetitions in our text.

The visit seems to have combined two objects on the part of Sewall, one being in reference to his own kindred and the property of his family in England, and the other a desire to be with Mr. Mather, the agent of Massachusetts, and other friends who sought to uphold the interests of the colony, now without a charter or a settled government, and to secure, if possible, a restoration of its privileges. It should be added that William L. Sachse, in his work, The Colonial American in Britain (1956), states that "the earliest diary to give a substantial account of sight-seeing in London by an American" is this record of Sewall's.

Thorsday, November 22, 1688. Set sail out of Boston Harbour about an hour by Sun [*before sunset*], with a very fair wind. *Friday, Nov. 23, mane,* the wind came up at North-East to our great discomfort. Benny Harris reads the 21 of the Proverbs, which is the first Chapter I heard read on Shipboard. I much heeded that verse, He that wandereth out of the way of Understanding shall remain in the Congregation of the dead. At night I read the first of the Ephesians, and go to prayer. *Saturday, Nov. 24,* wind holds North-East, we go away East-South-East and the like, hoping to shape clear of Nantucket Shoals. Mr. Clark reads the two first Chapters of Isaiah, and Capt. Clarke prayes. *Sabbath, Nov. 25,* Strong East wind. In the even reef the Mainsail. I read the 74th Psalm, being that I should have read at home in the family. Read four or five verses out of Dr. Manton on the first of James: very suitable for me. Sung the 23[d] Psalm. *Monday, Nov. 26,* sail generally East-South-East. Mate takes an Observation, and finds that we are in the Latitude of 40[D]· and 13[M]· *Tuesday Nov. 27,* sail East-South-East, and sometimes East and North. Ait my wives Pasty, the remembrance of whom is ready to cut me to the heart. The Lord pardon and help me. *Wednesday, Nov. 28*, rains hard in the morning, the other Tack is brought on board, and we sail North-North-East. Just at night the wind blows very hard, just in our teeth, so ly by under the Mizzen, the other sails being furled. Scarce any sleeping all night, things in the Cabbin were so hurled to and again. *Thursday, Nov. 29*, wind comes up at North, or thereabouts, so steer East-N.-East. This is the first day of a fair wind since our coming out; goe away with fore-sail on our course. Clouds and no observation. About 12 at night, the Ship being under a hard Gale of wind, the whipstaf is somehow loosed from the Gooseneck, which puts us into great consternation: and the word is given, Turn out all hands. Several go into Gunroom and steer there for awhile, and by God's blessing no great harm. Some of the men said if she had not been a stiff ship would have been overset. *Friday, Nov. 30ᵗʰ*, one Casement being left down and the wind astern, a Sea is shipped into the Cabbin to our great startling and discomfort. Mrs. Baxter, who lay athwart ships at the bulkhead, the most wet. Very high wind and by flaws, we ly under our foresail not quite hoisted, and sail East. 'Tis a very laborious day by reason of hail, snow, wind and a swoln sea all in a foaming breach. A little before night the foresail is reefed, and Main Top-Mast took down to prepare for the tempestuous night, which proves very stormy, sore flaws of wind and Hail. *Satterday, Decemb. 1*, wind very high, frequent storms of Hail and Rain in fierce Gusts. About an hour by sun we are put into great confusion, the iron of the Whipstaff coming out of the said Staff. Some goe down and steer below, but fain at last to take in the foresail and ly by till the staff was fitted. The good Lord fit us for his good pleasure in this our passage.

Sabbath, Dec. 2, goe with our fore–courses, and just before night hoist the Top-sail, sailing East-N.-E. Read out of Dr. Preston and Manton,³⁴ prayed and sung Psalms. *Monday, Dec. 3*, calm in the morn for some hours, then a South-west wind and Top-sails out. Rain at night. Reef the Mainsail because now the wind very high. Caught two Petterils which Mr. Clark intends to preserve alive. Note, my Erasmus was quite loosened out of the Binding by the breaking of the water into Cabbin when it did. Was comforted in the even by reading the 4. 5. 6. 7. verses especially of the Ephesians. About 8 at night the Mate tells me he saw three Corpressants [*corposants: St. Elmo's Fire*], upon the top of each mast one. *Tuesday, Dec. 4. mane*,

---

³⁴ Dr. John Preston (1587-1628) had been master of Emmanuel College. Dr. Thomas Manton (1620-1677), a Presbyterian, was scribe to the Westminster Assembly. Both men were voluminous authors.

a violent North-East storm rises, so all sails taken in and ly by: very troublesome by reason of the frequent seas shipt and throwing the things in the Cabbin into confusion. Mis. Mary's Chest broken and her things powred out. I put on a clean shirt this morn. Can't dress victuals to day. *Wednesday, Dec. 5.* wether is moderated: but the wind so contrary that we sailed E.S.E. and South-East. *Thorsday, Xr. 6th* wether is comfortable, but wind, E.N.E., so we sail N. or N. and by West. Mis. Baxter is taken ill with a Flux. Kill a Shoat. *Friday, Dec. 7th*, very fair day: sail N. East. Breakfast on one of my wive's Plum Cakes. Read Dr. Preston, Saints Support of sorrowfull Sinners. One of the Geese dyes yesterday, or to day. Mis. Baxter is better.

Satterday, Dec. 8, very mild wether. Sail N.E. and E.N.E. In the afternoon veer'd out about 100 Fathom of Line, but found no bottom. Suppose ourselves very near the Banks of New-found-Land, by reason of the multitude of Gulls. Gunner trims me. *Sabbath, Dec. 9.* South, and South-w. wind; very temperat whether. Just at night Rain and N.W. wind. Cloudy all day. *Monday, Dec. 10th* North Wind. *Tuesday, Dec. 11.* N. and N. and by W. Pleasant wether. Last night I prayed to God and was somewhat comforted. This day the Captain takes a List of 's Letters. *Wednesday, Dec. 12.* West wind. Very pleasant wether. *Thursday, Dec. 13.* Strong S.W. wind. Ship runs between 6 and 7 Knots. Cloudy, drisky day. *Friday, Dec. 14*, Fast wind. See Birds, and a number of Fishes called Bottle-noses. Some say they are Cow-fish, or Black-fish. *Satterday, Dec. 15.* N.W. wind. Very pleasant morn. A little before night is a calm, after that the wind comes up at South-East, or thereabouts. Sail East N. East.

Sabbath, Dec. 16. Very high wind and swoln sea, which so tosses the ship as to make it uncomfortable: wind after, so Cabbin shut up and burn Candles all day. Shifted my Linen this day, Shirt, Drawers, N. Wastcoat, Binder: only for course to sail with. *Monday, Dec. 17.* Strong N.W. wind. *Tuesday, Dec. 18,* wind N. N. West: many flaws: storms of Hail. Afternoon was a Rainbow. Killed the Sheep to day. Dream'd much of my wife last night. She gave me a piece of Cake for Hannah Hett; was in plain dress and white Apron. Methoughts was brought to bed, and I through inadvertency was got up into the uppermost Gallery, so that I knew not how to get down to hold up the Child. We are in about 48D. N. Latitude.

Wednesday, Dec. 19, pleasant, west and southwest wind. Have an Observation. Was a Rainbow in the morn, and in the even Mr. Samson set the Sun by the Compass. This morn was refreshed in prayer from the Instance of Jonah and God's profession of 's readiness to give his Spirit to those who ask.

Thorsday, Dec. 20, strong North wind. Are in 48 D. 36, M.

Lat. At night the wind veers a little to the Eastward of the North.

Friday, Dec. 21. Little wind and that is Northerly. See many Porpuses. I lay a [*wager*] with Mr. Newgate that shall not see any part of Great Britain by next Saterday senight sunset. Stakes are in Dr. Clark's hand. In the night wind at North-East. *Satterday, Dec. 22,* wind is at North-East, at night blows pretty fresh. This day a Gannet was seen, and a Purse made for him that should first see Land, amounting to between 30 and 40$^{s.}$ N. England Money. I gave an oblong Mexico piece of Eight. Starboard Tack brought on board, and sail, N.E., N.N.E. and North by E.

Sabbath, Dec. 23. Pretty strong East, N. East wind. Sail N. and by E. Saw a Ship about noon some two Leagues to Leeward of us. A Gannet seen this day. Towards night the Capt. sounds and finds a sandy bottom. The water between 70 and 80 Fathoms deep.

Monday, Dec. 24, wind remains right in our Teeth. See a Ship to Leeward most part of the day which stood the same way we did: but we worsted her in sailing. *Tuesday, Dec. 25,* see two Ships, one to windward, 'tother to Leeward. About 10, m. a Woodcock flies on board of us, which we drive away essaying to catch him. Wind at North-East. Ly by under the Mainsail all night. *Wednesday, Dec. 26.* This morn perceive the Rails of the Ships head and the Lion to be almost beaten off, which cost considerable time and pains to fasten again. Ly by with no Sails. A Rainbow seen this day. *Thorsday, Dec. 27,* begin to sail again a little, winding East, N. East. *Friday, Dec. 28,* wind contrary, yet keep sailing sometimes N. East, sometimes goe South and by West upon the other Tack. Saw three Ships in the Afternoon, which, suppose are bound for England as we are. *Satterday, Dec. 29.* Have an Observation; are in 49^{D} and 50   See a Ship.

Sabbath, Dec. 30th Spake with a Ship 7 weeks from Barbados, bound for London, tells us he spake with an English Man from Galloway, last Friday, who said that the King was dead, and that the Prince of Aurang [*Orange*] had taken England, Landing six weeks agoe in Tor-Bay. Last night I dreamed of military matters, Arms and Captains, and, of a suddain, Major Gookin, very well clad from head to foot, and of a very fresh, lively countenance—his Coat and Breeches of blood-red silk, beckened me out of the room where I was to speak to me. I think 'twas from the Town-house. Read this day in the even the Eleventh of the Hebrews, and sung the 46th Psalm. When I waked from my Dream I thought of Mr. Oakes's Dream about Mr. Shepard and Mitchell beckening him up the Garret-Stairs in Harvard College. *Monday, Dec. 31st,* contrary wind still, speak with our Consort again.

1689

Tuesday, January 1. [1688/9.] speak with one [*vessel*] who came from Kennebeck [*sic*] in Ireland 8 dayes agoe: says there are Wars in England. Pr. of Aurang [*Prince of Orange*] in Salisbury Plain, with an Army Landed with fourscore and 5 Men of War and above two hundred Fly–Boats, has took Plimouth and Portsmouth, &c. and is expected at London daily.[1] Read Hebrews 13th *Wednesday,*

[1] Some thirty years before, as the Puritan Commonwealth collapsed, England had joyously brought Charles II to the throne, and the fun and games of the Restoration era began, but at the end of the three decades few were happy. There had been the Great Plague of 1665 (seventy thousand died in London alone) and the Great Fire of 1666 (half of London's population was unhoused). The Clarendon Code had made things as bad as possible for the Dissenters, especially for their clergy. Charles began to itch for the absolute power enjoyed by his first cousin Louis XIV. The incredible Dover Plot was hatched: Charles was to declare himself a Catholic; and with money and troops lent by Louis he was to enslave England. The plot failed because Louis, who picked this time to conquer the Netherlands, received little help from England, and was beaten by William, Prince of Orange; and because Charles's Declaration of Indulgence to all proscribed and persecuted sects was at once seen as a move to free the Catholics. The cry of "No Popery" was raised, and the Test Act was passed by Parliament, expelling all Catholics from the service of the crown. Charles's brother James, Duke of York, a Papist, had a secret meeting of English Jesuits at St. James's Palace, and from this the lying Titus Oates stirred up the country over a Popish Plot. Charles frus-

Jan. 2. Last night about 12 aclock the Wind comes fair, so that by morning the word was, Steady, Steady. The Lord fit us for what we are to meet with. Wind veered from East to South, and so Westerly. This day eat Simon Gates's Goose. *Thorsday, Jan.* 3, wind comes East again. A gray Linnet and a Lark, I think, fly into the Ship. *Friday, Jan.* 4, wind not very fair. Some say they saw a Robin-Redbrest to-day. *Satterday, Jan.* 5th, wind is now come to be about Southwest. Sounded and found a red, blackish sand about 50 Fathoms deep. Have a good Observation. This day I finished reading Dr. Manton. Blessed be God who in my separation from my dear Wife and family hath given me his Apostle James, with such an Exposition.[2] Page 8. Honour God in your houses, lest you become the burdens of them, and they spue you out. The tendernes of God's Love! He hath a James for the Xns. of the scattered Tribes. Obj. My affliction for sin, not Christ. Ans. 'Tis an error in Believers to think that Xt. is altogether unconcern'd in their sorrows, unless they be endured for his Names sake. If you do not suffer for Xt, Xt. suffers in you and for you. We should with the same cheerfullness suffer the will of Xt, as we would suffer for the name of Xt. P. 15. Look then not to the earnestness of your motions, but the regularity of them; not at what you would, but at what you ought. Men think 'tis a disgrace to change their mind and therefore are unplyable to all applications made towards them. But there is not a greater piece of folly than not to

---

trated the outraged Whigs by dissolving Parliament, and an attempt by them to murder him on the highway (the Rye House Plot) was frustrated by accident. His closing years were relatively quiet, and he died 6 February 1685 in the arms of the Roman Church. James II was an incompetent blunderer and lasted just four years. Monmouth's rebellion was quickly crushed, but James tried to force Catholicism on the English. The Test Act was repealed, his Declaration of Indulgence stirred up a hornet's nest, and the seven bishops who protested and refused to read it were jailed, tried, and triumphantly acquitted. When James's wife bore him a son, this was the last straw: the possibility of a prolonged Stuart dynasty was too much for Englishmen. William, Prince of Orange, Stadtholder of Holland, the champion of Protestant resistance to Louis (he was grandson of Charles I and husband of Mary, daughter of James II), was appealed to by the English Whigs. He sailed in the Dutch fleet in November 1688, and landed at Tor Bay, South Devon, on Guy Fawkes Day. While Sewall was crossing the ocean, and James was dallying at Westminster or taking ineffective measures, William and his army were marching up through Somerset and Wiltshire and Berkshire to Abingdon and down the Thames to London. On 11 December James fled, dropping the Great Seal into the Thames. Louis welcomed him to France and gave him the palace of St. Germain-en-Laye for his home. Sewall was unaware of it, but he was on hand for the Glorious Revolution.

2 Dr. Thomas Manton, the Presbyterian divine, had published his *Practical Commentary . . . on the Epistle of James* in 1651.

give place to right reason. 409. Julian, the Apostat, was a very just, strict, temperat man. So [*Kaspar*] Swenkfield, a man devout and charitable, notable in prayer, famous for Alms: but of a very erroneous and fanatical spirit.[3] V. 17ᵗʰ Cap. 3. p. 400. Sorrow in Heaven a note above Elah, 482. God hath every way provided for the comfort of His people: He hath pity for their afflictions and pardon for their sins. Cap. 5. 11. P. 561. There is no time wherein God doth not invite us to Himself. 'Tis wisdom to perform what is most seasonable. There is a time to encourage Trust. At what time I am afraid, I will trust in Thee. Ps. 56. 3. Cap. 5, V. 13, P. 569. Doves Eyes, Doves peck and look upward: same V. P. 571. Paul's Thorn in the flesh meant of some racking pain, not of a prevailing Lust. Cap. 5. v. 14. P. 584. Must pray in Faith, either magnifying God's Power by counterbalancing the difficulty, or by magnifying his Love, referring the success to his Pleasure. Cap. 5. v. 15. P. 589. In some cases Profession may be forlorn, but not in time of publick contest, P. 622. Psa. chiefly respects the feeling of our Consciences. We dread them and God will set them at distance enough, 613. Free Grace can show you large Accounts and a Long Bill cancelled by the blood of Xt. The Lord interest us in this abundant Mercy through the bloud of Xt, and the sanctification of the Spirit. Amen. Intend to give my Book to the Ship, and so took out this Note or two. *Satterday, Jan. 5ᵗʰ 1688/9.* Sounded twice to day. Found 50 Fathom first, then about 70. odd. Wind Souwest. A flock of Sparrows seen today. Psa. 84, or some such small Birds.

Sabbath, Jan. 6. See Capt. James Tucker, Commander of the Betty of London, about 120 Tons, whom spake with, this day sennight. Saith he saw the Light of Silly last Thorsday night. We carry a light and keep company. *Monday, Jan. 7ᵗʰ*, Mr. Clark goes on Board our Consort, and brings Oranges and a Shattuck [*shaddock*]. So steer in the night E. and East and by South. We had no Observation. Capt. Tucker saith he had by a forestaff, and Latitude 49.30. Reckons we shall be abrest with the Lizard by morning. Wind So. west. *Tuesday, Jan. 8, mane*, a brisk west wind. We sound and have 55 fathom: speak with our Consort, who saith he had Lizard Soundings, and would now have us steer East and by N. They were a little to windward of us, and a little astern. By and by they all gathered to their Starboard side, and looking toward us made a horrid Outcry, Land! Land! We looked

---

[3] Schwenkfeld (1490-1561) embraced the Reformation with great enthusiasm, but he later developed ideas which brought him into conflict with the Reformers, and had a stormy career. Some of his followers, the Schwenkfelders, a Silesian sect, emigrated to Pennsylvania in 1734 and still maintain their identity there.

and saw just upon our Larboard Bow, horrid, high, gaping Rocks. Mr. Clark imagined it to be the French Coast. We asked our Consort. He said, Silly! Silly! Trim'd sharp for our Lives, and presently Rocks all ahead, the Bishop and Clarks, so were fain to Tack, and the Tack not being down so close as should be, were afraid whether she would stay [*i.e., not miss stays*]. But the Seamen were so affected with the breakers ahead that the Mate could not get it altered, or very little. But it pleased God the Ship staid very well, and so we got off and sailed in Bristow Channel toward Ireland, winding Nore, N. West, and N.N.W., westerly. Just when saw the Rocks it cleared a little, and when fix'd in our course thicken'd again. Blessed be God who hath saved us from so great a Ruin. Saw the Light-House, that look'd slender, about the height of a man, and a Rock with a cloven top, not altogether unlike a Bishops Mitre, which I therefore take to be the Bishop. Wind would have carried us between Silly and the Lands End, but durst not venture and could not speak to our Consort, who probably knew better than we. And we Tacking, he Tacked.[4]

Tuesday, Jan. 8, 1688/9. About Noon our Consort being astern, Tacked, and we then Tacked, and stood after him, hoping to wether Sylly and its Rocks. Just before night we were in much fear by reason of many Rocks, some even with and some just above the water under our Lee, very near us, but by the Grace of God we wethered them. In the next place we were interrogated by the Bishop and his Clarks, as the Seamen said, being a Rock high above the water, and three spired Rocks by the side of him, lower and much lesser, which we saw, besides multitudes at a remoter distance. The breach of the Sea upon which made a white cloud. So I suppose the former Rocks near the Land of Sylly not the Bishop. Sailed Souwest, and S.W. by S. At night our Consort put out a Light, and about 8 o'clock began to hall away South-East. We imagined we saw some Glares of the Light of Sylly, but could not certainly say.

Wednesday, Jan. 9th As soon as 'twas light the word was they saw a Man of War, which put us into as great a consternation almost as our yesterday's Danger. Puts out his Ancient [*ensign*]; coming nearer speaks with us: is a Londoner from the Canaries, who by dark wether for several days had not made the Land, and lost his Consort last night. We told him we came from Sylly last night. He told us that five weeks agoe a Ship told them the Prince of Aurange was Landed

---

[4] The Scilly Islands are some thirty miles west of Land's End, and navigation thereabouts has always been dangerous. Bishop Rock now has an excellent lighthouse. The Lizard, a promontory of Cornwall, is the southernmost point of the English mainland.

in England before they came from Portland. This was at Canaries. Said also, the King not dead. Suppose ourselves abrest with the Lizard. Our Gunner said he saw it. Sail along 3 of us pleasantly, *Laus Deo*.

In the night the Londoner carries two Lights, one in 's poop, the other in 's round Top.

Thorsday, Jan. 10, 1688/9. Very fast wind, sail along with four or five more ships. About Ten o'clock saw the Isle of Wight plain, which is the first Land next to Sylly that I have seen. Next to that saw high white Cliffs: but then Clouds and Fogg took away our Sunshine and Prospect. The Ile of Wight makes a long space of Land, Hills and Valleys.

Friday, Jan. 11. A pretty while before day, a vehement North wind comes up, so that fain to ly by, and great confusion by reason that the 6 or 7 Ships were so near together that ready to fall fowl one of another. In the morn see that we are over against Beachy [*Head*]. In a while Tack about to try to gain the Wight, but cannot. A little before night tack again; Seven Cliffs. Make thus cold wether.

Jan. 12. Meet with a Pink 14 days from Liverpool: tells us Prince of Aurange landed about the 29th Nov. [*he actually landed on the 5th*] in Torbay, with 50 Thousand Men, Six hundred Ships: Sea-Commanders all yielded to him: no bloud shed: King and Prince of Wales gone to France somwhat privatly. Bought three Cheeses of him. He sent us some Bottles of very good Beer, and we him one of my Bottles of Brandy. About 12 o'clock the wind springs up fair, and about 6 in the even we take our leave of Beachey. Saith the occasion of Prince's coming in, that apprehends King James has no Legitimate Son, that that of Pr. Wales is a Cheat.[5] Told us there were English-men found dead, drowned, tied back to back: so put us in great fear, because he intimated as if French Men of War were cruising with English Commissions. *Sabbath, Jan. 13.* Goe ashoar at Dover, with Newgate, Tuttle and Sister. Hear 2 Sermons from Isaiah, 66. 9.— Shall I bring to the birth?

Sabbath, Jan[r] 13, 1688/9. Through God's Grace landed at Dover about 9 or 10 aclock with Mr. Newgate, Mr. Tuthill and his Sister Mary and Monsier Odell. Mr. Newgate and I went and heard one Mr. Goff in a kind of Malt-House. In Afternoon all went. His Text Isa. ult. v. 9th, vid. Sermon-book.

Monday morn, Jan. 14th, view the fort at the west end of the Town and the Castle: went into the Kings Lodgings. The Town is like a

5 See our note to the entry of 16 August 1688.

Bow, only the two Ends the thicker parts and the back the thinner, being built as the Sea and Cliff would suffer it.

A small River runs that helps to clear the Dock of Shingle: the Peers also defending. Houses of Brick covered with Tile generally: Some very good Buildings. A handsome Court-House and Market-place, near which the Antwerp Tavern, where we drunk coming out of Town.

Got this night to Canterbury time enough to view the Cathedral, and Kentish Husbandry as went along.

Monday, Jan^r 14. Rode in a Coach to Canterbury, after had view'd at the West, King's Lodging &c. 'Tis a piece of work that at first cost Labour and Expence, but now much decay'd. Getting to Canterbury a little before night view'd the Cathedral, which is a very lofty and magnificent building, but of little use. Visited Aunt Fissenden,[6] her son John and three daughters Mary, Elisabeth, and Jane, as I take it. Cousin Jn° sup'd with us at the Red Lion. I should have said before that Dover is a large Town like a Bow, only the back is thinnest, reaching from the Fort to the Castle. A convenient Market-place and Court Chamber. The Harbour not altogether unlike Boston Dock but longer. Two Peers to keep off the small shingle or stones, and that also clear'd in some measure by a small River whoes head is several Miles towards Canterbury, on which two or three villages and Water-Mills for Corn. The Town built chiefly of brick. Houses, most of them old, some very fair buildings. Town built as the Cliff and Sea would admit back of the Bow toward the Cliff. A very handsom square of Warehouses, and another little range, both more newly built, on the Beach, which made a good shew as we came ashore in one of the Boats that came for a Pilot.

Jan. 15. To Chatham and Rochester, which make a Long Street of Good Houses. A fair Assize-House now building, just over against which we lodged at a Coffee House: no room in the Inn. Dined at Sittingburn.

Wednesday, Jan. 16th To Dartford, where had a good Goose to Dinner. 'Tis a considerable place. A river runs into the Thames under a Stone Bridge of four Arches. To Southwark, where we drink and reckon with the Coachman. Hire another Coach for 18^d to Cousin Hull's.[7] *Thorsday, Jan. 17th,* went to the Exchange. *Jan. 30th,* went to

6 Probably the mother of Hannah Fessenden, who married John Sewall, brother of the diarist. N.E.H.G.R. XVII, 304.
7 This was Sewall's arrival in London; the final leg of his journey was a drive of a couple of miles into the city over London Bridge, the only bridge spanning the

the Temple and to White-hall. Saw Westminster–Abby: Henry 7[ths] Chapel. Heard Dr. Sharp preach before the Commons, from Psa. 51. —Deliver me from Blood guiltinesse, &c[8] Saw St. James's Park.

Jan. 31. Heard Mr. Chauncy preach.[9] Writ to Mr. Flavell this day.

Feb. 1. Received one from Mr. Flavell inclosed in Mr. Mather's.[10]

Feb. 7. A Minister who lives at Abbington earnestly invites me to his House with Mr. Mather, and he will goe and shew us Oxford. Mr. Brattle[11] shewed me Gresham Colledge,[12] by Mr. Dubois his kind-

---

river there. Edward Hull, a nephew of Sewall's father-in-law, John Hull, conducted a haberdashery business at the Hat-in-Hand within Aldgate (*A.A.S.Proc.* 1936, N.S. XLVI, 211). Sewall made his headquarters with him while he was in London, and, as he reveals 19 July, had a room over the shop. In another place in the Diary Sewall made the following record: Wednesday, Jan'y 16, came to London. Wednesday, Feb. 13th, went out. Satterday, March 16, into London. Thorsday, March 28, went out. Monday, Apr. 15, came into London.

[8] John Sharp, D.D., Dean of Norwich, was later made Archbishop of York. By chance Sewall heard a sermon which stirred up a great controversy in the House; Macaulay has an account of it in his *History of England*, Chap. X.

[9] Rev. Isaac Chauncy (B.A. 1651) was the oldest of President Chauncy's six sons, all of whom were graduated from Harvard. He was an L.R.C.P. and at this time was practicing medicine and preaching to a small congregation of nonconformists in Mark Lane, Aldgate. (*Sibley* and *Calamy*). During his English stay Sewall naturally encountered many of the Puritan clergy who had been deprived of their church livings and silenced by the enactment of the Clarendon Code (the Act of Uniformity, the Five Mile Act, the Conventicle Act, and the Corporation Act) early in the reign of Charles II. We have been able to identify most of them in the modern work of A. G. Matthews, *Calamy Revised: Being a Revision of Edmund Calamy's Account of the Ministers and Others Ejected and Silenced, 1660-1662* (Oxford, 1934), a scholarly compendium based upon the five volumes resulting from the dedicated labor of the Presbyterian parson Edmund Calamy (1671-1732).

[10] Increase Mather had reached England in May 1688, and remained there as agent from Massachusetts at the courts of James II and William and Mary until he came back in May 1692 with the new Province Charter. The story of his English sojourn is told fully in Kenneth Ballard Murdock's biography. On the 17th of January, the day following his arrival, Sewall spent the evening with Mather; Mather recorded this in his diary, Sewall did not. The two men saw much of each other in England, but Sewall's entries give the impression that Mather kept his show pretty much in his own hands and was inclined to brush Sewall aside and lose his temper with him.

[11] Thomas Brattle (Harvard 1676), merchant of Boston, was in London on business, and he and Sewall enjoyed seeing the sights together; they returned on the same ship later in the year. Sewall had been present when Brattle's mother died suddenly at the wedding of Daniel Quincy and Anna Shepard, 9 November 1682. Brattle was treasurer of Harvard College from 1693 until his death in 1713; he was the principal founder of Brattle Street Church, and from him Brattle Street derived its name. *Sibley*.

[12] In addition to being the founder of the Royal Exchange and the propounder of

ness and Cost. Afterward went to Smithfield, and the Cloisters of the Blew Coat Boys [*at Christ's Hospital*]. Gresham-Colledge Library is about one Hundred and fifty foot long, and Eighteen foot wide.

Feb. 9, 1688/9. Guild-Hall I find to be Fifty yards long, of which the Hustings take up near seven yards, Measuring by the same yard jointed–Rule, Mr. Brattle and I find the breadth to be Sixteen Yards.[13]

Feb. 11th Mr. Brattle and I went to Covent-Garden and heard a Consort of Musick. Dined to-day with Madam Lloyd and Usher.[14]

Feb. 12. Saw three Waggons full of Calves goe by together. At the Star on the Bridge, Mr. Ruck's, saw the Princess pass in her Barge, Ancients and Streamers of Ships flying, Bells Ringing, Guns roaring.[15] Supped at Mr. Marshal's.

Sewall left London on a trip 13 February.

Feb. 18, 1688/9. Writt to Tho. Read of Gillingham desiring him and the Uncle, in whoes hand the Bond is, to give me a meeting at Salisbury. I can give an authentick discharge. Send me an answer by the first opportunity by Penton of Rumsey to be left with Mr. Jnº Storke of said Rumsey.

Feb. 18, 1688/9 Winchester

To a pr Boots Spurs Sasoons	0-15-0
To the Man	0- 0-6

Gresham's Law, Sir Thomas Gresham (1519?-1579) established Gresham College for the gratuitous instruction of all who chose to attend the lectures; it is still carried on.

[13] Guildhall, the hall of the Corporation of the City of London, dates from 1425. It was seriously damaged in the Great Fire of 1666 and the Great Fire of 29 December 1940, but each time restored. The great hall was formerly used for trials as well as important public meetings and banquets, which are still held there. The Sewall-Brattle measurements are confirmed in modern guide-books.

[14] Madam Bridget (Lisle) Hoar Usher had left her husband and her Boston home 12 July 1687 (*q.v.*) and was residing with her sister Madam Tryphena Lloyd in Devonshire Square without Bishop's Gate. Madam Lloyd later married a Grove; her daughter Elizabeth Lloyd married Lord James Russell, fifth son of the first Duke of Bedford. *Savage* and L.B.

[15] Mary, Princess of Orange, had just come over from Holland. She transferred to a barge and was being rowed to Whitehall. The following day William and Mary were offered the crown, accepted it, and were proclaimed King and Queen. Sewall wrote nothing about the historic event. John Evelyn (*Diary*, 21 February 1688/9) saw the royal couple proclaimed "with great acclamation and general good reception. Bonfires, bells, guns, etc. It was believed that both, especially the Princess, would have showed some (seeming) reluctance at least, of assuming her father's Crown . . . but nothing of all this appeared; she came into Whitehall laughing and jolly, as to a wedding, so as to seem quite transported." She was twenty-seven.

A Letter 0- 0-2
Tavern 0- 0-6

Bought a Bay Horse at Winchester-Fair for which am to pay four pounds. Cous. Storke Cr. for the sum £4-0-0

This day Feb. 18, Recd a Letter from Cous. Hull at Winchester which gives an acco. that my N.E. friends well; will send the Letters by the Carrier.

Febr. 19. Went to Winchester into the Hall and Arbour to see the choice of Knights of the Shire. Jarvis, Henly and Fleming stood. It came to the Pole, I offer'd my Voice, but was refus'd because I would not lay my hand on and kiss the book, though I offer'd to take my Oath.

My Rapier was broken short off, I suppose coming down the steps into Hall. View'd the king's [*troup?*] Deliver'd Mr. Goldwier the packet of Letters in the Hall.

Feb. 19. Bought a Bridle, Saddle, Saddle cloath of Cous. Gilbert Bear, for 0-6- 0
A new Girt 0-0- 6
Driver   0-0-10

Febr. 20th Went to Baddesly and Visited Mr. Goldwire Father and Son.[16] Mis Goldwire is gone to London. Visited Cousin Rider, but he not at home. Mr. Goldwire invited me to stay there all night.

Saw the Stone of my Aunt Rider's Grave. She died March 21 1687/8. Lies in Baddesly burying place.

Thorsday, Feb. 21. Cousin Jane Holt came in the morn to invite me to dinner. I went with my Aunt Alice and Cous. Nath[l]. Had very good Bacon, Veal, and Parsnips, very good shoulder of Mutton and a Fowl rosted, good Currant suet Pudding and the fairest dish of Apples that I have eat in England. From thence Cous. and I went to the Church, and then up the Street to a Hill where we saw Winchester and Hampton plain; they lye pretty near North and South. Bell was ringing for a Funeral, so Ch[h] open. View'd it. Have three good Bells. Sup'd at Uncle Nath[ls]

Friday, Febr. 22, 1688/9, rid to Stouthton[17] with Cousin Nath[l] View'd the City. Delivered Mr. Biles his Letter, and Mr. Rawling's his Letters to Mrs. Graunt, and to Mis Bernard who lives now with Mr. Lee the Son, she being remov'd from the Water Gate: So had

---

[16] John Goldwire, B.A. All Souls, Oxford, 1624, had been ejected as Vicar of Arundel, Essex, in 1662. His son John, M.A. New Inn Hall, Oxford, 1654, had been ejected as Vicar of Felpham, Sussex, two years before. They taught school at Broadlands, near Romsey, and afterwards at Baddesley, Hants. *Calamy*.

[17] Southampton.

a fair oportunity to see Mis Phoebe Lee formerly Goldwire: She entertain'd us with a great deal of Respect and kindness, Has three children, a Son and two Daughters, eldest ab^t six years old.

Visited Aunt Hills and Cousin Thomas Dummer, who is just setting up at his Mother's house. Saw also the House where Cous. served his time and a young Maid, comely enough, whom some allot for my Cousin. Din'd at the Dolphin before these visits, at least before all save Mr. Biles. Cousin treated me.

To the Barber £0-0-6

Enquir'd of Capt. Dummer as came home. He is rather worse than when we were there.

Satterday, Feb. 23, ride to Bushnet and get a Shoe set on upon my Horse 4^d.—This day Cous. Newman's Man comes and tells my Aunt that his Mistress is brought to bed of a Son.

February 23, In the Afternoon Cous. and I goe and see fair Oak where are about 7 or 8 Houses. Drank a Cup of Beer at the Angel. —To a Bag 2.2^d, Quire Paper at Winchester 3^d, which Unkle bought £0-2-5.

Sabbath, Febr. 24, Went and heard Dr. May preach from Eph. 5. 11, Have no fellowship &c. Made a good Sermon; among other things mentioned erroneous Worship as a work of Darkness. I went not in till they began to sing. Stoke People sing well. In the Afternoon heard Mr. Leadbeter at Otterburn; rid most part of the way. He Catechis'd and by that means was somewhat hamper'd in his Surplice and Common Prayer because had left some till after Catechising. Text was out of Deut. 32.36. Shew'd that when God's people lowest and the enemies highest God usually was wont to help. This day Scripture fulfill'd in your ears. God's People never have reason to despair; wicked never secure. Cous. Mary din'd with us.

Febr. 25, 1688/9. Went to Winchester in the morning, and there met with my Letters from my dear wife and New England Friends, dated January last. *Laus Deo.*

To a pair of Buckles for Cousin Sarah £0-3-3
Spent in my Journy 0-3-7

View'd Winchester Colledge, the Chapel, Library built in the midst of the Green within the Cloisters. Left my Indian Bible and Mr. Mather's Letter there.[18] Was shew'd also the Hall which is above Stairs. Cous. Bear din'd with me at the Checker.

---

18 The second edition of Eliot's Indian Bible (Cambridge, N.E., 1685), which Sewall presented, is still in the library of Winchester College; it bears Sewall's signature. His other gift, "Mr. Mather's Letter," probably Increase Mather's tract,

Febr. 26. Recd. of Cous. Nath. Dummer for acc° of John Edwards Cash £3-0-0 Three pounds Engl. Money.

Feb. 27. Lodg'd in Mr. Goldwire's best Chamber at Baddesly. *Febr. 27,* din'd there, then went to Rumsey. *Febr. 28,* Rid to Salisbury and paid Madam Sarah Woodward Nine Engl. Crowns in full for Ten pieces of Eight for William Brown, Esqʳ of Salem, as *per* Recᵗ writ by Mr. Chauncellors Clerk, said Chauncellor being at London £2-5-0

The Chancellor's clerk shew'd me the Cathedral, Chapter House and Cloysters. Chapter H. round with a Pillar in the middle to support the Roof. Got the Organist to give us some Musick. Bp. Davenant's Tomb. Shew'd as a strange thing (a Bishp I think) that lay North and South. The Cathedral is very neat and stately. Two Crosses in It. Candles on the Communion Table, so at Winchester. The Bells hang in a Steeple distant from the Chʰ. Tell us are Twelve small Chapels for Prayers every Hour. The Bible over the Passage that leads into the Chorus, that so Persons may hear on both sides. The Spire is excellent for height and beauty.[19] Din'd with the Chancellor's Clerk. His Lady gone to a Christening, that it was invited and could not stay, but shew'd us in a manner her whole House, first Plate, Library and Bedding. Her Daughter of 4 moneths old whom took out of the Cradle and kiss'd though asleep.

Febr. 28. Rid on the Powny to go to Shaftisbury but raind and wind very bleaky, so returnd to the Whᵗ Hart again. Abᵗ an Hour by Sun went out of the City at Fisherton Bridge to goe along the villages by the Bourn towards Mere. Reach'd to Chilmark. Lay at the Noggin just by the Chʰ on a Doust Bed; rested very well. Had the ringing of the four Bells. Pretty handsom Ch.; Steeple in the middle. Four Grave Stones like the roof of a House; written on the side.

Half Bush¹ oats and Supper, Breakfast £0-3-6
Salisbury 1-8
is a large place good streets, a very fair Market place besides a butter Cross.

From Salisbury to Wilton, and so on throw some other villages to

---

De Successu Evangelij apud Indos in Novâ-Angliâ (London, 1688, etc., Holmes 128), has not survived.

19 Puritan though he was, Sewall nevertheless found agreeable things to say about Salisbury Cathedral, one of the handsomest ecclesiastical structures in Christendom. It was built at one time, between 1220 and 1258, and the spire, the tallest in Britain (404 feet), was added between 1335 and 1365. The Chapter House is octagonal, with a central pillar. A belfry was built north of the cathedral about 1262, but this was removed in 1790 by a ruthless architect, James Wyatt, who committed additional mayhem on the cathedral itself.

Chilmark, where lodgd at the Noggin near the Ch. in a doust Bed.

March 1. From Chilmark to Hendon a Market Town, thence to Fonthill where the Springs rise so thick in the Gravelly high-way that in less than ¼ of a Mile the stream obtains the reputation of a little river, by Sir Edward Cottington's To Barwick, so to Mere where saw the like out of the Hill and high way. Mere is a compact Town, and the Ch. hath a good handsome Steeple with four Pyramids at top. To Gillingam a convenient place. Lay at the Red Lion. Deliver'd my Letters to mr. Richard and Jnº Pern. *Satterday March* 2ᵈ rid to Shaftisbury, a pretty fair Town built with stone, Chimnyes and all, some Houses thatcht, some covered with stone, Two Churches on the Hill, Trinity and St. Peters, great Market of wheat, Barley, Beans, Beef, Mutton, Leather, Cloaths &c. The part of the Town next Gillingam fetches water at the foot of the Hill out of Gill. Liberty in consideration of which pay a Calvs head, Pair fringe Gloves of a Noble.

Gillingham March 2ᵈ 1688/9, Recd. of Mr. John Pern One Guiney to give to Mr. Edward Rawson with a Letter.

With Bread and Beer, a Duz. or two Come dancing down the Hill the Monday before ascension day; i.e., the two persons last married whom they call the Lord and Lady, but now generally there is a stated Dancer, a merry arch jocose Man, who procures a Lady. A Horse carries abᵗ Sixteen Gallons in two Tuns, which is worth two pence, to some of the farthest Houses from the Wells. One well is for washing, the other for brewing. I saw a Horse load from the washing well; a furse keeps the water from flapping out. Lodg'd in the Crown at the red Lion in Shaftsbury.

March 4, Went to Gillingham and from thence to Meere, so to Wylie, lay at the Bull. *March* 5, to Winterburn Stoke a small village by a Bourn four miles from Wilie. When on the Downs abᵗ two mile from W. Stoke saw Yarnborough Castle, which hath abᵗ three ditches, the innermost deep and large qᵗ within a great quantity of ground, the ground hath such a descent that being rid in could not see the other Ditch on the contrary side, qᵗ a pretty many acres of ground, lies in an orbicular form. From thence to Stonehinge,[20] four

20 Stonehenge, on Salisbury Plain, near Amesbury, Wiltshire, has been standing about 4000 years. Although much has been discovered, it is not known definitely who built it, or why. Originally there were thirty massive slabs, 20 feet tall, in a circle 97 feet in diameter, capped by a continuous lintel. Sewall's sharp eye spotted the hemispherical tenons. These 40-ton stones were cut on the Marlborough Downs, twenty-four miles away, hauled, dressed, and erected by hand. Within the circle was a ring of slender upright stones brought from Pembrokeshire in Wales, a series of trilithons (two uprights with lintels) in the shape of a horseshoe, and an-

miles from W. Stoke are nine transverse stones, three of them together, the other single because I suppose their fellows fallen down
and so there is a discontinuance, rid through between some; but
others the supporters stand so close canot. Almsbury to the eastward
of this place. The supporters have round Tenons, and the transverse
pieces mortices. From Stonige rid to Lake and Durnford ab^t two
miles off upon a pleasant Bourn from Almsbury which runs to Salisbury. From thence four miles to Salisbury, went to old Sarum,[21] rid
up to the highest summit. Are very deep Ditches something like
Dover Castle, only Sarum's walls all gone save some little part or
fragment of Flint wall in one place and other stone in another. From
thence to the Plume of Feathers in Salisbury where were entertaincd
in the Lamb. From thence home ab^t Sunset. *Deo Gloria.*

Bought a whip at Salsbury 1.6^d, two p^r sizers for my Daughters
1.2^d   0-3-8
At Shaftsbury Gloves   0-3-6
two p^r for my Daughters, 18^d, p^r for Cous. Mercy.
Spent I suppose in the Journy ab^t 40 or 50^s. Bore Cous. Stork's
charges £2-10-0
Wensday March 6. Went to Lee. Saw my House, Barns and
Ground, there are Seven Closes, two very fair ones besides the Or-
chard Ground and Half an Acre just by mr. Nowes's house. Visited
him. He offers me four Hundred Pounds for my Bargain. The
Tenants wife teaches scholars, One was reading whom I markt and
gave them 6^d to buy Apples £0-0-6
Thorsday March 7th Recd. of Cous. Jno Stork, 8 half Crowns, Engl.

---

other horseshoe of the slender upright stones from Wales. Many are now missing.
Sighted through the opening between the uprights of the central trilithon, the sun
rises over the heelstone, 256 feet away, on the day of the summer solstice, and
that day only. R. S. Newall, *Stonehenge* (1955) and H. E. Edgerton and B. Hope-
Taylor, Stonehenge—New Light on an Old Riddle, *Nat. Geog. Mag.* June 1960,
cxvii, 846-866; see also G. S. Hawkins, *Stonehenge Decoded* (1965).
[21] The name Sarum apparently evolved from a misunderstanding of the paleo-
graphical abbreviation (Sa, plus the *-rum* sign) for Sarisburia (Salisbury); it is
now the ecclesiastical name of Salisbury. (*O.E.D.*) The original settlement of Old
Sarum was on a great mound, which had been fortified by the Romans, about a
mile north of the present city, and a cathedral was built there in Norman times.
The site was too windy, and the town became too crowded. In 1220 the cathedral
at New Sarum (the present Salisbury) was begun, and when the clergy moved
down, the townspeople followed. By the fifteenth century the old site was a deserted ruin. Old Sarum was subsequently famous as a rotten borough, and, though
without inhabitants, continued to return two members to Parliament; elections
were held there under a huge elm tree up to the passage of the Reform Bill in
1832. R. L. P. Jowitt, *Salisbury* (1951).

Money £1-0-0

Thorsday, March 7. Went from Rumsey to Redbridge just below which is the Landing place ab^t 4 miles from Rumsey. From thence throw Milburn to Southampton. Heard mr. Robinson[22] sitting in mr. Taylor's Pue. Text, as I remember, out of Rom. 6. 3. Know ye not &c. Said they who were call'd to teach were call'd to baptise though they were not settled Officers; They who hold forth the Covenant of Grace, may set the Seal to it. Philip the Deacon: Apostles not Apostles till after Christ's Ascension, for till then sent only to the Jews, yet they baptised. Seem'd to say must be a Sermon or the like at Baptisme. This day Mr. Tomlin[23] baptiseth Warner Newnam at Stoke, Preaches at Unkle Dummer's. After Sermon went into mr. Robinson's and sat with him, mr. Thornes, mr. Lee the Father, mr. Watts, mis Robinson. Went home with Jane Kirby, Cous. Tho. Holt's mistress; but I knew it not till he met her; it being late, and I observ'd a boy run parallel with us in the Grounds and ask'd her about it; I took him up; and when set him down by the Mill, Lent him half a Crown to buy Paper and Quills, told him if learnd to write and read well, 'twas his, if not, must have it again with I know not how much interest and put him to a great deal of trouble.

Friday, March 8, Unkle Richard, Cous. Nath. and I went to Hatterworth, there din'd with Fritters at Goodwife Galler's where Mehetabel Holt lives, thence to Rumsey and Lee, take Livery and Seisin of my Tenement. To Stoke.

Satterday, March 9. Ride to Tichfield, view the Church and mr. Oakes's Pulpit, removed from the Pillar where it stood in his time to the other side.[24] Sexton spake much in 's praise and enquired after his Children. Saw Mis. Bromfield's Monument who died 1618. Din'd with Cous. Tho. Dummer, bought the first pound of Tobacco which he sold in a Fair. Cous. Nath. accompanied me to Kirbridg, from thence alone, saw my Lord Southampton's seat by the way, is a small Town. From thence I rid alone to Gosport ab^t 6. miles. Gosport is compass'd with a form'd Bank and Ditch which I walkd all round. Is two or three good streets in 't but they are not long. Pretty good houses.

22 Nathaniel Robinson had been ejected as rector of All Saints, Southampton, in 1660. At this time he was pastor of a Congregational church at Southampton formed the year before. *Calamy.*
23 Samuel Tomlyns, M.A. Corpus Christi College, Cambridge, had been ejected as rector of Crawley, Hants, in 1662, and was now pastor of a congregation at Andover, Wilts. *Calamy.*
24 Urian Oakes (Harvard 1649) had been minister of Tichfield for ten years before he was silenced by the Act of Uniformity of 1662.

Mar. 10 would have heard mr. Goldwire, but mr. Beamont the Minister of Fareain preached from Ps. 45, 15. Doct. Interest and Duty of Christians to rejoice in Chs^t made good profitable Sermons; but I think might have been more so, if had us'd the Metaphor of Bridegroom and Bride, which heard not of. Sat in the Afternoon in mr. Lock's seat, who has the best House in Town.

Monday, March 11, Went to Portsm°, Mr. Barton shew'd me the Fortifications, with whom din'd, visited Cous. Dummer, saw the Dock, long Storehouse where Cables lye at length, Royal Charles 136 foot by the Keel, to the Sun at the Red Lion again and so to Tich-field, where lodgd at the Bull.

March 12. To Bussledon where a Pink leaving with Charcole out of Tichfield Park for Cornwall, to Itching Ferry after had viewd Peartree Chapel, Madam Mills Daughter and two or 3 more accompanying me, is a plain Chapel of Stone covered with Tile. Rails of Burying place are mostly fasten'd in a circle of living Trees: Is Service there but once a fortnight. Saw no Memorandum of Richard Smith Esqr the Builder. To Rumsey, visited Mr. Warren,[25] gave him Twenty Shillings, visited mr. Burbenk.—N. at Portsm° saw plenty of Shrimps which are took at Porchester.

March 13, 1688/9. Recd. of Amie Gales Fifteen pounds Money with some Abatements by reason of extraordinary Losses, and extream lowness of the price of Corn, is in full for One years Rent of my Tenement at Lee, ending this present Moneth the five and twentieth day 1689. Abatements relate to several years. S.S. Recd. XV£ £15-0-0. Recd of Cous. Storke 22 pr. Wom^s Stockins n° 30 at 24^s 6^d

per Duz.	£2- 5-0
Item 4 Duz. ditto at 20^s 6^d *per* Duz N° 24	4- 2-0
It^m 16 pr. wom^s at 1^s *per* pair N° 16	0-16-8
7 pr. Mens coloured at 3^s 6^d N° 20	1- 4-6
6 pr. Youths at 18^d pr. N° 24	0- 9-0
	8-17-2

8 Duz. 3 pr. in all.

March 14, 1688/9. Recd. of Cous. Nathl Dummer Hair

Buttons 21 Gross at 2^s 6^d *per* Gross	2- 9-0
9 Gross ditto	1- 1-0
Cash	2-12-6

Charges reckoning nothing for time: made two journeys to

[25] Thomas Warren, M.A. St. Catherine's, Cambridge, had lost the rectorship of Houghton, Hants, in 1662. He was preaching at Romsey and living on £16 per annum. *Calamy.*

Ashley near Limmington ab^t 30 miles off Feb. 26 .   .   -17-6

                                                              _____

                                                              7- 0-0

Which with 3£ before is in full of Jn° Edwards's ten pounds.
Recd. of Cous. Dummer on acc° of Bro^r Stephen Sewall
    Cash Engl. Money £0-11-2
Recd. of Cous. Dummer for Mrs. Batter to lay out in Silver
    Spoons   5-16-3
five pounds sixteen shillings and 3d.
            B
    Mark E M
Thorsday March 14, 1688/9. To Cous. Jane Holt a broad
pss £1-3- 6
Cousin Mercy Stork yesterday 5.6^d, and 18^d before in Shaf-
    tisbury Gloves 0-7- 0
To Cous. Jn° pr. Buckles 0-5- 0
Thomas, Cash   0-3-
3 little sons, Philip, —— and Sam 0-7- 6
Two Girls before had Primers 0-0- 6
March 15 To Cous. Sam. at Bp. Stoke Gold Crown .   .   .   0-5-10
Cous. Stephen 0-2- 6
Cous. Sarah ½ Crown and pr. Buckles before ab^t 3 or 4^s . 0-6- 0
Boy and Maid 0-2- 0
To Cous. Abigail, Unckle Nath's Eldest Daughter .   .   .   0-2- 6
    Din'd there with very good Beef, Bacon and rost fowls. Company
Unkle, Aunt, Aunt Alice, Cous. Stephen Winchester Butcher —
Left with Mr. Richard Dummer my Unkle ½ Crown for
    Deborah Rider, and ½ Crown to each of Aunt Sarah's
    Children   0-7-6
Deborah with Tears shew'd my last Letter to her Mother, who I
think was dead before it was writt.
    Friday, March 15, Unkle Stephen sick on bed with a Crick ins
Back. Unkle Richd. goes on foot to Winchester, Cous. Nath. and I
ride to see his house at Compton by the way which stands very con-
veniently ab^t ¼ mile from the Ch^h 2 from Wr.
    At the Checker have a Hogs Cheek Souct,[26] Send for Cous. Gilbert
Bear and Cous. Jn° Dummer; I treat them with Ale and Wine, but
Unkle Richd will Call for one Pint and indeed Cous. Mercy Stork
and he seem the most kind of all my Relations. At Winchester recd.
Mr. Thorner's Letter of Mrs. Widell, who is a Shipmasters wife and
with her Daughter Hunt and D'r. in law Widell, are going to meet

26 Soused, or pickled.

their Husbands, one Winchester Gentlewoman; From Farnum to Bagshet 5 women and one Man—there took in a Souldier instead of the woman. At Winchester had of Mr. Edward Grace by his man Edward Hooker a bill of £20 on Mr. Tho. Abney at the Crown in Cornhill for Twenty pounds 2^s 6^d paid there £20-2-6, Date March 15, 1688.

Sewall returned to London 16 March.

Satterday March 16. Capt. Widell was at Holburn with his Son and Son in Law to meet their Wives, I drunk a Pint wine with them and took leave. Mrs. Widell the Mother was very good Company and so the rest.

Sabbath March 17. The Ld. Mayor Chapman dyes in the morn.

March 18, wrote to my Wife. 2, to Cousin Quinsey, 3, to Bro. St[ephen] Sewall, inclosed in Sir William's into the Downs.

Monday March 18, Went and saw the Jews burying Place at Mile-End:[27] Some Bodies were laid East and West; but now all are ordered to be laid North and South. Many Tombs. Engravings are Hebrew, Latin, Spanish, English, sometimes on the same stone. Part of the Ground is improv'd as a Garden, the dead are carried through the keepers house. First Tomb is abt the year 1659. Brick wall built ab^t part. Ont 's two sides 5444, Christi 1684, Tamuz 21, June 23, as I remember.—I told the keep^r afterwards wisht might meet in Heaven: He answerd, and drink a Glass of Beer together, which we were then doing.

March 19. Writt to Cousin Storke to send me a perfect account, Dr. and Cr., and the Balance Money. I took up in Stockings 8, 17, 2 Am willing to allow what's reasonable for receiving my Money.

March 19. To Mrs. Elizabeth Mills, for Pole's Synopsis[28] entire, lacking nothing, will give £4. here.

[27] Jews had been forbidden to live in England since the time of Edward I, but they had come in nevertheless, recorded as Spanish and Portuguese Catholics, and duly went to màss every Sunday. An attack on Spanish Papists in Cromwell's time forced many of them to reveal their identity, and permission was granted in 1656 to hold services in Cree Church Lane and to purchase a burial ground at Mile End, Whitechapel. (N. G. Brett-James, *The Growth of Stuart London*, 1935, 484-485.) Sewall must have also visited the Bunhill Fields Burial Ground, near Finsbury Square, "the Campo Santo of the Dissenters," but he made no mention of it.

[28] Matthew Poole (1624-1679), M.A. Emmanuel College, Cambridge, 1652, published his *Synopsis Criticorum Aliorumque S. Scripturae Interpretum* in five folio volumes in London in 1669; it brought together in convenient form the labors of the previous biblical commentators, and had a large sale. Another edition,

March 19. Saw Paul's, which is a great and excellent piece of work for the Arches and Pillars and Porches. The Stairs are five foot ½ long and four Inches deep, winding about a great hollow Pillar of about six foot Diameter.[29] *March* 20. Went and saw Weavers Hall and Goldsmiths Hall. Went into Guild-Hall and saw the manner of chusing the Mayor. About 16 were put up, though I think but four were intended. Pilkington and Stamp had by much the most Hands, yet those for fatal Moor and Rayment would have a Pole, which the Court of Aldermen in their Scarlet Gowns ordered to be at four o'clock.[30] They sat at the Hustings. Sheriffs in their Gold Chains managed the Election. Common Sergeant [*counsel of the Mayor and Aldermen*] made a speech. When the People cry'd, a Hall, a Hall, the Aldermen came up two by two, the Mace carried before them, came in at the dore opposite to the Street dore out of another apartment. I stood in the Clock-Gallery.

March 20. Writt to Mr. John Richardson, of Bristow, to send me Mr. Sergeant's and my Account, and that I would however pay my own. Fear [I] shall never hear of Nath. Man, or the Fidelity any more.[31]

March 25. Writt to Mr. Brown inclosing Mrs. Sarah Woodward's original Receipt by Bant, Copy by Lason. Writt by Lason to Mr. Torry. Mr. Higginson inclosing Mr. Whitfield's Papers.

March 28, To my Wife, inclosing Mr. Henry Hatsel's 2d Receipt. 27 To Mother Hull, with a Case of Spectacles, Shagreen.

Sewall began another journey from London 28 March.

March 28, 1689. With Mr. Mather and his son Sam[*uel*] went in the Coach of Abbington to Hounslo, so to Colebrook and to Maidenhead 22 miles from London. Sam. and I went to Bray-Ch. and writt out 2 Epitaphs by Candlelight. Maidenhead belongs to the Parishes of Bray and Cookam. Is only a Chapel of ease at M. head. A Non-

---

made up of the same sheets but with new front matter by Johannes Leusden, was published at Leyden in 1684.

[29] Work on the present St. Paul's Cathedral did not get under way for nearly a decade after the Great Fire of 1666, and the building was not declared completed until 1711. The stairs Sewall describes are in the base of the southwest, or clock tower, and lead from the Dean's Door to the level of the nave. Above them rises the famous Geometrical Staircase, built after Sewall's visit.

[30] The candidates mentioned were Sir Thomas Stamp, Sir Jonathan Raymond, Sir John Moore, and Sir Thomas Pilkington, who was elected. M.H.S.EDS.

[31] Sewall refers to this business again 10 May; he had shipped cargoes in the *Fidelity* in 1686 and 1687. M.H.S.Proc. LII, 335-336.

conf. Minister Mr. Brice preaches in a Barn.[32] Outside the Hart is in
Bray, other side of the way is in Cookam. I din'd alone at Colebrook
with a Bullock's Cheek. Ab^t 6. aclock Mr. Mather, Son and I sup'd on
two Dunghill fowls. Mr. Mather prays and we get to bed just at nine.
Bray Ch. a mile off the nearest way.

Friday March 29, to Abbingdon. Lodge with Mr. Danson,[33] find He
has Mis Dulcibella Garbrand, mr. Dunches Grandch., by his Daughter Beck. She has a daughter Martha 4 years old a very desirable child.
Mis Jane Cave also lives in the House, a Border. *Satterday March 30*
Mr. Mather and we ride in the Coach to Oxford 5 miles, little ones,
costs us 12^s of which I pay 5 and mr. Mather the rest. See the Colledges and Halls, New-Colledge, Maudlin and Christ Ch. do most
excell. At New-Col. eat and drank Ale, wine, Lent Cakes full of Currants, good Butter and Cheese, by means of Mr. Benj. Cutler the
Butler, to whom D^r. Woodward sent a Letter on my behalf. Saw the
Theatre and Schools Congregation-House. To Abingdon. *On the
Sabbath March 31*, Mr. Danson preaches in the morn. Come to me
all weary. Mr. Mather in afternoon. All are sinners, which preach
before at Mr. James's, *vide*. *Monday Ap 1*, very windy, yet view Abingdon, the river Occe which gives name to Occ-street running at the
bottom of the Gardens of one side the street, there Pikes and Perch
are catcht, Occ Eels also are famous. On it stands a mill and just
where it falls into the Thames there is a Stone Bridge for Horse and
foot. Their flat Boat ly there which carry Seven Hundred Quarters of
Malts, which they count seventy Tun. Have Flashes to help them
over the Shallow places. *Tuesday Ap. 2*, View the Hospital, old Town-
Hall the place where the Abby was which in precedency next to
Glastenbury, and in Revenue above it. Ch. hath 5 Iles. Ab^t 300 Soldiers come to Town, so Horses press'd that could not get out. Mr.
Danson preaches to the Youth at his House, They that seek me early
shall find me.—

Wednesday, Ap. 3, went to Mr. Jennings, where had Ale and Cider,
thence to Oxford in the Rain. Mr. Gilbert, a Bachelour of Divinity

---

[32] John Brice, B.A. St. John's College, Oxford, was ejected as rector of Easthamp-
stead, Berks, in 1662. He was licensed as a Presbyterian in 1672, and was preaching at this time to a congregation of two hundred at Maidenhead, Berks. *Calamy*.
[33] Thomas Danson, M.A. New Inn Hall, Oxford, had been Fellow of Magdalen,
vicar of St. Mary's, Sandwich, Kent, and vicar of Sibton with Peasenhall, Suffolk,
where he was ejected in 1662. He settled at Abingdon, Berks, in 1679. His wife
was Anne, daughter of Tobias Garbrand, D.Med., principal of Gloucester Hall,
Oxford. *Calamy*. The Dunches seem to have been one of the county families at
Baddesley, Hants, where Sewall's father preached.

shew'd us the Bodleian Library which is an Ach, H, a very magnificent Thing. The Galleries very magnificent about 44 of my Canes in length and near 8 in Breadth. I lookt in one book, which in Cuts sets forth the Glory of Old Rome. Mr. Gilbert gives us a pint of wine. Lodge at the Bear Inn.[34]

Leave the Horse of William Matthews who keeps the Cross-Keys in Abbingdon, at the Roe Buck in Oxford. Am to pay 7ˢ for the Journey and 12ᵈ a day for every working day beyond seven working dayes. Give the Keeper of the Roe-buck 6ᵈ if I leave not the Horse with him on a Market day, Wednesday, Satterday. Agreed with Stiles on the same terms, am to leave his Horse at the Cross Keys in Oxford, to begin to morrow, Ap. 4ᵗʰ.

Ap. 4, 89, left my Cane cuzen [*with cousin*] and Box of Linen, silk stockings, Gloves, with Jnᵒ Wilmot of Oxford the Booksellers son.

Dr. Nehemiah Grew son of Dr. Obadiah Grew formerly of Baliol Colledg, Oxford, lives at Racket Court in Fleet-Street near Shoe-Lane.—Leave a Ps[*alm*] B[*ook*] there. Dine with Dr. Grew Ap. 8.[35]

Leave Bodicot ¼ mile left H.

Lodge at the Unicorn Mr. Stiles, where also the Lord Brooks Lodges in 's way to London, just by the Market House six Pillars of a side. Abbingdon has a stately market house on square Pillars, in the Town hall the Meeting is.

---

[34] Thomas Gilbert, M.A. and B.D. (Oxon.), was a learned nonconformist clergyman who attained great influence in Cromwell's time, but had his livings in Shropshire and Buckinghamshire taken away at the Restoration. Thereafter he lived quietly in Oxford until his death in 1694, writing Latin verse and epitaphs for dissenters. Calamy described him as "the completest schoolman" he ever knew, in his element among "crabbed writers." (*D.N.B.*) The *Carmen Congratulatorum* which he presented to Sewall on 14 April may have been a broadside; we do not find it listed among his works. Externally the Bodleian is little changed today; the interior was rebuilt in the 1960's and Duke Humfrey's Library carefully restored to its original state.

[35] Nehemiah Grew, B.A. Pembroke Hall, Cambridge, and M.D. Leyden, was a distinguished vegetable physiologist to whom Sewall later sent scientific information about the Indians of New England (*C.S.M.* xiv, 142f.). His father, Obadiah Grew, M.A. Balliol and D.D., was the greatly beloved vicar of St. Michael's, Coventry, but lost his living in 1662. He continued to preach in the vicinity. In 1682, after he had lost his eyesight, he was convicted of a breach of the Five Mile Act and imprisoned for six months in Coventry gaol. While in prison and later he dictated a sermon each week which was taken down in shorthand and read to other amanuenses who produced about twenty copies to be read to Dissenting congregations. Under James II's declaration for liberty of conscience he had been restored to his congregation and was preaching at Leather Hall at the time of Sewall's visit. *D.N.B.*

Ap. 4. Mr. Holland a Fellow of Corpus Christi shews me his Chamber Cellar, Library ab^t the bignes of our Chappel where saw Dr. Jn°
Reynolds Monum^t who was President of said College. Said Holland treated me very civilly though told him was a N. E. Man.[36]

Thorsday Aprl. 4. I ride to Kidlington   4 m.
                              Dedington 10
          Attlebury, through a bad Ford,   2

Warwick Apr. 5, 1689. St. Mary's Chappel. Richd Beucamp's Statue in Brass very lively, veins and nails of 's hands. died 1439. Robert Dudley in Alabaster. *Spe certa resurgendi in Christo hic situs est &c. Obijt* 7, 4, 1588. Earl of Leicester.

Ld. Brook, slain at Leicester, in another part with a stately Marble round the edge of which is engraven,—Fulke Grevil servant to Queen Elisabeth, Councillor to K. James, and Friend to Sir Philip Sidney. No Statue. But Marble Pillars ab^t the Stone.[37]

Satterday Apr. 6, Got well to Coventry about an hour by Sun. By mistake of the Christian name, I goe to a King that is member of the Ch. to which Mr. Blower preaches. He informs me of Dr. Grew and that they have the Lord's supper. I wait on the Dr. who receives me very candidly and kindly but refers me to Mr. Briant because He cant be abroad. Lodge at the K's Head.

Ap. 7. went to Leather Hall and heard my namesake [*blank*] Shewell preach in the morn. Mr. Briant administered the Sacrament, Eating and drinking first himself, then Mr. Shewell, then the Deacons, then every one, saying Take, eat this in remembrance of Chr^t. Might be 200 Communicants.

Mr. Briant preaches in the afternoon. I hear Mr. Blower between.[38]

---

[36] In another place Sewall records: "Apr. 4 was shew'd the Library and Chapel of Corpus Christi Colledge and the Cellar by Mr. Holland, a Fellow. Library may be ab^t the bignes of Harvard." Dr. John Rainolds (1594-1607) was one of the translators of the Prophets for the King James Bible; so was Dr. Thomas Holland (d. 1612). There was no one named Holland at Corpus Christi at that time; perhaps Sewall remembered the translator's name instead of his host's.

[37] Sewall had a good eye. The striking and realistic effigy of Richard de Beaumont, Earl of Warwick (1382-1439), famous diplomat and warrior, by John Massingham, sculptor, is starred in Baedeker. Beàuchamp Chapel, a separate structure attached to the church, erected under Richard's will, is double-starred, a choice example of English medieval art. John Harvey, *Gothic England* (1948), pl. 82; Joan Evans, *English Art 1307-1461* (1949), 181-183, pl. 82-83. The tomb of Sir Fulke Greville, first Baron Brooke (1554-1628), the poet and statesman, is in the Chapter House.

[38] Thomas Shewell, M.A. Magdalen Hall, Oxford, had been Curate of Leeds up to the time of the Act of Uniformity. He shared the Presbyterian preaching at Coventry with Jarvis Bryan, M.A. Emmanuel College, Cambridge, sometime rector

Monday Ap. 8. I view Bp Gate street. Mr. Tho. King is dead, was a great Persecutor and help'd to put Dr. Grew in prison. Just above Bp Gate there is a Cistern of ab^t 17 yards square, the water brought in a leaden Pipe ¾ mile off, depth 5 or 6 foot, from thence the water runs into Brewing Vessels just within the Gate. View'd the Water work, the Wheel is over-shot, 3 Suckers, the water brought from a Spring partly throug the Pool in Pipes. Pool serves only to drive the wheel, Water carried to the heart of the City. Went into St Michaels steeple which the Sexton tells me is higher by several yards than the Monum^t, a wager of 20^s laid ab^t it and a man sent on purpose to measure it.[39] The Cross is a noble thing, Gilded, and many Kings, but not high, but little higher than the Houses. Alderman Owen shew'd me the City Hall, where saw my gr^t Grandfathers name without any alias.[40] Shew'd me St. Mary Hall which is a fair Thing and good Accommodati. for publick Feasts and Treatments.

The Room at entrance of which the Maiors names are, is call'd the Maiors Parlour. Din'd with Dr. Obadia Grew and his Daughter and 2 Kinswomen.

Tuesday Apr. 9, Din'd with mr. Sam Blower and his wife, then went to Capt. King's in Mich-Park Street where was Prayer by Briant, a Bro^r mr. Wills, and mr. Blower preach'd, Mr. Shewel prayd too. No Singing. Visited Cousin Powers, and Cous. Lapworth, whose maiden name was Ann Lee, hath a son at London Bp. G[*ate*] Street near the Bull, a Daughter at Eltham in Kent and a Daughter Mary at home of ab^t 20 years old a handsom maid.[41] I perceiv two Pastures worth ab^t 40£ *per* anum are divided between that Powers and 2 daughters of which this Lapworth one. Powers's was first given to his Bro^r, is call'd Barn-

---

of Old Swinford, Worcs. Samuel Blower, M.A. Magdalen College, Oxford, had been chaplain in the household of Samuel Dunch of Baddesley, Hants, who died in 1667 and left him £20 for life. *Calamy.*

[39] The steeple of St. Michael's, Coventry, completed in 1433, rises 294 feet, about four times the height of the nave. The cathedral was struck by an incendiary bomb on the night of 14 November 1940, and the interior burned out. The Monument, a fluted Doric column near the north end of London Bridge, commemorating the Great Fire of 1666 and erected in 1671-1677 from plans of Sir Christopher Wren, is 202 feet high.

[40] The family name anciently had been Shewell, and the diarist's great-grandfather may have been the one in his line to change the spelling; in this case he would have written his name Sewall *alias* Shewell. His will (P.C.C., Barrington, 63) as published in H. F. G. Waters, *Genealogical Gleanings in England* (1901), I, 153-155, makes no use of the alias, however.

[41] We are glad to see that Sewall, just turned thirty-seven, had an eye for a pretty girl. It was a critical eye, too, for on 22 February he referred to another young maiden as "comely enough."

field hard by the City. Is more Land at Stoke given by my Aunt Randall as this was. Told them who I was and offer'd to confirm their Right. Lapworth said he would not give 3ᵈ.⁴² Anne his wife knew my father and Mother at Warwick. *Wednesday Ap. 10,* Had 3 of the City Waits bid me good morrow with their wind Musick.—Went to Warwick found Mis Tuckey still from home, tells me by a Letter that will come home on Friday morn: I sent a Letter to her by Wᵐ Claridge. *Thorsday Apr. 11ᵗʰ* good weather, pretty deal of sunshine and no Rain all day.⁴³ I went with one Charles Emms to Guy Cliff and saw his Cave, drank at his Well, saw the Cellars cut in the Rock.⁴⁴ By the way I found my Pilot was a Quaker. Abᵗ 200 Hundred Soldiers I saw drawn forth in the morn to the westward of the Town, which had their Drums, Cross a Horseneck and a Trumpet being all Horsemen. In the Lord's Hall Guy's Pot was filld with Brandy Punch; when in the field heard the volleys and Huzzas, the Pope carried abᵗ

People, Soldiers and many others exceedingly debauch'd. Was Trim'd by one Jnᵒ Jarvis near the Upper parish Church, call'd Sᵗ Mary as the Lower is call'd Sᵗ Nicholas, at which Mr. Butler used to preach: Many remembʳ him, all speak him a very good Man.⁴⁵ It seems Guy's Tower which I went up on to view the Town, is the very Tower my

---

⁴² Following his entry of 12 April, Sewall has some notes: "A copy of Mis Randall's tripartite Indenture that leads to the Use of her Fine and Recovery, dated Octobʳ 20, 1645.—Mr. [Henry] Sewall's Will was prov'd Junij ult. 1628, Cur. Prær. Cant. Lond.—To the said [daughter] Margaret [Randall] during her natural Life and after her decease to the Heirs of her Body issuing, and for want of such issue of her body, to remain to the right heirs of me, the said Henry the Testator, for ever.—[Great-] Aunt Randall's Will dated May 4, 1646." Sewall had evidently obtained copies of these documents. Margaret Randall, widow, had died childless, leaving her property to various nephews and nieces, not "Heirs of her Body," but apparently all of the Sewall blood. Sewall was technically a more correct heir, but his efforts to turn an honest penny were bluntly ended by Cousin Ann Lee Lapworth's husband. Abstracts of the wills and other details can be found in H. F. G. Waters, *Genealogical Gleanings in England* i, 153-156, 811.

⁴³ The coronation of William and Mary took place at Westminster on the 11th while Sewall was looking about the town of Warwick.

⁴⁴ Guy's Cliffe, once the home of the Percy family, is about two miles from Warwick on the bank of the Avon. There is a cave on the grounds in which Guy of Warwick is said to have lived after a pilgrimage to the Holy Land in 925; his legendary feats in slaying the Dun Cow and the Danish giant Colbrand are chronicled in a French poem of the thirteenth century. Guy's porridge-pot and other so-called relics are exhibited in the Great Hall of Warwick Castle. W. S. Shears, *The Face of England,* 419.

⁴⁵ Henry Butler was vicar of St. Nicholas, Warwick, from 1643 to 1662, when he was ejected. *Calamy.*

Ld. Capel was once Prisoner in.[46] I lodge at the Cross-Keys in Castle-street, in the yellow Chamber next the Castle, fronting to the Street. Effigies of the late Ld. Brooks hangs there. *Friday Ap. 12*, very pleasant fair morn.

Oxford, *April 13th* 1689. Rec^d of Samuel Sewall the Horse of Jn° Stiles of Abbingdon, in good condition, with Bridle, Saddle, Saddle-cloth and nine shillings 6^d in full for his Hire, I say Rec^d *per* me.

DANILL FORKNER.

Paid mr. Die five shillings Earnest to goe in his Coach next Monday morn, Fare Ten Shillings £0-5-0

Apl. 14. Heard Dr. Hall at St Ole's, Dr. Smith at St. Mary's, Dr. Lethbridge at Carfax.[47] Visit Dr. Tho. Gilbert who gives me his Carmen Congratulatorium. *Ap. 15*, Come to Wickam where dine in K. Ch. 2^d Bedchamb^r, 4 Men, so we pay for the 2 Maids 12^d apiece. Rid through Uxbridge where drunk some Kans of Ale, from thence to London ab^t 7 o'clock. Passengers shew'd me the House where Uxbridge Treaty was held and say 'tis now haunted that none dare dwell there.[48] A lovely Stream runs throw the Town-House compass'd with a Brick Wall: Great part of the House now pulled down.

Sewall returned to London 15 April.

April 20, 1689. Writt to Mrs. Mary Batter by Bant. Shipped a Duz. Silver Spoons of Mr. Samuel Layfield, wt 19 oz. 1 p., cost £5.13.3. Received of Cous. Nathl Dummer for your account £5.16.3, freight, 5.8, so will be somewhat more than I have in my hands.

Apr. 20. Writt to Cous. Nath. inclosing Cous. Nath.'s Bill for Mrs.

---

[46] Arthur Capel, first Baron Capel, M.P., was an active royalist leader in the 1640's and aided Charles I's escape from Hampton Court in November 1647; he was condemned by the parliament in 1649 and beheaded. *D.N.B.*

[47] Sewall does not appear to have suffered any pain in attending these three ancient orthodox churches, though he pointedly kept out of the Anglican church in Boston. John Hall, D.D., was Fellow of Pembroke College, rector of St. Aldate's Church, and Lady Margaret Professor of Divinity; in 1691 he became Bishop of Bristol. Sewall probably called the church St. Ole's because that was what he heard; there is other evidence in the diary that he was troubled with deafness. St. Mary's has been the University Church since the fourteenth century; the preacher was probably Thomas Smith, D.D., Fellow of Magdalen College. Only the tower of St. Martin's Church, Carfax, now survives. Thomas Lethbridge, D.D., was Fellow of Exeter College. Joseph Foster, *Athenae Oxonienses*.

[48] Negotiations were begun at Uxbridge, Middlesex, 30 January 1645, between commissioners of Charles I and of Parliament, but they were broken off on 22 February; a part of the Treaty House, in which they were carried on, still remains. Wickam, above, is High Wycombe.

Batter's Spoons by Bant. *April 22.* Went on foot to Hackney through Brick-Lane, about ½ a mile long, and dined with Mr. Tho. Glover his Son, Brad, Thomson, their wives, Mr. French, and several Grandchildren. Eat part of two Lobsters that cost 3.9ᵈ apiece, 7ˢ:6ᵈ both.

April 20, 1689. Mr. Thomas Gooding [*Goodwin*] would be glad to see me at Pinnor.⁴⁹

April 24. Writt to Dr. Grew, inclosing my Psalm-Book, in Turkey-Leather, and 4 of Mr. Cotton Mather's Sermons. Paid Cous. Hulls Bookseller in full, 15.6. and 2ˢ for Pasting and Cover of my Gazetts. Went this day to White-Hall to attend the Earl of Shrewsbury about New England: are referred to Friday next.

April 23. With Mr. Mather waited on the Lord Wharton, and Sir Edward Harly.⁵⁰

London, April 26, 1689.

Hat in Hand &c.

Honoured Sir, Necessity puts men upon hard Shifts to find out some pretence or other for making their addresses to those from whom they may expect relief. There was Capt. John Hull, of Boston in N. E., with whom in his life-time you had some Correspondence by way of Merchandise. He died in Septʳ 1683, leaving a Widow and a Daughter, who is my wife; by whom I had an Estate that might afford a competent Subsistence according to our manner of living in N. E. But since the vacating of the Charter, and erecting a Government by Commission, the Title we have to our Lands has been greatly defamed and undervalued: which has been greatly prejudicial to the Inhabitants, because their Lands, which were formerly the best part of their Estate, became of very little value, and consequently the Owners of very little Credit. Sir, I am glad that you are returned again to England, to your Country, Possessions, and dear Relations, and to a Seat in Parliament. I hope your former Distresses will help you to sympathise with others in the like condition. I, and several besides me, are here far removed from our Wives and Children, and have little heart to goe

⁴⁹ Thomas Goodwin Jr. was minister of Pinner, Middlesex. His father, Thomas Goodwin, D.D., had been removed as president of Magdalen College, Oxford, and considered emigrating to New England, but the move was successfully opposed by his wife. *Calamy.*

⁵⁰ Charles Talbot, twelfth Earl of Shrewsbury, was Secretary of State; he had been one of the leaders of the Revolution, contributing to William III's support in Holland, and had landed with him in England the previous November. Sir Edward Harley (1624-1700) had been Governor of Dunkirk; he was a member of the Convention Parliament, sitting for Hereford. Philip Wharton, fourth baron, was a Puritan and did much to foster Mather's efforts in England; he had introduced him to James II and William III. *D.N.B.*

home before some comfortable settlement obtained, whereby we might be secured in the Possession of our Religion, Liberty and Property. I am informed some favorable Votes have been passed in the House of Commons, wherein N. E. was mentioned. I intreat your forwarding of such Votes as you have Opportunity, in doing which you will be a Partner with God, Who is wont to be concerned in relieving the Oppressed. I shall not take up more of your time from your momentous Employments. My hearty Service presented to you, I take leave, who am, Sir, your humble Servant,

SAM. SEWALL.

Above is Copy of my Letter to Tho[s] Papillon, Esq.[51]

April 25. Writt to my Unkle Ste[*phen*] Dummer. Sent the News of yesterday's Acts. Sent John Heifford and Mr. Taylor's Letters.

April 27. Mr. Danson introduced me, and I visited Mis. Beck, Mr. Dunche's Daughter, and her daughter, and Madam Horsman, formerly Dulcibella Dunch, and her daughter, near fifteen years old: hath also a Son, and buried two Children. Hath been a widow above ten years. Lives in John's Street in Piccadilly near Jacob's Well.

April 29. went to Greenwich with Mr. Mather, Whiting,[52] Brattle, Namesake: Supped at the Bear. Went through the Park to Mr. John Flamsted's, who shewed us his Instruments for Observation, and Observed before us, and let us look and view the Stars through his Glasses.[53]

April 29. In the morn saw the Westminster Scholars; 3 of them made Orations in Hebrew, Greek, Latin, before the Dean and Delegates. Cambridg Delegates sat now on the right hand, for they take turns. Sub-Dean also had an Epistle; as did the Dean and Delegates. The grave Dr. Busby sat by.[54]

April 30. Come to Deptford, where breakfast with Cheescakes: from thence to Redriff upon the River's Bank, where Dr. Avery's Cousin had us to a Gentleman who showed us many Rarities, as to

---

[51] Thomas Papillon, merchant and politician of Huguenot antecedents, was M.P. for Dover and London. He fled to Utrecht in 1684 to avoid payment of £10,000 damages awarded against him by a packed jury, but returned at the Revolution. *D.N.B.* There were Papillons in Boston from 1679. *Savage.*

[52] Probably William Whiting of Hartford, who was at this time a merchant in London, and in 1686 had acted as agent for Connecticut, addressing the throne in regard to their charter. *Savage.*

[53] John Flamsteed (1646-1719) was the first Astronomer Royal, a self-educated genius who laid the foundations for modern astronomy but wrangled much with Newton, Halley, and other contemporaries. *D.N.B.*

[54] Richard Busby, D.D. (Oxon.), famous schoolmaster and zealous churchman, was head of Westminster School from 1638 to 1695. *D.N.B.*

Coins, Medals, Natural and artificial things: from thence by water to Tower-Stairs, about 10 o'clock.

April 30. Queen's Birth-Day. Streamers, Flaggs, Guns. Writ to Mrs. Dulcibella Horsman, inclosed Mr. Cotton Mather's Sermons bound up in good Calv's Leather. Hat in Hand, &c. Spent 4.3^d apiece in going to Greenwich.

May the 2^d went with Capt. Hutchinson, and saw the Crown, Scepter, Armory, Mint, (none to see the Milling) Lions, Leopard. Visited Dr. Annesly.[55] He entertained us standing in the Garden, we went not into the house; carried Mr. Mather's Letter with us. [*May*] 3. went to White-Hall, are referred till Monday. Went to the Glasshouse and visited Mr. Harwood in Prescot Street, Goodman's Fields. His wife speaks French.

May 2. writt to Unkle Richard Dummer, transcribed Copenhagen.

May 3. went to the end of Southwark toward Newington Butts; as returned went into St. Mary Overies, saw the monument of Lockier, who died 1672, in the 72^d year of his age.[56]

Sabbath, May 5, 1689. Went to Dr. Annesly's in little St. Helena's, with Capt. Hutchinson, where the Lord's Supper was administered. The Dr. went all over the Meeting first, to see who was there, then spake somthing of the Sermon, then read the words of Institution, then prayed and eat and drunk himself, then gave to every one with his own Hand, dropping pertinent Expressions. In our Pue said: Now our Spiknard should give its smell; and said to me, Remember the Death of Christ. The Wine was in quart Glass Bottles. The Deacon followed the Dr., and when his Cup was empty filled it again: as at our Pue all had drunk but I, and filled the Cup and then gave it me;

[55] Sewall should have mentioned that the sights Elisha Hutchinson took him to see were in the Tower of London. Samuel Annesley, D.C.L. (Oxon.) was ordained by presbyters as early as 1644 as chaplain to the Earl of Warwick, but he did not get on well with Cromwell and had a spotty ministerial career. After 1672 he preached to Presbyterians in Little St. Helen's Place. He married a daughter of Century White (John White, M.P., 1590-1645), by whom he had twenty-four children. One daughter, Susanna, was the mother of John and Charles Wesley; another married John Dunton (p. 99 n), and a third married the notorious Thomas Dangerfield, an accomplice of Titus Oates. *D.N.B., Calamy*.

[56] The Church of St. Mary Overie, Southwark, is now the Cathedral Church of St. Saviour and the seat of the Bishop of Southwark. It is just south of London Bridge, and is very ancient. John Harvard was baptized there, and graduates of Harvard College added a memorial chapel in 1907. Nearby is the elaborate tomb of Lyonell Lockyer, with a long doggerel inscription extolling the virtues of his pills and a reclining figure of the quack-doctor himself, which still amuses visitors. More significant characters buried there are Gower, Bishop Launcelot Andrewes, Massenger, Fletcher, and Shakespeare's brother Edmund.

said, as gave it—must be ready in new Obedience, and stick at nothing for Christ.

Tuesday, May 7th went to Windsor, [*May*] *8th* Eaton, Hampton–Court, and so home.

May 8, 1689.[57] Queen's Bed-Chamber, 24 foot sqr. King's publick dining R. 32 ft. and near square.

Council Chamber	44
Breadth	24

3 windows to the River almost the height of the Room. Blew Damask Curtains.

St. George's Hall 32 yards 2 foot long. Breadth eleven yards, Five steps of Marble to an ascent pav'd with Marble, at the end of the Hall Eastward, over, St George painted on the side of the wall. At the West four Men supporting a Gallery between whom enter into the Chapel. The Communion Table at the West End. The floor of the Hall pav'd with coarser stone by much. Abt 32 foot high, 7 narrow windows 14 foot deep looking into the Court where Charles 2d on Horseback. Over each window a square window from which the Light descends through an oval lying long ways of the Hall.

Eaton Colledge Library 69 Foot long, the Shelvs four.

Thursday, May 9, went to H[*ampton*] Court, to wait on the King and Council. Mr. Mather not there: said he was feverish, yet I perceive was at Change. Sir Robt Sawyer[58] spake of the Quo–warranto in Ch[*arles*] the First's time, and supposed we had no Charter; asked if any had seen it. I said I had seen a Duplicate. Dr. Cox craved Day; so are to appear agen next Thorsday, and just as we were going out, by Sawyer's means were called back, and then he spake of the Quo-warranto for Misdemeanors, and we are ordered to attend the Attorney General with our Charter. As came home, were entertained by Mr. Stephen Mason with Cider, Ale, Oysters and a Neat's Tongue, being ten of us, or 11. This house is at Clapham, wherein Col. Bathe did dwell.

May 10, writt to Mr. John Richardson of Bristow, that had paid

---

[57] The descriptions under this date are taken from Sewall's Almanack, and (except for the last line of the entry) refer, not to Eton and Hampton Court Palace, which he visited the 8th, but to Windsor Castle, which he saw on the 7th. St. George's Hall is among the state apartments at Windsor and should not be confused with St. George's Chapel.

[58] Sir Robert Sawyer (1633-1692) had been the "chamber fellow," or roommate, of Samuel Pepys at Magdalene College, Cambridge, and was afterward attorney general under James II. In June 1688 he appeared as senior counsel for the seven bishops. Early in 1689 he was elected to the Convention Parliament for Cambridge University. *D.N.B.*

Mr. Ive, £10.16.7, for owners of Fidelity and £10.6.0, for my own proper account, as also, £1.6.3, for Mr. Peter Sergeant's proper account—£22.08.10. If any vessel get away from Bristow, give me a hint of it. If any happen to goe before you can send to me, tell Mr. Sergeant his N. E. friends and I were well this day.

Satterday, May 11th Declaration of War against France comes out.[59]

Sabbath, May 12, Capt. Hutchinson and I watched with Mr. Wharton at his Sister Pack's in Kirby Street, Hatten Garden. *Monday morn, May 13,* heard Mr. Read preach.[60]

Tuesday, May 14th, Mr. Richard Wharton dyes about 10 *post merid.*[61] He rid to Town the Wednesday before in order to goe to Hampton-Court last Thorsday. Monday, May 6, was at Westminster pleading against Mr. Blathwayt, in behalf of N. E. Mr. Brattle and I came down by water with him. *Wednesday, May 15,* went and dined with Fish at Capt. Kelly's upon Mr. Partrige's Invitation. Capt. Hutchinson, Clark, Appleton, Brattle, Hull, in company. Went to a Garden at Mile End and drunk Currant and Rasbery Wine, then to the Dog and Partrige's, and plaid Nine–Pins. At the house a Souldier was shot by his drunken companion the night before. Sir Samuel Dashwood has by the Poll 1000 and odd, and Sir Wm Ashurst 1700 and odd, for a Citizen to sit in Parliament. Mr. Perry has a new maid come, called Anne, from Chichester.

Thorsday, May 16, went to the Old Baily, the Court was holden by Pilkinton, Mayor, Lord Chief Justice Holt, Lord Chief Justice Pollixfen, Chief Baron Atkins, and 7 more Judges. Sat till 3 o'clock, in which time the London Jury returned and brought in four Verdicts, which they were charged with at once.

[*May*] 18, goe to Hampton Court in company of Capt. Hutchinson and Jo. Appleton; Mr. Mather, Sir Sam. Tomson, Mr. Whiting, and Mr. Joseph Tomson ridd in another Coach. Cost 21s apiece, besides money to the Drivers. Were dismissed *sine Die.* Mr. Ward and Hook our Council. Entertain Mr. Humphrys too. Just now about a virulent Libel comes out against N. E., the day Mr. Wharton buried.

59 Known as King William's War in America, this universal war against Louis XIV continued until the Peace of Ryswick, 20 September 1697.

60 Joseph Read, B.A. Trinity College, Cambridge, was ejected as rector of Great Witley, Worcestershire, in 1661, and had been imprisoned and fined for preaching in conventicles. *Calamy.*

61 Wharton had been a manufacturer of tar, turpentine, resin, etc. in Boston and a large purchaser of Pejepscot lands. He was a member of the Council under Andros, but opposed him, and went to London in 1687, with others, to complain against his measures. *Savage.*

Monday, May 20. Meet to answer the Print, and in the evening another accosts us, called an abstract of our repugnant Laws, full of Untruths almost as the former.[62] To comfort me when got home, met with a Letter from my dear Brother, by the way of Bilbao, dated the 12 March; all friends and my wife and Children well, but New England bleeding.

May 21, writt to Mr. Flavell of our N. E. Affairs. Writt of the 20th to Cousin Bear and Cous. Nath. Enclosed in a packet ¼ Hundred of Mr. Cotton Mather's funeral Sermons.

May 22. writt to Unkle Nath. to tell him of my Brother's Letter from N. E., dated March 12, and of the Sermons sent to be left at Cousin Bear's *per* Waldern. Cous. Nath, give him two.

May 23. Green Goose Fair. Agreed to pay, as Cous. Hull does, for being trimmed by the Quarter. Begin today.

Monday, May 27. Saw the Dutch Embassadors make their public Entrance. Came up through Crouched Friars, were about 50 Coaches, with Six Horses apiece, besides Pages on foot, and youths on Horsback. The main streets thwacked with people, and yet little miss of people in Fen-Church and Lumbard Streets.[63]

May 30th went to the Funeral of Mr. Agust, Non-conf. Minister, who used to preach on the Sabbath where Mr. Alsop keeps his Lecture. Hath left some Thousands to a little Daughter of 2 or 3 years

[62] The New England agents met to answer an anonymous pamphlet (Sewall's "virulent Libel" above) which came out the 18th: *Considerations humbly offered to the Parliament, shewing that those Charters relating to the Plantations were taken away upon quite different reasons from those in England, these Charters being seized for the abuse of their Power, in destroying not only the Woollen and other Manufactures but also the very Laws and Navigation of England, and making themselves as it were Independent of this Crown.* It is reprinted in the *Andros Tracts* III, 1-9. The second item that accosted them was *An Abstract of some of the Printed Laws of New England which are either contrary, or not agreeable to the Laws of England, which Laws will immediately come in force, in case the Bill in Parliament for the restoring the Charters of the Plantations doth pass, and are not controllable, by any authority in England, as they pretend by their Charters.* This is reprinted in the *Andros Tracts*, III, 11-16. Within a few days Mather published an anonymous answer, without imprint or date: *New-England Vindicated, from the Unjust Aspersions cast on the former Government there, by some late Considerations, pretending to shew, that the Charters in those Colonies were Taken from them on Account of their destroying the Manufactures and Navigation of England* (Holmes 81; reprinted in *Andros Tracts*, II, 111-123). See our note on the Corporation Bill (17 July 1689).
[63] These streets are in Aldgate. Crutched Friars Street traces its name to the Convent of Crouched Friars, founded in the neighborhood in 1298. A. J. C. Hare, *Walks in London*, I, 384.

old. Buried at St. Giles' Church from the 3 Compasses, Kirby Street, Hatten Garden, Dr. Gilbert principal Bearer.[64]

May 31. Went to Mr. Papillon to speak to him in behalf of N. E., who entertains me candidly, and promises to promote our Interest, and would have me take off [*dissuade*] those who may think contrarily. *May* 31. Is a Fast kept at Dr. Annesly's: they began with singing and sang 4 or 5 times. After all, had a Contribution. When came home, found a Letter from Cousin Quinsey, giving an account of the Health of my Wife, Children and friends, on the 26 March. Came by Woodbery from Bristow. Five Ministers exercised, Mr. Kentish, Dr. Annesly, Mr. Sclater, Mr. Franklin, Mr. Williams.[65] Four first wear their own Hair.

June 1. Writt to Cous. Hull for the last at Portsmouth. Writt to Unkle Stephen Dummer acquainting him with our friends welfare, March 26.

June 3, 1689. Capt. Hutchinson, Mr. Brattle and I went to Newington to visit Mr. Saltonstall, at his son-in-law Horsey's. I gave him two of Mr. Cotton Mather's Sermons. As came home saw one Elisabeth Nash, born at Enfield, about 25 Years old, just about Three foot high, not the breadth of my little finger under or over. Her Hands show Age more than anything else. Has no Brests. By reason of her thickness and weight can goe but very sorrily. Can speak and sing but not very conveniently, because her Tongue is bigger than can be well

---

[64] Benjamin Agus (or Agas), M.A. Corpus Christi College, Cambridge, had been rector of Chenies, Bucks, from 1649 until his ejection in 1662, and was later chaplain to the Earl of Angelsey. In 1682 he was convicted of holding conventicles at his house or meeting-place in the parish of St. Giles in the Fields, London. Vincent Alsop, M.A. St. John's College, Cambridge, took holy orders as a conformist, but later received Presbyterian ordination. He was rector of Wilby, Northants, and after ejection in 1662 preached semi-privately and suffered imprisonment. At this time he was lecturer at Pinner's Hall. He published numerous writings, and it is probable that the sermon Sewall mentioned 6 and 30 November 1685 was one of his. *D.N.B.* and *Calamy*.

[65] This was an important group of nonconformist divines. Thomas Kentish, M.A. Pembroke College, Oxford, was rector of Overton, Hants, at his ejection in 1660. He was arrested and imprisoned various times for preaching in London. Dr. Annesley has been identified above (2 May). Samuel Slater, M.A. Emmanuel College, Cambridge, was ejected at Bury St. Edmunds, Suffolk, in 1661, and was prosecuted in London. "Mr. Franklin" is probably Robert Franklyn, of Jesus College, Cambridge, sometime vicar of Westhall, Suffolk, ejected 1662, who was preaching as a Presbyterian in London at this time. Daniel Williams, D.D. (Edinburgh and Glasgow), did not begin to preach until 1667, and was afterwards one of the leading ministers in London. By his will he established and endowed Dr. Williams's Library, now in Gordon Square, London. *D.N.B.* and *Calamy*.

stowed in her Mouth. Blessed be God for my Stature, unto which neither I, nor my Dear Mother, my Nurse, could add one Cubit.

June 4. Green Hastings, i. e. Pease, are cry'd at 6ᵈ a Peck, in little carts. Cous. Hull, Mrs. Perry and Bedford come from Portsmouth. I meet them at the Cross Keys in Gracious Street.

June 10ᵗʰ Gave the Ch. Wardens of Cree-church,[66] for the relief of the Protestants of Ireland, four Crowns—£1.0.0. Writt to Richard Cornish copies of Mr. Tho. Read's Bonds, and the Affidavit by Bant, for fear of miscarriage, that so he might understand how his business lay and not be cheated out of his Money by his Unkle. Cousin Robert Andrews brings me a Letter from my Cousin of Swathling, his Mother-in-Law. Dines with us on a good Line of Veal and Strawberries.

June 11. Green Hastings are cry'd for a Groat [*fourpence*] a pcck.

June 12. Went and dined with Cous. Allen, with Beans, Bacon, and a very good Line Veal roasted. Beans 5ᵈ a Quart. Cous. Sarah played on her Flute. Cous. Atwell sings well.

June 13. Last night dreamed of Mr. Adams. We sign a Petition for leave to goe home. Write to Unkle Dummer to tell him he must come up to London, if he will make a Letter of Attorney for N. England.

June 15. Being at Mrs. Calvin's alone in a Chamber, while they were getting ready dinner, I, as I walked about, began to crave a Blessing, and when went about it remembered my Cloaths I had bought just before, and then it came into my mind that it was most material to ask a blessing on my Person: so I mentally pray'd God to bless my Flesh, Bones, Blood and Spirits, Meat, Drink and Aparrel. And at Dinner, paring the Crust of my Bread, I cut my Thumb, and spilt some of my Blood, which word I very unusually, or never before, have used in prayer to my present remembrance.

June 16. Last night I dreamed of my Wife, and of Father Hull, that he had buried somebody, and was presently intending to goe to Salem.

June 20ᵗʰ Writ to Cousin Storke, answering his of the 10ᵗʰ *inst.* Last Sabbath day night dreamed of the death of my dear Wife, which made me very heavy.

June 20. Went to hear Mr. Alsop,[67] where, in the utter [*outer*] part I saw Madam Horsman, who spake very kindly to me. About 10,

66 St. Katharine Cree Church (1631), Leadenhall Street, Aldgate, escaped the bombings of World War II.
67 Probably at Pinner's Hall, where Vincent Alsop was lecturing. See 30 May.

mane, I visited Mr. Nathan[1] Mather, who lives now in Fan[*Fen*]-Church Street. Betty Ward and her husband visit us June 24. Eat and drink at the 3 Tuns. Mr. Burfort visits us.

June 25. The Statue of Edward the first is set up on the Royal Exchange.[68] See Mr. Lake.

Wednesday, June 26. Mr. Mather, his Son, Cousin Hull and self, set out for Cambridge, 45 miles: got thither by 7 o'clock, with one set 4 Horses. Lay at the Red Lion in Petit Curie.[69]

Thorsday, June 27, Mr. Littel, Fellow of Emmanuel Colledge, shows us the Gardens, Walks, New Chapel, Gallery, Library of the Colledge, in it a Bible MS. of Wickliffe's Translation. Mr. John Cotton and Hooker had been Fellows, as appeared by Tables hanging up. Dr. Preston, Head of it.[70] The Street where it stands is called Preacher's Street, from Black Friars formerly resident there. *Note.* Said Fellow had in 's Chamber, Sir Roger Le Strange, Jesus Salvator and K. Charles, 2[d], hanging up together. Saw St. John's Colledg, which stands by the River. Hath a good Library and many Rarities, among which was a petrified Cheese, being about half a Cheese.[71] Trinity Colledge is very large, and the new Case for the Library very magnificent, paved with marble checkered black and white; under, stately walk on brave stone;[72] the Square very large, and in midst of it a Fountain. In the Hall many Sparrows inhabit, which is not known of any Hall beside. At meal-Times they feed of Crums, and will approach very near Men. King's Colledge Chapel is very stately. Went on the

[68] This was the second building of the Royal Exchange, Cornhill, opened 1669. It was destroyed by fire in 1838, and replaced by the present one in 1844.

[69] The Red Lion is still providing food, drink, and lodging in Petty Cury, and this editor drank a glass of lager to Sewall's memory there on the afternoon of 30 August 1958.

[70] Thomas Little, D.D., was afterward prebendary of Norwich Cathedral from 1700 to his death in 1731 (J. Venn, *Alumni Cantab.* III, 91). John Cotton, B.D., vicar of St. Botolph's, Boston, Lancashire, and Thomas Hooker, M.A., rector of Esher, Surrey, and minister of the English nonconformist church at Delft, came to America together in the summer of 1633. Cotton became teacher of the First Church of Boston, and Hooker was the first minister of Hartford (*D.A.B.*) John Preston, D.D. (1587-1628), famous Puritan preacher and author, was Master of Emmanuel College 1622-1628. (*D.N.B.*)

[71] The petrified cheese was also seen by Zacharias Conrad von Uffenbach, who visited St. John's College 29 July 1710 (J. E. B. Mayor, ed., *Cambridge Under Queen Anne,* 1911, p. 129), but it had disappeared by 1958, when this editor inquired for it.

[72] The noble library of Trinity College, designed by Sir Christopher Wren and built 1676-1695, deserves a better appellation than "Case," and we feel that "stately" is a distinctly inadequate description of the great architectural masterpiece of Cambridge, King's College Chapel.

top of the inward Stone Roof, and on the top of the outward Lead-Roof, and saw the Town, and Ely about 10 miles off. Below, on the side, under little Arches, is the Library. Mr. Littel dined with us at our Inn: had a Legg Mutton boiled and Colly-Flowers, Carrets, Rosted Fowls, and a dish of Pease. Three Musicians came in, two Harps and a Violin, and gave us Musick. View the Publick Library, which is in form of an L, one part not fil'd with books, some vacant shelvs to bespeak Benefactors. Saw the Divinity School over which the Regent House is. The School fair and large. Public Acts are kept in St. Marie's Church, over against which the Schools are. Just before night our Landladie's Son had us along Bridge-Street, and shewed us Sidney-Colledg as I take it, and be sure Magdalen Colledg on the other side of the River, on which side there is none but that. Went to the Castle-Hill, where is a very pleasant Prospect, the Prison and Sessions House just by, which is very ordinary, like a Cow-House. Cattell having free egress and regress there. Gallows just by it in a Dale, convenient for Spectators to stand all round on the rising Ground. Then went in Trumpington Street, which with this makes a [*here S.S. draws a T on its side*]. Most of the Colledges stand on Trumpington Street, and the oldest of all, Peter–House, next to Trumpington. I saw the Chapel in the outside of which 'tis said There was a great deal of Rome in a little Chapel: but Mr. Mompesson, Cousin's friend, not being within, saw not the Inside. 'Tis a small Colledge. St. Maries is a fair Church. In sum Cambridge is better than it shows for at first; the meanness of the Town-buildings, and most of the Colledges being Brick.

June 28. Mr. Harwood and I step'd out and saw Queen's Colledge, which is a very good one, in the Garden a Dial on the Ground, Hours cut in Box. The River has there also a quicker Stream, being a little below the Mill: have several Bridges to go over to their Groves. Over against it stands Katherine Hall, the New Buildings of which are some of the goodliest in Cambridge. By it, the Printing Room, which is about 60 foot long and 20 foot broad. Six Presses. Had my Cousin Hull and my name printed there. Paper windows, and a pleasant Garden along one side between Katherine Hall and that. Had there a Print of the Combinations. As came Homewards, saw Audley Inn, or End. I can't tell which is the right name. 'Tis a stately Palace.[73]

---

[73] Audley End is a fine Jacobean mansion near Saffron Walden, Essex, on the Cambridge-Bishop's Stortford road. It was built in 1603-1616 by Thomas Howard, first Earl of Suffolk, and latterly was the seat of the Barons of Braybrooke. Thomas Wright, *Hist. and Topography of the County of Essex* (1836), III, 111-112.

Din'd at Safron-Walden: went out and saw the Safron Roots, which
are Ten Shillings a Bushel, about an Acre might yield an hundred
pounds and more. Were just dugg up to be planted at Abington, a
little place not far off. Have a fair Church. I writt out the Lord Audley's Epitaph. Went into the Vault and saw the Earl of Suffolk's
Coffin, who died January last: stands on Tressels, and may see it in
the outside at the Grate. Outside is black Velvet, and a small plate
of Copper, telling time of 's Death: rest is garnish'd.[74] Lodg'd at
Hockerhill, pertaining to Bishop-Stafford. In the even, Mr. Sam.
Mather and I viewed Tuesday's Well and Castle Hill. Set out on Satterday, about 4 *mane*, breakfasted at Epping. Got to Mr. Cropper's
about Eleven aclock. He keeps a Coffee House. While Mr. Mather
read the Votes I took Thorsdays Letter and read the News of Boston,
and then gave it Mr. Mather to read. We were surpris'd with joy. At
Change Capt. Hutchinson shew'd me Capt. Byfield's Letter, which
comes by Toogood. They had the News on Change that day we went
to Cambridge.[75]

*The news was joyful indeed: in April the Bostonians had carried out a
quiet, well-bred, and bloodless revolution. On the fourth John Winslow, a
young Boston merchant, arrived from Nevis with the news that William
of Orange had landed in England. On the morning of Thursday the 18th,
lecture-day, rumors went about that armed men were collecting at the
North End and the South End; drums beat through the town and an ensign was set up on the beacon. Captain Hill marched his company up
King (now State) Street escorting several of the former magistrates, who
went to the Council Chamber. Meanwhile Captain George of the Rose
frigate, ashore, Secretary Edward Randolph, and others of the Andros
party were apprehended and locked up. About noon the magistrates appeared on the eastern gallery of the Town House and read a declaration to
the assembled people narrating the oppressions suffered by the colony
since the vacating of the charter and portraying at some length the mis-*

[74] Thomas Audley, Baron Audley of Walden (1488-1544), founder of Magdalene
College, Cambridge, and Lord Chancellor of England, had been given the Abbey
of Walden at the dissolution of the monasteries; he constructed a tomb for himself there during his lifetime. His descendant, James Howard, third Earl of Suffolk and third Baron Howard de Walden, keeper of the King's house at Audley
End, had died in December 1688, and was buried 16 January 1688/9 at Saffron
Walden. (*D.N.B.*) "Bishop Stafford," below, is Bishop's Stortford, Herts.
[75] Nathaniel Byfield's *Account of the Late Revolution in New-England* was licensed 27 June and printed immediately by Richard Chiswell in London; it is reprinted in the *Andros Tracts*, 1, 1-10. See Sewall's entry for 1 July.

government of Andros. It concluded: "We do therefore seize upon the persons of those few ill men which have been (next to our sins) the grand authors of our miseries; resolving to secure them for what justice orders from his Highness, with the English Parliament, shall direct . . ." Cotton Mather is presumed to be the author, and there is evidence that the uprising had been long planned and that only a suitable opportunity was wanting to put it in execution. The signal on Beacon Hill had done its work, and by two o'clock, in addition to the twenty companies paraded in Boston, several hundred soldiers were waiting on the Charlestown side. A summons was then sent to Andros in the fort on Fort Hill to deliver up the government and fortification. The lieutenant in command of the Rose frigate made the ship ready for fighting and sent a boat to bring off Andros and his attendants, but the crew was overpowered and disarmed by John Nelson and his party from the Town House bearing the summons to the governor. Andros and his retinue went back into the fort. The Nelson party then managed to get possession of some cannon in an outwork and point them at the fort. The governor sent West to confer with the men at the Town House, and when he returned with the reply, Andros and his party came forth disarmed. Sir Edmund was placed under guard in Hezekiah Usher's house, and the rest of the party put in jail. The next day the Castle, in the harbor, was surrendered by order of Andros, who had been threatened that if he did not do so, he would be exposed to the rage of the people. The guns in the ships and batteries were then trained on the Rose frigate. Captain George, who detested Randolph as much as the New Englanders, begged that he might not be required to surrender his ship, for by doing so he and his men would lose their wages; the revolutionists obliged, and the sails were brought ashore and locked away. Governor Andros was transferred to the fort, Randolph was placed in the common gaol, and the rest of the hated officials were kept at the Castle. Dudley, who had been absent at Long Island, was captured in the Narragansett country and placed under house arrest in Roxbury. "A revolution had been consummated, and the government of the King of England in Massachusetts was dissolved." A council of safety was organized immediately, two conventions of delegates from the towns were soon held, and there was a provisional reestablishment of the old government in May; these men carried on until the arrival of the new charter in 1692. On the 10th of February 1689/90 the whole Andros crowd was shipped off to England. Palfrey III, 577f.

[*Upon his return from the Cambridge journey Sewall recorded his expenses in his almanac:*] Wednesday June 26. 1689. Journey to Cam-

bridge, Mr. Increase Mather, Sam Sewall, Edward Hull, Sam
Mather. Breakfast at Epping in Essex £0- 2-3
Dine at the Crown in Hoggerill, a Hamlet of Bp. Stafford.
Two young Ducks in Hartford-shire 0- 6-2
Cherries brought from London, 25 Miles 0- 0-4
have none at the place. Water of Tuesday's well. Ruins of
an old Castle In the way from Bp. Stafford to Cam-
bridge 0- 2-3
Friday, June 28. Paid at the Red Lion, Cambridge . . . 1-13-0
Safron-Walden, Diner 0- 7-0
and view of Audley House Hockerill, Supper, and Maid . 0- 7-0

———————

2-18-0

June 29, Breakfast at Epping 0- 2-0
So Journey Cost me ab^t 35^s besides what gave to persons that
shew'd us the Colledges and Audley H.

July 1. Writt to Cousin John Dummer by Walden, the Waggoner,
inclosing four of the N. E. Revolutions; one to Winchester, one to
Bishop-Stoke, one to Southhampton, and one to Rumsey. Paid him a
Groat. They come out publickly this day, by the Hawkers.

LONDON, July, 2. 1689.

HON'D SIR, I have just now read the noble Petition of the Citizens of
London, in the Common Hall assembled, the 24th past, whereby I hope
the honorable Commons of England will be effectually moved to expedite
the Bill for restoring Corporations to their Ancient Rights and Priviledges, in doing which I am very glad that yourself is so ready to bear a
part. I have met with a Letter written to the Queen when Princess of
Orange, in behalf of New England, which I intreat yourself and Lady
to accept of, from, Sir, your humble Servant, S. S.
To THO. PAPILLON, Esq.

July 2, 1689. Writt to Mr. Zech. Tuthill, of Yarmouth. Thanked
him and his Sister for their good Company in the America. Enclosed
N. E. Revolution, Guild Hall Petition, June 24, and 8 of Mr. Kick's
Letters to the Queen. Send by the Coach, Rich'd Oakman. 1^s 6^d

Disposal of Revolution, the Duz. Capt. Hutchinson deliver'd me
this day, *July 3. 1689 [in London].*

To Dr. Annesley . . . . One.
To Mr. Layfield . . . . One.
To Cousin Allen . . . . 1.
To Mr. Gilbert of Oxf. ⎫
and Mr. Danson . ⎬ . . . . . . 3.

To Dr. Grew of Coventry . . . . 1.
To Mrs. Tuckey, Warwick . . . . 1.
To Madam Horsman . . . . 1.
    Piccadilly
To Mr. Goldwire, Baddesly, Hampshire . . . . 1.
To Mr. Alsop . . . . 1.
Keep one for my self . . . . 1.
To Dr. Nehemiah Grew . . . . 1.
To Mr. Goodwin . . . . 1.
To Cousin Tho. Dummer, Portsmᵒ . . . . . 1.

July 4, 1689. Copy of a Letter to Dr. Obadia Grew, at Coventry.

HONOURED AND DEAR SIR, My Countrymen and dear Friends in New England, being animated, as I hope, by the Spirit of Life from God, have endeavour'd to write after your Copy here in England, which I counted myself oblig'd to give you an account of, and have accordingly inclos'd it, earnestly entreating your Prayers that God would establish the work of their hands upon them, and give them Light and Direction for every step they have to take. We have some hopes of getting home before winter. The dangers of the Passage are now multiplied. I crave your Remembrance of us that we may be preserved from them all, and carried securely to Boston, or, however, to a better Haven (if that be denied) even to Heaven, which will be the more so to me by reason of meeting yourself there. One of our New-England Gentlemen died the 14ᵗʰ of May last, herc in Town. The Survivers are in good health. Pray, Sir, present my Service to Mr. Briant, Mr. Blower, and my Namesake, your Assistants, to Mr. King and your own family. Accept the same to your self from him who is your obliged friend. I have inclos'd the Noble Petition of the Londoners, the answere of which we are waiting for, New England being much concern'd in 't. Inclosed also Mr. Kick's Letter to the Queen. Hat in hand, &c. SAM. SEWALL.

Writt yesterday to Dr. Tho. Gilbert of Oxford, enclosing the Print of N. E. Resurrection, and Mr. Kick's Letter.

July 4, Writt to Mrs. Hannah Tuckey, of Warwick, enclosing a Print of the Revolution in New England, four of Mr. Cotton Mather's Sermons, and Mr. Kick's Letter to the Queen. Hat in hand.[76]

[76] The letter from Abraham Kick, merchant of Amsterdam, to Queen Mary is dated from The Hague, 1 February 1689. This was a separate printing. Increase Mather included the letter in his *Brief Relation of New England* (see the note to 31 July).

July 6, '89.

To Mr. Tho. Goodwin,

SIR, Capt. Brookhaven did a pretty while since signify to me a desire you had to see me at Pinor [*Pinner*], which is to me very obliging, who am a Stranger in this Land. I hope before my return I may have an Opportunity to pay you a Visit. 'Tis little is here to be done, and yet for all that I find it inconvenient to be out of the way, one thing or other presenting of a sudden, wherein we that are here count it our Duty if we can in anything assist Mr. Mather. I have inclosed a printed account of what has lately happened in New England, which I would fain hope is their Resurrection, and not a *praeludium* of it only. What is there transacted seems to be well resented [*regarded*] at Court, and the King promises to doe what is in His power towards restoring our Liberties. If you come to Town, I should be glad to see you on the N. E. Walk, or at my Chamber. Desiring your Prayers that all things may work together for Good, respecting N. E. and me, I take leave, who am, Sir, your obliged friend and Servant,   S. S.

Hat in hand, &c.   Peny Post.[77]

[*July*] 5, 1689. Cousin Hull comes in with a Countenance concern'd, and tells me sad News for me, which was that had rated me as a Merchant, £10.0.0. 'Tis inconvenient, but I wish I hear no worse news.

[*July*] 7. Goe and hear Mr. Stretton,[78] and sit down with him at the Lord's Supper. He invites me to dinner. Text, Hosea, 2. 14. Before Sermon read the 32 Psalm, the 50th of Jeremiah, the 12th of Matthew. Had one plate of bread, about 5 Bottles of Wine, and two Silver Cups. At night about 10 aclock, a great fire breaks forth in Mincing Lane. I was hardly asleep between 10 and 11, before there was a sad Alarm and Noys of Carrs to carry away Goods. A Woman lately brought to Bed was fain to be remov'd to another House. I went and sat a little while with Mr. Mather in Fan [*Fen-*] Church Street.

July 8. Went with Mr. Brattle and swam in the Thames, went off from the Temple Stairs, and had a Wherry to wait on us: I went in

[77] Provision for a complete penny postal system was not made by the English government until 1711. The convenience which Sewall used was a private enterprise, devised in 1681 by Robert Murray, an upholsterer, who soon made it over to William Dockwra, a London merchant. M.H.S.EDS. and *D.N.B.*

[78] This is probably Richard Stretton Jr., who was minister at York Buildings, Strand, in 1688. His more famous father, Richard Stretton, M.A. New College, Oxford, was ejected at Petworth, Sussex, in 1660, and later pastor of a congregation which met in Shoemakers' Hall, London; however, in 1689 he was preaching in Oxford "at an antiquated dancing school outside the north gate." Wood, *Athenæ Oxonienses*, as quoted in A. G. Matthews, *Calamy Revised.*

in my Drawers. I think it hath been healthfull and refreshing to me.[79]

July 9. Cousin Brattle, his wife and Daughter, Mrs. Shinkfield, Mr. Crossman, were invited to Dinner by Cous. Hull. Afterward, He and I went to Stepney, saw Thomas Saffin's Tomb,[80] one end of 't joins to the wall. 50ˢ was given for the Ground. Tis a very large burying-place. Were to be ten buried this night: we saw several Graves open and the Bones thick on the Top. Saw a Bowling Green where is 3 or 4 Sets of Bowls. The Lord help me aright to improve my Flesh, Bones and Spirits, which are so soon to become useless, and it may be expos'd in one part or other of God's Creation.

Wednesday, July 10ᵗʰ. Between 12 and 1 it grows very dark, thunder, Lightening and Rain, much like a N. E. Thunder Shower: but the Thunder not so sharp.

July 11. 1689. Receiv'd of Mr. Samuel Layfield, by his Servant, £20.0.0.

July 12. This day two stood in the Pillory before the Royal Exchange for speaking against the Government. Shears was one. They were exceedingly pelted with dirt and Eggs. Another, that stood for forgery, had none thrown at him that I took notice of. Cousin Hull startled me again this day in the even, saying with a concern'd Countenance, there was bad News for me, which was, that my Suit of Cloaths was in danger of being Moth–eaten. Treated Jnᵒ Rawson at the Clubb to day. He belongs to the Pearl Frigot, a 5ᵗʰ Rate, 30 odd Guns.

July 13. Paid Joseph Cliffe, Collector of Poll Money, Ten pounds one Shilling. [A few lines are illegible.] Mr. Wotton gave me a very good Book, well bound and Lettered on the Back, of Mr. Flavell's.

Monday, July 15ᵗʰ. I rid to Tyburn, and saw Eighteen Persons, 16 Men and 2 Women, fall. They were unruly in the Prison, which hasten'd their Execution. Din'd in Great Russell Street, view'd the House and Walks of Lord Montague:[81] then ridd to Hemsted. Mon-

---

79 The Temple Stairs, a landing-place extending across two stone arches well into the river, within the Inner and Middle Temple Grounds, can easily be found on old London prints, but the exact site is now covered by the Victoria Embankment.

80 Thomas Saffin was the son of Judge John Saffin of Boston; he died of smallpox 18 June 1687 at twenty-three. His epitaph was copied and commented upon in Addison's Spectator, No. 518, 24 October 1712. N.E.H.G.R. IV, 109.

81 Montague House, Great Russell Street, Bloomsbury, the town house of Ralph Montague, third Baron Montague of Broughton, was a new building, replacing an earlier one destroyed in a fire 19 January 1685/6. It was purchased by the government and the British Museum established in it in 1753. (Wheatley and Cunningham, London Past and Present II, 555-556.) The present buildings of the Museum were erected on its site beginning in the mid-nineteenth century.

tague House makes a goodly Shew that way. Hempsted is a most sweet and pleasant place for Air and shady Groves. Bought the Gazett there. From thence ridd to Highgate, which is about a Mile. There drank at the Crown, and then came home by Islington. Then went to the funeral of Mr. Loves,[82] formerly an Assistant to Dr. Owen. Was buried in a Grave near the Dr.'s Tomb. A pretty many Men and Women there. Was carried from Armorers Hall in Coleman Street to the new burying Ground.

July 16. Saw London Artillery Company pass by about 2 aclock. Most had Buff Cloaths and Feathers in their Hats. Marched 5. 6. 7. and Eight in a Rank. The Pikes. Had Musick besides the Drums.

July 17. Mr. Mather, on Change, told Capt. Hutchinson and Sam. Appleton that he had put in their Names as Witnesses to Sir Edmund [*Andros*]'s raising Money without an Assembly. Ask'd where was Capt. Hutchinson. I shewed and went with him to him, and Mr. Mather ask'd him to be at Westminster at such a time, but said not a word to me. Afterwards I went home, and then went to Mr. Whiting's and told him that I could testify, and Mr. Walker that collected the Money was in Town. He seem'd little to heed it, and said I might be there: he knew not that I could testify: but he seems plainly to be offended, and for my part I can't tell for what. A Moneth or two agoe Mr. Mather spake something about it, and I said I could not tell whether 'twere so convenient then, because we hop'd every day for the Parliament Act to come forth, and thought Sir Edmund might have friends there, and such a thing as this might make them more desperately eger to hinder the Bill. But now the Bill is even despair'd of, and our friends in N. E. are in for Cakes and Ale, and we must doe all we may and swim or sink with them.[83]

July 18, 1689. Sent Cousin Mary Atwell one of Mr. Flavell's Books to Toothill, a place about 7 miles off, where she is for the benefit of the Aer. Mrs. Katharine Norcott of Hogsden, widow, makes her Will on March 11th 1683. Prov'd August 27, 1685. Mr. Tho. Rowe, John Rowe, and William Rowe are Executors. In the Will is this Clause.— *Item*. To my dear Kinswoman Mis. Jane Poole, in Boston, in New

[82] Isaac Loeffs, M.A. Peterhouse, Cambridge, was ejected at Shenley, Herts, in 1662 but remained there preaching locally until about 1675, when he removed to London. He died 10 July 1689. *Calamy*.

[83] The purpose of the Corporation Bill, a Whig measure, was the restoration of the town and plantation charters vacated during the last two previous reigns, which, if decided, carried with it the fate or fortune of Massachusetts. Though the bill was passed by the Commons, Parliament was prorogued in January 1690 before the Lords could take action upon it. T. J. Holmes, *Increase Mather* . . . *Bibliography* II, 374.

England, five pounds, if she be living, if not, I give it unto her Son Theophilus.[84]—Mr. Thomas Rowe, who shewed me the Will and executes it, lives in Ropemakers Alley in Morefields. Capt. Hutchinson, Mr. Sam. Appleton and I went to Westminster to give an Evidence for N. E., but there was not an opportunity. So must wait on Mr. Mather again another time. Writt to my Unkle Stephen, thank'd him for his Love, of which I was unworthy, will come down if I can. Writt him the News of the Gazett and the burial of Mr. Loves.

July 19. I was in the Shop to read a Print Cousin Hull had took in about Ireland, and Madam Owen and Madam Usher passed by, so I invited them and they kindly came up to my Chamber. I treated them with a Glass of good Cider. Gave Madam Owen one of Mr. Cotton Mather's Sermons, the Revolution of N. E., and Mr. Kick's Letter. Advis'd with Mr. Mather about Mis. Pool's Legacy. He would remit the Money by Bill of Exchange, if it were to Him.

July 19. Mr. Matthew Wotton, Bookseller, sends me by his Servant a parcell of Englands Duty, which are 25, the Sale of which in N. E. I am to warrant, if I doe well get there; not else. Are sent to Mr. Joseph Branning, at Boston, New England. I pay him the frait for them.

July 21. Went in the afternoon to Stepney, and heard Mr. Lawrence. He fears the Clouds returning after the rain as to Antichristian powers. His heart much upon the 1000 years. Something in this Sermon, and I perceive by them that know: few Sermons without. Gives notice that Mr. Crouch, the Minister, dead, and will be buried tomorrow, 5 aclock, from Armorour's Hall. Sat with Mr. Paice.[85]

July 22, 1689. Mr. Joseph Paice and I saw Mr. Increase Mather Sign, Seal and Deliver an Obligation to Mr. Stephen Mason for 150 pounds English Money with Interest this day 2 Moneth, as I take it. Two Bonds signed and sealed of the same tenor. Sealed at the N. E. Coffee house with my *Anchora Spei.*[86]

[84] Theophilus Pool was probably the son of William Pool of Dorchester, Massachusetts, and brother of Bethesda Pool, mentioned by Sewall 10 January 1676/7. William Pool and his sister Elizabeth are credited with being the founders of Taunton, Massachusetts. Sewall's entry of 3 August implies strongly that Theophilus was dead. M.H.S.EDS. and *Savage.*

[85] Richard Lawrence, M.A. Pembroke College, Oxford, was ejected from the rectorship of Trunch with Swafield, Norfolk, in 1660, and became pastor of a congregation in Amsterdam. Later he preached for nearly thirty years at Stepney. John Crouch was ejected as vicar of Alderbury, Wilts, in 1662 and had been fined in 1682 for preaching in his house in White's Alley, London. *Calamy.*

[86] Probably Sewall's seal ring. We have not been able to locate any surviving impressions from it.

To 2 ounces Mannæ 0.1.0

To 4 quarts Northall Water, by Dr. Morton's Directions—0.1.0.

Paid Mrs. Cooper in full for washing my Clothes and making up Linen—0.1.4.

July 23. The White Regiment marches into the Artillery Ground, of which the Lord Mayor is Colonel, and so they have the Preeminence. Consist of Eight Companies, 14 or 15 hundred in the whole, perhaps. Some had Silver Head-pieces: Mr. Layfield for one.

July 24. Benj. Hallawell visits me. I give him my frize Coat, and Right Thoughts, bound with Mr. N. M. Life.[87]

Wednesday, July 24. Dine at Cous. Brattles, in company of Cous. Brattle, his Wife, Cous. Hull, Mr. and Mis. Perry, Mr. Crossman, Mis. Shinkfield, Cousin Mary, and a Gentlewoman of Farnum. Had a Dish of Bacon with Pidgeons, Sauce, Beans and Cabbage. Then roast Veal. Tarts. After, walk'd with Mr. Brattle, Jenner, Nicholson, Cooper, Breading, to Blackwall. View'd Sir Henry Johnson's Dock, where the Ships ly afloat at Low water, the Gates keeping in the Water. A very great Ship building there now. From thence went on board the Mehetabel, and then on board the America, at Bugsby hole. So to Blackwall again, which has two little Streets like a Carpenters Square. Walk'd home. I fell down and hurt my right hand and left Legg on the Gravel. Standard out and Bells ringing for joy the Princes Anne is brought to Bed of a Son.[88]

[87] Nathaniel Mather (Harvard 1685), son of Increase, entered college at twelve and devoted himself so excessively to study that his frail body gave way before he was twenty. Sewall visited him in his last illness at Salem, 25 September 1688, and noted his death 17 October 1688. Cotton Mather wrote a biography of his brother, *Early Piety, Exemplified in the Life and Death of Mr. Nathanael Mather*, which was printed in London in 1689, his first book to be printed there. A sermon of Cotton Mather's, *Right Thoughts in Sad Hours*, had also been printed in London in 1689, probably at Sewall's expense. It is dedicated "To My very Worthy Friend, Mr. S.S." (T. J. Holmes, *Cotton Mather . . . Bibliography*, I, 286-293; III, 927-929). The Nathaniel Mather whom Sewall visited 20 June 1689 was an older brother of Increase. He was born in England, took his degrees at Harvard in 1647 and 1650, and returned to serve as parish minister under Cromwell. He was ejected in 1662 and went to Holland. In 1671 he succeeded his brother Samuel (Harvard 1643) as a Congregationalist pastor in Dublin, and when New England was devastated by King Philip's War, he was active in procuring a shipload of provisions sent by the Irish for the relief of the distressed here. (Boston reciprocated in 1847 and sent a shipment of provisions to the sufferers of the potato famine in Ireland.) Nathaniel Mather had come to London in 1688 to take charge of a congregation in Lime Street. *Sibley.*

[88] Princess (later Queen) Anne had married George, Prince of Denmark, in 1683; several children were born to them, but all died young.

July 24. paid my Barber 2^s 4^d, Man, 2^d—£0.2.6.

Borrow'd and rec'd of Samuel Sewall, Money of England, Twenty Shillings. I say, Borrow'd and rec'd *per* me

BENJAMIN HALLAWELL.

£1.0.0.

July 25. I begun on Tuesday to drink Northall Waters by advice of Dr. Morton, ½° Manna in the Water each morning. To day he adviseth me to leave off putting in Manna, and to hold on drinking the Water a week or fortnight.

July 26. Bought at Hoiburn a Greek Testament and Sheppard's Abridgment of the Laws—0.18.6.

Satterday, July 27 Writt to my Wife, to go by Dartmo[*uth*], Capt. Lewis advising that there was a vessel going to N. E. from thence.

Monday, July 29, Standing in the Shop about 7. *mane,* Mr. John Usher comes to the door, which surpriseth me. Foy is at Pezans. Mr. Usher came to Town Satterday night. Sir William [*Phips*] and Lawson arriv'd; all friends well. He knew not of his coming away till a day or two before. Is very confident, and hopes to be going home in seven weeks, or to be at home in little more than that time. I go and acquaint Mr. Mather, who had heard nothing of it. He hastens to tother end of the Town. The Lord save N. E. I spoke to Mr. Usher not to do harm, as knowing the great King we must finally appear before: because he spake of going to the King. King is proclaim'd at Boston. Mr. Cook had like to have been kill'd with a fall from his horse. This 29th July the Jews have great joy by reason of a Priest come to Town in the Harwich Coach, they having not had one a long time. Mr. Ekins his Wife and Daughter here.

July 30th Rec'd of Mr. Tho. Rowe, Five pounds English Money. This Money by order and [*illegible*] account of Mrs. [*Jane*] Pole, widow, of Boston. This five pounds is in full of a Legacy given said Pole by Mrs. Katharin Norcott de^{c}d, in her last Will and Testament; whereof said Rowe is one Executor £5.0.0. *Vide* July 18. at tother end of this Booke.

July 31. N. E. Convention printed her, 500 Copies.[89] Visited Mr. James, but found him not at home: Sat a little while with 's Daughter, but he came not in. Left Him N. E. Revolution and Convention.

---

[89] Sewall is referring to Increase Mather's *A Brief Relation of the State of New England* (Holmes 17), which was licensed 30 July 1689 and published anonymously by Richard Baldwine. It is reprinted in the *Andros Tracts,* II, 150-170.

July 31. To a Map of England, Scotland and Ireland 0.10.6. Large one of London 0.2.6.

Went and was Trim'd by Cousin Henry Ward, and gave his wife, who sat by him in the Shop ½ Duz. Silver Spoons, marked E. W. 1689. Cost 63^s of Mr. Layfield, weighing 10^{oz} 11^P—8^s fashion, £3.3.0.

Aug. 1. News Letter. A Ship is arriv'd at Penzans in Cornwall, from New England, and reports that that Government has in all their Towns and Cities proclaimed William and Mary their rightfull Soveraigns,[90] and caused all Processes of Law, and otherwise, to run in their Majesties Names, and are sending over two persons in the nature of Envoys, to have their Liberties confirmed and to pay fealty for the same. I read the above-written at Temple-Bar, at Cheapside and Algate, in the very same words. Capt. Hutchinson trails a Pike to day under his Cousin, in Sir Tho. Stamp's Regiment, the Green. His is the 3^d Company—i.e., the 6th, reckoning in the field–officers.

Aug. 1, 1689. To Mr. Wotton, for Baker's Chronicle, £0.17.6.

Aug. 3. Lent and paid [*John*] Rawson, five Shillings, as per Receipt. Mother-in-Laws Name is Margaret James, next the Dogg, on the Left hand, without Bishop Gate—£0.5.0.

Aug. 3, 1689. Writt to my Wife by Dartmo[*uth*], inclosing Thorsdays Gazett, this days Scotch Paper, telling of Gov. Bradstreet's Letter by Peck being come to hand from Berwick: though none from Foy, whoes Passengers have been in Town this week. Pay Mrs. Pole 6. 10. 0. for £5 received here, Mrs. Norcott's Legacy, with abstract of the Will. Mr. Mather presents his Respects, and says that Sir Henry Ashurst told him the Country had put as much honour on him in sending the Address to him as if the Emperour had made him his Envoy. Corporation–Bill sticks in the Birth. Mr. Ratcliff follows his business close. Capt. Nicholson, 'tis reported, will be Governour of New York. Many of us desirous to come home, but judge not fit to come without a Convoy. Service to Gov. Bradstreet, Mr. Willard, Moodey, thanks for their Labour of Love. Glad was a Fast at our

---

[90] The proclamation of William and Mary in Boston 29 May 1689 was attended by a joyous celebration such as never had been seen in the colony before. People flocked in from the surrounding towns; there was a great horseback procession of the government officials, the "principal gentlemen," and the military; "there was a great dinner at the Town House for the better sort; *wine was served out in the streets* [italics ours]; and the evening was made noisy with acclamations, till the bell rang at nine o'clock, and families met to thank God at the domestic altar for causing the great sorrow to pass away, and giving a Protestant King and Queen to England." *Palfrey* III, 589-590.

House in April. Duty to Parents, Love to Brothers, Sisters, and to thee and our dear Quaternion. S. H. E. J.[91]

Aug. 6. Writt to Cous. Quinsey by Faymouth, of Foy's Arrival and delivery of the Country's Letters. Writt to Eliakim to the same purpose.

Aug. 7th Went with Mr. Mather, Mr. Whiting, Mr. Samuel M[ather] and Mr. William Whiting. Saw the Hall Chapel, Council Chamber, and some of the Lodgings of Chelsey, about 26 in one Gallery. Very lovely Cellar, two rows of Pillars that support the upper floor. Saw the Physick Garden, and in it among other things, an Olive Tree, Orange Tree, Cortex Peruvianus.[92] Cost about 20ˢ. When was at Mr. Whiting's, Mr. Lobb came in and spake of hot discourse in Council last Sabbath-day, about sending a Governour to N. E. Sir William Waller, to prevent others as he says, has petition'd to be Governour.

Aug. 8. Writt to Cous. Nath¹ Dummer, inclosing Bro. Stephen's; bid him send by the first Post any Letters he intends for New England because Ships just ready to sail. Writt to the Widow Brunton of Whitehaven, and to Mr. Robert Johnson of Dunfrey in Scotland that [they] would remit to Mr. Ive for my Account of Money [they] have in their hands of Ketch Tryal, of which Mr. John Winslow own'd ⅛ and I ⅜: both made Mr. Ive our Attorney: Mr. Addington and Mr. Dan¹ Quinsey in my behalf, supposing I had been at Sea homeward bound, they being my Attorney: I approve of the Person they have pitch'd on and intreat them to apply to him. Have been great Losers, having receiv'd nothing of Ketch or hire. Am with Mr. Edward Hull, at the Hat in Hand, within Algate, London. If I am gon he will give Mr. Ive the Letters sent first Post.

Aug. 8. Writt to Mr. Zech. Tuthill inclosing a N. E. Convention.

Aug. 8. To 2 Pole's Annotations and 2 Catechises. £4.8.o. Leusden's Hebrew Bible—o.18.o.

Rec'd of Mrs. Rebeckah Barrett one Letter with a Token to Madame Leverett at Boston, her only Sister.

91 The quaternion consisted of the four Sewall children then living: Samuel, Hannah, Elizabeth, and Joseph.
92 The Garden for Medical Plants was instituted at Chelsea in 1673 by the Company of Apothecaries, and was the basis of the subsequent improvements in the interest of medical botany made by Sir Hans Sloane, who brought Peruvian bark into general use. Mr. Lobb was probably Richard Lobb, who married Nathaniel Mather's wife's sister (Mather Papers, 3 M.H.S. Colls. VIII, 468). Sir William Waller (d. 1699) seems to have been a person of as much elevation of character as Titus Oates. D.N.B.

Aug. 9. Visited Madam Usher, Loyd, Harfield, Cous. Bridget, Madam Blackwell, and took my leave of them. Mr. Mather came in.

Aug. 9. To 3 Bushels and 3 pecks very good boiling Pease—£0.13.

Madam Usher sends a small Book to Mr. Moodey by me.

Rec'd of Mr. Layfield—£16.17.0 Cash and the Spoons, July 31., now writt off, which come to £3.3.0—£20.0.0., which is, as suppose, in whole of my Bill.

To Mr. Increase Mather for New England £27.0.0.

Aug. 10. Writt to Mis. Pole that I had received her Legacy given by Mrs. Katherine Norcott: send Acquittances. My hearty service to Mr. Stoughton. Gave her full Instructions as to the Will. Bant [*shipmaster*].

Aug. 10. Writt to my dear Wife enclosing Mr. Mather's Receipt for £100, use of N. E. Bant.

Aug. 11. Sung, or rather wept and chatter'd, the 142 Psalm, in course. Mrs. Perry ill, kept her Bed yesterday.

In the Barrel, Aug. 12. '89., one Set Poles Synopsis Criticorum: Two pair Annotations, *ditto*.

Aug. 12. To 2 more Poles Annotations, put up this day, £4.8.0.

Left for Cousin Hull to pay Mr. Parker's Bill: Mr. Alford for my Watch, Mr. Dunton.

Paid 40£ to the Heirs of Mr. Stephen Winthrop for Releases of Meetinghouse Ground and my Warehouse: fain to take up the Money of Mr. Hall and give bond with Cousin Hull, and counter-bond to Cousin Hull, £40.0.0: was fain to doe it in a hurry, Capt. Willie not being come from sea till very lately. Gave Mrs. Perry Clarks Examples. To Mr. Walter Perry in full for Board from June 24 to this day at 8ˢ *per* Week—£2.16. Borrow'd of Mr. Perry, Seven Guineas in Gold—£7.10.6.

Gave a Note to Mr. Stephen Mason that if he would accommodate Madam Usher with £5., I would see it repaid. Left to Cousin Hull, to pay the Lines—£13.16.0. Hooks 0.11.6.

Paid of the Chees	0. 8.	0
Lines	13.16.	0
Hooks	0.11.	6
7 Guineas of Mr. Perry	7.10.	6
Mr. Parker	25. 2.	9
Mr. Alford, Stockings	3.15.	0
Borrow'd to Lend New-England	27. 9.	2

78.12.11

Hat, for Self and Son 2.7.0.

Muffs, Jarman Serge 5.15.0.

Cousin Hull, Dr. To Cash paid him, which rec'd of Mr. Whiting £5.0.0
Bill to pay Bennet, of Ipswich 5.0.0
for which sum of £10, Brother Stephen Sewall is to have Credit, I having rec'd it, or with 20ˢ of Cousin Nath Dummer, John Edwards Money.

Tuesday, Aug. 13. Came with Capt. Hutchinson, Mr. Brattle, Partridge, Appleton from Salutation at Billingsgate to Woolige, where din'd with Mr. Sam. Allen: saw the King's Ropeyard and the Canon in the Waren. Ropeyard nine score paces long. From thence to Graves-End in the even. Went on board the America about 10 aclock, hurting my shin against the end of a Chest going into the Cabbin, from which I suppose in the night issued a pretty deal of Blood, and stain'd my Shirt, which startled me when rose in the morning at Graves-End, where I lodg'd with Mr. Brattle.

Aug. 13. Cous. Samuel Sewall hath aboard the America, Wm. Clark, Commander:

Number S. S. 2 Punchin Books: No. 3 Punchin Cordage; 4 Barrel Cheese; 5. Barrel Pease: 6. 7. 8 Three small Trunks with his childrens Names, the first Letters of them and the year of their Birth. 9. Barrel of Books: A Map of England and London: A Sea-Chest: A Bed, Quilt, 4 Blankets; one large Trunk, mark'd with nails, H. S. one, (the 4ᵗʰ) small one, corded with Canvas: One old small Trunk; one Cheese in Lead, mark'd W. V. for Capt. Vaughan, of Portsmouth, with Thanks for his kind Entertainment of me at his house: one Cheese Store: one Deal Box of Linnen: one Box Biskets: 1 Small Case Liquors; 1 great Case Bottles (Liquors in Common): Three Pastboard Boxes, with Hats: One Angling Rod: 1 Hat in a Paper: Two Hampers, 1 Beer, 1 Ale: 1 Ladder. Memorandum, that this 13ᵗʰ August, '89, I drew a first and 2ᵈ Bill of Exchange on Cous. Sewall, for £5. payable to Henry Bennet, of Ipswich: which said £5, with Mr. Wᵐ Whiting's £5. make good Cousin St. Sewall's £10.

4 good Muffs £2.6: two of the best £1.14.0. Hats unpaid for. Above is Copy of what Cousin Hull writt at Gravesend.

Aug. 14ᵗʰ Mr. Mather comes down, and chides us severely that none staid for Him, and seeing the Ship not gone, goes to London again. I gave him my Letter by Cous. Hull, which had writt to inform him, not knowing of 's coming, and beg'd his pardon, thinking I might be more servicable here and at Deal, than at London.

Aug. 15. Write to Cous. Quinsey by Bant, with Invoice and Bill of Lading, Mr. Vaughan's Cheese, his and Bro. Sewall's Annotations: Muffs Stockings. Mr. Brattle and I ride to Chatham, dine at the Crown, see the Dock and 33 Spinners of Rope-yarn, goe on board the Britannia, so to Sittingburn, lodge at the George: rains hard in the night. In the morn a good Ring of 6 Bells entertains us: no wether for the Ringers to work.

Aug. 16. From Sittingburn to Canterbury in the Rain, dine at the Crown: Mr. Powell: send for Cous. Fissenden, his Sister dead since my being there, and my Landlady at the red Lion dead. Bought each of us a pair of Gloves of Mr. Chiever. From Canterbury to Sandwich with the Post. Sandwich a large place and wall'd about, 10 miles from Canterbury, in a very flat, level country; Creek comes up to it. From thence to Deal 5 miles, built on the Beach. Land we ride over is call'd the Downs, and the Castle, Sand-Down Castle. Lodge at the 3 Kings. Mrs. Mary Watts, a widow, our Lanlady.

Satterday, Aug. 17. Goe to the new Meeting house that is building for Mr. Larner[93] in the 3ᵈ and lower street of Deal, towards the north end, which is, within the Walls, 34 wide and 41 foot long: 2 Galleries, one at each end, of 4 Seats apiece. Roof is double with a Gutter in the middle: built with Brick covered with Tile. Went to see Sand-Down Castle: but a Coach was there to bring out a Corps. The little Sand-Cliffs and inner Sand Hills, something like Plum Iland little hills, give name no Question to that part of the Sea now call'd the Downs. Deal is built between the 2 forlands, about 5 mile from the North-forland, 3 parallel Streets, the uppermost built on the very Beach, daring the Sea.

Sabbath, Aug. 18. Hear Mr. Larner in a Barn. Morn read the 8ᵗʰ Romans.

Aug. 19. Mr. Brattle and I went and saw Deal and Sholden Church, about a mile off: the Church very old, but set off with a new brick Steeple. That part call'd old, and upper Deal, though some of the Ground between that and the very low Country, Houses and Gardens and Orchards almost all the way.

Deal, Aug. 19. To a pair Home-made Stockings, which weighed

11½ oz. at 3ᵈ	0.2.10
pair Mittins	0.0. 5
Quire Paper	0.0. 6

---

[93] Richard Lardner (pronounced and sometimes written Larner), 1653-1740, the Deal preacher, was educated at the school for Dissenters at Stoke Newington conducted by Charles Morton, later vice-president of Harvard. Nathaniel Lardner, D.D., his son, was a celebrated nonconformist scholar and divine. D.N.B.

To drink with Mr. Clark's Cousin, ... 0.0. 6

Aug. 21. Mr. Mather and my Namesake come in a Coach from Gravesend. Intended to have gone to Plimouth: but the Plimouth Coaches full.

Aug. 22. Writt to E[*liaki*]m by Clark inclosing a Bill of Lading, Invoice, and Copy of Cous. Hull's Note at Gravesend.

Aug. 20. 22. Writt to Mr. Flavell, inclos'd to Cous. Hull.

Aug. 22–26. Enclos'd in Cous. Hull's to me. Mr. Mather, Sam, Mr. Brattle and I came aboard first in a boat: gave 3ˢ: Others came aboard in the night.

Aug. 23. Writt to my Unkle St[*ephen*] Dummer, to take leave of him and friends in Hampshire from Deal. Writt to Mr. Zech. Tuthill, Mr. Perry, Cous. Hull. Exceter come. Exceter comes into the Downs. Mr. Mather, Brattle, Namesake and Self goe aboard the America. Call on Bant. Mr. Quarles dying there.

Aug. 24. Mr. Mather, Mr. Sam[1] and Self visit Mr. Larner, who desires Mr. Mather to preach for him tomorrow.

Aug. 24. To an English Testamᵗ Oxford Print, 0.1.2. To a Mans and Womans pair of Kid Leather Gloves, which gave Mrs. Lamin for her Brother Clarke, in consideration of his servicableness in dressing our Diet on Shipboard, cost—0.4.0. Gave Capt. Clarke two Guineas, one of the new Coin. In consideration of my Passage hether 2.3.0. To the Men on Shoar, to drink—0.1.0.

Aug. 25. Mr. Mather preaches for Mr. Larner in the Afternoon.

Aug. 26. Visit Mr. Larner.

Aug. 26. To a Bed of Straw to lay under my Featherbed—0.2.9.

Aug. 27. Tuesday. Exceter summons all aboard about 4. p.m. Came to us in the Ship-Arbour, Mr. Lamin. Got aboard between 6 and 7. The shifting the wind was unexpected. No publick Prayer in the even. Very sore night for Thunder and Lightening. Were about to sail at midnight and the wind chopt about, and blew so hard that were glad to drop another Anchor again.

Aug. 28. Mr. Mather reads the 3ᵈ Matthew: reads the epistle out of my Testament. Prays. Boat comes aboard and brings Gazett signifying Pope's Death [*Innocent XI*].

Aug. 28. To Mr. Brattle, for my Share of Disbursements towards the Cabbin—£4.11.4.

Paid it thus. Discounted his Barrel of Cheese 1.10.9

Cash in Guineas 3. 0.7

                                                            ————
                                                            4.11.4

Paid him at the same time, nine Shillings for two pounds of Quick

Silver, he hath in his hand for me; I paid him for my Wether-Glass before, 10^s—: in all, £0.19.0.

Satterday, Sept. 14th. Went on Board when the Ship under sail, but wind veer'd against us, so came again to Deal.

Sept. 15. Sabbath-Day. Went aboard: the Fleet sail'd, Wind N. West, veer'd fairer and fairer: in the Night was much Lightening and loud Thunder. Exceter convoy. Sail by Dover, Folkston, Rumney.

Monday, Sept. 16. is rainy, so can't well see the Land.

Tuesd. Sept. 17. Come up with Portland, wind at north, or thereabouts, and very strong. We are almost the farthest of all from the Shoar, and had lost the Exceter in the night: find her in the morning. Am ready to wish myself with Mr. Mather and my Namesake, recovering of the Small Pocks at Deal.[94] After, sail with the Barclay-Castle, and on Wednesday morning, between 8 and 9. fair wether. Came to an Anchor in Plimouth Sound, the Tide being made strongest against us, and the wind but bare.

Wednes. Sept. 18. About 6. p.m. the Ship being got up higher, we went ashoar. Mr. Brattle and I lodg'd together at the house of one Mr. John Jennings near the Key. *Note.* In coming up a Privateer fell foul of us, took off our Ancient-Staff, much discompos'd our wooden Guns, put Will's [*Merry's*] Thumb out of joint, and some other damage. Nf.L. [*Newfoundland?*] Convoy have an order not to goe, it being so late in the year.

Sept. 20. Writ to Mr. Mather at Deal, and to Cousin Hull at London, to pay ten pounds to Anne Searle, in Meeting house Alley. She is a Widow, daughter to my Landlord, John Jennings, of whom I am to receive the Money in way of Exchange.

Sabbath, Sept. 22. I goe and hear Mr. Jacobs.[95] In the morn he reads the 39th of Jeremiah. Preach'd a funeral Sermon from 1 Thess. 4. 17. —and so shall we ever be with the Lord. Begun thus—One being lately dead who did belong to this Congregation, but now, we hope, is gone to a better. Afternoon read the 4th John, and 1 John 3. 19, was his Text:—The love of the Saints with its genuine effects and fruits, is a good Evidence of real syncere Christianity.

Monday, Sept. 23. Last night Thundered for a great while together,

[94] Mather and his son Samuel (Sewall's "Namesake") had intended to return on the ship with Sewall, but on 3 September Samuel was taken sick and the next day was found to have smallpox. Mather stayed with his son, and the *America* sailed without them; they did not return to Boston until May 1692. K. B. Murdock, *Increase Mather*, 228, 284.

[95] Nathan Jacob had been ejected as vicar of Ugborough, Devon, in 1662. *Calamy.*

rains this day. Many Souldiers march away to make room for D. Bolton's Regiment lately come hether by sea.[96] Two Serjeants goe out of our house, and two other Souldiers come in.

Plymouth, Sep. 23. Borrowed of Mr. Thomas Brattle, Cash, Ten Shillings: fill'd 12 Bottles with Beer at the Ship, the same day £0.10.0.

Sept. 24. Mr. Brattle, Dr. Edwards and I walk to Stonehouse, 1½ Mile from Plimouth, a Cause[wa]y thither. Visit Capt. Hutchinson and Mr. Partridge, who lodge there in a very mean Chamber.

Sept. 25. Went with Mr. Bedford, who shewed us the Cittadel, and Sir Nicholas Stanning, the Lieut. Governour, who gave order that he should have us into his house, and then came in himself, and drank to us in a Glass of Ale, that being the drink I chose and Mr. Brattle. Two Men were laid Neck and heels. In the afternoon went aboard and fetch'd ashoar my Trunk: Landlady's Brother and Daughter went with us.

Sep. 25 paid Mrs. Elizabeth Jennings 3ˢ for our Chamber and Lodging to this day, ½ to me £0.1.6.

Sept. 26. Went with Capt. Hutchinson, Brattle and Partridge to Milbrook in Cornwall, and there din'd well for 6ᵈ apiece. Went by the Beach and came home the upper Way by Maker Church, which is a large fair one upon the Hill, and so a very good Mark for Seamen. Go over Crimble Passage to Mount Edgcomb. Milbrook is part in Devonshire and part in Cornwall. Dr. Edwards came after us, and overtook us coming home. Milbrook People goe to Maker Church.

Sept. 26. Plimouth, deliver'd to be wash'd 2 Shirts, 2 Handkerchiefs, 5 Crevats, 1 Cap, 1 Binder.

Plimouth 27ᵗʰ September 1689, at Mr. Jennings, neare the Key.[97]

An Account of Severall things on board the America, Wm. Clark, Commander, which Mr. John Edwards saith he put on board said Ship when he came down to Gravesend intending to have gon Chirurgeon to the said Ship, and therefore took no receipt for them.
I. E. store. 1 box of medicines, cost £15.15.7: 1 box with a jack in it, without any mark on't 2.10.0
1 fishing net call'd a Seyne, put up in a powther barrell, with a canvis over it, and not marked 3.0.0
I. E. store 1 box with Spice, fruit, &c, ... 2.9.3
                                                        £23.14.10.

---

[96] Charles Paulet (or Powlett) was created Duke of Bolton in 1689; both he and his son, the second duke, were active supporters of William of Orange. The M.H.S. editors credit the elder with raising a regiment of foot for the reduction of Ireland this year, but this fact is not recorded by the D.N.B.
[97] This entry is in another hand.

The day above-mention'd Capt Clark was here and told Mr. Edwards that whatever the said Edwards had aboard should be deliver'd to him or to his order, and that he would detain nothing, or words to the same effect, in presence of us, SAMUEL SEWALL, THO. BRATTLE.

Friday, Sept. 27. Landlord receives a Letter from 's Daughter giving an Account of £10, paid her for me by Cous. Hull, but I have no Letter from my Cousin.

Sept. 28. Mr. Brattle and I walk out and see the Course of the Water brought by Sir Francis Drake, Anno, 1591, as appears by an Inscription. We are told it is brought so winding about, that notwithstanding the Hilliness of the Country, no Troughs are used to carry it over Valleys. Many very good Overshut Mills driven by it. Upon another Conduit is engraven, *Redigit desertum in Stagnum*,[98] 1593. It's brought 9 or 10 miles, from Ruper Down, deriv'd from a River as one goes to Tavistock, commonly call'd Testick.

Sept. 28, paid for washing Linnen at Plymouth, £0.1.4.

Sept. 29. Sabbath. Heard Mr. Sherril [99] preach forenoon and afternoon, from the 11th Isaiah, 6–9, verses; of the taming Men's Dispositions by the Grace of God.

Sept. 30. Mr. Bedford invited Mr. Brattle and me to dinner to Mr. Daracot's. Had a dish of Fowls and Bacon with Livers: a Dish of Salt Fish, and a Piece of Mutton reaching from the neck a pretty way of the back, the Ribs reaching equally from the back bone, Cheese and fruit: no Wine. This evening we are told that 4 Frigots are come into the Sound which are to Convoy the Ships bound to the West Indies.

Octob. 1. Receiv'd Letters from Cous. Hull and Mr. Mather about N. E. Sèe one Mr. Tucker married at the New Church.

Oct. 1. Rec'd of Mr. John Jennings Ten pounds, in consideration of Ten pounds my Cousin Hull paid his Daughter, Anne Searl, in London, of which Mrs. Searl hath advised her Father, £10.0.0.

Octob. 2. Hear a Stranger preach at Mr. Jacobs's from Exod. 25. 15, from whence observ'd that God was not oblig'd to continue the Tokens of his favourable presence to any people. At the Fleece Capt. Clarke tells us that he hath this day put Six hundred weight of good Beef aboard, and what is there already is good. Make some essays to get Mr. Edwards again, but he seems resolv'd to the contrary.

[98] "He turneth the winderness into a standing water." Psalms 107:35.
[99] Nicholas Sherwill, M.A., sometime chaplain of Magdalen College, Oxford, was "notoriously disaffected to the Church of England in her discipline" and was silenced and imprisoned. Another record says he was "A Gentleman, and liv'd on his own Estate"; under the Declaration of Indulgence he was licensed as a Presbyterian. *Calamy.*

Oct. 2. paid my Landlady, Mrs. Jennings for my Chamber, 3ˢ,—½ —£0.1.6.

Oct. 3. Agree upon putting aboard 5 Shoats, fowls, &c.

Oct. 3. To a Urinal, which is in the great Drawer of my Trunk, 0.0.6.

Paid Mr. Partridge, for my Self and Mr. Brattle, 30ˢ each, to buy Shoats, &c, for the Voyage—£3.0.0.: my part, £1.10.0.

Paid Mr. Brattle three pounds ten shillings: which, with the 30ˢ above, makes five pounds, the sum Capt. Ezek¹ Hutchinson paid Cous. Hull on the said Brattle's Account.

Oct. 4. Write to Cous. Hull, which is at least my third Letter. Goe aboard the America: bring Will Merry ashoar. See the Ships in Catwater [*the estuary of the river Plym*], over against Onson Passage. Dr. Edwards goes aboard Capt. Weare, in order to leave us.

Oct. 5. The Ships inward bound sail for London. Dr. Edwards in Weare. Went to Crimble [*Cremil*] Passage. Spake to Mr. Jacobs when came home. Saw an Ensign buried. The Company was drawn up in one Rank, Pikes, next the House of Mourning. When ready to goe, rank'd six, came to funeral Posture: Colours cover'd with Mourning went after Pikes, then Captain, then Parson and Corps. Posted the Pikes *ex adverso*, mutually, when Service saying. Gave 3 Volleys, but saw not the Colours open all the while. The Tattoo with which the Watch is set goes thus:—

Dūrrera dūm

Dūrrera dūm

Dūrrera dūm

Dūrrera dūm

Dūm dūm Dūm dūm Dūrrera dūm

Dūm dūm Dūm dūm Dūrrera dūm

Dūrrera dūm.

About three Sets of Drums take it one after another.

Oct. 6. Goe to Mr. Jacobs's, and in the Afternoon sit down with him at the Lord's Supper: and so I goe from one Pit to another to see if I can find any Water to refresh me in my disappointments and discomforts. Dr. Edwards comes in again being put back by the wind: is now willing to goe. But, *Oct.* 7, the Captain and he are like to break off again for 20ˢ, and hear of a Frigot being taken by the French off of Silly, so that am wavering as to my going, or else would rather give the 20ˢ myself than goe without him. Were four Frigots of the English, and eleven of the French. The Lively taken.

Oct. 8, 1689. Rec'd of Mr. Jnᵒ Jennings, by the hand of his Wife,

Five pounds, for which have drawn a Bill on Cousin Hull of the same sum, payable to Mrs. Anne Searle, daughter of said Jennings.

Oct. 9. paid 18ᵈ, my proportion for the Chamber one week, Diet, and Punch last night, to drink with our Host and hostess, 1ˢ—0.2.6.

Thorsday, Oct. 10. Set Sail out of Plimouth Sound with a fair wind, East, N.E. Capt. Allen having left the Ship I was about to leave it too, but he returning I returned.

Oct. 11. Pleasant wether. Two Rogues to windward of us, which the Man of War keeps off but can't come up with them: in the night a meer Calm.

Oct. 12. Fair wether, wind East and somewhat Southerly.

Sabbath, Oct. 13. The Convoys leave us when scarce 40 Leagues from Silly. Night very tempestuous.

Oct. 14. Make a shift to sail West, and West and by South. A Scattering day. I broke my white Plate.

Tuesd. Oct. 15. Is a strong West wind, or West by South. Saw a Rainbow or two this day. Sail to the Northwest.

Oct. 16. The wind is just in our Teeth. Last night presently after going to bed, turn'd out in some Consternation because of a Squawl, and danger of running on 2 or 3 Ships. Many Porposes, or Herring Hogs seen this day.

Thorsday, Oct. 17. Foggy rainy wether, wind at South pretty strong: Several Ships in sight.

Oct. 18. *ditto. Oct.* 19. Wind westers. One of the Frenchmen complain'd yesterday and to day of a feverish distemper. Dumenee.

Sabbath, Oct. 20. About sunrise saw a pleasant Rainbow. Matt. 18. 20. This place is to be understood of the least meetings of true Christians in the name of Christ, as well as of the largest Councils. Preston, Pillar and Ground of Truth, 7. 11. 2 Kings 17. 33. 34. God will not own his own commanded Worship when mingled and compounded with another, *idem,* p. 16 at the bottom.

Monday, Oct. 21. Wind came at South-East some hours before day. By noon was little wind: a little before night it came at Norwest, so brought on board the other Tack, and laid the Ship's head the other way. Found out Mr. Mather's Cake.

Oct. 22. Wind comes contrary: calm.

Wednesday, Oct. 23. Wind N. Nor East since 10 last night. 6 or 7 Knots the Ship runs.

Oct. 24. See a Sail to windward. Capt. Dumenee remains very ill. Mr. Edwards took some blood from him to day. Sorted my Letters, giving what belong'd to Capt. Clark inside his bagg.

Oct. 25. Fair wether, but wind in our teeth.

Oct. 26. Fair warm wether, wind Southwest, sail N.W. by W.N.W.: are in 44^d 30^m Latitude. Tis suppos'd a Current sets us to the Southward, or else cant tell how came by this Latitude. Mr. Fannevol [100] sick yesterday: pain in 's ear. Have a very sick Ship. Read in Dr. Preston, of God's Attributes, from 7, A.M. The Lord comfort me by that His Name. Mr. Partridge has forborn coming into Cabin some days, looking on the disease to be contagious.

Oct. 27. Very rainy day: sun shines out pleasantly about an hour before setting: grows a Calm, which makes the Ship roll in a very irksome manner.

Oct. 28. Capt. du Menee very dangerously ill. See a Ketch ahead of us. Wind in our teeth. We goe to Prayer, and Eat in the Round house by reason of the Frenchman's illness.

Oct. 29. Last night sail'd briskly a good part of it: but this day the wind at South West, and a Swoln Sea. Fair wether.

Oct. 30. Wind N.W. At night Demenee is watch'd with, who has been delirious a great while.

Oct. 31. Strong West wind, so that we hardly have gain'd anything for a considerable time.

Friday, Nov. 1. Contrary Wind, but shifting. Mr. Partridge trim'd me. Will Merry has the Measles, as many have had before him.

Nov. 2. Strong West wind: last night much Lightening and Rain. In the afternoon saw a Ship standing to the Eastward, but when came nearer stood from us to the Southward; we ly N.N.W. Demenee grows better.

Nov. 3. Strong West Wind.

Nov. 4. Wind N.W. Mr. Simons has the Scurvy.

Nov. 5. Wind N.W. Rainbow. Dine in the Cabin again. Mr. Simons has a very bad Legg. Put on my Deal Stockings to day. *Nov. 6* Mod[*erate?*] Wind.

Nov. 7. Wind SS.E., S.W. and S.E. Last night Mr. Brattle was taken with his indisposition of Spitting Blood. Call'd the Doctor, and was about to breath a vein as lay in 's cabin: but it ceasing, defer'd. This day after a slender Dinner, was taken worse than in the night, and had Seven Ounces of Blood taken away.

Nov. 8. Last night about 12 or 1, Mr. Brattle calls me up, thinking

---

[100] It is likely that Mr. Fannevol (called Faneville 15 November) was one of the three Faneuil brothers admitted as inhabitants of the colony 1 February 1692; they were Huguenots from Rochelle in France. Andrew became wealthy as a merchant in Boston, John returned to Rochelle, and Benjamin settled in New Rochelle, New York province. Benjamin's son Peter, who inherited his uncle's fortune, gave to Boston the famous market-house known by his name. *Savage.*

to be let Blood again, to prevent his coughing it up: but Dr. Edwards gave him 4 Grains of Laudanum Opiatum dissolv'd in Plantan Water, with which he lies. In the day inclines to vomit, which doth about noon, without Blood. Eats Barly boil'd. Towards night the wind comes fast, but is very little of it.

Nov. 9. Wind is fair, being North, or better, make good way of it: the former part of the night uneasy: Ship passing in the trough of the Sea.

Nov. 10. Wind fair, but towards night veers to the Westward of the North. Capt. Walkington is so sick as to take his Cabin and keep it almost all day. Dr. gives him something to sweat at night.

Nov. 11. Fair Wind. So Tuesday.

Nov. 12. A fairer, but little of it. Strengthen the Bolt-sprit, the Gammon [*lashing*] of which was loosed.

Nov. 13. Are in 43. Latitude. Sound, but find no bottom; so suppose we are Southward of the Bank, 4. p.m. Birds and coldness of the Water are indications that we are near it.

Nov. [14.] Fair Wind and Wether. Sound, but find no bottom. Wether so mild that eat at the Table on the Deck, 4 or 5 times together.

Friday, Nov. 15, 9 *mane.* Sound, and find ground in 45 or 50 fathoms. Bring the Ship to and put out fishing Lines. Mr. Fanevill only catches a good Cod, which had several small Fish in him, suppose to be Anchovas, however, very much resemble that Fish. Very foggy wether. Judge are on the Southermost point of the Bank. And now we have tasted afresh of American Fare. Lord, give me to taste more of thyself everywhere, always adequately good. *Nov.* 16. N.W. NN.W. *Nov.* 17. North Wind. Calm.

Monday, Nov. 18. South Wind, run 7 Knots. See many Porpuses jumping.

Nov. 19. N.W. and North Wind. See two Ships astern, standing right after us.

Wednesday, Nov. 20. East Wind. Sail 6 and 7 Knotts. *Note.* Last night about 2 aclock, Mr. Partridge came into Cabin and told us the Ships were come up with us, which made several suspect them to be Rogues, and put us in fear lest they should be Enemies. The small Arms are charg'd. But in the morning, by putting out our Ancients, find them to be Jersy-Men, our Friends. The best Sailer spake with us: he shortens sail for his partner, who sails heavy and hath sprung a Leak. Thinks we are the hindermost of all the Fleet. So, by the good Hand of God, that which cause of Fear and thoughtfullness to us, is turned into matter of Pleasure and Comfort. Blessed be his

Name. Yesterday Observed: found the Latitude 41 and 25 Minutes.

Nov. 20, 1689. If it should Please God, who is Righteous in all his Ways, and Holy in all his Works, to put an End to my Life before I come to Boston, my Desire is that the Rev. Mr. John Hale, of Beverly, have given him the Sett of Pool's Synopsis which I bought of Mis. Mills, quarto 5 Volumes: And that Mr. Charles,[101] the Son of the Reverend Mr. Israel Chauncy, of Stratford, have given him another Sett of Mr. Pool's Synopsis Criticorum, in five Books: And that the Money laid out with the Winthrops, on account of the Land the South–Meetinghouse stands on, be given the persons concerned, that so if have done them no good, may doe them no hurt. Provided no damage happen by a Bond I have given the Winthrops, or one of their Husbands, a Copy of, which is in my Papers. And that my dear Brother, Mr. Stephen Sewall, have given him my new Cloath-colour'd suit with the Chamlet Cloak. And if I have not done it already in my Will, left at Boston, I desire that my Namesakes, Sam. Toppan and Sam. Sewall of Newbury, have Five pounds apiec given them by my dear Mother and Wife, unto whom my other Friends are equally known as to my Self. I desire my dear Wife to accept of my Watch as a Token of my Love. And as to the things mentioned on this and the other side of this Leaf, I leave them to the Discretion and good liking of my dear Mother and Wife, to doe them or leave them undone, because the Estate is theirs. As witness my Hand,   SAM. SEWALL.

Nov. 21. A great deal of Rain. Wind Shifts. Speak with the Jersy Men.

Nov. 22. Friday. Wind comes to Norwest and blows hard. Speak with the Jersy Men.

Nov. 23. Have an Observation and find are in 40 and 33 Minutes, more Southerly much than the Mariners supos'd: so Tack'd immediately, and by night the wind came to fair, about to ly N. West, and had very fresh way.

Nov. 24. Suppose are now in the Latitude of Cape Cod, or near it: Sound, but find no bottom: Wind at West, but by night veers to the Southward, so as to ly West Norwest. Very pleasant wether, but no Observation.

Monday, Nov. 25. About Break of Day the Wind carries away our

---

101 Charles Chauncy had recently been graduated from Harvard (1686); in 1695 he was ordained as the first minister of Bridgeport, and he was one of the twelve clergymen who formed the Saybrook Platform in 1708. His father, Reverend Israel Chauncy (Harvard 1661), was the son of President Chauncy, whose memory Sewall venerated. *Sibley.*

Main-Top Mast, breaking it off just above the Cap: about 8 Foot of the Mast lost. The day spent in fitting the piece, hoisting it into its place, and partly fixing it with Rigging. Intended to have set up a Purse to day [*for the one who should first get sight of land*]: but this evil occurrent hindred us. Wind comes to the Northward of the East, which makes us bring the other Tack aboard, and by Westward by South, hope the Wind will veer faster.

Tuesday, Nov. 26. Wind abaft; hails and snows, yet not very thick wether. The Main-Top Sail was brought to in the night. In the morn give two half Crowns, a Jacobus, and a Carolus Secundus to the Purse. Sounded in the night, and now about 10, *mane*, but fetch'd no ground: so judge are between the Bank and the Land. A flock of Isle a Sholes Ducks seen to day. When the Lead came up saw we had Ground about one hundred and 30 Fathom: in the night lay by, not knowing our Latitude.

Nov. 26. paid to the Mariners Purse, £0.5.0.

Nov. 27. Wind West and by South. Sail to the Norward: Sound and find all oose at 130 Fathoms. In the night Sound and find small, black, gritty Stones, so in the night stood to the Southward, because came to 70 and 50 Fathom, and had not an Observation.

Nov. 28. Stand to the Norward, N.W. and N.W. and by Nor. E. Have a good Observation: are in the Latitude of 42 and 50, which, it seems, is the Latitude of Cape–Anne. Hoist up the Top Sails, to see if can make the Northern Land. See a small Boat gone adrift. About 3. p.m. Sauny goes up the Shrouds and on the Topsail yard spies Land, and takes the Purse. The Mate Wallis and Gunner say 'tis Pigeon-Hill on Cape–Anne. Gunner, who is a Coaster, saith also that he sees Newbury Old–Town–Hills, and Rowly Hill. All see it plain on the Deck before Sunset. Pleasant wether, clear skie, smooth sea. Sail N.W. Blessed be God who has agen brought me to a sight of New-England.

Nov. 29. Most pleasant day. Find the Land we saw yesterday to be Agamenticus Hills. Cannot wether Cape–Anne, so goe into Piscataqua River: land at the Great Island: from thence to the Bank in the night. Càpt. Hutchinson and I lodge at Mr. Crafford's. Send Madam Vaughan her Cheese.

Satterday, Nov. ult. [30] Ride to Newbury. Friends there exceeding glad to see me, being surpris'd at my coming that way.

Sewall resumed his diary at home with a précis of his trip:

Nov. 22, 1688. Fast-day, set sail from Boston. Landed at Dover January 13. Sabbath. Came from London Augt. 13th 1689. From

Plimouth Octob. 10ᵗʰ. Landed at the great Island, Pascataqua, Friday, Nov. 29. 1689. Nov. 30. came to Newbury from the Bank. Spent the Sabbath at Newbury. Dec. 2. Came to Boston: Staid so long at the Ferry that it was between 9. and 10. before I got into my own House. Mr. Cook only came with me from Govʳ Bradstreets.

Dec. 4. paid Capt. Wᵐ Vaughan fourty shillings N. E. Money, which is in full of what I borrowed of Mrs. Margaret Vaughan at Portsmouth, Nov. 30.

Thorsday, Dec. 5. Capt. Hutchinson and I took our Oaths; Govʳ Bradstreet there: Deputies treated us at Wing's after Lecture, as Major and Capt. Appleton, Mr. Eps and others had done at Ipswich as came along.

1690

Friday, January 3 [1689/90]. I treated the Magistrates at James
Meers; viz: Dept. Governour, Mr. Winthrop, Richards, Russel, Johnson, Appleton, Hutchinson, Cook, Hawthorn, Smith, Philips, Shrimpton, Addington, Swain, with Mr. Willard, Belcher, Bromfield; I think
all these there.

Jan. 9ᵗʰ. Tho. Hawkins, Pirat, was Tried and found guilty.[1]

[1] On the night of 8 August 1689 Thomas Pound, pilot of the *Rose* frigate, which
had been interned at the time of the rising against Andros (p. 223), set off from
Boston with half a dozen men in Thomas Hawkins's fishing boat for Nantasket.
In the harbor five additional men boarded the boat, and Pound's plan to capture
a large ship and prey on the French in the West Indies was disclosed; Hawkins
agreed to go along as sailing-master. Within a matter of hours they had captured
the ketch *Mary* and sailed for Falmouth (Portland) where they were joined by
seven soldiers who deserted from Fort Loyal. On the 16th, off Race Point, Cape
Cod, a boatload of the pirates, armed, seized the sloop *Good Speed.* After plunder-
ing the brigantine *Merrimack* at Homes Hole, Martha's Vineyard, the pirates sailed
for Virginia, where they were joined by two adventurers, and captured a Negro.
They sailed directly for Massachusetts and anchored in Tarpaulin Cove, Naushon
Island, in Vineyard Sound. There they sold the Negro to the master of a Salem
bark. Pound then sailed for Race Point, Cape Cod; Hawkins went ashore there and
deserted the pirates, but was later brought to Boston and lodged in jail. Pound
continued to rob vessels in the vicinity of the Cape. On 30 September the Governor and Council commissioned Captain Samuel Pease to go to sea at once with
a crew of twenty to capture the pirates; they sailed that evening in the sloop
Mary. Four days later they discovered Pound at Tarpaulin Cove. In the ensuing
fight Captain Pease was mortally wounded, but the pirates were quelled after four
had been killed and twelve wounded. The *Mary* returned to Boston on the 18th
with fourteen prisoners who were securely jailed. All this occurred while Sewall

Jan. 10ᵗʰ. It falls to my Daughter Elisabeth's Share to read the 24. of Isaiah, which she doth with many Tears not being very well, and the Contents of the Chapter, and Sympathy with her draw Tears from me also. Mr. Dudley went home yesterday, or the night before; but it seems refuseth to pay the Guards except the Council will order the Sum.

Sabbath, Jan. 12. Richard Dummer, a flourishing youth of 9 years old, dies of the Small Pocks. I tell Sam. of it and what need he had to prepare for Death, and therefore to endeavour really to pray when he said over the Lord's Prayer: He seem'd not much to mind, eating an Apple; but when he came to say, Our father, he burst out into a bitter Cry, and when I askt what was the matter and he could speak, he burst out into a bitter Cry and said he was afraid he should die. I pray'd with him, and read Scriptures comforting against death, as, O death where is thy sting, &c. All things yours. Life and Immortality brought to light by Christ, &c. 'Twas at noon.

Monday, Jan. 13ᵗʰ Joseph Eliot goes to Mr. Wiswall at Duxbury, returns with a Letter on Tuesday.

Thorsday, Jan. 16ᵗʰ He and I ride thether in a very cold day with a Letter from the Council to invite him to goe to England with Mr. Cook.

Friday, 17. Return homward. Call and see Mr. Torrey and his wife; Cous. Hunt and her Sons Jnᵒ and Daniel. Lodge at Unkle Quinsey's, coming in the night from Weymouth for fear of Snow. Got home between 11. and 12. Went after dinner to the Town-House, to Mr. Addington, from thence to Mr. Browning's, from thence with Mr. Cotton Mather to the Prisoners who were condemned on Friday. Spoke to, and pray'd with Pounds and others; then with Coward, Johnson and others. Gave him [*Mr. Mather*] two Duzen Books

---

was abroad. Sewall resumed his place on the Court of Assistants 24 December 1689. Hawkins was put on trial 9 January 1689/90 and found guilty the same day; Pound and the rest of the indicted men were brought to trial the 17th and found guilty. Wait Still Winthrop, one of the magistrates, was dissatisfied with the verdict or sentence, and immediately made strenuous efforts to get the pirates reprieved; this is what Sewall is referring to on 27 January. The pirate episode is told fully in G. F. Dow and J. H. Edmonds, *The Pirates of the New England Coast 1630–1730* (1923), 54–72, the trial record is printed in *Records of the Court of Assistants . . . 1630–1692* (1901) I, 305–322, and there is an extensive account, by J. H. Edmonds in *C.S.M.* xx, 22–84, of Thomas Pound, who returned to England, published a map of New England with a very accurate chart of Boston Harbor in 1691, became a captain in the Royal Navy, and died as a retired gentleman in 1703 at Isleworth, Middlesex.

bound qt. Right thoughts. &c. Sermons to his Father Philips, and on the Ark.[2]

Monday, Jan. 27. Five were order'd to be executed, but, chiefly through Mr. Winthrop's earnestness in Reprieving, only Tho. Johnson dies. Had join'd in reprieving Pounds and Buck at the Governour's, and then got away; but Mr. Winthrop, Addington, Shrimpton followed me to my house with another Writing for Hawkins, which Winthrop and Shrimpton had signed, and got me to sign: He was ready to be turn'd off before it took effect, which gave great disgust to the People: I fear it was ill done. Governour, Winthrop, Shrimpton, Addington, Phillips, repriev'd Coward, and most seem'd to desire that he and his 3 companions might be spar'd. Some in the Council thought Hawkins, because he got out of the Combination before Pease was kill'd, might live as well as Coward; so I rashly sign'd, hoping so great an inconvenience would not have followed. Let not God impute Sin.

Jany 27 [16]89/90 Received of Jn° Edwards Chirugeon ten shillings: He discounted the other ten with Mr. Partridge in whoes behalf I lent it and charg'd it to his Account.

Feb. 1. Addresses and Letters are read over before the Court, and Agents in the Deputy's room, and Mr. Stoughton's Declaration. After, Mr. Winthrop mention'd the Reprievs; I spake for my self that, by Generall Court, intended that which was to sit on Tuesday, the day after Reprieve.

Feb. 2. at Even. Little Joseph sucks his last as is design'd, his Grandmother taking him into her Chamber in order to wean him.

Feb. 7th Court adjourned to Wednesday next, to meet at Charlestown, because of the spreading of the Small Pocks at Boston.

About Jan. 29. Sister Gerrishes daughter is buried, and Sister Moodey's Daughter known to have the Small Pocks.

---

[2] The volumes presented by Sewall to Cotton Mather were all of the latter's authorship. *Right Thoughts in Sad Hours, Representing the Comforts and the Duties of Good Men under all their Afflictions; And Particularly, That one, the Untimely Death of Children* (London, 1689) was probably printed at Sewall's expense while he was in that city. It has a lengthy dedication "To My very Worthy Friend, Mr. S.S." and there is evidence that the sermon was occasioned by the death in June 1686 of Sewall's son Hull. At the end of the book is printed a letter from Edward Taylor to Sewall, dated 14 August 1686, sending him his condolences and two verses from one of his poems. (This early printing of Taylor's work is discussed by T. H. Johnson in N.E.Q. xiv, 139–141.) The other Mather volumes were: *Small Offers Towards the Service of the Tabernacle in the Wilderness: Four Discourses, accommodated unto the Designs of Practical Godliness* (Boston, 1689) and *Work upon the Ark* (Boston, 1689). T. J. Holmes, *Cotton Mather . . . Bibliography,* 927–929, 986–988, 1271–1274.

Feb. 8. and 9th Schenectady, a village 20 miles above Albany, destroy'd by the French. 60 Men, Women and Children murder'd. Women with Child rip'd up, Children had their Brains dash'd out. Were surpris'd about 11. or 12 aclock Satterday night, being divided, and secure.[3]

In the Storm of Snow that then fell Skippar Dotey, his Son Jnº, and Elkana Watson, were cast away on Ba[rn]stable Bar. Bodies not found, and 'tis fear'd they are murder'd by a free Negro and Indians.[4]

Friday, Feb. 21. Charlestown, Generall Court adjourns to the 12th March.

Feb. 24. [*In margin:* Treat.] Monday, Govʳ Bradstreet and Lady, Mr. Stoughton, Major Hutchinson and wife, Mr. Willard, Mr. Moodey and wife, Mis. Mather, Maria, Mr. Allen and wife, Cous. Dummer and wife, Cous. Quinsey and wife, Mr. Cotton Mather, Mr. Tho. Brattle, who with Mother, wife and Self. made Twenty, Marshal Green waited: Sat all well at the Table. Mr. Cotton Mather returned Thanks in an excellent manner: Sung part of the Six and fiftieth Psalm, in Mr. Miles Smith's version, Thou knowst how long I have from home—to the End. Mr. Mather was minded to have that Translation: I set it to Windsor Tune. *N.B.* The bitterness in our Cups, was that, the Massacre at Schenectady by the French; the amazing news on't was by Post brought to Town this day. Govʳ Bradstreet brought the Papers and read them before and after dinner. At last, Mr. Danforth, Major Richards, Major General Winthrop, Col. Shrimpton, Mr. Addington came in, and dispatcht Orders to the

[3] The full, sickening story of the Schenectady massacre may be read in Francis Parkman's *Frontenac and New France.* On the 15th of February Mayor Pieter Schuyler and Dirck Wessell [Ten Broeck] of Albany and Kiliaen Van Rensselaer of Rensselaerswyck wrote to the Massachusetts government giving a graphic account of the attack; the original is preserved in the Massachusetts Archives, xxxv, 240, and printed in *The Andros Tracts,* III, 114–120. How Sewall hit upon the correct modern spelling of Schenectady (the Albany gentlemen wrote Shinnechtady, and there were dozens of other spellings) is something we do not attempt to explain.

[4] Sewall omitted here a significant piece of news which we can supply from the Diary of Lawrence Hammond (2 *M.H.S.Proc.* VII, 151–152): "February 10 This day sailed from Boston [the ship *Mehetabel*] bound for London, Mʳ [Gilbert] Bant & in him Sʳ Edmᵈ Andross, late Govʳ of Newengland, Mʳ Jos. Dudley, Mʳ [John] Palmer, Mʳ [Edward] Randolph, Mʳ [John] West, Mʳ [James] Graham & others, who are sent home to yᵉ King, as by his Letter arrived here in November last. Likewise Mʳ Richᵈ Martin sailed yᵉ same day, & in him Dʳ Elisha Cook Dʳ Thomas Oakes & Mʳ Icchabod Wiswall, who are sent by yᵉ Convention to Implead yᵉ aforesᵈ Gentlemen. They Anchored at Nantasket, yᵉ wind coming Southerly. Mʳ Martin Anchored not, but saild direct away."

Majors to stand upon their Guard, To Capt. Price, Senr Capt. in
Salem Regiment.

Just about dinner time Mr. Nelson comes in and gets me to subscribe 100. to the Proposals against the French. I thought 'twas time
to doe something, now were thus destroy'd by Land too. Mr. Danforth looks very sorrowfully. Mr. Stoughton thinks best to prosecute
vigorously the buisiness against the Eastern French.

Feb. 28. Capt. Vaughan, Mr. Martyn and Mr. Fryer are approved
Magistrates of the County of New-Hampshire: Mr. Vaughan Sworn.

March 1. I visit Mr. Eliot, who embraces me heartily, and calls me
Brother: I present him with Mr. Flavell's Book; England's Duty. Mr.
Walter sits with me all the while. Visit Madam Dudley. Was com-
ing away, and Mr. Hutchinson call'd after me, and I went in and saw
Mistress Hutchinson and Billy. Pray'd excuse for my unmindfullness
of them.[5]

Sabbath, March 2^d I pray'd in the Family, that might have an Interest in God, Signed, Sealed and Delivered, and that all that tended
to make it sure, might be perfected. And being in my Pue, I was praying that as God had dispos'd me to put up a Petition some way
unusual, so He would doe some unusual thing for me. While these
words were in my mind, in came Mr. Moodey, who preach'd from
2. Thes. 3. 1. Doct. Tis the Duty of all, especially of those who have
profited by the word, to pray that the Word of the Lord may run
and be glorified: And I hope I was included in the Blessing at the
Close; for if I know any thing in this matter, I know that I desire and
pray God's word may run and be glorified: which came in my mind
when the Blessing was given.

To the Constables of Boston,
and every of them.

You are Required in their Majesties Names to Walk through the several parts of the Town this day, and take effectual care to suppress and
dissipate all unlawfull Assemblies, or tumultuous gathering together of
people for the Skailing or throwing at Cocks, and such like Disorders,
tending to the disturbance of their Majesties Liege People, and breach of
the Peace, contrary to the wholsom Laws on that behalf made and provided, particularly, those entituled Cruelty, and Prescriptions. Hereof you

[5] On this trip to Roxbury Sewall gave his friend John Eliot, the Indian missionary, a copy of John Flavell's book, *England's Duty under the Present Gospel
Liberty* (London, 1689). Nehemiah Walter (Harvard 1684) was Eliot's colleague at the First Church. Rebecca Tyng Dudley was the wife of Joseph Dudley,
who had sailed the previous month with Andros. Eliakim and Sarah Shrimpton
Hutchinson were the parents of Billy (Harvard 1702).

may not fail. Dated in Boston the fourth day of March 1689/90. An-
noque Reg. and Reginæ Willielmi and Mariæ—Secundo.

> SIMON BRADSTREET *Gov*[r]
> WAIT WINTHROP
> ELISHA HUTCHINSON } *Assist*[ts]
> SAM SEWALL
> ISAAC ADDINGTON

I gave the preceding Warrant to Thomas Banister, Constable,
who said he would take effectual Care about it. Another was given
to Capt. Prout, to be deliver'd to a Constable at the North end of
the Town, only it was given on Monday night at James Meers's and
so the Governour had not sign'd it.

March 4, 1689/90. Sam. Haugh, 14 years old last February,
chuses me for his Guardian.[6] Solomon Raynsford introducing of him
with a pretty handsome Speech for my acceptance. Dept. Governour
was by and told him he must now hearken to me and take me for
his Father. George Monk brought in a Dish of Fritters, but Major
Hutchinson, Mr. Addington and my self eat none of them, only
Major Richards (of the Court) did eat.[7]

March 7th Mr. Stoughton gives Major General and my self a
Meeting, as cold as 'tis, and undertakes to give Lieut. Swift notice
to be here next Monday at one aclock at my House, with a discreet
person or two of Punquapaog Indians. I write to Capt. Noah Wiswall
to be here at the same time with one or two from Natick, with a
hint of the occasion.[8]

---

[6] Samuel and Atherton Haugh were sons of Samuel Haugh of Boston (who died
25 June 1679) and his wife Ann Rainsford, and grandsons of Rev. Samuel Haugh
of Reading. Savage says that Sewall was guardian for both boys, but there is no
evidence in the diary that Atherton was Sewall's ward. Sam was indentured to
Thomas Savage 6 November 1690. On 1 February 1695/6, his twentieth birth-
day, he was in trouble with Mrs. Savage's maid and Sewall lectured him but
"Could not discern that any impression was made on him." Sam and Atherton
were present at a dinner party at the Sewalls' 4 February 1696/7. On 30 September 1697 Sam was married to Margaret Johnson by Rev. Samuel Willard.
Sewall was a bearer at his funeral 9 June 1717. On 11 July 1699 Sewall was
present at Pulling Point when Atherton was married to Mercy, daughter of Deane
Winthrop.

[7] We omit here a copy of a letter of Wait Winthrop and Sewall to William
Stoughton, dated Boston, 5 March 1689/90, requesting a meeting with him
"about disposing of the Friend-Indians in such place and manner as may be most
expedient for the safety of the English and themselves." The letter was delivered
by Eliakim [Mather].

[8] A letter from Sewall to Mr. Joseph Webb, Clark of the Writts, 1 March 1689/
90, on court routine, copied into the diary here, is omitted.

March 10ᵗʰ 1689/90. Mr. Stoughton, Major Generall and my self met at my house, and there came to us Lieut. Swift with William Hahaton for Punkapaug; and Capt. Noah Wiswall with James Rumney Marsh, and Peter Ephraim for Natick. Enquired what might be most expedient for the present settlement of the Friend-Indians, so as may be for the safety of themselves and English; in order to passing a Law for them in the Generall Court.

March 17ᵗʰ. Capt. Blagge came to enquire if the Council's Letter were ready, so I invited him and Mr. Melyen to dine with me; which accordingly they did, and Marshal Green fell in.

March 18, 1689/90. I gave New-Roxbury the name of Woodstock because of it's nearness to Oxford, for the sake of Queen Elizabeth, and the notable Meetings that have been held at the place bearing that Name in England, some of which Dr. Gilbert inform'd me of when in England. It stands on a Hill, I saw it as went to Coventry, but left it on the Left hand. Some told Capt. Ruggles that I gave the name, and put words in his Mouth to desire of me a Bell for the Town.[9]

Friday, March 21 1689/90. Madam Bradstreet, Mrs. Moodey, Mrs. Mather and my wife ride in the hackney Coach to Dorchester, dine with Mr. Stoughton. It should have been on Wednesday, when the news came indistinctly in the afternoon of the Surprisal of Salmon Falls. This Friday morn before they went to Mr. Stoughton's, the dolefull news came that between 80. and 100. persons were kill'd and carried away, were taken by surprise about break of day: no Watch kept: are about half French, half Indians. Hopewood Capt. of the Indians, Artel [*François Hertel*] of the French. Hampshire General got 100. Men and came up with the Enemy about Sun-set and fought them till night took away the sight of them. One Frenchman taken making up his pack who gives an account as above.

[9] Roxbury, Massachusetts, outgrowing its bounds, petitioned the General Court in 1683 for a tract of land in the Nipmuck country west of the Quinebaug River, and this was granted the following year. Settlers from Roxbury took possession in 1686. Three years later a delegation was sent to the General Court requesting confirmation of the grant, a name, etc. This passed 12 March 1689/90 and the naming was referred to Sewall. C. W. Bowen, *History of Woodstock* (1926), 32–33; F. S. M. Crofut, *Guide to the History . . . of Connecticut* (1937), II, 871–872. It does not appear that Sewall ever gave the town a bell.

On 18 March 1689/90, Governor Bradstreet, Sir William Phips, Major-General Winthrop, Major John Richards, Major Elisha Hutchinson, Colonel Samuel Shrimpton, and Captain Samuel Sewall, or any three of them, were to issue such orders for setting forth the forces as the Council might do. This appointment stands on the Colony Records, although Sewall makes no mention of it. The Council Records of this date are missing. M.H.S.EDS.

This day Capt. Townsend is appointed Commander in Chief.

Satterday, March 22. Sir William Phips offers himself to go in person; the Governor sends for me, and tells me of it, I tell the Court; they send for Sir William who accepts to goe, and is appointed to Command the Forces; Major Townsend relinquishes with Thanks. Sir William had been sent to at first; but some feared he would not goe; others thought his Lady could not consent. Court makes Sir William free, and Swear him Major Generall, and several others. Adjourn to Boston, Wednesday 14 night one aclock.[10]

March 24, 1689/90. Eight Companies and Troops Train. I goe into the field, pray with the South Company, Exercise them in a few Distances, Facings, Doublings; before which Thanked them for their Respect in mentioning me when in England, warning the Company in my Name; and told them the place I was in required more Time and Strength than I had, so took leave of them.

March 25. Drums are beat through the Town for Volunteers.

April 2. Father Dana falls from a scaffold in 's Barn and dies.[11]

April 4, 1690. Major Richards, Hutchinson, Col. Shrimpton, Mr. Addington and my self went to the Castle to view what Capt. Fayerwether had done, and what was proper for him further to doe in making Batteries, and putting the place into yet a more defensible posture. Went to Dear-Island, and saw how the sea wash'd it away. Then went to Apple-Island, to the Castle again, and there din'd; suffer'd no Guns to be fired; but the Captain caus'd the Flagg to be hoisted all the while we were there, in token of Respect. Cost us 5ˢ 8ᵈ apiec. This day Capt. Theophilus Frary, Mr. Joyliff, Wyllys, Sergeant, Adam Winthrop, Mr. Jnᵒ Clark, Timᵒ Thornton are chosen Commissioners for the Town of Boston. Capt. Frary, who had most, had 24 Votes; several of them but 16, the Meeting was so thin. This

---

[10] Sir William's first expedition in 1690 was a complete success. The Bay Colony despatched under his leadership seven or eight hundred men in eight small vessels for an attack on Port Royal (afterwards Annapolis), in Acadia, from which place privateers had been fitted out to prey on her commerce. Port Royal, surprised and unprepared, surrendered at the first summons. Phips later captured and destroyed the French fort at the mouth of the River St. John and returned to Boston laden with loot (*Palfrey* IV,49). Phips and the Mathers had been drawn together in mutually-advantageous attachment. On 23 March Cotton Mather had baptized the forty-year-old general and received him into membership in the Second Church; later he wrote his biography, *Pietas in Patriam* (London, 1697). In the early days of the colony only church members were admitted as freemen, but under the prodding of Charles II, the General Court had removed this restriction 3 August 1664.

[11] Richard Dana, the progenitor of the Cambridge family.

day Mrs. Averys Shop, and Christian Herridges Shop shut, by reason of Goods in them Attached.

Satterday, April 5. A Post comes giving notice of a Saw-Mill and several Houses burnt at Wells the 3ᵈ Instant, and Sayers Garrison beset with the Enemy. Council order one hundred and twenty Men to be sent out of Essex for their relief. April 4, one Pond of Dorchester, who had several praying at his House and he conversant among them, yet died before the day and Duty was ended; so that they were fain to break off to lay him out.

April 14. Sam. has an Issue made in his left Arm to prevent the swelling in his Neck, which else 'tis feared may prove the King's Evil. Have the advice of Mr. Addington and Dr. Allen who made the Issue.

April 15. Capt. Willard's Letter comes to Town of the 9ᵗʰ Instant, giving an account of the danger they were in at Casco of an Assault from the Enemy, 30 Indian Canoes being seen, and Several Fires on the Land. Writt to my Father and Brother Stephen.

April 21, 1690. Mr. Stoughton and I set forward for New-York,[12] Tho. Mosely waited on Him; Joseph Cowell on me: Mr. Cooper and others in Company, refresh'd at Roxbury, Billinges, and from thence rid to Rehoboth; lodg'd at the Bear, which one Saunders keeps. Mr. Anger sup'd with us.

April 22. To Bristow, visited Mr. Saffin by the way and Mrs. Saffin; lodg'd at Capt. Byfield's.

---

[12] Following the revolutions in England and Boston and the collapse of Andros's Dominion of New England (which included New York), Jacob Leisler seized power by various steps in New York and ruled *de facto* for twenty months, assuming the title of lieutenant governor in December 1689. Accorded recognition by the Albany officials, Leisler devoted himself vigorously to the prosecution of the French War, and made the first attempt to create a military union of the colonies. In April 1690 he invited the governors of the colonies to meet in New York to concert measures for the common safety. Massachusetts sent Sewall and William Stoughton (Commission dated 15 April 1690 in Mass. Archives, xxxvi f.4, 5), Plymouth sent John Walley, and Connecticut sent Nathan Gold and William Pitkin. Rhode Island sent no delegate but promised to raise 300*l*. Maryland was not represented but promised a hundred men. The Jersies and Pennsylvania ignored the conference. The commissioners drew up a statement, 1 May 1690, pledging for the "Present Expedicon for the Strengthening of Albany the Pursuing and by the help of Almighty God Subduing the french and Indian ennemies" four hundred men from New York, one hundred and sixty from Massachusetts, one hundred and thirty-five from Connecticut and sixty from Plymouth. It was signed by Leisler, Peter De Lanoy, mayor of New York; Stoughton, Sewall, Walley, Gold, and Pitkin. E. B. O'Callaghan, ed., *Documentary History of New York*, quarto ed., ii, 134–135.

April 23. Perswaded Major Walley to goe with us, went to Newport, agreed with Tho. Brooks for his Sloop at 12ˢ per diem. Lodg'd at Mr. Hedges.

April 24. Set sail, leaving our Horses and taking our Bridles and Saddles in the Sloop.

Satterday, April 26. got into Oyster Bay [*Long Island*], the wind being Contrary, and there anchored.

April 27. Went ashore, rid to Hempsted through Jerico, to hear Mr. Hubbard,[13] but he was at York: Staid at Mr. Jacksons, read Chapters, and Mr. Stoughton prayed excellently.

April 28. Rid to Jamaica, there din'd with Mr. Prudden,[14] Pastor of the Church there. From thence to Brookland [*Brooklyn*], where Mr. Edsal met us with a File or two of Troopers, got to the Ferry about 12. aclock. Went over and din'd with the Governour. Lodg'd at Mr. Mariot's; but were so disturb'd that were overcome by the Governour's importunity and lodg'd at his House. Major Gold and Mr. Pitkin met us there for Connecticut.

May 1. Rose before the Sun some considerable time that might ease my burdened mind in Prayer.

May 4. Sabbath. Went to the Dutch Church in the morn.[15] Sung the 69ᵗʰ Ps. 2ᵈ Pause from the 24ᵗʰ v. to the end, which Capt. Lodowick[16] taught me the evening before, and lent me his Book, pointed to every syllable. At my Lodging, Mr. Mariot's (for took leave of the Governour on Satterday, not knowing but might sail.) Read, pray'd over, and sung the 25ᵗʰ Psalm which should have sung in course, if I had been at home this day; and is a Psalm extraordinarily fitted for me in my present Distresses, and by which have receiv'd comfort. Mr.

---

13 Jeremiah Hobart (Harvard 1650), minister of Hempstead, Long Island.

14 John Prudden (Harvard 1668) left the Jamaica church in 1692 to succeed his classmate Abraham Pierson as minister of New Ark, East Jersey. *Sibley.*

15 There was only one church in New York City in 1690, the Dutch Reformed Church of St. Nicholas, which stood inside the Fort, south of Bowling Green. Domine Henricus Selyns, a Netherlander sent over by the Classis of Amsterdam, opposed the Leisler regime, and at this time was being harried by the governor's snoopers and the governor himself, but he committed no overt act, and was allowed to remain at his post. Two years later he was able to preach a sermon rejoicing in Leisler's downfall. E. T. Corwin, *Manual of the Reformed Church* (1879), 457–458.

16 Charles Lodwyck was captain of one of the six militia companies and later mayor of New York. At the beginning of Leisler's rebellion, when the inhabitants rose 31 May 1689 and demanded the keys of the Fort from Lieutenant Governor Nicholson, it was Captain Lodwyck to whom they were delivered. *N.Y.Hist. Soc. Colls.* (1868), 288.

Selyns Text, Philip. 2. 12. Work out your own Salvation, &c. In the afternoon it rain'd hard, so staid at our Quarters, read Chapters, and I pray'd. Landlady desired to be present.[17]

May 5. Got on board our Sloop, leaving Capt. Du Peyster's Dinner.[18] Wind sprung up fair, got well throw Hell-Gate, went ashore at Dr. Taylor's near the White Stone, wooded and watered: Sailed again with a fair wind.

On *Wednesday Morn, May* 7th there was a Fogg, which put us to our shifts, not knowing which way to sail; but it pleased God to clear the Air, so as we saw our Course, Block-Island, Point-Judith, and got in about noon, being their Election day. Gov[r] Bull furnish'd us with Beds for the voyage; Din'd at Mr. Hedge's. Henry Bull chosen Governour, Major Green of Warwick, Dept. Governour. Rid to Bristow, lodg'd at Capt. Byfield's.

May 8. Rid to Billinges, where Mr. Lee met us in his way homeward, gave an account of the wellfare of my family, having din'd with my Mother and wife at Cous. Dummer's. Pray'd with us.

May 9. *Friday*, Rid to Dedham and there refresh'd, so home by 12. or thereabouts; visited Mr. Eliot and Mr. Walters by the way. Mr. Stoughton and I waited on the Governour and I on the Council with Gov[r] Leisler's Letter.

Found my Family all well, save Sam's sore in his neck, and Hannah droops as though would have the Small Pocks. *Note.* I have had great heaviness on my Spirit before, and in this journey; and I resolved that if it pleas'd God to bring me to my family again, I would endeavour to serve Him better in Self-denial, Fruitfullness, Not pleasing Men, open Conversation, not being solicitous to seem in some indifferent things what I was not, or at least to conceal what I was; Endeavouring to goe and come at God's call and not otherwise; Labouring more constantly and throwly to Examin my self before sitting down to the Lord's Table. Now the good Lord God of his infinite Grace help me to perform my Vows, and give me a filial Fear of Himself, and save me from the fear of Man that brings a Snare. At Billinges heard Sam. Haugh was dead, which made me sad: but it proves not so. At Roxbury Mr. Bennet tells me of the death and Burial of

---

[17] We suspect that Sewall's malaise may have been occasioned by the part he was forced to play in sending men off to risk their lives in war; also, he may not have been able to stomach the uncouth Leisler or the atmosphere of New York under a dictatorship. And of course, correct Bostonians have never felt at ease in New York.

[18] Captain Abraham De Peyster, a merchant and one of the leading citizens of New York, became mayor the following year and was later chief justice of the province. *D.A.B.*

John Alcock, died on Monday, and buried on Wednesday, May 7th E^m Mather one of the Bearers.

May 10. Hannah takes a Vomit, her Grandmother earnestly desiring it. Has the Small Pocks very favourably, keeps her Bed but three or four days; about 50 or 60 in her face; pretty many on her Wrists.

May 19th Begins to keep below with her Brother, and Sister Betty.

Wednesday, May 21, 1690. Mr. Eliot dies about one in the Morning; I visited him as I came from New-York: This puts our Election into mourning.[19]

May 22. We hear of the Taking Port-Royal by Sir William Phips; Mr. Moodey well; which something abates our sorrow for the loss of Casco, if that sad news prove true.

Mr. Walter preaches the Lecture, and so is the first who has such a publick opportunity to mention Mr. Eliot's Death, Ambassadour, Chariots and Horsmen [2 *Kings II.*].

Friday, May 23. Is a Fast at Charlestown. In the afternoon Mr. Danforth and I call'd out of the Meeting presently after it began, the certainty of Casco's destruction being now brought. After having sat in Council awhile went to Mr. Eliot's Funeral; Governour and Dept. Governour, &c. there. Bearers, Mr. Allin, Morton, Willard, Fiske, Hobart (Nehem.), Thacher. Mr. Torrey and Danforth not there. Mr. Dummer of York[20] there; He comes to ask help; 'Tis doleful news we have to celebrate Mr. Eliot's Funeral with. Casteen is said to head about 70. French, and Indians are above Two Hundred. Capt. Willard came away the very day before the Attack.

May 24th News is brought of Capt. Nicholson being come to his Government at Virginia, and Govr Slaughter to New-York: First comes by Water: Mr. Arnold, the Keeper, brings the second by Land. This day I goe over to Winisimmet and see my Brother St[ephen] Sewall.

May 25. *Sabbath.* Jane Toppan is taken very ill; give her a vomit: She brings up three great Worms, and much fowl matter.

May 26. Has many Symptoms of the Small Pocks, we count it the first day.

[19] John Eliot of Roxbury, the "Apostle to the Indians," was eighty-six. Sewall had visited him 1 March and 9 May. A Cambridge graduate of 1622, he came over in 1631 and for nearly sixty years was minister of the Roxbury church and tireless in his efforts to Christianize and civilize the aborigines of New England. His translation of the Bible into Algonquian (Cambridge, Mass., 1663) was the first Bible printed in North America.

[20] Shubael Dummer (Harvard 1656), minister of York, Maine, was killed by a body of Indians and French in an attack on that settlement, 25 January 1691/2.

May 26. Mr. Cotton Mather prays with Eliakim.

May 28. Small Pocks appear.

Sabbath, June 1. Betty and Joseph are taken. Betty very delirious. Mr. Moodey is known to have the Distemper.

Monday, June 9ᵗʰ Joseph hath a very bad night, as also the night before.

June 10ᵗʰ. He grows better and the Small Pocks doe apparently dye away in his face.

Wednesday, June 11ᵗʰ. We put Sam. to Bed, having the Small Pocks come out upon him, as the Physician and we judge. Betty is so well as to Goe into Mother Hull's Chamber, and keep Jane Company, between 9 and 10. *mane.*

Thorsday, June 12. After Lecture there is a Meeting of the Overseers of the Colledge: the Fellows are appointed to hold the Commencement. Mr. Nathaniel Gookin, and Mr. Cotton Mather were chosen Fellows, i.e. the Choice of the Corporation was confirmed.[21] About seven aclock I married Capt. Theophilus Frary and Mis. Mary Greenwood, at the house of said Greenwood.[22]

Satterday, June 14. Have all my family together at Prayer, which has not been for many weeks before. Mr. Danforth, Mr. Russel, Mr. Hawthorn, Major Hutchinson, S. Sewall and Mr. Corwin subscribe for the Albany Expedition, Complaint being made that the Council's not subscribing much hindred others.

About 4 or 5. P.M. June 14ᵗʰ Mrs. Winthrop dies of the Small Pocks.[23] About the same time Cyprian Stephens, and Nathˡ Williams, Son of Jnᵒ Williams, die. The Lord fit particular persons and me and New England for his good pleasure.

Monday, June 16ᵗʰ Notice is given by beat of Drum of the Sale of the Souldiers part of Plunder taken at Port-Royal, to be made next Wednesday: this between 3. and 4. P.M.

Monday, June 16. Between 7. and 8. in the Even Mrs. Mary Winthrop is buried: Mr. Stoughton, Col. Shrimpton; Sewall, Addington; Eliakim Hutchinson, Sergeant, Bearers. Intended Tuesday, but the Heat of the Weather compell'd the using this day. Had a double

---

[21] This meeting of the Harvard Overseers was not entered in the college records. *C.S.M.* xv, xxxiv.

[22] Sewall seldom made a diary record of the marriages he performed as magistrate. In 1690 ten of the twenty-nine marriages recorded in Boston were by him, and in the marriages listed in the *Boston Record Commissioners' Reports* of 1883 and 1898 we have counted 175 by Sewall between 1690 and 1728.

[23] Mary Browne of Salem, the first wife of Wait Still Winthrop.

Coffin. Capt. Torrey was buried last Thorsday; died the Tuesday before. Mr. Stoughton, Major Richards, there.

June 17ᵗʰ Tuesday. Sam. rises and sits up a good while very hearty and strong. Blessed be God. This day one of my Shirts goes to lay out a Man dead at Nurse Hurds of this distemper, being a Stranger.

June 23. Brother Emons buries a Daughter of a Consumption. Was a pious Maid, at Woman's Estate.

June 27ᵗʰ John Lake dies at his Mother's, of the Small Pocks. Col. Shrimpton loses a very good Servant. William Parson, Mr. Joseph Parson's only Son and Child, was buried of the Small Pocks yesterday, June 26.

Friday, July 4. Mistress Tyng, wife of Mr. Edward Tyng, is buried. Mrs. Parson dies this day of a Consumption and Fever.

June 30. My wife and I ride to Braintrey in the Coach, carrying sick Cousin Quinsey with us: ly there all night.

July 2. Go to Cambridge by Water in the Barge, wherein the Governour, Major Generall, Capt. Blackwell, Mr. Addington, Allen, Willard and others: Had the Tide homeward. Thirty Commencers besides Mr. Rogers, Sir Mather, and Mr. Emmerson. Sir Mather in England yet had a Degree conferred on him. Mr. Rogers and Emmerson should have Commenc'd last year, but were hindred by Sickness.[24]

Sabbath-day July 6. When we are at the Funeral of Mrs. Parson the News comes in of the Engagement at Oyster-River, and that in probability two Captains slain.

July 7ᵗʰ Brother Stephen Sewall goes out with Sixty or Seventy Dragoons, and several others to the number of 150. or thereabout; The Lord God of Hosts goe along with them.

July 8. Are alarm'd by a Post who brings a Relation of Frenchmen being Landed at Cape-Cod, and marched within ten miles of Eastham.

July 14ᵗʰ 1690. Mis. Rebecka Taylor dies of the Small Pocks.

July 16. Mis. Taylor buried. William Taylor principal mourner. Bearers, Major Richards and Col. Shrimpton, Sewall, Eᵐ Hutchinson, Middlecot, Serjeant. This day Cousin Quinsey comes from Braintrey in Sam. Marshal's Boat, lands at Gill's Wharf, rests at our House, then gets home. Is worse than when he went. Mrs. Green

24 Samuel Mather, who had left Harvard in the last quarter of his sophomore year, at age thirteen, and sailed for England with his father, Increase Mather (p. 164), received his B.A. degree *in absentia*, "doubtless on the theory that his private studies with the Rector [Increase] had kept him up to the standard of his Class" (*Sibley* IV, 67). Nathaniel Rogers of 1687 received his M.A. in course; John Emerson, B.A., was a member of the Class of 1689.

the Printer's wife dies this day.[25] Jnᵒ Conney's only Son and Child, buried this day. Mr. C. Mather prays with Cousin Quinsey, and after at our house.

Sabbath, July 20. When Mr. Willard was in his first Prayer, there was a Cry of Fire, which made the People rush out. 'Twas said Mr. Winslow's Chimney was on fire. Just about the same time, the House next the Old Meetinghouse, the Chimney smoaked so, and beat into the House that made great disturbance there.

July 25. Major Nath¹ Saltonstall, and Major Tho. Henchman apply themselves to the Council, shewing that if so many be press'd for Canada as the Order mentions, the fronteers will draw in, and they themselves profess they will do so. Major Saltonstall comes no farther than Charlestown, because of the Small Pocks. Major Generall, Mr. Addington, and self goe over and give him a visit.

Tuesday, July 29, 1690. This is a day of much Thunder and plenteous Rain which prevents the Souldiers for Canada their mustering as was intended. Cous. Quinsey as I sat with him bid me shut the door, and ask'd if I had done that, meaning his Will. Mr. Moodey visited him this day. He is very low.

July 30. Eliakim Mather sets out for Eastham. Mr. Edw. Rawson and I have hot words about Deeds he shews me relating to the Salmon-Falls Sawmill: Capt. Wincoll having in '86. made a Deed to George Broughton, and Acknowledg'd it in April last, of his Right in the Salmon-Falls: Of which Deed said Rawson writ out a Copy before he went away and gave me.

Satterday, Augt. 2. News comes of our Agents having presented Addresses to the King and Queen; of the King's intention to go into Ireland, and an Act framing to enable the Queen to govern in the mean time. Sloop that went for Ammunition, her arrival at Silly. *Væ malum!* about 2. aclock after midnight a fire breaks out on tother side the Mill-Crick, which gets over to this side and consumes about fourteen Dwelling Houses besides Warehouses; Madam Leverett, and Mrs. Rock are great Sharers in the Loss.

Monday, Augt. 4. Cousin Quinsey signs, seals and publishes his Will, Capt. Jacob Eliot, Theophilus Frary and my self Witnesses. Then went with Major Walley to Dorchester to meet Govʳ Hinkley, Commissioner for Plimouth, but Connecticut and Rhode-Island failing, nothing could be done to purpose: but urgd Govʳ Hinkley to furnish us with a hundred Men: hope he will send fifty. Din'd

---

[25] Hannah, the wife of Samuel Green Jr., with whom Sewall was associated as public printer. Green died the same month. The family of Green, a remarkable dynasty of printers, is recorded in *N.E.H.G.R.* civ, 81–93.

with Mr. Stoughton. Went and saw Capt. Withington's Company, 16 files, 4 deep, drawn up by the Meetinghouse, gave them a French Crown to drink. Took Mrs. Mills's Acknowledgment of a Deed as she lay abed. Mrs. Pierce buried near the Tomb of her Grandfather Cotton.

Friday, Augt. 8, 1690. Dept. Governour, Major Generall, Major Richards, Mr. Russell, Major Hutchinson, Major Phillips, Mr. Addington and self went to Nantasket to see the Lieut. Generall Muster his Souldiers on Georges Island; went on board the Six Friends; urgd that might sail by the first opportunity; came up to Town. And about 11. or 12. at night Major Hutchinson, Mr. Addington and S. S. with Mr. Eyre went down again carrying Carriages for field-picces. Anchor'd at Nantasket about 3. When day, *Augt. 9ᵗʰ*, was come, went on board; the Generall persuaded Him to make Signs of Sailing; then with the Lieut. Generall visited the Ships of War and other Vessels, directed as to the number of Souldiers each vessel was to have and order'd to make Signs of Sailing. Wind comes fresh from Sea; Go and dine at Hull with Sir William [*Phips*] and his Lady and Mr. Hale: Come on board, order is given to unmore, to be in a readiness if the wind should spring up. About 6. wind veer'd and the Fleet came to sail, Four Ships of War, and 28 other. Brought up my Lady from Hull. Got up to Town about 9. at night;[26] call'd at Cous. Quinsey's whom I found very ill.

[26] Sewall's interesting record of the departure of the Phips expedition recalls his presence at the intercolonial congress in New York in April when plans were made for the conquest of Canada. A diversion was to be made by an assault on Montreal by a force of English from Connecticut and New York, and of Iroquois Indians. Captain Benjamin Church was to lead an expedition into Maine to threaten the hostile eastern tribes. The contribution of Massachusetts was to be a great assault by water on Quebec. Sir William Phips was made general and John Walley of Barnstable lieutenant general. The thirty-two vessels Sewall noted carried 2000 men. The whole enterprise was unsuccessful. Captain Church's diversion made no real contribution to the descent upon Canada. The overland expedition to Montreal came to a standstill at the southern end of Lake Champlain. When Phips arrived before Quebec with his fleet, his energy and courage deserted him; he delayed his attack, did not press it home when he made it, and abandoned it at the moment when it might have succeeded. Some of his ships were lost on the return voyage and the casualties numbered two hundred. The colony, hopefully expecting reimbursement from enemy spoils, had borrowed the money for the expedition. Some £50,000 had been sacrificed and the treasury was empty. To pay the returning soldiers, paper currency was issued. It fell in value at once, and was a source of trouble for the colony for two generations. *Palfrey* IV, 51–59; Edward Channing, *Hist. of the U.S.* II, 530–531. Two contemporary accounts of the second Phips expedition, one anonymous, and one by Rev. John Wise of Ipswich, are printed in 2 *M.H.S. Proc.* xv, 218–320.

Sabbath, Augt. 10ᵗʰ Went to see Cous. Quinsey; read the 102. Psal. and begin 103. pray'd, and so went home. Put up a Bill at his request. Just after Contribution in the Afternoon, was call'd out, Cousin being very bad, so far as I could perceive. He desired me to pray, which I did: Afterward sent for Mr. Willard, and He pray'd, then Cousin pull'd his hand out of the Bed, and gave it to Mr. Willard. Seem'd to pray himself; but I could hear little except Jesus Christ; breath'd quick and hard, till at last abated and He quietly expired about Seven aclock. Mother Hull and I being there. I have parted with a cordial fast Friend, such an one as I shall hardly find. The Lord fit me for my Change and help me to wait till it come. Cousin was concern'd what he should doe for Patience, but God graciously furnish'd him, and has now translated Him to that State and place wherein He has no occasion for any.

Tuesday, Augt. 12. About 7. P.M. we lay the Body of Cous. Daniel Quinsey in my Father's Tomb. Mr. Serjeant, Dummer, H. Usher, Davis, Williams, Conney, Bearers. I led the Widow, then the Children, next, Mr. T. Brattle, Mis. Shepard, H. Newman, Mistress Margaret, Mr. Willard, Mother Hull, Mr. Parson, my wife and so on. *Note.* My wife was so ill could hardly get home, taking some harm in going in Pattens, or some wrench, so had a great flux of Blood, which amaz'd us both, at last my wife bad me call Mrs. Ellis, then Mother Hull, then the Midwife, and throw the Goodness of God was brought to Bed of a Daughter between 3. and four aclock, Aug. 13ᵗʰ 1690. *mane* Mrs. Elisabeth Weeden, Midwife. Had not Women nor other preparations as usually, being wholly surpris'd, my wife expecting to have gone a Moneth longer.

Wednesday, Augt. 13, 1690. Eliakim Mather goes away about 10. at night for Eastham, and so for Jamaica before his Return.

Augt. 16. Capt. Cyprian Southack comes in, saith he saw not the Fleet.

Augt. 17. Mr. Willard keeps his Sabbath at Roxbury, and so the Baptism of my little Daughter is deferred to the next Lord's Day.

Sabbath-day, August the four and twentieth, 1690. I publish my little Daughter's name to be Judith, held her up for Mr. Willard to baptize her. She cried not at all, though a pretty deal of water was poured on her by Mr. Willard when He baptized her: Six others were baptized at the same time; Capt. Davis's Son James, and a grown person, Margaret Clifford, two of them. I named my Daughter Judith for the sake of her Grandmother and great Grandmother, who both wore that Name, and the Signification of it very good: The Lord grant that we may have great cause to praise Him on her ac-

count and help her to speak the Jews Language and to forget that
of Ashdod. Nehem. 13. 24. And that she may follow her Grandmother Hull, as she follows Christ, being not slothfull in Business,
fervent in Spirit, serving the Lord. Her Prayers and Painstaking for
all my Children are incessant, voluntary, with condescension to the
meanest Services night and day: that I judg'd I could in justice doe
no less than endeavour her remembrance by putting her Name on
one of her Grand-Daughters. I have now had my health and opportunity to offer up Nine Children to God in Baptisme. Mr. Tho.
Thacher baptized the two eldest; John and Samuel; Mr. Samuel Willard baptized the Seven younger. Lord grant that I who have thus
solemnly and frequently named the name of the Lord Jesus, may
depart from Iniquity; and that mine may be more His than Mine,
or their own.

Augt. 28. Publick Fast. Letters are brought to the Governour in-
forming that the Maquaws [*Mohawks*] failing to join the Christians
at Wooden [*Wood*] Creek about 100 miles above Albany, they were
coming back again, which puts a great damp upon us here, to think
that our fleet should be disappointed of their expected Aid.

Aug. 29ᵗʰ. We hear by a vessel 9. weeks from Bristow of King
William's being in Ireland with a great Army and vast Preparations
of War. Sail'd from High-Lake [*Hoylake*] the 11ᵗʰ of June 1690. Mrs.
Davis buried this day, who died of the Small Pocks in Child-Bed.

Augt. 29, 1690. I watch at night with about 30. men. Word was
Skenectady. Nathan[1] Clarke of Newbury buried this week, died Augt.
25.

Sept. 1, 1690. Eight Companies Train. Governour dines at Mr.
Pain's with the South Company. Capt. Frary exercises the Company. Joseph is carried into the Common to take the air and see
the men.

Friday, Sept. 5ᵗʰ I went to Cambridge in the morn to visit Brother
Stephen Sewall and his wife, and come down with the Dept. Governour and Marshal.

Sept. 9. Mrs. Jane Pole, widow, a Mother in our Israel, died at
River-House in Boston, Sept. 9ᵗʰ and was buried at Dorchester Sept.
11ᵗʰ 1690.[27]

---

[27] Jane was the widow of William Pole (or Poole), B.A. Oxford 1612, son of
Sir William Pole of Colcombe, Devon; Captain William Pole and his sister Eliza-
beth were founders of Taunton, Massachusetts, and he was later schoolmaster at
Dorchester, where he died 24 February 1674/5. The Pooles were proprietors of
the ancient iron works in Taunton. *N.E.H.G.R.* xxxviii, 266, xlviii, 490f.;
Morison, *F.H.C.*, 396.

Thorsday Sept. 11th Being crowded in the Pue, by reason Mr. Hutchinson and Sergeant constantly sit there and claim Propriety, so Mr. Usher is forced to take my place; having also found that sitting so near the out-side of the House causeth me in Winter-time to take cold in my head, I removed into Gallery, and sat with Dept. Governour, Mr. Russel, Major Hutchinson, where had very convenient sitting.

Sept. 13th. Sister Emons buried. This Week we hear of a sore fight between the English and French Fleets.[28]

Sept. 14th I Watch, Word was Salmon-Falls, had a very comfortable night; only between 3. and 4. were disquieted by Guns fired at Charlestown, and Drum beat: But I did not observe a continual Beat of the Drum, so caus'd not an Alarm; and about day a Messenger was sent over who told us the occasion was some Indians seen in their back fields. Run-away Servants they appear to be; by which means the Town was generally rais'd: But throw God's goodness Trouble at Boston prevented.

Tuesday, Sept. 16th. About eleven at night a Fire breaks out at the House of Jn° Allen, Worsted Comber, in which his Apprentice, Sam. Worster, was burned, with the House of Lieut. Reynolds, Mr. Bligh, Langden and a great part of Savil Simson's. The wind being Sou-west the South-Meeting-House was preserv'd with very much difficulty, being in a flame in diverse places of it. Capt. Cyprian Southack, and Lieut. David Mason did very worthily, hazarding themselves with many others on the Lead for a great while.

Sept. 17th. Fast at Mr. Mathers.

Sept. 18th. Mr. Willard's Edward dies of a Convulsion Fit.

Sept. 20. Is buried at Roxbury in Mr. Eliot's Tomb, I was at the Funeral. Rain and Thunder this day after a great deal of dry wether which made it extream dusty. Mr. Walter went to Prayer: Mrs. Willard sick, and not at the Grave. My little Judith languishes and moans, ready to die.

Sabbath, Sept. 21. About 2 *mane*, I rise, read some Psalms and pray with my dear Daughter. Between 7. and 8. (Mr. Moodey preaches in the Forenoon,) I call Mr. Willard, and he prays. Told Mr. Walter of her condition at the funeral, desiring him to give her a Lift towards heaven. Mr. Baily sat with me in the Afternoon. I acquainted Him. Between 7. and 8. in the evening the child died, and I hope sleeps in Jesus.

Sept. 22. In the even, Mr. Moodey, Allen, Mather come from Mrs.

[28] The Dutch and English were defeated by the French in the Battle of Beachy Head, off the coast of Sussex, 29 June.

Clark's Funeral to see us. Mr. Moodey and I went before the other came, to neighbor Hord,[29] who lay dying; where also Mr. Allen came in. Nurse Hord told her Husband who was there, and what he had to say; whether he desir'd them to pray with him: He said with some earnestness, Hold your tongue, which was repeated three times to his wive's repeated intreaties; once he said, Let me alone, or, be quiet, (whether that made a fourth or was one of the three do not remember) and, My Spirits are gon. At last Mr. Moodey took him up pretty roundly and told him he might with the same labour have given a pertinent answer. When were ready to come away Mr. Moodey bid him put forth a little Breath to ask prayer, and said twas the last time had to speak to him; At last ask'd him, doe you desire prayer, shall I pray with you, He answer'd, Ay for the Lord's sake, and thank'd Mr. Moodey when had done. His former carriage was very startling and amazing to us. About One at night he died. About 11. aclock I supposed to hear neighbour Mason at prayer with him, just as I and my wife were going to bed. Mr. Allen prayed with us when came from said Hord's.

Sept. 23. Tuesday, between 5. and 6. Sir Moodey carries the Body of my dear Judith to the Tomb, Solomon Rainsford receives it on the Stairs and sets it in. On the Coffin is the year 1690. made with little nails. Govʳ Bradstreet and Lady, Mrs. Moodey, Mather the Mother, Mr. Winthrop, Richards here, with many others; Ministers, Willard, Moodey, Mather.

As we were going, one [*blank*] of Watertown came up with the Bearer, and talk'd to him on horseback, Mr. Moodey bid him be gon about his business; at that he was in a rage and threaten'd to strike him, and said he was a pittyfull Dogg and we were all pittyfull Doggs. I thought of David and Shimei and said nothing to him. The Lord prepare me to undergo evil Report, and to be vilified by men; but not for evil-doing. I led my wife, Sam. his Grandmother, Hannah Betty, Jane Toppan managed Joseph. Before we went, Children read the 18. 19. and 20ᵗʰ Chapters of John, being in course for family reading.

Sept. 24. Between 5. and 6. P.M. Jnᵒ Hord buried; None of our House there save Mother Hull.

Sept. 25. A printed sheet entituled publick Occurrences comes out, which gives much distaste because not Licensed; and because of the passage referring to the French King and the Maquas.[30]

---

29 John Hurd, a tailor, had been made freeman in 1640. Mary, his wife, "Nurse Hord," was occasionally called in to minister to the Sewall family. *Savage.*
30 Only one issue of America's first newspaper, *Publick Occurrences Both For-*

Sept. 30. Going to Muddy-River, I meet Simon Gates and his Wife bound for Dorchester Lecture, so turn back and goe with them from D[*eacon*] Eliot's plain by Bearsto's. Mr. Danforth preached and pray'd very well. Text 18. Luke—and shall not God:—shew'd that God would certainly hear and deliver his people at their Importunity. Mr. Torrey there, with whom din'd at Mr. Danforth's, and with Mr. Nehem. and Gershom Hobart. I sat in Mr. Stoughton's Pue; His family not well.

Oct. 1. Print of the Governour and Council comes out shewing their disallowance of the Public Occurrences.

Oct. 2. Mr. Mather writes a very sharp Letter about it.

Oct. 3. John Marion jun^r is chosen Clerk of the South-Company and Sworn, had 23 Votes.

Oct. 7. Mrs. Cook aged 75 years died.

Oct. 9. Buried in the new burying place. Maj^r Richards, Maj^r Generall, Maj^r Hutchinson, Col. Shrimpton, Sewall and Addington, Bearers. Buried after the Fast.

Oct. 14. Fast at Roxbury, I go thether on foot; Lady Phipps there, is come to Town again it seems, the Small Pocks being at Charlestown.

Oct. 15. Had Sam. over to Winnisimmet to see his Unkle Stephen, Mr. Evans carried him home behind him from the Ferry.

Oct. 19th. Mrs. Goose dies of an Apoplexy.[31]

Oct. 21. Is buried in the new burying place, Sewall, Addington; Eliot, Frary; Townsend, Allen; Bearers. Is a rumor in Town that Sir Edmund is to come Governour of New-York, and Col. Slâter our Governour. Tories are flush'd, and 'tis said were drinking Sir Edmund's Health last night at Neh. Pierce's. Capt. Hammond refused last week to deliver the Records.

Tuesday, Nov. 4. Accompanied Mr. Stoughton to Col. Paige's. He

reign and Domestick, was published, and the sole surviving copy is in the Public Record Office in London; it appears in Samuel Abbott Green, *Ten Facsimile Reproductions relating to Old Boston* (1901) and in L. H. Weeks and E. M. Bacon, *An Historical Digest of the Provincial Press* (1911). The journal was suppressed by proclamation of the Governor and Council on 29 September; their broadside (*Massachusetts Broadsides*, No. 169) reached Sewall 1 October. Benjamin Harris was the publisher; he was a London printer and bookseller who worked in Boston from 1686 to 1695, and was a shipmate of Sewall on his crossing in 1688–1689 (*D.A.B.* and Worthington Chauncey Ford in *M.H.S. Proc.* LVII, 34–68). Victor Hugo Paltsits, in New Light on "Publick Occurrences", *A.A.S. Proc.* LIX, 75–88, prints a favorable letter of Cotton Mather written 17 October.

31 Mary (Balstone) Goose was the wife of Isaac Goose (or Vergoose) of Boston. *Savage.*

sent his Coach to the Ferry for us. Found at 's house Col. Gedney, Major Brown, and my brother Sewall; had a sumtuous Feast. Col. Gedney presses earnestly that Volunteers may be encouraged Eastward.

Thursday, November the Sixth 1690, at my House in Boston Samuel Haugh and Mr. Thomas Savage mutually sign'd, seal'd and deliver'd Indentures to each other; Sam. to serve him from 7th Octʳ last, Seven years and Six Moneths. Witnesses, S. S. Joseph Wheeler, Jnᵒ Cole, Thomas Banister.

Friday, Nov. 8, 1690. Read Govʳ Leisler's extream sharp Letter.[32] Jnᵒ Hoar comes into the Lobby and sais he comes from the Lord, by the Lord, to speak for the Lord; Complains that Sins as bad as Sodom's found here. Pass 20. Rates, a Bill to encourage Volunteers. Head money to be but 12ᵈ for each of the 20 Rates. About 8. at night, Governour and Magistrates goe into the Deputy's Room, Governour prays that Mountain of the Lord's House may be established in the top of the mountains, &c. Adjourns the Court to the 10th of December at 9. *mane.* Between 9. and 10. at night, Governour sends to me and enforms of the defeat at Canada; and that Urrumbee, Hawkins, and other chief Indians sued for peace. News of Canada came from Salem. Shute comes into Boston that night or next morning, hath thrown over aboard more than Sixty persons since his going hence, most Indians of Plimouth. Town much fill'd with the discourse, and some cast blame on Major Walley; were nine weeks getting thether and landed not before the 7th or 8th of October.

Satterday, Nov. 8. Council meets. Send away Major Hutchinson, Capt. Townsend and others to Wells to treat with the Indians, and commit the care of the sick on board Shute, to the Select-Men. Two lie dead on board at this time, the Small Pocks and Cold kills them.[33]

Friday, Novembʳ 21, 1690. Mr. Samˡ Willard, Mr. Edw. Rawson, Capt. Joshua Scottow, Deacon Jacob Eliot, Deacon Theophilus Frary and Samuel Sewall met together, at said Sewall's House in Boston. Mr. Edward Rawson in regard of his Age, and dwelling out of Town desired that Mrs. Judith Winthrop's Deed of the Meeting-house Land in Boston, her Receipt, Mr. Leveret's Release, Mrs. Norton's

---

[32] This entry should have been dated 7 November. Leisler had written in a rage to Governor Bradstreet 15 September 1690, complaining about the "treachery and cowardice" of Major Fitz-John Winthrop, etc. The letter is quoted in *Hutchinson* (1936) I, 338n.

[33] A truce was made at Sagadahoc, 19 November, by Captain John Alden, appointed by the Governor and Council for this purpose, and six Indian chiefs; in consequence of this truce, the land enjoyed rest for the winter. *Hutchinson* (1936), I, 342.

Deed of Gift 1669, Mrs. Norton's Deed of Gift 1677, An Instrument of Mr. Edw. Rawson, Capt. Joshua Scottow, and Capt. Jacob Eliot to Sam¹ Sewall and others, being Six Writings in all, should be put into a Chest to be provided for that purpose, on which a Copper plate to be fastened with this Engraving, *South Church,* and Mr. Peter Sergeant to be entreated to keep the said Chest in his house, being of Brick and conveniently situated; and that, if can conveniently do, also put the Church plate in said Chest; and said Edward Rawson committed the above-mentioned writings to said Eliot to be disposed of as above with as great Speed as conveniently may be, according to this Agreement.

Signed by—   EDWARD RAWSON.

SAM SEWALL.

J. SCOTTOW.

JACOB ELIOT.

THEO. FRARY.³⁴

Nov. 21. I accompanied Capt. Hill to the Funeral of Joseph Asgood, or Asbud, of Almsbury, a souldier of about 18 years old who died at Fort-hill of the Small Pocks. Mr. Laurence, Capt. Davis's Son-in-Law, is buried this day; so that Five own Sisters are now Widows. 'Twas Tuesday, the 18ᵗʰ of November, that I heard of the death of Capt. Stephen Greenleaf, Lieut. James Smith and Ensign Wᵐ Longfellow, Serjᵗ Increase Pilsbury, who with Will Mitchell, Jabez Musgro, and four more were drown'd at Cape Britoon on Friday night the last of October. [*In margin:* Unkle Longfellow with several others Drowned at Cape Britoon.]

Satterday, Nov. 22. Went to the burial of Major Sam¹ Ward; was buried a very little to the Westward of our Tomb. Major Walley, Savage, Townsend; Capt. Wing, Greenough, Barnard, Bearers. Govʳ Bradstreet and 's Lady went next the Herse. Was buried from Mr. Skinner's, a Relation. Major Hutchinson with about 13 files 4 deep, attended the funeral. One Volley only, because of the scarcity of Powder.

Wednesday, Nov. 26ᵗʰ. Mr. Willard and I rid to Dorchester, from thence with Mr. Stoughton and Danforth, the Minister, to Braintrey, where met Mr. Torrey. I sign'd a Lease to Nehem. Hayden; Mr. Stoughton, Unkle Quinsey and his Son Witnesses. Mr. Torrey is for a Fast, or at least a Fast first. Mr. Willard for a Thanksgiving first. Mr. Torrey fears lest a Thanksgiving should tend to harden people in their carnal confidence. Cousin Gookin grows worse of her brest rather than better. Were wet coming home; met Mr. Caleb Moodey

³⁴ The actual signatures of these men appear in the diary.

and N. Gooding on Crane's plain, riding to meet the Son of said Moodey, who came home in Jarvis and landed at Cape-Cod Harbour. When came home went to Capt. Hill's to the Meeting. I read the 11th Sermon of Mr. Flavell to the end of the 3^d Excellency; 6 first Lines I composed with my own hand in London concerning God's being the Centre and Rest of the Soul. No body ask'd for the Meeting, so I invited them to our house.[35]

Nov. 27. As 2^d Bell is begun to be rung for Lecture, the Cleper falls out, the staple that held it being broken. At night Goodm. Williams rings the South-Bell for 9 aclock, at which many people started, fearing there had been fire. No ringing at the Old Meeting-House on the Sabbath, Nov. 30, nor 9 aclock Bell since Thorsday, that I have heard.

Nov. 29. Menval had a hearing before the Council as to Money of his in Sir William's hand: very fierie words between Sir William and Mr. Nelson. When Sir William went out seemed to say would never come there more, had been so abus'd by said Nelson, and if Council would not right him, he would right himself.[36]

Nov. 30. Tis extream cold and poor Cous. Savage is still aboard at Nantasket, not being able to be brought up yesterday, wind so high, he so low brought by wound and sickness.

Dec. 1, 1690. The Pink Eagle 80 Tuns, Joseph Buckly Master, Loaden for Jamaica, was burnt in the Harbour, very little sav'd besides a new Cable; came by Carelessness. Owners, Capt. Checkly, his Brother Sam. Mr. Foxcroft.

Dec. 1. Went to the Funeral of John Hews of Newbury, a Souldier from Canada, died of the bloody flux. Mr. Moodey and his Son went next the Corps, Major Richards and Hutchinson next, Sewall and Thornton, Capt. Hall, &c.; about 30 or 40 Men and Women: Extream Cold. Visited Sir William, so home.

Dec. 2. Lieut. Ephr. Sale dies.

Dec. 3. Brother Needham dies and Goodw. Deacon. I was with Brother Needham on Tuesday about 11. aclock and had comfortable

---

[35] The lines in Flavel's sermon, composed by Sewall, are as follows: [Communion with God] "is the centre which rests the motions of a weary soul; 'tis the rest and refreshment of a man's spirit. Psal. 116, 7. *Return unto thy rest, O my soul.* When we attain perfect communion with God in heaven, we attain to perfect rest; and all the rest the spirit of man finds on earth is found in communion with God." John Flavel, *Works* II, 542. M.H.S.EDS.

[36] Meneval, the governor of Port Royal, had been brought to Boston by Phips as a prisoner of war. He was complaining that Sir William and his lady had refused to return to him the money and articles he had given into the general's hands for safekeeping. Alice Lounsberry, *Sir William Phips* (1941), 211–214, and Massachusetts Archives, XXXVI, f.233 and 262 as cited by M.H.S.EDS.

discourse with him; I had much adoe to persuade him to let me help him on with his Jacket; he was much affected with the kindness.

Satterday, Dec. 6. Brother Wm Needham is buried about 3 aclock: Bearers, Deacon Eliot, Frary, Allen, Tomson, Bridgham. Had Rings and Gloves. Executors sent me a Ring.

Wednesday, Dec. 3, 1690. A Church is gathered, and Mr. John Whiting Ordained Minister at Lancaster. Mr. Sam Whiting gives him his Charge, Mr. Estabrooks gives the Right hand of Fellowship; Mr. Brinsmead and others there.

Monday, Dec. 8. Din'd with me at the Royal Exchange, Sir William Phips, Isaac Addington Esqr., Mr. Saml Willard, Capt. Joshua Scottow, Capt. Nathl Byfield, Mr. Peter Sergeant, Samson Sheaf, Thomas Brattle, Jno Eyre, Henry Dering, Capt. James Hill. Twelve in all.

Dec. 16, 1690. Very cold. I visit the Major Generall in the even, who has kept house ever since Wednesday last, through pain and Indisposition by putting his Anklebone of his right legg out of joynt. Advised him of the Fast to morrow.

I spoke with Mr. Partridge about Kittery Grant, that if he cut any Masts there, he should give me an account of them, and I would use him well. He said he got Masts at Exeter, and not there this winter: and would be sure to wrong no man, much less me.

Wednesday, Decemb^r 17, 1690. A Day of Prayer is kept at the Townhouse, Mr. Allen prays, Mr. Moodey preaches, Mr. Willard prays. 'Tis so cold and so much Ice in Charlestown River, that neither Dept. Governour, Treasurer, Mr. Morton, nor Charlestown Deputies could get over. Mis. Russel hath the Small Pocks which stays him. Mr. C. Mather is ill, and can't come. Major Generall has put his Ankle out of joynt, he not there. Col. Shrimpton and Deacon Eliot were there. This morning we have the sad news of the death of Mr. John Clark, our beloved Physician, between 4. and 5. *mane.*

Dec. 19, 1690. Heard Mr. Thacher preach at neighbour Herridges; then went to the Funeral of Mr. Jno Clark; Bearers, Richards, Hutchinson, Addington, Middlecot; Townsend, Turell. Governour [*Bradstreet*], Sir William, Major Johnson, Treasurer [*Phillips*], and Sewall went next the Relations. Warm Southerly wether. Three desirable Men now dead; one out of each Church. Our Mr. Pain, the oldest, being about 68.

December 23, 1690. Major Pike tells me in the Townhouse of Eliakim Mather's being come. Came with Mr. Cotton about noon, but I saw him not till night, being detained at the Townhouse all day.

Dec. 29, 1690. Mr. Addington and I goe to Sir William Phips's, where Mr. Moodey and Mr. Mather in his Border: had very sharp discourse; Mr. Mather very angrily said that they who did such things as suffering Sir William to be arrested by Meneval, were Frenchmen, or the people would say they were, &c.

Dec. 30. Council orders the Writt against Sir William to be null.[37]

Dec. 31. Visit Cousin Savage at Reading, who keeps his Bed, and can hardly stir, yet is cheerly.

[37] This is the Meneval affair again. Governor Bradstreet wrote a private letter to Phips, 7 January 1690/1, saying that the Council made an order 30 December for the delivery to Meneval of his chest and clothes, "taken into custody by your order when he was brought up from on board the vessel." But as Meneval has not received them, and is in great want of his clothes, Bradstreet reminds Phips of that order, and hopes he will execute it. M.H.S.EDS.

1691

TRAGIC FIRE AT MUDDY RIVER / COTTON MATHER VINDICATES
PERRIWIGS / LEISLER'S REBELLION / TRIP TO NEWBURY / PRIVATE
FAST / RESIGNATION AS CAPTAIN OF THE SOUTH COMPANY / JOHN
ALDEN'S SHIP CAPTURED BY THE FRENCH / MARY SEWALL BORN /
CHURCH COUNCIL AT LYNN

Jan. 1 [1690/1]. Visit Capt. Clap. Mr. Allen preaches against minding our own things, &c. His house broken up in Lecture time and above 40£ in Money stolen.

Jan. 2. Eliezer Russel buried.

Jan. 3. Josiah Grice, a very usefull man and good Christian, died last night. Mrs. Ruck buried this day, Sam. Clark's Aunt; outliving her Son but a very little while.

Jan. 7*th*. Mr. Addington and I went to Mr. Cotton Mather, and expostulated with him about the discourse at Sir William's, and the Remonstrance brought to the Council by Capt. Greenough and Mr. Coleman the Tuesday following: and hope 'twill tend to promote Charity and Peace.

Satterday, Jan. 10, 1690/1. Betty with her Sister and others were riding in a sled, and the Indian who drove it struck Betty with his Goad on the side of the head so as to make it bleed pretty much and swell, but thanks be to God, no danger now the fright is over, and heals.

Sabbath, Jan. 11*th*. At night the House of Joshua Gardener, at Muddy-River, is burnt, and two of his Children; the Lord help us to repent that we do not likewise perish. Twas my turn to Watch. I sent Eliakim; the north watch saw the light of the fire.[1]

Jan. 21, 1690/1. Meeting at Mr. Woodmancies in Major Wallies house. A cry of fire was made which much disturb'd us in the middle of Sermon; it prov'd to be Mr. Pole's Chimney, which made a great light. Snow on the houses which prevented danger. Sermon, Brother Emons read, was about Hungering and Thirsting after Righteousness. Mr. Burroughs on the Beatitudes. Sung 2*d* part 45. Psal. Mr. Burroughs referring to the time of the new Jerusalem. Very Cold.

[1] See Sewall's entry for 21 December of this year.

Satterday, Jan. 24, 1690/1. Wear comes in; came from Cows Decr 1; brings Mr. Dudley, Mr. [*William*] Brenton and others.

Jan. 26. Mr. Brenton exhibits his Commission, under the Broad Seal, for exercising the Office of Collector, Surveyor and Searcher.

Jan. 27th. Major Generall comes not, so that had much adoe to persuade Major Hutchinson to hold the Court, it seeming so odd for only three freshmen to hold it where seven or more of the chiefest and ablest used to keep Court; by that means begun not till past noon.

Feb. 2. This morn Capt. Roger Clap dies, about 86 years old. Capt. Brown arrives at Marblehead, came from Plimouth 19th December.

Feb. 3. This morn, or last night, Capt. Johnson dies suddenly, a very old Man, between 86 and 90.[2] On Sabbath-day night, Feb. 1. Col. Shrimpton's Sign, the Royal Exchange, is blown down, the Keeper of it run away on Satterday.

Friday, Feb. 6. Mr. Stoughton and Dudley call here, which is the first time since his coming from England when I was at home.

Sabbath, Feb. 15. 9. mane, at the desire of Annis Hill, I give a Warrant to search for her Husband, Tho. Hill the Tanner, who has been missing ever since last night. This day is taken up drown'd. This morn, Elisabeth Dixie (now Pemberton) is taken into Church before the Sacrament.

Feb. 12. I watch with Mr. Bannister and Peter Wear; Sit at James Meers's between while because of the Rain, darkness and slippiriness. Had a good night.

Tuesday, Feb. 17. Went in Mr. Shiprev's Boat to Hog-Island, to see what Wood the Tenant had cut. Passage has been open about a week, and Crooked Lane a 14 night.

Feb. 18. Mr. Willard and Capt. Frary came to our House.

March, 3, 1690/1. About noon Marshall Generall Green dies of the Fever about noon.

March 4. Buried in the evening.

March 5. After Lecture Mr. Saml Gookin is Appointed by the Governour and Council to be Marshal Generall till the sitting of the Generall Court; and the Oath administred to him in open Court accordingly.

March 9, 1690/1. Town-Meeting. Select-Men chosen, Mr. Jn° Joyliff, Tho. Walker, John Foster, Penn Townsend, Tim° Prout, Bozoon Allen, Jeremiah Dummer, Jn° Marion sen^r, Obadiah Gill. Town-Treasurer, chosen by papers, Mr. James Taylor. Select-Men last year, now passed by, are Capt. Turell, James Hill, Mr. Richard Middlecot.

---

2 Captain Francis Johnson, who was made freeman at Salem in May 1631.

Constables, Joseph Belknap, Elizur Holyoke, Joseph Grant, William Rouse, Jnº Borland, Benj. Bream, Samson Duer, George Clark, Timº Wadsworth. Fin'd Jacob Melyen, Jnº Mico, Jnº Borland. Overseers of the Poor, Nathᶦ Williams, Benj. Walker, William Coleman, Sim. Stoddard.

March 10*ᵗʰ* Four Deputies for Boston, Capt. Penn Townsend, Capt. Theophilus Frary, Timº Prout, Mr. Adam Winthrop, 27 Votes. Mr. Serjeant, Taylor, Eyre had several votes.

March 10, 1690/1. Cousin Anna Quinsey removes to Charlestown with her Children and Goods.

Monday, March 16. I watch, accompanyed by Serjᵗ Jnº Bull, and Corpᶦ Peter Wier: had a very comfortable night. Gave money to each Guard.

March 19, 1690/1. Mr. C. Mather preaches the Lecture from Mat. 24., and appoint his portion with the Hypocrites: In his proem said, *Totus mundus agit histrionem.* Said one sign of a hypocrit was for a man to strain at a Gnat and swallow a Camel. Sign in 's Throat discovered him; To be zealous against an innocent fashion, taken up and used by the best of men; and yet make no Conscience of being guilty of great Immoralities. Tis supposed means wearing of Perriwigs: said would deny themselves in any thing but parting with an opportunity to do God service; that so might not offend good Christians. Meaning, I suppose, was fain to wear a Perriwig for his health. I expected not to hear a vindication of Perriwigs in Boston Pulpit by Mr. Mather; however, not from that Text. The Lord give me a good Heart and help to know, and not only to know but also to doe his Will; that my Heart and Head may be his.

March 25, 1691. I walk on foot to Roxbury, and visit Mr. Bowls, who lies very sick of the Small Pocks, this the 7ᵗʰ day. Mr. Walter pray'd with him before I came away.

March 28, 1691. A Post comes to Town from New York, and brings a Letter from Henry Sloughter, Governour there, who arrived the 19ᵗʰ Instant, on Thorsday. Messenger tells us that on Tuesday, and Wednesday before, Capt. Leisler fired upon the Town, and killed Six persons; some went to fire a great Gun at the fort, and by accident, five persons were slain, of whom Mat[*thew*] Gregory was one. On Friday, the fort was surrendered, out of which 400 marched. Col. Bayard took out of Prison, and Capt. Leisler put in his room, and Bayard's chain put on 's Legg. Governour had six weeks passage from Barmudas, so that some began to think he might have been cast away.

March 27. Mr. Moodey visited us in the even, pray'd hard for Assurance. I was at Charlestown Lecture, where Mr. Morton Preach'd well about the Light of God's Countenance desired by the Saints— very thin Assembly. Mr. Russel and I prov'd one Greenland's Will. The L. hear the Prayer of Mr. Morton and Moodey for them and me. Mr. Moodey talked with me about resisting unto blood, the Subject he was to treat of next Sabbath: and witnesses not being slain.

April 5*th*. At night, about 12. or 1. set sail in the Prudent Mary Bark, Daniel Lunt Master, for Newbury; sail'd through Squam, so to Ipswick Bar and Newbury Sound. Mrs. Hannah Moodey and Jane Toppan with me; fell aground at Sandy Beach an hour by Sun, Apr. 6.

Apr. 9*th*. Ride and visit Mr. Simms and Ward, take Livery of Jn° Kent's Lot.

Apr. 10*th* Drive a Nail in Abiel Sommerby's House.

Apr. 11. Ride to the Falls to visit Sister Longfellow; To Peter Cheyny's Mill.

Apr. 13. To Salem, visit little Sam. Sewall, my Namesake.

Apr. 14. Home, find all well, blessed be God.

Apr. 20*th* 1691. Being pressed with the sense of my doing much harm and little good, and breach of Vows at my return from New York, this time twelvemonth, that is, not heedfully regarding to go at God's Call, I kept a Fast to pray that God would not take away but uphold me by his free Spirit. When I came to look, I found it to be the very day of the week and year as much as could be that I set out for New York, which made me hope that twas a token for good that God would pardon that Sin and Sins since committed. Pray'd for Sister Dorothy, my family, New England, that God would fit me for his good pleasure in doing and suffering. Treaty with Indians to be the 1st May, &c.

Apr. 27. Went with Mr. Moodey on foot to the Ferry, and with Major Phillips accompani'd him to Mystick, where left him with Mr. Allen the Scholar and other Company at the Widow Wade's; as return'd saw Mr. and Mrs. Morton at their Farm. This Afternoon had Joseph to School to Capt. Townsend's Mother, his Cousin Jane accompanying him, carried his Horn-book.

Apr. 27, 1691. Din'd at Cous. Dummer's with the Select-Men.

May 4. Eight Companies Train; I went not into field; in the evening Major and Captains came hether to desire me not to lay down my place, Mr. Cotton Mather being here, set in with them. Mr. Mather staid and went to prayer with us, and had the very expressions us'd by the Dept. Governour when He deliver'd me my Commission; viz: Let us serve our Generation according to the Will of God, and afterwards fall asleep.

Satterday, May 16. Between 3. and 4. P.M. South-Company is warned to attend on the Election day, by Solomon Rainsford, in the Rain.

May 19, 1691. mane, Mr. Richardson visits me. I ask whether he receiv'd my Letter I sent him before my going for England. He answered, yes. I tried to reinforce it, as to what concern'd his faithfull fullfilling his Ministry. What effect twill have God knows.

May 20th. Election-day, very fair and comfortable wether. Led the South-Company into the Common, there pray'd with them, so march'd with Capt. Hill to the Governour's. Guard consisted of two Files on each Flank, &c.; had but four Drums, made extream bad Volleys at night. After being treated by the Governour, the 122. Psalm was sung, Mr. Allen got me to set the Tune, which was Windsor; it brought to mind the Psalm sung in that very Room in 1686, which Mr. Nowell read. *Note.* Throw what heartlessness I scarce know, but I went not for Mr. Morton to bring him to the Meetinghouse, nor to fetch him from Mr. Eyre's to dinner, which now I look upon it, troubles me much. Mr. Hutchinson and Addington not sworn this day.

May 21. Dept. Governour, Major Generall and I went to speak to Mr. Stoughton, desiring him to accept of the place he is called to. I bought two answers of Church of England Address of Mr. Wilkin, and gave Mr. Stoughton one. Major Pike, my self, Matthew Jn°son, Sam¹ Partrigg, and Joseph, are a Committee to consider how Money may be got in for present Exigencies. Just as was at our Gate with them and a crowd of other people, about 7. aclock, Ben. Harris comes to me, and tells that Capt. Leisler and Mr. Millburn were executed last Satterday, that Mr. Fannevil brought the news: whereas most were pleasing themselves that there was like to be no such thing, and that Govr Sloughter begun to think him an honest man and entertain him at his Table.[3]

---

[3] Following the Glorious Revolution in England and the Boston revolution of April 1689, Fort James was seized in Manhattan, 31 May 1689, and Captain Jacob Leisler usurped complete control of southern New York. An energetic executive, he devoted himself to the French war and a military union of the colonies, but lack of co-operation from the other colonies and his own tactlessness prevented success. When Colonel Sloughter, commissioned Governor of New York by William and Mary, arrived, Leisler was tried for treason. He and his son-in-law and chief lieutenant, Jacob Milborne, were hanged. In 1695 Parliament

May 29ᵗʰ. Mr. Addington and I wait on Mr. Stoughton at Dorchester.

May 30ᵗʰ. Mr. Stoughton takes his Oath.

June 1. Mr. Taylor, Mr. Pierpont and Mr. Walter dine with me; Mr. Walter tells me of a small Paraphrase of Mr. Eliot's upon Ezek. 37., written about half a year before his death.

June 2ᵈ 1691. Mr. Edward Taylor puts his Son James to Mr. Steward, Shopkeeper of Ipswich, for Seven years, to serve him as an Apprentice, Term to begin the first of July next. Mr. Taylor desires me to represent himself in making the Indenture, if Mr. Steward desire the accomplishment of it befor He comes down again.

June 3, 1691. Sister Sewall of Salem comes to see us; 5ᵗʰ, Brother comes, tells me Ezekiel Northend is like to go to Sister Dorothy again. 6ᵗʰ, goe home.[4]

June 10ᵗʰ 1691. I goe to Salem, visit Mr. Higginson, dine with Him, after his Lecture; view the fortifications.

June 16ᵗʰ. Brother sends me word of the arrival of Jnᵒ Ingersoll, well laden with good Salt. Sister Dorothy's being come thether the night before, intends hether shortly.

June 17. Fast at the Townhouse, Magistrates, Ministers: Mr. Hale, Bayly, Brinsmead, Torrey, Moodey, Willard pray, Mr. Lee preaches. Mr. Fisk, Thacher, Gookin, Jnᵒ Danforth sup here.

June 19ᵗʰ 1691. The Reverend Mr. John Wilson, Pastor of the Church at Medfield, came before me, and seal'd and published a certain Writing to be his last Will and Testament, to which accordingly I subscribed my name in the place of the Witnesses; Bromfield, Clark, Sharp having subscribed before.

Monday, June 22. Sam. Toppan brings Sister Dorothy to Town. Tom. Hitchborn's Son drowned this day. I watch at night in the Ensign's turn with Serjᵗ Bull and Corpˡ Weare.

June 29. Went to the Island, had my Daughters Hannah and Elisabeth with me. Went to see about building a room for Goodw. Balchar to doe her work in. Cornelius Creek and Jnᵒ Wells row'd us in Mr. Shiprevs Boat. Yesterday Rainsford arriv'd with 17 Men that remained alive on Antis Coti [*Anticosti*]; 4 dead of Small Pocks since the Longboat's coming. They saw Ten Sail of Frenchmen standing for Canada River, many of them suppos'd to be of 3. and 2 hundred Tuns.

---

reversed Leisler's attainder and restored property to his family; in 1702 the New York Assembly voted an indemnity to his heirs. *D.A.B., Dict. Amer. Hist.*

[4] Sewall's sister Dorothy was married to Captain Ezekiel Northend of Rowley 10 September 1691, and this is reported in the entry of 17 September.

July 20. Much Lightening in a Cloud toward the Castle, which many observ'd and talk'd of.

Wednesday, July 22. Brought the Major Generall, going to Jamaica, and under the Oak over against the Schoolhouse took leave. Is at last gon to New London to settle his affairs; which Journey he has a very long time talk'd of.

Wednesday, Augt. 5*ᵗʰ*. The death of Govʳ Sloughter[5] is talk'd of through the Town. News came last night or this morning. Capt. Scottow told it here as was at Breakfast with Mr. Torrey and me. Cousin David Hobart here.

Thorsday, Augt. 6. Very great Thunder and Lightening last night between 1. and 4. past midnight, from the Southward first, and then from the Northward. Hear already that a Barn at Malden is burnt by it.

Augt. 11, 1691. Sentenc'd Francis Allen and two Frenchmen: admonish'd Humfry Johnson of Hingham and his wife for living apart. Mr. Payson din'd with us. Adjourn'd to this day 14 night, 1 P.M.[6]

August 14. Went to Charlestown-Lecture, from thence walk'd to Cambridge with Mr. Addington to visit the Deputy Governour, who has kept his Bed these three days, having an inward Fever. Visited the Colledge and so came from thence about Sunset in the Shadow of the Evening. Mr. Moodey preached the Lecture from Acts 16. 29, 30. Shew'd that such an anxious Speedy Enquiry after Salvation, was a good step towards it.

Augt. 19, 1691. Sent Jane to Newbury by Timᵒ Burbenk, to help tend her Brother Sam. Toppan, who is there taken ill of the Small Pocks.

Augt. 23, 1691. Sabbath-day, about 3 P.M. The Revᵈ Mr. John Wilson of Meadfield dies, being 70. years of age wanting a moneth. *vid.* June 19ᵗʰ.

Augt. 28. *Friday.* Fast at Charlestown, where I am. After my coming home when 'tis almost dark, Jane Toppan comes in from Newbury and brings the very sorrowful News of the death of Cous. Sam.

5 Colonel Henry Sloughter, Governor of New York province, died 23 July after only four months in office.

6 On 12 August 1691, Samuel Sewall, Merchᵗ, became surety to the town for Bethulia Mighell, widow, and her family (*Boston Record Commrs. Report* x, 80). This was Bethia Weld, widow of Rev. Thomas Mighill of Scituate (Harvard 1663) who died 26 August 1689. In his will he entreated "the worshipfull Mʳ Samuel Seawell Mʳ Isaac Addington of Boston and my loving Cousin Mʳ John Wells Senʳ of Roxbury to take the oversight of this my last will and to Assist my wife with their best Counsell advice and Direction" (*Pilgrim Notes and Queries* v, 61). Sewall made no mention of Mrs. Mighill in the diary.

Toppan last Tuesday night about nine of the Clock; buried the Wednesday night following, because of the Heat. No Minister with him: Mr. Shove prayd not with him at all, went not to him till was just dying: suppose might be afraid of 's school. Sam. bewail'd his not minding Spiritual things more, and that times were such as that things of that nature were scoff'd at. About Monday night last as Joseph was going into Cradle, He said, News from Heaven, the French were come, and mention'd Canada. No body has been tampering with him as I could learn. The Lord help us to repent that we may not perish, as probably Eliakim and those with him have done; and now poor Cousin Sam.[7]

Sept. 1, 1691. Went to a Fast at Dorchester, Mr. Danforth pray'd and preach'd. Mr. Moodey pray'd in the Afternoon, Mr. Torrey preach'd, pray'd, had a comfortable day. Before came home, supp'd at Mr. Stoughton's in company of Mr. Danforth and wife, Mrs. Hannah Moodey, Mr. Edw. Rawson, Mr. Moodey, Torrey, Bondet, Mr. Sam. Moodey.

Sept. 2, 1691. Went with Mr. Moodey and visited the Dept. Governour, Mr. Stoughton and Russel came in. Mr. Moodey pray'd. Dame Mitchelson present, earnestly desiring prayers. Mrs. Danforth tells me that Goodw. Luxford was buried yesterday, died of the Fever after four years Torment or more, of a Chronical Illness. Deacon Cooper died a little while agon, a very good Man.

Sept. 5. I went over the water with Sam. Haugh to his farm to view the Carpenters Work.

Sept. 14, 1691. Mr. Parker comes to me by my desire; tells me there was no Rigging on the Mast he saw; at the [?] he called and said, did think it was Condey's Mast, there was no Rigging on it: Condey is his Sister's Son. Saith there is now a report from Barbados that Condey is cast away on Cuba, and all the men safe. *Utinam.*

Sept. 14, 1691. Nine Companys Train, Capt. Smith of Winnisimmet making one. The Troop also in Arms led by Lieut. Swift, Capt. Eliot being sick of the Fever and Ague. South Company chose two Corporals; Tho. Banister who had nineteen Votes, and Thomas Walker jun[r] who had Twenty Votes. They who came next, were Tho. Wallis, who had fifteen votes, and John Mason, who had Nine. By reason of Capt. Smith, drew into Three Divisions: South Company, Major Savage and Smith made one: Horse charg'd each Division twice or thrice, and so drew off.

[7] Samuel Toppan, Sewall's nephew, died of the smallpox 25 August at the age of 18. *Savage.*

Din'd at Mrs. Man's; had the Governour, Mr. Willard, Bayly, Capt. Dummer.

After the Training Edward Cowell was buried; died at Hingham; Corps brought hether by water. Mr. Baily on a White Horse prayd at finishing the Exercise. Thanked God that no evil accident had been this day.

Sept. 17ᵗʰ 1691. Capt. Scottow's Sappho tells me that Sister Dorothy was married last Wednesday sennight and was gon to Rowley.

Sept. 25ᵗʰ 1691. Elisabeth Clements of Havarill is tried for murdering her two female bastard children.

Sept. 26. She is brought in guilty by the Jury, Mr. Crisp Foreman. Mr. Stoughton was not in Court on Friday afternoon when the Trial was; and went off the Bench on Satterday morn when the Jury were call'd to give in their verdict. Persons present were, Govʳ, Russel, Johnson, Hathorn, Hutchinson, Sewall, Addington, Phillips.

Friday, Oct. 9. Mr. Baily preaches the Lecture at Charlestown; After Lecture Mr. Morton dines in his new House, one Room being clos'd. Were at Table, Mr. Morton and Mrs., My Lady Phips, Mr. Moodey and Mrs., Mr. Allen, Mr. Baily, little Jnᵒ Bailey.

Monday, Oct. 12ᵗʰ, 1691. Eight Companys Train; exercise single in the morn. I dine in the late Mr. Thacher's Study, have there Major Richards, Major Generall Winthrop, Mr. Addington, Mr. Willard, Capt. Scottow, Mr. Waldron. It seems Major Richards serv'd his time in the House, to Major Gibbons. Capt. Scottow told us that one of his Squadrons did now make two Captain's Companies. Exercise Regimentally in the Afternoon; when concluded, Mr. Mather prayd.

Oct. 16. Ordered the Clark to warn the Officers to meet me at Sergᵗ Bull's. After the meeting at Mr. Willards went thether. Serjᵗ Bull, Rainsford, Odlin; Corpˡ Wheeler, Weare, Banister, Jnᵒ and Isaac Marion there. I acquainted them with my inability to serve longer as a Captain, and my desire the Company might be setled.

This day a Dutchman comes in with a French Prize taken in Lat. 25. to the Eastward of Barmudas, bound for Brest. Elisa. Emmerson was brought to the Bar to be sentenc'd, she deliverd a Petition to the General Court, so she was sent back to Prison again.

Satterday, Oct. 18. P.M. Had my four children to Mr. Robert Saunderson to receive his Blessing as he lay on his Bed; hath not been at Meeting these two Sabbath-days; his Right Eye is grieved with a Rheum, &c.

Oct. 19, 1691. Mr. Cotton Mather visits me; we meet Mr. Willard, and He comes in also. Talk of parting. This day news is brought of Capt. Alden's being Taken by a French Frigot at St. John's, Mr. Nelson carried to Quibeck;[8] Col. Tyng and Mr. Jn° Alden jun' kept Prisoners till Articles made for Capt. Alden's coming home be fullfill'd. There is Loss to Boston Merchants about 18.000 pounds; besides what prejudice may come by the Intelligence the French may extort from our Men. This day the Marshal General tells me that above fifty Sheep were kill'd at Cambridge last night, having their Throats bitten, and blood suck'd.

Thorsday, Oct. 22. Mr. Nehemiah Walter marries Mrs. Sarah Mather before John Phillips, Esqr.

Sabbath, Oct. 25. Capt. Frary's voice failing him in his own Essay, by reason of his Palsie, he calls to me to set the Tune, which accordingly I doe; 17, 18, 19, 20, verses 68th Psalm, Windsor Tune; After the Lord's Supper, 6, 7, 8, 9, verses 16th Low-Dutch. P.M. 2½ staves of 141. Ps. St. Davids, Jehova, I upon Thee call. After Evening Exercise, 2d part 84th Ps. Litchfield; I knew not that had the Tune till got to the 2d Line, being somewhat surprized, though design'd that Tune. I would have assisted Capt. Frary but scarce knew what Tune he design'd; and the Tune I guess'd at, was in so high a Key that I could not reach it.

Sabbath, Oct. 25, 1691. Boston, N. E. I pray'd this morn that God would give me a pardon of my Sins under the Broad Seal of Heaven; and through God's goodness have receiv'd some Refreshment and Light; I hope I doe thirst after Christ; and sensible of my own folly and Loathsomness that I value Him no more, and am so backward to be married by Him.

Wednesday, Oct. 28, 1691. My wife is brought to Bed of a Daughter about 8. in the morning; Elisabeth Weeden, Midwife. Rose about 4. m.

Sabbath. Novembr 1. A very pleasant day. Mr. Willard baptiseth my Daughter Mary, was enlarged in Prayer, none else baptised. Capt. Eliot not being abroad, I set the Tune again; Martyr's, St. Davids, Oxford.

Mis. Richards dies this day.

Monday, Nov. 2. I ride to New Cambridge to Mr. Neh. Hobart's to see his Dwelling, and prepare a place for Sam. Visit Mrs. Oakes as I come home, at her Cousin Chaney's. Visit Mr. Fitch at Mr. Bailyes. Mr. Dudley.

Nov. 3, 1691. Mr. James Lloyd marryes Mrs. Rebecka Leverett.

Wednesday, Nov. 4, 1691. Went to the Funeral of Mrs. Richards.

---

[8] Captain John Nelson had brought to Boston the news of the landing of the Prince of Orange, and he was one of the leaders in the revolt against Andros. He was long imprisoned in Quebec and France. *Hutchinson* (1936), I, 319–322.

Mr. Stoughton, Major General Winthrop, Mr. Russel, Sewall, Addington, Phillips, Bearers. Was put in a new Tomb in the North-burying Place. Bearers had Scarvs and Rings. Saw not Mr. Dudley there. Governour went thether on foot in the wet and dirt, and home again. Much Rain fell last night and this morning; fair wether at the Funeral. Sir Robert Robison there. No Minister out of Town that I saw, save Mr. Morton. Mr. Moodey at Portsmouth.

Yesterday had the News that Mr. Hatches Sloop, burthened 40. Tuns, was run away with by Rogues we heard were drownd. Sloop was richly laden, which makes the stroke the greater, especially to Hatch, who was removing to dwell at Connecticut.

Satterday, Nov. 7th 1691. Mr. Shove sets out for Marlborough in his way to Simsbury, Joseph Strickland and others accompanying him.

Sabbath, Nov. 8. Is a Contribution for the Fronteer Towns; Capt. Eliot, though abroad on the Day of the Thanksgiving, is now ill again, of the bloody Flux, it seems; I set the Tune; York, Windsor, 119th Ps., on the two last Staves of the 34th Psalm.

Nov. 10, 1691. Council of Churches meet at Lin. From Boston, Mr. Willard, Sewall, Frary; Allen, Hutchinson, Bridgham; Mather, Foster, Keech: Malden, Wigglesworth, Sprague, Green; Salem, Noyes, Hathorn, Corwin, Gardener, Lindon. Had much adoe to prevail with the Church to own us as a Council, but did do it at last; heard what was to be said, drew up our Advice by Mr. Cotton Mather; wherein all parties blamed; They accepted of it and thank'd us heartily for our visiting them. Bell was rung both times before went into Meeting-house. Mr. Wigglesworth Moderator.

Thorsday, Nov. 19th 1691. Sam. goes to Cambridge with Mr. Henry Newman, who is to carry him to morrow Nov. 20. to Mr. Neh. Hobart's at New Cambridge.

Nov. 18th. Last night the Governour was taken with the Stone, so the Council meet at his House; He was at the Town-house yesterday but then the Wether hinder'd the Council's meeting.

Tuesday, Dec. 1, 1691. Brother Wm Moodey brings Sister Gerrish to see us; she is great with child, looks to ly in the latter end of February, with her eighth.

Dec. 2. Very stormy day of Snow and Rain; by the fire I speak earnestly to Sister to make sure of an Interest in Christ, being alone.

Friday, Dec. 4. Brother Moodey and Sister Gerrish take their journey homeward, intend to call at Salem, notwithstanding the Small Pocks.

Monday, Dec. 7th. I ride to New-Cambridge to see Sam. He could hardly speak to me, his affections were so mov'd, having not seen me for above a fortnight; his Cough is still very bad, much increas'd by his going to Cambridge on foot in the night. Mr. Hobart not at home. Mr. Lawson was by accident there, and so had the benefit of his Company home. Got well home before 6. aclock, set out from home after 12. Staid there about 1½ hour. *Laus Deo*.

Monday, Dec. 21, 1691. I went with Mr. Addington and his wife to Muddy-River, to the House of Joshua Gardener, where came Mr. Walter and his wife, Mr. Denison and wife, Sir Ruggles and Mrs. Weld the Mother. Had a very good Dinner. Mr. Walter crav'd a Blessing, Mr. Denison return'd Thanks, mentioning the sad Providence that befell them last January, and God's present smiles in their new House and children; Mr. Walter pray'd that God would double their Mercies. Sung the 23. Ps. and 18th v. 51. Mr. Walter desired me to set the Tune, which I did; St. David's. Twas so late before Mrs. Weld came, that got home by Moon-Light. Wife was invited, but went not by reason of the Cold. Was glad of this opportunity to converse with Mr. Walter, Denison and their wives. The Lord give me to believe on his Son, and fit me for His Entertainment in Heaven.[9]

December 25, 1691. General Court passes an order for prohibiting Frenchmen being in the Seaports or Frontier Towns, except by License from the Governour and Council; and pass an order for Laying a Duty on things exported and imported, to defray the charge of a Guard-Ship. Adjourn to the 8th of March.

The marriage of Hanna Owen with her Husband's Brother, is declar'd null by the Court of Assistants. She commanded not to entertain him; enjoin'd to make a Confession at Braintrey before the Congregation on Lecture day, or Sabbath, pay Fees of Court and prison, &c. and to be dismiss'd. Governour not abroad to day.

Mr. Moodey takes his journey towards Portsmouth this day. Cold and Snowy. Shops open and business carried on as at other times.

[9] Sewall had recorded the burning of Joshua Gardener's house on the night of 11 January 1690/1 and the loss of two of his children in the fire. The December housewarming was something of a family gathering. Mrs. Gardener was Mary Weld, grandniece of Dorothy (Whiting) Weld ("Mrs Weld the Mother"), whose daughter, Dorothy (Weld) Denison, was present with her husband, William Denison of Roxbury (Harvard 1681). Nehemiah Walter (Harvard 1684) was the Roxbury minister; on the 22d of October Sewall had recorded his marriage to Sarah, daughter of Increase Mather. Sir Ruggles was Thomas Ruggles (Harvard 1690), not yet M.A. and not entitled to be called "Mr."

1692

January, 2, 1691/2. Tim° Dwight dies about 10. *mane.*[1]

Boston in N. E. January 2, 1691/2. I had been at Mrs. Collucott's, and coming home between 12. and 1. I call'd to see Tim° Dwight, and as I stept into the Room, saw him laid out under the sheet.

Monday, Jan. 4th Went to the Funeral of Tim. Dwight. Cous. Dummer, Capt. Jn° Walley, Capt. Wing, Rowse, Tho. Savage, Goldsmith, Robt Saunderson, Bearers. Mr. Joyliff and I went next the Relations; by the Dock-head Mr. Willard struck in: no Minister before; buried at the new burying place; somthing troublesom going, by reason of the great Snow fell yesterday. 38 years old. Lord grant that I may be ready, when the Cry shall be, Behold, the Bridegroom cometh.

Tuesday, Jan. 12, 1691/2. Major Hutchinson and I visit Major Johnson, Mr. Hez. Usher and Sol. Phips in Company. He is very glad to see us. Call'd at Betty Gardener's as came back. This week's Rain and Sun have thaw'd the ways as if it were March. Major Johnson has kept house about 18 weeks. Takes his disease to be the burning Ague mentioned in the Scripture. This night [*blank*] Hamlen, formerly

---

[1] Sewall's entry of 12 August 1676 records Timothy Dwight's Swoun that evening, brought on, Sewall feared, by a maiden he passionately loved. Timothy recovered quickly when John Hull permitted his apprentice to go to her. No record of Dwight's marriage has survived, but his wife, designated affectionately in his will, was Elizabeth. Dwight's bearers included four master goldsmiths, Jeremiah Dummer, William Rouse, Thomas Savage, and Robert Saunderson, whose work, along with Dwight's, is highly cherished by museums and collectors after nearly three centuries for its beauty and excellence of craftsmanship. Boston Museum of Fine Arts, *Colonial Silversmiths, Masters and Apprentices* (1956).

Plats, before that, Crabtree, a middle-aged woman, through some displeasure at her Son whom she beat, sat not down to Supper with her
Husband and a Stranger at Table: when they had done, she took
away, and in the Room where she set it, took a piece of grisly meat of
a Shoulder of Mutton into her mouth which got into the top of the
Larynx and stopt it fast, so she was presently choak'd. Tho. Pemberton and others found it so when they opened her Throat. She gave a
stamp with her foot and put her finger in her mouth: but Pemberton
not at home, and di'd immediately. What need have all to Acknowledge God in whose Hand their breath is, &c. Sam. Worden, and another woman, die the same night, and widow Oliver de Sweet, the
next day. *Attonitus tamen est, ingens, discrimine parvo committi
potuisse nefas.* [*Ovid, Met., vii. 426.*] 1 Cor. 10. 31.

Jan. 19*ᵗʰ* 1691/2. Visited Mrs. Pool, who lies sick on bed, and has
been there this Moneth; gave her one of Mr. Willard's Cordials; was
very glad to see me. Speaking about Widow Hamlen, she mention'd
1 Cor. 10. 31. Mrs. Elisa. Pool has buried five Sisters, Eliot, Gard,
Sanford, Brown, Burton. Sanford, Gard, have left no Children.[2]

Jan. 24*ᵗʰ* 1691/2. Govʳ Bradstreet comes to Meeting this Afternoon,
which as I remember has not done in January till now.

Tuesday, Jan. 26, 1691/2. News comes to Town by Robin Orchard,
of Dolberry's being arrived at Cape Cod; Sir William Phips made
Governour of the Province of New England.[3] Foy (in whom went Mr.
Lee) taken into France; Quelch and Bant also. Six weeks passage from
Plimouth. This day, almost at the same Time, news was brought of
an Attack made by the Indians on York.

Jan. 25, 1691/2. I asked Mr. Willard at Mr. Eyre's whether the
Times would allow one to build an house; answer'd, I wonder you
have contented your selvs so long without one; but I little thought
what was acted that day at York. Got Mr. Eyre to come home with
me about 8. at night to advise me.

[2] It was not a drink that Sewall gave Mrs. Pool, but a copy of Rev. Samuel Wil-
lard's book, *The Mourners Cordial Against Excessive Sorrow Discovering what
Grounds of Hope Gods People have concerning their Dead Friends* (Boston,
1691). Elizabeth Pool was the daughter of Governor William Brenton of Rhode
Island and the wife of John Pool of Boston, merchant. The five sisters were Sarah,
wife of Rev. Joseph Eliot (Harvard 1658) of Guilford; Martha, wife of John
Card (or Carder) of Warwick; Mary, wife of Judge Peleg Sanford of Newport;
Mehitable, wife of Joseph Brown (Harvard 1666) of Charlestown; and Abigail,
wife of Stephen Burton of Bristol. *Savage.*

[3] The nomination of Sir William Phips was undoubtedly mainly due to Increase
Mather, as Cotton Mather states impliedly in his Life of Phips. It is there called
the work of the agents, Sir Henry Ashurst and Increase Mather, but no one in
that generation doubted to whom the suggestion was due. M.H.S.EDS.

Feb. 8, 1691/2. Gillam arrives, and a Copy of the New Charter comes to Mr. Secretaries hand, about which there is much discourse.

Feb. 12, 1691/2. Joshua Atwater dies, falling off the outward Wharf; he was drowned about 2. or 3. in the morning, intangled in the wood as the Jury brought it in; was going on board the Sloop Mary. Was excommunicated.

Feb. 19, 1691/2. Major Hutchinson begins his journey Eastward against the Enemy. Mr. Stoughton, Major General, Mr. Addington and I brought him going to the Ferry, went not over, the wind was so high. The Horse he intended to have being lame, he took mine.

Feb. 26, 1691/2. News comes to Town of Wear's Arrival last night at Marblehead. Jn° Hayward brings me a Letter and news of it, as were at Breakfast with Unkle Quinsey, Mr. Weld and Brother Stephen. Mis. Maccarta goes to her Husband, ill of the Gout. Mr. Whittingham got to Town by 5. *mane* and brought the News.

Satterday, Feb. 27. Between 4. and 5. *mane,* we are startled at the roaring of a Beast, which I conjectur'd to be an Ox broken loose from a Butcher, running along the street, but proved to be our own Cow bitten by a dog, so that were forc'd to kill her; though calved but Jan. 4ᵗʰ and gives plenty of Milk. Happy are they, who have God for their Spring and Brest of Supplies. Exceeding high wind this day at North East.

Sabbath, Feb. 28. Day is so Stormy that Governour went not to Meeting. Madam Bradstreet not well.

March 11ᵗʰ 1691/2. Mrs. Townsend, wife of Capt. Pen Townsend, died this morn. about 2 aclock; by which means Mr. Addington came to the Governour and Assistants and ask'd excuse as to his attendance at Court, and desir'd that I might supply his place. Made an order as to Joseph Mason, Constable, Watertown. Adjourn'd to the last Tuesday in April, at one P.M. Capt. Wincoll brought us the Jury's verdict about Baker Nason's killing his elder Brother Jonathan Nathan [*sic*] with his Oar in the Canoe in Pascataqua River: and asks advice whether to keep him there, or send him to Boston-Prison. Seems to have done it in 's own defence March 1. 1691/2.

Monday, March 4ᵗʰ 1691/2. Mis. Sarah Townsend buried between 5. and 6. Bearers, Sewall, Dummer, Bromfield, Hill, Winthrop, Eyre. Went to Mr. Davies Gate, and then turn'd about, and so went into the old burying place, out of the Schoolhouse Lane. Was about 39 years old. Set in a brick'd Grave.

March 14ᵗʰ 1691/2. Anniversary Town-Meeting. Select-Men, Tho. Walker, 78—Capt. Bozoon Allen, 75—Capt. Jer. Dummer, 74—

Capt. Pen Townsend, 70—Jnº Maryon, 69—Obadia Gill, 68—Mr. Jnº Foster, 47—Capt. Timº Prout, 32—Mr. Joseph Bridgham, 30. Mr. Joyliff left out.

Mr. Joyliff also lays down his Recorder's place, his sight does so much fail him. Overseers of the Poor, Mr. Samuel Checkly, Mr. Samuel Lynde, Mr. Edmº Brown, Mr. Wᵐ Robie. The Treasurer was chosen next after the Select-Men, had 87. Votes, and not one Vote for any body else that I saw.

March 23, 1691/2. Capt. Alden sails with Capt. Converse for Redemption of Captives [*from Canada*], and fetching home Col. Tyng and Mr. Alden the Son. About 5. P.M. Moses Bradford, essaying to draw a youth out of the Water at Capt. Wing's Conduit, fell in himself and was drown'd, many people round about trying to save him. Boy was taken out alive.

March 24ᵗʰ 1691/2. Governour not at Lecture, being indisposed.

April 11ᵗʰ 1692. Went to Salem, where, in the Meeting-house, the persons accused of Witchcraft were examined; was a very great Assembly; 'twas awfull to see how the afflicted persons were agitated. Mr. Noyes pray'd at the beginning, and Mr. Higginson concluded. [*In the margin*], Væ, Væ, Væ, Witchcraft.

This is Sewall's first mention of the Salem witchcraft affair. Examinations of those accused or suspected had been going on for several weeks before the local magistrates, and many had been committed to jail. On this occasion the deputy governor, Thomas Danforth, and six members of his council were present: James Russell, John Hathorne, Isaac Addington, Samuel Appleton, Sewall, and Jonathan Corwin. The record is printed in Thomas Hutchinson's History of Massachusetts-Bay (1936), II, 21–23, and there is an account in Charles Wentworth Upham's Salem Witchcraft (1867), II, 101–113. John Proctor, his wife Elizabeth, and Sarah Cloyse were examined by Samuel Parris, and testimony was taken in all seriousness from the "afflicted"—the young girls whose wild imaginations, hysterical antics, and screaming fits had precipitated the delusion. Sewall's comment here is the reaction of a sensitive man who took the proceedings at their face value.

One of the major disappointments of the Sewall diary is the scantiness of his record of the witchcraft episode. Some diarists omit disagreeable occurrences from their pages, and Sewall's omissions may be accounted for by the revulsion of feelings of a man of warmth and kindness, and by doubts about the affair, doubts which ripened by the time of his recantation in 1697. Of Sewall's belief in witchcraft there can be no doubt: he was a man of his time, and the learned and the ignorant of 1692 no more questioned the existence of witchcraft than we question the passage of radio waves through the air today.

In the dismal and interminable winter of 1691–92, a group of bored teenage girls, and younger—the daughters, relatives, and neighbors of the Rev. Samuel Parris of Salem Village (now Danvers)—idled often in the kitchen of the parsonage to listen to the tales of Tituba, the half-Carib, half-Negro slave, and to learn voodoo tricks and spells from her. Before many of these forbidden gatherings had taken place they had worked themselves up into mass hysteria, and would put on an act of screaming, writhing, and swooning whenever there was an audience. The parents, the clergy, the doctors, had only one explanation: the girls were possessed. Next the girls accused various crones of bewitching them and torturing them by spectral means. A special court was convened in Salem to deal with this outbreak. Feeling their power as the venerable judges attended in all seriousness to their rantings, the girls went on to accuse scores of persons, some on the basis of family and church feuds which they heard about at home, and before the summer was over nineteen of the convicted had died on the gallows.

Salem and its environs, and indeed New England, were in a state of malaise at this time: the colony charter had been revoked, the Phips expedition had resulted in death, failure, and debt; from the frontier settlements constantly came news of fresh horrors perpetrated by the Indians; there were broken families, homeless children, footloose ex-soldiers. The stress and social disorganization finally produced a community hysteria which found its catharsis in the witch trials and executions.

Belief in witchcraft was once universal in western society, and is not totally unknown today. The English settlers carried it to the new world with the rest of their intellectual baggage. Church and civil law followed the biblical injunction that a witch must not be suffered to live (Exodus xxii, 18). Prior to 1692 there had been six executions for witchcraft in Massachusetts. In the seventeenth century in England the number is estimated in the hundreds; in Scotland the figure is 3,400 between 1580 and 1680; on the Continent, where a complicated and systematized doctrine formed the basis for inquisitorial proceedings, the victims from the fourteenth to the seventeenth century are reckoned at half a million. Most of these were burned; no witches were burned in English America.

It is not possible to compress the history of witchcraft into an editorial note; those who desire the background should consult George Lyman Kittredge, Witchcraft in Old and New England (1929). For the Salem Village episode, Marion Lena Starkey's book, The Devil in Massachusetts (1949), will be enough to satisfy most readers; her list of the sources and

*the multitude of earlier books on the subject is the best available. A later
discussion, Perry Miller's chapter, The Judgment of the Witches, in his
The New England Mind: From Colony to Province (1953), is enlighten-
ing.*

April 13th 1692. A Church is gathered at Wrentham, and Mr. Man
Ordained.[4] Mr. Brinsmead gave the Charge and Mr. Gookin the Right
Hand of Fellowship. The Church of Mendon also sent to and ap-
peared.

Apr. 25, 1692. Eight Companies Train for the first time; considerable heat, and hurt done in skirmishing just at night. Mr. Lawson
concluded with prayer; saluted one another with a general volley, gave
the South Company a Piece of 8/8 [*a Spanish dollar*] to drink.

May 2. No Artillery Training, so near the Election.

May 4. Election-Day, Major Hutchinson and Capt. Greenough's
Companies attend, Mr. Moodey preaches. Dine at Wing's. At the
Election Capt. Johnson of Wooburn is left out, and Major Richards
chosen again. Sir William Phips had the most votes, viz: 969. No
Treat at the Governour's but Beer, Cider, Wine.

May 14th 1692. Sir William arrives in the Nonsuch Frigat: Candles
are lighted before He gets into Townhouse. Eight companies wait on
Him to his house, and then on Mr. [*Increase*] Mather to his. Made no
volleys because 'twas Satterday night.

Monday, May 16. Eight Companies and two from Charlestown
guard Sir William and his Councillors to the Townhouse, where the
Commissions were read and Oaths taken.[5] I waited on the Dept. Governour to Town, and then was met by Brother Short and Northend,
who inform'd me of the dangerous illness of my father, so I went with
them, and was not present at the Solemnity; found my father much
better. At Ipswich, as we were going, saw a Rainbow just about Sun-
set, in Company of Brother Northend.

May 24th 1692. First general Council, Saltonstall, Major Gedny,

[4] Samuel Man (Harvard 1665) had been teaching at Dedham since his graduation and preaching to a small society at Wrentham; the church, as gathered at
this time, consisted of ten persons. Horace Mann was one of his descendants.
Sibley.

[5] Sir William Phips had been commissioned Governor by William and Mary 12
December 1691. He brought with him the new Province Charter, dated 7 October 1691, which was read and proclaimed at this meeting. Sewall was one of the
twenty-eight named to the Council. Because of his absence, as explained, Sewall
did not take the oath until the 24th (*C.S.M.* xvii, 44–46). In his entry of 24
June 1721, Sewall gave Increase Mather the credit for putting his name in the
charter.

Walley, Hutchinson, Lothrop, Alcot, Sewall took their Oaths together, presently after Major Appleton took his. Justices of the Peace
were nominated for the Province.

One of the first matters to come to the attention of the new governor
was the witchcraft affair; already about a hundred of the accused were in
jail awaiting trial. The Governor's Council met for the first time 24 May,
as Sewall recorded. The next day Phips instituted a Court of Oyer and
Terminer "to enquire, hear and determine all manner of crimes and
offenses perpetrated within the counties of Suffolk, Essex and Middlesex . . ." The commissioners were William Stoughton (Harvard 1650),
the lieutenant-governor, who presided; John Richards, Nathaniel Saltonstall (Harvard 1659), Wait Still Winthrop (Harvard ex-1662), Bartholomew Gedney, Samuel Sewall (Harvard 1671), John Hathorne, and Peter
Sergeant, or any five of them. Saltonstall soon retired and was succeeded
by Jonathan Corwin. The clerk was Sewall's brother Stephen. The court,
sitting in the town house at Salem, met 2 June. Bridget Bishop was tried,
convicted, and sentenced; she was hanged 10 June. On the 30th of June
the court sat again, according to adjournment. Sarah Good, Elizabeth
How, Sarah, the wife of John Wilds; Susanna Martin, and Rebecca Nurse
were tried, convicted, and sentenced; they were executed 19 July.

July 13, 1692. Eight Companies in Arms on the Common. Right-
hand File of each Company drawn off for the Service.

July 14ᵗʰ. At night, Sister Hannah Toppan and Sister Mehetabel
Moodey being here on a visit, give me the following account of my
Father's family, in the several branches of it.[6]

1. Hannah—Jacob, Jane, John, Hannah, Elisabeth, Abraham,
Anne. 7.

Samuel—Samuel, Hannah, Elisabeth, Joseph, Mary. 5.

John—Hannah, John, Henry, Stephen, Samuel, Nicholas a
Twin, 6.

Stephen—Margaret, Samuel, Susanna. 3.

Jane—Joanna, Jane, Joseph, Sarah, Elisabeth, William, Moses. 7.

Anne—William, Anne, Stephen, Elisabeth, Nathan. 6.

Mehetabel—Mary, Dorothy, Samuel, Mehetabel. 4.

Eight and thirty in all.

Hannah buried 1; Samuel 5; John 2; Stephen 3; Jane 1; Anne 3. Fifteen in all.

[6] The names tabulated here are the children of Henry and Jane (Dummer)
Sewall, followed by lists of their living children. Full information on these families is given in our Genealogical Appendix.

July 20ᵗʰ 1692. Fast at the house of Capt. Alden, upon his account.[7] Mr. Willard pray'd. I read a Sermon out of Dr. Preston, 1ˢᵗ and 2ᵈ Uses of God's Alsufficiency. Capt. Scottow pray'd, Mr. Allen came in and pray'd, Mr. Cotton Mather, then Capt. Hill. Sung the first part 103. Ps., concluded about 5. aclock. Brave Shower of Rain while Capt. Scottow was praying, after much Drought. Cous. Daniel Gookin sups with us, and bespeaks my marrying of him to morrow.[8]

July 27, 1692. A plentifull Rain falls after great Drought.

July 30, 1692. Mrs. Cary makes her escape out of Cambridge-Prison, who was Committed for Witchcraft.[9]

Thursday, Augt. 4. At Salem, Mr. Waterhouse brings the news of the desolation at Jamaica, June 7ᵗʰ. 1700 persons kill'd, besides the Loss of Houses and Goods by the Earthquake.

The Court of Oyer and Terminer sat 5 August and six were tried, convicted, and sentenced: Rev. George Burroughs (Harvard 1670), John Proctor and his wife Elizabeth; George Jacobs Sr., John Willard, and Martha Carrier. Thirty-five residents of Ipswich, headed by Rev. John

---

[7] Captain John Alden, shipmaster, had been accused by some of the afflicted Salem Village girls as their tormentor. He was a son of John and Priscilla Alden of Plymouth, the Pilgrims. For over thirty years he had been a leading and respected citizen of Boston; he was one of the founders of the South Church in 1669, and as a brave and efficient seaman in command of the armed vessel of the colony he had done noble service in the wars against the French and Indians. He was about sixty-five years of age. It is a pleasure to read of his resolute temper and the indignation in behavior and speech which he exhibited when, to his amazement, he found himself before the magistrates at Salem on 31 May, charged by a group of "wenches, playing their juggling tricks," with tormenting them, as they had never before seen each other. On this occasion he is said to have used the strong language of an old sea dog. The magistrates sent him to the Boston jail, and he was there when Sewall, one of his judges, took part in the fast at his home. After a confinement of fifteen weeks, with the aid of friends he made his escape to Duxbury, where relatives secreted him until the delusion was spent. He was discharged of "suspition of Witchcraft" by the Superior Court of Judicature 25 April 1693 (*C.S.M.* x, 25). In June 1693 Sewall records a visit to Captain Alden and his wife to tell them of his sorrow for Alden's imprisonment and his pleasure at his "Restauration." On 14 March 1701/2 Sewall went to visit the ailing captain, and was present when he died. M.H.S.EDS., *Hist. Catalogue of the Old South Church* (1883), 223–225.

[8] The following day Sewall married Daniel Gookin (Harvard 1669), minister of Sherborn, to Bethia Collicott of Boston.

[9] Elizabeth, the wife of Nathaniel Cary of Charlestown, had been committed to prison in Boston, but her husband had her transferred to Cambridge jail, where she was kept in irons. After her escape they fled to New York, "where Governor Fletcher entertained them very courteously." Hutchinson, *Hist.* (1936), II, 36.

Wise, sent a petition to the Court of Assistants at Boston, certifying the unblemished character of John Proctor and his wife, and twenty neighbors of Salem Village testified in their behalf; these actions saved the life of Elizabeth Proctor, who was enciente, but the other five were executed 19 August. Sewall made a record of this execution.

Wednesday, Augt. 10. I carried my Mother, Mrs. Jane Sewall to visit Sam. at Mr. Hobart's at Newton.[10] Mr. H. Newman there, who came with us as far as Roger Adams's.

Monday, Augt. 15. Mr. Joseph Eliot comes in and tells me the amazing News of the Revd. Mr. Nathan[1] Gookin's being dead; tis even as sudden to me as Mr. Oakes's death. He was one of our best Ministers, and one of the best Friends I had left.[11]

Augt. 16, 1692. I went to the Fast at Roxbury and from thence to the Funeral of Mr. Gookin. Mr. Mather, Allen, Morton, Willard, Bayly, Hobart, Bearers. Has left a widow, a Son and Daughter. Capt. Ruggles also buried this day, died last night, but could not be kept.

Augt. 19th 1692. This day the Lieut. Governour, Major Phillips, Mr. Russel, Capt. Lynde and my self went to Watertown. Advis'd the Inhabitants at their Town-Meeting to settle a Minister; and if could not otherwise agree, should first have a Town-Meeting to decide where the Meetinghouse should be set. Many say Whitney's Hill would be a convenient place.

This day [*in the margin*, Dolefull! Witchcraft] George Burrough, John Willard, Jn° Procter, Martha Carrier and George Jacobs were executed at Salem, a very great number of Spectators being present. Mr. Cotton Mather was there, Mr. Sims, Hale, Noyes, Chiever, &c. All of them said they were innocent, Carrier and all. Mr. Mather says they all died by a Righteous Sentence. Mr. Burrough by his Speech, Prayer, protestation of his Innocence, did much move unthinking persons, which occasions their speaking hardly concerning his being executed.

Augt. 25. Fast at the old [*First*] Church, respecting the Witchcraft, Drought, &c.

Augt. 27. About 4. P.M. Cous. Fissenden comes in and tells the sad news of Simon Gates being dead of the Fever; died yesterday and is buried to day. I heard not a word of it, and so neither saw him sick,

[10] The name of New Cambridge, or Cambridge Village, had been changed to Newton 8 December 1691.
[11] Nathaniel Gookin (Harvard 1675) had been minister of the church in Cambridge since 1682; he was thirty-five.

nor was at his Burial. The Lord grant the Landlady and her Children may be also ready.[12]

Thorsday, Sept. 1, 1692. Major John Richards marries Mistress Anne Winthrop before Wᵐ Stoughton Esqr. the Lieut. Governour, at the House of Madam Usher.

Sept. 4ᵗʰ. Major Richards accompanies his Bride to our Meeting, morning and evening. *Note.* Mr. Randolph came to Town last Friday.

The special Court of Oyer and Terminer met again the 9th and 17th of September. On the first day six were tried, convicted, and sentenced, and on the second day nine were condemned. Of this number, eight were hanged 22 September on Gallows Hill: Martha, wife of Giles Corey; Mary Easty, Alice Parker, Mary Parker, Ann Pudeator, Willmot Reed, Margaret Scott, and Samuel Wardwell. There were no further executions for witchcraft.

Monday, Sept. 19, 1692. About noon, at Salem, Giles Corey was press'd to death for standing Mute; much pains was used with him two days, one after another, by the Court and Capt. Gardner of Nantucket who had been of his acquaintance: but all in vain.[13]

Sept. 20. Now I hear from Salem that about 18 years agoe, he was suspected to have stampd and press'd a man to death, but was cleared. Twas not remembred till Anne Putnam was told of it by said Corey's Spectre the Sabbath-day night before Execution.[14]

[12] In a marginal note Sewall says that Simon Gates died at Muddy River.

[13] In an open field near the Salem jail, Giles Corey, about 80 years of age, was put to death by officers of the law, who placed heavy stones on his supine body, adding them until his life was extinguished. This was in strict accord with English law, but the case stands alone in American annals; *peine forte et dure* was the punishment for standing mute and refusing to plead to an indictment. The details of Corey's "unsettled and impulsive character, of his ill-repute, perhaps unjustly grounded, among his neighbors, and of his troubled life" as well as of his execution can be found in Charles Wentworth Upham, *Salem Witchcraft* (1867), I, 181–191; II, 334–343. Corey felt that he had no chance of acquittal of the charges of witchcraft standing against him; he also bethought his not inconsiderable land holdings which might be forfeited if he were convicted as a felon. He therefore executed a deed in Ipswich jail conveying his property to his sons-in-law, William Cleves and John Moulton, who had stood by him in his troubles. When called to court to answer the indictment of the grand jury, he stood resolutely silent.

[14] Cotton Mather printed Thomas Putnam's letter to Sewall in his *Wonders of the Invisible World.* Ann Putnam, 12, was one of the aptest pupils of Tituba in the Parris kitchen, and with her mother, one of the chief accusers of the witches.

Sept. 20, 1692. The Swan brings in a rich French Prize of about 300 Tuns, laden with Claret, White Wine, Brandy, Salt, Linnen Paper, &c.

Sept. 21. A petition is sent to Town in behalf of Dorcas Hoar, who now confesses: Accordingly an order is sent to the Sheriff to forbear her Execution, notwithstanding her being in the Warrant to die to morrow. This is the first condemned person who has confess'd.[15]

Sept. 21. Brother and Sister St[*ephen*] Sewall come to see us.

Putnam wrote: "The Last Night my Daughter Ann was grievously Tormented by Witches, Threatning that she should be Pressed to Death, before Giles Cory. But thro' the Goodness of a Gracious God, she had at last a little Respite. Whereupon there appeared unto her (she said) a man in a Winding Sheet; who told her that Giles Cory had Murdered him, by Pressing him to Death with his Feet; but that the Devil there appeared unto him, and Covenanted with him, and promised him, He should not be Hanged. The Apparition said, God Hardened his Heart, that he should not hearken to the Advice of the Court, and so Dy an easy Death; because as it said, 'It must be done to him as he has done to me.' The Apparition also said, That Giles Cory was carry'd to the Court for this, and that the Jury had found the Murder, and that her Father knew the man, and the thing was done before she was born. Now Sir, This is not a little strange to us; that no body should Remember these things, all the while that Giles Cory was in Prison, and so often before the Court. For all people now Remember very well, (and the Records of the Court also mention it,) That about Seventeen Years ago, Giles Cory kept a man in his House, that was almost a Natural Fool: which Man Dy'd suddenly. A Jury was Impannel'd upon him, among whom was Dr. Zorobbabel Endicot; who found the man bruised to Death, and having clodders of Blood about his Heart. The Jury, whereof several are yet alive, brought in the man Murdered; but as if some Enchantment had hindred the Prosecution of the Matter, the Court Proceeded not against Giles Cory, tho' it cost him a great deal of Mony to get off." (Reprinted from Mather's book in G. L. Burr, *Narratives of the Witchcraft Cases*, 1914, 250). The court record of Giles Corey's offense has been preserved, and is published in *Records and Files of the Quarterly Courts of Essex Co., Mass.* VI (1917), 190–191. On 18 July 1676, "Giles Cory, presented upon suspicion of abusing the body of Jacob Goodell by beating, was fined, and ordered to pay witnesses, Mr. Endecott, Elisha Cabee, Lott Kellom, Wm. Benett, Jon. Proctor and Samll. Pope." Elisha Kebee testified that "a little before Jacob Goodall's death, he saw Gills Core unreasonably beat said Jacob with a stick of about an inch through and that with the great end of the stick he struck him nearly a hundred blows which so grieved deponent that he ran to Corie and told him he would knock him down if he did not forbear."

[15] By reason of a strange inversion of jurisprudence which prevailed in the witchcraft court, confession insured immunity from trial or imprisonment or execution. Some fifty-five of the accused confessed their complicity with the Evil One and were allowed to go free. Dorcas Hoar had been tried and sentenced, and her hanging was imminent before she confessed; she would have gone to the gallows except for the petition gotten up for her by influential friends, including John Hale, minister of Beverly. M.H.S.EDS.; M. L. Starkey, *The Devil in Massachusetts*, 205–206.

Thorsday, Sept. 22, 1692. William Stoughton, Esqr., John Hathorne, Esqr., Mr. Cotton Mather, and Capt. John Higginson, with my Brother St., were at our house, speaking about publishing some Trials of the Witches.[16] Mr. Stoughton went away and left us, it began to rain and was very dark, so that getting some way beyond the fortification, was fain to come back again, and lodgd here in Capt. Henchman's Room. Has been a plentifull Rain, blessed be God. Mr. Stoughton went away early in the morn so that I saw him not. Read the 1 Jn° 1. before went to bed.

Thorsday, Sept. 29ᵗʰ 1692. The Major Generall sets out for Elisabeth's Iland and Marthas Vinyard. Governour comes to Town.

Friday, Sept. 30. Go to Hog-Island with Joshua Gee and sell him 3 white oaks for thirty shillings; I am to cart them to the Water side.

Satterday, Oct. 1. I ride to Newton to see Sam., dine with Mr. Hobart, his wife, Mrs. Prentice, and 2 or 3 Cambridge Scholars; bring home some Chesnuts in the Burs to set. First went to George Bearstow's and the widow Gates's. Rains at night Oct. 1.

Friday, Oct. 7ᵗʰ. Mr. Willard and I visit loansom Mr. Torrey;[17] we meet my Unkle entring Crane's Plain in his way to Boston; He turns back with us and accompanies to Weymouth. Mrs. Fisk is very dangerously ill. Got home rather before seven aclock very well, blessed be God. Mr. Torrey took our visit very kindly. Din'd in his Kitchin Chamber. He made Mr. Willard crave a Blessing and return Thanks, which He perform'd excellently. To morrow will be a moneth since

16 Cotton Mather had written to Stephen Sewall, Clerk of the Special Court of Oyer and Terminer, on 20 September requesting "what you kindly promised, of giving me a Narrative of yᵉ Evidences given in at yᵉ Trials of half a dozen, or if you please a dozen, of yᵉ principal Witches, that have been condemned." In a postscript he added that "his Excellency, the Governor [Phips], laid his positive commands upon mee to desire this favor of you" (*N.E.H.G.R.* xxxiv, 108). The material was used by Mather in a book discussed at this gathering; he called it *The Wonders of the Invisible World.* The book was rushed through the press and appeared about the middle of October, but bears the date 1693 on the title-page. Following Mather's breviates of the trials there is a statement over the names of William Stoughton and Samuel Sewall, dated at Boston, 11 October 1692, that "Upon Perusal thereof, We find the Matters of Fact and Evidence Truly Reported." The book is treated exhaustively in T. J. Holmes, *Cotton Mather . . . Bibliography* (1940), iii, 1234–1266.

17 Loansom Mr. Torrey was Samuel, the Weymouth parson. He was educated at Harvard in the Class of 1656, but when the Corporation extended the years of study for the B.A. from three to four years, he was one of the seventeen who "went off, and never took any Degree at all." In 1681/2 he declined a unanimous election as president of the college. Mrs. Torrey was Mary, daughter of Edward Rawson, secretary of the colony. Torrey remarried in 1695. *Savage; Sibley* 1, 564–567.

Mrs. Torrey died, Sept. 10th 1692. Mr. Torrey seems to be of opinion that the Court of Oyer and Terminer should go on, regulating any thing that may have been amiss, when certainly found to be so. Fine rain after our getting home.

Oct. 10th 1692. The Court of Oyer and Terminer is opened at Boston to trie a French Malatta for shooting dead an English youth.

Oct. 11, 1692. Went to the Funeral of Mrs. Sarah Oliver, widow, aged 72. years; buried in the new burying place; a very good, modest, humble, plain, liberal Matron. Bearers, Sam. Sewall, Major Jnᵒ Walley, Capt. Joshua Scottow, Capt. James Hill, Capt. Jacob Eliot, Capt. Theophilus Frary. Scarvs and Gloves.

Read Mr. Willard's Epistle to Mr. Mather's book, as to Cases of Conscience touching Witchcraft.[18]

Oct. 11, 1692. Set two Chesnuts at Mr. Bromfield's Orchard, and three at our own, hoping they may come up in the Spring.

Satterday, Oct. 15th Went to Cambridge and visited Mr. Danforth, and discoursed with Him about the Witchcraft; thinks there cannot be a procedure in the Court except there be some better consent of Ministers and People. Told me of the woman's coming into his house last Sabbath-day sennight at Even.[19]

[18] Subsequent to the first witch execution, that of Bridget Bishop on 10 June, the Governor and Council requested the opinion of the principal ministers upon the state of things as they then stood, and on 15 June twelve of them submitted a body of rules formulated for the guidance of the Salem court. Although they judged that "there is need of a very critical and exquisite caution, lest by too much credulity for things received only upon the devil's authority, there be a door opened for a long train of miserable consequences, and Satan get an advantage over us" the court paid more attention to their recommendation of "the speedy and vigorous prosecutions, of such as have rendered themselves obnoxious, according to the directions given in the laws of God and the wholesome statutes of the English nation, for the detection of witchcrafts." (Hutchinson, *Hist.*, 1936 II, 38–39.) After 19 July, when five more persons were executed, doubts apparently assailed the leading ministers. On 1 August Increase Mather and seven others met at Cambridge to discuss the witch trials, and Mather was asked to prepare in the form of a book a more forceful presentation of the principles laid down by the clergy in June. Mather's book, *Cases of Conscience concerning Evil Spirits*, was printed by November, though the title-page carried the date 1693. By early October a manuscript copy had been presented to Governor Phips, and other handwritten copies had been circulated. By 11 October Sewall had read Samuel Willard's prefatory address, which was printed in all editions, attested by fourteen clergymen. By 15 October the remarks of Thomas Danforth to Sewall indicated that the ministers and people were opposed to a continuation of the trials. By the end of October the court had fallen. T. J. Holmes discusses the *Cases of Conscience* at length in his *Increase Mather . . . Bibliography* (1931), I, 106–138.

[19] Thomas Danforth of Cambridge, "through a long life was one of the most

Friday, Oct. 21. Went to Salem and visited my sick Brother, who has had a Fever all this moneth; Is very desirous to live, and makes vows to serve God better, if his life be spared: was much affected at my coming in.

Oct. 23. At night, Mr. Cook, Oakes and Wiswall arrive,[20] got to their houses almost before any body knew it; have been 8 week and 5 days from Plimouth. Went and saw my Landlord and Landlady Jennings; their Son in Jamaica has a Plantation spoiled by a Mountain thrown upon it by the late Earthquake.

Oct. 26, 1692. A Bill is sent in about calling a Fast, and Convocation of Ministers, that may be led in the right way as to the Witchcrafts. The season and manner of doing it, is such, that the Court of Oyer and Terminer count themselves thereby dismissed. 29 Nôs. and 33 yeas to the Bill. Capt. Bradstreet and Lieut. True, Wm Huchins and several other interested persons there, in the affirmative.

Oct. 27th. Mr. Cotton Mather preaches from James, 1. 4.

Oct. 28th Lieut. Governour coming over the Cause[wa]y is, by reason of the high Tide, so wet, that is fain to go to bed till sends for dry cloaths to Dorchester; In the Afternoon, as had done several times before, desired to have the advice of the Governour and Council as to the sitting of the Court of Oyer and Terminer next week; said should move it no more; great silence, as if should say do not go.

Oct. 29. Mr. Russel asked whether the Court of Oyer and Terminer should sit, expressing some fear of Inconvenience by its fall. Governour said it must fall.[21] Lieut. Governour not in Town today. Several

---

energetic and useful citizens of the town and the Colony." He had been deputy governor, treasurer of the college, and on 6 December 1692 was chosen a justice of the Superior Court of Judicature (L. R. Paige, *Hist. of Cambridge*, 1877, 530). In his letter of 8 October 1692, Thomas Brattle named him as one of "several about the Bay, men for understanding, Judgment, and Piety, inferiour to few, (if any,) in N.E. that do utterly condemn the said [witchcraft court] proceedings, and do freely deliver their Judgment in the case to be this, viz. that these methods will utterly ruine and undoe poor N.E." (G. L. Burr, *Narratives of the Witchcraft Cases*, 1914, 184). We have been unable to identify his female visitor.

20 Elisha Cooke, Thomas Oakes, and Rev. Ichabod Wiswall were returning from England, where they had been agents of the colonies: Cooke and Oakes from Massachusetts-Bay and Wiswall from Plymouth. Evidently Wiswall went on to his home in Duxbury without delay, for he was not present at the festivities at Cooke's on 15 November.

21 In fact, the Court of Oyer and Terminer had fallen of its own weight. The charter of 1691 granted power to the General Court or Assembly to establish courts of record for all purposes. Another section empowered the Governor and Council to appoint "Judges Commissioners of Oyer and Terminer Sheriffs Pro-

persons drowned on Friday 28ᵗʰ. Major General comes home Oct. 28. even, having been gon a Moneth. Deputies doe this day Treat the lately returned Agents Oct. 28.

Nov. 4, 1692. Law passes for Justices and Ministers Marrying persons. By order of the Committee, I had drawn up a Bill for Justices and such others as the Assembly should appoint to marry: but came new-drawn and thus alter'd from the Deputies. It seems they count the respect of it too much to be left any longer with the Magistrate. And Salaries are not spoken of; as if one sort of Men might live on the Aer. They are treated like a kind of useless, worthless folk.

Nov. 5. No disturbance at night by Bonfires.

Nov. 6. Joseph threw a knop of Brass and hit his Sister Betty on the forhead so as to make it bleed and swell; upon which, and for his playing at Prayer-time, and eating when Return Thanks, I whipd him pretty smartly. When I first went in (call'd by his Grandmother) he sought to shadow and hide himself from me behind the head of the Cradle: which gave me the sorrowfull remembrance of Adam's carriage.

Tuesday, Nov. 15ᵗʰ 1692. Mr. Cook keeps a Day of Thanksgiving for his safe Arrival. Mr. Bradstreet and Lady, Major Richards and wife, Major General, Mr. Danforth, Col. Shrimpton, Mr. Oakes and wife, Mr. Sergeant and wife, Mr. Eᵐ Hutchinson and wife, Mrs. Elisha Hutchinson, Mr. Chiever and wife, Mr. Morton, Mr. Willard and wife, Mr. Allen and wife. Mr. Allen preach'd; from Jacob's going to Bethel. Sung twice after my being there, which was late, and once before. Sung after Dinner. Mr. Bayly and Mrs. Bayly there. Mr. [*Increase*] Mather not there, nor Mr. Cotton Mather. The good Lord unite us in his Fear, and remove our Animosities!

Satterday, Nov. 19ᵗʰ. I drove a Treenail in the Governour's Briganteen; and invited his Excellency to drink a Glass of Brandy, which was pleas'd to doe with Capt. Greenough, Mr. Jackson Elliston, and

---

vosts Marshalls Justices of the Peace and other Officers to our Councill and Courts of Justice Belonging." This witchcraft court was established before the legislature met, and before any system of courts had been arranged by its authority. Emory Washburn (*Judicial History of Massachusetts*, 1840, 140–141) discusses this matter, arriving at the conclusion that the Commission was illegal. However this may be, as soon as the legislature exercised its undoubted powers, and established, by Chapter 33 of the Acts of 1692–3, a superior court over the whole province, the temporary court ceased without any formal act of extinction. Occasionally afterwards Commissioners of Oyer and Terminer were appointed, nine cases being cited in W. H. Whitmore's *Massachusetts Civil List* (1870), 75–76. M.H.S.EDS.

his little Son. Saith 'tis the first time has been in the House since my Father's days, who was one of his Owners to the Wreck.

Nov. 20. Mr. Dudley at our Meetinghouse P.M. Uproar in N[orth] M[eeting] House by Cry of Fire, in first Prayer, Afternoon Exercise.

Nov. 21, 1692. Mr. Joseph Eliot, of Guilford, visited, supped and prayed with us, went not away till half an hour after nine at night.

Nov. 22, 1692. I prayd that God would pardon all my Sinfull Wanderings, and direct me for the future. That God would bless the Assembly in their debates, and that would chuse and assist our Judges, &c., and save New England as to Enemies and Witchcrafts, and vindicate the late Judges, consisting with his Justice and Holiness, &c., with Fasting. Cousin Anne Quinsy visited me in the Evening, and told me of her children's wellfare. Now about, Mercy Short grows ill again, as formerly.[22]

Nov. 25. Mr. Mather sent for to her. Bill for Courts pass'd.

Mrs. Brown, wife of Major Wm Brown, is buried this day; is much lamented in Salem. Died on Monday about Sunset. Mr. Bartholomew died about the same time. Extraordinary foggy and dark wether almost all this week.

Nov. 24. Sam. comes to see us from Newton. Give him 16^d, a Groat having engraven, *Salvum fac Regem Domine*, which he construed to me, &c.

Tuesday, Dec. 6. A very dark cold day; is the day Apointed for chusing of Judges. Wm Stoughton, Esqr., is chosen Chief Justice, 15 Votes (all then present.) Tho. Danforth Esqr. 12—Major Richards, 7—Major Genl Winthrop, 7—S. S. 7—I last voted for Mr. Hathorn, who

---

[22] Mercy Short was living at Salmon Falls, New Hampshire, when the Indian massacre took place there 18 March 1690. Her parents and other kindred were brutally murdered and she and five siblings were carried off to Canada as prisoners. She was redeemed and brought back in the Phips fleet in November 1690 to Boston, where she probably went into domestic service. In the summer of 1692 she was sent by her mistress on an errand to the prison where some of the Salem witches were confined. Sarah Good (who was executed 19 July) asked Mercy for some tobacco, "and she affronted the Hag . . . by throwing a Handful of Shavings at her and saying, That's Tobacco good enough for you. Whereupon that Wretched Woman bestowed some ill words upon her, and poor Mercy was taken with just such, or perhaps much worse, Fits as those which held the Bewitched people then Tormented by Invisible Furies in the County of Essex." Fasting and prayer were used as remedial measures, and after several months of fluctuation, Mercy's diabolical molestations ceased completely. Cotton Mather's account, A Brand Pluck'd Out of the Burning (1693) was first published in G. L. Burr, *Narratives of the Witchcraft Cases* (1914), 253–287. See also W. F. Poole, Witchcraft in Boston, in *Memorial Hist. of Boston* (1882), II, 146–152.

had 3—when Major Gen¹ Winthrop chosen, so I counted it probable that he might now carry it: but now Major Gedney had more than he. I esteemed Major Gedney not so suited for the place, because he is Judge of the Probat of Wills. This was in Col. Page's Rooms, by Papers, on Wednesday, December 7ᵗʰ 1692. Tuesday was spent about Little-Compton business and other interruptions. Were at last about 18 Assistants present.

Dec. 8. Mr. Danforth is invited to Dinner, and after press'd to accept his Place. Mr. Morton and Mather dine with us; Governour should have said first.

Thorsday, Dec. 22, 1692. After Lecture, the Governour delivers Mr. Stoughton his Commission as Chief Justice of the Superior Court, and to Major Richards, Winthrop, Sewall as Justices, and the Secretary gave each of us an Oath singly, that would impartially administer Justice according to our best skill. I would have stayed till Mr. Danforth took his; but the Governour granted it not.[23]

Major General tells me, that last night about 7 aclock, he saw 5. or 7 Balls of Fire that mov'd and mingled each with other, so that he could not tell them; made a great Light, but streamed not. Twas our privat Meeting; I saw nothing of it. Order comes out for a Fast. I carry one to Mr. Willard. Mis. Willard talks to me very sharply about Capt. Alden's not being at the Lord's Supper last Sabbath-day.

Dec. 22. Betty being sick, lyes abed and sweats.

Dec. 23. She takes a vomit, and brings up two Worms; one above six inches, and the other above eight inches long; a third about eleven inches in length.

Tuesday, Dec. 27, 1692. I meet the Lieut. Governour at Col. Dudley's, and wait on Him to Watertown, falling in with Major Phillips, Mr. Russel, and Capt. Lynde at Cambridge. Got to Watertown Meetinghouse about eleven aclock. Mr. Lawson went to Prayer. Spent several hours in Debate between three parties relating to a place for publick Worship, and settleing a Minister. At length, Voted unanimously, 1. That would leave the determination of these Differences to a Committee; and would abide by their determination.

2. Do pray the Governour and Council to choose the Committee.

3. Do desire Mr. William Bond and Lieut. Benjamin Garfield to move the Governour and Council for obtaining a Committee for the ends abovesaid.

These three Votes were written one by one by Mr. Lawson and

[23] Sewall continued as Justice of the Superior Court of Judicature until his resignation on account of age in 1728; he was made Chief Justice 16 April 1718.

voted. I think, in the first, one or two held up their hands for the negative, and no more.

After this went to Nevison's[24] and took a very good Repast provided for us by the Select-Men; by which time 'twas past Sunset. Got home well about 7 aclock, in the dark, over the Neck alone. *Laus Deo.*

Satterday, Dec. 31, 1692. I went to Newton to see Sam. Mrs. Hobart is not well, has been very sick: went out about 11. and came in about 5. Staid more than two hours there.

[24] John Nevinson, son of Rev. Roger Nevinson of Hambledon, co. Surrey, kept a public house in Watertown before 1685 and until his death in 1695. Henry Bond, *Genealogies of . . . Watertown* (1855), I, 375.

Augt. 19th 1692. This day the Lieut Gour
-Major Phillips, mr. Russel, Capt. Lynde
& my self went to Watertown. Advis'd
ye Inhabitants at yr Town-Meeting to settle
a Minister; and if could not otherwise
agree, should first have a Town-Meeting
to decide where ye Meetinghouse should
be set: Many say Whitney's Hill
would be a convenient place.

This day George Burrough, John
Willard, Jno Procter, Martha Carrier &
George Jacob were executed at Salem
a very great number of Spectators be-
-ing present. Mr. Cotton Mather was
there, Mr. Sims, Hale, Noyes, Chiever
&c. All of ym said they were inocent,
Carrier & all. Mr. Mather says they all
died by a Righteous Sentence. Mr. Bur-
-rough by his Speech, Prayer, protestati-
-on of his inocence, did much move un-
-thinking persons, wch occasions yr speaking
hardly concerning his being Executed.
Augt 25. Fast at ye old church respecting
ye Witchcraft, Drought &c.

Augt. 27. abt 4 p. m. Cous. Fissenden
comes in & tells ye sad News of Simon
Gates being dead of ye — Fever
died yesterday & is burred to day. I
heard not a word of it, & so neither
saw him sick; nor was at his Burrial.

Dolefull!
Witchcraft

Simon
Gates m.e.
Dies. at
muddy River

The Lord grant y^e Lassmody & her
children may be also ready.

Thursday, Septr 1. 1692. Major John Ri:
Nuptiæ Major Richard chards marries M^rs. Anne Winthrop be=
fore Wm Stoughton Esqr y^e Lieu^t Govr,
at y^e House of Madam Usher.

Septr 4th Major Richard accompanies his Bride
to our Meeting, morning, & Evening.

N. Mr. Randolph came to Town last Friday. ———

Giles Corey pressed to Death Monday, Septr 19. 1692. ab^t noon, at Salem,
Giles Corey was press'd to death for standing Mute
much pains was used with him two days, one after
another by ye Court & Capt Gardner of Nantucket
who had been of his acquaintance: but all in
vain. ^r 20. Now I hear from Salem that ab^t
18 years agoe, he was suspected to have stamp'd
and press'd a man to death; but was cleared. Twas
not remembred till Ane Putnam was told of it
by ye Corey's Spectre ye Sabbath-day night
before ye Execution.

Septr. 20. 1692. The Swan brings in a rich
French Prize of ab^t 300. Tuns, laden w^th
Claret, w^t Wine, Brandy, Salt, Linen,
Paper &^c.

Septr 21. A Petition is sent to Town in behalf of Dorcas Hoar, who now confesses: Accordingly an order is sent to ye Sheriff to forbear
her Execution, notwithstanding her being in
ye Warrant to die to morrow. This is ye first
N. condemned person who has confess'd.

Septr. 21. Bror & Sister St. Sewall come to
us.

1693

Although the special court of Oyer and Terminer had ceased to exist
the previous October, there were further trials for witchcraft this year,
none of which Sewall records. On the third of January 1692/3 the Supreme
Court of Judicature sat at Salem for the County of Essex: present were
William Stoughton, chief justice; Thomas Danforth, Wait Winthrop,
John Richards, and Samuel Sewall. Of more than fifty cases that came before it, the grand jury ignored the majority, but indicted twenty-one persons for felony by witchcraft.[1] Of these only three were found guilty by
the jury, and all three escaped death.

Jan. 16, 1692/3. Serj^t Solomon Rainsford is buried. Wm Gilbert
and he died the last week.

Sabbath, Jan. 22, 1692/3. A very extraordinary Storm by reason of
the falling and driving of the Snow. Few Women could get to Meeting. Our two Maids and my self there. A child named Alexander was
baptized in the Afternoon. Major General not abroad in the Afternoon. Govr Bradstreet very sick.

Jan. 27, 1692/3. Mr. Elisha Cook, Mr. Isaac Addington and I saw
and heard Simon Bradstreet Esqr. sign, seal and publish a Codicil
now annexed to his Will, written by said Addington at said Bradstreets direction, and read to him several times. Signd and seald it
sitting up in his Bed. After told us that if his Estate should exceed
Two hundred pounds more than was mentioned in the Will, would

[1] In his book, *More Wonders of the Invisible World* (1700; reprinted in G. L.
Burr, ed., *Narratives of the Witchcraft Cases*, 1914), Robert Calef gives different
figures, but we follow John Noble's extracts from the records of the court in
C.S.M. x, 23–24.

have his Executors distribute it according to the direction of his Overseers, and Wife, I think. Said, the reason why would sell the little
farm, was because 'twas a ruinous thing, and yielded but 8£ *per* annum in Country-pay. Call'd for Ale and made us drink.

Jan. 28. Went in with Mr. Cotton Mather to Mr. Bradstreets, and
heard him pray.

Sabbath, Jan. 29, 1692/3. A very sunshiny, hot, thawing day. *Note.*
Just as we came out of the Meetinghouse at Noon, Savil Simson's
Chimny fell on fire, and blaz'd out much, which made many people
stand gazing at it a pretty while, being so near the Meetinghouse.

*On 31 January 1692/3 the Superior Court met at Charlestown for the
County of Middlesex, with Justices Stoughton, Danforth, Richards, Winthrop, and Sewall present. The following day, "All but yᵉ Chief Justice
Present," five women were tried for witchcraft, and all were found not
guilty.*

Sabbath, Feb. 5, 1692/3. Three Williams baptized; Elisabeth Wis-
endunk and Abigail Winslow taken into Church, and Elisabeth
Monk (formerly Woodmancy) Restored, having made a satisfactory
Confession.

Feb. 8ᵗʰ 1692/3. Capt. Checkly Tells me at Charlestown, that my
Brother Stephen's wife was yesterday about 11. aclock brought to bed
of a Son. Major Gedney and Mr. Hathorn confirm the same when
I come over to Boston. Mr. Torrey came to Town yesterday to see if
he could get the last clause in the Law relating to Ministers,[2] taken
away, or alter'd: is highly concernd about it.

Feb. 28. Went to Roxbury Lecture. Just before went to the Burial
of Nathanˡ Brewer.

Copy of a Letter to Major Nathˡ Saltonstall Esqr. [Harvard 1659] at
Havarhill, March, 3. Friday, 1692/3.

Dicere quæ puduit, scribere jussit Amor.

SIR, Not seeing you in the Assembly, to speak to you and for the reason
forementioned, I am put upon writing my Salutations to young Mr. Ward,
your self, and good Lady: and telling, that I have sympathised with you
and your family, as to the report that went of some being afflicted by a
person in your shape, and that I fully believe the Letter asserting your
Innocence. Allow me also to intimate that I was grieved upon this day

---

[2] The act which disturbed Samuel Torrey was passed 17 February 1692/3 and
is printed in the Province Laws. *Acts and Resolves* ı (1869), 102–103.

was fortnight, when I heard and saw that you had drunk to excess; so that
your head and hand were rendered less usefull than at other times. You
may remember, you were sitting in the South-side of the Council-chamber,
on the bench; I drew near to you, and enquired concerning Mr. Ward;
you answer'd, He was better, which made you so merry: you also told me
of the breaking up of the Ice of the River Merrimack, having received the
account from your son[-*in-law, Rowland*] Cotton. That is the time I intend. Let me intreat you, Sir, to break off this practice (so 'tis rumourd
to be) not as the River; but obstinatly and perpetualy to refuse the Yoke.
As to your being deny'd a Judges place by the Governour, I no ways influ-
enc'd Him in the matter, neither do I know who did. And I was surpris'd
to hear any Talk of the North Regiment of Essex being put under any
other Major. Don't furnish your Enemies with Arms. I mention this that
you may believe, I write not of prejudice but Kindness; and out of a sense
of Duty, as indeed I doe. Take it in good part from him who desires your
everlasting wellfare, S. S.

March 7, 1692/3. Not having had an opportunity to send my Letter, I was this day surprised to see Major Saltonstall in the Court.
I came home at noon, and took my Letter and deliver'd it with my
own hand just at night, desiring him to read it at his Lodging: but
He being impatient, sat down in the very place mentioned, and discours'd me, gave me Thanks and desired my Prayers. God give a good
effect. This day there is a sore storm of snow after much unusually
warm wether and settled ways.

March 9, 1692/3. Joseph puts his Grandmother and Mother in
great fear by swallowing a Bullet which for a while stuck in his
Throat: He had quite got it down, before I knew what the matter
was. This day in the Afternoon One of Mr. Holyoke's Twins falls into
the Well and is drownd, no body but a Negro being at home; was a
very lovely Boy of about 4 years old.[3] Satterday, March 11, about Sun-
set He is buried. When I come home from the funeral, my wife
shows me the Bullet Joseph swallowed, which he voided in the Orchard. The Lord help us to praise Him for his distinguishing Favour.

March 10, 1692/3. Gwin arrives, 9 weeks from Liverpool; the great
news we had of Dunkirk's being besiegd comes to just nothing; tis so
far from being Taken.

Sabbath, March 12. Bant arrives in the America 9. weeks from the
Isle of Wight; Capt. Thomas Dudley comes in him, first I heard or

[3] The other twin son of Elizur Holyoke was Edward, who became the ninth
president of Harvard College.

saw of him was at Meeting in the Afternoon, sat in his Unkle Allen's Pue.

March 13th 1692/3. Anniversary Town-Meeting. Select-Men, Mr. Tho. Walker, 92—Capt. Bozoon Allen, 87—Obadia Gill, 81—Saml Checkly, 74—Tim^o Thornton, 73—Jno Maryon, 66—Ephraim Savage, 52—Nathl Williams, 29—James Hill, 28. Constables, Capt. Tim^o Clark, 86—Mr. Tho. Cooper, 74—Joseph Russel, 63—Jacob Malyne, 61—Richard Chievers, 49—Enoch Greenlef, 43—William Parkman, 36—Hezekia Henchman, 35. Capt. Ephraim Savage, Town-Clerk. Mr. James Taylor, Treasurer. No Constable fined this year. Very quiet Meeting. Capt. Pen Townsend, Capt. Jer. Dummer, Mr. Jno Foster, Mr. Timo. Prout, Mr. Joseph Bridgham left out. Did not see cause to choose any Overseers of the Poor this year, supposing the work might be better done without such an office.

March 15. Govr Bradstreet's pains return.

March 17. Mr. Willard is sent for, who prays at the breaking up the Assembly; then Mr. Secretary acquaints the Deputies that the Governour accepted their endeavours, and what heat might have appear'd in any debate twas overlook'd. Mr. Speaker in behalf of the Representatives, thank'd the Governour for his Acceptance of their poor Endeavours. Then Mr. Secretary in the Governour's name, declared the Court to be dissolved. This was about one of the Clock. The Lieut. Governour and Major General not present. This Even Mr. Dudley and his Son, Capt. Tho. Dudley, visit me.

Sabbath, March 19, 1692/3. Benjamin Hallawell, late captive in Algier, and his Infant daughter, Mary, were baptized. When I first saw him in London, I could hardly persuade myself that he could live over the Sea, and now I see him and his daughter baptized. Lord let it be a Token that Thou wilt revive thy work in the midst of the years. In London, twas some discouragement to me to think how hardly 'twould come off for the father to pay me for the English Money I had disbursed for the Redemption of a dead Son: but God has given him a new life.[4]

Wednesday, March, 22. 1692/3. Our kitchen chimney fell on fire about noon, and blaz'd out sorely at top, appeared to be very foul: the fire fell on the shingles so that they begun to burn in several places, being very dry: but by the good Providence of God, no harm done. Mr. Fisk was with us, and we sat merrily to dinner on the West-

---

[4] We omit here a letter dated 21 March 1692/3 which Sewall copied in part into his diary; it is a friendly letter of family news and health to an unnamed recipient, probably in Newbury.

field Pork that was snatch'd from the fire on this Occasion. Mother was exceedingly frighted; and is ready to think we are called to remove. This very morning had as 'twere concluded not to build this Summer; because my wife is loath to ly in at another place. What we shall now doe, I know not.[5] Rid to Dorchester.

March 28, 1693. Mr. Cotton Mather has a Son born, which is his first; it seems was without a Postern for the voidance of Excrements; dies Satterday, Ap. 1.

March 28, 1693. I have six little Pines planted in my Pasture by the North-burying Place.

April 4, 1693. I wait on the Lieut. Governour to Watertown, Mr. Russel and Capt. Lynde meet us at Cambridge: I rode with a Watertown man and saw the place by Whitney's where some would have the Meetinghouse stand. At the Meetinghouse heard the Allegations *pro* and *con*, took in their Papers. Came home in the Rain.

Apr. 13. Brother Toppan comes to Town.

Apr. 14. Carries home Jane to see her friends.

Apr. 15. I ride with Capt. Gookin, and take a further view of Watertown that might the better consider the pleas about the place for a Meetinghouse; went about as far as Samuel Begelos near the end of the great Plain. At our coming back, refresh'd our selvs at Mr. Remington's. Call'd at Justice Bond's, who gave us special good Cider.

The first Superior Court of Judicature for the County of Suffolk was held at Boston, 25 April 1693. Justices Stoughton, Danforth, Richards, and Sewall were present. Captain John Alden of Boston appeared, as we have noted, and was discharged of "suspition of Witchcraft" by proclamation.

Apr. 26, 1693. Wednesday. The old Kitchen is pulled down.

Satterday, Apr. 29. The little Hall is Removed, and joind to Matthias Smith's house.

In May, 1693, the Superior Court held a session at Ipswich, Essex County. Justices Danforth, Richards, and Sewall were present. Five women

---

[5] Within a few weeks the decisions had been made by Mother Hull and the Sewalls, and preparations were begun for a brick addition to their house by 26 April. The construction took many months and Sewall recorded numerous details. At the time of the great hailstorm 29 April 1695 the house was still unfinished, but the fast kept in the new chamber 13 August 1695 after Mother Hull's death seems to have been a housewarming.

*indicted for witchcraft were tried and found not guilty. No further cases
of witchcraft are to be found in the records of the court.*

Friday, May 5. Alexander Millar and Frank, Cous. Savages Negro,
begin to digg the Cellar. Mrs. Goose is brought to bed of a daughter.

Satterday, May 6. Widow Sarah Hurd dies.

Tuesday, May 16, 1693. The first stone is laid in the new building,
being the great Stone that lay at Capt. Wyllys's Corner, and is now
our Corner-Stone next Father Walker's.[6]

May 20. The Corner stone next Fort-Hill is laid; The Corner next
Wheeler's Pond had the other half; being the white split Rock on the
Common.

May 20. The Governour comes home from Sea. Major Converse
went out after the Enemy with 200 and odd men, yesterday was sennight; designd for Tackonnick.

Tuesday, May 23, 1693. The Corner Stone next Cotton-Hill is laid,
which fell as it were cheerfully and willingly into his place. I gave the
workmen a piece of Eight.

Satterday, May 27. The foundation of the Cellar is finished, by
stones gotten out of the Common.

Wednesday, May 31. Stoughton, 31—Danforth, 64—Pynchon, 57
—Richards, 60—Winthrop, 65—Saltonstall, 39—Russell, 64—Gedney, 49—Pike, 39—Cook, 31—Hathorn, 35—Hutchinson, 39.

Left *out*—Bradstreet, Hinkly, Appleton, Mason, Lynde, Heman,
Joyliff, A. Winthrop, Middlecot, Alcock.

Wednesday May 31, 1693. Election. Addington, 37—Sewall, 77—
Phillips, 55—Corwin, 46—Foster, 38—Sergeant, 38—Brown, 41—
Bradford, 72—Lothrop, 65—Walley, 24—Thomas, 70—Saffin, 28—
Frost, 66—Hook, 44—Donnell, 27—Silvanus Davis 34.

New—Stoughton, Danforth, Pynchon, Addington, Brown, Thomas,
Frost, Hook, Saffin, Peirce.

Mr. Elisha Cook was refused by the Governour on Thorsday, and
the day following Capt. Daniel Peirce was chosen by 19 votes. Col.
Shrimpton had 17, and Col. Dudley 18.[7]

On Satterday, June 3. Mr. James Taylor was chosen Treasurer by

---

[6] The Hull-Sewall house was on the east side of what is now Washington Street,
in the large block, then undivided, between Summer and Bedford Streets. Robert
Walker's house was across the street and somewhat farther south. Sewall's other
points of orientation are easy, but remote: Fort Hill was east, Wheeler's Pond
south, and Cotton Hill north. 2 *M.H.S.Proc.* 1, 314, 317.

[7] K. B. Murdock has extensive comment on the council election of 1693 in his
Increase Mather (1925), 314–316.

28. votes; Major Phillips had 22; I had 5. I was told before I should have votes and endeavoured to prevent it.

Thorsday, June 8. Elisabeth Emerson of Havarill and a Negro Woman were executed after Lecture, for murdering their Infant Children. Mr. Cotton Mather preached from Job, 36. 14: made a very good Sermon to a very great Auditory.[8] Mr. Danforth labours to bring Mr. Mather and Cook together, but I think in vain. Is great wrath about Mr. Cook's being refused, and 'tis suposed Mr. Mather is the cause.[9]

June 9. Mr. Rawson, *quondam* Secretary, breaks his Fast with us.

Monday, June 12, 1693. I visit Capt. Alden and his wife, and tell them I was sorry for their Sorrow and Temptations by reason of his Imprisonment, and that was glad of his Restauration.[10]

June 13. Several of the Frigots come up above Long-Island. Sir Francis [*Wheler*] came to Noddles-Island yesterday.[11]

Tuesday, June 20. John Barnard lays our Cellar Floor.

[8] Cotton Mather reported in his *Diary* (1, 164): "Many and many a weary Hour, did I spend in the Prison, to serve the *Souls* of those miserable Creatures . . ." His sermon, A Holy Rebuke to the Unclean Spirit, was published in his *Warnings from the Dead* (Boston, 1693; Holmes 440).

[9] Increase Mather is referred to here. Dr. Elisha Cooke had been elected a member of the Council at this time, but was negatived. The quarrel between him and Mather was political, as well as personal. After the overthrow of Andros, the General Court sent over two of its members, Elisha Cooke and Thomas Oakes, to act as agents of the Colony with Mather and Sir Henry Ashurst. Plymouth Colony sent at the same time Rev. Ichabod Wiswall of Duxbury. All three, especially Cooke, were zealous for the revival of the old charter. Mather seems to have shown the most worldly wisdom, and to have secured all possible advantages in a new charter. But the contest among the agents was bitter. Between them the prosecution of Andros was dropped, and hard words exchanged (*Andros Tracts*, ii, xxiii). Cooke was not named in the list of councillors, and when elected in 1693 was dropped. He was elected in 1694, and served annually till 1703, when he was negatived by Dudley; he died 31 October 1717. Dr. Cooke's son Elisha (Harvard 1697) was also a prominent politician, speaker, and councillor, and died in 1737. M.H.S.EDS.

[10] See our note on Captain John Alden under 20 July 1692.

[11] In response to repeated requests from the colonies for a naval force to be sent from England to join with land forces from New England and New York for the reduction of Canada, Admiral Sir Francis Wheler was sent out early in 1693. The expedition was a tragic failure: Sir Francis had orders to capture Martinique first, and while they were in the West Indies fever broke out among his men. When the fleet reached Boston, 11 June 1693, 1300 of the 2100 sailors had died, and 1800 of 2400 soldiers. Hutchinson (*Hist.*, 1936, ii, 54) reports that the fleet-fever "spread in Boston and was more malignant than ever the small pox had been, or any other epidemical sickness which had been in the country before . . ."

Friday, June 23. Sir Francis and several other Capts. of Frigotts are Treated at Cambridge by the Governour and Præsident.

Monday, June 26. The Brick-Work is begun; the South-end of the house being carried up several foot high.

Last night Tim° Wadsworth's man dies of the Fever of the Fleet, as is supposed, he having been on board and in the Hold of some ship. Town is much startled at it.

Monday, July 3, 1693. Mrs. Howchin is buried. Bearers, Major Richards, Mr. Cook, Major Hutchinson, Sewall, Mr. Addington, E^m Hutchinson.

July 11, 1693. Mr. Cotton Mather prays at the opening of the Council. Plentifull Shower of Rain after much Drought.

Before dinner, Mr. Danforth and I go in to the Deputy's about the Bill relating to the Treasurer.

Satterday, July 15, 1693. Mr. Cotton Mather prays in [*the Council*] in the morn. About noon Mr. Willard prays, the Assembly-men being sent for in. Presently after the Governour stands up and dissolvs the Assembly. Was much disgusted about the old Treasurer, and about the not passing of the Bill to regulat the house of Representatives.

July 15, 1693. I went to Mr. Goose, and told him his wife could not conveniently sit any longer in my wives Pue, and therefore desired her to look out another place.

July 24. Capt. Turell is buried. Mr. Joseph Dasset was buried yesterday, being much lamented. Jn° Shove and [*Samuel*] Saxton died before, all of the Fleet-Fever, as is supposed; besides others. The Town is much startled. Capt. Byfield speaks of removing his wife and daughters to Bristow. One of the Fleet-Women dies this day, July 24, 1693, at David Johnson's, over against the Town-house.

July 25. Three Carpenters die.

July 26. Dr. Pemberton dies. Persons are generally under much consternation, which Mr. Willard takes notice of in his Prayer.[12]

July 27th Preaches excellently from—Luke 12. 4. Be ye therefore ready. Caleb Rawlings falls from the top of the Steeple of the North Church, and breaks his Leg, Arm and Neck. Mr. Tho. Pemberton buried. This day we send Joseph to Mr. N. Hobart's to Newton: He rides on the Saddle before Hannah Trowbridge, who guides the Horse, and steadies him.

---

12 Dr. Thomas Pemberton, Boston surgeon, had been present at the dissection of 22 September 1676. He was the brother of Rev. Ebenezer Pemberton, who was ordained as colleague with Rev. Samuel Willard at the South Church, 28 August 1700.

Friday, Augt. 4ᵗʰ 1693. The Governour sets sail for Pemmaquid, goes off at Scarlet's Wharf about 8. in the Even, with Major General, Mr. Addington, Mr. Foster. Capt. Colton's overtaking the enemy who did the Spoil at Squabaog July 27, and killing 5 or 6 of them, bringing back 2 Captives, &c. comes to our hand just now about.

Sabbath, Augt. 6ᵗʰ at 6 P.M. There is a Rainbow about South South-East; has been no Rain. Govʳ Bradstreet is indispos'd, and goes not abroad in the Afternoon.

Sabbath, Augt. 6, 1693. Capt. Wᵐ Greenough died about 4. this morn, buried about nine at night. Three Vollies past nine at night. Neither Major General nor Major Hutchinson in Town. Bright Moonshine. This evening I hear that Mr. Steward of Ipswich is dead.

Monday, Augt. 7. About 4. *mane* I go for the Midwife; About 4 P.M. My Wife is brought to Bed of a Daughter. Thanks be to God. This day Sarah Noyes a young woman of about 21 years dies. Tis very cool and comfortable wether after about a weeks time of excessive Heat. Clouds gather thick, and a little Rain in the Evening.

Wednesday, Augt. 9. There falls a plentifull Rain after a long distressing Drought. *Laus Deo.*

Friday, Augt. 11. I visit Mr. Thacher of Milton who is very glad to see me. Sir Flint conducts me whom I met on the Road.[13]

Monday, Augt. 14. Mrs. Nowell dies. Samson Waters, just building a great House, Roof up, Moses Draper, a very hopefull young man, and 2 more.

Augt. 15. Tuesday. Mrs. Mary Nowell buried. Mr. Cook, Major Hutchinson, Sewall, Allen, Willard, Baily, Bearers. Was laid in Mr. Usher's Tomb.

Augt. 14. The plates and summers [*summer beams*] of the lower Chamber Floor are laid.

Satterday, Augt. 12. Capt. [*and Deacon, Jacob*] Eliot comes sick from Muddy-River.

Wednesday, Augt. 16. Dyes about 2. at night.

Augt. 17. Is buried. Major Hutchinson, Sewall, Joyliff, Walley, D. Allen, Bridgham, Bearers. Buried in the new burying place. Tis a sudden and very sore Blow to the South Church, a Loss hardly repaired. On the Sabbath, Mr. Willard being in before me, I did not mind D[*eacon*] Eliot's absence, and wondered I heard not his voice beginning the Ps., and Capt. Frary waited when I should begin it. We

13 Undoubtedly this was Henry Flynt, who had taken his first degree in July, and as Tutor Flynt or Father Flynt, was a famous Harvard teacher and college character for half a century.

shall hardly get another such a sweet Singer as we have lost. He was one of the most Serviceable Men in Boston, condescending to his friends. One of the best and most respectfull Friends I had in the World. Lord awaken us. Scarce a Man was so universally known as He. Dyed in the 61. year of 's Age. Was one of the first that was born in Boston.

Satterday, Augt. 19. Governour returns from Pemmaquid, and Counsellors all in good health. Concluded a Peace with the Indians on Friday, Augt. 11. They were very desirous of a Peace and professed themselves ready to do what the Governour desired; have sent 3 Hostages.

Sabbath, Augt. 20. Mr. Willard propounds a Church Meeting on Friday next 3. P.M. that may elect a Deacon or two, Capt. Frary not being able to officiat at the Lord's Table, which we are invited to this day sennight.

Augt. 21. I visit Mr. Torrey, who is much better, and very glad to see me: is yet very weak. Coming home Deacon Swift tells me that Mr. Loyd dyed this Afternoon. Visited my Unkle and Aunt. Unkle brought me going till came into Milton bounds. When come home, find the South-East windows of the first Chamber set up.

Satterday, Sept. 9. I return from Point-Judith, having been gon from home ever since the 28. of August. At my return, find little Jane not well.

Sept. 21. Call Mr. Willard to pray with little Jane. Went to Roxbury-Lecture, Mr. Hobart came home with me, who also pray'd with Jane; both excellently. By Dr. Oakes advice, I give her a little Manna. Methinks she looks like Henry in his Sickness. The good Lord prepare her and us for the issue, and help us to choose the things that please Him. Nurse Judd watches.

Sept. 13, 1693. Between 12. and 1. at night following that day, Little Jane expires, much as Henry did, in neighbour Smith's lap, Nurse Hill and I being by.[14]

Sept. 15, 1693. The body of Jane Sewall was laid in the Tomb, between 4. and 5. P.M. John Willard carried the Corps. Lord teach me to profit. I led my wife; Cous. Dummer, Mother; Sam. his Sister; Jane, Elisabeth.

[14] Sewall inserted here a list of his children, with dates of birth, baptism, and death. This information has been incorporated in our Genealogical Appendix. "All the above-named Eleven Children [the author added] have been by their father, Samuel Sewall (holding them in his arms) Offered up to God in Baptisme, at the South-Meeting-House in Boston. The Rev^d Mr. Thomas Thacher baptised Jonh [*sic*] and Samuel; and the Rev^d Mr. Samuel Willard baptised the other Nine, upon the Sabbath Day in the Solemn Assembly of God's Saints."

Sept. 25. Mr. Wm Winthrop dies of the bloody Flux.

Sept. 27. Mr. Joseph Winthrop dies of the same disease. Two children of Major Winthrop.

Sept. 28. Both are buried together, being a very affecting sight. Ministers and Physicians had all Scarvs and Gloves, and many others.

Oct. 5, 1693. By Warrant from the Major, the South-Company is warned to Train on Monday and Tuesday next; words run, *late under the Command of Capt. Samuel Sewall.* John Maryon warned.

Oct. 7th Mr. Cotton Mather's Daughter Maria, of about 2 years old, is buried in the North burying Place; Mr. Pierpont, Willard, Jer. Allen, Winthrop, Bearers. Died on Thorsday night or Friday morn.

Oct. 7th 1693. Mr. Robert Saunderson dies.

Oct. 11th Carried my daughter Hannah to Salem in Company of Mr. Hathorne and Sam. Wakefield; got thether about 8. at night.

Oct. 12. Carried her to Rowley, Wm Longfellow rid before her; I staid Lecture at Ipswich, where unexpectedly heard Mr. Edward Tomson preach a very good Sermon from Felix's procrastination.

Oct. 13. Rid home, having much adoe to pacify my dear daughter, she weeping and pleading to go with me.

Wednesday, Oct. 18. Jn° Barnard raises the Roof of the brick House, no hurt done, through God's goodness.

This day, Mrs. Hunt, Mr. Torrey's Sister, is buried. Alass! that it should be so.

Friday, Oct. 20. The Ship at Bull's Wharf of Four Hundred Tuns, named the Lere-Frigot was Lanched. Yesterday's Storm hindered her being Lanched then. Mr. Eyre's child buried this Afternoon.

Monday, Oct. 30th. I ride to Newton to see Sam and Joseph.

Tuesday, Nov. 21, 1693. Our House is covered and defended against the wether.

Nov. 24. The first Snow falls.

Nota. Nov. 21. Governour bids the Deputies goe chuse a new Speaker; which they pray excuse for. Governour alledges as a reason, Speaker's adjourning their House from Friday till this day without acquainting Him. By mediation the matter is compos'd, and Wednesday morn, the Governour sends to them by the Secretary, to desire them to go on with the business of the Court. Mr. Secretary is directed to enter their Acknowledgment of their Error, and asking Pardon, and that would not practise in like manner for time to come.

Nov. 25. Representatives vote that none be chosen Representatives but persons resident in the Towns for which they are chosen, and having Free-Hold there, &c.

Tuesday, Nov. 28, 1693. The Bill for regulating the choice of Representatives was brought in with the clause relating to Residency of the Persons to be chosen, in the Towns they are chosen for. The Dissent also of 21 Deputies was brought in with it, alledging the vote was contrary to Charter, Custom of England, of the Province, hindred men of the fairest estates from Representing a Town where their Estates lay, except also resident; might prove destructive to the Province. Persons subscribing, Nathan¹ Byfield, Benjᵃ Davis, Francis Foxcroft, Pen Townsend, Daniel Allin, Richard Sprague, Jahleel Brenton, Timᵒ Clark, Stephen Pain, Ebenezer Brenton, Joseph Brown, Jonathan Prescot, John Brown, Giles Dyer, Isaac Little, John Cutler, Timᵒ Thornton, John Legg, Sam¹ Blocket, Stephen Francis, Ebenezer Prout. The clause was read, and the Dissent 2 or 3 times by the Secretary, and then put to the Vote, Governour not being there.[15]

Content.	Not Content.
1. Thomas Danforth	Wᵐ Stoughton, Lt. Govʳ
2. John Richards.	Bartholomew Gedney.
3. Wait Winthrop.	John Walley.
4. James Russell.	Isaac Addington.
5. John Hathorne.	Peter Sergeant.
6. Samuel Sewall.	Samuel Donnel.
7. Jonathan Corwin.	Nathan¹ Thomas.
8. John Foster.	Charles Frost.
9. Daniel Pierce.	

Governour came in presently after had done voting.

---

[15] Sir William Phips had not been a popular governor, and was opposed by a strong faction who wanted him removed. Following certain high-handed actions which had increased the alienation, his partisans proposed and carried in the House an address to the king praying that the governor might not be removed. Of the 50 members present in the House, 24 voted against it, most of them inhabitants of Boston who represented towns in the country. Phips's partisans, "to prevent further trouble if there should be further occasion for any thing to be done in favor of the governor," then brought in the bill with the residence requirement, obviously aimed against the Boston influence, which was passed 25 November. The bill was approved in the Council by a 9–8 vote, Sewall voting in favor, though he had been a non-resident representative from Westfield in 1683.

The residence requirement has generally prevailed in American legislative procedure since that time, restricting the powers of the electors by contracting the limits within which they can choose their public servants. The M.H.S. editors remark, and we agree, that perhaps no other detail in our form of government has had so extensive and pernicious an influence as this restriction of offices to persons inhabiting the districts to be represented. *Hutchinson* (1936), II, 56–60; Robert Luce, *Legislative Assemblies* (1924), 218–228.

ORDINATION.

Wednesday, Nov. 29. Rode to Dedham and saw Mr. Joseph Belchar Ordained. He preached very well from Exod. 4. 12. Mr. Neh. Hobart ask'd the Objections; Mr. Sam¹ Torrey Solemnly prayed and gave the Charge, Mr. N. Hobart and Mr. Jn° Danforth joining in laying on of Hands. Mr. Moses Fisk gave the right Hand of Fellowship. 118. Psalm sung from the 25ᵗʰ v. to the end; St. David's Tune.

Tuesday, Dec. 12, 1693. Rode to Salem with Lieut. Governour and Mr. Danforth, issu'd the Court on Wednesday. Thorsday a great Storm of Rain: so stay'd there still. Din'd at Brother's. Were there in Company afterward, Lieut. Governour, Mr. Danforth, Noyes, Gedney, Major Brown, Hathorne, Capt. Higginson, Mr. Leverett, Paul Dudley, Mr. Newton, Sewall, Sam, Stephen. Supped at Major Brown's; Sung the 122. Ps. &c.

Dec. 15. Very pleasant wether, came home.

Dec. 20. Mr. Barthol. Chever is buried. Capt. Cullimer and 5 others drown'd coming from Scituat last Satterday in a Boat. A Briganteen cast away on Tinkers Island, about 6 drowned, among which an only son sent by his father from Nevis. There is a great Snow on the ground, most of it fallen within these 7 days.

Dec. 21. Publick Thanksgiving, very moderat Comfortable Wether.

Dec. 22. Judge How dies who came from Barbados.

Dec. 23. Governour sails Eastward.

Dec. 27, 1693. Went to the Funeral of Judge How, being invited. Went back at the Gate, and proceeded not to hear the Sermon. Mr. Addington, Foster, Walley, Williams went with Mr. Sergeant to his House.

Dec. 28ᵗʰ. Mr. Ward of Havarill is buried. 87 years old.[16]

---

[16] John Ward (Emmanuel College, Cambridge, 1626/7) was minister and physician in Haverhill from 1641 until his death.

1694

Friday, Jan. 5th. Being in the chamber of the new House next
Tiler's, I fell down, and razed off the skin of my right Legg upon
the shin bone, putting my self to much pain; I was fain to fall across
the Joysts, to prevent falling through, which I was in great danger of.

Satterday, Jan. 13, 1693/4. The Floor of the lower Chamber towards the North-East, is laid; I drove a Nail.

Monday, Jan. 15, and *Jan. 16,* the Floor of the Hall-Chamber is
laid. The Ice is clear gon out of the Docks as in March.

Jan. 17. The Governour and Major Phillips return, and come to
Town by Land from Salem, having been gon near a Moneth. This
day John Mountford marries Mr. Bridgham's wives Daughter [*Mary
Cock*].

Jan. 19, 1693/4. Kitchen floor is finished. This day Mrs. Prout dies
after sore conflicts of mind, not without suspicion of Witchcraft.

Satterday, Jan. 27. The Hall Floor is finished.

Jan. 30, 1693/4. The Kitchin Casements are Glazed and set up.

Wednesday, Feb. 7. Major Townsend has a Daughter still-born and
buried this day. Richard Cornish is buried this week.

Friday, Feb. 23, 1693/4. Council Day for chusing Commissioners
for the Chancery. In the Afternoon chose Mr. Stoughton, 17. Votes,
Mr. Winthrop 16, Major Richards 13, Danforth 7. One and Twenty
present. Lieut. Governour declares his Non-acceptance. Governour
adjourns the Council till morning for Consideration.

This day Henry Ems the Baker has his name put into a Commission to be a Messenger to the Representatives when sitting, and Commission deliver'd to him in the Council-Chamber.

Satterday, Feb. 24, 1693/4. Mrs. Margaret Thacher, widow, dies.
This day our Stairs in the new House are finished.

Wednesday, March 7, 1693/4. I went to Mr. Cook's and offered
him £100. for his old Debt relating to Capt. Wincoll, as I had offer'd,

before I went to England. Had lately promis'd Mrs. Cook to make her some offer before the end of winter.

Monday, March 12, 1693/4. Waited on the Chief Justice and Mr. Danforth to Plimouth.

Thorsday, March 15. Came home; good wether all four days.

Friday, 16. A great Snow falls.

March 27, 1694. Governour, Mr. Danforth, Winthrop, Russell, Sewall, Addington, Foster, Sergeant, Walley, Lieut. Alford, Goodwin, Mason, and Atkins, Carpenter, went to the Castle to view the works in order to Reparation. Mr. Secretary read there the dialogue between Whig and Torey, while it rained.[1] As came up, Capt. Clark saluted us with 3 Huzâs and Guns from his Briganteen.

April 2, 1694. Monday. Artillery Training; Bastian and I set seeds of White-Thorn at Saunders's Pasture, north end. In the Afternoon, all the Town is filled with the discourse of Major Richards's Death, which was very extraordinarily suddain; was abroad on the Sabbath, din'd very well on Monday, and after that falling into an angry passion with his Servant Richard Frame, presently after, fell probably into a Fit of Apoplexy, and died. On Tuesday night was opened and no cause found of his death; noble Parts being fair and sound.[2]

Friday, April 6. Major Richards is buried in his Tomb in the North Burying Place; Companyes in Arms attending the Funeral. Bearers, Stoughton, Danforth; Russell, Brown; Sewall, Addington; Major General and Mr. Foster led the Widow. Mr. Torrey was not there because 'twas Friday. Coffin was covered with Cloth. In the Tomb were fain to nail a Board across the Coffins and then a board standing right up from that, bearing against the top of the Tomb, to prevent their floating up and down; sawing and fitting this board made some inconvenient Tarriance.

Apr. 26. Major Brown marries Mrs. Rebecka Bayly.

Tuesday, May 1. Mr. [Josiah] Woolcot marries Mrs. [Mary] Freak.

Wednesday, May 2. Major Brown has home his Bride; I went as far as Bride-Brook and then returned; many Salem Gentlemen being come to meet Him; though would have been many more but that the

---

[1] A *Dialogue Betwixt Whig and Tory, Aliàs Williamite and Jacobite. Wherein the Principles and Practices of each Party are fairly and impartially stated; that thereby Mistakes and Prejudices may be removed from amongst us, and all those who prefer English Liberty, and Protestant Religion, to French Slavery and Popery, may be inform'd how to choose fit and proper Instruments for our Preservation in these Times of Danger* (No place of publication; 1693).

[2] John Richards of Dorchester is called by Savage "a high friend of liberty"; he was named to the Council in the 1692 charter, and the same year appointed, along with Sewall, a justice of the Superior Court.

day was doubtfull and prov'd very rainy. I came over the ferry with Capt. Legg of Marblehead, his Son and Daughter Brattle, &c: had a very fair wind, but great rain. Visited Hannah Hett, now Parkman, and went to the Funeral of Hezekia Henchman, who died yesterday; was a Jury-man at the last Superiour Court. N[ote]. As went over in the ferry-Boat my Horse kick'd my knee and put me to considerable pain. Brother tells me Sister fears she shall have the Dry Belly-Ache.

May 30. Election.

Mr. Joshua Gee, sometime Captive in Algeer, tells me *June* 11, 1694, that the Turks observe an Hebdomadal Revolution as we do; Our first day of the week is their first day of the week; And they call the days by their Order in the Week; one, Two &c. If they have any notable piece of work to doe, they chuse to begin it upon the first day of the Week, bec. God began his Works on that day.

July 4, 1694. Waited on the Governour to the Commencement. In the forenoon Exercise, Mr. Coleman brings news of the Arrival of Eldridge and that Bennet parted from him about a week ago. Mr. Secretary said that the Packet relating to the Governour are in him. After coming from the Governour at night, Mr. Sam¹ Gaskill, our neighbour's, coming home is told me, comes in Bennet; came up from Nantasket about 8. or 9. at night.

July 5. Mr. Gaskill tells me that orders for the Governour's going to England are sent in the Ship by Mr. Maxfield, a Scotchman, who, he supposes deliver'd the Governour's Packet last night. Said Maxfield gave a receipt for them at London.

July 16, 1694. Town-Meeting at Boston. Chose Assessors, Capt. Foster and I gave them their Oathes. Brother brings Betty to Town.

Wednesday, July 18, 1694. Oyster-River is surprised and 90 odd persons kill'd and captivated, 13 Houses burnd, much Cattel killed and Corn stroy'd.

Friday, July 27. Groton set upon by the Indians, 21 persons kill'd, 13 captivated, 3 badly wounded. About 9. night, Mr. Lodowick comes to Boston. Between 10. and 11. there is an Alarm through the Town kept up till near day-break. Mr. Brattle was arriv'd at Col. Shrimpton's, there he told me of Mr. Lodowicks unhappiness in coming just then. During the Alarm, Mr. Willard's little daughter Sarah dies, buried on Sabbath-day a little before Sunset.

Augt. 6, 1694. Set out with Major Townsend for Albany. Return Augt. 31.

Our diarist has let us down at this point, with no details whatever about an interesting trip to Albany. Fortunately Benjamin Wadsworth (Har-

vard 1690), who went along as chaplain, kept a journal, which was published in 4 M.H.S. Colls. I, 102–110. Mr. Wadsworth was then assistant at the First Church of Boston; later he was teacher of that church for thirty years, then became the eighth president of Harvard, where his house still stands in the College Yard.

Captain Sewall and Major Penn Townsend, who had been commissioned by the province to treat with the Five Nations, set out on Monday August 6. At Watertown they were met by Lieutenant John Hammond with thirty troopers to guard the party to Springfield. They followed the Bay Path and spent the night at Marlboro. Tuesday they dined in the woods, saw a bear, and lodged at Quabaug (Brookfield). Wednesday they reached Springfield and spent the night at Westfield, where they were joined by Colonel John Pynchon, another Massachusetts commissioner, and Colonel John Allyn and Captain Caleb Stanley, Connecticut commissioners. Captain Joseph Wadsworth of Hartford appeared with sixty dragoons for a guard. The next two days they had bad riding through a "hidious, howling wilderness" and camped each night. On the 11th they reached Kinderhook, where they kept the Sabbath, using the Dutch meeting-house. About twenty families lived there, and there were two forts; provisions were very scarce and the party was obliged to pay twelve pence a score for eggs and twelve shillings a piece for lambs. Monday they reached Greenbush easily and crossed the Hudson to Albany.

Albany was a small, compact, well-fortified city entirely encompassed by a palisade of pine logs a foot thick, standing eight or ten feet above ground and sharpened at the tops. There were six gates to the city. At the top of the hill at the west stood the fort, mounting fifteen or sixteen great guns which commanded the entire area. The houses were built with a tall lower storey, "but very few of them have an upright chamber"; many were built of brick with tile roofs. The gable end faced the street.

The day appointed for the treaty with the Five Nations (Mohawks, Oneidas, Onondagas, Cayugas, and Senecas) was the 15th of August. "His Excellency the Governour of York" [Colonel Benjamin Fletcher], five of his council, Colonel Nicholas Bayard, Colonel William Smith, Colonel Stephen Van Cortlandt, Chidley Brook, Esq., and Major Peter Schuyler; and Colonel Andrew Hamilton, "Governour of New-Jersays", were present with the Massachusetts and Connecticut commissioners already mentioned to treat with twenty-five sachems from the Five Nations. "The treaty was held in the street, that runs East and W. [now State Street], a little above the meeting-house. The Sachims were attended with many other Indians. When they came to the place where the treaty was held, they came two in a rank, Rode, the Sachim of the Maquase [Mohawks] being the leader, singing all the way songs of joy and peace. So, likewise, when they were sat

down, they sang two or three songs of peace before they began the treaty.
Nothing was said in this treaty, for the first three days, scil. 15, 16, 17, of
Aug., but what was said by the Indians: the treaty was finish'd Aug. 22."

"We keept the Sabbath, Aug. 19, 1694 [Wadsworth continues]. There
was but one meeting house in the town. Four sermons were preached in it;
the 1 and 3d were preached by Domine [Godfriedus] Dellius, in Dutch;
the second and 4th were preached in English, the former by Mr. Joshuah
Hubbard [Joshua Hobart, Presbyterian minister of Southold, L.I., Harvard 1650], (who came to Albany to see his son, who was a Livetenant
there,) the latter by myselfe, out of 12 Rom. 1. His Excellencie's Chaplain, Mr. [John] Millar, read Common Prayer before each of the English
sermons, tho neither of the English ministers who preached were present
at the same."

The New England party left Albany the 22d and lodged at Kinderhook.
They continued southward through Claverack into the Livingston Manor.
"At Turconnick [Taghkanic], (which is a very stately farm of Mr. Levi-
stone's,) we baited, and refreshed horse and man". Probably this was one
of the settlements of Robert Livingston, first lord of the Manor of Livingston, which had been created eight years before. There was rough travelling, some of it by moonlight, through what we now call the Berkshires,
until Woodbury, Connecticut, was reached. They went on through
Waterbury and reached Farmington, where they kept the Sabbath (the
26th), listening to sermons by Samuel Hooker (Harvard 1653) and
Thomas Buckingham (Harvard 1690). Two days were spent at Hartford;
on Wednesday the 29th, accompanied by six troopers, they went on to
Woodstock, formerly New Roxbury, which Sewall had named. Thursday
four men guarded the party as far as Mendon, and left them to proceed by
themselves to Medfield that night. The next day (31 August) they reached
Boston at noon. Wadsworth reflected on the peculiar hand of Providence
that was over them on the long and hazardous journey: "neither man nor
beast had any broken bone, nor bruise that was dangerous"; they were not
hindered by bad weather, and though they rode part of sixteen days, they
were caught in only one small shower, but had "very plentifull showers
when at our stages, scil. Kindarhook, Albany, Harford."

Of the conference, Palfrey wrote (1, 153) that it had no result beyond
some general assurances of good-will on the part of the Indians.

Oct. 5, 1694. Mr. Willard, Mrs. Willard, Mrs. Noyes, Hannah and
Joseph ride in the Coach to Newton, to visit Mr. Hobart; Sam. and I
goe on Horsback. This day Mr. Oakes's Urian is buried; and Cous.
Mary Dummer dies about break of day.

Fifth Day, Oct. 11, 1694. I have Sam. to Michael Perry to live with him upon Trial. Mr. Torrey prayed earnestly for him at my desire; went a little before eleven aclock.[3]

Fourth-day, Oct. 17, 1694. Mrs. Margaret Shepard, Sam. Phillips's Son, and Mrs. Elisa. Pole dye.

Oct. 19. Mrs. Pole buried. Bearers, Mr. Cook, Sewall, Addington, Oakes, Byfield, Oliver. Was laid in the old burying place.

Oct. 20. This week the upper Floors are laid with boards that had only this Summer's seasoning.

Oct. 22, 1694. Capt. John Wincoll mounting his Horse to ride with Major Hook and others, from Newitchewannuck to the Point, falls off his Horse; in falling cries, Lord have mercy upon me, and dies immediately.

Oct. 24. Sending an Agent from hence voted in the negative by the Council.

Sabbath, Oct. 28, 1694. There is a very High boisterous and cold Norwest Wind, my dear Mother Hull for fear the wind should bear her down, does not put on her Cloak: but wears two Scarvs and so catches cold; however, grows indispos'd so that cannot eat nor sleep; kept from the Catechising and lecture. I left word with Mr. Oliver that mother desired his Brother to come and see her, which he did Nov. 1. and left directions. Mr. Moodey prays with her.

Nov. 1, 1694. Capt. Dobbins refusing to give Bail, the Sheriff was taking him to Prison, and Sir William Phips rescued him, and told the Sheriff He would send him, the Sheriff, to prison, if he touch'd him, which occasioned very warm discourse between Him and the Lieut. Governour.

Nov. 2 Mr. Willard visits her [*Mrs. Hull*] and prays; speaks to her to be very carefull lest should have a sore fit of sickness.

Nov. 3, 1694. 1. past m. Mr. Willard prays and the Governour adjourns the General Court to the last Wednesday in February next, P.M. Several of the Council desired a dissolution, lest some Emergency should require the Calling of an Assembly, and this Adjournment bind our hands; but the Governour would not hearken to it. Onset of the Enemy, Packets from England, were mention'd. Before the Adjournment, Governour expostulated with the Speaker about copying out and dispersing a Letter of Sir H. Ashurst's; then said, This Court is dissolv'd to such a time: being put in mind of his mistake, said, I mean Adjourn'd.

[3] Michaël Perry was a Boston bookseller with a shop "over against the Town House"; Sam was placed with him to learn the business, but during the winter the luckless Sam's feet became sore and swollen from standing in the cold shop, and Sewall brought him home 14 January 1694/5.

Wednesday, Nov. 7. First day of the Court's meeting this week, Capt. Dobbins is call'd. He utterly refuseth to give Bail, confesseth himself to be in the Sheriff's Custody. Between the Sheriff and Keeper is carried to Goal, which makes great Wrath. He pleaded Justification for it, produced two Warrants under the Governour's Hand and Seal, and an Act of Parliament: Court adviseth.

Sixth-day, Nov. 9, 1694. Lieut. Governour and Council dine at James Meers's; The Treat was intended for the Governour; but is so offended at Capt. Dobbins Imprisonment, that He comes not, nor Mr. Mather the Father, nor Son, nor Capt. Foster; so chair at the upper end of the Table stands empty. *Note.* Mr. Cotton Mather was sick of a grievous pain in his facc, clse He had been there, as He told me afterward.

Fifth-day, Nov. 15ᵗʰ. Is a Council at the Governour's House about taking Mr. Jackson's Affidavits; defer it till after Lecture that Capt. Byfield may have notice to be there.

Mr. Walter preaches a very good Sermon from Ps. 73. 27. They that are far from Thee shall perish: shewd the misery of the unregenerat: and Happiness of Believers, by reason of their manifold Nearness to God. Governour did not go to Lecture. After Lecture was much debate at the Townhouse, and at last Mr. Jackson's Affidavits were all read over, and his Oath given him by the Lieut. Governour and Council.

Seventh-day, Nov. 17ᵗʰ 1694. Just about Sunset or a little after, the Governour goes from his House to the Salutation Stairs, and there goes on board his Yatcht; Lieut. Governour, many of the Council, Mr. Cotton Mather, Capts. of Frigatts, Justices and many other Gentlemen accompanying him. 'Twas six aclock by that time I got home, and I only staid to see them come to sail. Guns at the Castle were fired about seven: Governour had his Flagg in main Top. *Note.* Twas of a seventh day in the even when the Governour came to Town, and so tis at his going off, both in darkness: and uncomfortable, because of the Sabbath.[4]

---

[4] Hutchinson (*Hist.*, 1936, II, 57–59) gives a sketch of the closing months of Phips's administration. The Governor became involved in various personal disputes, arising partly from his interpretation of his official powers, partly from his character. "He was of a benevolent, friendly disposition; at the same time quick and passionate."

One quarrel was with Captain Short, of the *Nonesuch* frigate, whom he at last caned in the street. Finally, he was ordered to leave his government, and to answer in England the complaints made against him. On his arrival in London, he was sued by Joseph Dudley and Jahleel Brenton for £20,000. Sir Henry Ashurst bailed him, but he laid his arrest so much to heart that it was supposed to

Nov. 20, 1694. The Dial is set up at the South-West end of the house. Mr. Torrey lodges here.

Nov. 21. My wife grew so ill that I got up between three and four in the morn. Call Mrs. Weeden; proves a rainy day.

Nov. 21, 1694. My wife is brought to bed of a Daughter between 9. and 10. of the Clock in the morn. Mr. Torrey prayd with Mother and me in the Kitchen of the new house for that mercy; Mother desiring Him, saying that my wife was in great and more than ordinary Extremity, so that she was not able to endure the Chamber: I went also to acquaint Mr. Willard, and as I came back, I met Mrs. Perce, who wish'd me joy of my Daughter, as came in at the Gate. Mr. Torrey was prevail'd with to go into Chamber and Return Thanks to God. Women din'd with rost Beef and minc'd Pyes, good Cheese and Tarts. Grows to a very great Storm.

Nov. 22. I put up a Bill for to Thank God for delivering my wife in childbearing; there was no other. Mr. Cotton Mather preached from Isa. 32. 2. taking occasion from the Storm. Lieut. Governour not at Meeting. Mr. Torrey and Fisk lodge here.

Nov. 23. They go home, though the wether is still cloudy, drisky and uncomfortable.

Sabbath, Nov. 25, 1694. I named my little Daughter Sarah, Mr. Willard baptiz'd her. Lydia Cornish, and Joseph Scot were baptiz'd at the same time. Mr. Torrey said, call her Sarah and make a Madam of her.[5] I was strugling whether to call her Sarah or Mehetabel; but when I saw Sarah's standing in the Scripture, viz: Peter, Galatians, Hebrews, Romans, I resolv'd on that side. Also Mother Sewall had a sister Sarah; and none of my sisters of that name.

Dec. 4, 1694. Lieut. Governour calls at 's entrance into the Town; I told him I had spoken to Mr. Willard to pray; tells me of his intended Treat at Mr. Coopers, and enquires whom He had best to invite. Between 2. and 3. P.M. we meet at Mr. Secretaries, from thence go to the Townhouse; viz. Lieut. Governour, Mr. Danforth, Gedney, Russel, Cook, Phillips, Brown, Hathorne, Addington, Sewall, Lynde, Hook, Sergeant. Mr. Willard prayed. Then Lieut. Governour made a brave Speech upon the occasion of the Government's being fallen on Him.[6] After this, Col. Hutchinson came in and made 13.

---

have brought upon him or increased the sickness of which he died, the 18th of February, 1694/5. M.H.S.EDS.

[5] Sarah, in Hebrew, means lady, mistress, or dame.

[6] The Lieutenant-Governor was William Stoughton, who succeeded on the departure of Phips. 17 November 1694, and acted as Governor until the arrival

After twas debated, and several Acts of Parliament view'd, gave the Lieut. Governor an Oath for his due Execution of the Acts referring to Navigation, so far as they concern the Plantations. Voted a Letter to be sent to the Government of Rode-Island that they would discountenance Capt. Tu's [Tew's] proceedings. Voted Capt. Hammond, of Kittery, Register and Clerk in the room of Capt. Wincoll, deceased; at the Instance of Major Hook. Lieut. Governour invites, and we go to Mr. Cooper's, where a Splendid Treat is provided, most cold meat. Councillors, Ministers, Justices there, and Col. Shrimpton, Mr. Eᵐ Hutchinson, &c. Mr. Increase Mather Crav'd a Blessing; Mr. Willard return'd Thanks.

I mov'd Mr. Willard and Mr. Cotton Mather, that, seeing the Old and South Church fell short in their singing on the Thanksgiving-day, might make it up now, if they saw meet: Mr. Willard said would sing what He intended then, prevented by the night: Ask'd Lieut. Governour and read the 47. Ps. Clap hands.—Spake to me and I set it. Lieut. Govʳ Usher was invited, but not there; He is gon to Prison this afternoon, as tis said, upon Mr. Shrimpton's Execution.

Dec. 7, 1694. Col. Gedney tells me that Brother Gerrish is dead. It seems he died Dec. 4. and was buried the day following. Capt. Noyes's Company in Arms.

Tuesday, Dec. 25. Shops are open, men at work; Carts of Pork, Hay, Coal, Wood come to Town as on other days. Mr. Maccarty's shop is open.

---

of the Earl of Bellomont, 26 May 1699. When Lord Bellomont went to New York, in May 1700, Stoughton was again acting Governor, and so continued until his death, 7 July 1701. The Council then became the supreme power in the Colony, acting until the arrival of Governor Joseph Dudley, 11 June 1702. M.H.S.EDS.

1695

SEWALL OBSERVES A DAY OF PRAYER / QUEEN MARY DIES OF
SMALLPOX / CHURCH DISPUTES IN CHARLESTOWN, SALEM VILLAGE,
AND WATERTOWN / SEWALL PLANTS SOME TREES / GREAT HAILSTORM
DAMAGES THE NEW SEWALL HOUSE / SUDDEN DEATH OF SIR WILLIAM
PHIPS IN LONDON / GENERAL COURT PASSES A BILL AGAINST INCEST /
DEATH OF JUDITH QUINCY HULL / WILLIAM OBBINSON'S
MISTREATMENT OF HIS WIFE / FAST IN THE NEW CHAMBER / FORMER
GOVERNOR BRADSTREET MOVES TO SALEM / THOMAS MAULE PRINTS A
DISPLEASING BOOK / DAME WALKER'S DEATH

Seventh-day, Jan. 5. [1694/5]. I waited on the Lieut. Governour to
Braintrey, and visited Unkle Quinsey. Was somewhat exercis'd about
my dream the last night, which was that Mr. Edward Oakes, the
Father, was chosen Pastor of Cambridge Church. Mr. Adams and I
had discourse about the Oddness of the matter, that the father should
succeed his Son so long after the Son's death. I excus'd my not voting,
as not pertaining to me; though I had other reasons besides. Thus I
was conversing among the dead.

Unkle Quinsey brought us going as far as Mr. Wilson's house. Got
home about an hour by Sun. *Laus Deo.*

Had Capt. Thomas's Company from Tho. Walkers to Unkles Gate,
by accident.

Fifth day, Jan. 10. Major Hook dies, being much wanted and
lamented. Had a Letter from him Dec. 31. It seems was taken but
that day Sennight before he died. The Lord save New England. Dr.
Doel of Newbury died a little while ago, one of my Schoolfellows, as
was also Brother Gerrish; heard not certainly of said Doel's death till
Mr. Emmery told it me Jan. 15, in the Street.

Jan. 16. Lieut. Governour, Mr. Cook, Mr. Secretary, Mr. Sergeant
and S. S. went over to Charlestown and visited Mr. Morton and Mr.
Graves; to see if could bring over Mr. Graves, &c. that so another
Minister and God's Ordinances might be setled there in peace, but
see little likelihood as yet. Went to the Meeting, at Mrs. Noyes's bid-

ding, in Mr. D. Oliver's new brick house. The weather was so extream rainy and snowy that very few were there. Sung the 30th Psalm.

Second day, Jan. 14. I goe to Mr. Perry and speak to him to send home Sam. from the Shop, that so his sore and swoln feet might be cured; which standing in the cold shop would prevent. He sends him home. Had no Coler.

Feb. 9, 1694/5. Jacob Mason, the Instrument-maker, died last night very suddenly, as he sat in a chair at the widow Hannah Cowell's, where he was instructing a young man in the Mariner's Art. This day there is a very extraordinary Storm of Snow. It seems Jacob Mason was in Drink.

Feb. 12, 1694/5. Mrs. Moodey is stricken with the Palsie in her right side, and is made speechless. Mr. Moodey is sent for. The last night and this day, Feb. 12, the wether is extream Cold which Mrs. Moodey always hardly bears.

Feb. 15. Bastian fetches Sam's Chest from Mr. Perry's. It falls out so that neither he nor Mrs. Perry are at home. I gave the maid 12^d and Robin a Real.

Lord's Day, Feb. 17, 1694/5. James Meers's Daughter was taken sick last night and dyed this morning; which Suddenness Mr. Willard mention'd with a great deal of Affection in the morning-Prayer. A Note was put up. She was more than Twenty years old.

Third-Day, Feb. 19, 1694/5. Salem-Chamber [*prayer*], Samuel to be disposed to such a Master and Calling, as wherein he may abide with God. Jane, and Fathers family. [*In margin:* Private Fast.]

Assembly that is to sit next week, that may be directed and succeeded by God, to doe for the Salvation of the Province. That a Man after God's own heart may be chosen for a Judge. Fronteers from Albany and Kinderhook, to Pemmaquid. Spring. England.

This day in the evening, I hear of the desolating Earthquake that has been in Italy near Naples, the last Fall. Archbishop of Canterbury [*John Tillotson*] dead. Wait Newman dyd between the Groin and Plimouth. Is 3,000£ Loss in Fifield's being Taken.

Fourth-day, March 6, 1694/5. I had got a printed List of all the Councillors names except the Judges, that might serve for a Nomination, and indented them with Scissers, and so every one took as it pleas'd him, and put into Mr. Secretaries Hat. Elisha Cooke, Esqr. had Twenty Votes. Barthol. Gedney, John Hathorne, Elisha Hutchinson, John Foster, and Nathanael Thomas Esqrs. had One Vote apiece; which made up the whole number of Electors: for the Lieut. Governour voted not, sustaining the place of Governour; Col.

Pynchon was not here, and Major Hook dead. So there remained 25. This day Joseph Belknaps little Son of about 4 years old, falls into scalding Wort and is kill'd. On the Sabbath a Roxbury Woman fell off her Horse and is since dead: On the day before, one Trusedal, of Newton, was pulling Hay from an undermined Mow in the Barn, which fell upon him and kill'd him. Mr. Wheelwright is chosen to succeed Major Hook as to the Probat of Wills, and Mr. Peperill as a Justice of the Inferiour Court. Mr. Elatson buryed his wife this day. Bearers had Scarfs and Rings; was buryed from Mr. Colemans.

March 11, 1694/5. Went to Plimouth to keep Court; 13*th* Came to Hingham; 14*th* home, *vid* Almanack; 15*th* Voted the Writt for calling an Assembly to be conformable to the Law, Nov. 8, 1693, a further Tax of 3000 and odd pounds granted, and an additional Impost for a fund of 4000. Bills of Credit.

This day, *March* 15, young Tim° Clark, of about 14 years old, falls down into the Hold of a Ship on the Kilson, and dies, to the great Sorrow of all that hear of it. At night Deputies make the Lieut. Governour and some of the Council drink at the Exchange Tavern.

March 16. Deputies vote for Mr. Torrey to preach the Election Sermon, and that 25th April be a Fast. Lieut. Governour makes a Speech to the Deputies; Mr. Willard prays. Lieut. Governour desires Mr. Secretary to declare that the Court is dissolv'd. Gives the Speaker &c. a Glass of Wine at Mr. Epaphras Shrimptons. Upon the 14th of March Mr. Mitchell dies, is buried upon the 16. A Storm of Snow this day.

Sabbath, March 17. Is a very sore Storm of Snow. When After-noon Exercise is over, Mr. Willard stays the Church and Major Wal-ley, Capt. Williams, and Checkly are chose to accompany our Pastor to Salem-Village on the 3ᵈ of April next; that Church calling a Council, to see if can put an end to their contentions.

March 18, 1694/5. Last night I dream'd that all my Children were dead except Sarah; which did distress me sorely with Reflexions on my Omission of Duty towards them, as well as Breaking oft the Hopes I had of them. The Lord help me thankfully and fruitfully to enjoy them, and let that be a means to awaken me. This day Tim. Clark is buried, a great Funeral. He never spake after his Fall. Great Snow on the Ground.

March 17, 1694/5. Mr. Woodbridge of Newbury dies in a good old Age, more than 80; buried March 19th as Capt. Hill tells me, March 21. after Lecture.[1]

[1] John Woodbridge had been at Oxford before emigrating to Newbury with his uncle Thomas Parker and James Noyes in 1633/4. He was deputy to the General

March 23. Very sore Storm of Rain. Mr. Woodbridge was a Good Man, and a constant attender upon God in his publick worship on the Sabbath-day, though he himself preached not. I saw Him when last at Newbury.

March 29, 1695. Went to the Meeting at Mr. Olivers: Major Walley sat next me, and presently after the Exercise, ask'd me if I heard the sad News from England, and then told me the Queen was dead, which was the first I heard of it. It seems Capt. Allen arriv'd yesterday at Marblehead, who brought the News, and fill'd the Town with it this day. It seems the Queen died on the 27ᵗʰ of December, having been sick four days of the Small Pocks. C. Allen was at Corunna about the Groin,² when the Pacquet came thether that brought the News of it: Whereupon the Fleet performed their usual Ceremonies, and the Merchants went into Mourning. Mr. Willard preached from Jnᵒ 21-21, 22. to prepare men to acquiesce in the Soveraign Disposal of God as to mens honouring of Him in Doing, or Suffering, or both.

April 1, 1695. Joseph speaking about my sending two Frenchmen to prison upon the Act relating to them, said, If this Country stand when I am a Man, I'll drive them all out.

April 1. Three of Watertown came to me and gave an account of their Town-Meeting; which was Wednesday last, but could do nothing: so adjourned to the 28ᵗʰ Inst. and then chose Select-Men; Though the Farmers voted with the East-End; yet the Middle outvoted them and have chosen Select-men to their mind, and Capt. Garfield Town-Clerk, in stead of Capt. Prout, who has endeavour'd much to obstruct their proceedings about the New-meetinghouse. Parties were so combin'd on either side that 'twas a continued Duel in each, One to One; and Four Score and odd Votes apiece. The Lord give a peacable Settlement to that Church and Town, so as may be most for the advantage of His Interest and Glory.

April 3, 1695. I planted Two Locusts, two Elms at Wheelers pond, and one in Elm-Pasture near the Line over against the Middle-Elm. The middle Locust-Tree at Wheelers pond was set there the last year.³

Court and a schoolmaster prior to his ordination over the church at Andover in 1645. Returning to England in 1647, he was minister of Andover, Herts, and Barford St. Martin, Wilts, until his ejection at the Restoration. His later years were spent back in Newbury, where he had extensive landholdings. His wife was Mercy, daughter of Governor Thomas Dudley. Woodbridge, New Jersey, was named for him. Morison, *F.H.C.*, 409–410; *N.E.H.G.R.* xxxii, 292; *Calamy.*

² Corunna, a seaport in northwest Spain, is called in Spanish La Coruña, and in French La Corogne; British sailors corrupted the latter into "The Groyne."

³ The Boston Town Records of 25 March 1695 have the following entry: "Whereas Capt Samuell Sewall hath been at charge in severall Essays to plant

Apr. 5. There is pretty much Thunder and Lightening about break of day. Thunder seem'd to me like Great Guns at first.

Apr. 7. Capt. Hill has a Grandson James baptiz'd.

Tuesday, Apr. 9, 1695. Piam Blower and others from Virginia and Barbados bring a Confirmation of the Queens death: and Report that the French King is dead; and his Gen¹ Luxemburg;⁴ that two other duelled for the honour of his place, one fell, and the other went over to the Confederats. Ketch arrived that came from Plimouth the Tenth of February. This day father Daws makes my little Bridge.

Apr. 10. When I rise in the morn I find the Ground and houses covered with Snow. Be it that Lewis the 14ᵗʰ be indeed dead &c. yet we may have a sharp, though short winter in New England still. God defend.

Apr. 16, 1695. My Appletree which I nourish from a kernel, has the growth of 1694 and is now scarce Ten inches high; removd it this Spring into the room of a young Appletree that dyed.

Apr. 23. Neighbour [*Edward*] Ellis dies.

Apr. 24. We are told from Madera, that one of the Mast-Ships is Taken and that Lewis 14 is yet alive. Very wet and Rainy Wether.

Monday, April 29, 1695. The morning is very warm and Sunshiny; in the Afternoon there is Thunder and Lightening, and about 2 P.M. a very extraordinary Storm of Hail, so that the ground was made white with it, as with the blossoms when fallen; 'twas as bigg as pistoll and Musquet Bullets; It broke of the Glass of the new House about 480 Quarrels [*squares*] of the Front; of Mr. Sergeant's about as much; Col. Shrimpton, Major General, Govʳ Bradstreet, New Meetinghouse, Mr. Willard, &c. Mr. Cotton Mather dined with us, and was with me in the new Kitchen when this was; He had just been mentioning that more Ministers Houses than others proportionably had been smitten with Lightening; enquiring what the meaning of God should be in it. Many Hail-Stones broke throw the Glass and flew to the middle of the Room, or farther: People afterward Gazed upon the House to see its Ruins. I got Mr. Mather to pray with us after this awfull Providence; He told God He had broken the brittle

---

trees at the south end of the town for the shading of Wheelers Pond therefore it is Ordered that the said Sewell and his Heires and none else shall have Liberty from time to time to lop the trees so planted or to be planted and to cut them down and Dispose of them, he or they planting others and causing them to grow in stead of those cut down." *Boston Rec. Commrs. Report,* VII, 221.

⁴ A few hours after King William had lost his beloved wife, he was delivered from the most formidable of his enemies, the great French general François-Henri de Montmorency-Bouteville, duc de Luxembourg. Lewis the 14th continued to enjoy life at his roomy establishment at Versailles for another twenty years.

part of our house, and prayd that we might be ready for the time when our Clay-Tabernacles should be broken. Twas a sorrowfull thing to me to see the house so far undon again before twas finish'd. It seems at Milton on the one hand, and at Lewis's [*the ordinary at Lynn*] on the other, there was no Hail.

I mentioned to Mr. Mather that Monmouth made his discent into England about the time of the Hail in '85, Summer, that much cracked our South-west windows. Col. Archdell, Governour of Carolina comes to Town from Portsmouth this night.[5]

Apr. 30. Col. Archdell waits on the Lieut. Governour in the Council-Chamber just after the breaking up of the Court. Came from London the 10. of January, from Falmouth the 24th to Madera, and from thence to Portsmouth in Mr. Olivers Briganteen, and so hether by land. The Queen died the 27. Dec.r, was laid in State. Parliament ordered Money for the Funeral which was like to be sumptuous. Parliament, Lord Mayor, &c. waited on the King with their addresses of Condolance. News of French King's death was contradicted. D[*uke*] Luxembourg dead. Dr. [*Thomas*] Tennison Archbishop. Has brought no Gazett nor Print. Courtiers and Merchants were in Mourning.

May 1. A vessel arrives from Barbados giving an account of the notice taken there of the Queen's Death in Guns and Colours, by order of the Governour; which with the News from Col. Archdell caused the Lieut. Governour to give order to the Captain of the Castle for firing of Twenty guns about 3. P.M., to take it from the Frigots below; Captains having been spoken with.

I visit Mr. Loring who lies sick of 's Cut-Toe at Pilgrim Simkins. Coming back with Mr. Secretary, Major Walley meets us, and tells us of good News, which was the Escape of Hezekia Miles from the Indians where he had been captive several years; saith they are sick at St. John's. Mr. Hobarts Son Gershom is well at a new Fort a days Journey above Nerigawag, Masters name is Nassacombêwit, a good Master, and Mistress. Master is chief Captain, now Bambazeen is absent. Hezekia got to Saco last Thorsday.

May 5, 1695. About 3 hours News comes to Town of the death of Sir William Phips, Feb. 18th at which people are generally sad.[6] Lay

---

[5] John Archdale, a brother-in-law of Ferdinando Gorges, had been in Maine thirty years before, pressing the latter's claim to the ownership of that area. At this time he was on his way to Carolina, sent by the proprietors to be governor. *D.N.B., D.A.B.*

[6] Sir William died in London and was buried in the church of St. Mary Woolnoth, Lombard and King William Streets. Lady Phips had a handsome white

sick about a week of the new Fever as 'tis called. Cous. Hull says
the talk is Mr. Dudley will be Governour. Tis said the King goes over
Sea again, and Seven persons are to have the Regency in his absence.

May 6. The mourning Guns are fired at the Castle and Town for
the Death of our Governour. Representatives the same as before,
chosen this day.

May 8, 1695. I visit my Lady, who takes on heavily for the death
of Sir William. Thinks the Lieutenant and Council were not so
kind to him as they should have been. Was buried out of Salters
Hall. This day, May 8, we have News of the Taking of Seven Vessels
by a Small French Pickeroon. One is a Briganteen, Mr. Greenwood,
Master, out of which had 1000£ Money. Neither of the Frigats is
yet got out.

Monday, May 13, 1695. Set out with John Trowbridge for Newbury, visit my Brother by the way; visit Sister Northend: lodge at my
Father's.

Tuesday, 14. Goe to the Ferry and meet Mr. Danforth, Cook, Col.
Hutchinson, Jnᵒ Hubbard, drink at my Father's, I sup with them at
Mrs. White's. [*In margin:* Kittery Court.]

Wednesday, May 15. Set out for Portsmouth, have a Guard of Six
men from Newbury. Capt. Smith of Hampton meets us with 12. by
Govʳ Usher's order, long Arms. At Hampton Major Vaughn and Mr.
Waldron's Letter meets us to invite us to their Houses, they being
at the Council. Find Mrs. Redford very sick, taken the day before.

Thorsday, May 16. Went up the River to Mr. Shaplighs and there
held the Court just over against Dover. Went down in the night, and
found Mrs. Redford dead.

Friday, May 17. Drive a Pin in Major Vaughans Grist and fulling-
mill. Capt. Walbon carries us down to Govʳ Usher's Treat; after go
to the Fort, and are saluted by the Ordinance at going in, and coming
out. Interceded for an Ensign of Hampton then in hold in the Fort,
upon which was presently dismissed.

May 18. Din'd with Mr. Penhallow. Go to the funeral of Mrs.
Redford.

May 19. Mr. Moodey preaches both parts of the day, in the afternoon partly a funeral Sermon on the suddenness of Mrs. Redford's
lamented death. Great Rain in the Afternoon.

May 20. Ride to Newbury. I treat Mr. Danforth, Cook, Hutchin-

---

marble monument erected in the church (inscription in *N.E.H.G.R.* iv, 290),
but the building was replaced by the present edifice of Nicholas Hawksmoor in
1716, and the monument is gone.

son, Moodey, &c. with Salmon at Capt. Serjeant's. I lodge at Newbury.

May 21. Ride to Ipswich in Company Capt. Sergeant, Mr. Mayo,
Plaisted. It seems Cous. Hobart of Hingham was buried this day.
Sent Joanna Gerrish home. Lodge at the Widow Appleton's with
Major Epps.

May 24. Friday. Walk to Argilla, and visit Madam Symonds, who
sits up in her chair, but is weakly.[7]

May 25. In our way home divert to Col. Appleton's, who keeps
house by reason of a Sore Legg. The day is very hot, which makes us
almost faint by that time we reach Lewis's; there refresh very Comfortably. Got home seasonably and found my family well, except
Sarah, blessed be God.

Wednesday, May 29, 1695. Election. Stoughton 71. Danforth 79.
Winthrop 74. Pynchon 41. Gedney 74. Cook 69. Hathorn 58. Pike
48. Hutchinson 70. Brown 55. Corwin 70. Foster 64. Russell 66.
Sergeant 49. Addington 78. Phillips 76. Perce 69. Sewall 77. Voted but
for 18. at first. Col. Saltonstall had 39. as 1693, and was left out.

Plimouth. Bradford 57. Lothrop 64. Thomas 59. Saffin 59.

Main[e], Wheelwright 71. Frost 72. Mr. E^m Hutchinson 34. in
stead of Major Hook, deceased.

Zagadahock, Lynde 50.

Vagum [*at large*], Shrimpton 28. Thacher 32.

Thacher had 46. when voted for Plimouth, yet there lost it.

Voters, Depts. 56, Councillors 26: 82. *Note.* Every One of the
Council living, was there; but the Lieut. Governour did not vote.

Friday, June 14. The Bill against Incest was passed with the
Deputies, four and twenty Nos, and seven and twenty Yeas. The
Ministers gave in their Arguments yesterday in Writing; else it had
hardly gon, because several have married their wives sisters, and the
Deputies thought it hard to part them. 'Twas concluded on the
other hand, that not to part them, were to make the Law abortive,
by begetting in people a conceipt that such Marriages were not
against the Law of God.[8]

[7] Argilla was the estate of Deputy Governor Samuel Symonds at Ipswich. He
died 12 October 1678. Rebecca, his widow, whose death Sewall records 21 July
1695, was Symonds's third, or possibly fourth, wife, and had been the widow
previously of Henry Byley, John Hall, and Rev. William Worcester. *Savage.*

[8] Chapter 2 of the Acts of 1695–6, An Act to Prevent Incestuous Marriages, lists
among the many degrees of kindred forbidden marriage that of a man with his
wife's sister or with his wife's niece (either her brother's or sister's daughter);
it did not forbid the corresponding marriage of a woman with her husband's
brother or nephew. This law remained on the statute books until 1785. The

Mr. Secretary treats the Lieut. Governor, Council, Ministers; Major Townsend and Mr. Bromfield, at James Meers's. Mr. Allen in returning Thanks, mentioned the passing of this Act, and that relating to Ministers.

At night, reading in course in the family the Eleventh of the Revelation, it brought fresh to my mind what I had said to Mr. Mather a pretty while agoe, that if we could pass the Law against Incest, might help to finish our Testimony.

June 16, 1695. Lord's Day. Mrs. Willard is brought to bed about noon, and her Daughter Eunice baptised. Four Males baptised; Robert, John, John, William. Mother goes to Church in the afternoon, and so is at the Baptisme. Last night were comfortable Showers after much dry wether.

Friday, June 21. My dear Mother Hull tells me of Capt. Daviss Invitation, and bids me to remember to be at the Meeting. Mr. Willard preaches excellently. At home, at prayer, we read the 16. of the Revelation; I spake somthing to the Sixth Vial, but little thought how presently those awfull Words, Behold I come as a Thief! did concern me and my whole family: And then, and at prayer with my Wife in the Chamber, was wofully drowsy and stupid. About one at night, Jane comes up with an unusual Gate, and gives us an account of Mothers Illness, not being able to speak of a considerable time. I went to Capt. Daviss and fetched some Trecle Water and Syrup of Saffron; Dame Ellis made a Cake of Herbs to try to strengthen

penalties were severe: the marriage was declared null and void; children of such a marriage were "forever disabled to inherit by discent [sic], or by being generally named in any deed or will by father or mother"; those convicted were to be "set upon the gallows by the space of an hour, with a rope around their neck and the other end cast over the gallows, and in the way from thence to the common goal [sic] shall be severely whipped, not exceeding forty stripes each; also every person so offending "shall forever after wear a capital I of two inches long and proportionable bigness, cut out in cloth of a contrary colour to their cloaths, and sewed upon their upper garments on the outside of their arm or on their back in open view . . ." (The misspelling of *gaol* above was common in official and general use from the 16th to the 18th century; the O.E.D. found it difficult to say whether *goal* was merely an erroneous spelling of *gaol*, after this had itself become an archaism, or was phonetic.)

The arguments of the ministers, mentioned by Sewall, i.e. the deliberations of the Cambridge Association, were printed for the public as *The Answer of Several Ministers in and near Boston, To that Case of Conscience, Whether it is Lawful for a Man to Marry his Wives own Sister?* by Bartholomew Green in 1695 as an eight-page pamphlet. It is signed by Increase Mather, Charles Morton, James Allen, Samuel Willard, James Sherman, John Danforth, Cotton Mather, and Nehemiah Walter. Sewall had it reprinted in 1711. Diary, 13 April 1711 and T. J. Holmes, *Increase Mather . . . Bibliography* I, 17–20.

Mrs. JUDITH HULL,

Of *Boston,* in *N. E.* Daughter of Mr. *Edmund Quincey* ; late Wife of *JOHN HULL* Efq. deceafed.

A Diligent, Conftant, Fruitfull Reader and Hearer of the Word of GOD, Refted from her Labours, June, 22. 1695. being the feventh day of the Week, a little before Sun-fet ; juft about the time She ufed to begin the Sabbath.

Anno Ætatis fuæ 69.

Epitaph

GReat *Sarah*'s Faith ; joind with Good *Hannah's* Prayer ;
For Hearing of the Word, glad *Maries* Care ;
Aged *Elizabeths* Juft Walk ; To dwell
Nigh Prophets, a true *Shunamitifh* Zeal ;
An *Humble* Soul, *Trim'd* with an *High* Neglect
Of *Gay Things,* but with *Ancient Glories* deck't;
All thefe Expir'd at once ! Array'd with *Them,*
Our HULDAH's gone to Gods *Jerufalem* :
Without a *Figure* fo, with her *Laft Breath*
Shee Triumph'd o'er that *Holophernes,* DEATH!
Perfect in *Thoughts, Words, Deeds,* She foars on high,
Performing what her *Name* did fignifie.

Mothers Stomach. In the morn Roger Judd is sent to Cambridge for Dr. Oliver, mother chusing to speak with him and no other.[9] When he comes he advises to a Plaister for the Stomach, which is applied; and a Potion made of Bezar [*bezoar*] to be taken in Syrup of Saffron and Treacle water; of which took once or twice. About 8. or 9. I call'd Mr. Willard at her desire, who prays with her. Finding the room free once, and observing her very great weakness; I took the opportunity to thank her for all her Labours of Love to me and mine, and ask'd her pardon of our undutifullness; She, after a while, said, GOD PITY 'EM; which was the last prayer I heard her make. About six I ask'd if I should call Mr. Willard, (for had said to him that he should come again if he could). As far as I could perceive, she said, Not so soon. But I called, or sent; yet could not discern any attention to the prayer, her disease had prevail'd so far, and a little before Sunset she expired, to our very surprising Grief and Sorrow. Roger Judd was here about noon, and said, that when some in the next room spake about who should Watch, my dear Mother answer'd, She should need no Watchers, she should be above at Rest.

June 24. About Seven aclock, my dear Mother is entombed. Bearers, Mr. Danforth, Russell, Cooke, Elisha Hutchinson, Addington, Sergeant.

July 7. Gov[r] Bradstreet is seised again with his old pains.

July 15. I discourse Capt. Sam[1] Checkly about his taking Sam. to be his Prentice. He seems to incline to it; and in a manner all I mention it to encourage me. The good Lord direct and prosper.

July 12, 1695. Kept a Day of Prayer in secret Respecting my dear Mother's death; and Sam's being to be placed out, &c.

July 21. Madam Symonds of Ipswich dies.

July 23. Council at Charlestown: Was at Watertown this day Sennight.

July 26, 1695. Poor little Mary falls down into the Cellar of Matthias Smith's house, and cuts her head against the Stones, making a large orifice of more than two inches long; 'twas about 6 post meridiem. The Lord sanctify to me this bloody Accident.

July 30, 1695. Mr. Cook and I ride to Cambridge, there with Mr. Justice Danforth to hold the Court.

Judith Shepard of Charlestown is Tried for her Life for firing the house of Mr. Richard Foster; clear'd by the Jury; but bound in a Bond of an hundred pounds to answer for other Crimes at the next Superiour Court and to be of the good Behaviour. Trial held so long

[9] Dr. James Oliver of Cambridge (Harvard 1680) was one of the most esteemed physicians of his day. His house stood between Mount Auburn and Arrow Streets.

that 'twas nine aclock ere we got out of the Meetinghouse; and then dark and like to rain, so lodg'd at Mr. Danforth's.

July 31. Issued the Court. Came home by Charlestown. Went to the Meeting at Capt. Alden's and invited the Meeting hether this day fortnight.

July 30. Jane sails for Newbury in Benajah Titcomb's Sloop, loosed from the wharf past ten the night before.

Augt. 6, 1695. Mr. Obinson's wife comes to me and complains of her Husband's ill usage of her; kick'd her out of bed last night; lets her have nothing but water to drink, won't let her have Cloths or victuals. This was 2 post meridiem.[10]

Fifth-day, Augt. 8, 1695. About 9. M. little Sarah has a Convulsion Fit; I and Mr. Torrey were sent for to see it. It lasted not long. When all quiet, Mr. Torrey went to Prayer. A little after Lecture, Sarah has another sore Fit. My wife and I take her to bed with us.

Augt. 8, 1695. About six in the Morn. Sarah has another sore Fit in her Mother's arms presently after she was brought down.

Third-day, Augt. 13, 1695. We have a Fast kept in our new Chamber. Mr. Willard begins with Prayer, and preaches from 2 Chron. 34. 27. Mr. Allen prays. P.M. Mr. Bayly begins with prayer, preaches from Luke 1. 50, and then concludes with prayer. Sung the 27 Ps. 7-10. I set Windsor Tune and burst so into Tears that I could scarce continue singing. Mr. Thornton was here, but went away when Mr. Allen was at Prayer. Mr. Cook, and Mr. Addington here, Mr. Sergeant was diverted. *Note.* Had better have invited all the Council in Town, at least. I appointed this day to ask God's Blessing after the death of my dear Mother, and in particular to bless Sam. with a Master and Calling and bless us in our new house. The Lord pardon and doe for us beyond our hopes, contrary to our Deserts.

Augt. 17, 1695. The Court is Adjourned to the 20th of November. A Duel was fought this day upon the Common between Peggy and one Capt. Cole; Lieut. Governour has spoken to Mr. Cook to bind them over to the Sessions.

Augt. 25. Robt Williams the Bell-Ringer, Publisher [*crier*] and

---

[10] William Obbinson was a tanner. Savage places him in Boston in 1675 and reports him to be "of unknown derivation; may have been that year driven by the Indian war from some outlying settlement." The wife's name was Mary, and they had no children. She is probably the Mrs. Obinson mentioned in Thomas Brattle's Letter of 8 October 1692 (G. L. Burr, ed., *Narratives of the Witchcraft Cases*, 1914, 179–180) as having "afflicted" a child in Boston; the father applied to the Boston justices for a warrant against her, but the warrant was denied. By his will, Obbinson dealt his wife a final blow by bequeathing his estate to the wealthy Paul Dudley.

Grave-digger died this morn. He was suddenly stricken the fifth-day before, just after his ringing the five-a-clock Bell; fell down as essayed to go up his own stairs, and I think so continued speechless till death. Mr. Baily took notice of the Suddenness of it in his prayer. The Flag is out almost all day at the Castle for Pincarton, comes in in the even, brings word that the Lord Bellamont is coming over our Governour in the Unity Frigat; [New] Hampshire to be annexed. Mr. Ives's Son is come over, and several other Passengers.

Third day, Augt. 27, 1695. Went to Dorchester Lecture. Lieut. Governour came to Boston, whom met on the road, yet went on; in his Pue sat Mr. Alford, Mrs. Hutchinson Elisha, Mrs. Foster, Mrs. Nelson, Mrs. Danforth and I. Went to Mrs. Flints, whether came Mr. Weld, Mr. Thacher, Mr. Walter, Mr. Denison, with whom sat down to dinner. Several young Gentlewomen sat down afterward.

Mr. Danforth's Text was Ps. 111. 7. All his Commandments are Sure. That was, their Doctrine; shew'd that not an iota could fail, but all the Threatenings and Promises firm and binding; therefore ought with aw to keep God's Law.

Augt. 27, 1695. In the morn I had Joseph to Mrs. Kay's to School at Mr. Trott's house.

Sept. 2, 1695. Artillery Training. Dine at George Monk's, invited by Col. Paige; Mr. Moodey and Mr. Chiever there, Addington, Foster.

This day Mr. George Badcock, Ship-Carpenter, falls from a Ship he was helping to build at Charlestown, breaks his Neck and three of 's Ribs, of which he dies. His Brother dyed in the Spring at Milton, by a like fall; which renders it very awfull. George Badcock married Ruth Ruggles Nov. 19, 1691.

Sept. 4, 1695. Wm Longfellow brings Jane down from Newbury. This day there is a Fast at Cous. Dummers; Mr. Allen preaches in the morn, Mr. Cotton Mather in the Afternoon. Mr. Bayly began with Prayer. Mr. Russel began in the Afternoon, Mr. Moodey concluded. Two last Staves of the 146. Ps. Sung.

Second day, September 9, 1695. Set out for Bristow, with Mr. Danforth and Mr. Cook. Baited at Neponset, din'd at Billenges, where were also Mr. Newton and Mr. Cary; went to Woodcock's, refresh'd there, so to Rehoboth; lodgd at the Bear, Sheriff was there to meet us; Major Generall also lodged there in his way home from New-London.

Third-day, Sept. 10. To Bristow by the Bridge. Had two Actions concerning Land. Sup at Mr. Saffin's. I lodgd at Mr. Wilkins's. Major Church is sick, I visit him; came with Mr. Danforth to Taunton, there din'd; from thence to Bridgewater, visited Mr. Keith.

Lodg'd at our Landlord Hayward's, who, by Mr. Danforth's procurement, pray'd with us very well in the evening. Mr. Cook was sick and scarce slept all night.

In the morn, Sept. 12, set out about Sunrise; din'd at Mr. Pain's at Braintrey, got home a little after one of the Clock, and find all well, blessed be God.

Sept. 17, 1695. Govr Bradstreet has the remainder of his Goods put on board Mr. Graften; The house being empty, I prevail with him and his Lady to walk to our house, and wish us joy of it. They sat there near an hour with Mrs. Corwin and Wharton. Govr Bradstreet drank a glass or two of wine, eat some fruit, took a pipe of Tabacco in the new Hall, and wish'd me joy of the house, and desired our prayers; came to us over the little Stone–bridge; went away between 12. and 1. in Madam Richards's new Coach and horses. About three, the Lieut. Governour, Mr. Secretary, Sergeant and Sewall waited on them at Madam Richards's, to take leave; in the way the Letter met us giving an account of ten men shot at Pemmaquid, out of 24. going to get wood: four of whom are dead. Hugh March, George's Son, was killed at the first shot. This was Monday was Sennight. This day, Sept. 17, was a great Training at Boston: many Gentlemen and Gentlewomen dine in Tents on the Common. Colonel had a Standard: Great firings most of the day. I should have remembered that Govr Bradstreet this day sent the Halberts, Copies of the Records, and a Loadstone belonging to the Publick, to the Secretary, who caus'd them to be lodg'd at present in the Town-house Chamber; where I saw them when went to write Letters to Capt. March.

Sept. 18. Govr Bradstreet sets sail for Salem about Six aclock in the morning.

This day Mr. Torrey and his wife, Mr. Willard and his wife, and Cous. Quinsey dine with us; 'tis the first time has been at our house with his new wife; was much pleas'd with our painted shutters; in pleasancy said he thought he had been got into Paradise. This day, Sept. 18, Mr. Cook enters the Lists with Col. Paige, and sues for Capt. Keyn's Farm again.[11] Govr Bradstreet arriv'd at Salem about 3 P.M.

[11] The full details of the Richard Cooke-Nicholas Paige litigation, also mentioned in the diary 5 August and 20 December 1686, 17 November 1701, and 28 February 1702, may be found in Mellen Chamberlain, *Documentary Hist. of Chelsea* (1908) I, 635–668; II, 1–84. Most readers, however, will prefer the account by Edmund Sears Morgan in his entertaining article, A Boston Heiress [Anna (Keayne) Lane Paige] and Her Husbands: A True Story, in *C.S.M.* xxxiv, 499–513.

Sixth-day, Sept. 20. Mr. Borland's Briganteen arrives, 6 weeks from Falmouth, in whom comes Mr. Edward Brattle, Mr. Governeur, &c. The Lord Bellamont is made our Governour. Hardly will come over before the Spring. Confederats have had success against Namur, Cassal, &c. Venetians have gained a great Victory over the Turks in the Morea.

Oct. 11, 1695. I received a letter from Cous. Storke giving an account of the death of my dear Unkle, Mr. Richard Dummer. Meeting at Mr. Serjeants.

Oct. 12. Jn° Cunable finishes the Stairs out of the wooden house to the top of the Brick house. Little Mary grows a little better after very sore illness.

Oct. 7ᵗʰ Jn° Brown's family, of Turkey hill, are led captive. All are brought back save one boy that was kill'd; knock'd the rest on the head, save an infant.

Oct. 14, 1695. I visit Mrs. Saunderson and pray God to grant her Mercy and Grace to help in time of need. *Oct. 15.* She dies. *Oct. 17.* Buried, so that house is emptied of its ancient Inhabitants. Sewall, Dummer, Frary, Butler, Hill, Maryon, bearers. Lord teach me to abïde in, and to go out of the world. Mr. Moodey at the Funeral.

Seventh day, Oct. 19, 1695. Pray'd for God's Favour towards Sam. That might duely wait on Christ at his Table to morrow &c., with fasting.

Oct. 23, 1695. My dear Mother visits us; rides behind Joseph Gerrish from Rowley this day.

Oct. 26. Mr. Banistar watches, and calls me about break of day to see the Comet, which seems to point from East to West.

Sewall's next entry is Copy of a Letter to Capt Frary Xr.12.95. We omit this letter written 12 December 1695 to Captain Theophilus Frary, deacon of the South Church, entreating him "by all means, to have No more to do with this Oath," which is unexplained. See the entry of 4 February 1695/6.

[*In margin:* Thomˢ Maule. Book.]

Whereas there is lately printed and published a Pamphlet in Quarto, containing Two hundred and Sixty pages, entituled, *Truth held forth and maintained &c. by Thomas Maule. Printed in the year* 1695. Which is stuff'd with many notorious and pernicious Lies and Scandals, not only against particular and privat persons, but also against the Government, Churches, and Ministry; And against those Worthies who first followed

Christ into these uttermost ends of the Earth; as if they had therein loosed themselves from His Yoke, and shaken off his Burden: As also many corrupt Expressions in point of Doctrine, perverting the Scriptures, and subverting the True Christian Religion.

The Representatives of this His Majesties Province humbly pray, that the Premises may be enquired into, and some suitable Testimony born against the author and his Evil Work.

Dec. 14ᵗʰ 1695. Read and Voted in the house of Representatives, and pass'd in the affirmative, and sent up to the honᵇˡᵉ Lt. Govʳ and Council for a Concurrence.

NEHEMIAH JEWETT, Speaker.
Vera Copia S. S.

[*In margin:* Maul's censure.]
Adjourned to the 26ᵗʰ of February.

The Lieut. Governour, before the Adjournment, sent for the Deputies in, and told them He could not pass the Bill for the Tax, without His Majesty was made the Grantee; and could not pass an Act to conform the precept to that against Non-Residents; and gave them this time to consider of it. Capt. Bond went home from Court very sick, and then Mr. Jewett was chosen Speaker in his room.

Sabbath, December 15. Capt. Bond dies—18ᵗʰ is buried.

Dec. 19. Thomas Maule, Shopkeeper of Salem, is brought before the Council to answere for his printing and publishing a pamphlet quarto, 260. pages, entitled Truth held forth and maintained, owns the book, but will not own all till sees his Copy which is at N. York with [*William*] Bradford who printed it. Saith he writt to the Governour of New York before he could get it printed. Book is order'd to be burnt, being stuff'd with notorious Lyes and Scandals, and he Recognises to answer at next Court of Assize and General Goal Delivery to be held for the County of Essex. He acknowledg'd that what was written concerning the circumstance of Major General Athertons death, was a mistake: p. 112, 113. was chiefly insisted on against him; which believe was a surprize to him, he expecting to be examined in some point of Religion, as should seem by his bringing his Bible under his Arm.¹²

¹² Thomas Maule, a tailor, and afterward a prosperous merchant of Salem, came from Warwickshire, where he was born in 1645. In May of 1669 he was sentenced by the Essex County Quarterly Court "to be whipped ten stripes well laid on" for saying that Rev. John Higginson "preached lies and that his doctrine was of the devil." Maule remained an outspoken, fearless, and public-spirited man of strong opinions all his life; by 1672 he had become a Quaker. He built up a large business in general merchandize, and his "success and popularity in trade

I was with Dame [*Sarah*] Walker, and Sam. came to call me to take
T. Maule's Recognisance; I told her Sam. was there: she pray'd God
to bless him, and to bless all my posterity.

Dec. 20. Dame Walker is very restless; said she was past all food
now, had quite lost her Appetite. Said, why does living man complain, man for the punishment of his Sin? Justified God, and pray'd
Him to help her, and enable her to bear what He laid on her; spoke

---

were in no small measure due to his practice of charging no interest on obliga-
tions due to him." Between 1690 and 1694 Maule wrote his book *Truth held
Forth and maintained;* it is mainly "an exegesis of Maule's views of religion in
general and a defence of Quaker tenets in particular, together with a cordial lam-
basting of the Puritan Theocracy for its hatred and persecution of that sect."
Understandably he was not able to get it licensed or printed in Boston, so he
obtained a license in New York and sent the manuscript to William Bradford;
printed copies reached New England in the fall of 1695. Lieutenant Governor
Stoughton and the Council, meeting on 12 December 1695, ordered that Maule be
arrested and brought before the Council and that his house and the bookstores
should be searched, and all copies of the book seized. Sheriff George Corwin (Cur-
wen) acted promptly; on 14 December he made return that he had seized thirty of
the books in Maule's house and had arrested the author and lodged him in Salem
gaol. The same day the House of Representatives took the action which Sewall
copied into his diary above. Maule was brought to Boston by the jailer and
deputy sheriff for the hearing on 19 December, which Sewall describes. The next
day (according to the Suffolk Court files, 3327A) Maule appeared before Judge
Sewall and gave bond in the sum of £200 to appear at the next session of the
court in Essex County, his sureties being Thomas Bannister of Boston, shop-
keeper, and Robert Calef of Boston, clothier. The records of the next session of
the criminal court for Essex County, held in May 1696 at Ipswich, contain only a
brief formal reference to the matter; Maule was bound over to the fall session
of the court at Salem under a bond of £200, John Loder and John Woodwell
becoming his securities. Sewall sat on this court, but made no mention of Maule
in the diary. Maule gives a detailed account of the hearing in his book *New
England Pesecutors* [sic] *Mauled With their own Weapons* [New York, 1697].
He was outspoken and unyielding, and so angered the court that at the Salem
term before the same judges in November he was indicted not only for publishing the book, but for "saying what he did before the honorable court at Ipswich
in May last." Maule was represented at Salem by Benjamin Bullivant, the Boston
apothecary, who argued several formal pleas; Anthony Checkley, the King's attorney, argued briefly in reply, and the court promptly overruled all the pleas. Maule
was then "left to say for himself," and he did this so effectively that the verdict
was Not Guilty. This note is heavily indebted to the excellent and detailed article
on Maule by Matt Bushnell Jones (*Essex Inst. Hist. Colls.* LXXII, 1–42), who
writes that Maule's trial was forty years earlier than the famous trial of John Peter
Zenger in New York in 1735, and says that "it must be conceded that the Salem
Quaker won the first victory for freedom of the press in America under conditions
that reflect great credit upon the puritan jury that set him free." It may be added
that the M.H.S. editors were wrong in identifying Matthew Maule of *The House
of the Seven Gables* with Thomas Maule.

how hard twas to comply with that Text, Thy will be done; we would fain have our own Wills; but God could of unwilling make us willing. Last night she pray'd that God would take her to Himself. When I took leave this morn, she Thank'd me for all my Visits, and acknowledged the kindness of me and my family. After I was gon, in the Afternoon, Dec. 20. Mehetabel [*Thurston*] sais she heard her Grandmother say, How long Lord, how long? Come Lord Jesus! Mehetabel asked what she said to her, she reply'd, How good is God.

Seventh day, Dec. 21. Between 8. and 9. I went to see Dame Walker, and found her very weak and much alter'd. Mehetabel told her I was there, she said with a low voice, I thank him. Afterward Mehetabel ask'd her if should pray, she said, I stand in need. Twas the last day of the Week, and so I went to prayer, insisting on God's being a present help in time of need, and pray'd that God would strengthen her Faith, that so she might enter into his Rest. I ask'd her if she heard, her Answer was, I thank God, I did. I went home to Prayer, Intending after that to go to Mr. Willard to pray him to give her one Lift more heaven-ward. But before I could get away, a Girl came running to call me. And by that time I could get thether, the Good woman had expired, or was just expiring, being about Ten of the clock in the morning. God fulfilled his good Word in her and kept her Leaf from withering.

She had an odd Conceipt all the last night of her life, that she was in Travail; and though she ceas'd groaning and gave attention to me when at prayer; yet one of the last words I heard her say, was, My child is dead within me; which were indeed some of the very last.

Second-day, Dec. 23, 1695. Dame Walker is buried. Bearers, Mr. Ezek. Chiever, Capt. Theophilus Frary, Capt. James Hill, William Daws *pater*, Jnº Maryon *pater*, Deacon Joseph Bridgham, beside a 2ᵈ set of Bearers; Odlin, Wheeler, Butcher, Jnº Maryon *fil.*, Joseph Brisco. Major General Winthrop, Mr. Cook, Mr. Sergeant, Mr. Addington, Sewall were there, of the Council; Mr. Willard, Mr. Allen, Mr. Oakes, Physician, &c. Women, Mrs. Sergeant, Mrs. Willard, Mrs. Noyes, Mrs. Williams, Mrs. Pierson, my Daughters, *cum multis alijs*; very comfortable Wether over head, somthing dirty under foot. *Note.* After Sam. came home, he was exceedingly affected, shed many Tears, and is even overwhelmed with Sorrow: The Lord grant that the removal of one of his best friends may put him upon seeking unto God betimes and making Him his Hiding Place. Was buried just about Sun-set.

1696

BETTY SEWALL'S CONCERN ABOUT ORIGINAL SIN / SAM HAUGH IN
TROUBLE WITH A MAID / YOUNG SAM SEWALL'S DIFFICULTIES ABOUT
HIS CALLING / JACOBITE PLOT DISCOVERED / COMMOTION UPON THE
ARRIVAL OF THE MAST FLEET / PEMAQUID FORT SURRENDERS TO
THE FRENCH / SEWALL GIVES LODGING TO THE CONTROVERSIAL
JOSEPH BAXTER / TWO HARVARD UNDERGRADUATES DROWNED SKATING
AT FRESH POND / FAST-DAY BILL / DEATH OF THE INFANT SARAH
SEWALL

Secund day, Jan. 6ᵗʰ 1695/6. Kept a Day of Fasting with Prayer for
the Conversion of my Son, and his settlement in a Trade that might
be good for Soul and body. *Uxor prægnans est.* Governour's expected
Arrival, which will bring great changes. Supply for the South-Church.
Three Courts sit to morrow. Lord's Supper the next Sabbath-day. Mr.
Moodey's Entanglements, Watertown. Church of England. New
England. My Hair. Read Epistles to Timothy, Titus, Philemon, Hebrews. Sung the 143, 51, and 130. Psalms. I had hope that seeing God
pardon'd all Israel's Iniquities, He would pardon mine, as being part
of Israel.

Seventh-day, Jan. 4ᵗʰ. The Revd. Mr. Edward Bulkly, of Concord,
dies at Chelmsford in a good old Age; is buried at Concord.[1]

Jan. 7ᵗʰ. Deacon Henry Allen dies. Col. Gedney's wife is dead
within this week.

Jan. 8ᵗʰ. Unkle Quinsey lodged here last night, having received a
Letter from Mr. Gookin to desire him, agrees to bind Daniel Gookin
to Cous. Dummer for 8 years from the 10ᵗʰ of March next. Not being
able to stay, desires me to see it effected. Bulkley and Edmund Quinsey dine with us.

[1] Edward Bulkeley was the son of Peter Bulkeley, M.A. (Cantab.), the wealthy
rector of Odell, Bedfordshire, who brought his family over in the *Susan and Ellen*
in 1635 and the same year became one of the pioneer settlers and the first minister of Concord. Edward attended the University of Cambridge and became minister of Marshfield in 1642; after the death of his father in 1659 he succeeded
him as minister of Concord. They were direct ancestors of Ralph Waldo Emerson. Morison, *F.H.C.*, 369–370.

Jan. 11. 1695/6. I write a Letter to Mr. Zech. Walker acquainting him with his Mother's death and Funeral;[2] that some Recompence ought to be made to Mehetabel and Mary for their faithfull and Laborious Attendance on their Grandmother. Altho' I reckon my self abundantly satisfied for any little Service I did or could doe for our dear friend, by her desireable Company and harty Thanks; yet I earnestly desire your Prayers, that my aged Father and Mother may live and die with such like Faith and frame of Spirit as this our Sarah did. I delivered this Letter to be given to the Post on Second day morning, Jan. 13, 1695/6.

About 10. aclock *Jan. 13, 1695/6.* Cous. Dummer came to invite me to goe along with him to Cambridge to visit Mr. Danforth. About Noon we set out, and at Mr. Danforth's Gate, meet with Mr. N. Hobart and Trowbridge; Mr. Danforth made us dine there; then after awhile, Mr. Hobart was called in to Pray, which he did excellently, Mr. Morton being by, who came with us from the Colledge. *Note.* When were there at first, Mr. Danforth bad me look on the Cupboard's head for a book; I told him I saw there a Law-book, Wingate on the Common Law. He said he would lend it me, I should speak to Amsden to call for it; and if he died, he would give it me. Again when took leave after prayer, He said he lent me that Book not to wrap up but to read, and if misliked it, should tell him of it. By that time Cous. and I could get to the Ferry twas quite dark. Capt. Hunting told us the River was full of Ice and no getting over. But I went to Sheaf and he hallowed over Jnº Russell again. Boat came to Ballard's Wharf below the lodg'd Ice, from whence had a very comfortable Passage over with Madam Foxcroft.

When I came in, past 7. at night, my wife met me in the Entry and told me Betty had surprised them.[3] I was surprised with the abruptness of the Relation. It seems Betty Sewall had given some signs of dejection and sorrow; but a little after dinner she burst out

[2] Sewall had recorded Sarah Walker's death 21 December 1695; she was the widow of Robert Walker, linen-webster, who had known Sewall's father and grandfather in England (pp. 39, 141). Rev. Zachary or Zechariah Walker was minister of Woodbury, Connecticut.

[3] Betty Sewall was fifteen. In the editor's opinion, this entry, the one of 10 January 1689/90 (when she was eight), and the entries of 22 February, 3 May, and 12 November of this year concerning her, reveal the real horrors of the Calvinist religion. The rationale is set forth in Sandford Fleming, *Children and Puritanism* (New Haven, 1933). It is pleasant to record that Betty survived these experiences, in due time married Grove Hirst, took her place in Boston society, and was the mother of eight children: Samuel was a Harvard graduate; Mary became Lady Pepperrell, Elizabeth married Rev. Charles Chauncy of the First Church, and Jane married Rev. Addington Davenport of Trinity Church.

into an amazing cry, which caus'd all the family to cry too: Her
Mother ask'd the reason; she gave none; at last said she was afraid she
should goe to Hell, her Sins were not pardon'd. She was first wounded
by my reading a Sermon of Mr. Norton's, about the 5ᵗʰ of Jan. Text
Jnº 7. 34. Ye shall seek me and shall not find me. And those words in
the Sermon, Jnº 8. 21. Ye shall seek me and shall die in your sins, ran
in her mind, and terrified her greatly. And staying at home Jan. 12.
she read out of Mr. Cotton Mather—Why hath Satan filled thy
heart, which increas'd her Fear. Her Mother ask'd her whether she
pray'd. She answer'd, Yes; but feared her prayers were not heard because her Sins not pardon'd. Mr. Willard though sent for timelyer,
yet not being told of the message, till bruised Dindsdals [?] [4] was given
him; He came not till after I came home. He discoursed with Betty
who could not give a distinct account, but was confused as his phrase
was, and as had experienced in himself. Mr. Willard pray'd excellently. The Lord bring Light and Comfort out of this dark and dreadful Cloud, and Grant that Christ's being formed in my dear child,
may be the issue of these painfull pangs.

Feb. 1. 1695/6. Sam. Haugh came to speak about Frank's burial:
I sent Atherton away before and spake to Sam as to his Mistress'
Maid being with child, and that she Laid it to him, and told him if
she were with child by him, it concerned him seriously to consider
what were best to be done; and that a Father was obliged to look after
Mother and child. Christ would one day call him to an account and
demand of him what was become of the child: and if [he] married
not the woman, he would always keep at a distance from those whose
temporal and spiritual good he was bound to promote to the uttermost of his power. Could not discern that any impression was made
on him. I remark'd to him the unsuitableness of his frame under a
business of so great and solemn Concern.[5]

Third-Day. Feb. 4. Mr. Willard, Major Walley, Capt. Frary and
Seth Perry *pater*, met here about the difference between said Frary
and Perry. Capt. Frary seems now again to justifie his Oath, and
what he did before was out of Surprize. Major Walley desired Mr.
Elliot and Holyoke to meet on Lecture day, Feb. 6. which they did,

---

[4] These two words are not clear in the MS, though they resemble the words
printed. We have not been able to make any more sense out of them than the
earlier editors.

[5] Sam was twenty that day. He and his brother Atherton had been left fatherless
in infancy, and Sam became Sewall's ward. Sewall records Sam's choice of him
as guardian 4 March 1689/90, *q.v.*

and sent for Mr. Perry. This day Sennight is assigned him to bring in his account.

Sixth-day, Feb. 7ᵗʰ. Mrs. Alden is buried.[6] Bearers were Mr. Chiever, Capt. Hill, Capt. Williams, Mr. Walley, Mr. Ballentine.

Capt. Frary was pass'd by, though there, which several took notice of. *Note.* Last night Sam. could not sleep because of my Brother's speaking to him of removing to some other place, mentioning Mr. Usher's. I put him to get up a little wood, and he even fainted, at which Brother was much startled, and advis'd to remove him forthwith and place him somewhere else, or send him to Salem and he would doe the best he could for him. Since, I have express'd doubtfullness to Sam. as to his staying there.

He mention'd to me Mr. Wadsworth's Sermon against Idleness, which was an Affliction to him. He said his was an idle Calling, and that he did more at home than there, take one day with another. And he mention'd Mr. Stoddard's words to me, that should place him with a good Master, and where had fullness of Imployment. It seems Sam. overheard him, and now alleged these words against his being where he was because of his idleness. Mention'd also the difficulty of the imployment by reason of the numerousness of Goods and hard to distinguish them, many not being marked; whereas Books, the price of them was set down, and so could sell them readily. I spake to Capt. Checkly again and again, and he gave me no encouragement that his being there would be to Sam's profit; and Mrs. Checkly always discouraging.

Mr. Willard's Sermon from those Words, What doest thou here Elijah? was an Occasion to hasten the Removal.

Feb. 10. Secund-day. I went to Mr. Willard to ask whether had best keep him at home to day. He said, No: but tell Capt. Checkly first; but when I came back, Sam was weeping and much discompos'd, and loth to goe because 'twas a little later than usual, so I thought twas hardly fit for him to go in that Case, and went to Capt. Checkly and told him how it was, and thank'd him for his kindness to Sam. Capt. Checkly desired Sam. might come to their house and not be strange there, for which I thank'd him very kindly. He presented his Service to my wife, and I to his who was in her Chamber. Capt. Checkly gave me Sam's Copy-book that lay in a drawer.

Just before I got thether, I met Mr. Grafford who told me that Mumford said I was a knave. The good Lord give me Truth in the

[6] Elizabeth (Phillips) Everill was the second wife of Captain John Alden Jr. See our note to 20 July 1692.

inward parts, and finally give Rest unto my dear Son, and put him into some Calling wherein He will accept of him to Serve Him.

Feb. 12. 1695/6. I rode to Brooklin with one Ems, a Carpenter, to view the widow Bairsto's house, in order to repairing or adding to it. From thence to G. Bairsto's agen, to Devotions, to treat with him about a piece of ground to sell it me and issue the Controversy about a way. From thence to Cambridge, to Mr. Wadsworth's Chamber, where found Govr Usher, Mr. Secretary, &c. with them came home, got to Mr. Allen's by 4. P. M. Supp'd. Sung two Staves of the 132^d Ps. begin at the 13th verse. Went to the Meeting at Mrs. Noyes's.

Sabbath, Feb. 16. 1695/6. Mr. Emmerson preaches twice in the new Meetinghouse at Watertown, which is the first time. Capt. Checkly's Son Samuel is baptized with us. I was very sorrowfull by reason of the unsettledness of my Samuel.

Feb. 22. 1695/6. Betty comes into me almost as soon as I was up and tells me the disquiet she had when waked; told me was afraid should go to Hell, was like Spira, not Elected. Ask'd her what I should pray for, she said, that God would pardon her Sin and give her a new heart. I answer'd her Fears as well as I could, and pray'd with many Tears on either part; hope God heard us. I gave her solemnly to God.

Feb. 26. 1695/6. I pray'd with Sam. alone, that God would direct our way as to a Calling for him.

It seems John Cornish essay'd yesterday to goe to carry Cloth to the fulling-mill, and perished in the Storm; this day was brought frozen to Town, a very sad spectacle.

By reason of the vehemency of the Storm yesterday, but ten Deputies assemble, so that the Lieut. Governour questions whether the Court be not fallen, because 40. Constitute a House.

Fifth-day, 27th. 32 Deputies appear.

Sixth-day. Have fourty or upward. Chuse Major Townsend Speaker. Lieut-Governour was much disturb'd as fearing the Court could not legally be held, because was not that appearance the first and second day as the Law præscribes.

Sabbath, Apr. 12, 1696. About 8 m. it begins to snow; by noon the houses and ground were covered, and at 5 P.M. I saw an Isicle seven inches long. This new Snow was plentifully to be seen on the Ground for about three days space.

Fifth-day, Apr. 23, 1696. News is brought of several of our men killed at Tartooda [*Tortuga*], and Six Vessels Taken.

Mr. Daniel Oliver marries Mrs. Elisabeth Belchar.

Apr. 24. Lydia Moodey visits me, and tells me that Mr. Phillips of Rowley dyed the last Wednesday, the same morn we read—The prophets do they live for ever? in Zech. 1. The Lord help me to re-deem the time.

Sabbath, May 3, 1696. Betty can hardly read her chapter for weep-ing; tells me she is afraid she is gon back, does not taste that sweetness in reading the Word which once she did; fears that what was once upon her is worn off. I said what I could to her, and in the evening pray'd with her alone.

Fifth-day, May 7, 1696. Col. Shrimpton marries his Son to his wive's Sisters daughter, Elisabeth Richardson. All of the Council in Town were invited to the Wedding, and many others. Only I was not spoken to. As I was glad not to be there because the lawfullness of the intermarrying of Cousin-Germans is doubted; so it grieves me to be taken up in the Lips of Talkers, and to be in such a Condition that Col. Shrimpton shall be under a temptation in defence of Himself, to wound me; if any should happen to say, Why was not such a one here? The Lord help me not to do, or neglect any thing that should prevent the dwelling of brethren together in unity. And, Oh most bountifull and Gracious God, who givest liberally and upbraidest not, admit me humbly to bespeak an Invitation to the Marriage of the Lamb, and let thy Grace with me and in me be sufficient for me in making my self Ready. And out of thy Infinite and Unaccountable Compassions, place me among those who shall not be left; but shall be accepted by Thee here, and Taken into Glory hereafter. Though I am beyond Conception Vile! Who may say unto Thee, What doest thou? Thou canst justify thy self in thy proceedings. And O, Lord God forgive all my unsuitable deportment at thy Table the last Sabbath-Day, that Wedding Day; and if ever I be again invited (In-vite me once again!) help me entirely to give my self to thy Son as to my most endeared Lord and Husband. And let my dear Wife and all my children, partake in this priviledge, and that not as Umbrâs, but on their own account.

May 11ᵗʰ 1696. Joseph falls down and breaks his forhead so as bleeds pretty much.

May 11ᵗʰ 1696. Town-Meeting to chuse Assembly-men, 134. there; Mr. Eyre had 88. Major Townsend 85. Capt. Byfield 82. Mr. Oliver 74. Mr. Tho. Brattle had 67. Left out Mr. Bromfield, Thornton, Frary.

May 12, 1696. Cous. Dummer, Mr. Eyre, Bromfield, went with me to Mr. Increase Mather and acknowledged that his Preaching the Lecture once or twice was very pleasing to us, and that we were thankfull for it, and desired more; that He would please to preach in course, as being as diffusive a way of doing good, as any in our Little

Israel. He treated us with Respect and some Encouragement, I hope.

Fourth-day, May 13, 1696. Mr. Willard, Capt. Wyllys, Capt. Frary, and Mr. Sheaf met at my house about the difference between said Frary and Mr. Perry; Wyllys, Sheaf and I told him plainly that it had been well the matter had been issued by their mutual Confession to each other at their privat Meeting, as was once intended. He persisted and said he knew certainly that what he had sworn was true; I told him the less was said of that nature, the better twould be, 'twas so long agoe; and if Mr. Eliot was possess'd, Mrs. Eliot his Mother must be his Tenant; whereas the father's Will made him her Servant, and nature too, he being under age; and the Scripture saith the Heir under age differs little from a Servant.

May 18. By reason of the Major Generall's illness, I am forced to go to Ipswich Court; and being to go, my wife desir'd me to go on to Newbury; I went with Brother on Wednesday night. Visited Father, Mother, Friends, return'd to Salem, got thether about Nine. Sup'd well with the Fish bought out of Wenham Pond. Between eleven and noon, Tho. Messenger comes in, and brings me the amazing news of my Wive's hard Time and my Son's being Still-born. We get up our Horses from the Ship, and set out by Starlight about 12, yet the Bells rung for five before we got over the Ferry. Found my wife as well as usually; but I was grievously stung to find a sweet desirable Son dead, who had none of my help to succour him and save his Life. The Lord pardon all my Sin, and Wandering and Neglect, and sanctify to me this singular Affliction. These Tears I weep over my abortive Son.

> *Causa parata mihi est, et vitæ, et mortis, ibidem;*
> *In tredecim, Solus denegor, ire foras,*
> *Spes tamen hæc maneat,[7] stimulante dolore, parentes,*
> *Ad memet Jesus introijsse potest.*

Fourth day, May 27, 1696. Election. Rainy day, which wet the Troops that waited on the Lieut. Governour to Town. Mr. Cotton Mather preaches. Powring out Water at Mispeh, the Text.

Votes.—Stoughton 60—Danforth 65—Pynchon 61—Russel 55—Gedney 69—Winthrop 58—Hathorn 62—Hutchinson Elisha 79—Sewall 70—Addington 71—Cook 72—Brown 55—Phillips 58—Corwin 46—Shrimpton 57—Foster 62—Perce 53—Sergeant 45. Major Pike had 32, so Col. Shrimpton comes in his room.

Plimouth—Bradford 65—Lothrop 67—Thomas 66—Thacher 41.

Main[e]—Eᵐ Hutchinson, Frost, Wheelwright, votes so unanimous that they were not parted.

[7] Over this word Sewall interlined *sanet*, perhaps as a variant reading.

Sagadahoc—Joseph Lynde 41. *Note.* Mr. Tho. Brattle had 21.

At Large. Vagum. Walley, 39. Saffin 39. *Note.* Capt. John Appleton had 26. I have fallen 7 since last year; the Lord advance me in real worth, and his esteem.

May 28. Our two old Nurses got my Wife on the Pallat-Bed, which much discomposed her, put her in great pain, and all in great fear. Grows better by morn. May 29.

Sabbath, May 31, 1696.

Mr. Willard is so faint with his Flux, that is not able to come abroad, and so there is a disappointment of the Lord's Supper, which should otherwise have been celebrated this day. Mr. Cotton Mather preaches, exhorts us to examine our selves, whether we were prepared for that Ordinance. And said that Humiliation for the disappointm^t, and mourning after Christ, God might make as profitable to us as the Ordinance.

May 30. Post brings from New-York a confirmation of the News about the Plot,[8] and a printed Proclamation for the Thanksgiving in England: It seems the Governour has a Packet.

Second-day, June 1, 1696. Mr. Wigglesworth preaches the Artillery sermon, from Ephes. 6, 11. Put on the whole Armour of God, that ye may be able to stand against the wiles of the Devil. In the Applications, said 'twas necessary we should doe so by reason of the evil of the Times or else of Popery, or something as bad as Popery should come to be set up. What should we doe? Mentioned Rev. 16, 15, said the Garments there and Armour in the Text were the same. About Dinner Time the Guns were fired at the Castle and Battery for joy that the Plot was discovered.

June 11, 1696. I strove with my might that in stead of Tuesday, Thursday, and Satterday in every Week, it might be said, Third, fifth and seventh day in every week: but could not prevail, hardly one in the Council would secund me, and many spake against it very earnestly; although I asked not to have it chang'd in the Fairs. Some said twas the speech of the English Nation; mend it in the Fasts; mend it every where or no where, others said persons would scarce know what days were intended; and in England would call us Quakers. I urg'd that the Week only, of all parcells of time, was of Divine Institution, erected by God as a monumental pillar for a memorial of the Creation perfected in so many distinct days.

June 19. News is brought to Town of Capt Berries being slain.

[8] The assorted villainies of the Jacobite plots to do away with William III, their discovery and punishment, and the public reaction, make fascinating reading in Chapter XXI of Macaulay's *History of England.*

June 20th. Wm Veisy is bound over for plowing on the day of Thanksgiving &c. News comes that the embargo is kept strictly in England.[9]

Sewall neglected to record here that on 6 July 1696, he and his wife Hannah gave to Harvard College a farm of 500 acres in Petaquamscot (Kingston, R.I.) in the Narragansett country, the income to be applied "for and towards the support and education at the said College of such youths whose parents may not be of sufficient ability to maintain them there, especially such as shall be sent from Petaquamscot aforesaid, English or Indians, if any such there be." This farm was sold in 1828 for $6,014.83. Harvard reported in 1964 that the book value of the Sewall Scholarship Fund was $21,125.00.

Legendum.

At Edinburg Octr 27, 1695, in the Colledge, it being the Sabbath, and their Sacrament day, One Mr. John Moncrife, preaching on that Text, Jer. 3, 22, Return you backsliding children, and I will heal your back-slidings: Behold we come unto Thee for thou art the Lord our God,—Between the hours of 10 and 11, there came such a down-powring of the spirit of God on the whole Congregation (supposed to be 3 or 4000), that they all cryed out, not being able to contain themselves: So that the Minister could not be heard; but was forced to give over preaching to the people; and sung a Psalm to compose them. A person present adds, that he and 100. more never saw Heaven on Earth before, being like Peter on the Mount, or Jacob in Bethel, or Paul in a Rapture. For the Lord came down with the Shout of a King among them, so that they could have been content to have built Tabernacles there; which has dash'd the Jacobite party more than all the Kings forces could doe.

From London by the ships that arrived July 12, 1696.

July 12, 1696. By reason of fire on Mrs. Phillips stone house over against the Town house, the morn. Exercise was tumultuously interrupted, both at the old meetinghouse and ours.

[9] William Veazey of Braintree was called by Lord Bellomont "the most impudent and avowed Jacobite . . . known in America" (*N.Y. Col. Docs.* IV, 581). For plowing on the day set apart for public thanksgiving for the preservation of King William from assassination, Veazey was indicted for "High Misdemeanour, in open Contempt of His Maj[es]ties Royal person and Government here established," and brought to trial before the Superior Court of Judicature 27 April 1697. He pleaded guilty and was fined 10*l* and ordered to be set in the pillory in the market place in Boston the next day for an hour (*C.S.M.* III, 65). Sewall deals with Veazey's son in his entry of 26 July.

The North [Church] who had no impression from this, were much disturbed by the Alarm from the Castle, which a man rashly told them of as were celebrating the Lds Supper. About One the Drums beat throw the Town, all goe into Arms. Nantasket Beacon began. Had order it seems on the sight of 2 great ships to fire it, because of the 2 who lately took Capt. Paxton. In the Afternoon some went to Meeting; abᵗ 30. men in all at ours. North met not till abᵗ 5 P.M. when our exercise was over; went to the Townhouse and after a while by Mr. Whittingham rec'd the Packet which makes void many of our Laws; viz. Courts, Colledge, Habeas Corpus, Forms of Writts &c. and Confirms many others.[10]

July, 23. In the Evening were much startled by a Letter from Govʳ Usher, of many ships seen off and their Province in Arms upon it. Lt. Govʳ came in his Charet to my house, and sent for the Council. Majʳ Genˡ, Mr. Cook, Mr. Secretary, Mr. Foster, Serjeant, Majʳ Walley came, Majʳ Townsend also sent for and came: After a while, the Captain of the Castle comes in, and informs us that twas the Mast-Fleet from Engl'd, so were comfortably dismiss'd between 9 and 10 of the Clock.

July 26. We hear that Mr. Bullivant and Mr. Myles are come.[11]

27ᵗʰ At the Council the Lt. Govʳ reads the Letters that give notice from the Lords[12] of a French Squadron intending for America: they will afford us what Assistance they can under the present Circum-

10 By the new Charter (1691), all "orders, laws, statutes and ordinances" made by the General Court were required to have the written consent of the Governor; they were then to be transmitted by the first opportunity for the royal approval. If rejected within the space of three years after they were presented to the Privy Council, they became void; but a failure to reject within that time was equivalent to a confirmation. Abner Cheney Goodell's edition of the Province Laws, *The Acts and Resolves, Public and Private, of the Province of Massachusetts Bay, 1692–1780* (Boston, 1869–1904), has exhaustive annotations on the history of the rejected acts (M.H.S. EDS.) See our note for the entry of 12 October 1696.

11 Benjamin Bullivant came to Boston about 1685, an apothecary and physician from London. He was made clerk of the Superior Court, 9 November 1686, and was one of the first churchwardens of King's Chapel. He was a partisan of Andros and was imprisoned at the uprising in 1689, but was detained in Massachusetts when Andros and his following were deported. A journal of events in New England from 13 February to 19 May 1690, sent to London by Bullivant, and now in the Public Record Office, is published in 1 *Proc. M.H.S.* XVI, 103–108. H. W. Foote, *Annals of King's Chapel*, 1, 46–48.

Samuel Myles (Harvard 1684), rector of King's Chapel, had gone to England in 1692 to obtain aid for the chapel; he returned with furnishings given by the late Queen Mary. *Sibley.*

12 The Commissioners of the Board of Trade and Plantations, revived by William III in December 1695.

stance of Affairs. Reads also Mr. Blathwayts Letter recommending the subscribing the Association by all in publick place and Trust, with one drawn for that purpose.[13] This day also receiv'd an Express from Col. Pynchon, of Count Frontenac's coming ag^t the 5 Nations, or Albany, or N. E., or all, with 2000 French and 1000 Indians: Casteen with 4 or 500 to hold us in play the mean while. The wind coming North last night ships arrive at Nantasket this morn. Mr. Myles and Bullivant come to Town.

July 26. Mr. Veisy preach'd at the Ch. of Engl'd; had many Auditors. He was spoken to to preach for Mr. Willard; but am told this will procure him a discharge.[14]

Third day Augt 4. Pemmaquid Fort is summond by the French: the two ships which took the Newport Gally, and said Gally; besides many hundreds by Land.

Fourth day Augt 5th summond them again, and for fear of their Guns, Bombs and numbers, Capt Chub surrendred, and then they blew up the Fort. This News came to Town Augt 10. Capt. Paxton brought it; just after publishing the Act referring to Navigation.[15]

Fourth-day Augt 12, 1696. Mr. Melyen, upon a slight occasion, spoke to me very smartly about the Salem Witchcraft: in discourse he said, if a man should take Beacon hill on 's back, carry it away; and then bring it and set it in its place again, he should not make any thing of that.[16]

[13] Following the discovery of the great Jacobite plot to assassinate King William, it was proposed in the House of Commons that the members should enter an association for the defence of their sovereign and their country. An instrument was drawn up by which the members, each for himself, recognized William as lawful king, and bound themselves to stand by him and each other against James and James's adherents. The Association was first signed in the House 25 February 1695/6, and generally thereafter throughout the kingdom (Macaulay, *Hist. of England*, Chap. XXI). The Massachusetts legislators subscribed the Association 18 September 1696, *q.v.*

[14] William Vesey Jr. (Harvard 1693) was studying theology with Samuel Myles. Evidently it was felt that preaching at the South Church might impair his standing with the Church of England. Later in 1696 he was called by the "Churchwardens and Vestrymen of the City of New-York" to officiate over the new church they were establishing. He went to England, was given an M.A. at Oxford, and received Anglican ordination. On Christmas day 1697 he was inducted as the first rector of Trinity Church. His stormy career in New York politics is fully told in C. K. Shipton, *Sibley's Harvard Graduates* IV, 173–179. Two Manhattan streets were named for him: Rector and Vesey.

[15] Probably Statutes 7 and 8 William III, Chap. 22. M.H.S. EDS.

[16] The M.H.S. editors felt that the allusion here was to the case of the Rev. George Burroughs, whose "preternatural strength" came in as evidence against him on his trial and condemnation for witchcraft.

Seventh-day, Augt 15th Bro^r St. Sewall comes to Town; Gets an order to Col. Hathorne for erecting a Beacon on Pigeon hill on Cape-Anne, and for pressing 20. men at Marble-head. This day vessels arrive from Barbados, bring news of 10. great ships at Petit Quavers, of between 60 and 90 Guns. Mr. Williams, the physician, and his wife are both dead. Mrs. Hatch and her children in Tears for the death of her husband, which was brought to her about an hour by Sun. We are in pain for Saco fort. Guns were heard thrice on fifth day all day long. One Peters and Hoyt scalp'd at Andover this week; were not shot, but knock'd on the head.

Augt 24. Betty rides to Salem, to sojourn there awhile: Sam carries Joanna Gerrish to Newbury.

7^r 5th Little Mchetabel Fifield dies, being about 8 weeks old.

Septr 7th Jane sets sail for Newbury with little Sarah; suppose got thether the next day.

Septr 8 Mr. Benj^a Wadsworth is ordain'd pastor of the first Church. Mr. Allin gave the charge, Mr. I. Mather gave the Right Hand of Fellowship: Spake notably of some young men who had apostatized from New England principles, contrary to the Light of their education: was glad that he [*Mr. Wadsworth*] was of another spirit. Mr. Willard was one who joined in laying on of hands.

Septr 9. Purchase Capen had been gunning, or shot a fowl by the by as was at work: charg'd his Gun which others knew not of, laid it down as was about to go home at night; a Lad took it up in sport and held it out, it went off and killed the Owner.

Septr 10. Mr. Walter preaches the Lecture, made a very good sermon. The fear of the Lord is to hate Evil.

Letter. Mrs. Martha Oakes. Not finding opportunity to speak with you at your house, nor at my own, I write, to persuade you to be sensible that your striking your daughter-in-law before me, in my house, is not justifiable: though twas but a small blow, twas not a small fault: especially considering your promise to refrain from speech it self; or at least any that might give disturbance. As for New England, It is a cleaner Country than ever you were in before, and, therefore, with disdain to term it *filthy*, is a sort of Blasphemie, which, by proceeding out of your mouth, hath defiled you. I write not this to upbraid, but to admonish you, with whom I sympathize under your extraordinary provocations and pressures; and pray God command you freedom from them. S. S.[17]

---

[17] Martha was the wife of Dr. Thomas Oakes (Harvard 1662), Representative and physician of Boston, who had been agent of the Colony in England, and brother of President Urian Oakes. She was evidently an English woman with a stepdaugh-

7^r *14. 1696.* Went with Mr. Moodey, and visited Mrs. Collins, John Soley, and Mr. Wigglesworth and his Wife, dined with them; I furnished New England Salt.

7^r *16.* Keep a day of Prayer in the East end of the Town-House, Govr, Council and Assembly. Mr. Morton begun with Prayer, Mr. Allin pray'd, Mr. Willard preached—If God be with us who can be against us?—Spake smartly at last about the Salem Witchcrafts, and that no order had been suffer'd to come forth by Authority to ask Gods pardon.

Mr. Torrey pray'd, Mr. Moodey; both excellently: All pray'd hard for the persons gon forth in the expedition.[18] 7^r 17th Mr. Moodey preacheth the Lecture from Act. 13. 36. For David after He had served his own Generation &c: made a very good Sermon; Din'd with Mr. Danforth, Winthrop, Gedney, Russel, Sewall—about 10, at Meers's.

7^r *18, p. m.* The Council and Representatives subscribe the Association.[19] In the morn had warm discourse whether the Court could sit or no, because the writ by which twas call'd was made void; at last spake round and were then quiet. Govr said he was resolved to hold the Court if so many would abide with Him as were capable.

7^r 25th *1696.* Mr. John Glover is buried. Col. Pynchon, Mr. Cook, Mr. P. Sergeant and Mr. Oakes were there. Drew up a Letter to the Duke of Shrewsbury.

Octr 3. David Edwards is buried. The Revival of Courts is published; and the Court adjourned to the 18. Novr 1, p. m Some mov'd for a Dissolution, saying fear'd we were not on a good bottom, which anger'd the Lt Govr Septr 29. 1696. Mr. Wigglesworth and his wife lodge here.

---

ter. Sewall's rebuke is quite revealing. Mrs. Oakes does not appear in the diary again until 1719, when Sewall went to Cambridge to be one of her bearers.

[18] Captain Pascoe Chubb had surrendered the English fort at Pemaquid (above, 5 August) with the condition that his command should be protected from harm and sent to Boston, but the French could not enforce the agreement and the Indians put many of the English to death. When the news reached Boston five hundred men were raised and despatched to the Penobscot. On 16 September the ministers of Boston and environs were invited to meet the General Court, and the day was spent in religious exercise. When the forces reached the Penobscot the French squadron had sailed for St. John; there was no engagement, and the troops and ships returned to Boston. *Palfrey* IV, 154–155.

[19] This is the document referred to at the end of our footnote of 27 July 1696; we omit the text, which was printed in full by the M.H.S. editors from the manuscript in the Massachusetts Archives.

Octr 3. 1696. Mr. Joseph Baxter[20] lodges here, being to preach for Mr. Willard on the Sabbath: Deacon Frary came to me on Friday; told me Mr. Willard put him upon getting help on the fifth day at even, because disappointed of Mr. Sparhawk. He sent that even to Braintrey; but for fear of failing rode thether himself on Sixth-day morn and secured Him: After the Meeting at Bro^r Wheelers, came and told me of it, and earnestly proposed to me that He might lodge at my house; which I thought I could not avoid except I would shut my doors against one of Christ's servants; which I also inclin'd to, only was afraid lest som should take offence. And my Library was convenient for Him.

Octr 10. Bro^r Pemberton dies. *Oct^r* 12. Lt Governour goes to Cambridge, Mr. Secretary, Major Wally and I goe to Dorchester and wait on his Honour from thence; Mr. Cook, Mr. Hutchinson, Foster, Russel, Lynde there: Mr. Williams made an Oration (Mr Pemberton should have done it but was prevented by his fathers death). Lt Govr complemented the President &c., for all the respect to him, acknowldg'd his obligation and promis'd his Interposition for them as become such an Alumnus to such an Alma Mater: directed and desired the Presd^t and fellows to go on; directed and enjoined the students to obedience. Had a good dinner: came home: Mr. Danforth not there. Mr. Cotton Mather took off Mr. Chauncy and Oakes's Epitaphs as I read them to him.[21]

Oct. 13 Govr goes to view the Castle, I went not because of a Flux. Mr. Simms dined with me to day, spake of the assaults he had made upon periwiggs; and of his Repulses. Seem'd to be in good sober sadness.

[20] Baxter had been graduated from Harvard in 1693 at seventeen; at this time he was in the middle of a controversy in the church at Medfield over his ordination.
[21] Harvard was in a state of no little embarrassment at this time, being without a charter or any other instrument of legal existence. The abrogation of the Massachusetts Bay charter in 1684 had been interpreted as repealing the Harvard charter as well. The legislature under the new royal government had passed an act incorporating Harvard College 27 June 1692, but on 12 July 1696 news had arrived that the Privy Council had disallowed the college charter and other legislation. Lieutenant Governor Stoughton assumed the responsibility of reorganizing the college government, and at the meeting that Sewall recorded, Stoughton "desired & appointed the Rev^d m^r Jncrease Mather to continue as president of the Colledg . . . & the [other college officers] to proceed in the Jnstitution & Goverm^t of the house, & in the Managemen[t] of the Estate of the Colledge according to the late Rules of said Colledg, until his Maj^tys further pleasure shall be known, or a legall settlement of said Colledge shall be obtained." Harvard College Records, 12 October 1696, in *C.S.M.* xv, 355; Josiah Quincy, *Hist. of Harvard University* (1860), I, 82.

4 d. Octr 21. 1696. A church is gathered at Cambridge North-farms;[22] No Relations made, but a Covenant sign'd and voted by 10 Brethren dismiss'd from the churches of Cambridge, Watertown, Wooburn, Concord for this work. Being declar'd to be a church, they chose Mr. Benj. Estabrooks[23] their Pastor, who had made a good Sermon from Jer. 3. 15. Mr. Estabrooks, the father, managed this, having pray'd excellently: Mr. Willard gave the charge; Mr. Fox the Right hand of Fellowship. Sung part of the 4 Ps. From the 9th v. to the end, O God, our Thoughts. Mr. Stone and Fisk thanked me for my Assistance there. Cambridge was sent to though had no Teaching officer; they sent Elder Clark. Hasting, Remmington.

Sabbath, Octr 25. Towards the latter end of Mr. Mathers Prayer, a dog vomited in the Ally [*aisle*] near the corner of Mr. Willards Pue, which stunk so horribly that some were forc'd out of the house; I and others could hardly stay; Mr. Mather himself almost sick. Just about duskish we know there is an house on fire, it proves Peter Butlers, just by my Ladies [*Phips*], where Mr. Nowell once dwelt. Mr. Green, who married Mr. Mathers daughter, is one of the Tenants: He and his family were at Charlestown, keeping Sabbath there.

Fifth day Octr 22. Capt. Byfield Marries his daughter Debora to James Lyde, before Mr. Willard. Mr. Sparhawk would have had her.[24] *Octr 29th* Clouds hinder our sight of the eclipsed Moon; though tis apparently dark by means of it.

Octr 30. Mr. Wigglesworth tells me that one John Bucknam of Malden, above 50 years old, has been perfectly dumb near 18 years, and now within about 3 weeks has his understanding and speech restored. He is much affected with the Goodness of God to him herein.

2^d day, Novr 2. Mary goes to Mrs. Thair's to learn to Read and Knit.

3^d d. Novr 10. Ride to Salem with Mr. Cooke, get to Lewis's ¼ of an hour before Mr. Danforth; were met there by Mr. Sheriff, Mr. Harris and Brown; Mr. Howard went with us; in the Even visit Govr Bradstreet, who confirms what had formerly told me about Mr. Gage

---

22 Now Lexington.

23 Benjamin Estabrook (Harvard 1690) died the following July, nine months after his ordination. His wife Abigail was the daughter of Sewall's pastor, Samuel Willard. The father, Joseph Estabrook (Harvard 1664), was minister of Concord. *Sibley.* See our note for 18 April 1700.

24 Sewall was in error here. Deborah Byfield, the daughter of Judge Nathaniel Byfield of Bristol and Boston, became the second wife of *Edward* Lyde of Boston. They were the parents of Byfield Lyde.(Harvard 1723). Rev. John Sparhawk of Bristol (Harvard 1689) was the unsuccessful suitor. *Savage;* H. W. Foote, *Annals of King's Chapel* I (1882), 178n.

his being in the Expedition against Hispaniola and dying in it. Nov^r
11. Grand jury present Tho. Maule for publishing his scandalous Book.
Jury of Tryals, of whom Capt. Turner and Capt. King were two, bring
him in Not Guilty, at which he Triumphs. Mr. Bullivant spake for
him, but modestly and with respect.[25] In the even visited Major Brown,
there sung First part of 72 ps. and last part 24th. But first visted
Mr. Higginson, though had din'd with us. He tells me that the pro-
tector, Oliver Cromwell, when Genl, wrot to Mr. Hook of Newhaven,[26]
and therein sent comendations to Mr. Cotton; upon which Mr. Cotton was writt to by Mr. Hook and desir'd to write to the Genl, which
He did, and advis'd him that to take from the Spaniards in America
would be to dry up Euphrates; which was one thing put Him upon
his Expedition to Hispaniola, and Mr. Higginson and 3 more were
to have gone to Hispaniola if the Place had been taken. O. Cromwell
would have had Capt. Leverett to have gone thether Govr, told him
twas drying up Euphrates, and He intended not to desist till He came
to the Gates of Rome. This Mr. Cook said He had heard his father
Leverett tell many a time. Govr Leverett said, My Lord let us make
an end of one voyage first, and declin'd it; at which Oliver was blank.
One told Mr. Leverett, Jamaica was the Protectors Darling, and he
had disadvantaged himself in not consenting to goe.

Novr 12. Dine with Fish and Fowls at Major Brown's. Col. Gedney
went out of Town, so that we saw him not all the Court. Major
Brown, Mr. Benj. Brown, Brother, Mr. Emmerson, Col. Hathorn
brought us going as far as the Butts. Mr. Cook ask'd me which way
would goe, I said we will goe [with] Mr. Danforth as far as the
[blank], so came home by Charlestown very comfortably. I set Betty
to read Ezek. 37, and she weeps so that can hardly read: I talk with
her and she tells me of the various Temptations she had; as that [she]
was a Reprobat, Loved not God's people as she should. Intends to
come home when she has don her Cusheon. Find all well at home.

Novr 13. Mr. Addington comes to me, and tells me I was sum-
moned to Dorchester by the Lt Govr to dine. I told him of Mr. Simon
Wainwright, and ask'd his Advise about putting his name out of the
Commission, He made me no Answer; At which I was a little disap-

25 Maule's acquittal (see our note for 19 December 1695) obviously displeased
Sewall; although he lived until 1724, Sewall never mentioned him again in the
Diary.
26 William Hooke, M.A. (Oxon.), first minister of Taunton, was settled in New
Haven from 1645 to 1656. He returned to England, became domestic chaplain
to Oliver Cromwell and court preacher, and was silenced for nonconformity in
1662. His wife was Jane, sister to Edward Whalley, the regicide. Morison, *F.H.C.*
381–382.

pointed and look'd on him: He stood up and said he was very ill: I reach'd the elbow chair to Him and with my Arms crowded him into it; where he presently became like a dying man: I sent for Mr. Oakes, who was not at home: But he quickly reviv'd and said He was in a Sweat, would sit a little and then goe: Said twas well I got him into the chair, else should have fallen. He gave me an Almanack in Mr. Ushers name, desir'd me to present his Duty to the Lt Govr and went home. I fear twas a fit of the Apoplexy. Went with Maj^r Wally and Capt Southack to the Lt Gov$^{r's}$, where dined; Capt Kiggin, Jesson, Eyre, Fayerwether, Tho. Brattle, Belchar, Dudly, Southack, Davenport, Edw. Turfry, Maccarty, Mr. Leverett, Danforth, Major Townsend, Major Walley, Sewall; Govr Usher, Lt. Governour and Mr. Usher sat at the end of the table, Capt Kiggin next on the Lt Gov^{rs} side, then Capt Jesson, Mr. Eyre. Sewall sat next on Mr. Usher's side, then Major Wally, Major Townsend. 'Twas about sunset by the time we got home. *Novr 20 6th day*, Madam Saml Bellingham, Capt Thomas, Mr. Willard and their wives, Mr. Woodbridge and his Kinsman Brockherst dined here.

Novr 25. 1696. Bro^r brings home Elizabeth, who is well, blessed be God. Went thither Augt 24.

Novr 25. Mr. Wm Brattle was Ordained at Cambridge. He and Mr. Mather, the President, preached. Twas first order'd that Mr. Brattle should not preach, but many being troubled at it, twas afterward altered. Mr. Brattle also procured the Church to order that Elder Clark should not lay his hand on's head when he was ordain'd; and he refrain'd accordingly. So that Deacon Gill coming home, said he liked all very well except the Bill of Exclusion. I was feverish by reason of Cold taken the day before, and so abode at home.

Wednesday, Novr 25. 1696. As I sat alone at home in the old Room, I had the Notion first; Tis when Martyrs *Seen*, not *slain* [*as a fulfilment of Prophecy*].

Second-day, Novr 30. Many Scholars go in the Afternoon to Scate on Fresh-pond; William Maxwell, and John Eyre fall in and are drown'd. Just about Candle-lighting the news of it is brought to Town, which affects persons exceedingly. Mr. Eyre the father cryes out bitterly.[27] *Decr. 1.* The body of Jno Eyre is brought to Town. Dec^r

[27] The lads were Harvard undergraduates. Maxwell was from Barbados and Eyre was the son of Katharine (Brattle) Eyre, afterwards the Widow Winthrop, whom Sewall unsuccessfully courted. President Mather preached a sermon on the occasion, *A Discourse Concerning the Uncertainty of the Times of Men* (Boston, 1697), and John Gibbs, sometime vicar of Newport-Pagnell, Bucks, a relative of Maxwell, preached a funeral sermon on him there, which was published in London in 1697. *C.S.M.* xxvi, 279.

3. is buried. Ministers of Boston had Gloves and Rings, Counsellors Gloves, of Boston. Bearers, Hutchinson, Dudley, Sim. Bradstreet, Dummer Jer., Jn° Winthrop, Belchar. Maxwell was buried at Cambridge. Paul Miller, his 2 sons, and about 4 more drowned last week; vessel and corn lost coming from Barstable.

Decr 2. 1696. Now about Capt. Byfield brings in a long Bill from the deputys for a Fast and Reformation, written by Mr. Cotton Mather, to which a Streamer was added expressing that Partiality in Courts of Justice was obvious; with a Vote on it that 500 should be printed, should be read; and sent up for Concurrence: 'twas deny'd; and our Bill for a Fast was sent down; Dept^s deny'd that. Govr told them the way was unusual, they had taken, sending out a Committee, calling the Ministers, voting all, and never letting the Council know: that it pertain'd principally to the Govr and Council to set forth such orders with a motion from them. A while after Capt. Byfield came in, and said 'twas no new thing, and they had taken no wrong step. Little was said to him. It seems this message is enter'd in their Booke. The Council were exceedingly grieved to be thus roughly treated.[28] About Decr 18, Mr. Mather, Allen, Willard, C. Mather give

---

[28] "During the fall and winter of 1696–97 there existed a widespread public foreboding, a sense of distress and impending disaster. Failure of crops, losses at sea, widespread sickness, raids by the Indians and failures of expeditions against the French, all seemed to indicate to the New England mind the frown of God's displeasure. Memories of the witchcraft tragedies hung like a black cloud over the community. A general repentance was demanded by leading men." (T. J. Holmes, *Cotton Mather . . . Bibliography* II, 493.) Cotton Mather was requested to draw up a proclamation for a day of general fasting and prayer. "This Instrument, was read and pass'd in the House of *Representatives;* but thro' some unhappy Influence, they added an Article unto it, which was not of my Composure [the Streamer mentioned by Sewall]; and that Article gave such Offence unto the *Councellors,* that the whole Instrument there met with Opposition, and *all* come to *Nothing.*" (Cotton Mather, *Diary* I, 211). The text of this document is printed in *Acts and Resolves* VII, 523–533 and in William De Loss Love Jr., *The Fast and Thanksgiving Days of New England* (1895), 266–268. Not only the Streamer, but Mather's swipes at the judiciary and his exaggerated views of New England's moral decline outraged the Council, and the proclamation was rejected 11 December 1696. On the same day, a condensation of Mather's text, prepared by Sewall (Love, p. 269; Holmes, II, 496) was voted in Council and sent down for concurrence. Since this led up to one of the most important actions in Sewall's life, we print the full text:

By the Honble the Lt Govr, Council & Assembly of his Maj^tys Province of ye Massachusetts Bay; in General Court Assembled.

Whereas the Anger of God is not yet turned away; but his Hand is still stretched out against his people, in manifold Judgments; particularly in drawing out to such a Length, the Troubles of Europe, by a perplexing War. And more Especially, respecting our selves in this Province, in that God is pleased still to go on in diminin a paper subscribed by them, shewing their dislike of our draught for the Colledge Charter, and desiring that their Names might not be entered therein. One chief reason was their apointing the Govr and Council for Visitor.[29]

Decr 19. Mr. Allin prays, and the Court is prorogued to the 17th Febr. at 1. p m. Lt Governour said that hop'd by praying together, our Love to God and one another should be increased. This is the first Prorogation that I know of.

---

ishing our Substance, cutting short our Harvest; blasting our most promising Undertakings; more ways than one, Unsettling of us; and by his more immediat Hand, snatching away many out of our Embraces by suddain & violent deaths; even at this time when the Sword is devouring so many; both at home and abroad; and that after many Days of publick and Solemn addressing of Him. And althô, considering the many Sins prevailing in the midst of us, We cannot but wonder at the Patience and Mercy moderating these Rebukes; yet we cannot but also Fear, that there is something still wanting to accompany our Supplications. And doubtless there are some particular Sins, which God is angry with our Israel for, that have not been duely seen and resented by us, about which God expects to be sought; if ever He turn again our Captivity.

Wherefore its Command^d & Appoit^d. that Thursday the Fourteenth of January next be observed as a Day of Prayer and Fasting throughout the Province; strictly forbidding all Servile Labour thereon, That so all God's people may offer up fervent Supplications unto him for the preservation and prosperity of his Maj^tys Royal person & Governm^t and Success to attend his Affaires both at home & abroad: That all Iniquity may be put away, which hath stirred Gods holy Jealousie against this Land; that He would shew us what we know not, and help us, wherein we have done amiss, to doe so no more; And, Especially, that whatever Mistakes, on either hand, have been fallen into; either by the body of this People, or any Orders of Men, referring to the late Tragedie raised amongst us by Satan and his Instruments, through the awfull Judgment of God; He would humble us therefore, and pardon all the Errors of his Servants and People that desire to Love his Name; And be attoned to His Land. That He would remove the Rod of the Wicked from off the Lot of the Righteous; That He would bring the American Heathen, and cause them to hear and obey his voice.

Decr 11. 1696. Voted in Council and sent down for concurrance. Is^a ADDINGTON, Secr'y.

Dec. 17, 1696. Voted a concurance. PENN TOWNSEND, Speaker.
    I consent.   Wm STOUGHTON.

(*Acts and Resolves*, VII, 132; 5 *M.H.S. Colls.*, v, 440n.)

[29] This entry and Sewall's statements on the charter in his second *Nota* of 19 December are explained in S. E. Morison's *Harvard College in the Seventeenth Century* I, 511–512. In September 1696 the House prepared a bill for a new charter for the college, which the Council rejected and replaced by another which required the president to live at the college and vested the power of visitation in the Governor and Council. The charter bill was approved by the Governor 17 December 1696, but never went into effect because certain officers named in it (the Mathers, James Allen and Samuel Willard) objected to its terms and sent a letter of protest.

Nota, Deputies voted our Bill for the Fast at length. Mr. Byfield brought it in, said, They would have *doubtless* instead of *probably.* And would have those words—*and so revive that joyful Proverb in the world, One flock, one Shepherd*—Left out. Their reason was because Gods conversion of the American Heathen did not make it good. Therefore would have the word *Obey* added after our *hear,* and let that be the close.

Nota. I had by accident met with and transcribed Mr. Strongs Notes on Rev. 12ᵗʰ about the slaying of the witnesses, the evening before this fell out: The last words were, prepare for it. I doe not know that ever I saw the Council run upon with such a height of Rage before. The Lord prepare for the Issue. I dont rememb' to have seen Capt. Byfield or Oliver at prayers. And the Ministers will go to England for a Charter, except we exclude the Council from the Visitation. Allege this Reason: because the K[*ing*] will not pass it, and so shall be longer unsettled. *Note* Dec' 12. 1696. Capt. Davis's eldest Daughter dyes very suddenly. Was a great Funeral next week.

Dec' 21. A very great Snow is on the Ground.³⁰ I go in the morn to Mr. Willard, to entreat him to chuse his own time to come and pray with little Sarah: He comes a little before night, and prays very fully and well. Mr. Mather, the President, had pray'd with her in the time of the Courts sitting. *Dec'* 22. being Catechising day, I give Mr. Willard a note to pray for my daughter publickly, which he did. *Note,* this morn Madam Elisa. Bellingham came to our house and upbraided me with setting my hand to pass Mr. Wharton's acc° to the Court, where he obtain'd a Judgmᵗ for Eustace's farm. I was wheadled and hector'd into that business, and have all along been uneasy in the remembrance of it: and now there is one come who will not spare to lay load. The Lord take away my filthy garments, and give me change of Rayment. This day I remove poor little Sarah into my Bed-chamber, where about Break of Day Dec' 23. she gives up the Ghost in Nurse Cowell's Arms. Born, Nov. 21. 1694. Neither I nor my wife were by: Nurse not expecting so sudden a change, and having promis'd to call us. I thought of Christ's Words, could you not watch with me one hour! and would fain have sat up with her: but fear of my wives illness, who is very valetudinarious, made me to

---

³⁰ "The winter of 1696 was as cold as had been known from the first arrival of the English; slays and loaded sleds passing great part of the time upon the ice from Boston as far as Nantasket. Greater losses in trade had never been known, than what were met with in this year; nor was there, at any time after the first year, so great a scarcity of food; nor was grain ever at a higher price." *Hutchinson, Hist.,* (1936), II, 76n.

lodge with her in the new Hall, where was call'd by Jane's Cry, to take notice of my dead daughter. Nurse did long and pathetically ask our pardon that she had not call'd us, and said she was surprizᵈ. Thus this very fair day is rendered fowl to us by reason of the general Sorrow and Tears in the family. Master Chiever was here the evening before, I desir'd him to pray for my daughter. The Chaptʳ read in course on Decʳ 23. m. was Deut. 22. which made me sadly reflect that I had not been so thorowly tender of my daughter; nor so effectually carefull of her Defence and preservation as I should have been. The good Lord pity and pardon and help for the future as to those God has still left me.

Decʳ 24. Sam. recites to me in Latin, Mat. 12. from the 6ᵗʰ to the end of the 12ᵗʰ v. The 7ᵗʰ verse did awfully bring to mind the Salem Tragedie.[31]

6ᵗʰ day, Decʳ 25, 1696. We bury our little daughter. In the chamber, Joseph in course reads Ecclesiastes 3ᵈ a time to be born and a time to die—Elisabeth, Rev. 22. Hannah, the 38ᵗʰ Psalm. I speak to each, as God helped, to our mutual comfort I hope. I order'd Sam. to read the 102. Psalm. Elisha Cooke, Edw. Hutchinson, John Baily, and Josia Willard bear my little daughter to the Tomb.

Note. Twas wholly dry, and I went at noon to see in what order things were set; and there I was entertain'd with a view of, and converse with, the Coffins of my dear Father Hull, Mother Hull, Cousin Quinsey, and my Six Children: for the little posthumous was now took up and set in upon that that stands on John's: so are three, one upon another twice, on the bench at the end. My Mother ly's on a lower bench, at the end, with head to her Husband's head: and I order'd little Sarah to be set on her Grandmother's feet. 'Twas an awfull yet pleasing Treat; Having said, The Lord knows who shall be brought hether next, I came away.[32]

Mr. Willard pray'd with us the night before; I gave him a Ring worth about 20ˢ. Sent the President one, who is sick of the Gout. He prayᵈ with my little daughter. Mr. Oakes, the Physician, Major Townsend, Speaker, of whoes wife I was a Bearer, and was join'd

---

[31] *Quod si nossetis quid sit, misericordiam volo, et non sacrificium, non condemnassetis inculpabiles* (If ye had known what this meaneth, I will have mercy and not sacrifice, ye would not have condemned the guiltless).

[32] The Hull-Sewall tomb sounds from Sewall's description like a great mausoleum, but it was an excavation, undoubtedly lined with brick, in the New, afterward the Granary, Burying Ground. It is covered by a brown stone superstructure or sarcophagus, inscribed HONL. JUDGE SEWALL'S TOMB NOW THE PROPERTY OF HIS HEIRS PHILIP RIDGWAY 1810 RALPH HUNTINGTON 1812 NO. 185 RALPH HUNTINGTON. Burials therein are listed in *L.B.* II, 310–312.

with me in going to Albany and has been Civil and treated me several times. Left a Ring at Madam Cooper's for the Governour. Gave not one pair of Gloves save to the Bearers. Many went to the Church this day, I met them coming home, as went to the Tomb. 7*th day Decr 26.* Roger Judd tells me of a ship arriv'd at Rhode Island from England, and after, that Mr. Ive has written that most judged the King of France was dead, or dying. Ship comes from New Castle, several weeks after the Falkland.

1697

SEWALL PUBLICLY RECANTS HIS PART IN THE WITCHCRAFT TRIALS /
SOUTH CHURCH DISPUTE OVER MR. BRADSTREET / VISIT FROM
HANNAH DUSTIN / TRIP TO NEWBURY / DROWNING OF RICHARD
WILLARD / SALT WORKS ESTABLISHED / LIMESTONE DISCOVERED AT
NEWBURY / PARSON WHITING SLAIN BY INDIANS AT LANCASTER /
OUTING AT HOGG ISLAND / PLYMOUTH CHURCH ADVISED TO DISMISS
PARSON COTTON / FOREST FIRES / SEWALL PUBLISHES HIS PHÆNOMENA
QUÆDAM APOCALYPTICA

Jany 1. 6th day 1696/7. One with a Trumpet sounds a Levit at our
window just about break of day, bids me good morrow and wishes
health and happiness to attend me. I was awake before, and my wife,
so we heard him: but went not to the window, nor spake a word. The
Lord fit me for his coming in whatsoever way it be. Mr. Willard had
the Meeting at his house to day, but We had no Invitation to be
there as is usual.

On the 22th of May I buried my abortive son; so neither of us
were then admitted of God to be there, and now the Owners of the
family admit us not: It may be I must never more hear a Sermon
there. The Lord pardon all my Sins of Omission and Commission:
and by his Almighty power make me meet to be partaker of the In-
heritance with the S^ts in Light. *Secund-day Jan^y* 11, 1696/7 God
helped me to pray more than ordinarily, that He would make up
our Loss in the burial of our little daughter and other children, and
that would give us a Child to Serve Him, pleading with Him as the
Institutor of Marriage, and the Author of every good work. *Jan^y* 15.
Gridley's wife dies in child-bed.

Copy of the Bill I put up on the Fast day; giving it to Mr. Willard as he pass'd by, and standing up at the reading of it, and bowing when finished; in the Afternoon.

Samuel Sewall, sensible of the reiterated strokes of God upon himself and family; and being sensible, that as to the Guilt contracted, upon the opening of the late Commission of Oyer and Terminer at Salem (to which the order for this Day relates) he is, upon many accounts, more concerned than any that he knows of, Desires to take the Blame and Shame of it, Asking pardon of Men, And especially desiring prayers that God, who has an Unlimited Authority, would pardon that Sin and all other his Sins; personal and Relative: And according to his infinite Benignity, and Soveraignty, Not Visit the Sin of him, or of any other, upon himself or any of his, nor upon the Land: But that He would powerfully defend him against all Temptations to Sin, for the future; and vouchsafe him the Efficacious, Saving Conduct of his Word and Spirit.[1]

Jany 26. 1696/7 I lodged at Charlestown, at Mrs. Shepards, who tells me Mr. Harvard built that house. I lay in the chamber next the street. As I lay awake past midnight, In my Meditation, I was affected to consider how long agoe God had made provision for my comfortable Lodging that night; seeing that was Mr. Harvards house: And that led me to think of Heaven the House not made with hands, which God for many Thousands of years has been storing with the richest furniture (Saints that are from time to time placed there), and that I had some hopes of being entertain'd in that Magnificent Convenient Palace, every way fitted and furnished. These thoughts were very refreshing to me.[2]

[1] The fast-day was 14 January 1696/7. In the margin beside this entry Sewall wrote: "Mr. Daniel Neal's Hist. N. England p. 536. Names of the Judges, p. 502, vol. 2." These notes were written many years later, after Sewall had read Daniel Neal's *History of New England*. See the entry of 3 May 1720.

[2] Little was known of John Harvard when the original edition of this diary was published, but the M.H.S. editors found "something very touching and impressive in the tenderness and devoutness of this entry." Since that time researches of Henry Fitz Gilbert Waters, J. Leslie Hotson, and others, have brought new facts to light, and these appear in S. E. Morison, *The Founding of Harvard College* (1935), 103–107, 210–227. Harvard took his M.A. from Emmanuel College, Cambridge, in 1635, married Ann Sadler in 1636, came to America in the summer of 1637, and in August of that year was admitted an inhabitant of Charlestown. He died there of consumption, 14 September 1638, leaving his library and half of his estate to the new college that had been opened at Cambridge earlier that summer. The following March the General Court ordered that the institution should be called Harvard College.

Harvard's widow married Thomas Allen, M.A. (Gonville & Caius College,

Jany 28. 1696/7 Mr. Palmer marries Mrs. Abigail Hutchinson. *Febr. 4* Bro^r Hawkins and his wife, the Thurtons, Sam. and Atherton Haugh, Joseph Gerrish and Wm Longfellow dine with us. *Febr. 5.* Extream cold, which discern not when Joseph went away. This evening Mr. Willard, Bromfield, Eyre, Sergeant, Frary, Hill, Williams, Oliver, Checkly, Davis, Wally, Stoddard, met at my house. Mr. Willard pray'd. Then discours^d what was best to be done relating to the desires of some for a ch meeting; whether twere best to call one, or no. Mr. Willard shew^d his resentments of the disorderly carriage in striving to bring in Mr. Bradstreet,[3] after only thrice preaching [*as a candidate for the South Church*], and that in that way, he should not be settled with us till he Mr. W. was in his Grave. That he had a Negative, and was not only a Moderator. Shew'd his dislike of the Person and his Preaching, inferiour to the ministerial Gifts of others. Before the Meeting broke up, I said his Preaching was very agreeable to me, I thought not of him, had no hand in bringing him to preach, had prejudices against him, was ready to start at first when any spake of fixing on him; yet as often as he preached, he came nearer and nearer to me. Spake this chiefly because all that Mr. Willard had said of Mr. Bradstreet, had been exceedingly undervaluing: and because Mr. Willard said No body had been with him to speak to him about Mr. Bradstreet but Mr. Stoddard. Mr. Oliver said if Mr. Willard were so averse, had rather let it rest. Sometimes said were now ready for a new Meetinghouse. Some, Let us call Mr. Baily. At last agreed to mention the matter to the church after the Afternoon Exercise. *Febr. 7.* Mr. Willard recapitulats how long he had been our Pastor; near 20. years; and near 18. years alone, had to his measure

---

Cambridge), minister of Charlestown from 1638 to 1651. Allen was succeeded in that pulpit by Thomas Shepard Jr. (Harvard 1653), who served from 1659 to 1677. The latter's successor was his son, Thomas Shepard III (Harvard 1676), who died in 1685. Sewall's host was Anna Tyng, the widow of Thomas Shepard Jr.; their daughter Anna had married Daniel Quincy, the goldsmith, cousin of Mrs. Sewall. Mrs. Shepard died 5 August 1709 at her granddaughter's home in Milton, but the remains were brought by water to "her own House" in Charlestown where Sewall attended the funeral August 6. The Harvard-Shepard house was on Town Hill; if it survived until the American Revolution, it must have been consumed in the conflagration which destroyed Charlestown 17 June 1775.
[3] Simon Bradstreet (Harvard 1693), grandson of the governor, was being considered for a ministerial post at Charlestown and at the South Church; though a quiet, learned, pipe-smoking man, he was the occasion for bitter disputes in both churches. In October 1698 he was ordained and settled at Charlestown. He and Sewall became close friends, and he appears frequently in the diary. *Sibley*; H. A. Hill, *Hist. of the Old South Church* 1, 301f; W. I. Budington, *Hist. of the First Church, Charlestown* (1845), 111.

served God faithfully, was desirous of Help, lay not in him, that had none; if what he propounded more than a year ago had been attended, might have made for the Glory of God. Ask'd if now were ready to pitch on any; if were, then must have a Fast. None speake; at last Capt. Ephr. Savage desired might meet in som dwelling house, many were there present which were not of us. Mr. Willard assented, and on Mr. Sergeants motion, appointed to meet at his house, 15. Ins^{tt} at 2 p.m. When at our house, some said Charlestown being before us, to call a Fast after they had call'd Mr. Bradstreet would be evil spoken of: the person of their desires being gon. Some said that Fasting now at Charlestown and here was but a Trick; not just so: but tending that way. Mr. Willard said Charlestown would be before us, do what we could; and if they call'd him 'twas not fit for us to meddle till he had given his Answer: som look'd at this as Artifice in the Ministers to prevent the South Church. For when Mr. Willard propounded Mr. Pemberton by name, 1695, No Fast preceded. If Mr. Willard had not so propounded, believe the thing had been issued at that time: but many look'd on it as an Imposition and tending to infringe their Liberty of choice. I had been with Mr. Willard the day before, and told him some scruples that I was not just ready to act till had enquired further.

Feb. 8. Mr. Bromfield and Eyre call me, and we visit Mr. H. Usher, who is now brought to Town about a week ago; Lay at Malden some time by reason of a fall from 's horse last 4th day five weeks. *Febr.* 9. I visit Mr. Willard: spake with him after he began, about our conference last 6th day, told him the reason of my speaking as I did; because had heard he should say, I forc'd the Church Meeting: whereas I intended not so; but as we had engaged silence, I told him my heart; as I said I always did when he confer'd with me and enquired of me in such cases. He said was sorry he propounded Mr. Pemberton as he did. Seem'd to resent my saying; That the Negative was a high point, and better not to talk of it then (which at the conference) term'd it a check, I think parted good friends. Much vilified Mr. Bradstreet; hardly allowed him any thing but a Memory, and the Greek Tongue, with a Little poesy. I said what shall Charlestown doe? Answer was, Let them do as they please. Mr. Willard is to assist on the Fast Day, which proves very cold, 4th day Feb. 10.

Feb^r 10. 4th *day* 1696/7 Goodw. Duen putting on a Rugg and going into our house much scares the children; so that come running to me throw the old Hall, with a very amazing Cry. I was sawing wood; and much surpris'd. Wife came and all. The Lord save me and his people from astonishing, suddain, desolating Judgm^{ts}; pardon all my folly and perverting my way, and help me to walk with a right foot. This was between 10 and 11. aclock. m. Deacon Maryon went from hence but a little before.

March 8. 1696/7 went to Plimouth in compᵃ of Majʳ Genˡ, Mr. Cook; visit Mrs. Cushman. *March* 12. Mr. Cook and I came to Barkers. 13. home; wether was extream cold.

March 15*ᵗʰ*, 1696/7. L't Thomas Mumford informs me that about eighteen years ago the eldest daughter of Nimerad, being regent after her father's death, during the minority of her Brother, that she might cleanse herself from her Mourning for her deceased father, gave notice that she had a mind to wash herself from her mourning and be clean, and for that reason appointed a Dance to be held upon such a day. To which many resorted at 40 miles distance to a very large house prepared for that solemnity. When the Assembly was full she stood up and acquainted them that she had had much adversity and now hoped for prosperity; that Wenoquaspouish was now her name, and then set a Tune and began a Dance, then call'd a person and gave him a string of Peag, then he made a speech desiring that she may have long prosperity of her Name, mentioning it; and then shouted three times and gave thanks for her Gift and sat down. Then the Queen set another Tune, call'd out another man, and *sic deinceps*. When a woman was call'd, she only after receiving the gift makes three shouts and sits down.

Note. When a person desires to have a new name they propound several to the Elders, and that which is allowed and ratified by them, that Name the person is called by, and no other. Psalm 30.11. Jer. 31.13. Lam: 5.15. Luke 15.25. Wenoquaspouish signifies as much as bright Lady.

March 24. 1696/7 went to Watertown to an Ordination; but was disappointed, the West and East not agreeing. Came home by Cambridge; Eat at Mr. Remington's[4] with Mr. Phips and wife, Sheriff Philips and wife. Call'd in to see Mrs. Danforth; but it seems it was not convenient. *March* 26. 1697. Mrs. Danforth dies.[5] This day Mr. Leverett was by the Council denyᵈ to be of the Corporation for the Colledge. How the Deputies will resent it, I know not. Day was appointed for nominating Justices, but the heat about what way should do it in was so great, that did nothing.

March 27, 1697. I read to the Lieut-Governour my *Phænomena Apocalyptica*, what had written of it. He Licences the printing of it.

[4] Lieutenant Jonathan Remington kept the Blue Anchor tavern in Cambridge.
[5] Mary (Withington) Danforth, the wife of Thomas Danforth.

About 10. at night Govr Bradstreet dyes; which we are told of March, 29th at Cambridge, where we were upon the account of Mrs. Danforth's Funeral. Madam Leverett, Madam Cook, and my wife and I rode together in the Coach. Major Genl Winthrop, Mr. Cook, and Sewall were Bearers on one hand; and Mr. Russell, Hathorne, and Phillips on the other hand. Rings and Scarvs. Col. Winthrop, Hutchinson, Sergeant, Lynde, Thomas were there.

Sixth-day, Apr. 2. 1697. Lieut-Governour, Mr. Secretary, Col. Shrimpton, and Sewall ride to Salem. It rain'd most of the way, and yet, a little beyond the Butts, Col. Gedny met the Govr with a small Troop; and in the Rain led us along through the Town to the Fort, to view it and see what condition 'twas in; and also the Brest-Woik: From thence went back to Col. Gedney's. Governour, Mr. Secretary, Col. Phillips and Sewall dined there: From about two *post meridiem*, the wether clear'd and was warm. About 3 was the Funeral; Bearers, Mr. Danforth, Major Gen. Winthrop, Mr. Cook, Col. Hutchinson, Sewall, Mr. Secretary: Col. Gedney and Major Brown led the Widow; I bore the Feet of the Corps into the Tomb, which is new, in the Old Burying place.

Mr. Willard, Capt Checkly, Capt Hill, Capt Williams Capt Belchar &c. there.

Mr. Bromfield, Mr. Eyre. Probably very many would have assisted, had not the wether been discouraging. Three Volleys, but no Great Guns, by reason of the Scarcity of Powder. Came home comfortably in the Sunshine; which prov'd well; for the next morning was a set Rain. Ministers at the Funeral, Mr. Willard, Mr. Shepard, Mr. Chiever, Mr. Higginson, Noyes,[6] Mr. Hale, Mr. Gerrish, Mr. Hubbard of Ipswich, which are all I took notice of.

Second-day, Apr. 5th. No Artillery Training, and consequently no choice of a Minister as is usual. Last night and this morning were very cold, possibly that might be the reason. Street of earth and water was hard frozen.

Apr. 8. 1697. Mr. Cotton Mather gives notice that the Lecture hereafter is to begin at Eleven of the Clock, an hour sooner than formerly: Reprov'd the Towns people that attended no better; fear'd twould be an omen of our not enjoying the Lecture long, if did not amend.

In the Morning agreed with Mr. Wilkins about Sam's living with him. Unkle Quinsey is here.

6 Nicholas Noyes (Harvard 1667) did not take his M.A. degree until 1716; Sewall punctiliously omitted a title for him in this list.

Second-day Apr. 12. 1697. Sam. begins to go to Mr. Wilkins;[7] Sold some of the Joy of Faith and some of Dr. Goodwin's 3ᵈ volum. At night we read Gal. 6. 9.—in due season we shall reap, if we faint not. Lord furnish father and Son with Faith.

This day Artillery meets: chuses.

Cold put them by this day sennight. Jnᵒ Marshal that waited on the Council and Selectmen and us'd to enquire after New–comers, is buried, and Braintry-Harris.

April 29. 5ᵗʰ day is signalised by the Atchievment of Hannah Dustun, Mary Neff, and Samuel Lennerson; who kill'd Two men [*Indians*], their Masters, and two women and 6. others, and have brought in Ten Scalps.

May 1. 1697. The first Sheet of *Phænomena Apocalptica* is wrought off. 3ᵈ *day May 11.* Elisabeth Sewall, and Joanna Gerrish set sail for Newbury in Edward Poor, between 10. and 11. a-clock, fair wind. Sent my Father a cheese and Barrel of Flower by him. Aunt Quinsey, and Cousin Edmund here. *Fourth-day, May 12.,* very brisk Southerly wind; so that hope Betty is got well to Newbury. This day wrought off the first half-sheet of the *Phænomena;* which I corrected my self. Hannah Dustun came to see us; I gave her part of Connecticut Flax. She saith her Master, whom she kill'd, did formerly live with Mr. Rowlandson at Lancaster:[8] He told her, that

---

[7] Sam had been placed with Michael Perry, the bookseller, in October 1694, but he had to leave the following January because of sore and swollen feet from standing in the cold shop. This time he went to work for Richard Wilkins, the bookseller commemorated by John Dunton in his *Letters from New England.* Sam was still at the Wilkins shop 20 October 1701, the day Cotton Mather erupted there in a loud verbal attack on our diarist.

[8] If the reader is somewhat startled to find the Sewalls entertaining a murderess, there is a ready explanation. On the 15th of March 1696/7 a band of Indians invaded the town of Haverhill and murdered or carried off about forty of the inhabitants. Hannah (Emerson) Dustin, who had lain-in a week before, was at home with her infant and the nurse, Mary (Corliss) Neff. Thomas Dustin, her husband, and seven other children were some distance from the house; he guided those children to a place of safety, but was unable to rescue his wife and baby. As the Indians marched Hannah and the nurse off with the rest of the captives, Hannah saw her infant brutally murdered and her house in flames. When the party reached an Indian settlement on an island at the confluence of the Contoo-cook and Merrimac rivers, Hannah and Mary were assigned as servants to an Indian family of twelve. Samuel Lennardson, a boy captured at Worcester the year before, was also in the ménage. Terrified by threats of being taken northward hundreds of miles and being stripped and forced to run the gauntlet, Hannah and the boy concerted a desperate plan. One night as the Indians were sleeping, they seized hatchets and dispatched ten of them. An old squaw, and a small Indian boy not marked for their attentions, escaped. The three English then started for Haver-

when he pray'd the English way, he thought that was good: but now he found the French way was better. The single man shewed the night before, to Sam[1] Lennarson, how he used to knock Englishmen on the head and take off their Scalps; little thinking that the Captives would make some of their first experiment upon himself. Sam. Lennarson kill'd him.

May 17. 1697. I accompany the Maj[r] Gen[l] and Mr. Cook to Salem, and so to Ipswich. Before I got to Mrs. Appleton's she was gone to Bed: So Mr. Rogers having invited me, I lodged there.

May 20. ride to Rowly, Newbury, lodge at my Fathers, who is indispos'd by a Rheum in his eyes; Much Rain at Newbury: Little or none at Salem. *May*. 23. I lead my dear Mother to Meeting, and hear Mr. Tappan preach.

May. 24. I perswade Father to make a settlement of Land and Marsh on Bro[r] J. Sewall: I take the Acknowledgm[t] *May* 25. Bro[r] St[ephen] S[ewall] Records it. Mr. Noyes and I dispute about the Fifth Seal. Come to the Blew Bell, refresh there; visit Mr. Wigglesworth, meet with Mr. Tappan from Reading, and ride with him to Charlestown.

May 26, 1697. Election-day: Capt Foster Guards the Governour to the Town-house, where the Court had a Treat. Mr. Danforth preaches. Dine at the stone house.

Massachusetts. W[m] Stoughton Esq. 64. Tho Danforth 77. Col. Pynchon 61. Wait Winthrop 54. J. Russell 69. Col. Cedney 66. Elisha Cook 57. Col. Hathorn 76. Elisha Hutchinson 80. S. Sewall 78. Isaac Addington 63. Major Brown, 57. Jn[o] Foster 70. Peter Sergeant 64. Col. Phillips 74. Jon[a] Corwin 58. Col. Wally 36. Col. Pierce 64.

Plimouth—Lothrop 73. Jn[o] Thacher 69. Thomas 54. Saffin 39.

Election, May 26, 1697 Main[e] Hutchinson, Frost, Wheelright,

---

hill, but the methodical Hannah, wishing to have proof of her exploit, went back and secured the ten scalps. At Haverhill they found the rest of the family safe. Hannah and her husband came to Boston in April to petition the General Court for relief, and the court voted 5*ol* in June, half to Hannah, and the other half to be shared between the Widow Neff and Lennardson. Hannah was lionized in Boston (not everyone was invited to the Sewalls') and showered with gifts, one coming from the Governor of Maryland. Cotton Mather took down her story, which was printed in his *Decennium Luctuosum* (Boston, 1699) and reprinted in the *Magnalia*. The story has been retold many times, with considerable variation of detail, e.g. in *Hutchinson* (1936), II, 80–81; G. W. Chase, *Hist. of Haverhill* (1861), 185–194; Timothy Dwight, *Travels in New-England and New-York* (1821–22), I, 411–414; *Palfrey* IV, 156. J. G. Whittier wrote Hannah's story in his *Hist. of Haverhill* (1832), on the title-page of which the editor, B. L. Mirick, substituted his name for that of the author. Savage gives the genealogical details of the Dustin and Neff families. Hannah is commemorated in the *D.A.B.*

untold. Zagadahock, Col. Joseph Lynde, untold. At Large Major Bradford, and Col. Shrimpton.

June 1, 1697. I goe to the Funeral of my Tutor, Mr. Tho. Graves;[9] accompanied Col. Pynchon, Mr. Cook, Addington, Sergeant, Saffin. Bearers were, Capt. Byfield, Mr. Leverett; Capt. Sprague, Capt. Hammond; Mr. James Oliver, Mr. Simon Bradstreet. Charlestown Gen^t had Gloves; Mr. Danforth had none that I observ'd. Mr. Morton is very short-breath, sat upon a Tomb in the burying-place, and said, for ought he knew he should be next. Mr. Willard, Pierpont, N. H., Mr. Brattle C. and Mr. Angier, Mr. Wadsworth there. Mr. Graves was a godly Learned Man, a good Tutor, and solid preacher: His obstinat adherence to some superstitious conceipts of the Common-Prayerbook, bred himself and others a great deal of Trouble: yet I think he kept to the Church at Charlestown as to his most constant attendance; especially on the Lords Day. Has left one Son by Mr. Stedman's daughter.

My Tutors are gon; the Lord help me to do worthily while I stay here; and be in a readiness to follow after!

June, 9. 1697. I have my Wife to Newton to take the Aer, Mr. Oliver, his wife and little daughter ride with us. Dine at Mr. Hobart's; Mr. Eyre and wife ride in their Calash. Mr. James Oliver and wife, Mr. Dudley and Mrs. Mico, Mr. Pemberton, and Mrs. Betty Oliver; Mr. Noyes and Sarah Oliver there too. Mr. Gershom Hobart was there. After Dinner sung the 113. and 24. Psalms, View'd the new frame of their Meeting House. Mrs. Jackson there. Walk'd out before dinner and gather'd my wife a handfull of strawberries. Call'd at B. White's coming home. *June* 11. about 5 p.m. My wife is taken with extream Pain and Illness, Vomiting and Flux. Told me when I came home, was afraid should never have seen me more. Took a Pill in the night: Disease abates.

June 12, 1697. Betty gets her Mother a Mess of English Beans; which she makes a shift to eat. These are our First Fruits.

Second-Day, June, 28. 1697. I visit my sick languishing Unkle Quinsey; who is oppressed with Difficulty in voiding his Urine. Was very glad to see me.

Cous. Edmund was at home. Visited Madam Dudley in coming home, and condol'd her loss of her Sons. She startled me in telling that I had not heard the sad News from Boston; which was that

---

9 Thomas Graves (Harvard 1656), tutor of Sewall's class (1671) at college, was a physician, judge of the inferior court and justice of the peace in Middlesex County; he had been at odds more than once with the church and the government. See Sewall's entry of 16 January 1694/5.

Rich⁴ Willard was drown'd at Cambridge. Alas! As went to Braintry, I saw the Neals reaping down a good field of French Barly: I desire to bless God for giving me to see the First fruits in such a time of Scarcity.

June, 29. I went and saw more than twenty Bushels of Salt raked, which is the most hath been raked in any one day yet. Rich⁴ Willard is buried. He went to Cambridge and was admitted; and then went into the River, and was drowned with his Admission in his Pocket. His father and Mother mourn sorely.[10]

July, 7. 1697. I ride with my wife and Mr. Stoddard and his wife to the Commencement. Mr. Willard, Wᵐ Hubbard, Cotton [of] Plimouth, Whiting, Brinsmead not there. *Note.* Mr. Moodey was buried the day before; was a very great Funeral. Many Ministers and Magistrates there. 'Twas celebrated with the discourse of Major Frost's death. Had him laid in our Tomb. *Friday, July, 16. 1697.* Lᵗ Govʳ went to the Castle, had with him Mr. Usher, Col. Pym, Majʳ Genˡ, Mr. Cook, Elisha Hutchinson, Mr. Secretary, Foster, Sergeant, Sewall, Mr. Allen, Mr. S. Mather, Capt. Byfield, Mr. Eyre Mr. Bridgham, Capt. Legg. Many Guns fired: about 10, at a mark with Bullets. Coming back, touched at Noddle's Island, and saw Col. Shrimpton. Capt. Clark hoisted his Flagg; and about our entrance within the Wharf, fired 9. Guns, very smart ones. *Note.* Dined in their chapel, and after that sung the 2d part of the 24ᵗʰ Psalm. Col. Hutchinson, Majʳ Townsend, Mr. Eyre, Mr. Bridgam, Capt. Legg and S. S. dined at a little Table by our selves.

When got home went to Mr. Burroughs's Meeting: Mr. Willard had begun his sermon, preached excellently from those Words, But the wise took Oyle in their vessels with their Lamps. D[*octrine*]. They who would always be in a readiness for Christs uncertain coming; must see that they have Grace in their hearts, and that they always keep it in exercise. Propounded 3 especial Graces necessary in order to our being ready; Faith, Fear, Love.

Rains sweetly at night, is a Rainbow in the morn as Mr. Goose tells me. Mr. Hezekiah Usher died at Lin, July 11ᵗʰ was brought to Boston, and laid in his father's Tomb, July 14, 1697. Bearers W. Winthrop, Cook, Sewall, Addington, Sergeant, Eli. Hutchinson; Mr. Willards Bearers for Richard, were Mr. White, Mather, Pemberton, Burr, Bradstreet, Williams.

[10] Richard was the thirteen-year-old son of Rev. Samuel Willard, minister of the South Church. The diary of John Marshall (2 *M.H.S. Proc.* xiv, 17) makes it clear, as Sewall's entry does not, that the boy had gone to the Charles to swim, not to end his life.

Sixth half sheet, July 17, wrought off the Letter D. of my *Phæn.* Went to the Neck, and Col. Hutchinson laid out the Land for their Salt Works.[11]

Fourth-day, Augt 11. 1697. Johnson's ship was burnt in Charlestown Rode, a great ship of [*blank*] Tuns, loaden with Lumber.

This day a Fast was kept at Cousin Savages for his sister Thacher. Mr. Willard and Thacher Pray'd and preach'd excellently. Mr. Cotton Mather pray'd; my wife and I sup'd there.

Fourth-day; Septr 8. 1697. The Governour and Council first meet in the Council-Chamber, as it is now fitted with Cieling, Glazing, Painting, new Floor that brings it to a Level; New Hearth even with it. Deputies sent for in; Lt Governour made a Speech, that as they saw by the many Prorogations, He hoped my Lord should have now receiv'd them. I presented his Honour with the view of a half-sheet, which begins *In quatuor angulis terræ.* Col. Pierce gave an account of the Body of Lime-Stone discover'd at Newbury, and the order of the Select–men published by James Brown, Dept Sheriff, to prohibit any persons from carrying any more away under the penalty of 20^s. It seems they began to come with Teams by 30. in a day: The Town will have a Meeting, and bring it to some Regulation. Our Momford saith tis good Marble. Ens. James Noyes found it out.[12]

Sam. and Hannah and Betty ride to Braintrey and Weymouth; Joseph and Mary go over to Charlestown.

Sixth-day, Septr 10. 1697. Court passeth an Act about supplies to other Provinces, of Men, if occasion be; to continue till the end of next May Sessions. Twas dark, and a Candle was brought in: Mr. Woodbridge went to Prayer, which is the first hath been made in the Council Chamber since its being very well fitted up and made new. Pray'd that our Land-defiling sins might be pardon'd; and Land-destroying Judgments remov'd. Pray'd that God would be favourably

[11] By Chapter 18 of the Province Laws of 1695/6, passed 7 March 1695/6, Elisha Cooke, Elisha Hutchinson, John Foster, and their associates, received a monopoly of making salt in the province "after the manner as it is made in France" for fourteen years; they were required to produce one hundred hogsheads of good merchantable salt before the end of the year 1700. The salt works was in the marshes on Boston Neck outside of the line of fortifications. M.H.S. EDS.

[12] Joshua Coffin cites this passage in his *History of Newbury* (1845), 164–165, and adds that for nearly a century vast quantities of lime of the best quality were annually made in Newbury for export as well as for home use. This appears to have been the first limestone discovered in Massachusetts; previously lime had been obtained only from oyster and clam shells. Sewall noted this discovery in his *Phænomena* (1697), p. 64. M.H.S. EDS.

with us at our next Meeting. Court was prorogued to fourth-day Oct^r
13. 9. *mane.*

Sabbath; Sepr 12. 1697. We hear of the slaughter made at Lancaster yesterday.

Septr 13. At Roxbury Mr. Danforth tells me that Mr. Whiting, the
Minister, was dead and buried: Indians shot and scalped him about
noon. We rid to Dedham and refreshed there: Dined at Billenges.
Lodged at Childs's, at Rehoboth.

Septr 14. Went to Bristow over the Ferry, Bridge being down.
Lodge at Mr. Wilkins; were met by sundry of Bristow Gentlemen.
Issued our Business to good Satisfaction to our selves; Fourth-day
was a storm, else might have husbanded it so as to have come to
Rehoboth that night: But are glad of the Rain after so sore a
drought.

Septr 16. *fifth-day,* Mr. Danforth and I and our men, set out to
come home, Not one creature accompanying us to the Ferry. Had a
very comfortable Journey. No Dust moving. Visited Mr. Greenwood.
Din'd at Woodcocks with boil'd venison: Discours'd with a Lin
Quaker removing to Philadelphia, one Burrel; Advis'd him to read
the 35th of Jeremiah: The Contents in that Bible mentioned Pride,
which he was guilty of. Go by Wrentham; visit Mr. Mann, who hath
11. children. From thence to Medfield, Lodge at Capt Barbers, visit
Mrs. Wilson in the even; give her 4 p^s 8/8 [*pieces of eight, Spanish
dollars*].

Septr 17. I view Mr. Baxters House and the Orchard Capt Frary
hath given to the Ministry, which lies very convenient; A living Brook
running by it; and throw Mr. Baxters. Visit Capt. Thurston, who
was glad to see me. When at Dedham visit Mr. Belchar; Mr. Whitman is there, are going to Connecticut. Got home a little before one
post meridiem. Is a Rumor at Rehoboth that Col. Gibson is gon
into Canada. One Jamison brought on the news of our Armys Engagement. Blessed be God who hath carried us out and brought us
home safely and that preservs so many of our Towns like Flocks of
Sheep in a howling Wilderness, naked and defenceless.

Sixth-day, Octr 1. 1697. Jer. Balchar's sons came for us to go to
the Island.[13] My Wife, through Indisposition, could not goe: But I

[13] The young and old who went on this picnic to Hog Island are all easily identified. Jeremiah Belcher, a prosperous farmer in Rumney Marsh, was the father of
three sons: Edward, 28; Joseph, 22; and Ebenezer, 18. Sewall brought along five
children: Sam, 19; Hannah, 17; Elizabeth, 16; Joseph, 9; Mary, 6; and a niece,
Jane Tappan, 23. Samuel Willard was minister of the Old South; his children

carried Sam. Hannah, Elisa, Joseph, Mary and Jane Tappan: I prevail'd with Mr. Willard to goe, He carried Simon, Elisabeth, William, Margaret, and Elisa Tyng: Had a very comfortable Passage thither and home again; though against Tide: Had first Butter, Honey, Curds and Cream. For Dinner, very good Rost Lamb, Turkey, Fowls, Applepy. After Dinner sung the 121 Psalm. *Note.* A Glass of spirits my Wife sent stood upon a Joint-Stool which, Simon W. jogging, it fell down and broke all to shivers: I said twas a lively Emblem of our Fragility and Mortality. When came home met Capt Scottow led between two: He came to visit me and fell down and hurt himself; bruis'd his Nose, within a little of our House.

Upon the fourth day of the Week Septr 29, 1697, A Council met at Plimouth:

Septr 30. fifth day, They published their Advice, that Mr. Cotton should make an orderly secession from the Church. Advis'd the Church to dismiss him with as much Charity as the Rule would admit of; and provide for themselvs. This was for his Notorious Breaches of the Seventh Commandment, and Undue Carriage in chusing Elders. Thus Christs words are fullfilled, Unsavoury Salt is cast to the Dunghill. A most awfull Instance! [14]

---

were Simon (Harvard 1695), 21; Elizabeth, 22; William, 11; and Margaret, 10. Elizabeth Tyng, about 11, was the daughter of Edward Tyng, brother of Mrs. Willard. *Savage, Sibley,* and *N.E.H.G.R.* lx, 250–253.

[14] John Cotton (Harvard 1657) was the son of the great John Cotton of Boston. After his dismissal he went to Charleston, South Carolina, where he was minister until his death in a yellow fever epidemic in September 1699. Arthur Lord, devoted Plymouthean and editor of the Plymouth Church Records (*C.S.M.* xxii and xxiii) refused to believe Sewall's record of Cotton's adultery. In his preface to the church records (pp. xxxi–xxxii) he by-passed it, omitting a citation to this entry, but citing the milder entry of 8 March 1697/8. At the April 1924 meeting of the Colonial Society Mr. Lord triumphantly read a letter of Thomas Coram to Rev. Dr. Benjamin Colman, written from Liverpool, 23 September 1735, stating: "mr. Cotton . . . was in or about the year 1697 or within a year or two after Charged with attempting to be too Familiar with one of his Church Members Wife for which mr. Stoughton then Lt. Governor Displaced him from his Church w'ch Drove him to Carolina where he Dyed. I happened then to be building ships at Taunton in Plymouth Colony and well understood from those who had no friendship for that mr. Cotton, That all that affair was a Base piece of villainy that the man was no more Guilty of that Crime Charged on him than you or I was; I happened to speak of it severall Times in Plymouth Colony and in Boston, but at that time it was looked on a Sort of Blasphemy to Suspect mr. Stoughton could do anything Wrong . . ." (*C.S.M.* xxvi, 80–81, quoting Coram's letter from *M.H.S. Proc.* lvi, 30–31). Mr. Lord then remarked that although the incident has little importance or interest today, "it seems to me desirable in order to complete the record that some reference to this letter from

Fourth day Oct[r] 6. 1697. A Church is gathered at Watertown, East-end, and Mr. Gibbs Ordained. Mr. Fox ordains, Mr. Sherman gives the Right Hand of Fellowship. This was done in the Afternoon in the open Aer though a cold day. The Western party, having the Select-Men on their side, got possession of the Meetinghouse, and would not suffer the Assembly to enter there. The Lord be mercifull to his people, pardon our Sins and heal our gaping wounds! Mr. Torrey tells me that Mr. Mather declar'd among the Ministers Oct[r] 7. that they had dealt too favourably with Mr. Cotton. *Fourth-day, Oct[r] 13. 1697.* The Company of young Merchants Treat the Gov[r] and all of the Council in Boston, at George Monk's. Cap[t] Tuttle and L[t] Winthrop invited the evening before. Came between 12 and 1. to the Townh. Chamber and Guarded the Governour and Council to the Anchor.[15] Mr. Sam[l] Mather is the Chaplain. No other Minister there. Mr. Noyes is ensign. After Dinner They Guarded his Honour and the Council to the Council-Chamber again; and then gave three very handsom Volleys.

This day I printed off my last half sheet and told the Governour I might safely deliver it his Honour, being under so good a Guard; twas at G. Monk's. In the Evening Mat. 26. is read in the family in course, O my Father, if it be possible &c.

Seventh-day Oct[r] 16. K. being alter'd, and composed anew, is wrought off. The Fires make great Havock of Hay, Medow, Fence, Timber &c. Aer hath been fill'd with smoke for above a week.

Col. Gedney had his wife to Ipswich as he went to Newbury Court, and she falls sick and dyes there in about 3 weeks time. Died on Friday night last; heard not of it till this day Oct[r] 17. 1697.

Mr. Coram, which is persuasive if not conclusive as to the injustice of the charges by Sewall against Mr. Cotton, should be noted in the Transactions of this Society . . ."

This editor feels that there is no reason to disbelieve Sewall. It is of record that Cotton, "for lacivious uncleane practises with three women and his horrid lying to hide his sinne" was excommunicated from the First Church in Boston, 1 May 1664, though by reason of his "penitential acknowledgement openly Confessing his sinnes" he was restored to membership 12 June 1664 (*C.S.M.* xxxix, 60, 61). Mr. Lord, a lawyer trained in the rules of evidence, should have been more critical of Coram's letter, written by an old man many years after the event, especially the statement that Cotton was displaced and driven to Carolina by Stoughton. A church council from the churches of Weymouth, Duxbury, Bridgewater, Taunton, and Barnstable "Judged it best that the Pastor should cease his worke amongst them & the chh dismisse him with such expressions of their love & charity as the Rule called for" (*C.S.M.* xxii, 180), which is just what Sewall wrote. On 5 October 1697 the Plymouth Church voted to release him.

15 The Blue Anchor tavern on Washington Street, kept by George Monk.

Aer is full of smoke by reason of the Fires. *Octobr* 20. 1697. I wait on the Lieut Governour at Dorchester, and there meet with Mr. Torry, breakfast together on Venison and Chockalatte: I said Massachuset and Mexico met at his Honour's Table. When I first saw the Lieut. Governour He was Carting Ears of Corn from the upper Barn. At Noon visit Mr. Morton, and Mrs. Collins, at Charlestown.

Satterday, Octr 30. 1697. Several Acts are published; particularly that against Atheisme and Blasphemie.[16] Mr. Allen prays; Lieut. Governour Prorogues the Assembly to Dec. 15. 9 *mane*. Mr. Cook and I write a Warrant for the Adjournm't of Salem Court to the 16th November, because of the Thanksgiving. Mr. Jewet much for it.

Fifth-day, Novr 4th Guns fired with respect to the King's Birth-day. At night great Illumination made in the Town-house; Governour and Council and many Gentlemen there. About 8. Mr. Brattle and Newmen let fly their Fire–works from Cotton-Hill; Governour and Council went thither with a Trumpet sounding. *Note.* Governour, Mr. Secretary and I went to see Mr. Morton; before these works began, Had the Epistle to his Honour, a proof of it, in my pocket: but had not opportunity to shew it: was taken this day. I went and visited Mr. Baily, who discoursed pretty cheerily. There is News that the D[*uke*] of Saxony is turned Roman, and chosen King of Poland.

Third-day, Novembr 9th The Epistle to the Lieut-Governour, which is the last half-Sheet, is wro't off, and the Book is set to sale in Mr. Wilkins's shop. One is sold. Could not be wrought off last week, nor yesterday; because of the Laws.[17] Mr. Flint of Norwich came in to the Printing-Room: I gave him a Book stich'd up, which is the first perfect Book I have given away. Novr 8. I was mourning and praying to God; and it seems my dear Bror was sorrowing in the Burial of his little Hannah which I receiv'd an account of this day.

In the even met at Mr. Bridghams about the Bridge; Before came away sang all the ordinary Tunes. Sung 2d part 24. Ps 48. PS 147.

[16] The act against Atheisme and Blasphemie (Chapter 20, Province Laws of 1697) included among the punishments "boring through the tongue with a red hot iron." Chapters 17 (against Murder) and 18 (against Ravishment or Rape) carried the punishment of death; Chapter 19 (against Buggery) required not only the punishment of death but also the slaying and burning of the beast.

[17] All authors will appreciate Sewall's delight in seeing the first copies of his first book to come from the press. His entries in the previous months, beginning in May, show how eagerly he followed the book through its various stages of production. At the end, Sewall ran into a priority, and had to wait while Green and Allen printed *Acts and Laws, Passed by the Great and General Court . . . Begun and Held at Boston the Twenty-sixth of May, 1697. and continued by Several Prorogations until Wednesday the Thirteenth of October following* (Boston, 1697).

Phænomena quædam

APOCALYPTICA

Ad Aspectum NOVI ORBIS configurata.

Or, some few Lines towards a description of the New

HEAVEN

As It makes to those who stand upon the

NEW EARTH

By *Samuel Sewall* sometime Fellow of *Harvard* Colledge at *Cambridge* in *New-England.*

Psalm, 45. 10, *Forget also thy own people, and thy fathers house.*
Isai 11 14. *But they shall fly upon the shoulders of the Philistins toward the west.*
Act. 1. 6 -- 8 *Lord, wilt thou at this time restore again the kingdom to Israel?*
---- - *ye shall be witnesses unto me unto the uttermost parts of the earth;*
hasta lo ultimo de la tierra. *Spanish Bible.*
Luke, 15. 24 *For this My Son was dead, and is alive again; he was lost, and is found.* V 32. *For this thy Brother &c.*

Ille non deerit Promissis; restituet Regnum *Israeli*; sed suo modo, loco, ac tempore. *Bullinger.* Nequis illa a me dicta, aut adducta accipiat, quasi contendendi, aut adversandi studio; ac non discendi potius, ac conferendi gratia. *Ex* Med. Apoc. p. 371. *ad Phialam Sextam.*

MASSACHUSET;

BOSTON, Printed by *Bartholomew Green, and John Allen,* And are to be sold by *Richard Wilkins,* 1697.

Part of the 46. 2ᵈ part 102. Majʳ Wally, Mr. Bridgham, Capᵗ Hill, Capᵗ Wing.

Fourth-day Novʳ 10ᵗʰ Lᵗ Governour and Council met at the Council Chamber, were warn'd by Maxwell the day before. I took that opportunity to present the Lᵗ Governour with seven *Phænomena!* I said the Records and References were laid before his Honʳ as it were in open Court; and pray'd that his Honour would judge of the Cause according to its own Merits, and not according to the deficiency of the Attorney, who had fallen short as to the duely urging of many proper pleas. His Honour said it should be favourably judged of. In the evening, not having a Thanksgiving sermon at hand, I resolv'd to read in course, not thinking what the Chapter might be, and it prov'd to be Luke, 1. I applied Marys question to the business of the Natives; Though means fail'd, God could easily convert them: Sung the song of Zecharia and Simeon.

In the morn. *Novʳ 12ᵗʰ* Sung in course the 24ᵗʰ Ps., which was not aware of till my Son named it. Much Rain fell this day and night following; which was extreamly needed, for the Wells, for Cattell to drink, and for the Mills.

Novʳ 13 being at Mrs. Hillers to present her with a Print, and having only one left about me, Mr. Nehemia Willoughby came to the door, and I sent it to my Broʳ to Salem by him, with Condolance for the burial of his Daughters. *Tuesday, Novʳ 16. 1697.* I ride to Salem with the Major General. As went along in Boston, I saw Sheriff Bradford; and gave him one of the *Phænomena* for his Father, as was on horse back. *Fourth-day Novʳ 17.* Lecture-day. Mr. Noyes preached excellently from Ps. 122. 6. Pray for Jerusalem, her peace &c. Mr. Higginson dined with us; I gave him a Booke, which he kindly accepted. Desired me to come to him; I went next day in the Even. He gave me a Treatise against Perriwigs, and left it to me to do with it as I pleased. I mention'd Printing it. He said would not have it done while he liv'd however.[18]

Sixth-day, Novʳ 19. Mr. Higginson coms as far as Brothers to see me; which I wonder'd at. Mr. Hale and I lodg'd together: He discours'd me about writing a History of the Witchcraft;[19] I fear lest he go into the other extream. Came home with the Majʳ General, din'd at Madam Paiges; there found Hancock, Allen, and Sam. Haugh.

[18] John Higginson (1616–1708), minister of Salem, is the subject of a long biographical sketch by Simeon Eben Baldwin in 2 *M.H.S. Proc.* xvi, 478–521. The Treatise on Perriwigs does not appear among his publications.
[19] Rev. John Hale of Beverly published his book, A *Modest Enquiry Into the Nature of Witchcraft*, in 1702.

Found all well, *Laus Deo*. At Col. Paiges was told of the Death of Mrs. Thatcher. When came home, Mr. Cooke told me of the death of Mr. Hooker of Farmington.

*Nov*r 20. rid with Mr. Willard, Allen, Wadsworth, Bridgham to Mrs. Thachers Funeral—Mr. Allen pray'd. Gave Gloves, Mr. Torrey, Fisk, Danforth, Belchar were also there. Din'd after the Funeral, and came home. Mr. Willard told me of the falling out between the President and him about Chusing Fellows last Monday. Mr. Mather has sent him word, He will never come to his House more till he give him satisfaction. Got home before sun-set. He tells me that he had preached upon the Seals, and concluded those Sermons the last Lecture, and now I have put a Treatise into his hand relating to them.

*Nov*r 24, I visited Unkle Quinsey, met Mr. Torrey there. [*Read in?*] Flying Post or Post-Master, *Nov*r 27.—30 On Friday night last, Mr. Timothy Cruso, an eminent Non-Conformist Minister in the City [*of London*] departed this Life; and will be this day interr'd.

*Dec*r 7*th* went on foot to Cambridge, alone, visited Mr. Clark and his wife. He shews me Dr. Goodwin—God can, God will, give an Answer of Peace. Widow Alice Whiting, Widow Corlet. Mr. Brattle. Came down with Capt. Williams, Capt. Stoddard, Mr. Simeon Stoddard. Had a very comfortable journey. When came home my son presented me with Mr. Mathers Dead Faith. Lord help me to believe and repent.

*Fifth-day Decemb*r 9. 1697. Mr. Willard preacheth from 1 Jn° 2. 1. My little children, these things write I unto you that you Sin not. Doct. The proper tendency of the most evangelical Doctrines of the Gospel is to keep men from sinning. Mr. Fisk and Mr. Belchar dine with us. This day about 3 p.m, Gillam arrives at Marble-head, Capt. Balston, a Passenger, comes to Town that night. Early in the morn. *Dec*r 10*th* Sixth-day, Capt. Clark tells me of it. Letters are at the Posthouse. Mr. Jn° Willard brings the Order for proclaiming the Peace here, which was done between 3 and 4. p.m. Eight or 10 Drums, Two Trumpets: Prisoners released.[20] Mr. Cotton Mather was at the Townhouse Chamber pretty merry and pleasant: but was made sad by Col. Hutchinsons telling him of the death of his Unkle Mr. N. Mather, a very worthy Friend of New England. Visited the President in the evening. He is sorrowful. It seems Mr. Cole, and Mr. Vincent are also dead: very worthy persons. The ships set sail from Cows Second day Novemb*r 8. 1697, at Noon. A very extraordinary Passage.

*Lords-day Dec*r 12. 1697. about 3. p.m. just the time he should

[20] The Peace of Ryswick ended King William's War in America. The Treaty between France, England, Spain, and Holland was signed 20 September 1697.

have stood up to preach for Mr. Willard, Mr. John Bayly dieth, after much pain and illness by the Gout and other distempers. *Secund-day, Decr 13. 1697.* I ride to Braintry to visit my Unkle Quinsey: He speaks pretty freely to me. Saith he must run with open arms to a dying Saviour. I mention'd the publick Interest: He said if we were a holy and humble people, God would save us. Pray'd God to bless my children and family. I offer'd to have staid all night: but he desir'd me to goe home.

Fifth-day, Decr 16. Mr. Bayly is buried. Mr. Cotton Mather preach'd a funeral sermon from Psal. 31. 5. Great Assembly though a very Cold day. *Decr 17.* The Deputies chuse Major Townsend their Speaker: Council chuseth Wait Winthrop, and Elisha Cooke, Esqrs, to goe to New-York to congratulate his Excellencys Arrival, when shall receive certain advice of it.

Decr 18. Address and Instructions are agreed on.

Decr 22. 1697. A Law against Exportation of Money is published, and the Court prorogued to March 16. at one in the Afternoon. No Prayer this Court that I hear of in the Council. It hath been extream cold. *Seventh-day, Decemb^r 25. 97.* Snowy day: Shops are open, and Carts and sleds come to Town with Wood and Fagots as formerly, save what abatement may be allowed on account of the wether. This morning we read in course the 14, 15, and 16th Psalms. From the 4th v. of the 16th Ps. I took occasion to dehort mine from Christmas-keeping, and charged them to forbear. Hannah reads Daniel, 6. and Betty, Luke, 12. Joseph tells me that though most of the Boys went to the Church yet he went not. By the Intercession of his Mother, and his brothers Concession, he begins to read the Psalm.

1698

UNCKLE QUINSEY'S DEATH / SEVERE WINTER IN BOSTON / DEATH OF
COLONEL SAMUEL SHRIMPTON / INDIAN ATTACK ON ANDOVER / VISIT
TO PLYMOUTH / THE LAST HOURS OF CHARLES MORTON / INDIAN
COLLEGE AT HARVARD TORN DOWN / FIRE IN SALEM / VISIT FROM
EDWARD TAYLOR / HOLDS COURT AT SPRINGFIELD AND REHOBOTH /
EBENEZER PEMBERTON ELECTED MINISTER OF SOUTH CHURCH /
EXECUTION OF SARAH THREENEEDLES

Sixth-day, Jany 7. [1697/8], went over Charles River on the Ice, to
Charlestown–Lecture and came back on the Ice. Mr. Brattle, Mr.
D. Oliver, Mr. Mico, Newman, Welsteed in Comp^a. Mr. Bradstreet's
Text was Mat. 7. 21, an awfull Scripture.

Seventh-day, Jany 8, between ten and 11. m. Parmiter comes in,
and tells us that Unckle Quinsey died between 7 and 8 last night. A
true New England man, and one of our best Friends, is gon.

Fourth-day, Jany 12. 1697/8 went to the Funeral of my dear
Unckle. Went in the Coach, our horse failing us, Took in Madam
Dudley, sending Mr. Newman before, to tell her; she seem'd to
be glad of the Invitation and were mutually refreshed by our Company. Had my wife, Cousin Quinsey, and Madam Dudley. Bearers
were Col. Paige, Lt Col. Hutchinson, Mr. Addington, Mr. E^m Hutchinson, Major Townsend, Capt. Dummer, Major Hunt, and Ens.
Penniman; had Scarves. Ens^n Penniman was the only Commission
Officer of Braintry that could come abroad. Ministers there, Mr. Torrey, Mr. Willard, Mr. Fisk, Thacher, Danforth, Baxter; I saw from
Boston Capt. Hill, Mr. Eliot, Mr. Tay, Bennet; Mr. Palmer waited
on his father and Mother Hutchinson.

By reason of the severity of the wether, and a great Cold, I went
not to the catechising Jany 18. nor to the Lecture Jany 20th.

Jany 21. Sixth-day, Mr. Willard comes to visit us; though He himself also is very much indisposed by the Cold: prays with us. Speaks
as if had heard Capt. Scottow was dead: but was not very certain.
But before he went away, Jno Roberts came to invite me to be a

Bearer to morrow. It seems Capt. Scottow died the last night. Thus the New England Men drop away.

Seventh-day, Jany 22. 1697/8. Capt Joshua Scottow is buried in the old burying place; Bearers, Maj^r Genl Winthrop, Mr. Cook, Col. Hutchinson, Sewall, Sergeant, Walley: Extream Cold. No Minister at Capt. Scottow's Funeral; nor wife, nor daughter.

Jany 23, 1697/8 Very Cold. Mr. Fitch preacheth with us and pro-nounceth the Blessing, Mr. Willard not being there, by reason of illness: Text was, The Lord is my shepherd &c. Mr. Willard comes abroad in the Afternoon, and preacheth excellently; baptiseth a child and a woman. Very thin Assemblies this Sabbath, and last; and great Coughing: very few women there. Mr. Willard pray'd for mitigation of the wether; and the south Wind begins to blow with some vigor. My clock stood still this morning, and yesterday morn, which has not done many years.

Third-day, Jany 25. Rid to the Court over Charles River upon the Ice, directly from Broughton's Warehouse to the Ferry-place. Had no Minister in the Court or at Dinner; Mr. Morton sick at home. We sent a Plate to him from Table, and visited him in the Afternoon.

Fourth-day, Jany 26. Rid over to Charlestown on the Ice which had much Water on it by the Thaw, the South Wind having blown very hard all night: I consulted Mr. Gee before I ventured; and in the morn. look'd out and found that the Ice between us and the Castle was not broken. Mr. Danforth not there. Jury kept up all night about the Case between Annesley and Tucker; brought in a special verdict, and the Court presently gave for Annesly; I was against it; Major Generall and Mr. Cooke for it: Major General proposed Advisement bill next term. I aproved it; but Mr. Cooke turn'd his minde. Visited Mrs. Shepard, and Cousin Quinsey.

Jany 26. 1697/8 Mrs. Ruth Carter dys.

Jany 27. I was sent for to the house; it seems she hath nominated Mr. Addington and me as executors in Trust with her Husband, on behalf of her little Son. Is agreed the Funeral to be on the 7th day.

Seventh day, Jany 29. 1697/8 Mrs. Ruth Carter is buried; Bearers Sewall, Addington, Byfield, Belchar, Legg, Borland. Ministers had scarvs, and Mr. Chiever, Mr. Oakes, Physician, Mr. Sergeant, Mr. Eliakim Hutchinson, Major Walley there. Got home by four oclock. 'Tis a very cold day. Joseph Perce and the widow Windsor, Capt Scottos sister, lye dead.

Febr. 2. I ride over the Ice to Charlestown, visit Mr. Russell, Mr. Danforth and dine with him; Go to Mr. Olivers for Betty, to George Bairsto's, visit Mr. Walter and his wife, and go home about 6.

Febr. 3. I saw Walter a little below the Castle. I hope the Ice will now begin to remove. Neither President nor Mr. Cotton Mather at Lecture. Mr. Willard preached excellently from Rev. 2. 11. He that overcometh shall not be hurt of the second Death. Day warm though blustering; the sun very much qualifying the Aer. More at Lecture than formerly, and little Coughing.

Febr. 4. 1697/8. Mrs. Lynde buried; Bearers Mr. Cooke, Addington, Bromfield, Capt. Williams, Capt. Foxcroft, Mr. Maccarty.

Febr. 5. 1697/8 Deacon Swift calls here and earnestly thanks me for the *Phænomena* I gave him, hopes it will doe good. This day I prayd for it, for Betty. Preparation for the Lords Supper.[1]

Fourth-day, Febr. 9. Last night, about nine of the clock, Col. Shrimpton dyes of an Apoplexy. Capt. Ichabod Plaisted told me of it. He was seen at his door the last Sixth–day. I gave my Letters to Capt Plaisted to carry to Newbury. *Second-day, Febr.* 14. 1697/8 Col. Sam¹ Shrimpton was buried with Arms; Ten Companies, 8, Muddy River and Sconce:[2] No Horse nor Trumpet: but a Horse led—Mr. Dyers, the Colonel's, would not endure the cloathing: Mourning Coach also and Horses in Mourning: Scutcheon on their sides and Deaths heads on their foreheads: Coach stood by the way here and there and mov'd solitarily. Bearers Majʳ Genˡ Winthrop, Mr. Cook, Lᵗ Col. Hutchinson, Mr. Addington, Capt. Foster, Majʳ Walley. Mr. Eᵐ Hutchinson and Mr. Allen led the widow, Capt. Clark fired twelve great guns at the Sconce, began as march'd to the New-burying place where the Corps was set int [*sic*] to the two wives. Very fair and large Paths were shovel'd by great pains and cost, three in the Burying place, one direct to the Tomb, the other compassing by the sides in which the souldiers stood Drawn up. Wᵐ Scovel being well and having on his new Coat, I fitted him with my Musket, Rapier, mourning, Ammunition, and he serv'd in the South-Company.

Febr. 15. Remarkable Sun-dogs and a Rainbow were seen. *Febr.* 16. Mr. Chr. Tappan comes hether. Sam. reads the 2ᵈ Habakkuk out of course at evening prayer; next morn reads the 90ᵗʰ Psalm in course. Secret sins in the light of thy countenance, pained me. *Feb.* 19. I go over the Ice and visit Mr. Morton, who keeps his bed.

Febyr. 21. I rid over to Charlestown on the Ice, then over to

---

[1] At this point Sewall inserted a list "of some I have been a Bearer to." These funerals are recorded in the diary under the dates attended, with four exceptions: Mrs. Mary Thompson, 44, 5 July 1699 (scarf); Mrs. Mary Balston, 75, 21 July 1699 (scarf); Mr. Theoder Atkinson, 90, 16 August 1701 (scarf); Madame Penelope Bellingham, May 1702 (scarf).
[2] The Sconce was the fort at Fort Hill, commanding Boston Harbor.

Stowers's, go to Mr. Wigglesworth: The snow was so deep that I had a hard Journey, could go but a foot pace upon Mystick River, the snow was so deep. Mr. Wigglesworth preach'd Jan.ʳ 23. from those words, Who can stand before his Cold? Then by reason of his own and peoples sickness, Three Sabbaths pass'd without publick worship. *Feb.* 20. a very cold day, He preached from those words; He sends forth his word and thaws them; which began 21 and especially 22, and has thaw'd much and yet moderately.

Febr. 24. 97/8. Febr. 22. at break of day, Andover is surprised. Lᵗ Col. Bradstreet's house rifled, his kinsman Wade slain: Capt. Chubb and his wife slain and three more. Some Houses and Barns burnt, and in one a considerable quantity of corn, and twenty head of Cattel. Pulpit cushion taken away, Meetingh[ouse] fired, but quenched.

Febr. 24. I would fain have had the condition of Gods people put into the order for the Fast, in some such expression; As we hope to rejoice with them, so we desire to sympathise with the Brethren of our Lord Jesus in France, Germany, Greece and other parts of the world under the Oppressions. But could by no means prevail; and the general Clause was hardly got in; the order being drawn up without it.

Febr. 26. I ride to George Bairsto and the widow Gates: They complain their sheep, having been so long kept from the ground, are sick, some dye. Others will not own their Lambs.

Febr. 26. A considerable quantity of Ice went away last night: so that now there is a glade of water along by Governor's Island about as far as Bird Island. Easterly wind all this day.

Febr. 28. A guard is set upon Charles River to prevent persons venturing over on the Ice for fear of drowning; and the Ferrymen are put upon cutting and cleaving the Ice, which they do so happily, that I think the Boat passeth once this day. *March the first,* I walk on purpose, and see the wharf at Henchmans clear, and the Ferryboat passing very comfortably.

Second-day, March 7. Set out for Plimouth about 10. *mane.* Get to Barkers and lodge there. Majʳ General set out about Noon and came to us at Barkers in the night.

March, 8. Get to Plimouth about Noon, Are entertain'd at Cole's. Send two mile for Mr. Little, who prays at the opening of the Court: invite him to Dinner: Speak not to Mr. Cotton. I lodge at Cole's, the house was built by Govʳ Winslow and is the oldest in Plimouth. *March, 9.* Word is brought us that our Horses are broke out of themselves, or else are taken out of the stable; viz. four, Majʳ Generals, Mr. Cooks, mine, and Mingo's. Sent presently to their flat-house, but hear nothing of them. Court rises. Capt. Byfield goes home. Mr. Cook and I linger hoping to hear of our horses and trying to get more. *Fifth-day, March,* 10. I walk out in the morn. to see the Mill, then turn up to the Graves, come down by the Meetinghouse, and seeing the door partly open, went in and found a very convenient Opportunity to pray, the wind being cold; for my self and family, for Plimouth, Bp Stoke, the Province, &c. Maj^r General, Mr. Sherriffe, Mr. Ward, Master of a Connecticut Sloop, and I Dine together at Coles. I pay for Ward because invited him, and Maj^r General for the Sheriffe. Had large discourse in the even with Mrs. Cotton, Mr. Cotton, Mr. Rowland. I told Mr. Cotton, a free confession was the best way; spake of Davids roaring all the day long and bones waxing old whilest he kept silence. I spake with Deacon Fance[3] today, sent for him to Mr. Cotton's: It seems upon the 5th of October, The Church, by speaking one by one, declared their Mind was to Release Mr. Cotton from his office-bond as Pastor; sent to Mr. Cotton to meet them (they were at Shirtly's, 25 in number, some that could not come sent their minds to the same effect: and New Society ready to do it). Mr. Cotton to come to the Meeting-house, thither they goe, and there Deacon Fance declares what the church had done. Mr. Cotton was at Cole's: when ready to come away March, 11. I said his danger was lest catching at shadows, he should neglect the cords thrown out to him by Christ and so be drown'd. Some of my last words to him was, Kisse the Son, lest he be angry! This was in the house between him and me alone. Just as was mounting, He desired me to pray for him till I heard he was dead.

As came along, went a little out of our way and came to Duxbury houses; so then resolv'd to visit Mr. Wiswall, who had been long sick of the Gout, and was very glad to see us. Gave us a very good Goose to Dinner. It rained, and got but to Barkers that night. My horse flounder'd in a bank of Snow, and threw me off; but had no hurt. *Laus Deo.* Dine at Cushings, Get home a little before Sunset and find all well, blessed be God.

Second-day, March 14. 1697/8 Anniversary Town-Meeting, Mr. Cotton Mather prays excellently: I being present, am chosen Moder-

3 Deacon Thomas Faunce (1647–1746) was town clerk and later ruling elder of the Plymouth church. In 1741 in his 95th year he was brought to the waterfront and there he pointed out the rock which his father had assured him was the one which had received the footsteps of the Pilgrim fathers. This is the basis of the present identification of Plymouth Rock. Rose T. Briggs, *Plymouth Rock* (1954). "The honour'd ancient Elder Fânce" paid a visit to Sewall at Plymouth 2 May 1726.

ator;[4] Voted that would have but seven Select men; which are Samson Stoddard 122, Mr. Walker, Capt. Bozoon Allen, Capt. Tho: Hunt, Mr. Isaiah Tay, Mr. Obadiah Gill, Mr. Jn° Marion jun^r; Jn° Maryon sen^r and Mr. Barns left out.

Voted that in chusing Jury men should chuse those present as well as absent. Voted a committee to consider what might be beneficial for the Town to set Poor to work, &c. Concluded with Prayer. A candle was lighted before we had done. Select-men invited me to sup with them at the stone-house; Thither word was brought of our Horses being found and brought to Town.

Third-day March 15. Foggy day, at night between eight and 9 aclock it Thundered and lighten'd several times and rain'd very hard. As went into Town about 11 aclock, Met Mr. Hungerford and Cooper on Horseback, who told me the Governor was at Barbados in Jany last. This day Capt Frary tells me he is going to deal with his Bro^r Perry, who call'd him all to naught this day 7 night; as Rogue, pittifull Rascal, &c. Took occasion to say that my Letter put him into such a condition almost as the poor creatures were in at Salem, that he read a little of it, and threw it in the fire and burnt it. I met him near the door, as he was going into Town, or else I think he had not come in.

Fourth-day, March 16. 1697/8. I sent to the college Library my *Phænomena*, well bound in calvs Leather, with Mr. Oakes's election sermon, and Mr. Willard's Tract about Swearing; by Josiah Cotton.

March, 23. 1697/8 Rode to Braintry with Cous. Ephraim Savage, to a Fast kept there. Mr. Fisk pray'd and preach'd in the Forenoon and Mr. Torrey, in the Afternoon. Lodg'd there with Mr. Torrey. *March, 24.* came home by 5. p.m. Rain'd in the forenoon and most part of the day. *April, 2.* 1698. Went to Hog-Island with Mr. John White in his Birch Canoe: I see how the sheep are dead, it seems ten since last Thorsday, 3 drown'd, and more so sop'd in the water, that they dyed. Lost his horse this day sennight. I perceive his son

---

[4] Sewall served several times as moderator of the town meeting in Boston, but did not always make a record of the fact. The other dates are 3 June 1702, 16 February 1702/3, 1 June 1703, 11 March 1705/6, 14 May 1706, 29 April 1709, 13 March 1709/10, 3 August 1711, 7 December 1715, and 28 September 1720. He declined election as moderator 9 May 1711. There is no record that he ever served as selectman, but he held other town offices: 8 April 1700 town auditor (one of five); 10 March 1700/1 and 9 March 1701/2 overseer of the poor (one of five), 16 February 1702/3 overseer of the poor (one of eight); 13 March 1709, 12 March 1710/11 and 10 March 1712/3 school inspector (one of five), 9 March 1718/9 and 15 March 1719/20 school inspector (one of seven). R. F. Seybolt, *The Town Officials of Colonial Boston 1634–1775* (1939).

Joseph Belchar married Jonathan Bills' Daughter last January; which knew not of till now; that I cheapen'd a Duck,[5] and they told me his wife knew the price. Their Net Cattel have stood well, not one dead. Mr. White kill'd an Eagle flying, and a shildrake. No News of the Governour from N. York by the Post: Speak of sixty persons dead at Fairfield.

Thursday Apr. 7ᵗʰ. 1698. I acquainted Mr. Brenton that I had sold my 600. Acre Lot at Narraganset, as supposing he had no mind to hire it, but was cold in the matter, going away to Rode-Island and not perfecting the Lease, nor offering me any to sign, nor desiring me to stay till he should come back, that I remember. Broʳ St[ephen] Sewall visits us this day; lodges here Thorsday night and Friday night.

Sixth day, April 8. I visited Mr. Morton.[6] I was told he was asleep, but went in, and when I drew nigh his Beds side, he earnestly streach'd out his flaming hand to me, and strove to speak, but could not. I think the first I heard him say was, Sir, I asked him how he did in such long illness. He at first said, *That which can't be cur'd must be endur'd.* But seem'd presently after to correct himself and say, *I desire patiently to submit to the hand of God.* A while after I said, you cannot speak to me, but you can speak to God, which is a thousand times better; I pray that God would help you to speak to him, and that he would graciously hear you when you doe speak. He seem'd to ly still in a listening posture, and made a little pause, and said, *Excellent things! If I could receive them and live up to them!* Before this He said something about his man Tiler, that he heard he was become a new man. When I took leave, He said, *I wish you well and all your family.* I told him I doubted not but that I should fare the better for his Blessing. *Second-day, Apr. 11.* Mr. Willard and I having appointed it before, went to see Mr. Morton. He was in his Agonies, but Mr. Willard pray'd with him, and he seemed to be sensible by the motion of his eye. He died between two and three of the clock, Fowl, that us'd to tend him, clos'd his eyes; and Mr. Willard spake to them to close his under Jaw, which they did. Deacons desired us to go and see Mr. Bradstreet, which we did: but he was not at home, was gon to Cambridge.

Third-day, Apr. 12. 1698. By a sloop from thence we hear that the Governour [*Lord Bellomont*] arrived at Sandy-hook Apr. 1. and was receiv'd magnificently at New-york Ap. 2. Capt. N. Williams told me first of it in the Meeting-house, after Catechising.

[5] Sewall bargained or haggled over the price of the fowl; this sense of the word has disappeared from our language.
[6] Charles Morton, vice-president of Harvard College.

Apr. 13. Capt. Frary and Bro^r Perry desire Mr. Sergeant and me to issue their difference.

Apr. 14. Go to the funeral of Mr. Morton. President, Mr. Allen, Willard, Brattle, Bradstreet, Wadsworth Bearers. Lt Governour and about 12 of the Council there. Had Gloves, and so had the Ministers. Scholars went before the Herse. It seems on Monday morn a Lad was kill'd by a hogshead of sugar falling on him as it was hoisting into a Boat in which the boy stood. Ap. 14. Mr. Wadsworth's Text was from James, 4. 14. One use was of Comfort against Persecution: insisted pretty much on it, that the life of persecutors was as a vapor. When came from the funeral, went to the Town-house, and there the Lt Governour deliver'd Maj^r Genl Winthrop, &c, their Commission for going to N-York.[7]

Apr. 15. Post comes to Town. *Apr.* 16. His Excellencies Letter to the Lt Governour and council is read, dated Ap. 4. N. York. Thanks for Praying for Him, which saw by the order for the Fast; doubts not but fâr'd the better. Shall write more by the next, was now in pain by the Gout. Agreed upon One hundred £ here, and another at N. York for the Agents. As were looking on the seals, and guessing at the birds, swans, Ducks—I guess'd Coots, which consented to. And I made a shift to read the Motto, *Vincit veritas*, which was consented to; though given over before, as not legible.[8]

Mr. Sergeant is prevail'd with, that his Excellency be rec'd at his house. A hundred pounds are ordered towards the expense.[9]

Ap. 15. I got some Trees at Roxbury and Muddy River and brought them home in Bristos cart. White-Oak got out of Palsgrave

[7] The Council had commissioned Wait Still Winthrop, Elisha Cooke, and Penn Townsend, speaker of the house, with John Rogers for a chaplain, to go to New York to pay the new Governor their respects. *Memorial Hist. of Boston* II, 181.
[8] Sewall was correct. The governor of New York, Massachusetts, and New Hampshire, was Richard Coote, Earl of Bellomont. His arms, as stamped on the seals, were: argent, a chevron sable between three coots proper; crest, a coot; motto, *Vincit veritas*. An engraving of his seal, showing his arms quartered with those of his wife Catherine Nanfan, is given in *Heraldic Journal* I, 166, and in *Historical Magazine* IX, 176. M.H.S. EDS.
[9] The stately and comfortable mansion of Peter Sergeant on the west side of Washington Street, south of School Street, was built in 1679. Lord Bellomont resided there from May 1699 until he returned to New York in July 1700. Sewall owned a coach-house and stable nearby which he rented to the province for the governor's use (2 *M.H.S. Proc.* II, 122–131). After Sergeant's death, 8 February 1713/4, the mansion was purchased by the province as a residence for the governor, and was thereafter known as the Province House. The Indian archer weather vane by Shem Drowne, which surmounted the cupola, is now one of the choice possessions of the Massachusetts Historical Society.

Alcock's Lot; he was there and gave leave: set it when came home in the Pasture in the Common, and the Poplar to the street and the Platan at the upper corner next to Charlestown. *Ap.* 16. Set the rest.

Ap. 18. Chose Mr. Noyes to preach the Election sermon.

Ap. 19. Mr. Danforth and I sign'd a Writt for adjourning the Superior Court to the 14th of June.

Apr. 19. Accompanied the Gentlemen in the way towards [*New*] York as far as Lions; then Mr. Secretary, Leverett and I came back: Others went as far as Dedham. Mr. Rogers of Ipswich and major Wainwright is with them.

May, 4. Sign'd a writt for adjourning Ipswich Court to June 21.

May, 5. Mr. Brinsmead lodges here.

May, 6. Speaking of the uncertainty of the conversion of Adam and Eve, I shew'd him Dr. Goodwin and Owen's Notions. He told me of a converted Turk, and of strange Visions at Meccha, in the year 1620, to be seen in Clark's Examples. It being the same year with Plimouth it affected me. Gave him the Fr. King's adnulling of the Edicts made in favour of the Protestants.[10]

May, 9. 1698. Town-Meeting for choice of Assembly-men warn'd by printed Tickets: Number present 340.

Chosen

Mr. John Eyre	218.
Capt Sam¹ Legg	200.
Capt. Nath¹ Byfield	196.
Majʳ Pen Townsend	172.

Next

Foxcroft	156.
Thornton	124.
Bromfield	119.
Frary	113.

Joseph Royal chosen Constable in Capt. Goff's room, who fin's.

May, 10. Mr. John Brown has home his Bride to Salem, Mrs. Sarah Burroughs. Very cold blustering day after the pleasant warm Rain yesterday, and Rainbow near night, south E and by East. *Fourth-day, May,* 11ᵗʰ As I lay in my bed in the morn, this verse came into my mind,

> To Horses, Swine, Net-Cattell, Sheep and Deer,
> Ninety and Seven prov'd a Mortal yeer.

---

[10] Sewall's guest, William Brinsmead, or Brimsmead (Harvard ex-1655), was minister of Marlboro. The document Sewall gave him was a copy of the revocation of the Edict of Nantes, proclaimed by Louis XIV, 22 October 1685.

May, 11. 1698. I, my wife, Hannah, Elisabeth Joseph, Mary rode in the coach to Muddy-River, and in the new Room with the widow Gates and her daughter Sparhawk, sung the 114th Psalm. Simon catch'd us a Bass. Call'd at Bairsto's as came back. When came home met with news of a ship from England, 8 weeks Passage.

Sam chose to goe to Cambridge with Josiah Willard. Lords day *May*, 15th 1698. Very dark day, plentifull Rain and some Thunder. *May*, 16, 1698. Capt. Nicholas Down comes from Topsham. April, 14. brings news of the probability that the King of Spain is dead. Updike arrived a little before at Marblehead, and brings the news of the Joseph Gally being cast away on the coast of Ireland and all the persons in her lost. Madam Bellingham one: Sail'd from hence the 8th of November. 58 drowned in the Tilt boat, Febr 3. 1. p.m., and near 30 out of two Wherries.

In the beginning of this Moneth of May, the old Brick Colledge, commonly called the *Indian* Colledge, is pull'd down to the ground, being sold to Mr. Willis the builder of Mr. Stoughtons colledge.[11] *May* 25. Mr. Secretary, Major Walley and I went to meet the Governour, who rid to Town in his Coach. Mr. Noyes preaches.

For the Election, see the List.

Mr. Tappan lodges here with Sam.

May, 31. Jnᵒ Alden comes from Holland, last from Cows; viz. Apr. 18th: brings word that John Foy arriv'd in the Downs Apr. 9th Are Letters from Mr. Ive giving an account of the Receipt of Letters by Foy. Ships are fitting out. Broʳ Steph. Sewall comes to Town, May 31. 1698. *Second-day, May 30. 98.* Inhabitants meet to chuse a Representative in Majʳ Townsends room. Voters 318. Andr[ew] Belchar 175. Fr. Foxcroft 138. Bromfield 3. Frary 1. Thornton 1. I have not taken notice of such a close adherence to each side before.

June, 10. 1698. Mr. James Allin comes into the Council Chamber, and presents an Address from the Fellows of Harvard Colledge sign'd by himself as Senior Fellow, which was to ask concurrence and Assistance in sending the President to England, to solicit for a Charter,

11 The Indian College, a two-storey brick structure, was built in the Harvard Yard about 1656 with funds supplied by the Company for the Propagation of the Gospel in New England. But Harvard's efforts to give a university education to the natives were unsuccessful and the building was not kept in proper repair. After 1692, when the college press, which had occupied one of the rooms, was given up, the edifice was deserted. Thomas Willis used the bricks in the new Stoughton College, the gift of the Lieutenant Governor, which was completed in 1699 and torn down in 1781. The present Stoughton Hall (1805) perpetuates the name. Morison, *H.C.S.C.* I, 340–360; II, 518–521.

as supposing the Law sent will not be approv'd in England, because
the Council was join'd with the Govr in the Visitation. And Mr.
White, who was sent to N. York by the college, being returned, the
Governour's Letter was read manifesting an utter improbability of
passing the Law as it was, because the Lords had directed the Governours being Visitor alone. Address was read and sent down. Representatives sent it up again, desiring the council to act on it first.
When twas read with us I asked whoes the Colledge was; because
twas said Our Colledge—

Sixth-day, June 12. 1698. 4 p.m. Mrs. Elizabeth Jeffries dieth, and
the shop of her Father, Mr. John Usher, is shut up upon it. It is affecting that an only child should be snatched away so soon. Has left
8 children.

Tuesday, June, 28. 1698. Court at Salem, Major Brown praesident;
were remov'd to the Ship Tavern and candles lighted; a cry of Fire
was made. A Girl drawing Rum in a little Warehouse of Mr. Lyn-
don's, or looking after a cask that leak'd, the candle fired it, which
took the cask and broke it up with a Report, so catch'd Cotton and
fired Mr. Willoughbys house in the Garret of which was a Barrel of
Powder, that taking fire blew off the Roof and very much dispersed
the flaming partickles; much of which was thrown on Major Brown's
house over the way, the wind carrying it thither so that and his warehouse were quickly burnt down, and much Money and Goods lost
with the Buildings. Five houses in all burnt, Mr. Hirst's for one. This
is the first considerable Fire that ever was in Salem. It seems the
stroke makes a deep impression on Maj^r Brown. Has lost 3 or four
Thousand pounds.[12]

Commencement day, and next, Mr. Tappan was here.

July, 13. 1698. divided the Haugh's Tenement. When came home
rec'd Sir Henry Ashhurst's Letter, wherein He thanks me for my
kind Present of the *Phænomena* sent him. This is the first notice I
have had of their being in England. This day Roger Judd tells me
that Col. Lidget is dead.[13]

July, 15. 1698. Mr. Edward Taylor comes to our house from West-

[12] Major William Browne, a leading merchant of Salem, and councillor from
1693, was nevertheless able to leave 100*l* to Harvard at his death in 1716. Josiah
Quincy, *History of Harvard University* (1860) I, 418.
[13] Colonel Charles Lidget had appeared frequently in the diary; he was a Bos-
tonian, the son of Peter Lidget, a partner of John Hull. He took the side of
Governor Andros, and was one of the founders of King's Chapel in 1686. He
sailed for England in February 1689/90 and was living in London at the time of
his death. *N.E.H.G.R.* xxxiii, 406.

field.[14] *Monday July* 18. I walk'd with Mr. Edward Taylor upon Cotton Hill, thence to Becon Hill, the Pasture, along the Stone-wall: As came back, we sat down on the great Rock, and Mr. Taylor told me his courting his first wife, and Mr. Fitch his story of Mr. Dod's prayer to God to bring his Affection to close with a person pious, but hard-favoured. Has God answered me in finding out one Godly and fit for me, and shall I part for fancy? When came home, my wife gave me Mr. Tappan's Letter concerning Eliza, which caus'd me to reflect on Mr. Taylor's Discourse. And his Prayer was for pardon of error in our ways—which made me think whether it were not best to overlook all, and go on. This day John Ive, fishing in great Spiepond, is arrested with mortal sickness which renders him in a manner speechless and senseless; dies next day; buried at Charlestown on the Wednesday. Was a very debauched, atheistical man. I was not at his Funeral. Had Gloves sent me, but the knowledge of his notoriously wicked life made me sick of going; and Mr. Mather, the president, came in just as I was ready to step out, and so I staid at home, and by that means lost a Ring: but hope had no loss. Follow thou Me, was I suppose more complied with, than if had left Mr. Mather's company to go to such a Funeral. [*In margin:* Cambridge Mr. Ive's son Dies suddenly]

July, 26. By reason of the fowlness of the wether Mr. Cook and I rid in the Coach to Cambridge. Maj[r] Generall, Cook and I rid together in it to Charlestown, and laid it there.

Augt 12. Tis told all about the Town that Major Generall courts Mary Howard. [*In margin: Amor.*] [15]

Augt. 15, Second-day, Set out for Springfield, lodg at Marlborow.

Augt. 16. To Quaboag, with a guard of 20 Men under Cornet Brown. Between Worceser and Quaboag we were greatly wet with Rain; wet to the skin.[16] Got thither before twas dark. A Guard of 20 from Springfield met us there, and saluted us with their Trumpet as we

[14] Sewall did not often see his classmate and roommate, the busy parson, doctor, poet, and binder of books from western Massachusetts. *D.A.B.,* Supp. 1.

[15] There is a biography and portrait of Major General Wait Still Winthrop in L. S. Mayo, *The Winthrop Family in America* (1948), 97–111. His first wife, Mary Browne of Salem, died in 1690; he did not take a second wife until 13 November 1707, when he married Katharine (Brattle) Eyre. The Sewalls did not attend the wedding, but Winthrop sent them gloves.

[16] Umbrellas were unknown here in Sewall's lifetime. As late as 1750 Jonas Hanway, the eccentric traveler and philanthropist, was ridiculed for carrying one in the streets of London. *D.N.B.*

Quaboag is now Brookfield.

alighted. *Augt. 17.* very fair day in which we went to Springfield. *Augt. 18.* Open'd the Court, present Winthrop, Cooke, Sewall. Gave a Bill to the Grand-Jury, Mr. John Holyoke, Foreman. They found the Bill. Inpanel'd a Jury of Trial; upon her Arraignment, she having at last pleaded Not guilty, Adjourn'd to the morning, when court Open'd, Mr. Taylor of Westfield prayed. *Augt. 19.* Jury, Mr. Parsons foreman, brought in Sarah Smith Guilty of murdering her Bastard daughter. Adjourn'd till Noon. Court met and the Maj^r Generall pronounced the sentence. She had been kept at Derefield about a Moneth's time, by reason of the extremity of the Winter, was brought down to Springfield Jail Febr. 18.

Augt. 20. Went to the Long Meadow to bring the Maj^r Generall going towards Hartford. Meet with Jno Noble, with him went to Westfield and kept Sabbath with Mr. Tailor, *Augt. 21.*

Augt 22. Return'd to Springfield; Mr. Tailor with me. Rain'd hard in the Afternoon and night, and part of the morn. *Augt. 23.* By which means were not able to reach Quaboag; and twas thought could not pass the Rivers. So went to Northampton, a very Paradise. Lodg'd at the ordinary, getting to town in the night. *Augt. 24.* very fair day, Mr. Cook and I went with Mr. Stoddard and heard Mr. I. Chauncy preach his first Lecture at Hadley. Made a very good sermon. Invited us to dinner. Went over to Hatfield. Mr. Cook being importun'd to see Benj Wait's wife; it was late and lodg'd all night with Mr. Williams.

Augt. 25. Went early in the morn to Hadly, and from thence with a Guard of ten men to Quaboag. *Augt. 26.* to Marlborow. *Augt. 27.* Home, not wetting our foot; though the height of the Rivers was so much feared. Found all well at home through the abundant goodness of God, to whom be the Praise. Upon the Neck the Lieut. Governour met us in his New Coach and read us out of the Governour's Letter the News that New-Spain had Revolted from the Crown of Spain and had crowned the Vice-Roy of Mexico their King.[17]

[17] Although this revolt turned out to be a sham, as Sewall reported 17 September, Cotton Mather's imagination was stimulated: "Understanding that the way for our Communication with the *Spanish Indies*, opens more and more, I sett myself to learn the *Spanish Language* . . . a few liesure Minutes in the Evening of every Day, in about a Fortnight, or three weeks Time, so accomplished mee, I could write very good Spanish. Accordingly, I composed a little Body of the *Protestant Religion*, in certain Articles, back'd with irresistible Sentences of Scripture. This I turn'd into the Spanish Tongue; and am now printing it . . . The Title of my Composure is, *La Religion Pura* . . ." (*Diary* 1, 284–285). The composure appeared as part of his *La Fe del Christiano*, printed in Boston in 1699.

Augt. 29. I send Mr. Noyes's sermon and a *Phænomena* to the Governour by the Post, sermon was the first that was bound.[18]

Sept'r 12. Danforth, Cook, Sewall set out for Rehoboth. Capt. Byfield with us very brisk and generous; I lodg'd with him. *Sept'r 13.* To Bristol. Benjᵃ Allin's Sentence was confirm'd, He appearing notoriously Naught. The Judgm't of the Court in the Writt of Error was not declar'd till Sept'r 15. which was for Blagrove ag't Byfield, at which Capt. Byfield swell'd grievously. In a case of Saffin *vers.* Curtis, which Capt. Byfield was concern'd for Curtis, Jury brought in for Curtis.—Capt. Byfield, with a remarkable Air, thank'd the Jury for their Justice and sentence. For their Justice, and with a voice a little Lower said, He had none before. I told him he deserv'd to be sent to prison. He disown'd the words; And alleged; He said he had none to thank any body for. Mr. Cook seconded me. Mr. Danforth heard not. Capt. Byfield declin'd coming home with us. Rain hinder'd our setting out that day. So after dinner at Mr. Saffin's, Not knowing better how to bestow my time, Look'd on Mr. Saffin's Books, and lit on Dr. Fullers History of the Worthies of England, and in p. 116. 117. found mention made of the Inundation at Coventry, on Friday April, 17. in the Majoralty of Henry Sewall my Father's Grandfather. Mention is made p. 134. of Wᵐ Dugdale's Illustrations of Warwickshire.

Sept'r 16. Dined at Woodcocks, visited Mr. Man, Lodg'd at Meadfield. *Sept'r 17th.* got home just about Noon, very comfortable and well, and find all well at home. Blessed be God. Mexican Revolt is a sham, as Mr. Tho. Brattle saith: Report is taken from John Bant, which as far as I can see is rather Negative, than any thing else. He in his wilder'd condition heard, though in stead of going to Barbados, fell near Jucatan.

Copy of a Letter to His Excellency, the Governour, Sept'r 19. 1698, by the Post:

MAY IT PLEASE YOUR EXCELLENCY:

I come to offer your Excellency five more of Mr. Noyes's Sermons, praying your Lordships favourable Acceptance of them. Here is one John Bânt, who sail'd from this Port last May, bound for Barbados: but missing that, and the Neighbouring Islands, fell into the Bay of Mexico, and came within sight of Jucatan. From thence he went to the Havanna, where he

---

[18] *New Englands Duty and Interest, To be an Habitation of Justice, and Mountain of Holiness* . . . This was the election sermon preached by Sewall's friend Nicholas Noyes (Harvard 1667) on May 25th. It was dedicated to the Earl of Bellomont, the governor. Sewall sent five more copies later with a letter which is printed below.

arrived upon the Lords day, about eight weeks agoe. Was had before the
Governour, and in two or 3 hours was commanded thence, not being permitted to stay to fit his vessel. Said Bant turned up to the Bay of Metansis
to Water; where he spent some days and conversed with the people. And
yet heard not a word of the Mexican Revolt. Which makes the Truth of
it to be questioned here. However it be, God will work in the fittest season and place, for the Help of his people and distress of their Enemies.
The ships that came out with Capt. Cliffe, are not arrived. I crave leave
to add that I am (though unknown) your Excellency's most humble and
obedient serv't.   S.S.

First Letter was Augt. 29; sent the first and only book that was
then bound in red Leather.

Octobʳ 11. 1698. Mr. Joseph Webb buried. Bearers. Cook, Elisha
Hutchinson, Sewall, Addington, Eliakim Hutchinson, Dummer. Mr.
Allin and Wadsworth there. I saw no other Ministers. *Sixth-day,
Octobʳ 14. 1698.* Church Meeting at the South church. Put in votes
for election of a Minister. Mr. Ebenezer Pemberton had Thirty seven
votes, and Mr. Jabez Fitch, Twenty three. I think Mr. Oliver and
Davis did not vote. In the Nomination September, 30. Mr. Fitch had
Thirty six, and Mr. Pemberton Twenty one. *Fourth-day, Octobʳ 19.
1698.* Mr. Bullivant was with me to take leave, and desired my favour
on behalf of Dr. Chip, that he might dwell in part of Mr. Gouges
house at Cotton Hill: And that might have it all, if said Gouge left
it. Said he had an estate, was a very ingenious civil person: would
send him to me. *Seventh-day; Octobʳ 29. 1698.* Thomas Savage junʳ,
shopkeeper, and Sarah Threeneedle were brought face to face in a
very great Audience: She vehemently accused him, and he asserted
his innocency with vehement Asseverations. She said he had ruin'd
her; if he would have promis'd her any thing, it had not come to this.
Said She forgave him, Judgment of God hung over him if did not repent.

Seventh-day, Octobʳ 29. 1698. Last night a strange body of fire
was seen in the sky, which gave an unusual Light: Davis, the Bell-
man, told me of it when he was coming to call me to Court, and met
me by the way.

Fourth-day, Novembʳ 9. Mr. Cushing is ordain'd at Salisbury. Mr.
Higginson preaches a Sermon, Text, Eternal Judgment.

Fifth-day, Novʳ 10ᵗʰ 1698. A Church is gathered at the West end
of Newbury, and Mr. Samˡ Belchar ordained their Minister.

Fifth-day, Novʳ 10. Mr. Green is ordained at Salem Village, and
likelihood of a stability of Peace and settlement there. *Fifth-day,*

Novr 17th Very fair serene wether; Mr. Cotton Mather preaches at the South-Meetinghouse: Sarah Threeneedles is an Auditor; is a very vast Assembly, and the street full of such as could not get in; 51. Psalm 2^d verse sung, 9–15 verses. Mr. Willard read the whole, and I set the Tune. After Lecture Sarah Threeneedles is executed. Mr. Woodbridge went to the place of execution and pray'd with her there.[19]

Sabbath, December 4. 1698. Last night lying awake, but with my eyes fast shut, Lightening flash'd in my face, I could not certainly tell what Light it should be; but presently heard a loud clap of Thunder. This day between the ringing of the morning Bells, it Thundered several times, but with a more confused and rumbling noise. Much Rain, Mist.

Decemb^r 6th. 1698. Our cherubims heads are set up.[20] Sister Gerrish here with her son Joseph. *Decr 9.* Go homeward.

Decemb^r 10. Mr. Wadsworth prays, and the Court is dissolv'd about 4 p.m.

Decr 8. Capt. Belchar invites all the Deputies to his daughters Wedding. The speaker, Mr. Eyre, and Mr. Oliver, Dep^t for Cambridge, were of a committee with Mr. Secretary and me to acquaint Mr. Mather with the Courts desire of his removal to Cambridge, and carry him an Order for 200£ per annum so long as he should reside there.[21] By reason of the Wedding, twas near 7 in the even

[19] Sarah Threeneedles, daughter of Bartholomew and Damaris (Hawkins) Threeneedles, was born in Boston, 9 November 1679. She had been convicted of "murdering her Base-born Child." Cotton Mather made the most of his opportunity. He wrote (*Diary*, 17 November 1698): "The *General Court* then sitting, ordered the [Thursday] Lecture to bee held in a larger and a stronger [meeting] House, than that *old* one, where tis usually kept. For my own part, I was weak, and faint, and spent; but I humbly gave myself up to the *Spirit* of my Heavenly Lord and Hee assured mee, that Hee would send His *good Angel* to strengthen mee. The greatest Assembly, ever in this Countrey preach'd unto, was now come together; It may bee four or five thousand Souls. I could not gett unto the *Pulpit*, but by climbing over *Pues* and *Heads*: and there the Spirit of my dearest Lord came upon mee. I preached with a more than ordinary Assistence, and enlarged, and uttered the most awakening Things, for near two Hours together. . . ." Mather called his sermon *Reflections on the Dreadful Case of Sin Punished with Sin*, and published it in his *Pillars of Salt* (Boston, 1699) and in part in his *Magnalia. Savage*; T. J. Holmes, *Cotton Mather . . . Bibliography* (1940), II, 818–822.

[20] These were carvings on the gateposts in front of Sewall's house. The southernmost one was blown down in a great windstorm 26 January 1724/5, and the other was taken down 1 February.

[21] The General Court wanted Increase Mather to resign as minister of the Second Church in Boston and reside at the college, where he had served as president since 1685. Mather declined to do so in a letter to Lieutenant Governor Stoughton

before we got thither. I began, and ask'd excuse for our being so late. The reason was, most of us were come from a Wedding; However I hop'd, it was a good omen, that we were all come to a Wedding. Mr. President expostulated with Mr. Speaker and Mr. Eyre about the votes being alter'd, from 250, as the Council had set it, and also his name being left out and making him a five–years president. *Note.* By a conference the Bill was made as ours at first, saving fifty pounds less. We urg'd his going all we could; I told him of his Birth and education here; that he look'd at Work rather than Wages, all met in desiring him, and should hardly agree so well in any other. Mr. Speaker, in behalf of the House, earnestly desired him. Objected want of a House, Bill for Corporation not pass'd, Church [*his attachment to it*], Must needs preach once every week, which he prefered before the Gold and Silver of the West-Indies. I told him would preach twice a–day to the students. He said that (exposition) was nothing like preaching.

Sabbath, Dec 11. 1698. I went to see Capt. Wyllys, he ruttled much at first coming in; Mrs. Wyllys bid me sit, and would speak to him by and by: He made a little noise and fetch'd his breath deep once or twice or thrice and expired between 8 and 9 m, just before our first Bell rung. No body there then but the family and my self.

[*December 13*] Capt. Edw. Wyllys buried in the new burying place, at the upper end. Bearers, Maj^r Genl Winthrop, Sewall, Col. Phillips, Lt Col. Lynde, Mr. Oakes, Mr. Eyre. Cold blustering day. Mr. Fisk there.

Tuesday, Dec 20. 1698. Hannah, sitting on one of the Lether chairs, fell on the rest, Joanna went to her and was surprised; I went to her and help'd to raise her up; seem'd to have a short Convulsion Fit. Mr. C. Mather and his wife were here. As brought them going, desired Mr. Mather to remember her in his Prayers. The Providence put me and the family into great Consternation. The Lord fit for the Issue.

This week have News of Some of the Fleet of the Scotland Company being at Jamaica; and tis rumor'd they intend to settle on the American Isthmus, or on Golden Island just by it. Makes much Discourse in Town. I gave Mr. [*John*] Borland a Duz. *Phænomena*, and half a Duz. of Mr. Noyes's Sermons, to send them to welcom them into the New World, to go by Bant.[22]

---

dated 16 December 1698. Sewall copied the letter into his diary the following March, but we omit the text, which is available in Josiah Quincy's *History of Harvard University* (1860), I, 499–500.
[22] The Company of Scotland Trading to Africa and the Indies was chartered by

Tuesday Dec 27. 1698. Col. Romer is treated at the Castle.[23] Capt. Fairwether ask'd me not to goe: so I went to Roxbury Lecture. Saw

---

the Scottish parliament in 1695 at the urging of William Paterson (1658–1719), founder of the Bank of England, and a promoter of the modern type, "whose whole capital consisted of an inventive brain and a persuasive tongue." A settlement was to be made on the Isthmus of Darien (Panama); here in a great free port was to be concentrated not only the wealth produced on its own soil, but the greater wealth which would be produced by trade with China, India, the East Indies, Africa, and America. Enormous enthusiasm was stirred up for the project in Scotland, and vast sums were invested in the company's stock by the nobility, the city corporations, and lesser people who turned over their life-savings. "The whole kingdom seemed to have gone mad. Paterson had acquired an influence resembling rather that of the founder of a new religion, that of a Mahomet, that of a Joseph Smith, than that of a commercial projector." Macaulay describes the mania vividly in Chap. XXIV of his *History*. Even the Bostonians participated. The extent of Sewall's involvement cannot be determined, but funds raised there were placed in his hands 27 December 1698. A portion of his day of prayer 25 January 1698/9 was devoted to the Company of Scotland, and on 8 April 1700 he wrote a letter of enthusiastic encouragement to the ministers on the expedition (*L.B.* I, 227–229). See also Sewall's entry following 8 May 1699.

The Scots settlers, some 1200 in number, landed in Darien 1 November 1698, took possession of a small peninsula which they named Caledonia, made friends with the local chieftains, and began to build their great trading-center of New Edinburgh. Word of their progress and rosy descriptions got back to Scotland, and a second expedition of 1300 emigrants set out. Meanwhile everything had gone wrong. Provisions were inadequate and ill-chosen, Scots who had never known a warm day in their lives collapsed and died laboring under the tropical sun; disease made fearful havoc. Finally the survivors set off in three ships to return; the voyage was a horror and men died by the score. A pitiful remnant, including Paterson, finally reached New York.

Four months after the first settlers had fled, the second expedition arrived; expecting to join a prosperous colony, they were worse provided with necessities than their predecessors. After making a feeble effort to restore what had perished, and much infighting, they agreed to evacuate the settlement when a fleet of Spanish vessels anchored off New Edinburgh. The Articles of Surrender (in Latin; none of the Scots knew Spanish) were copied by Sewall in his Letter-Book (as printed, I, 242–244). Francis Borland (Macaulay calls him John), Scots clergyman educated at Glasgow, who accompanied the second expedition, survived to write an account of it: *Memoirs of Darien* (Glasgow, 1715; reprinted 1779). Modern studies are: Francis Russell Hart, *The Disaster of Darien* (Boston, 1929) and George Pratt Insh, *The Company of Scotland* (London and New York, 1932).
[23] Castle Island, southeast of Boston, had been fortified from the earliest days of settlement, but had fallen into disrepair. Colonel William Wolfgang Römer, "chief military engineer to their royal majesties in North America," who had come over with Bellomont, completely rebuilt the fortification between 1701 and 1703; it was then named Fort William, or Castle William, for William III. In 1776 it became Fort Independence. N. B. Shurtleff, *Topographical and Historical Description of Boston* (1891), 477f.; *D.N.B.*

as went, Jn° Lion's daughter buried, of 12 years old. Mr. Walters Text was out of the 19ᵗʰ Psalm,—cleanse thou me from secret sins. Godly men had a Soul-concern that God would pardon their Secret sins and cleanse them from them.

Major Townsend there, visited Mr. Walter and Madam Dudley, Mr. Hubbard, White, Newman came home with us by moonshine, I shew'd them the Scotland Acts, Subscriptions, Contributions; which Mr. Jackson left with me this day.

Decʳ 24. 1698. Read and sung in course in the Family the 3ᵈ part of the 77ᵗʰ Ps., which I hôp'd was going to be partly fullfill'd by the Company of Scotland. Decʳ 29ᵗʰ After Lecture I invite Major Vaughan and Mr. Partridge to Dinner, such as it was. At the Town-House with Mr. Justice Danforth, Winthrop, Cooke, took the New Oath made last sessions. And took an oath relating to the Special Court to try Jacob Smith; Mr. Danforth gave the commission to Mr. Cook. Voted some Money for Major Walley. Went to Vaughan and Partridge at Dering's, as told them I would, while in the chamber. Had only a piece of rost Beef, Minct pye and Tarts to Dinner. It seems the Lᵗ Govʳ invites the Council to Dinner to morrow at his house. After Dinner, Major Winthrop, Mr. Cook, Col. Hutchinson, Capt. Foster, Mr Sergeant, Mr. Hutchinson came in to discourse with Mr. Partridge and Vaughan, and staid till about 6 aclock, or past. Mr. Cook ask'd me whether I was bidden. I told him I knew nothing of it. Major Genˡ look'd upon me in good earnest, and almost angrily, at going away, and told me I must goe; but I heard nothing of it since, and tis now Decʳ 30th. past 3 *tempore pomeridiano*.[24]

The Grievousness of this prætermission is, that by this means I shall be taken up into the lips of Talkers, and shall be obnoxious to the Governour at his coming, as a person deserted and fit to be hunted down, if occasion be; and in the mean time, shall goe feebly up and down my Business, as one who is quite out of the Lᵗ Govʳˢ favour. The Lord pardon my share in the abounding of Iniquity by reason whereof the Love of many waxes cold.

I had the pleasure this day to read in course the 37. of Ezekiel. I

[24] I.e., 3 p.m. Stoughton's failure to invite Sewall to his dinner-party for the Council, of which he was a member, illustrates his cold, obstinate nature. They were both judges at the witchcraft trials. In January 1697, Sewall had made his penitential confession in public for the sin of his complicity in the affair; Stoughton seems never to have repented, but Sewall's action must have troubled him. Justin Winsor, *Narrative and Critical History of America*, v, 99; D.A.B.

could not but think of the Expedition of the Scots. Hannah read the 4th of Ephesians. How hard it is to practise the Duties there laid down, especially about Anger and Malice. Betty read the 20th of Revelation, all in course.

1699

BETTY SEWALL REJECTS A SUITOR / PROPOSED MARRIAGE OF
BASTIAN AND JANE, NEGROES / COUNCIL ESCORTS LORD BELLOMONT
FROM NEWPORT / TWO PIRATES ESCAPE FROM PRISON /
HOUGH-WINTHROP WEDDING AT PULLING POINT / SEWALL SWORN
IN AGAIN AS JUDGE OF THE SUPERIOR COURT / THE SEWALLS TAKE
LADY BELLOMONT TO COTTON HILL / JOURNEY TO BRISTOL AND
NEWPORT / DEATH OF JUDGE THOMAS DANFORTH / SEWALL'S
SISTER HANNAH TAPPAN DIES / THE MANIFESTO CHURCH /
DINNER-PARTY FOR THE BELLOMONTS

2ᵈ Day, Janʸ 2ᵈ [1698/9]. I speak to Mr. Mico about 8 m. at his
house, largely about Capt. [*Zechariah*] Tuttle. Saith he never heard
any ill of him, in answer to my asking if he had any blot. Saith knows
not his estate but thinks it may be about 6 or 700£. Is in good Business, and like to be in better. If he had a sister here to whom his
Father order'd 1000£ portion, he would bestow her upon Mr. Tuttle,
if he ask'd her.[1]

Just about this time Mrs. Moodey was seisd with the palsie on her
left side also, and made speechless.

Janʸ 3ᵈ After Roger Judd's being here, Mr. Willard and I went to
see Mrs. Moodey, Mr. Willard prays with her. Methinks fetcheth
her breath much shorter than when I saw her the evening before.

4ᵗʰ day, Janʸ 4. Mrs. Moodey dyes about Sun-rise. Roger Judd
comes into my house this morning, and talking about Mr. Willards

[1] Zechariah Tuthill was an unsuccessful suitor for the seventeen-year-old Betty
Sewall, and there is no record that he married anyone else. He was one of the
founders of the Brattle Street Church in 1699, and for nearly two decades captain
at Castle William. He died 7 January 1721/2, "a Gentleman entirely and universally esteemed of, and favoured by, all Degrees of People . . ." (*Boston News-
Letter*, 15 January 1721/2). Captain Tuthill became Sewall's tenant in the
latter's Cotton Hill house about the end of March, 1699, evidently taking the
house for his mother, Mary (Holyoke) Tuthill, and his sisters Sarah, Susannah,
and Mary. When Sewall took Lady Bellomont to Cotton Hill, 25 July, the Tuthill
daughters gave her a glass of wine. Mrs. Mary Tuthill, the widow of John, died of
injuries 19 September 1704, and Sewall was a bearer at her funeral.

sending for him yesterday, I ask'd him, if Mr. Myles [*Rector of King's Chapel*] should send for him, whether he would not reckon it his duty to go to him. At first, he said yes; but presently after said If I please. I told him that he made himself his own Judge. He said, If should now call a church-Meeting and send for him, he would not go to them; for he was none of them. Said he came not into church but [*by*] the importunity of Deacon Eliot and others; told him then he was for the church of England. And told me now twas his Conscience to go to the church of England, and he had sin'd in staying away from them so long. If he was persecuted for it, he could not help it.

Fourth-day, Jany 4th. Mrs. Moodey dies about Sun-rise. About 11 m. Daughter Elisabeth reads to me the second of Genesis in course. In the evening between seven and eight Capt. Zech. Tuthill speaks with her. This day I spake with Mr. Newman about his partaking with the French church[2] on the 25. December on account of its being Christmas-day, as they abusively call it. He stoutly defended the Holy-days and church of England. *Jan^r 6. 1698/9.* I received a Letter from Mr. Taylor giving account of Mrs. Woodbridges death at Harford: was brought to bed Dec. 18. died 21. Is much lamented.[3]

Jan^y—at night Capt. Tuthill comes to speak with Betty, who hid her self all alone in the coach for several hours till he was gon, so that we sought at several houses, till at last came in of her self, and look'd very wild.

Jany 9 speaks with her in my presence.

Jany 10. dine at Mr. S. Stoddard's, Had a great Treat. Major Vaughan, Mr. Secretary, Foster, Sewall, Townsend, President, Mr. Willard, Allin, Cotton Mather, Mr. Woodbridge, Bromfield, there: besides Select-Men.

Jany 10. at night sent Mr. Tuthill away, because company was here, and told him was willing to know her mind better. *Jany 18. 1698/9*

[2] A number of Huguenot families settled in Boston following the revocation of the Edict of Nantes in 1685. In the summer of 1686 several arrived in great sickness and poverty from the islands of St. Christopher and Eleuthera, and the Council voted 5 August to supply their necessities, requesting Captain Elisha Hutchinson and Captain Samuel Sewall to receive and distribute relief among them. Sewall made no mention of this in the diary. The French gathered a church which met first in the town school-house in School Street, and Rev. Pierre Daillé was minister for over twenty years. Sewall visited him in his last illness in 1715. C. C. Smith, The French Protestants in Boston, *Memorial Hist. of Boston*, ii, 249f.

[3] Mehitable (Wyllys) Russell Foster, wife of Timothy Woodbridge (Harvard 1675), minister of the Hartford church and a founder of Yale. Sewall wrote "Harford."

Court of Oyer and Terminer sits. Capt. Nath. Williams foreman. Capt. Wing had a son under the circumstances of the person to be tried: Bill was indors'd *Ignoramus*.[4] There din'd with us Mr. Hutchinson E^m, Mr. Sergeant, Capt. Jno. Brown, Capt. Jn° Turner that the Court paid for. I motion'd to invite Mr. Brown, and Maj^r Genl of his own accord invited Capt Turner as his cousin Brown's Companion.

Friday, Jany 20. Capt. Brown and Turner breakfast here: Betty came in afterward, and serv'd Almonds and Raisins, and fill'd a Glass of Wine to us; and it fell to her to drink to Capt. Turner. She went out of the way at first, after I had spoke to her to fill wine: which surpris'd me: and I contrived that of the Raisins on purpose to mend the matter. *Sabbath-day Jany 22,* Bro^r Roger Judd is cast out of the Church for his contumacy in refusing to hear the Church, and his contemptuous behaviour against the same, and Mr. Willard the Pastor. Refus'd to be there.[5]

Second-day, Jany 23. 1698/9 I carry my two sons and three daughters in the Coach to Danford, the Turks head at Dorchester: eat sage Cheese, drunk Beer and Cider and came homeward. Call'd at Madam Dudley's, then visited Mr. Walter; told him there was all my stock, desired his Blessing of them; which he did.

Jany 24. Went to Roxbury Lecture: Mr. Addington, Sergeant, E^m Hutchinson, Major Townsend and others there. Mr. Walter exhorted to privat Duties, and dehorted from privat sins, from the Consideration of God's seeing in secret. *Fourth-day, Jany 25. 1698/9* [Prayer] Company of Scotland, South-church. Children, especially daughter Elisabeth. France.

Thursday, March, 2. 1698/9 Mrs. Catharin Phillips buried, Mr. Danforth, Major Genl Winthrop, Russel, Cook, Elisha Hutchinson, Foster, Bearers. I think all the Council had gloves sent, and Rings there. Lt Govr was not there, by reason of the marriage of his Nephew, Mr. William Taylor, with Mrs. Sarah Byfield, this day. Govr Winthrop was at the Funeral.

[4] This was the first special court of Oyer and Terminer, under the act against piracy and robbing on the sea, to which Sewall had been appointed 22 December 1698. The complete record is printed in 1 *M.H.S. Proc.* xx, 321–324. The verdict of the grand jury, *Ignoramus*, meant that there was not evidence to support the charges, and by this endorsement all proceedings were stopped and the accused person discharged.

[5] Roger Judd was a refractory member of the church who had decided to join the Anglicans. He was chosen town scavenger in 1692/3 and became sexton of King's Chapel in 1701. His case is recorded in H. A. Hill, *Hist. of the Old South Church* (1890), I, 304–307.

March, 4. 1698/9 Foy arrives, came out of Faymouth in November, in him comes an Assistant [*Rev. Christopher Bridge*] to Mr. Myles who preaches March, 5.

March, 27. 1699. Mr. Middlecott desires his son Pain may be released as to Cotton-House.[6] *March, 28. p.m.* Capt. Tuthill comes and desires to take it. *March, 30. 1699.* I had the innermost Tooth save two on the lower left jaw, pulled out by Robert Ellis. It was in two pieces. It was loose and put me not to much pain. *March, 31.* Mr. Willard visits me and prays with the family. All present. *April, 1. 1699.* Mr. Jn° Wait was here and express'd his earnest desire that Bastian might have Jane, Mr. Thair's Negro. I spake to Jane on Monday.[7] *Apr. 6. 1699.* The President, Mr. Cotton Mather and Mr. Willard visit me. It seems a day or two ago there was a great Funeral of a Barbados Gentleman; Usher, Foster, Dyer, Maccarty, Harris, Newton, Bearers. Funeral sermon, and great crowding to it.

Apr. 8. Mrs. Eunice Wait comes to our house and expresses her desire that Sebastian might have Mrs. Thair's Jane; and would have me promote it; though she said 'twould be to their prejudice in some respect. Govr's speech is brought to Town of March 27, at the open-of the Assembly at New York. *Apr. 10.* The Spanish sheet is printed off. Bradish brought to Town. Was taken at Deerfield.

Apr. 13th. Orders are issued to Lt Col. Hutchinson to prepare for my Lords [*Lord Bellomont's*] coming as to the Regiment. *Apr. 13.* Council din'd at the Exchange Tavern.

Lords-Day, Apr. 16. Many Swallows do proclaim the Spring. *Apr. 15. 7th day,* Shute arrives from Salt-Tarbooda [*Tortuga*].

Apr. 18. Went to Neponset to meet Capt. Fayerwether. Took Roxbury Lecture in our way home.

Third-day, April 25. 1699. Madam Usher's case is committed to the Jury, whereof Jacob Nash is Fore-man. Mr. Willard pray'd, and afterward dined with us.

Fourth-day, April 26. The Jury brings in their verdict for Madam Usher. Mr. Leverett and Newton crave a Chancery. John Rainsford arrives, 8 weeks passage from the Downs. Mr. Secretary waits on the Lt Govr and comes into the Council-chamber after the Adjournment in the evening, and tells Mr. Winthrop, Mr. Cooke and me

---

[6] William Payne (Harvard 1689), Commissioner of Impost and Excise, evidently had been a tenant of Sewall's in his house on Cotton Hill. He was the son of Tobias Payne and Sarah Winslow, who was in succession the wife of Myles Standish Jr., Tobias Payne, and Richard Middlecott. *Savage.*

[7] Negotiations for the nuptials of Bastian (Sebastian), John Wait's Negro, and Jane Lake, servant to Nathaniel and Deborah Thayer, had been going on for some time. They were finally married by Sewall 13 February 1700/1.

that the Act for Courts is disannulled [*disallowed?*], and that of the Colledge, &c: so that our Court is like to die and sink in the midst.[8] The Lord be our King, and Lord, and Law-Giver. Pardon our Court-Sins, and sanctify our frequent Deaths. [*In margin*: Law for Courts Null'd.]

Fifth-day, April, 27. 1699. The Bell is toll'd in the morn: but go not in. After Lecture the Lt Govr shews us the Allowance and Disallowance of Laws. After Dinner Bell is toll'd again: go in. Mr. Danforth tells the people, Had such news from England as that could not hold the Court any longer; which they would hear published by and by: call'd for what papers the Jury had, out of their hands.

Drum is beat, and Allowance and Disallowance of the Acts is published, Lt Govr and Council standing in the Gallery. Great many Auditors below.

Second-day; May 8 1699. Boston Town-Meeting.

Number of Voters	323.
Capt. Andrew Belchar	239.
Mr. John Eyre	178.
Mr. John White	175.
Capt. Theophilus Frary	165.
Bromfield	156.
Legg	146.
Byfield	122.
Foxcroft	86.

Extract of Mr. William Paterson's Letter, dated at Fort St. Andrew, Febr. 18th. 1699. Sent to Mr. John Borland.

I have read the two books you sent, for which I thank the Author and you; and am glad to see the Spirit and Hand of Almighty God at this time in so eminent a manner, as it were moving in the minds of so many men, and inclining and preparing them (although in so many and various circumstances, and different and distant places) to this great Work, that, I hope we, though unworthy, are made the happy Instruments to begin.

Extract of this Letter, drawn by Mr. Steel, was printed at Boston, May, 15. 1699.[9]

8 Chapters 9 (An Act for Establishing of Courts) and 10 (An Act for Incorporating Harvard Colledge, at Cambridge, in New England) of the Province Laws of 1697 were disallowed by the Privy Council 24 November 1698.
9 William Paterson was the projector of the Darien scheme described in our note for 20 December 1698. John Borland was a Boston merchant, brother of Rev.

See my Journal of meeting the Gov[r] June, 7th.[10] Mr. Willard prays in the Council, and tis said did so yesterday. Gov[r] dines at Roxbury, four coaches. Capt. Byfield gives the Committee a Treat.

June, 5. 1699. Mr. Willard preaches an excellent Election Sermon.[11] Gov[r] dines at Monks. Major Walley chosen Capt., Capt. Byfield Lieut. Tho. Hutchinson Ens. Gov[r] Bellomont delivers the Badges, saying that He approv'd of the choice.

Mr. Wigglesworth and his wife lodge here. M. T. Wednesday nights.

Friday, June, 9, 1699. Capt. Natha. Byfield is sworn Judge of the

---

Francis Borland, one of the two Scots parsons on the second Darien expedition. The letter was published as *An Abstract of a Letter From a Person of Eminency and worth in Caledonia* [Darien] *to a Friend at Boston in New England* (No date. 2 pages. Evans 892; *Massachusetts Broadsides*, 224). The published text does not include the paragraph quoted by Sewall. Appended to the letter is another item: *Caledonia. The Declaration of the Council Constituted by the Indian and African Company of Scotland; for the Government, and direction of their Colonies, and Settlements in the Indies* (4 pages. colophon: Boston, Printed May, 15th 1699. Signed by Hugh Ross, Sec., New-Edinburgh, December 28, 1698; Evans 892, *Massachusetts Broadsides*, 225). Mr. Steel is not mentioned elsewhere in the diary and does not appear as a regular resident of Boston; we suggest that he may have been a Scottish agent for the Darien enterprise. An anonymous promotion piece by Paterson is listed by Evans (893): *Observations of a Person of Eminence and Worth in Caledonia, written to his friend in Boston, N.E. on their Scots settlement, New Edinburgh, at Darien, in America; with an account of the nature and condition of the country, and good disposition of the natives toward them, and of their addressing the President of Panama.* Dated at Fort St. Andrews, Feb. 18th. 1698, 9. (Boston: Printed by B. Green and J. Allen, 1699. 76 pages). No copy is now known.

[10] Not found. Writing to Governor William Burnet, 10 July [1728], Sewall says: "It was in the year 1699, the later end of May, when with many of the Council, I went to Newport to meet my Lord Bellomont, arriving there in the Province Gally from New York." In a letter to John Ive, 27 June 1699, Sewall gives additional details: "The Earle of Bellomont, our Governour, came to this place the 26 day of May last past; was then pretty much excersised with the Gout, but is now so far recovered as to be able to Walk, and his Lordship sits in Council almost every day and presides in a manner very satisfactory to the whole General Court." *L.B.* II, 244; I, 212.

[11] This was the Artillery Election Sermon. Willard called it *The Man of War*, and it was printed in Boston within the year. On 31 May Increase Mather delivered what is correctly called the Election Sermon—on the day of the election of the councillors—"In the Audience of His *Excellency* the Earl of BELLOMONT, Captain General and GOVERNOUR in Chief, and of the COUNCIL, and Representatives of the General Assembly of the Province of the *Massachusetts Bay*." He entitled the sermon, *The Surest way to the Greatest Honour*, and it was printed in Boston in 1699. T. J. Holmes, *Increase Mather . . . Bibliography* (1931), II, 562–566.

Admiralty, Capt. Lawrence Hammond Register, Franklin, Marshal. This was done before the Gov[r] and Council.[12]

Second-day, June 12, 1699. The Gov[r] goes to the Castle with Col. Romer and several of the Council: Was saluted by the Fort and Ships as passed by, and at the Castle. Afterwards Col. Romer desired a Shot might be made; the Gun broke, and kill'd Nathan[l] Homes, the Under-Gunner, who was buried at Roxbury next day, just before Lecture. One Proctor, an old man, was dangerously wounded: and the Governour's Butler, so as to lose much Blood.

In the Afternoon, June, 12. 1699. I went to Hog Island with Cous. Savage, to view the Barn whose Roof is blown off. No Guns were fired at the Governour's coming off from the Castle: but about six, many were fired as came to the Harbour to Land. Came from the Island just about 7 or after, and Landed on my own Wharf about Nine at night.

For the story of Sewall's involvement at this time in the affairs of Captain Kidd, which he saw fit to omit from his diary, see our note for 6 February 1699/1700.

Wednesday, June 21. A Pack of Cards are found strawed over my fore-yard, which, tis supposed, some might throw there to mock me, in spite of what I did at the Exchange Tavern last Satterday night.

Midsummer Day, 1699. Mr. Secretary, Capt. Belchar, Capt. Mason, and S. are invited, and dine with my Lord and Lady at Mr. Sergeants. At 9. at night Bradish and Witherly get out of Prison and make their escape with the Maid that help'd them out.[13]

Monday, June, 26. I visit the Lieut Govr His Honour kept house yesterday, had now his left Leg lying on a Chair.

June, 30. 1699. Writt to Mr. Nathanael Higginson at Fort St. George near Ceylon in Asia, with a *Phænomena* and several other Prints; persuading his Return to N. E. hope to see him Governour of this Province.[14]

---

[12] Not much is known of the history and personnel of the Massachusetts Court of Vice-Admiralty, but the available documents were gathered by H. H. Edes in C.S.M. x, 379–386.

[13] Joseph Bradish and Tee Witherly, pirates, had escaped by the aid of Kate Price. The jailer was a kinsman of Bradish (5 M.H.S. Colls. VI, 4n). They were captured and locked up again 26 October 1699, as Sewall records.

[14] Nathaniel Higginson (Harvard 1670) was the son of Rev. John Higginson of Salem. He went to England, where he was employed by Lord Wharton as steward and tutor of his children, and also in the mint at the Tower of London. In 1683 he established himself as a merchant at Fort Saint George, now Madras, India,

Third-Day, July, 11. 1699. I went with Mr. Willard to Pulling-Point
to Mr. Dean Winthrop's, (77) *annorum.* Between one and two, Mr.
Willard married Atherton Haugh and Mercy Winthrop: Said, Mr.
Atherton Haugh, Mrs. Mercy Winthrop; forbad all unlawful com-
munion with other Women and *vice versa.* Gave very good Advice
and Exhortation; especially most solemnly charged them never to
neglect family Prayer. Between 3 and four Major Gen¹ and Mr. Adam
Winthrop came and many with them, when we had almost din'd.
Sang a Psalm together, I set St. David's Tune: Sung part of two
Psalms, concluded with the 4 last verses of the 115.

When Mr. Willard ask'd Mr. Winthrop's consent, he also complemented me respecting Atherton Haugh: I said I was glad that had
found so good a Family and so good a wife. And after, when saw the
Bridegroom and Bride together after the Wedding: I praid God to
bless them, and give them such an Offspring wherein the Name of
Haugh and Winthrop might flourish.

Mr. Dean Winthrop liv'd there in his fathers days, and was
wont to set up a Bush when he saw a ship coming in; He is now 77
years old. In his Fathers time, his house stood more toward Dear
Island.[15] Wind was against us coming home; so that twas nine aclock
before landed. Were four hours in the passage. Maj^r Gen¹ &c bid there
all night, and pass'd it but uncomfortably.

*On 13 July 1699 the General Court agreed to a new charter for Harvard
College, naming Sewall a fellow. Governor Bellomont refused his consent
on the 18th, and Sewall was named to the committee to acquaint the
House of Representatives of this action. C.S.M. xv, xlix–l.*

Wednesday; July, 19. The Lady Bellomont and Madam Nanfan
visit us.[16]

July, 20. Deputies are sent for to Mr. Sergeant's, and in his best
Chamber, the Governour declares his Prorogation of the Court to
the 11th of Octob^r next, 9 *mane.* This was done about Noon, and
then the Lecture began about Later than is now usual.

---

where he succeeded Elihu Yale as governor of the factory under the East India
Company in 1692. We will encounter Higginson again in November 1708. *D.A.B.*
[15] Deane Winthrop's house is still standing on Shirley Street in Chelsea. L. S.
Mayo, *The Winthrop Family in America* (1948), 72; photograph in Mellen
Chamberlain, *Doc. Hist. of Chelsea* (1908), I, 121.
[16] Lady Bellomont was Catherine, daughter of Bridges Nanfan of Birtsmorton,
Worcestershire. Madam Nanfan was probably the wife of Captain John Nanfan, a
cousin, who was lieutenant-governor of New York province at this time.

July, 24. 1699. About 6 *mane*, my wife with Elizabeth, Joseph, Mary and Jane Tappan, set sail for Newbury in Titcomb. Rid down to the Boat in Mr. Simson's Coach.

Third-Day, July, 25. 1699. My Lord Bellomont deliver'd me my Commission for Judge of the Superiour Court. And the Chief Justice, Mr. Stoughton, Mr. Cooke and my self were sworn in Mr. Sergeants best chamber before the Governour and Council. And all of the Council present were sworn as Justices of the Peace; Only Mr. Eliakim Hutchinson declined taking his Oath. The Great God of Heaven enable us, and me in particular, to keep these solemn Oaths. When I came home Sam, Hannah and Joanna being gon to Dorchester with Madam Usher to the Lecture, I found the House empty and Lock'd. Taking the key I came in and made a shift to find a solitary Dinner of bak'd Pigeons and a piece of Cake. How happy I were, if I could once become wise as a Serpent and harmless as a Dove!

Council advis'd that the Governour give Mr. Mather some Authority relating to the College, pursuant to the Vote of the Representatives.

July. 25. Madam Usher, Sam, Hanna and Joanna ride to Dorchester Lecture in Mr. Simsons Coach.

Between 6 and 7, I have my Lady up upon Cotton Hill, and shew her the Town; Madam Sergeant, Nanfan, Newton there; and Maj^r Genl and Mr. Sergeant. Mrs. Tuthills Daughters invited my Lady as came down and gave a Glass of good wine.

As came down again through the Gate I ask'd my Lady's Leave that now I might call it Bellomont Gate. My Lady laugh'd, and said, What a Complement he puts on me! With pleasancy.

During this long hiatus in the diary Sewall lost his brother John Sewall of Newbury, who died 8 August aged 45. L.B. 1, 212.

Septr 11. 1699. Mr. Danforth, Cook, and my self set out for Bristow; I had a flux; Lodge at Childs's.

Septr 12. To Bristow. *13.* Court breaks up. *14.*[17] Mr. Newton and I bring Mr. Danforth and Cook going as far as the way that leads over the bridge. When got back the wind was so high that could not get over the ferry. Din'd at Howlands. Lodg'd at Mr. Wilkins's. *Friday Septr 15.* Mr. Newton and I ride to Newport, see aged John Savage,

[17] Sewall wrote in the margin: "Mrs. B. Oliver married." In the Boston town records there is an entry of the marriage of Samuel Keeling to Elizabeth Oliver by Mr. Samuel Willard on that date. She was the daughter of Nathaniel Oliver and Elizabeth Brattle. *Savage.*

(now Earl), by the way. Her husband, Ralph Earl, was born 1606. and his wife was 10. or 11 years older than he. So she is esteemed to be one hundred and five years old.[18] I pass over the ferry to Narraganset; by the time landed, twas almost quite dark. Got to Capt. Willet's, and lodg'd there. *Satterday* 7ʳ 16—went to Tho Hazard's, and with him to Niles's Mill, from thence to Point Judith. Find his son gon to Block-Island. So I went back to go to Newport, lodg'd at Joseph Morey's on Canonicut.

Sabbath-day. 7ʳ 17. Jos. Morey carrys me over; I hear Mr. Clap, who prays and preaches very well. Dine and lodge at Tho. Mallet's.

Second-day, 7ʳ 18. I ferry over to Canonicut, tis so late before I get over that am forc'd to lodge at Capt. Arnold's.

19. Went over with Briggs. Goe with Tho. Hazard to Mattoonuck, view the bounds and add to the heaps of Stones at 3 Corners. Go back and lodge on Boston Neck at Tho. Hazard's. (20) Ferry over to Rode-Island, Get to Newport about one.

I stand at Tho. Mallet's and salute his Excellency as he rides in his Coach into Town.

Septʳ 21. Governour[19] invites me to dine with him at Mr. Clark's. Mr. Saffin lodges with me.

Septʳ 22. N[athˡ]. Niles brings over Block-Island Harry [*an Indian*] to me. Have some Talk about a Release for Point Judith: puts it off till next day.

23. Agree for 15£ and draw a rough of it and take his hand to it. (24) *Lords Day*, Hear Mr. Clap. Govʳ Winthrop, Majʳ Genˡ, Col. Hutchinson, Capt Foster, Mr. Saffin, Sewall, Capt. Mason, Mr. James Noyes, Mr. G. Saltonstall there, besides some others, Strangers.

Septʳ 25. Ninnecraft [*in margin*: Ninnegret] executes a Release of Mr. Addington's drawing. Gov. Winthrop, Majʳ Genˡ Winthrop, Capt. Foster, Joseph Stanton, and Block-Island Harry, witnesses. N. Niles goes with him, and he Acknowledges it before John Green, dept.-Governour; Joseph Hull also present. I deliver it to Weston Clark, Recorder. (26) He brings it in the morn Recorded, give him 2.6ᵈ (27) Governour sets out for Boston, Pole of the Calash broken by the Horses frighted with a Pistol. The making of a new one takes up an hour or two. Dine at Mr. Brenton's at Bristow. Lodge at Rehoboth. (28) Set out at 7 *mane*. Dine at Billinges. Set out at 2. Get to Dedham by 5. After a little Recruit leave the Calash there. Governour rides on Horseback. Get home by Seven in good health

[18] G. Andrews Moriarty spoils this story in *N.E.H.G.R.* xcⁱⁱⁱ, 361–362; Joan was baptized 18 February 1609/10 at Widford, Herts, making her 89 at this time.
[19] The governor of Rhode Island was Samuel Cranston.

though the day was very hot. Find my family in health, only disturb'd at Betty's denying Mr. Hirst, and my wife hath a cold. The Lord sanctify Mercyes and Afflictions.

Seventh-day, Octob^r 14. I meet with the Governour, Lt Govr, Mr. I. Mather, &c about the Indian Affair, which is the first time, The Lord make me faithfull and usefull in it. Govr Ashurst's Letter was read wherein Mr. Cotton Mather, Mr. Neh. Walter, S. Sewall, Jn° Foster, Mr. Peter Sergeant, and Mr. Thomas Bannistor were added.[20]

Octobr 16. Pray for Sam. and my daughters Hannah and Eliza. and others of my Children. Mr. Torrey lodges here and tells me of the wofull Distance between Lt Col. Hunt, and himself. [*In margin:*] Mr. [*Ephraim*] Little ordain'd at Plim° Octr 4. 1699. Mr. [*John*] Cotton dyed, Septr 17. fol 206.

Octr 17. The President visits me and gives me one of his Books of Sermons, printed in London, 1699.[21]

Octr 23. The amazing news of the (See fol. 206) [*under date of 22 April, 1700*] dismal Mortality at Charlestown in Carolina comes to Town and is spread all over it: 150 dead in 6 days time: Draw the dead to the Grave in Carts. Mr. Cotton is dead among the rest.[22] Infection was brought from Providence. This made us the rather put Plantations in the plural number in the Bill this day order'd for Thanksgiving.

Octr 24. Mr. Wm Hirst comes and thanks my wife and me for our

[20] These men were made commissioners of the New England Company, an association of prosperous London merchants chartered in 1649 by the Long Parliament as the Society for Propagation of the Gospel in New England, the purpose of which was to convert the savages to Christianity. It was rechartered after the Restoration, 7 February 1661/2, as the Company for the Propagation of the Gospel in New England and the Parts Adjacent in America, but was always referred to as the Corporation or the New England Company. It should not be confused with the Society for the Propagation of the Gospel in Foreign Parts, established in 1701, which conducted the foreign missionary work of the Anglican church in the American colonies and other English possessions overseas. In 1699 Sir William Ashurst was governor of the Corporation. Sewall was most active in the work of the organization, and held the posts of commissioners' secretary 1700–1724 and commissioners' treasurer 1701–1724; his services are fully recorded in William Kellaway's history, *The New England Company 1649–1776* (London, 1961), and in George Parker Winship, Samuel Sewall and the New England Company, *M.H.S. Proc.* LXVII, 55–110. See also Frederick L. Weis, The New England Company of 1649 and its Missionary Enterprises, *C.S.M.* XXXVIII, 134–218.

[21] This was Increase Mather's *Two Plain and Practical Discourses concerning I. Hardness of Heart . . . II. The Sin and Danger of Disobedience to the Gospel* (Holmes, 171).

[22] See our note on John Cotton, 1 October 1697.

Kindness to his Son in giving him the Liberty of our house. Seems to do it in way of taking Leave. I thank'd him, and for his countenance to Hannah at the Wedding. Told him that the wellwishers to my daughter and his son had persuaded him to go to Braintry and visit her there &c.; said if were hope would readily do it. But as things were, twould make persons think he was so involved that he was not fit to go any whether else. He has I suppose taken his final Leave.[23] I give him Mr. Oakes Sermon, and my Father Hulls Funeral Sermon.[24]

Octob^r 26. 1699. Joseph Bradish, Tee Witherly, and Kate Price are brought to Town and sent to Prison, from whence they escaped June, 24. Fast is warned to be next Thorsday for the Afflicted church abroad.

Octr 27. Lt Govr Treats the Governour and his Lady and many more: Two tables. Capt. Crow breaks a Glass Bottle of Madera as it stood on the floor, so that it run about with its Sanguin Colour; Capt. Crow mention'd its not being able to be gathered up again. Mr. Danforth crav'd a Blessing; Mr. Bridge return'd Thanks. Before Dinner rid with the Governour to the end of Dorchester Neck. This day news comes to Town of Mr. Man's House being burnt last night. Capt. Foxcroft informs us at Dorchester of his Father Danforth's Sickness. Mr. Hirst and Sam. come home from Braintry where they lay the night before.

Octr 28. I visit Mr. Danforth who is very sick; his Daughter Foxcroft tells me he is much troubled with the Palsie. Was *much* indisposed the 22. inst, which was the beginning of his sickness; yet would go to Meeting which did him hurt; especially going out in the Afternoon. I wish'd him Refreshings from God under his fainting Sickness.

Seventh-day, Novr 4. Capt. [*John*] Appleton of Ipswich dies. He was an Israelite indeed, a great Ornament of that Church and Town. Died of the Jaundies. 77 years. This day the Govr Treats the Council and sundry other Gentlemen in Mr. Sergeants best chamber. Guns fired upon account of the King's Birth-day. At night Governour and Mr. Newton made an Illumination.

Lord's Day, Novr. 5. Tho. Danforth Esqr dies about 3 *post merid.*

[23] The reluctant Betty had sent away her suitor Grove Hirst, and was in Braintree. Sewall wrote her a stern letter 26 October 1699: "It ought to be seriously considered, that your drawing back from him after all that has passed between you, will be to your Prejudice; and will tend to discourage persons of worth from making their Court to you . . ." (*L.B.* 1, 213). The situation improved in the summer of 1700, and they were married the following October.

[24] Both of these sermons were printed for Sewall when he was in charge of the press in Boston and have his name in the imprint: Urian Oakes's *The Soveraign Efficacy of Divine Providence* (1682) and Samuel Willard's *The High Esteem which God hath of the Death of his Saints* (1683).

of a Fever. Has been a Magistrat fourty years. Was a very good Husbandman and a very good Christian, and a good Councillor: was about 76. years old.

Third-day, Novr 7. Mr. Stoughton, in his Speech to the Grand-Jury, takes great notice of Judge Danforth's Death. Saith he was a Lover of Religion and Religious Men; the oldest Servant the Country had; zealous against vice: And if had any Detractors; yet was so much on the other as to erect him a Monument among this People. Mr. Willard in his Prayer mention'd Gods Displeasure in his Removal; and desired the Judges might act on the Bench as those who must also shortly go to give their Account. Indeed it is awfull, that while we are sitting on the bench, at the same time the ancientest Judge should be lying by the Wall dead in his house. I can't tell how it came about, but I told Mr. Danforth at Bristow, I thought he would never come thither again, which made him take a more particular Leave than otherwise he would have done.

Sixth-day, Novr 10. 1699. Mr. Danforth is intombed about a ¼ of an hour before four p. m. Very fair and pleasant day, much Company. Bearers on the right side Lt Govr, Mr. Russel, Sewall: Left side, Mr. W. Winthrop. Mr. Cook, Col. Phillips. I help'd lift the Corps into the Tomb, carrying the feet. Had cake and cheese at the house. Col. Hathorn, Mr. Corwin, Bro^r Sewall, were there from Salem. Councillors had Rings, Ministers Gloves, Mr. Mather and Brattle Scarfs and Rings: so had the Bearers. Cambridge Burying Placc is handsomely fenced in with boards, which has not been done above a Moneth or 6 weeks.

Seventh-day, Novr 11th about the middle of the night following, my dear Sister Hannah Tappan dies of a Fever. Mr. Addington told me of it first upon Novr 13 in the Council-Chamber, from Mr. Gerrish of Wenham. At 7. at night I received a Letter from Bro^r Sewall of it, and that the Funeral is to be the 14. Our notice is so lame and late, that I persuade Jane to stay at home, it being almost impossible to get thither time enough. Besides all this, the Court at Salem keeps me there, and Bro^r Sewall also. We had liv'd eight of us together Thirty years; and were wont to speak of it (it may be too vainly). But now God begins to part us apace. Two are taken away in about a quarter of a year's time; And me thinks now my dear Bro^r and Sister are laid in the Grave, I am, as it were laid there in Proxy— The Lord help me to carry it more suitably, more fruitfully, toward the Five remaining; and put me in a preparedness for my own Dissolution. And help me to live upon Him alone.

Fifth-day, Novr the last. [30] 1699. The Rain freezes upon the branches of the Trees to that thickness and weight, that great havock is thereby made of the Wood and Timber. Many young and strong Trees are broken off in the midst; and multitudes of Boughs rent off. Considerable hurt is done in Orchards. Two of our Apple-trees are broken down, Unkles Tree, two thirds of it, are broken down. Peach Trees at Mrs. Moodeys are almost all spoil'd. And my little Cedar almost quite mortified. Some think the Spoil that is made amounts to Thousands of pounds. How suddenly and with surprise can God destroy!

I was at Capt. Foster's upon the 29. November, and was there saying, November is almost out, yet we dont know what may happen before tis quite out, alluding to the drowning of Mr. Eyres Son upon the 30. Novr 96. and Mr. Maxwell.

Sixth-day Dec. 1. Was at Mr. Hillers to enquire for my wives virginals:[25] Mrs. Sarah Foster came to the Door.

Decr 8. 1699. Capt. Tho. Gullock and Col. Paige dine with me. Capt. Gullock told of 800 French Refugees being settled at Cape Bon Sperance. And at dinner, I objecting the Inconvenience that would be to America, if the Dauphin should be King of Spain: He answer'd, that America would ruine him; For New Spain would certainly Revolt &c.

Decr 9. Mr. Colman visits me: I Expostulat with him about the 3^d Article in the Manifesto,[26] that had shew'd no more Respect to N. E. Churches. I told him Christ was a Bride-Groom, and He lov'd to have his Bride commended. Philomela[27] would have found out some words: at which he smil'd. He satisfied me as to Baptisme and said the word [Adopted] was left out. I told him he was the more in danger, and had need to be more upon his Guard; lest any hard sharp words he had met with should tempt him to do what he intended not. Warn'd him of the Cross in Baptisme, &c. Said he was of our mind. Because I told him meerly saying *Conform*, did not express such an Approbation of the N. E. way as I desired: Many in England conform'd to things they professedly disliked.

At his going away, I told him, If God should please by them to hold forth any Light that had not been seen or entertain'd before;

[25] The virginal was a keyed musical instrument, common in England in the 16th and 17th centuries, resembling a spinet, but set in a box or case without legs; the word was generally used in the plural form, applied to a single instrument. *O.E.D.*

[26] See our note on the Manifesto Church, 31 January 1699/1700.

[27] The poems of Philomela (Elizabeth Singer Rowe, 1674–1737), published in 1696, delighted the pious of that generation, and were enthusiastically praised by Klopstock, Wieland, and Dr. Johnson. *D.N.B.*

I should be so far from envying it, that I should rejoice in it: which he was much affected with.

Thorsday, Decr 14. Lay abed all day and took Physick for the Ague in my face. Mr. Willard, C. Mather, Fisk, Cheever, visit me. Mr. Willard prays. Presently after their going away, I had ease, and was Let out of the Stocks. *Dec. 17.* Cold day, so went not to the publick Worship. *Third-day, Dec. 19.* My Lord Bellomont, his Lady, Madam Nanfan, din'd with us in the New Hall, and with them Mr. Cook, Mr. Secretary, Mr. Sergeant, Mrs. Sergeant, Major Walley, Lt Col. Lynde, Lt Col. Townsend, Capt. Dummer, Mr. Brumfield, Mr. Stoddard, Mr. Newton, Mr. Jackson, Mr. Campbell, who with Madam Usher, my wife and self, make just 19. in all. Invited that were not here, Lt Govr, Mr. Oakes, cous. Savage, Col. Romer, Madam Hamilton, Madam Shrimpton. Sat down a little before Two, and Rose about Three. It happened to be Catechising day, which was not aware of, being disappointed the Wednesday before, which intended, by Mr. Eyre's Treat; and Friday by my sickness. So miss'd the company of Mr. and Mrs. Willard. Was fain my self to crave a Blessing and Return Thanks. I left off my Muffler but this day and yet find no inconvenience, Blessed be God. I told the Govr of the Fort-fight 24 years ago; and a great fight in France Dec. 19. 1562 [*at Dreux*].

Æneas Salter went to Dorchester for me, to speak to the Lt Govr I had invited Him my self against the day of our disappointment.

Decr 21. 1699. Went to Lecture, wearing my black cap.[28]

Sabbath-day, Decr 24. 1699. Mr. Colman and his Society meet in the New Meeting house, this being the first time. Our Meeting was pretty much thin'd by it.

Dec. 28. 1699. Mr. Thacher marrieth Mrs. Bayly: and Mr. Wells, a Taylor, marries cous. Savage's Eldest Daughter.[29]

[28] Sewall had reached the age of 47 and was losing his hair; this exposed him to the cold, especially in the meeting-house. He detested periwigs, and the black cap —not just a skull-cap, but a fitted one covering the top and back of his head— which appears in all his portraits, was his solution.

[29] This was a second marriage for Rev. Peter Thacher of Milton, Sewall's classmate. Susannah Bailey was the widow of Rev. John Bailey of the First Church. Joshua Wells was married to Sarah, daughter of Ephraim Savage. According to the town records, both marriages were performed on 25 December by Rev. Samuel Willard. *Savage.*

1700

FIRE IN CHARLESTOWN / CAPTAIN KIDD AND HIS TREASURE / COURT
HELD AT PLYMOUTH / YOUNG SAM HAS A NARROW ESCAPE FROM
DROWNING / TRIP TO PORTSMOUTH AND KITTERY / DEATH OF HENRY
SEWALL, FATHER OF THE DIARIST / SEWALL PUBLISHES HIS
ANTI-SLAVERY TRACT / ORDINATION OF EBENEZER PEMBERTON /
MARRIAGE OF BETTY SEWALL / COURT AT SALEM

Jan. 14. 1699/1700. Elder Jonas Clark, of Cambridge, dies, a good man in a good old Age, and one of my first and best Cambridge friends. He quickly follows the great Patron of Ruling Elders, Tho. Danforth, Esqr.

15. This day fortnight Lawrence Copeland of Braintry was buried; 't is counted that he liv'd to be at least one hundred and ten years old. *Teste Arnoldo octogenario olim ejusdem vicino.*[1]

*Jan*ʸ 17. 1699/1700. A great fire brake out at Charlestown last night though very rainy. Three Houses burnt; viz. the widow Cutlers and two more: on the left hand of the way as one goes to Cambridge, upon the side of the hill. Other Houses on the opposite side of the Ally very narrowly escaped. Elder Clark is buried this day. Snowy all day long.

Gave to Mr. Willard two volums of Rivets works.[2]

*Jan*ʸ 17 about 5 p. m. Dame Hannah Townsend dies in the 93ᵈ year of her Age. Cook, Hutchinson, Sewall, Addington, Chiever, Maryon *pater*, Bearers. Janʸ 19. 1699-1700.

*Jan*ʸ 24ᵗʰ The Lᵗ Govʳ calls me with him to Mr. Willards, where out of two papers Mr. Wᵐ Brattle drew up a third for an Accommodation to bring on an Agreement between the New-Church [*Brattle Square*] and our Ministers; Mr. Colman got his Brethren to subscribe it.

[1] Savage discusses the age of Lawrence Copeland, who died 30 December 1699; another contemporary record gives his age as 100. Sewall's informant was Joseph Arnold of Braintree, an octogenarian.

[2] André Rivet, a Poictevin (1572–1647), D.D. Oxford 1621, was known to scholars as Andreas Rivetus; he was a professor in the theological faculty at Leyden, a rigid Calvinist, and a voluminous author.

This day Janʸ 24. was a Council at the Goveners. Assembly is proroug'd to the 13 March.

Janʸ 25ᵗʰ Mr. I. Mather, Mr. C. Mather, Mr. Willard, Mr. Wadsworth, and S. S. wait on the Lᵗ Govʳ at Mr. Coopers: to confer about the writing drawn up the evening before. Was some heat; but grew calmer, and after Lecture agreed to be present at the Fast which is to be observed Janʸ 31.

Janʸ 30. Lᵗ Govʳ [*Stoughton*], Winthrop, Cooke, S. S. hold the Court in Sommers's great Room below stairs; finish the Court by 7. at night: Note, good going over the ferry as in Summer almost, no Ice. [*In margin:*] Court at Charlest[*own*].

Janʸ 31. Fast at the New Church.[3] Mr. Colman reads the Writing agreed on. Mr. Allin Prays, Mr. Colman preaches, prays, blesses. *p.m.* Mr. Willard prays, Mr. I. Mather preaches, Mr. Cotton Mather prays, Sing the 67 psalm without reading. Mr. Brattle sets Oxford Tune. Mr. Mather gives the Blessing. His Text was, Follow peace with all men and Holiness. Doct. must follow peace so far as it consists with Holiness. Heb. 12. 14.

Mr. Colman's Text was Rom. 15. 29. Mr. Fisk, Hobart, Belchar and many Ministers and Scholars there. Mr. Torrey absent by reason of sickness and the bad wether yesterday. Of the Council, Lᵗ Govʳ, Mr. Russell, Mr. Cooke, Col. Hathorne, Sewall, Addington, Sergeant (Foreseat) Col. Foster, Lynde, Saffin, Eᵐ Hutchinson, Walley, Townsend, Byfield. Mr. Willard pray'd God to pardon all the frailties and follies of Ministers and people; and that they might give that Respect to the other churches that was due to them though were not just of their Constitution. Mr. Mather in's Sermon, and Mr. Cotton Mather in's prayer to the same purpose. Mr.

---

3 The Church in Brattle Square was established in 1699 by a few Bostonians who wished to liberalize certain of the church practices of the day. Benjamin Colman (Harvard 1692), then preaching in England, was invited to become the first pastor, and accepted. It was necessary to establish fellowship with the other churches, hence the proceedings in which Sewall participated. The organizers of the church printed a three-page *Manifesto* or declaration of principles dated 17 November 1699, and from this the institution became known as the Manifesto Church; the document is reproduced in *Records of the Church in Brattle Square* (1902). Although the Mathers participated in the Fast, they by no means endorsed the platform of the New Church, and attended merely to maintain harmony among the Boston churches. Increase stirred up a controversy the same year by the publication of *The Order of the Gospel*; this fracas is recorded in detail in T. J. Holmes's *Increase Mather . . . Bibliography* II, 385–397, and in his *Cotton Mather . . . Bibliography*, I, 317–320. See also James De Normandie, The Manifesto Church, in *M.H.S. Proc.* XLVII, 223–231.

Willard and C. Mather pray'd excellently and pathetically for Mr. Colman and his Flock. Twas a close dark day.

Febr. 1. A pretty deal of Thunder Rain and Hail the last night. Col. Hambleton comes to Town this day from Pensilvania.[4]

Cousin Wm Savil died last night of a Fever.

Febr. 2. Cous. Savil is buried. Tis so very cold that none of us venture to goe. Visit my Lord [*Bellomont*].

Seventh-day, Febr. 3. 1699/1700. Capt. Win, in the Advice, a 4th Rate, arrives from England 6 weeks passage from the Spit-head. Govr heard nothing of him till he came and deliver'd his Packets. Came to Nantasket the day before; on Friday. He says, the King redeems all the Captives at Maccaness [*Mequinez, in Morocco*]. Peace.

Tuesday, Febr. 6. A Council is held at my Lord's. The Advice of Councillors asked about sending the Pirats on Board.[5] I motioned

---

[4] Andrew Hamilton was the last governor of East and West New Jersey under the proprietors. He established the first postal system in the colonies. *D.A.B.*

[5] Without a preliminary word, Sewall plunges us here into the later affairs of the celebrated pirate, Captain William Kidd. The entry relates to a discussion of the right to ship off Kidd and other prisoners for trial in England. (On this point, see *Memorial Hist. of Boston* II, 182–183).

William Kidd was a respected ship-owner and sea-captain with a family and a fine house in Manhattan; more than once he had rendered useful service to the government in chasing enemy pirates from the coast. In 1695 William III, urged by the East India Company, and with no warships at liberty, determined to send a private vessel against the pirates in the Red Sea and the Indian Ocean. Robert Livingston of the manor of Livingston in New York was in London defending his political and land interests. Captain Kidd was there on business. The Earl of Bellomont was being considered for the governorship of New York province. Livingston recommended Kidd to Bellomont as a suitable commander for a privateering expedition against the pirates, and a syndicate was formed in October 1695. Bellomont and four other noblemen (the Duke of Shrewsbury; Baron Somers, the Lord Chancellor of England; Admiral Sir Edward Russell, after 1697 the Earl of Orford; and the Earl of Romney) underwrote four-fifths of the costs of the expedition, while Livingston and Kidd provided the remainder. The net profits were to be divided in this way after a tenth part had been given to the king. (J. Judd, Lord Bellomont and Captain Kidd, *N. Y. Hist. Soc. Quarterly* XLVII 67–74; L. H. Leder, *Robert Livingston* [1961], Chap. VI). Bellomont was commissioned governor of New York, Massachusetts, and New Hampshire, 18 June 1697.

Meanwhile Kidd had procured the *Adventure Galley*, launched at Plymouth in December 1695, and sailed the following April for New York. There he completed his crew with a desperate set of men who were to receive no pay except a share in the booty. Kidd sailéd in September 1696; by December he had rounded the Cape of Good Hope. In February he reached the Comoro Islands, where one-third of his crew died of cholera and the ship began to leak. Threatened by a mutinous crew, Kidd now crossed over from legal privateering to piracy, and began to plunder the ships he had been sent to protect. In October 1697 he refused to attack a

Dutch ship; this provoked a small mutiny, in which he struck one of his gunners with a bucket, killing him. Kidd captured his richest prize, the *Quedagh Merchant*, in January 1698, and sailed to Madagascar, arriving in May; there he scuttled his own ship, took over the *Quedagh Merchant*, divided the booty with his crew, and entered into friendly relations with some of the pirates he had been sent to capture. Turning up at Anguilla, B.W.I., laden with loot, in April 1699, Kidd discovered that he and his crew had been proclaimed pirates and that a squadron had been sent in search of them. In a secluded cove off Hispaniola, Kidd left the *Quedagh Merchant* under guard, and with a portion of his treasure sailed north in a sloop, the *Antonio*. He reached Oyster Bay, Long Island, in June and sent James Emott, the New York admiralty lawyer, to talk with Bellomont in Boston. The perplexed earl sent Duncan Campbell, Scottish bookseller in Boston, with Emott, and they joined Kidd on his sloop off Block Island. Campbell returned to Boston 19 June with a written statement from Kidd protesting his innocence.

Now we get to Sewall. On the same day a meeting of the Council was held, at which Bellomont announced for the first time the return of Captain Kidd, and read Campbell's report. The Council approved a letter of safe conduct for Kidd. Sewall was present, but made no record of this meeting. Leaving much of his valuable cargo with John Gardiner on Gardiner's Island (in the fork of Long Island), Kidd sailed to Boston and appeared before Bellomont and the Council 3 July. Kidd requested time to prepare a narrative of his proceedings. He was then directed to give a "summary accompt of the lading on Board his Sloop now in port, and also on board the Ship he left in Hispaniola"; after giving this account verbally he was granted time until the next day to bring his narrative in writing and an invoice of the lading on board his ships. On 4 July Kidd appeared with five of his company who presented affidavits in writing, but Kidd requested a further extension of time. At the next meeting of the Council, 6 July, Kidd produced no report. He withdrew, and the governor acquainted the board of his orders from England to seize Kidd, his accomplices, and their vessels and goods. Warrants were thereupon ordered. Kidd and several of his company were then brought before the board and examined. The following day Kidd was again examined by the Council, then committed to prison. At the same meeting, 7 July, Sewall, Nathaniel Byfield, Jeremiah Dummer, Lawrence Hammond, and Andrew Belcher were "appointed and authorized to require and receive into their Custody all the Goods, Merchandizes and Treasure, imported in the Sloop Antonio by Captn William Kidd, lately Commander of the Adventure Gally and his Accomplices, with the said Sloop, and to take a particular Inventory thereof, and to secure the same in such safe place and places as they shall think fitt, until his Maj^ty's pleasure shall be known for the disposal thereof."

Not a word of this appears in the diary. Sewall did not go to Gardiner's Island, as his presence in Boston is accounted for continuously in the diary or the Council records, but the other commissioners did. An inventory, dated Boston, 25 July 1699, of the "Gold, Silver, Jewels and Merchandise, late in the Possession of Capt William Kid, which have been seized and secured by us underwritten, Pursuant to an order from his Excellency Richard Earl of Bellomont . . . bearing date July 7th, 1699," presented by Sewall, Byfield, Dummer, and Belcher, "Lodged in the Secretary's Office at Boston. Exam^d Is^a Addington, Sect^y", is printed in C. C. Gardiner, *Lion Gardiner and his Descendants* (1890), 100–101, and in *New York History* xxv, 517–521, from an original still in the possession of the Gardiner family. This was the receipt sent to John Gardiner; no copy is to be

that by that time the Prisoners could be got from N. York, Connecticut, Rode-Island: the Assembly might sit if his L^dship saw meet, and they would willingly rid themselves of them. Govr seem'd displeas'd. I had ask'd before, What Pirats, and the Govr said them and their Associats. Govr mention'd Kid, Gillam, Bradish, Witherly, to be sent aboard presently for better security. Council voted to leave it to the Gov^{rs} Discretion whom to send aboard: only the Govr had said to some that enquired, He intended not [*to let*] them out upon Bail. I think only I, Col. Townsend and Capt. Byfield were in the Negative. I said I was not clear in it. The grounds I went upon were because I knew of no power I had to send Men out of the Province. Capt. Byfield said, He was for their going aboard: but reckon'd twas not so safe to send them presently as to keep them in Goal. Voted also the Treasure to be deliver'd to such as the Govr should appoint. Govr nominated Lt Hunt and Capt. Win, capt. of the Advice. Present Mr. Cooke, Col. Hutchinson, Mr. Secretary, S. S., Mr. Russel, Col. Lynde, Capt. Foster, Mr. Sergeant, Mr. Saffin, Mr. E^m Hutchinson, Col. Townsend, Capt. Byfield, Major Walley. Have reckon'd them as came to mind. Lt Govr, Maj^r Genl Winthrop, Col. Phillips, not there.

High Wind, and very cold at Nwest.

Febr. 7th Council is called to advise about the Indians, being Rumors of a War by the Maquas. One Tobie, who murder'd several at Oxford, stirs them up, and brings Wampam to our Indians. On Wednesday night, Jan^y *ult*, the night it Thundered, Sixteen Men with women and children ran away from Woodstock. Govr Win-

---

found in the Massachusetts Archives. It should be added that no suspicion of complicity ever rested on the proprietor of Gardiner's Island.

As for Kidd, he was continued in jail in Boston for eight months, then shipped off with three other pirates in the *Advice*, as Sewall records 16 February. He was kept in Newgate for over a year, tried for the murder of his gunner and on various indictments for piracy, found guilty in each case, and hanged 23 May 1701 at Execution Dock, Wapping.

The literature on Captain Kidd, both fact and fiction, is enormous, and archival documentation is abundant. To the citations of the *D.A.B.* we would add Morton Pennypacker, Captain Kidd, *New York History* xxv, 482–531; G. F. Dow and J. H. Edmonds's chapter in *Pirates of the New England Coast* (1923), 73–83, and E. E. Hale's chapter in *Memorial Hist. of Boston* ii, 173–186. J. F. Jameson prints several documents in *Privateering and Piracy in the Colonial Period* (1923); some rough copies from English archives are printed in *N.E.H.G.R.* vi, 77–84, and the M.H.S. has two volumes of scrupulous English transcripts in the Frederick Lewis Gay collection.

throp has sent 40 Men thither. Have writt a Letter to answer his with Thanks; and to desire him to surprise Tobie if he can.

Friday, Febr. 9th. Will, formerly Capt. Prentices Negro, now living with Maylem, a Horse run away with him, threw him upon the hard frozen Ground, or Timber, near Houchins's corner, and kill'd him; died in a little while. I saw him panting as came from visiting Capt. Foxcroft. He was much delighted in Horses, and now dies by a Horse. About 1664. he sav'd his Master Prentice from a Bear. Went with Col. Townsend and me to Albany. Rid Post one while.

Capt. Belchar was at the Meeting, come home from burying his daughter Vaughan, who died in child bed. Child died first. Wast the most beautifull of all his Daughters. I wonder'd to see him at Mr. Bromfield's, the wether had been so excessive cold. Said, I was sorry for the cropping of his desirable Flower.[6]

Febr. 6, 7, 8. were reputed to be the coldest days that have been of many years. Some say Brooks were frozen for carts to pass over them, so as has not been seen these Ten years. Ground very dry and dusty by the high wind.

Febr. 12. A considerable snow falls. Jany 11th was a storm of Snow; which occasiond Mr. C. Mather to take for his Text, White as the snow of Salmon: Quickly melted away. Have not as yet had any path to make upon the Lords Day.

Febr. 12. Justices met with the Selectmen at the Stone-House, Davis's, to take away some misunderstandings between us; and to agree to take Lists of each quarter of the Town to reform and prevent disorders.

Tuesday, Febr. 13. I got up pretty early, being forc'd to it by a laxness. Had sweet communion with God in Prayer, and in reading the two last Sermons I heard in London, about Assurance &c. This came to my hand by accident, the book being fallen upon my wood in the closet. Had read before, my own Notes upon Ephes. 5. 15, 16, 7^r 16. 1679. at Mrs. Oliver's. The Lord inlighten my Understanding, and incline my Will.

Febr. 14. I visit Mr. Tho. Thornton in the Afternoon between 3 and 4. He made a shift to say he was willing to dy, but wanted Patience. Hop'd should dy next night. I spake to him what I could. Holp him up while he drank something comfortable.

[6] We like Sewall's warm remarks on Mary, one of the six daughters of Andrew Belcher of Cambridge and sister of Jonathan Belcher. Sewall had attended her wedding on 8 December 1698 to George Vaughan (Harvard 1696) of Portsmouth, New Hampshire. She was nineteen when she died.

At three past midnight he alter'd much.

Febr. 15, 3 *p.m.* Mr. Tho. Thornton dyes very quietly; which Mr. Gee acquaints me with. Is very near 93 years old.[7]

Febr. 16. pleasant wether. Kid, Bradish, Gillam, Witherly are sent on board the Advice Frigat. Warrant was dated Febr. 13. but no mention of the Council in it. But the Gov^rs name only, in pursuit of the King's Command.

Febr. 22. I had thoughts of sitting up to see the eclipse: but the cloudy thick sky discouraged me: yet kept a candle burning, and went to the Window at two of the clock; the wether was still thick with clouds, that I could see nothing: only seem'd very dark for a full Moon.

In the evening I visited Mrs. Williams in her Languishing. Am invited to a Fast there on Friday.

Wednesday, Febr. 28. We ship off the Iron chest of Gold, Pearls &c., 40 Bails of East-India Goods, 13 hogsheads, chests and case, one Negro Man, and Venturo Resail, an East-Indian born at Ceilon. Wether was doubtfull in the morning, which made us irresolute: but at last we set about it, and accomplish'd it very happily. I look upon it as a great Mercy of God, that the Store-house has not been broken up, no fire has happened. Agreed in the Weight of the Gold with our former Weight, and had so comfortable a day at last to finish our work. Mr. Bradstreet, and Capt. Winn's Clerk took an account at the Crane; but Capt. Winn would not give a Rec^t till had them on board the sloop Antonio, which ridd off just without the Outward Wharf. Gave a Rec^t for the Gold at Capt Belchar's as soon as it was weighed.[8] Cousin Wells and his wife visit us. I went to his L^dship to speake to Him about some paym^ts to be made of about £16.

March, 4. 1699. Capt. Gullock is sent to Prison for his contempt of the Governm^t in giving in to the Govr and Council an Insolent writing under his hand, and justifying it.[9]

---

[7] Thomas Thornton, silenced and ejected from the ministry by the Bartholomew act of 1662, came soon after to New England, and was minister of Yarmouth on Cape Cod. He spent his last years in Boston, where his son Timothy was a merchant and representative. *Savage.*

[8] Sewall's relief at being rid of the responsibility of Kidd's treasure is evident. Kidd's effects were forfeited to the Crown, and provided the sum of £6471, which Queen Anne gave towards the establishment of Greenwich Hospital (Pennypacker, *op. cit.*, 513). We hear no more of the *Quedagh Merchant,* which contained far greater treasure.

[9] The following day Captain Thomas Gullock presented a petition to the Council in person craving pardon for his miscarriages, whereupon he was discharged and freed.

March 5, Tuesday, 1699/1700. Mr. Sergeant, Capt. Frary, Capt. Hill, Capt Checkly and my self goe to Cambridge over the Ferry, and acquaint Mr. Pemberton with the Church's Call, and their desire of his Acceptance. He makes a very sensible Answer as to the Weight of the Work, his own inability; hôp'd God would hear his earnest Prayer, and help him to make a right Answer. Din'd at Remington's, Mr. Flint, Fitch, and Blower din'd with us: visited Mr. Brattle, came home round: Saw a man plowing at Muddy River; breaking up a Pasture with two oxen and a horse.

March 7*th* Mrs. Williams dies.

March, 11*th* 1699. 1700. Town-Meeting, chose Seven Select-men; Mr. Daniel Oliver, Mr. Isa. Tay, Mr. Joseph Prout, Mr. Jn° Maryon jun^r Capt. Tim° Clark, Mr. Elizur Holyoke, Mr. Obadia Gill, Mr. James Taylor Treasurer, Wm Griggs Town-Clerk. 5 overseers of the Poor; Elisha Hutchinson esqr. 38, Mr. Saml Lynde, 33, Mr. Jn° Eyre 31, Mr. Nathl Oliver 30. Capt. Nathl Byfield, 23. Constables, Benja Fitch, 90. Henry Hill, 83. William Man 63. Wm Welsteed 61. Joseph Billing, 57. Wm Clark jun^r 45. James Gooch, 40. Joseph Dowden 67. Jose Winthrop constable of Rumney-Marsh.

Surveyors of High Ways. Tho Walker, Stephen Minott, Jacob Melyen, Jn° Goodwin sen^r

Voted to raise Money;

Stock to set poor on work	£500
To maintain impotent poor	400
Schools, Bells, &c.	300
To mend the Way over the Neck	200
	£1400. 0. 0

Capt. Byfield was Moderator; had Candles, broke up at 8. Began at 10 m. Mr. Colman began with Prayer. Capt. Byfield dismiss'd the Assembly with Prayer.

Tuesday, March, 19. 1699/1700. Three young men: viz. Robert Cunable, Wm Salter, and Tho. Comer, went in a Canoo a Gunning before day-light, and were drowned. Wind high, and wether cold. Only James Tileston was saved.

March 21. Mrs. Martha Collins dieth.

March, 23. She is buried between 5 and 6. p.m. Bearers Lt Govr Stoughton, Mr. Russel, Sewall, Lynde, Byfield, Hayman. Mr. Cooke was at the funeral. Col. Phillips not well. Had Gloves and Rings. The under-bearers were honest men. I took my cousin Moodey, minister of York, over with me. Mr. Leverett there. Mr. Bradstreet the minister. Snow'd hard as we came home.

Monday, March, 25, 1700. Set out with Mr. Cooke for Plimouth, visited Mr. Torrey, staid near 3 hours, then to Mr. Norton's where Maj^r Genl Winthrop came to us late, so got late to Sittiate to Mr. Cushings, lodg'd there just by the ruins of Mr. Chauncey's house. Maj^r Genl had appointed to visit said Cushing. Were so belated that fail'd Maj^r Thomas, who with some other Gentlemen waited for us at the old Ferry on Marshfield side.

Tuesday, March 26. The wind is very bleak that it was ready to put me into an Ague, having rid late the night before. Had a noble Treat at Maj^r Thomas's. Mr. Sheriff and his Gentlemen were so wearied that they were afraid of some Miscarriage at the Ferry. Began the Court about five. Wednesday and Thorsday were extravagantly stormy. On Friday Mr. Cooke comes home but the wind was strong in my face, and cold that I durst not venture. Satterday was also very cold and chose rather to keep the Sabbath at Plimouth than by the way. Staid at Plimouth. At Noon was a Contribution for one that had his house burnt. Mr. Little invited me to sup with him, which I did.

Monday, April, 1. I was in a great quandary whether I had best, to avoid the wind, come home by water and leave my Horse, or no. At last I went on board Elisha Hedge's decked sloop laden with Oyle. He put in there in the storm from Yarmouth and lay till now for a wind. Came aboard about 2 hours by Sun, and landed at Mrs. Butlers Wharf before 3 p.m. Having had a very speedy and pleasant Passage, wherein I have experienced much of God's parental pity towards me, and care over me. I could not have got home to day by Land: and I fear my health would have been much impair'd, if I had come but part of the way. Jonathan Wheeler ridd in the Rain from Milton. I have now kept one Sabbath with those who first kept Sabbaths in New England;[10] *viz.* March, 31. 1700. At coming ashoar I met with the Lt Govr at Mr. Secretarys, and had their welcome.

Apr. 8. 1700. Mr. Turfrey is made Capt of Saco-Fort, and Truckmaster with the Indians, in stead of Capt. Hill.

Apr. 9. 1700. Snow covers the Ground.

---

[10] The M.H.S. editors wrote: "We must interpret this remark as merely meaning that Sewall spent the Sunday at Plymouth. To take a literal meaning, we should infer that he had met some survivor of the Pilgrims; but this seems improbable." We can add that Mary (Allerton) Cushman, a *Mayflower* passenger, survived until 28 November 1699, and that Sewall called on her in Plymouth 8 March 1696/7. Captain Peregrine White, born on the *Mayflower* after it had reached Cape Cod Harbor in December 1620, lived until 20 July 1704 at Marshfield, but there is no record that Sewall ever met him.

Sabbath, Apr. 14. I saw and heard the Swallows proclaim the Spring.

Fifth-day, Apr. 18. 1700. Mr. Cooke, Mr. Addington, Mr. Willard, Mr. Estabrooks and his Son Daniel come to my house and here adjust their Matters in difference relating to Mrs. Abigail Estabrookes and her Father—and brother in Law. Mrs. Abigail pass'd a Deed to Daniel last Summer, and he a Mortgage to her: Abigail being dissatisfied in the Mortgage, makes a Deed of the same Land to Capt. S. Checkly and Records it: It was a surprise to me to see it, and I express'd my Dislike of it in Terms that Mr. Willard could hardly bear. Said twas contrary to all Goodness, or words to that purpose. However I press'd that Daniel would give up his Deed, and Abigail her Mortgage; and that Capt. Checkly should give Daniel a Deed; that so this Fraudulency might not remain to be seen. It rain'd hard, and Mr. Estabrook and his son lodg'd here. *Ap. 19.* I gave Mr. Estabrooks 20ˢ to buy his Grandson Benjamin a Coat.[11]

Apr. 19. Sam. is sent for to be a Bearer to Mr. Eyre's Son, a very likely child, who dyed yesterday. I had that very day, Ap. 18, accidentally lit upon, and nail'd up the verses on Jnº; who dyed Novʳ 30. 1696.

April, 22. 1700. Mr. Sheriff Gookin, by Execution, delivers me and Cous. Anna Quinsey, Mr. H. Usher's House and Ground on the Common, And we introduce Madam Usher, *mane. Ap. 23, 24.* Tenant Wiar goes out. *Apr. 26.* Mrs. Usher removes thither to dwell. I send her a Cord of Wood that came from Muddy-River.[12]

Monday, Apr. 29, 1700. Sam. Sewall, Josiah Willard Jnº Bayly, Sam. Gaskill, and *[blank]* Mountfort goe into the Harbour a fishing in a small Boat.[13] Seeing Richᵈ Fifield coming in, some would needs

[11] Abigail Estabrook was one of the twenty children of Sewall's pastor, Samuel Willard. She had lost her husband, Rev. Benjamin Estabrook of Lexington (Harvard 1690) in 1697. The entry gives the impression that Abigail's lawless deeding of a piece of land for the second time was settled amicably, for her father-in-law, Rev. Joseph Estabrook of Concord (Harvard 1664) remained at Sewall's overnight and went off the next day with a gift for Benjamin junior. Abigail married the Rev. Samuel Treat of Eastham (Harvard 1669) 29 August 1700. *Sibley* IV, 56.

[12] At this point Sewall copied into his diary an extract from a letter of Hugh Adams (Harvard 1697), minister in Charleston, South Carolina, to his brother John Adams, shop-keeper in Boston, dated 23 February 1699/1700, describing the ravages of the plague in Charleston. He noted the death of John Cotton (see 1 October 1697) and that of his mother, Avis Adams, "being infected by means of tending Mr. Cotton all the time of his sickness, which was but three days."

[13] Josiah Willard (Harvard 1698) was the son of Samuel Willard of the South Church. Ebenezer Mountfort (Harvard 1702) became a merchant in Boston.

meet the ship and see who it was: Ship had fresh way with a fair wind; when came neare, Capt. call'd to them to beware, order'd what they should doe. But they did the clear contrary, fell foul on the ship, which broke their Mast short off, fill'd the Boat with water, threw Willard and Gaskill into the River. Both which were very near drown'd; especially Gaskill, who could not swim. It pleas'd God Fifield's Boat was out, so he presently man'd it and took them in. Gaskill was under water, but discover'd by his Hat that swam atop as a Buoy. Sam, Jn° Bayly and Mountfort caught hold of the Ship and climbed on board in a miserable fright as having stared death in the face. This is the second time Sam has been near drown'd with Josiah Willard. Mother was against his going, and prevented Joseph, who pleaded earnestly to go. He sensibly acknowledged the Good Providence in his staying at home, when he saw the issue.

1. A Narrative of the Portsmouth Disputation between Presbyterians and Baptists at Mr. Williams's Meetinghouse.

2. Bp. of Norwich's Sermon of Religious Melancholy.

3. Amintor, a defence of Milton with Reasons for abolishing the 30th Jan.

4. An Account of the first Voyages into America by don Barthol de las Casas   4s.

5. Account of a Jew lately converted and baptis'd at the Meeting near Ave Mary-Lane.

The President desires me to send for the above mentioned Books.[14]

Monday May 13. 1700. Mr. Wheelwright dies. This day p.m. I set out towards Kittery, Lodge at Salem.

May 14. Get to Newbury a little before sunset, visit my sick Father

---

[14] On 1 July 1700 Sewall wrote to John Love in St. Lawrence Lane to order the books requested by Increase Mather (*L.B.* I, 239). We have been able to identify all the titles except the last. 1. *A True Narrative Of the Portsmouth Disputation, Between some Ministers of the Presbyterian, and others of the Baptist, Persuasion, concerning the Subjects and Manner of Baptism: Held in Mr. William's Meeting-place there on Wednesday, Feb. 22. 1698/9*. The Third Edition (London, 1699). 2. Two editions were published in 1692 of Dr. John Moore's sermon, *Of Religious Melancholy*, preached before the Queen at Whitehall, 6 March 1691/2. 3. *Amyntor: Or, A Defence Of Milton's Life*, by John Toland, published in London in 1699, undertakes to prove that *Eikon Basilike* was written by John Gauden, Bishop of Worcester, and not by Charles I, who was executed 30 January 1649. 4. *An Account Of the First Voyages and Discoveries Made by the Spaniards in America. Containing The most Exact Relation hitherto publish'd, of their unparallel'd Cruelties on the Indians, in the destruction of above Forty Millions of People . . . By Don Bartholomew de las Casas, Bishop of Chiapa* (London, 1699).

in bed, call in the Major Gen¹ whom Father salutes. Kiss'd my hand, and I his again. Mr. Tappan came in and pray'd with him and us.

May, 15. Walks into the west end of the house with his staff, breakfasts there. I read the 17ᵗʰ Luke, and went to Prayer. My father would have stood up but I persuaded him to sit still in his chair. Took leave and went on to Portsmouth. Majʳ Gen¹ and I lodge at Col. Parkers. Most Gentlemen out of Town, some at Mr. Wheelrights funeral and som abᵗ Business. Mr. Hirst and Geoffries welcom'd us to Town. *May 16ᵗʰ* goe to Spruce-Crick and hold Court at Mr. Curtis's. Cousin Moodey comes thither and tells me of his son born that morn when sun about 2 hours high. Return in the night to Portsmouth.

May, 17ᵗʰ Benj Moss junʳ is sent to me to acquaint me that my dear Father died the evening before. It rains hard. Holds up about 5 p.m. I ride to Hampton, lodge at Mr. Cottons, where am very kindly entertained.

May, 18ᵗʰ ride to Newbury in the Rain; when breaks up, Broʳ and Sister come from Salem. Bury my Father, Bearers, Col. Peirce, Mr. Nich. Noyes, Mr. Sam. Plummer, Mr. Tristram Coffin, Major Dan¹ Davison, Major Thomas Noyes, had 8 Underbearers.

Sabbath, May. 19. Mr. Tappan in the afternoon preach'd a funeral Sermon from Prov. 19. 20. Said my Father was a true Nathanael: Mention'd 3 or four other deaths which occasion'd his discourse: gave a good character of most of them. *May,* 20. Rains hard, holds up in the afternoon. Major Gen¹ and Mr. Cooke come to Newbury in the night.

May 21, ride to Ipswich: Sheriff, Mr. Harris, and Major Epes meet us at Rowley. Give no Action to the Jury till after dinner. Lodge at Mr. Rodgers's where am very kindly entertain'd.

May 23. Mr. Rogers preaches very well of the Divine Efficiency in Mans Conversion, from Philip. 2. 13. Invite the Ministers to dinner, There are Mr. Hubbard, Rogers, Mr. Gerrish, Mr. Payson, Mr. Capen, Mr. Green, Mr. Rolf; last did not dine.

May 24ᵗʰ set out for Salem about an hour by sun, Mr. Joseph Woodbridge with me, Got to Brothers a little before Nine, met there Mrs. Anne Woodbridge. Proved my Fathers Will. *May* 25. 1700 went homeward in company Mrs. Anne as far as Col. Paiges. Got home about 3 aclock, found all well, Blessed be God. My Wife provided Mourning upon my Letter by Severs, All went in mourning save Joseph, who staid at home because his Mother liked not his cloaths. Sister Short here, came from Newbury the morn father died, and so miss'd being at the funeral. It seems about a 14night before, upon discourse of going to Meeting, my Father said, He could not goe, but hôp'd to goe shortly to a Greater Assembly. The Lord pardon all my sin of omission and commission towards him, and help me to prepare to Dye. Accept of any little Labour of Love towards my dear Parents. I had just sent four pounds of Raisins, which with the Canary were very refreshing to him.

Worthy Mr. Hale of Beverly was buried the day before my father. So was Mr. John Wadsworth of Duxbury, who died May, 15th 1700. I used to be much refreshed with his company when I went to Plimouth; and was so this last time. He gave me an account of the beginning of their Town, and of his Fathers going over to fetch Mr. Partridge.[15]

Friday, June, 7th 1700. mane, the Govr nominates Major Jno Walley for a Judge of the Superr Court, gives time of consideration till after dinner, Then give in Yes and No in papers. Said Walley had all present save his own and one No. Col. Hathorne was absent. I think had 25 Papers written YES. Chose Mr. John Clark a Justice Peace in Boston and many other; Justices of Inferior Courts, Coroners &c. Mr. Jno Wheelwright chosen Justice of Peace at Wells. Things were carried with Peace and comfortable unanimity.

Lords-day, June, 16, 1700. Mr. Daniel Oliver has his son Daniel baptised.

June, 17. Mr. John Eyre makes his Will in the morning, and dies in the Afternoon, an hour or 2. before Sunset. Born Febr. 19th 1653/4. I visited him on Satterday in the Afternoon: He was sitting up in his little Room, Took me by the hand at first coming in, Desired me to pray for him when took leave.

Fourth-day, June, 19. 1700. Mr. Jno Eyre is entombed in the new burying place. Nine of his children are laid there to handsel the new Tomb: Bearers, Sewall, Addington, Townsend, Byfield, Dummer, Davis: Scarvs and Rings. Lt Govr and many of the Council there. Mr. Thomas Brattle led his mourning widowed Sister. When I parted, I pray'd God to be favourably present with her, and comfort her in the absence of so near and dear a Relation. Having been long and much dissatisfied with the Trade of fetching Negros from Guinea; at last I had a strong Inclination to Write something about

---

15 Ralph Partridge (M.A. Cambridge 1603) had been curate of Sutton-by-Dover, Kent. He arrived in Boston in November 1636 and in 1638 became pastor of Duxbury, where he died in 1658 (Morison, *F.H.C.*, 393). John Wadsworth's father, Christopher, was an inhabitant of Duxbury as early as 1632 (*Savage*); if he went abroad to fetch Mr. Partridge, as the entry seems to say, this was a very unusual occurrence.

it; but it wore off. At last reading Bayne, Ephes.[16] about servants, who mentions Blackamoors; I began to be uneasy that I had so long neglected doing any thing. When I was thus thinking, in came Bro^r Belknap to shew me a Petition he intended to present to the Genl Court for the freeing a Negro and his wife, who were unjustly held in Bondage. And there is a Motion by a Boston Committee to get a Law that all Importers of Negros shall pay 40^s *per* head, to discourage the bringing of them. And Mr. C. Mather resolves to publish a sheet to exhort Masters to labour their Conversion. Which makes me hope that I was call'd of God to Write this Apology for them; Let his Blessing accompany the same.[17]

July, 8. 1700. Hannah rides in the Coach with her Mother to Mr. Thachers at Milton, to stay there awhile. Sister and Betty come to Town from Salem: *July,* 10th They go home. Waited on Mr. Mather this day, at three in the Afternoon. I told him the Honor of Athanasius, *Maluit sedem quam Fidei syllabam mutare:* Worthies of N. E. left their Houses in England, and came hither where there were none to preserve Religion in its Purity. Put him in mind how often God had renewed his Call to this work which was to be consider'd. That were 19 in the Council; and had every vote.[18]

Seventh-day, July, 13. My dear Mother comes hither by water from Newbury in one of the Poors. Set sail on Thorsday morning, and lodg'd aboard two nights in Marblehead Harbour: Capt. Norden and others would have had her come ashoar: but the wind was high and chose to keep on board. Jonathan Woodman jun^r waited on her to my house about 5. *p. mer^m.* Saw her not till just night; when brought in Mr. Cooke, Mr. Sergeant, E^m Hutchinson to drink, as they came from the Neck.

July, 17th The Ld Bellomont our Govr sets sail for New-york. [*In margin:* Exit Bellomont]

July, 25th 1700. Went to the Funeral of Mrs. Sprague, being invited by a good pair of Gloves.

Augt 2. 1700. Betty comes to Town from Salem. *Aug^t* 3. Bro^r comes to Town in the morning. I bring him going to the Ferry. About 2 *post merid,* Mr. Adam Winthrop dies. Between 3 and 4 I

[16] Paul Baynes, A *Commentarie Vpon The First Chapter of the Epistle of Saint Pavl, written to the Ephesians* (London, 1618).
[17] Here Sewall is referring to his anti-slavery tract, "The Selling of Joseph," which was printed 24 June 1700.
[18] This refers to a further attempt of the legislature to get Increase Mather, the President of Harvard, to reside at the college. The story can be found in Josiah Quincy, *Hist. of Harvard University* (1860) 1, 109f and K. B. Murdock, *Increase Mather* (1925), Chap. XIX.

receiv'd a Letter from the Justices of Northamptonshire, i. e. Partrig, Parsons, and Hawley to notify us that there is no Business requiring our going to Springfield this hot wether. We are very glad to be thus fairly discharged from this long and tedious journey.

Boston, 5th Augt 1700.

MADAM,—I present you with my greatest Respects and (nothing unknown intervening) will wait on you between the hours of eight and Nine this evening. Subscribe not my Name, you are not unacquainted with the hand: for as formerly, so I will remain an admirer of your person and Virtues. I expect the favour of your presence, as I am Madam your humblest Serv^a   STREPHON.[19]

Augt 7th 1700. Mr. Adam Winthrop is buried. Bearers Col. Hutchinson, Middlecott, Foster, El^m Hutchinson, Col. Townsend, Capt. Dummer. I rode with the Lt Govr in his Coach.

Lords day Augt 18. 1700. Henry Cole, Joseph's Schoolfellow, dies about 3 aclock *post mer.* of vomiting, Flux and Fever. Has been sick 12 or 13. days. His Father sent for me, and I pray'd with him in the morning. At 2 aclock I look'd on him and pray'd God to grant him that Favour and Loving Kindness of his that was better than Life. He thank'd me. In the morn, I ask'd him what I should pray for, He answer'd, that God would pardon all his Sin. Neighbour Cole had two Cows, and one of them is dead also. Henry was a forward towardly Scholar, and used to call Joseph every morning to goe to School.

Augt 30. 1700. A young hopefull Scholar is buried, Edward Mills's son by [*Mehitable*] Minot.

Wednesday, Augt 28. 1700. Mr. E[*benezer*] Pemberton is ordained [*minister of the South Church*]: He preached; then Mr. Willard Preached: Mr. Willard gave the charge: He, Mr. I. Mather, and Mr. Allen laying on Hands. Mr. I. Mather gave the Right Hand of Fellowship. Mr. Wigglesworth and Mr. Torrey were in the Pulpit, Mr. Hubbard of Ipswich and many Ministers below. A very great Assembly. All was so managed, as I hope does bode well, that the Blessing of God will accompany Him and us.

Septr 4th. 1700. Capt. Byfield and I took with us Peter Weare, and

[19] This letter, which has undoubtedly occasioned much speculation, some of it not flattering to Sewall, would have been stripped of its mystery if the M.H.S. editors had printed the marginal note added by the Rev. Samuel Sewall of Burlington, the last family ower of the diary. Mr. Sewall wrote: "Suppos'd a Letter from Mr. [Grove] Hirst to his [i.e. Sewall's] daughter Elizabeth. Vid. p. 212. Octr 17." On that MS page is Sewall's record of the marriage of Betty Sewall to Grove Hirst.

went to Mr. Gouge to warn him to leave my house at Cotton Hill. He acknowledged I had spoken to him about the 12 of Aug^t, and he would quit the house by the 12 or 14th of November next.

Thursday Septr 26th 1700. Mr. John Wait and Eunice his wife, and Mrs. Debora Thair come to Speak to me about the Marriage of Sebastian, Negro serv^t of said Wait, with Jane, Negro servant of said Thair. Mr. Wait desired they might be published in order to marriage. Mrs. Thair insisted that Sebastian might have one day in six allow'd him for the support of Jane, his intended wife and her children, if it should please God to give her any. Mr. Wait now wholly declin'd that, but freely offer'd to allow Bastian Five pounds, in Money per annum towards the support of his children per said Jane (besides Sebastians cloathing and Diet). I persuaded Jane and Mrs. Thair to agree to it, and so it was concluded; and Mrs. Thair gave up the Note of Publication to Mr. Wait for him to carry it to Wm Griggs, the Town Clerk, and to Williams in order to have them published according to Law.   As attests Sam Sewall J.

Lords Day Septr 29th 1700. Mr. Willard, by reason of sickness keeps house, and Mr. Pemberton preaches forenoon and Afternoon.

Note. from 11 to 2 p.m. it snows hard, covers the Houses and Ground, lodges on the Trees. Was very cold yesterday and to day.

Octr 2. Hanna comes home.

8^r 8th 1700. Is a Fast at the New-Meetinghouse to pray for Mr. Willard's Life. Mr. Colman, Wadsworth pray. Mr. Pemberton preaches: Philip. 1. 24. Mr. Allen, Cotton Mather Pray. 20th Psalm two staves and ½ sung L. Lt Govr, Mr. Russel, Cook, Addington, E^m Hutchinson, Townsend there. Mr. Fisk, Danforth, Walter, Brattle, out of Town. Pretty considerable congregation, it being so sudden, and first intended in privat.

8^r 10th 1700. Mr. Hirst asking my pardon, I told him I could forgive him, if he would never forgive himself; He fully assented to the condition: and said moreover that if ever he did the like again he would not expect or desire to be forgiven.[20]

---

[20] Hirst had apparently broken an appointment with his father-in-law to be. Sewall copied into his diary a letter written on the 6th: Sir, Speaking with my Son after your being here, I understand it will be inconvenient for you to come abroad this evening by reason of the solemnities of the day preceding. Besides, there is a Meeting of some of the South Ch[urch] occasioned by Mr. Willards Sickness; at which I am obliged to be. Therefore I shall not expect you, neither would I have you come till to morrow night. I thought good to signify thus much to you, who am, Sir, your friend and Servt

S.S.

To Mr. Grove Hirst, Merch^t in Boston, at Capt Ballentine's.

Octr 17th 1700. Capt. Theophilus Frary expires about 3 aclock past midnight.

In the following Evening Mr. Grove Hirst and Elizabeth Sewall are married by Mr. Cotton Mather. Present, I and my wife, Mr. Hirst and his wife, Bro^r St[*ephen*] Sewall of Salem and his son Sam, Brothers and Sisters of Bridegroom and Bride. Madam Usher, Capt. Ephra. Savage, Capt. Dummer and wife, Capt. Ballentine, Mrs. Mary Clark, Esther Wyllye, Margaret Stewart &c. Sung the 128. Psal. I set York Tune, not intending it. In the New Parlor.

Octr 18. Mr. Pemberton and Mr. Colman and his wife dine with us. Sent and Spent 21. Cakes.

Octob^r 20. 1700. In the Afternoon I and my wife, Mr. Hirst and his Bride, Sam. and Eliza Hirst, Will. Hirst and Hannah Sewall, James Taylor and Esther Wyllie, Joseph and Mary Sewall, walk to Meeting together.

Octr 30th Mr. Hirst comes and carries his daughter Betty to Salem. Mr. Grove Hirst and his wife accompany them.

Novemb^r 4th 1700. A Council was called at the Town-House. Present, The honorable William Stoughton Esqr. Lt Govr, Elisha Cooke, Elisha Hutchinson, Saml Sewall, Isaac Addington, Jno Foster, Peter Sergeant, John Walley, Eliakim Hutchinson, Penn Townsend, Nathanael Byfield, esqrs. Lt Govr ask'd Advice whether Benjamin Bedwell should be tryed by Commissioners of Oyer and Terminer; or at the Court of Assize and Genl Goal Delivery, to be held at Plimouth next March. Twas carried for the latter. A Proclamation was ordered to prevent endangering the Town by Fire-Works.[21]

Francis Hudson, Ferry-man, dyed last Lords-Day, Novr 3. Was one of the first who set foot on this Peninsula.[22]

Novr 10. 1700. Lords-day Madam Elizabeth Sergeant died in the Afternoon, half an hour past three. Was taken last Thorsday Sennight at night. Hath been delirious a great part of the Time, and hardly sensible since Friday.

Novr 11th Salem Court is adjourned by reason of Mr. Cooks Indisposition of Body.

Novr 12. Last night a considerable Snow fell which covers the

[21] The next day being the anniversary of the Gunpowder Plot.

[22] Francis Hudson, aged about sixty-eight years, made a deposition 10 June 1684 before Simon Bradstreet, Governor, and Samuel Sewall, Assistant, regarding the purchase of "his Estate and right in any Lands lying within the s^d neck of Land called Boston" from the first settler, William Blaxton (Blackstone), M.A. The deposition is printed in N. B. Shurtleff, *A Topographical and Historical Description of Boston* (1871, 1891), 296-297. The other deponents were John Odlin, William Lytherland, and Robert Walker (*ante* p. 141).

Ground several Inches thick. This morn Mr. Thomas Broughton expires about 87. years old: once a very noted Merchant in Boston, Select-man &c. About 3 years agoe he join'd to the North church. On Satterday-night I was with him when the President pray'd with him.

Novr 14. Madam Eliza. Sergeant is entombed, Bearers, Cooke, Hutchinson Elisha, Sewall, Addington, Foster, Walley. She was born Apr. 11. 1660. Maj^r Genl Winthrop was at the Funeral. He came last night from New-London.

Novr 14. 1700. about ½ hour past one in the Afternoon, Mr. Joseph Eliot dieth.[23] He was abroad on the Lords day at Meeting. I saw him in the street near his own house, about 8 in the morning. The Lord fit us for his good pleasure.

Novr 15th 1700. Mr. Tho. Broughton buried in the old burying place. Bearers, Sewall, Foster, E^m Hutchinson, Byfield, Howard, Fayerwether. No scarf. No Gloves. Went back again to the house.

Novr 16. Mr. Joseph Eliot was buried. Bearers, Capt. Alford, Capt. Checkley, Mr. Danl Oliver, Mr. Bennet, Mr. Cutler, Mr. Gibbs. 38. years old.

This day John Soams, the Quaker, dies. Was well this day sennight.

Novr 20th Mrs. [*Mary*] Lynde (formerly Richardson) was buried: Bearers, Cook, Sewall, Addington, Dummer, Dering, Gibbs. Scarf and Ring.

Novr 21. 1700. Day of publick Thanksgiving. At 3. *post merid^m* Mr. Willard comes abroad and Prays to the great Refreshment of the Congregation. This the first time since his sickness. In the evening I made these verses on it, viz,

> As Joseph let his brethren see
> Simeon both alive, and free:
> So JESUS brings forth Samuel,
> To tune our hearts to praise Him well.
> Thus He with beams of cheerfull light,
> Corrects the darkness of our night.
> His Grace assists us in this wise
> To seise, and bind the Sacrifice.

Monday, Novr 25th 1700. Prime brôt me a horse to Winnisimmet, and I ridd with him to Salem.

---

[23] Joseph Eliot (Harvard 1681), son of Deacon Jacob Eliot, was 36; he left a wife, Silence, and four children. *Sibley.*

Upon Mr. Samuel Willard, *his first coming into the Assembly, and Praying, after a long and dangerous Fit of Sickness;* November 21. 1700. *at* 3. *in the Afternoon, being a Day of Publick* THANKSGIVING. *Mr.* Pemberton's *Text,* Psal. 118. 27.

AS *Joseph* let his Brethren see
    Simeon both alive, and free :
So *JESUS* brings forth *Samuel,*
To tune our hearts to praise Him well.

Thus He with beams of cheerful Light
Corrects the darkness of our Night :
His Grace assists us in this wise
To seise and bind the Sacrifice.

Distressing Fear caus'd us to Pray *
God help'd us; He will help us aye.
Let's then our Ebenezer raise,
And honour GOD with endless Praise.

    * *October,* 8*th.* 1700.

Novr 26th Sup'd at Mr. Hirst's in company of said Hirst, his wife, Mrs. Betty Hirst, Mr. Noyes and my Brother. *Novr 28.* Court rose. Mr. Higginson was not at Lecture nor abroad this Court; so miss'd the pleasure of dining with Him. Visited him at his house and his sick wife. Madam Bradstreet, Mrs. Batter in Bed. Mrs. Jn° Higginson the 2^d Set out to come home about ½ hour past two in the Afternoon: came by Charlestown. Very cold going, abiding there, and Returning. Yet hope have taken very little hurt through the Goodness of God.

Major Walley has a swell'd face that keeps him from Meeting on the Sabbath xr. 1. 1700.

Novr 30th My Aunt Quinsey dieth of the Jaundice befôr break of day.[24]

Thorsday, xr. 5th 1700. Sam. and I ride to the Funeral of Aunt Eli. Quinsey. Because of the Porrige of snow, Bearers—Mr. Torrey, Fisk, Thacher, J. Danforth, Wilson, Belchar—rid to the Grave, alighting a little before they came there. Mourners, Cous. Edm^d and his Sister rid first, then Mrs. Anna Quinsey, widow, behind Mr. Allen; and cous. Ruth Hunt behind her Husband; then Sam. and I. None of the Gookins there. Mr. Torrey prayed. Bearers had Rings and Wash-Lether Gloves. I had Gloves and a Ring. Cous Edm^d invited us; so I lodg'd there all night, with Mr. Torrey, Sam. with his Cousin. All else went home. Cousin Savil was at Weymouth and came not. Funeral about 4. p.m.

Decr 6th Mr. Torrey and I and Sam. about 12 set forward and ride home; Find all pretty well, about 2 or 3 aclock, and good satisfaction as to our Lodging there. It Rain'd quickly after our getting home. Very foggy thawing wether.

Justice [*Daniel*] Cushing of Hingham died on Tuesday and, as is said, was buried this Thorsday.

[24] Aunt Quinsey was Elizabeth (Gookin) Eliot, the second wife of Edmund Quincy, Mrs. Sewall's uncle.

1701

WELCOMING THE EIGHTEENTH CENTURY / DEATH OF SEWALL'S
MOTHER / NEWS OF GOVERNOR BELLOMONT'S DEATH / JOSIAH
WILLARD PUTS ON A WIG / ARTILLERY ELECTION / LIEUTENANT-
GOVERNOR STOUGHTON'S LAST DAYS / JOURNEY TO THE EASTWARD
TO HOLD COURT / TRAINING DAY / LADY PHIPS MARRIES PETER
SERGEANT / COTTON MATHER DENOUNCES SEWALL / SALEM COURT /
SEWALL ABSENTS HIMSELF FROM SOUTH CHURCH

Jany 1. 1700/01. Just about Break-a-day Jacob Amsden and 3 other
Trumpeters gave a Blast with the Trumpets on the common near
Mr. Alford's [*in margin:* Entrance of the 18th Century]. Then went
to the Green Chamber, and sounded there till about sunrise. Bell-
man said these verses a little before Break-a-day, which I printed and
gave them. [*In margin:* My Verses upon New Century.] [1]

> Once more! our God vouchsafe to shine:
> Correct the Coldness of our Clime.
> Make haste with thy Impartial Light,
> And terminate this long dark night.
>
> Give the poor Indians Eyes to see
> The Light of Life: and set them free.
> So Men shall God in Christ adore,
> And worship Idols vain, no more.
>
> So Asia, and Africa,
> Eurôpa, with America;

[1] At the beginning of the twentieth century a similar observance was held in
front of the State House in Boston. Shortly before midnight of 31 December
1900, trumpeters gave a blast from the balcony, a chorus from the Handel and
Haydn Society sang Old Hundred, Sewall's verses, and America, and Dr. Hale
read part of the 90th Psalm. As the King's Chapel bell began to strike twelve,
trumpeters blew twelve blasts to welcome the new century (E. E. Hale, Jr., *Life
and Letters of Edward Everett Hale*, 1917, II, 372–373). On the facing page
we reproduce the enlarged version of Sewall's verses, a broadside appended to his
Proposals Touching the Accomplishment of Prophecies (1713).

WEDNESDAY, *January* 1. 1701.
A little before Break-a-Day, at *Boſton* of the *Maſſachuſets*.

ONCE more! Our GOD, vouchſafe to Shine:
Tame Thou the Rigour of our Clime.
Make haſte with thy Impartial Light,
And terminate this long dark Night.

Let the tranſplanted **Engliſh** Vine
Spread further ſtill :   ſtill Call it Thine.
Prune it with Skill :   for yield it can
More Fruit to Thee the Huſbandman.

Give the poor **Indians** Eyes to ſee
The Light of Life :   and ſet them free ;
That they Religion may profeſs,
Denying all Ungodlineſs.

From hard'ned **Jews** the Vail remove,
Let them their Martyr'd J E S U S love ;
And Homage unto Him afford,
Becauſe He is their Rightfull L O R D.

So falſe Religions ſhall decay,
And Darkneſs fly before bright Day :
So Men ſhall G O D in C H R I S T adore ;
And worſhip Idols vain, no more.

So **Aſia**, and **Africa**,
Europa, with **America** ;
All Four, in Conſort join'd, ſhall Sing
New Songs of Praiſe to CHRIST our K I N G.

All Four, in Consort join'd, shall Sing
New Songs of Praise to Christ our King.

The Trumpeters cost me five pieces 8/8. Gave to the College-Library Dr. Owens two last Volumes on the Hebrews. Sent them by Amsden. When was about to part with Dr. Owen, I look'd, to read some difficult place; pitch'd on v. 11th of the 8th Chapter—Know the Lord—I read it over and over one time and another and could not be satisfied: At last this came in my mind Know the Lord, i.e. Know the Messiah, to whom the word Lord is very much appropriated &c. *vide locum.* Now my mind was at quiet, and all seem'd to run smooth. As I hope this is Truth, so I bless God for this New-years Gift; which I also writt in a spare place, and gave it with the Book to the College.[2]

Jan[y] 2. 1700/01 Went afoot to Dorchester, carried Mr. Willard's Fountain open'd.[3] Eat Yokeheg[4] in Milk. L[t] Gov[r] orders me to wait on him next Tuesday morn.

Satterday, Jan[y] 4. 1700/01 Mrs. [*Deborah*] Thair is this morn taken with an Apoplexy after she had been up and employ'd a while; was at our pump for water. Dies about six in the Evening.

Between 2 and 3 in the Afternoon Mr. Sergeant, Col. Townsend, and I take the Affidavits of Batrth[*olomew*] Green, Jn[o] Allen and Tim[o] Green.[5] Present Mr. T. Brattle, Mr. Mico, and Tuthill notified.

[2] Dr. John Owen's four folio volumes of *Exercitations on the Epistle to the Hebrews* were published in London between 1668 and 1684. All of Sewall's donations to the library perished in the Harvard College fire of 24 January 1764. Amsden lived in Cambrdge and was a glazier; he died 11 June 1701. L. R. Paige, *Hist. of Cambridge* (1877), 480.

[3] Sewall was very fond of this work by his pastor, Samuel Willard, which was first published in 1700 with the title: *The Fountain Opened: Or, The Great Gospel Privilege of having Christ exhibited to Sinfull Men. Wherein Also is proved that there shall be a National Calling of the Jews From Zech. xiii. 1.* The first edition was printed in Boston by Bartholomew Green and John Allen for Samuel Sewall Jr., who was conducting a book business at this time. A second edition was printed in 1722 with a nine-page Appendix by our diarist, who appended a third edition of the work to the second edition of his *Phænomena Quædam Apocalyptica*, published in 1727, with an Appendix by himself dated 1 November 1727.

[4] Yokeheg (yokeage, rokeage) was an Indian dish made of Indian corn parched, pulverized, and mixed with sugar. *Dict. of Americanisms.*

[5] An anonymous tract, *Gospel Order Revived*, was printed in New York in 1700 in reply to Increase Mather's *Order of the Gospel* (Boston and London, 1700), mentioned in our footnote of 31 January 1699/1700. The author stated that "the Press in Boston is so much under the aw of the Reverend Author whom we answer, and his Friends, that we could not obtain of the Printer there to Print the following sheets . . ." Bartholomew Green, the Boston printer, **replied**

Mr. Nath¹ Oliver, Mr. Hern, Mr. Keeling: Mr. Hirst and my Son. I do not remember any more. Mr. Keeling, upon enquiry, what he call'd for pen and Ink for, whether twas to take notes or no: He own'd it was. Then I said I would also send for one to write, naming Mr. Barnard; so he forbore, and said he would not write.

Janʸ 7ᵗʰ Mrs. Thair is buried: By reason of the Court, Stars were seen before we went; but comfortably Light by remains of the Day. Moon-shine and Snow.

Bearers, Cook, Sewall, Addington, Oakes, Melyen, Maryon Jnᵒ. Buried in the new burying place, close to the Alms-house [*Granary*] Ground.

Friday, Janʸ 10. 1700/01. Mr. John Wait camc to me, and earnestly desired me to hasten consummating the Marriage between his Bastian and Jane, Mrs. Thair's Negro.⁶ This day I waited upon the Lᵗ Governour at Dorchester and spent about two hours in looking over and ordering Corporation Bonds, but brought none away with me. I shewed Mr. Green's paper, and asked his Honor's Leave to use his Name. Shew'd it in the morn to Col. Townsend at his own house, and to Mr. Sergeant at his, the night before. I had promised that nothing should be tack'd to their Names, but they should first have a sight of it.

BOSTON, Janʸ 13 1700/1701.

MADAM,—The inclosed piece of Silver, by its bowing, humble form, bespeaks your Favor for a certain young Man in Town. The Name [Real] the Motto [Plus ultra] seem to plead its suitableness for a Present of this Nature. Neither need you to except against the quantity: for you have the Mends in your own hand; And by your generous Acceptance, you may make both it and the Giver Great.   Madam, I am

Your Affectᵗ Friend   S.S.⁷

Janʸ 14ᵗʰ Having been certified last night about 10. oclock of the death of my dear Mother at Newbury, Sam. and I set out with John Sewall, the Messenger, for that place. Hired Horses at Charlestown: set out about 10. aclock in a great Fogg. Din'd at Lewis's with

---

to this statement with a handbill. The affidavits mentioned relate to this squabble, which is explained fully in T. J. Holmes, *Cotton Mather . . . Bibliography*, I, 317–320, and *I. Mather . . . Bibliography*, II, 385–397.

⁶ After almost two years of delay and red tape, "Bastian, Negro Servent to John Wait & Jane Lake, Negro Servent to Mr. Thair" were finally married by Sewall on 13 February 1700/01. *Boston Record Commrs. Report* XXVII, 2.

⁷ We take it that Sewall was playing Cupid for Samuel Junior, and that this letter was sent to Rebekah Dudley, whom the son married 15 September 1702. The square-brackets are Sewall's.

Mr. Cushing of Salisbury. Sam. and I kept on in Ipswich Rode, John went to accompany Bro[r] from Salem. About Mr. Hubbard's in Ipswich farms, they overtook us. Sam. and I lodg'd at Cromptons in Ipswich. Bro[r] and John stood on for Newbury by Moon-shine. *Jan*[y] 15th Sam. and I set forward. Brother Northend meets us. Visit Aunt Northend, Mr. Payson. With Bro[r] and sister we set forward for Newbury: where we find that day appointed for the Funeral: twas a very pleasant Comfortable day.

Bearers, Jn[o] Kent of the Island, L[t] Cutting Noyes, Deacon William Noyes, Mr. Peter Tappan, Capt. Henry Somersby, Mr. Joseph Woodbridge. I follow'd the Bier single. Then Bro[r] Sewall and sister Jane, Bro[r] Short and his wife, Bro[r] Moodey and his wife, Bro[r] Northend and his wife, Bro[r] Tappan and sister Sewall, Sam. and cous. Hannah Tappan. Mr. Payson of Rowley, Mr. Clark, Minister of Excester, were there. Col. Pierce, Major Noyes &c. Cous. John, Richard and Betty Dummer. Went ab[t] 4. p.m. Nathan[l] Bricket taking in hand to fill the Grave, I said, Forbear a little, and suffer me to say That amidst our bereaving sorrows We have the Comfort of beholding this Saint put into the rightfull possession of that Happiness of Living desir'd and dying Lamented. She liv'd commendably Four and Fifty years with her dear Husband, and my dear Father: And she could not well brook the being divided from him at her death; which is the cause of our taking leave of her in this place. She was a true and constant Lover of Gods Word, Worship, and Saints: And she always, with a patient cheerfullness, submitted to the divine Decree of providing Bread for her self and others in the sweat of her Brows. And now her infinitely Gracious and Bountifull Master has promoted her to the Honor of higher Employments, fully and absolutely discharged from all manner of Toil, and Sweat. My honoured and beloved Friends and Neighbours! My dear Mother never thought much of doing the most frequent and homely offices of Love for me; and lavish'd away many Thousands of Words upon me, before I could return one word in Answer: And therefore I ask and hope that none will be offended that I have now ventured to speak one word in her behalf; when shee her self is become speechless. Made a Motion with my hand for the filling of the Grave. *Note,* I could hardly speak for passion and Tears. Mr. Tappan pray'd with us in the evening. I lodg'd at sister Gerrishes with Joseph. Bro[r] and Sam. at Br. Tappans. *Jan*[y] 16th The two Brothers and four sisters being together, we took Leave by singing of the 90th Psalm, from the 8th to the 15th verse inclusively. Mr. Brown, the Scholar, was present.[8] Set out ab[t]

[8] Richard Brown (Harvard 1697) was schoolmaster at Newbury but did not get

11. for Ipswich, got time enough to hear Mr. Rogers preach the Lecture from Luke 1. 76. about ministerial preparation for Christ. Sung the nine first verses of the 132. Psalm. Mr. Rogers prai'd for the prisoner of death, the Newbury woman who was there in her chains. This is the last Sermon preached in the old Meeting-house. Eat Roast Fowl at Crompton's. Delivered a Letter to the Widow Hale; got very comfortably over the Ferry to Brothers, whether Mr. Hirst quickly came to welcome us and invite us to dine or breakfast next day, which we did, the morning being cold: Visited Madam Bradstreet and Major Brown, and told them of the death of their fellow-passenger. Rec'd me very courteously. Took horse about one p.m. Baited at Lewis's; Stop'd at Govr Usher's to pay him a visit.[9] He and his Lady being from home, we pass'd on, and got to Charlestown about Sun-set, very comfortably. Found all well at home through the Goodness of God.

Lords-Day, Jany 19th 1700/01 Ipswich people Meet the first time in their New- Meeting-House, as Deacon Knowlton informs me at Cousin Savages Meeting Jany 22th

Jany 29th 1700/01. Sam. and I went to Dedham Lecture, and heard Mr. Belchar preach excellently from Mat. 9. 12. Dined at said Belchars. Gave him and some young men with him my New-years verses: He read them and said Amen. Said twas a good Morning's Work.

Jany 30. Mr. Willard preaches from Eccles. 9. 2.—he that sweareth and he that feareth an Oath. Spake very closely against the many ways of Swearing amiss.[10] Great Storm.

Febr. 1. 1700/01 p.m. Waited on the Lt Govr and presented him with a Ring in Remembrance of my dear Mother, saying, Please to accept of the Name of one of the Company your Honor is preparing to go to. Mr. Baily, Oliver, and Chip were there when I came in.

Febr. 3. 1700/01. Little Richd Fifield, a child of ½ a year old, died very suddenly last Friday, and was buried this day. Mr. Simon Willard, and S. Sewall [the son] Bearers. Very windy and cold after the Rain.

---

on well with the townspeople; he was finally settled in the ministry at Reading.
[9] John Usher was treasurer of Massachusetts, councillor under Joseph Dudley, and lieutenant-governor of New Hampshire. His house in Medford, subsequently enlarged by Isaac Royall, merchant of Antigua, and his son Colonel Isaac Royall, is still standing and open to the public.
[10] Willard's sermon, published in Boston in 1701, was entitled The Fear of an Oath. Or, Some Cautions to be used About Swearing, If we would approve our selves Truly Godly. Sewall gave away five dozen of them 1 January 1703/4.

Satterday, Febr. 15 1700/01. News comes by Myles from England in a Gazett of Decr 2^d of the D[*uke*] of Anjou, the new K[*ing*] of Spain, taking his journey for Spain setting out from Versalles. Cardinal Albani, born 1650, is made Pope, takes the name of Clement the Eleventh. Gazett is printed here this day. Just about 3 in the Afternoon I went to the Maj^r General's; look'd upon Mingo who lies extream sick; then discoursed him in the Hall on the right hand where his pictures hang.

Tuesday, March, 4. 1700/01. Mrs. Anne Woodbridge is buried at Roxbury.

Satterday, March. 8. 1700/01. Ballard, from Barbados, brings News of the death of James Taylor at Barbados; Capt. Crow writes also of the Report they had that Jamaica was Sunk; which much saddens the Town.

Thorsday, March, 13. Turin,[11] that was blown off to Barbados, arrives. Was at Mr. Taylor's funeral Jany the last, Friday, (the day little Fifield died) And gives a more distinct account of the fears of Jamaica being sunk: and of Rumors of Wars between England and France: the Preparations at Martinico; and sending six Companies to St Christophers.

Satterday, March. 15th 1700/01 The Town is fill'd with the News of my Ld Bellomont's death, last Wednesday was sennight.[12] The Thorsday after, a Sloop set sail from N. York to Say-Brook; Mr. Clark, a Magistrate, carries it to New-London; from thence Mr. Southmayd brought it by Land last night, Capt. Belchar acquainted Mr. Secretary with it about 9 aclock last night. Upon this the Assembly is prorogued to Wednesday, the 16th April, at 9 *mane*.

Tuesday, March, 18th Last night I heard several Claps of Thunder: Great Fogg to day.

Wednesday, March, 19. We hear by the way of Virginia, that War is proclaimed between England and France.

Satterday, March 22. 4. *p.m.* The awfull News of the Lord Bellomont's death March 5th, 6. in the morn, 1700/01; is confirmed by Letters received by the Posts! The Town is sad.

Apr. 7th 1701. Last Satterday News was brôt by the Post of my Lord's Interment, March 27: So 46. Guns were ordered to be fired at the Castle, and 22. at the Sconce: were fired about 6. p.m. Have

[11] One of the Turrells, a seafaring family of Boston; the name is spelled Turin, Turinge, and Turrell in the town records.

[12] The unhappy Lord Bellomont died in Manhattan 5 March 1700/01. His remains are now interred in St. Paul's Churchyard, but no monument commemorates him.

warm discourse about the sitting of the Court. Lt Govr would have it dissolv'd; most of the Council are for its sitting. The Artillery Company gave three Volleys in the middle of the Town when they came out of the field, with regard to my Lord. Col. Townsend wears a Wigg to day.

Monday, Apr. 14th I ride and visit Mr. Trowbridge, who is still very feeble, and has been many months confin'd. From thence to Mr. Hobart's, with him to Sudbury, where we dine at Mr. Sherman's. From thence to Mr. Brinsmead's. He was much refresh'd with our company. Day was doubtfull: But got very well thither, and when by Mr. Brinsmead's fire, it Rain'd and hail'd much. Lodg'd at Mr. How's.[13]

Apr. 15th Mr. Torrey, Mr. Danforth of Dorchester, Mr. Swift came to us from Framingham to visit Mr. Brinsmead: He said twas as if came to his Funeral: If he were ready wish'd it were so. After dinner Mr. Hobart and I come home.

I staid and baited at the Greyhound, and got home between 8 and 9 very comfortably.

Satterday, May. 3. Mr. Daniel Olivers little Son is buried.

May, 28. 1701. Mr. Cooke, Addington, Walley, and self goe in my Coach and meet the Lieut Govr; met the Guard and his Honor near the first Brook. Mr. Belchar preaches; Lt Govr, notwithstanding his Infirmities, was an Auditor.

May, 29th The election [*of Councillors, or Magistrates*] is sent in. Lt Govr Approves all but Mr. Corwin, and to him he demurrs, taking some time of Consideration. Mr. Corwin said he acquiesced in it, and quickly went away, saying I humbly take my leave.[14] Mr. Eliakim [*Hutchinson*] pray'd he might be excused; he could not accept, He had sold most of his Interest in the Province of Main; and perceiv'd there was a desire among the Deputies that persons on the place might serve. In the evening Mr Cooke, Secretary, major Brown, Mr. Sergeant and I waited on Mr. Eliakim Hutchinson, and perswaded him not to decline serving. He treated us with Canary.

All the rest were sworn that were present. Major Walley and I wait on Mr. Belchar at Mr. Wadsworth's and give him the Thanks of Lt Govr and Council for his Sermon, and desire a copy.[15] This day

---

[13] Howe's Tavern at South Sudbury, built in 1686, has been called the Wayside Inn since Longfellow's time. William Brinsmead Jr. (Harvard ex-1655) was minister of Marlborough; he died 3 July 1701.

[14] The election of Jonathan Corwin was finally approved 3 June.

[15] Joseph Belcher of Dedham preached the election sermon; he called it *The Singular Happiness* (Boston, 1701).

a Burlesque comes out upon Hull-street, in a Travestie construing my Latin verses.

Mr. Howard's Daughter [*Sarah*] is married.[16] The President refused to be among the Ministers at their annual Meeting.

Monday, June. 2. 1701. Mr. Pemberton preaches the Artillery Sermon, from Luke. 3–14. Dine at Monk's. Because of the Rain and Mist, this day, the election is made upon the Town-house, Sewall. Capt.;[17] Tho. Hutchinson Lieut.; Tho. Savage junʳ, Ensign.; Tho. Fitch, 1 Sergt.: Oliver Noyes 2: Hab. Savage 3: Charles Chauncy 4. Call'd down the Council out of the Chamber, set their chairs below; Col. Pynchon gave the Staves and Ensign. I said was surpris'd to see they had mistaken a sorry pruning Hook for a Military Spear; but paid such a deference to the Company that would rather run the venture of exposing my own inability, than give any occasion to suspect I slighted their call. To Sergᵗ Fitch, Doubted not but if I could give any thing tolerable words of command, he would mend them in a vigorous and speedy performance: was glad of so good a Hand to me and the Company (Mr. Noyes abroad in the Gally). To Hab. S[*avage*] The savages are souldiers *ex Traduce*; in imitation of his honrᵈ father, Uncle, and Grandfather, hop'd for worthy performances from him. To Ch. Chauncy, Had such a honor for your Grandfather and father, that was glad was join'd with me in this Relation. Drew out before Mr. Ushers, gave 3 volleys. Drew into the Townhouse again; sent Sergᵗ Chauncy for Mr. Pemberton, who said he was glad to see the staff in my hand; pray'd with us. Had the company to my house, treated them with bread, Beer, wine Sillibub. ——They order'd Capt. Checkly and me to Thank Mr. Pemberton for his Sermon, which we did on Tuesday, desiring a copy. *June, 4.* Broʳ comes to Town, I Treat him at Tilyes: goes home.

Tuesday, June, 10ᵗʰ Having last night heard that Josiah Willard[18] had cut off his hair (a very full head of hair) and put on a Wigg, I went to him this morning. Told his Mother what I came about, and she call'd him. I enquired of him what Extremity had forced him to

16 Sarah Howard became the wife of Daniel Wyborn.
17 Sewall was now captain of the Ancient and Honorable Artillery Company, an organization founded and chartered in 1638, which is still flourishing. Pemberton's sermon, *The Souldier Defended & Directed*, was printed in Boston in 1701 by B. Green and J. Allen for Samuel Sewall Jr.
18 Willard (Harvard 1698) was the son of Sewall's minister. Six months later, when Josiah was invited to preach in his father's pulpit, Sewall showed his displeasure by attending the Brattle Square Church that day.

put off his own hair, and put on a Wigg? He answered, none at all. But said that his Hair was streight, and that it parted behinde. Seem'd to argue that men might as well shave their hair off their head, as off their face. I answered men were men before they had hair on their faces, (half of mankind have never any). God seems to have ordain'd our Hair as a Test, to see whether we can bring our minds to be content to be at his finding: or whether we would be our own Carvers, Lords, and come no more at Him. If disliked our Skin, or Nails; 'tis no Thanks to us, that for all that, we cut them not off: Pain and danger restrain us. Your Calling is to teach men self Denial. Twill be displeasing and burdensom to good men: And they that care not what men think of them care not what God thinks of them. Father, Bro⟨r⟩ Simon, Mr. Pemberton, Mr. Wigglesworth, Oakes, Noyes (Oliver), Brattle of Cambridge their example. Allow me to be so far a *Censor Morum* for this end of the Town. Pray'd him to read the Tenth Chapter of the Third book of Calvins Institutions. I read it this morning in course, not of choice. Told him that it was condemn'd by a Meeting of Ministers at Northampton in Mr. Stoddards house, when the said Josiah was there. Told him of the Solemnity of the Covenant which he and I had lately enterd into, which put me upon discoursing to him. He seem'd to say would leave off his Wigg when his hair was grown. I spake to his Father of it a day or two after: He thank'd me that had discoursed his Son, and told me that when his hair was grown to cover his ears, he promis'd to leave off his Wigg. If he had known of it, would have forbidden him. His Mother heard him talk of it; but was afraid positively to forbid him; lest he should do it, and so be more faulty.

June, 12. Mr. Willard marries Mr. Pemberton and Mrs. Mary Clark. All Mr. Willard's family there, as I am informed, and many others. Come to our Meeting the next Sabbath.

Monday, June, 30. L⟨t⟩ Gov⟨r⟩ said would go to the Commencement once more in his life-time; so would adjourn the Court to Friday, and did so. But was very much pain'd going home. Mr. Nelson, Secretary, and I visit him on Tuesday to disswade him from going, lest some ill consequence should happen. He consented, and order'd us to present his Bowl.[19] After Dinner and singing, I took it, had it fill'd up, and drunk to the president, saying that by reason

---

[19] There is every reason to believe that the Stoughton Cup, a handsome two-handled silver cup with cover, ten inches high, made by John Coney of Boston, presented by Lieutenant Governor Stoughton, and still at Harvard, is the vessel to which Sewall refers. It is illustrated in Morison, *H.C.S.C.* II, 469.

of the absence of him who was the Firmament and Ornament of the Province, and that Society, I presented that Grace-cup *pro more Academiarum in Anglia*. The Providence of our Soveraign Lord is very investigable[20] in that our Grace Cups, brim full, are passing round; when our Brethren in France are petitioning for their *Coup de Grace*. President [*Mather*] made no oration.

Friday, July 4. The court understanding the Lt Govr's growing illness, were loth to press him with business, and sent Mr. Secretary, me, Mr. Speaker and Mr. White to discourse his Honor, and propound an Adjournment. He agreed to it very freely. I said the Court was afflicted with the sense of his Honors indisposition; at which he rais'd himself up on his Couch. When coming away, he reach'd out his hand; I gave him mine, and kiss'd his. He said before, Pray for me! This was the last time I ever saw his Honor. *July 7th*, Mr. Cooke, Walley and I set out for Ipswich. About the time got thither the Lt Govr died.

July 8. Went to Newbury, eat Sturgeon at Major Davison's. Went to Hampton; from thence, having time, Major Walley and I with our Men, Bairsto and Hasting, went to Exeter; eat at Capt. Gilmans, Lodg'd at Mr. Clark's. *July 9*. Mr. Clark piloted us to Squamscot, where saw Govr Bradstreets daughter, Mrs. Wiggins. To Portsmouth. Lodg'd at Packers. In the Room where was told of my Fathers death, Govr Partridge told me of Mr. Stoughtons death Wednesday p.m.[21] Mr. Epaphras Shrimton writt it by the post. *July, 10*. Went to Kittery, Major Vaughan accompanied us. Lodge there at Spruce-creek. *July 11*. Major Wally and I ride to the [*Strawberry*] Bank. *July 12*. Bairsto and I alone goe to Newbury betime, over Carr's Bridge. Dine at Bro^r Toppans visit Arch. Woodman; lodge at sister Gerrishes.

July 13. *Lords-day*, Major Noyes shews me the Proclamation of the 10th publishing the Lt Governours death, and confirming Military officers.

July. 14, p.m. Mr. Cooke and Walley being now come to Town, rid towards Ipswich; I turn'd off to Cousin Dummers, visited her. Then to the Falls, Bro^r piloting us, lodge in Sister Moodey's Brick House; which has an excellent foundation.

[20] In this place Sewall wrote "2." The entry, though it begins 30 June, could not have been written before Wednesday, 2 July, the day commencement was held. *C.S.M.* xviii, 330–331.
[21] The cold-blooded William Stoughton (Harvard 1650) had been made lieutenant-governor and chief justice of the Superior Court of Judicature by the new charter of 1692 and served until his death, 7 July 1701.

July, 15*th* Funeral-day of L*t* Gov*r*. To Ipswich; Try Esther Rogers. Jury next morn ask'd advice, then after, brought her in Guilty of murdering her Bastard daughter. *July*, 17. Mr. Cooke pronounc'd the sentence. She hardly said a word. I told her God had put two Children to her to nurse: Her Mother did not serve her so. Esther was a great saviour; she, a great destroyer. Said did not do this to insult over her, but to make her sensible.

18. Rid to Salem in a little time, Sun almost down when went from Ipswich; yet got thither before the Bell rung. Lodg'd at daughter Hirst's. 19*th* ride home with my wife in a Calash with Joseph. Were in great danger by the pin of the Axeltree traping out, but Sam and Bairsto spied it and cried out before the wheel was quite worn off. 22. rid to Dorchester Lecture, only I was in the L*t* Governours Pue. 27. Go into mourning for the L*t* Gov*r* 30*th* Court sits.[22]

*Aug*t* 1. Choose Major Gen*l* [*Winthrop*] chief-justice, Mr. Saffin Justice, Mr. Cooke Judge Probats, without any mentioning the inconvenience of that authoritye resting in one mans breast. Capt. Byfield judge of Bristol-Court. Mr. Saffin had 14. They that sign'd his Commission are W. Winthrop, James Russell, Elisha Cooke, Jn° Hathorne, W*m* Browne, Elisha Hutchinson, Jonathan Corwin, Jn° Higginson, Peter Sergeant, Jn° Foster, Joseph Lynde, E*m* Hutchinson, Penn Townsend, Benj*a* Browne, John Thacher.

Have much adoe to get a number to sign the Maj*r* Gen*ls* Commission. If had not withdrawn his paper, suppose he would not have had a number; 'tis said Several Deputies have entered their dissent against the Agency.

*Aug*t* 11. Go down to the Castle to try to compose the differences between the Capt. and Col. Romer: Order that the Line next the Channel be presently finished with the Brick-Work. I told the young men that if any intemperat Language proceeded from Col. Romer, twas not intended to countenance that, or encourage their imitation: but observe his direction in things wherein he was Skillful and ordered to govern the work: or to that effect. Lest should be thought the Council had too much wink'd at his cursing and swearing, which was complained of.

*Aug*t* 19*th* Sign an order for Capt. Crow to cruise to Tarpolin Cove

---

[22] Sewall wrote in the margin: "Council has the Goverm*t*." By the death of both the governor (Bellomont) and the lieutenant-governor (Stoughton) the Council was placed in supreme control; it held power from 7 July 1701 until the arrival of Governor Joseph Dudley, 11 June 1702. John Saffin was chosen to fill the vacancy in the Superior Court caused by Stoughton's death, and Wait Still Winthrop was made chief-justice.

because of some suspected vessels there, as Govr Cranston informs.

Mr. Saffin takes his Oath, Mr. Secretary administers it, and Mr. Russel and Col. Hutchinson attest it. This morning, *vae malum*, Capt. Hunting accidentally shoots himself dead.[23]

Mr. E^m Hutchinson cut his hand last Satterday between his left Thumb and fore finger; It bled pretty much today. Came to Council but would not sign, because his right hand was occupied in holding his Left, to prevent bleeding. Mr. Sergeant sign'd for him at his Request.

Septr 8. rid to Rehoboth with Mr Cooke, Major Walley; Mr. Saffin went last week.

Sept. 9. to Bristow. Mr. Saffin and others met us near the Ferry. Peter Walker charg'd Mr. Saffin with urging a man to swear that which he scrupled to swear.

Septr 11. Mr. Saffin tampered with Mr. Kent, the Foreman, at Capt. Reynold's, which he denyed at Osburn's. Connived at his Tenant Smith's being on the Jury, in the case between himself and Adam [*a Negro*], about his Freedom. 7^r 12. Broke fast at Mr. Brenton's. Mr. Cooke and I rid to Billinges, near ½ the way in the night. 7^r 13. home between 12 and 1. Vessel arrives from England that brings News of Sir Henry [*Ashurst*] opposing Col. Dudley's being Govr: 4 of the Council; viz: Winthrop, Cooke, Hutchinson Elisha, Sergeant are said to have written to him.

Septr 17th. Wentworth arrives, in whom comes Capt. Richards and wife, Dudley Woodbridge, N. Henchman, Martin, Bonus, &c. Brings a Letter to the Lt Govr with a Bill of Lading for 50 Barrels powder given by the King.[24]

---

[23] Samuel Hunting of Charlestown was a sea-captain and the owner of the brigantine *Hannah and Mary*. Sewall recorded 20 July 1687 an affray at Charlestown in which he was stabbed.

[24] On this date Sewall wrote to Rev. James Pierpont of New Haven in reply to a letter from Israel Chauncy, Thomas Buckingham, Abraham Pierson, Gurdon Saltonstall, and Pierpont. These men, Harvard graduates and Connecticut parsons, were endeavoring to establish a collegiate school in that colony, and had asked Sewall's advice. He felt that they "should not be eagre in building a College [edifice] . . . But let the Scholars board in the Town, as it is in Holland . . ." In Academical Learning, the college should be like Harvard under Charles Chauncy. The president should "ground the Students in the Principles of Religion by reading to them or making them Recite the [Westminster] Assemblys Confession of Faith which is turned into good Latine, as also the Catechises; and Dr. Ames's Medulla." On 6 October 1701 Sewall and Isaac Addington wrote to Thomas Buckingham enclosing a draft of An Act for Founding a Collegiate School. The General Court of Connecticut later that month granted a charter to the school embodying much of the phraseology of the Sewall-Addington draft.

Monday, 7ʳ 29. Training of the Foot Company: In the Afternoon, I waited on Mr. Mather to desire his Appointmᵗ of a Meeting of the Commissioners [*of the Company for Propagating the Gospel*]. He tells me he is going to Lin tomorrow; and shall not return till next week: I tell him I will wait on him then.

Monday, Octʳ 6. 1701. Very pleasant fair Wether; Artillery trains in the Afternoon [*Sewall in command*]. March with the Company to the Elms; Go to prayer, March down and Shoot at a Mark. Mr. Cushing I think was the first that hit it, Mr. Gerrish twice, Mr. Fitch, Chauncy, and the Ensign of the Officers. By far the most missed, as I did for the first. Were much contented with the exercise. Led them to the Trees agen, perform'd some facings and Doublings. Drew them together; propounded the question about the Colours; twas voted very freely and fully. I inform'd the Company I was told the Company's Halberds &c. were borrowed; I understood the Leading–staff was so, and therefore ask'd their Acceptance of a Half-Pike, which they very kindly did; I deliver'd it to Mr. Gibbs for their Use.

They would needs give me a Volley, in token of their Respect on this occasion. The Pike will, I suppose, stand me in fourty shillings, being headed and shod with Silver: Has this Motto fairly engraven:²⁵

> *Agmen Massachusettense*
> *est in tutelam Sponsæ*
> *AGNI Uxoris.*
> 1701.

The Lord help us to answer the Profession. Were treated by the Ensign in a fair chamber. Gave a very handsome Volley at Lodging

---

Pierpont wrote to Boston at once (15 and 16 October) to announce the passage of the act, and Sewall replied 29 October telling him of the pleasure this gave to him and Addington. Sewall's letters are in the University Archives at Yale, and are printed in F. B. Dexter, ed., *Documentary History of Yale University* (1916), 7–9, 15–19, 26. Aside from a donation of books in October 1707, Sewall seems to have taken no further interest in the Collegiate School. It was Cotton Mather who suggested to Elihu Yale the donation which caused his name to be given to the institution. *Doc. Hist.,* 163–164.

²⁵ The silver ferule of this pike was in existence in 1910 and was the subject of a paper by Dr. Samuel Abbott Green in *M.H.S. Proc.* XLIII, 491–492. Sewall omitted the last two lines of the inscription, engraved by the silversmith as "Ex dono Honorabilis SAMUELIS SEWALL Armigeri." Dr. Green translates it: "The Massachusetts Company is for the protection of the Bride, the Wife of the Lamb [i.e., the church] 1701 By gift of the Honorable Samuel Sewall Esquire"; the scriptural reference is to Revelation, xxi, 9.

the Colours. The Training in Septr was a very fair day, so was this.

Thorsday, Octob^r 9th. 1701. Peter Sergeant Esqr. marries my Lady Mary Phips.[26]

Octr 10th Send my wife and me Gloves and Cake. Col. Hutchinson, Mr. Addington, Foster, Townsend, Bromfield, Stoddard, Burroughs, visit the Bridegroom and Bride, and sup there with Roast-Beef, Venison Pasty, Cake and cheese. Betty came yesterday to see us. Bro^r and his daughter came, and go home to day. Mr. Sergeant dwells at my Ladies house and Major Hobbie comes into his [*afterwards the Province House*].

Wednesday Octr 15. Court meets, draw up a new Address; send that and their former with the Memorial to Mr. Constantine Phips, with 100£ Sterling Money of England, for to recompence his former service.[27]

Octr 18., or thereabout, Mr. Foster and Cooke had a hot discourse about Mr. [*President*] Mather; Capt. Foster moving for a Quarter's Salary. I spake that he might have it.

.8^r 18. The Court is prorogued to the tenth of Decemb^r at 9 *mane.*

Octr 19. Mr. Sergeant and his Bride come to our Meeting forenoon and afternoon.

Octr 20. [*In margin:* Opprobrium. Mr. Cotton Mather speak hard words of me.] Mr. Cotton Mather came to Mr. Wilkins's shop, and there talked very sharply against me as if I had used his father worse than a Neger; spake so loud that people in the street might hear him. Then went and told Sam, That one pleaded much for Negros, and he had used his father worse than a Negro, and told him that was his Father.[28] I had read in the morn Mr. Dod's saying; Sanctified Afflictions are good Promotions. I found it now a cordial.

---

[26] Lady Phips, the widow of Sir William, was the daughter of Captain Roger Spencer of Saco, mariner. Her first husband was John Hull of Boston, a merchant, who was called junior to distinguish him from Sewall's father-in-law, the mint-master. *Savage.*

[27] Constantine Phipps, barrister of Gray's Inn, was agent of the Bay Colony in England from 1693 to 1710. He was knighted and made Lord Chancellor of Ireland in 1710. *D.N.B.*

[28] The full story of the ouster of Increase Mather from the presidency of Harvard by the Council can be read in Murdock's biography, Chap. XIX, The First Defeat. Cotton was fighting his father's battles, and he had heard rumors that Sewall's speech in the Council had been hostile to Increase. Sewall wrote Cotton a most irenic letter (*L.B.* 1, 263) asking him to meet with Major Walley and Captain Checkley at Richard Wilkins's bookshop on the 22d. When the Mathers had a chance to read exactly what had been said in the Council, they cooled off, and the breach was healed. K. B. Murdock, *Increase Mather*, 376.

And this caus'd me the rather to set under my Father and Mother's Epitaph,—Psal. 27. 10.

It may be it would be arrogance for me to think that I, as one of Christ's Witnesses, am slain, or ly dead in the street.

Octr 9. I sent Mr. Increase Mather a Hanch of very good Venison; I hope in that I did not treat him as a Negro.

8^r 20. Mr. Pemberton and his wife visit Daughter Hirst; pray with her.

Octob^r 22. 1701. I, with Major Walley and Capt. Saml Checkly, speak with Mr. Cotton Mather at Mr. Wilkins's. I expostulated with him from 1 Tim. 5. 1. Rebuke not an elder. He said he had consider'd that: I told him of his book of the Law of Kindness for the Tongue, whether this were correspondent with that. Whether correspondent with Christ's Rule: He said, having spoken to me before there was no need to speak to me again; and so justified his reviling me behind my back. Charg'd the Council with Lying, Hypocrisy, Tricks, and I know not what all [*in margin:* Surreptitious]. I ask'd him if it were done with that Meekness as it should; answer'd, yes. Charg'd the Council in general, and then shew'd my share, which was my speech in Council; viz. If Mr. Mather should goe to Cambridge again to reside there with a Resolution not to read the Scriptures, and expound in the Hall: I fear the example of it will do more hurt than his going thither will doe good. This speech I owned. Said Mr. Corwin at Reading, upbraided him, saying, This is the man you dedicat your books to! I ask'd him If I should suppose he had done somthing amiss in his Church as an Officer; whether it would be well for me to exclaim against him in the street for it. (Mr. Wilkin woud fain have had him gon into the inner room, but he would not.) I told him I conceiv'd he had done much unbecoming a Minister of the Gospel, and being call'd by Maxwell to the Council, Major Wally and I went thither, leaving Capt. Checkly there. 2 Tim. 2. 24, 25. Went to the Council, Sign'd Mr. Mather's order for £25. Hammer'd out an Order for a Day of Thanksgiving.

Thorsday, Octr 23. Mr. Increase Mather said at Mr. Wilkins's, If I am a Servant of Jesus Christ, some great Judgment will fall on Capt. Sewall, or his family.

Octr 24. Rainy Day, yet Judge Atwood comes from Rehoboth to Boston. 25. Visits several, and me among the rest. This day in the morn. I got Mr. Moody to copy out my Speech, and gave it to Mr. Wilkins that all might see what was the ground of Mr. Mather's Anger.

Writ out another and gave it to Joshua Gee. I perceive Mr.
Wilkins carried his to Mr. Mathers; They seem to grow calm. (On
Friday received Mr. Fitch's Letter and Blessing.) Receive the News
of Sister Sewall's being brought to Bed of a Son, which is the Sixth;
and the fifteenth Child. Messenger came in when Judge Atwood
here. Son Hirst comes to Town. Was in danger to be cast away
coming over the Ferry, the wind was so very high. Mr. Chiever visits
me this Afternoon.

Octob^r 28. 1701. Mr. William Atwood Takes the Oaths and sub-
scribes the Declaration and Association, to qualify himself to exercise his Authority here as Judge of the Admiralty.[29] He ask'd for a
Bible: but Mr. Cooke said our Custom was to Lift up the hand;
then he said no more, but used that Ceremony. His Commission was
first read before the Council. At going away, he thanked me for,
The Selling of Joseph, saying twas an ingenious Discourse.

Thus a considerable part of Executive Authority is now gon out
of the hands of New England men.[30]

Novr 1. 1701. Bastian has a Daughter born, he being at the
Castle; He calls her Jane. *Novr 2.* She is baptised by Mr. Allen;
Bastian holds her up. Deacon Isa. Tay is Ordained at the same
time; Mr. Allen and———Wadsworth [*Rev. Benjamin Wadsworth,
colleague minister of the First Church*] lay their hands on him.
Joseph went to that Meeting in the Afternoon, and brought us this
word. Hannah Davis, and Bumsteds daughter are taken into our
Church. *Monday, Novr 11. 1701.* Maj^r Genl Winthrop, Mr. Cooke,
Sewall, Saffin set out for Salem to keep Court. Going in the Calash
and benighted, I lodge at Hart's and go thence in the morning early.
Major Walley is released, and promises not to ask to stay at home
again, till I have had my Turn.

A complaint was prefer'd against Woodbridge at Newbury Court,
Jury cleer'd him. James Wise, the Complainant, Appeals. Action was
dismiss'd; because a man being Acquitted by a Jury, ought not to

[29] The M.H.S. editors noted that very little had been written about the officers
of the Crown during the colonial period. In Emory Washburn's *Judicial History
of Massachusetts,* 175, 185, it is stated that the first Judge of Admiralty was Wait
Still Winthrop, commissioned in 1699. Atwood succeeded him, with Thomas
Newton for deputy. In 1703 the district seems to have been divided, Roger Mompesson taking New York, and Nathaniel Byfield, Massachusetts, Rhode Island,
and New Hampshire. In 1715 Byfield was superseded by John Menzies, a Scots-
man, who died at Boston, 20 September 1728.

[30] A sentence burdened with much sad feeling for the writer as he marked the
steady transfer of authority to crown officials, while local government was im-
paired. M.H.S.EDS.

be Try'd again. Rioters that were fined Ten pounds apiece, were now fined twenty shillings, great pains having been used to bring them quite off; but the Jury confirm'd their former Judgment and were directed by the Court only to say Guilty. The Salem Justices were much disgusted at this management and sentence: I dissented from it as too small a Plaister for so great a Sore.

Satterday, Novr 15^*th*^ Went home. Major Genl Winthrop, Mr. Cooke, Saffin, Mrs. Anne, by Charlestown, I was forced to go to Winnisimmet; because my Horse was to be had back by Cous. Sam. Sewall. Had very comfortable going and coming home. Find all well. I lodg'd at my Son and Daughter Hirst's. *Laus Deo.*

Boston, N. E. Novr 19. 1701. The Court gave Sentence that the Law for Reviews bars Mr. Cooke &c. their Action against Col. Paige, Mr. Saffin was of that opinion also. Super. Court adjourn'd to Friday respecting Mr. Pain. In the Court held at Boston July 27. 1686, When Col. Paiges case was Tryed: Jury

Gervase Ballard	Francis Foxcroft
Benj. Alford	John Bird
Tho Clark	
Tobias Davis	
Willm Blake	
Joseph Crosby	
John Hersey	
Tho. Fuller	
Edw. Adams	
Nathan^l Stearns	

At the Court of Appeals, Novemb^r 2. 1686.

Joseph Lynde	
Samson Sheaf	Dudley
Francis Burroughs	Stoughton
William White	Bulkley
Daniel Brewer	Wharton
John Breck	Gedney
John Minott	Randolph
Peter Woodward	W. Winthrop
William Dean	Jno Usher
Samuel Goff	Edw. Tyng.
John Hammond	
John Morse	

Novr 23. 1701. John Joyliffe Esqr. dies. He had been blind, and laboured under many Infirmities for a long time. Mr. Brunsdon died the night before: and one Birds-eye a few days before; 3 men. Jno Arnolds wife is also dead. I wish it do not prove a sickly time after long Health.

Mr. Nicholas Noyes of Newbury, aged about 86 years, died on the Lords-Day 9^r 23. 1701. Mr. Oliver Purchas, late of Lin, now of Concord, is to be buried this week. Bearers of Mr. Joyliffe; Mr. Cooke, Addington, Sergeant, Anth. Checkly, El^m Hutchinson, Mr. Saffin.

Sabbath, Novr 30. I went to the Manifesto church to hear Mr. Adams; Mr. Coleman was praying when I went in, so that I thought my self disappointed. But his Prayer was short; When ended, he read distinctly the 137, and 138th Psalms, and the seventh of Joshua, concerning the conviction, sentence, and execution of Achan. Then sung the second part of the Sixty ninth Psalm. Mr. Brattle set it to Windsor Tune. Then Mr. Adams pray'd very well, and more largely: And gave us a very good Sermon from Gal. 4. 18. Doct. It is just and commendable &c. Mr. Adams gave the Blessing.

In the Afternoon Mr. Adams made a short Prayer, read the 139th Psalm, and the six and twentieth chapter of the Acts; Then Agrippa said——Sung. Mr. Coleman made a very good Sermon from Jer. 31. 33.—and will be their God, and they shall be my people.

Pray'd, sung—Contribution. Gave the Blessing. I spent this Sabbath at Mr. Colman's, partly out of dislike to Mr. Josiah Willard's cutting off his Hair, and wearing a Wigg: He preach'd for Mr. Pemberton in the morning; He that contemns the Law of Nature, is not fit to be a publisher of the Law of Grace: Partly to give an Example of my holding Communion with that Church who renounce the Cross in Baptisme, Humane Holydays &c. as other New-English Churches doe. And I had spent a Sabbath at the Old Church, and at Mr. Mathers. And I thought if I should have absented my self in the *forenoon* only, it might have been more gravaminous to Mr. Willards friends than keeping there *all day*. I perceive by several, that Mr. Coleman's people were much gratified by my giving them my Company, Several considerable persons express'd themselves so. The Lord cleanse me from all my Iniquity &c. Jer. 33. 8. and 16. which chapter read in course xr. 5th 1701.

Decr 24. 1701. Sam sets out for Newbury with Capt. Somersby; went away about ½ hour past 12.

1702

Jany 2. 1701/2. My Wife had some thoughts the Time of her Travail might be come, before she went to bed: But it went over. Between 4 and 5 m. I go to prayer, Rise, make a Fire, call Mrs. Ellis, Hawkins. Mary Hawkins calls Midwife Greenlef. I go to Mr. Willard and desire him to call God. The Women call me into chamber, and I pray there. Jn° Barnard comes to me for Money: I desire him to acquaint Mr. Cotton Mather, and Father.

Jany 2. 1701/2. My Wife is well brought to Bed of a Daughter just about two p.m., a very cold day: Was got into Bed without a fainting Fit.

Sabbath-day night my wife is very ill and something delirious. Pulse swift and high. I call Mr. Oakes about Two aclock or before. Grows a little better.

Jany 6. 1701/2. Nurse Hill watch'd last night. Wife had a comfortable night.

MEMORANDUM.

Sarah Sewall was born Novr 21. 1694. Baptised *per* Mr. Willard Novr 25. Died Decr 23. Was buried xr. 25. 1696.

A dear amiable Son of Samuel Sewall and Hannah his wife, was Still-born May, 21. 1696.

Judith Sewall was born upon Friday, Jany 2. at two in the Afternoon, Hannah Greenlef Midwife, Judd Nurse. Lords-Day, Jany 4. p.m., Was baptised by the Rever^d Mr. Ebenezer Pemberton. It being his Turn: because The Rev^d Mr. Willard administered the Lord's supper just before. So is a New Midwife, and a New Baptiser. What through my wives many Illnesses, more than ordinary, her fall upon the stairs about 5 weeks before; from which time she kept her chamber; her thoughtfullness between whiles whether she were with child or no; her Fears what the issue would be, and the misgiving of our Unbelieving hearts, GOD hath been wonderfully Merciful to us in her comfortable Delivery; which I desire to have Recorded.

Note. This is the Thirteenth Child that I have offered up to God in Baptisme; my wife having born me Seven Sons and Seven Daughters. I have named this little Daughter Judith, in Remembrance of her honoured and beloved Grandmother Mrs. *Judith Hull.* And it may be my dear wife may now leave off bearing.[1]

Jany 8. 1701/2 Mr. Incr. Mather preaches the Lecture from Gen. 18. 24. Doct[*rine*] The Wicked many times fare the better for the sake of the Godly, Hopes for England and N. E. because many Righteous ones in both. About 4. Alice Macdonnel is buried. Mr. Lynde and I were there as Overseers of the poor. This day agreed with Nurse Randal to suckle Judith.

Friday Jany 9. 1701/2 Buy a Wicker Cradle for Judith of Tho. Hunt; which Cost Sixteen Shillings.

My wife puts on her Cloaths, and sits up in the Bed.

Jany 10. My Wife gets on to the Pallat Bed in her Cloaths, and there keeps, while Linen Curtains are put up within the Serge; and is refresh'd by it.

Jany 12. 1701/2 The Harbour is open again, and pretty well freed from the Ice. *Jan^y* 13. *m.* I pray'd earnestly by my self and in the family for a Nurse; Went and expostulated with Mr. Hill about his daughters failing me; in the chamber: In the mean time, one of his family went and call'd the Nurse and I brought her home with me; which was beyond my expectation. For Mr. Jesse huff'd and ding'd, and said he would lock her up, and she should not come. I sent not for her, So I hope twas an Answer of Prayer.

Friday, Jany 16. My Wife Treats her Midwife and Women: Had a good Dinner, Boil'd Pork, Beef, Fowls; very good Rost–Beef, Turkey-Pye, Tarts. Madam Usher carv'd, Mrs. Hannah Greenlef; Ellis, Cowell, Wheeler, Johnson, and her daughter Cole, Mrs. Hill our Nurses Mother, Nurse Johnson, Hill, Hawkins, Mrs. Goose, Dem-

---

[1] Sewall, editorially and bibliographically punctilious, as befitted a former librarian of Harvard College and public supervisor of printing, here entered a reference to the list of his "former Children" recorded on an earlier page (13 September 1693). We have placed this material in our Genealogical Appendix.

ing, Green, Smith, Hatch, Blin. Comfortable, moderat wether: and with a good fire in the Stove² warm'd the Room.

*Jan*ʸ 17. We hear that Mrs. Sam. Brown of Salem is dead, and the first child she had. She earnestly desired a child, having been a pretty while married. Col. Turner's sister.

*Jan*ʸ 18. Storm of snow: but not very cold.

*Jan*ʸ 20. between 11 and 12. Farnum the Father, was pecking Ice off the Mill-wheel, slipt in and was carried and crush'd, and kill'd, with the wheel. Elder Copp and Mr. Wally came to call Cousin Savage at my house.

Note. Last night were under awfull apprehensions, lest the House was on fire, there was such smoke and smell in the cellar like as of a Colepit. Got Joseph Clark to view it and neibour Cole. Could find nothing. Cole suppos'd twas a Steem by reason of the cold. Many watch'd but found nothing. And blessed be God, the House is still standing.

*Jan*ʸ 22. 1701/2 Sam. comes home in company of his unkle Moodey, Broʳ and Sister Hirst. *Jan*ʸ 23. Broʳ Moodey goes home.

*Satterday, Jan*ʸ 24. 4 *post meridiem*. Mary Bowtel of Cambridge was burnt to death in her own fire, being in a Fit as is suppos'd. Her right arm, and left Hand, were burnt quite off; her bowels burnt out, &c. Coroner Green told us this at Charlestown, Janʳ 27. Tis very remarkable that two such awfully violent Deaths should fall out in one and the same week at Boston and Cambridge.

*Jan*ʸ 30. 1701/2 Cousin Moodey of York comes to see me: upon enquiry about a Hebrew word, I found he had no Lexicon; and I gave him my Buxtorf.³

*Jan*ʸ 31. 1701/2 William Parsons of 88 years, is buried. Was in the fifth-monarchy fray in London: but slipt away in the Crowd.⁴

2 This is the earliest American record of a stove; it is quoted in the *O.E.D.*

3 Parson Samuel Moody (Harvard 1697) had married Hannah Sewall, daughter of the diarist's brother John. Usually he did not leave Sewall's house empty-handed. The *Lexicon Hebraicum et Chaldaicum* of Johannes Buxtorf the elder of Basle was first published in 1607; as late as Sewall's time the London edition of 1646 was one of the requisites of Harvard students. *C.S.M.*, xxviii, 396.

4 Parsons had been fortunate to escape intact. Thomas Venner, sometime wine-cooper at Salem and Boston, had gone to London in 1651. A strong character, he had gradually attained leadership of a band of religious fanatics worshipping in a Coleman Street conventicle. They were called Fifth Monarchy men "be-cause they held the belief that the four great kingdoms, Assyrian, Persian, Mace-donian and Roman, which had successively possessed the dominions of earth, has passed away, and that their duty was to proclaim and establish the new King-dom of Christ upon earth, or the Millenium, according to the mystical chapters in the Book of Revelation." Stirred up to a frenzy early in January 1661, about

Febr. 1. William Willard and William Blin were baptised by Mr. Willard. At the funeral Mr. Chiever told me he enter'd his 88th year 25. Jan^r, and is now the oldest man in Boston.

Feb^r 2. Very sore storm of Rain and Hail and Snow. Hunting is cast away on the Rocks of Marblehead. Comes from the Bay; his company and he lost.

A man drownd in the Cellar of the Queens-head Tavern: went to take out the plug, and dropt in. It seems had the falling sickness. No Sun-shine this day.

Wednesday, Feb^r 11th The Gazette that Andover Adress presented Octob^r 9th relating to the Pr[*ince of*] Wales, I read it at Col. Hutchinson's in hearing of 12 or 13 of the Council, were there waiting for the Maj^r Gen^{ls} Rising. This Gazett comes by way of New-York. *Febr.* 14. This last week has been a week of extraordinary cold Wether. Last night I dream'd I was in company with Mr. Stoughton and Mr. N. Higginson.

Thorsday, Febr. 19. Mr. I. Mather preached from Rev. 22. 16— bright and morning Star. Mention'd Sign in the Heaven, and in the Evening following I saw a large Cometical Blaze, something fine and dim, pointing from the Westward, a little below Orion.

Febr. 21. Capt. Tim° Clark tells me that a Line drawn to the Comet strikes just upon Mexico, spake of a Revolution there, how great a Thing it would be. Said one Whitehead told him of the magnificence of the City, that there were in it 1500 Coaches drawn with Mules. This Blaze had much put me in mind of Mexico; because we must look toward Mexico to view it. Capt. Clark drew a Line on his Globe. Our Thoughts being thus confer'd, and found to jump, makes it to me remarkable. I have long pray'd for Mexico, and of late in those Words, that God would open the Mexican Fountain.

Febr. 21. This day Goodw[*ife*] Pope, and John Wait dye.

Febr. 22, 1701/2 My Wife goes to Meeting in the Afternoon, after long Restraint.

Febr. 23. Goodw. Pope is buried. Capt Byfield and I and the Select-Men, and about 12 women there; Cowel, Wheeler, Calef &c. One or two Bacons, her Grandsons, followed next.

---

fifty of them emerged at midnight of the 6th and with the war cry "Live King Jesus" rushed about creating panic and murdering innocent citizens. London was taken by surprise, and it was four days before the desperadoes were finally cornered and captured by the city militia. They were tried the 17th and despatched the 19th. Venner and another leader were drawn, hanged, and quartered. C. E. Banks, Thomas Venner, N.E.H.G.R. xlvii, 437–444.

Febr. 25. Archibald Macquerry has a son born at Charlestown without Arms.

Jn⁰ Wait is buried; Gen¹ Court Sat, and I think none of the Council at the Funeral.

Febr. 26. Sixteen of the Council sign an order for making Dracot a Town.

Feb. 28. Yesterday Mr. Cookes Petition to enable him to sue Col. Paige for his Farm, was brought forward. I moved that Col. Paige might be Notified and 4 more. Mr. Cooke seemed displeas'd, and in way of Displeasure said twas to delay his Business: was sorry I was so far engag'd *in it*. For this, and because of Sherbourn case, I chose to stay from Council this Forenoon; that might avoid being present when suspected, or charg'd with Prejudice. Sam. brings word of a Ship from England 19 weeks; last from Fayall, In whom is Mr. Brenton.

Capt Scott arrives, in whom comes Mr. Brenton, Febr. 28. 1701/2.

March, 11. 1701/2. In the Afternoon, there are great Southerly Gusts and Showers; Considerable Thunder and Lightening. Last night between 10 and 11, A great Fire brake out in Mr. Thomson's Warehouse upon the Dock: Seven or Eight of the chief Warehouses were burnt and blown up. 'Tis said the Fire began in that part which Monsr. Bushee hires. About half a Ship's Loading was lately taken into it.

Satterday, March, 14. 1701/2 at 5 p.m. Capt. John Alden expired; Going to visit him, I happened to be there at the time.

In April 1702 Sewall made a trip to Cape Cod and Martha's Vineyard as commissioner of the Society (or Company) for the Propagation of the Gospel among the Indians. As usual, he kept the record separate from his diary. The following fragment, ending with the entry of 10 April, was presented to the Massachusetts Historical Society by John S. H. Fogg, M.D., of South Boston, a manuscript collector, and appeared at the end of the published Diary.

[April 4] * * * Before which time one [Thomas] Crocker comes up, who married the widow of young Mr. [John] Lothrop, and becomes our Pilot. Saw Lieut. [John] Howland upon the Rode, who tells us he was born Febr. 24. 1626, at our Plimouth. Visit Mr. [Isaac] Robinson, who saith he is 92 years old, is the Son of Mr. [John] Robinson pastor of the Church of Leyden, part of which came to Plim⁰. But to my disappointment he came not to New-England till the year [1631] in which Mr. [John] Wilson was returning to England after the settlement of Boston. I told him was very desirous to see him for his Father's sake, and his own. Gave him an Arabian piece of Gold to buy a book for some of his grand children. Pass on to Melatiah Lothrop's, his wife very ill of a Chronical disease. Dine there. Barnabas Lothrop Esq[r] comes thither and earnestly invites me and my Son [*Samuel*] to lodge at his House. His Kinsman is glad of it because of his wife and the approaching Court. Dine at Melatiah's. Leave our Horses there. Visit Mr. Russel, Mr. Hinckley.[5] Madam Hinckley reads to us a very pious Letter of her daughter [*Abigail; Mrs. Joseph*] Lord: and Gov. Hinckley of his daughter [*Thankful; Mrs.*] Exper[*ience*] Mayhew. View the burying place, See Mr. Walley's Epitaph on a Rail broken off, and tumbled about; so well as could read the worn Letters, 'twas this: "Here lieth the body of that blessed Son of Peace, and Pastor of the Church of Christ, Mr. Thomas Wally, who ended his Labour, and fell asleep in the Lord, 21 March, 1677." [6] Saw Mr. Whippo and his wife and children;[7] repair to our Lodgings. Burying place is just by the Windmill. Much Ice remained till Noon.

Sabbath, April 5. Very cold still, but fair: much Ice. Mr. Russell preaches morning and Evening. As go home at night, Gov[r] Hinckley invites me to breakfast with him next day.

Monday, April 6. Goe and see the Court-house, Salt-pond, Crick where Mr. Lothrop lays his vessel; take leave of Mr. Lothrop. Breakfast with Gov[r] Hinckley. Set out with Mr. Russell about ½ hour past 7. Upon a small hill in Barnstable, he shows me both Seas. Brings us going to Cotuit, then he takes Leave. We miss our way a little and go up to a great Pond and small Orchard. Go back and then pass on. Call at Mr. Robinson's, they give us good Small Beer. Go to the Ferry-house; his Boat is at little Woods's hole; travel thither, there embark, and have a good passage over in little more than an hour's time. Refresh at Chases, from thence ride to Tisbury. First man I speak with is Joseph Dogget: he tells me Mr. Kithcart keeps an Ordinary; we go thither, the Day-Light being almost spent. Mr. Robinson's Son helps us and bears us company awhile. Milton visits us. Go to Week's about 1 p.m.

[5] Jonathan Russell (Harvard 1675) was settled as minister of Barnstable in 1683 and died there 20 February 1710/11. Thomas Hinckley was the last Governor of Plymouth Colony, serving from 1681 to 1692.

[6] Thomas Walley, B.A. (Oxon.), had been vicar of Rickmansworth, Herts, and rector of St. Mary's, Whitechapel, London. He lost his rectorship for nonconformity, came to New England in 1663, and was minister at Barnstable until his death, 24 March 1677/78. *Calamy.*

[7] Experience, daughter of Governor Hinckley, was the wife of James Whipple.

Tuesday, April 7. Mr. Sheriff Allen[8] having visited us over night, in his way from old Town, comes to us this morn, Apr. 7. From thence we pass to his House, see his wife and little daughter. Then visit Major Mayhew, then Exper[*ience*], whose wife lyes in of a Son. Dine at Maj^r Mayhew's, then ride to the Gay-head Neck, to Abel's Wigwam, where was pleased with the goodness of his house, especially the Furniture, demonstrating his Industry, *viz*, Two great Spinning Wheels, one small one for Linnen, and a Loom to weave it. When Abel came in from his sowing of Wheat, I discoursed him to mutual satisfaction. He gave us very good Milk and Water to drink. As came back saw an English House of Harry, but he not at home. Saw four good Oxen which belongd to one Indian. *Nota*. Abel says there are Fifty-Eight houses in the Gay-head Neck. Maj^r Mayhew says 'twill Entertain 58 more, and less than fourty Rod of Fence takes it in—q^t 1,000 Acres. Two Schoolmasters chiefly for Winter, Jonas Hassawit, the Anabaptist preacher, and Peter Chânin. No-Man's-Land is an Island of about 1½ mile long, ½ broad, better than a League from the main Island, well waterd and wooded, and inhabited by 7th day Indians. No-Man's-Land and the Gay-head are the only certain places for Fishing for Cod, which this Week they have begun to be successfully engaged in. Visit Mr. Thacher in our return. Tis a pretty while within night by that time we get from our Quarters at Mr. Allen's, where sup with Sheriff, his wife, Maj^r Mayhew, Mr. Torrey, Exp. Mayhew. Have a very good Chamber and Bed to lodge in, one of the best in Chilmark.

Wednesday, April 8. Japhet, Jonathan and Stephen come to me. I have much discourse with them, try to convince Stephen of his Anabaptistical Errors. Jonas and he have a Church of about 30, ten men. I perceive by Mr. Exp. Mayhew and Japhet 'tis hardly feesible to send any to the Eastward to convert the Indians, their Language is so different. Gave Japhet two Arabian pieces Gold, and Stephen two pieces 8/8 to buy Corn. Mr. Exp. Mayhew proposes to me as a thing very expedient that some short Treatise be drawn up and translated into Indian to prevent the spreading of the Anabaptistical Notions. Mr. Thacher and Mr. Thomas Mayhew and Mr. [*Simon*] Athern accompany me in my way towards Edgartown. Dine at Mr. Athern's, his wife not 14 when he married her. Mrs. Thacher on her death-bed troubled at her Marriage to Mr. Kemp, her first husband, some smell of Relation between them.

On the Rode, first Mr. Mayhew, and then Japhet, tell me the story of Japhet's birth. Get to the Town about 3 p.m. Visit Mr. Dunnam.

8 Ebenezer Allin, sheriff of Dukes County.

Go aboard and visit Capt. Jonas Clay, sick of the Gout. Lodge at Sarsons.

Thorsday, April 9. Breakfast at Major Mayhew's. Major Mayhew and his Brother accompany us to Chase's, where we meet with Mr. Exp. Mayhew and Mr. Allen the Sheriffe. Chase's Boat not come. By that time I got over 'twas near sunset. Madam Hinckley embarked in the boat and brought us over to visit her daughter Lying-in. Lodge at Lt Hatches with [*Rev. Samuel*] Shiverick.

Friday, April 10. Sam. and I rode alone to Sandwich, very good Rode. Bait at Mr. Chipman's. Taken in the Rain. Lodge at Capt Morey's. One Bears our Pilot from Sandwich to Plim°. Dine at Barker's. Bait at Cushing's. Drink at Mills's. Got home about 9 too late; were well and found all well. *Laus Deo.*

May, 1. Whitehorn arrives: Came from Falmouth March, 12. Ld Cornbury[9] came out with. Rains in the Afternoon, after much Drought. *May* 2. Great storm, very fierce Wind. A Briganteen is driven up the Harbour, and into the Mill-Crick with such Fury that she carrys away the Drawbridge before her.

May. 4, 1702. Artillery Comp^a Trains, Rainy day; So we exercise on the Town-House in the morn. Mr. Pitkin, Capt Whiting, Commissioners for Connecticut about Running the Line, Dine with us. Mr. Colman and Adams, Major Hobby, Capt. Pelham, Southack, Ephr. Savage, Mr. Paul Dudley, Will Dummer, Edw. Hutchinson, &c. In the Afternoon went into Common; Major Hobby, Will Dummer, Ned Hutchinson, Oliver Williams and another, Listed. Major Hobby was introduced by Col. Hutchinson, He and I vouch'd for him. Mr. Elisha Cooke jun^r mov'd to be dismiss'd, which when he had paid his Arrears, was granted by Vote with a Hiss. Went to Pol-

---

[9] Edward Hyde, Viscount Cornbury, was grandson of the first earl of Clarendon (Lord Chancellor and historian of the Civil War), and first cousin to Queen Anne. He arrived in May 1702 to be governor of New York, and when the East and West Jersey proprietorships were united under the crown as New Jersey, he became governor of that province also. His administration was a complete failure. He was called "a spendthrift, a 'grafter,' a bigoted oppressor and a drunken, vain fool." "We never had a governor so universally detested," wrote William Smith, the Tory historian. A transvestite, he appeared publicly in woman's attire, perhaps imagining that he resembled his royal cousin; or perhaps endeavoring actually to represent Queen Anne. Sewall had heard of his practice of "that abomination"—*Muliebri veste uti* (letter of 21 February 1708/9 in L.B. 1, 380–381). Cornbury was recalled in 1708, but his numerous creditors caused his arrest, and he remained in the custody of the Sheriff of New York until the death of his father (in 1709) made him Earl of Clarendon and enabled him to return to England. Lady Cornbury had died in New York in 1706 and is buried beneath Trinity Church. *D.A.B.*

lards to avoid the Rain. March'd out and shot at a Mark. Before
they began, I told the Company that I had call'd them to shoot in
October, and had not my self hit the Butt; I was willing to bring
my self under a small Fine, such as a single Justice might set; and
it should be to him who made the best Shott. Mr. Gerrish and Ensign John Noyes were the competitors, At Pollards, by a Brass Rule,
Ens. Noyes's Shot was found to be two inches and a half nearer the
centre, than Mr. John Gerrishes; His was on the right side of the
Neck; Ensign Noyes's on the Bowels a little on the Left and but
very little more than G. on the Right of the middle-Line. When I
had heard what could be said on both sides, I Judg'd for Ensign
Noyes, and gave him a Silver cup I had provided engraven

May. 4. 1702.
Euphratem Siccare potes.[10]

Telling him, it was in Token of the value I had for that virtue in
others, which I my self could not attain to. March'd into Common
and concluded with Pray'r. Pray'd in the morn on the Townhouse,
Praying for the Churches by Name. After Dinner, We Sung four
staves of the 68th PS. viz. first Part and the 9. and 10th verses of the
2d with regard to the plentifull Rain on the 1 and 2 May and now,
after great Drought; Mr. Dering mov'd we might sing. Some objected against our singing so much; I answer'd, Twas but *Four Deep.*
Were Treated at Major Savages.

Satterday, May 9. 1702. By this days Post we hear that my Lord
Cornbury arriv'd, a Thorsday was sennight, at New York. *May, 9.*
This day, several of the Gentlemen of the Council go to the
Castle. As they came up, Miller was going down. And a little after
they pass'd him his ship overset. A Swisse Boy drown'd.

Visit Sister Moodey twice in Kittery Circuit. *May 19th* Mr. James
How, a good Man of Ipswich, 104 years old, is buried. Died I think
on Lords-Day night, just about the time the News of the Kings
Death was brought from Madera.

May, 28. Burrington from New-found-Land brings Prints of the
King's death March, 8. at 8 m.[11] Queen's Speech to her Lords at St
James's. Lords Spiritual and Temporal, their Address; Queen's
Speech to the Parliament; Several Addresses; and at last the Gazette

---

[10] The drying-up of the river Euphrates, as a prophetic symbol, continued to
engage Sewall's interest. See p. 60.
[11] William III died in consequence of a violent fall from his horse at Hampton
Court the previous month. Queen Anne, his successor, was his sister-in-law, the
second daughter of James II.

containing the Proclaiming the Queen, came to Hand: Then we resolv'd to proclaim her Majesty here: Which was done accordingly below the Town-house. Regiment drawn up, and Life-Guard of Horse; Council, Representatives, Ministers, Justices, Gentlemen taken within the Guard; Mr. Secretary on foot read the order of the Council, the Proclamation, and Queen's Proclamation for continuing Commissions. Mr. Sheriff Gookin gave it to the people. Volleys, Guns. Went into chamber to drink, and there had the sad news of the Taking of 3 Salem Catches by the Cape-Sable Indians; one of them Col. Higginson's: David Hills, and one of the Masters kill'd. This arrived at Salem this day, and was sent per Express, one of the men swore it before the Council. Proclamation was made between 3 and 4.

May 29. At 5. p.m. Madam Bellingham dies,[12] a vertuous Gentlewoman, *antiquis Moribus, prisca fide,* who has liv'd a widow just about 30 years.

May, 31. 146. Ps. sung, and Mr. Pemberton preaches a Funeral sermon for the King, from the 3ᵈ and 4ᵗʰ verses of that Psalm.

June, 1, 1702. Artillery election-Day. Mr. Colman preaches from Heb. 11. 33. Sermon is well liked of. Had much adoe to persuade Mr. Willard to dine with me. Said Ministers were disgusted because the Representatives went first at the Proclaiming the Queen; and that by order of our House. But at last he came: I went for him, leaving my Guests. No Mather, Allen, Adams there. But there were Mr. Torrey, Willard, Simmes, Thacher, Belchar and many more. No Mr. Myles, Bridge, [*ministers of King's Chapel.*] No Capt of Frigot Tho the last were invited. *June. 10. 1702.* Committee Tryes Powder, and firing so much and long distempered me; that partly by that, and partly by my Wives intolerable pains, I had a most restless night.

June, 11. *Thorsday,* before I was dress'd, Sam. Gave the Word the Govʳ [*Joseph Dudley*] was come. Quickly after I got down, Maxwell summoned me to Council, told me the Secretary had a Letter of the Governours Arrival yesterday, at Marblehead. Mr. Addington,

---

[12] Penelope Pelham was the second wife of Governor Richard Bellingham, the last survivor of the patentees named in the Massachusetts Bay Charter. Their romantic marriage in 1641 was something of a scandal: "The young gentlewoman [about 22; he was 50] was ready to be contracted to a friend of his, who lodged in his house, and by his consent had proceeded so far with her, when on a sudden the governor treated with her, and obtained her for himself. He excused it by the strength of his affection . . ." (John Winthrop, *Journal,* 1908 ed., II, 43–44). Bellingham not only neglected to publish his intentions, but solemnized the marriage himself. *Savage, D.A.B.*

Joseph Dudley

Margaret Mitchel Sewall

Eliakim Hutchinson, Byfield and Sewall, sent per the Council, go with Capt Crofts in his Pinace to meet the Governour, and Congratulat his Arrival. We get aboard a little before got within Point Alderton; Capt Heron introduced us; After had all saluted the Govr I said,

Her Majesty's Council of this Province have commanded us to meet your Excellency, and congratulate your safe Arrival in the Massachusetts Bay, in quality of our Governour: Which we do very heartily; not only out of Obedience to our Masters who sent us; but also of our own accord. The Cloaths your Excellency sees us wear, are a true Indication of our inward Grief for the Departure of K. William. Yet we desire to remember with Thankfullness the Goodness of God, who has at this time peacably placed Queen Anne upon the Throne. And as Her Majestys Name imports Grace, so we trust God will shew Her Majesty Favour; and Her Majesty us. And we look upon your Excllency's being sent to us, as a very fair First-Fruit of it, for which we bless God and Queen Anne.

I was startled at 2 or 3 things; viz. The Lt Governour [*Thomas Povey*] [13] a stranger, sent, whom we knew nor heard anything of before: When the Govr first mention'd it, I understood him of Mr. Addington. I saw an ancient Minister, enquiring who it was, Governour said, twas G[*eorge*] Keith, had converted many in England, and now Bp. London had sent him hether with Salary of 200. Guineys per annum. I look'd on him as Helena aboard.[14] This man crav'd a Blessing and return'd Thanks, though there was the chaplain of the Ship, and another Minister on board. Governour has a very large Wigg. Drink Healths, About one and Twenty Guns fired at our leaving the Centurion; and Cheers, then Capt Scot and another Ship fired. Castle fired many Guns; Landed at Scarlet's Wharf, where the Council and Regiment waited for us; just before came at the North-Meetinghouse Clock struck five. Was the Troop of Guards, and Col. Paige's Troop. March'd to the Townhouse. There before the Court;

---

[13] Povey, a captain in the Queen's own regiment of footguards, returned to England in 1705.

[14] George Keith, M.A. (Aberdeen 1658), was first ordained in the Church of Scotland, then became a Quaker and was a schoolmaster and preacher in Philadelphia. He instituted a separatist faction among the Quakers, and for this he was disowned by the Society of Friends. Returning to England, he became an Anglican and was ordained priest by the Bishop of London in March 1702; this time he came over as one of the first S.P.G. missionaries, and preached chiefly in New Jersey and Virginia. Sewall's reference to Helen may mean that he foresaw in Keith the cause of ecclesiastical discords in the future (M.H.S.EDS.), but what trouble he caused here was for the Quakers, and by 1705 he was settled quietly in a Surrey vicarage. *A.A.S.Proc.* LXVI, 250; *D.A.B.*

Ministers, and as many else as could crowd in, the Governour's and
L[t] Gov[rs] Commissions were published; they took their Oaths laying
their hands on the Bible, and after Kissing it. Had a large Treat.
Just about dark Troops Guarded the Gov[r] to Roxbury. He rode in
Major Hobby's Coach Drawn with six Horses richly harnessed. By
mistake, my coachman stayed in the yard, and so Joseph and I went
alone. Foot gave 3 very good Volleys after the publication of the
Commissions, and were dismiss'd. Mr. Mather crav'd a Blessing and
Mr. Cotton Mather Return'd Thanks.

June 12. as Governour came to Town, he alighted and call'd at my
House, Thank'd me for my Kindness to his family. I was much indispos'd by my Throat being sore, and I feverish.

June. 13. Ships Sail.

June. 28. Gov[r] partakes of the Lords Supper at Roxbury: In the
Afternoon goes to Boston to hear Mr. Myles, who inveighed vehemently against Scism. *June.* 29. Refused to let us give our Yes and
No in Papers. *June,* 30. War is proclaim'd.[15] Address sign'd a 2[d] time,
which I again declined. New Justices are much talk'd of.

Satterday, July, 4. It is known in Town that the L[t] Governour
has his Commission for Captain of the Castle; and Charles Hobby,
for Colonel of Boston Regiment. *July,* 6. Col. Hutchinson, by order, delivers the Castle to the L[t] Gov[r]. In the afternoon Paul Dudley esqr. [*the governor's son*] is Appointed the Queen's Attorney.
Judges of Middlesex and Suffolk sworn. And Justices of Suffolk
(Mr. Sergeant, Hutchinson, Belcher Swear Not.) L[t] Gov[r] laying his
Hand on, and kissing the Bible. Council is adjourn'd to Wednesday. *July,* 9. Waited on the Gov[r] to Marblehead, to Salem. Were
Treated at Sharp's. *July.* 10. Went to Ipswich, in the Rain part of
the Way. Troop met us. I and Mr. White lodg'd at Mr. Rogers's,
as had done at Son Hirst's the night before. *July* 11. about 10. Gov[r]
sets out for Newbury, and I for Boston; Serene, windy day. Came
with B. Marston and Wakefield to Phillips's. Dined there with Capt
Winthrop, his lady, Madam Wainwright, Mrs. Belcher of Newbury.
Little Colman; Mrs. Anne Winthrop Lyes in there. Capt Adam
Winthrop accompanied me home. Find all well. *Laus Deo. July,* 14.
1702. A man is killed on board her Majesty's Ship the Swift, by a
Gun from the Castle. *July,* 15. Goe to Dedham Lecture, come home
with Maj[r] Gen[l] and his Son and Daughter from Connecticut.

July. 17. Visit Madam Dudley: Sup with her, cous. Dummer and

15 In May the English, the Dutch, and the Holy Roman Emperor had jointly
declared war on France, the War of the Spanish Succession; in America it was
called Queen Anne's War.

wife, daughter, Col. Townsend, Bromfield and wife, and Kate Dudley.

July, 20. Sam. visits Mrs. Rebecka Dudley.

July, 21. Mr. Borland's House, the Raising of it is begun. *July*, 20. Mr. Paul Dudley dined with us. I ask'd him if he had any service for Sam. to Roxbury: He told me he would be welcom there. *July*, 22. I went with the Major Gen¹ Winthrop to the Lieut Govʳ. At our privat Meeting I read the first sermon of Mr. Flavel's Fountain of Life.¹⁶

July, 24. 1702. When I had read to Mrs. Mary Rock¹⁷ the 2ᵈ half of Dr. Sibbs's 3ᵈ Sermon Glance of Heaven, In discourse about her father and Mother, She told me her Mother had not been with child in eight years ½. Was very fearfull about coming to N.-E. but at last had a day of Prayer, many Ministers: and she resolv'd to follow their advice, come what would. And about 12-moneths after her arrival here, she had this daughter viz. 7ʳ 1633. which was her last. *July*, 30. I, my wife, Sam. Hannah visit Madam Dudley, Mrs. Rebekah to whom Sam. gives a Psalm-Booke. *Augᵗ* 4. 1702. Govʳ Dudley invites me and my wife to Dinner and Lecture, Sends his Coach for us; Mr. Whiting and his cousin Foxcroft dine there, Mrs. Willard. Mr. Walter preach'd a solid Sermon from the days of Darkness. Exhorted to prepare for death.

Augt. 8. 1702. My dear sister Moodey dies a little before sun-rise. I and cous. Dummer dine at Roxbury.

Augt. 9. I put up a Note. *Augt.* 10. I goe to Winnisimmet and there meet Broʳ. Goe with him to Salem: lodge at Son Hirst's. *Augᵗ* 11. Set out from Salem as the School-Bell rung. Baited at Crompton's. *Note.* at Wenham pond Reproved David Simons for being naked about his Flax; threatened to Fine him. He submitted.

When came to Rowley, our Friends were gone. Got to the Falls about Noon. Two or three hours after, the Funeral was, very hot sunshine. Bearers, Woodman, Capt. Greenlef, Dea. Wᵐ Noyes, Jnᵒ Smith, Jonᵃ Wheeler, Nathan¹ Coffin. Many Newbury people there though so buisy a time; Col. Pierce, Major Noyes, Davison, Tristram

---

¹⁶ John Flavell, *The Fountain of Life Opened* (London, 1673).

¹⁷ Mrs. Rock was the widow of Joseph Rock, a wealthy merchant and one of the founders of the South Church; her first husband was Rev. Samuel Danforth (Harvard 1643) of Roxbury. She was the daughter of Rev. John Wilson of the First Church. Her mother did not come over with her husband in the *Arbella* in 1630, but on a subsequent voyage with him in 1632 (*N.E.H.G.R.* LXI,41). Richard Sibbes, D.D., preacher at Gray's Inn and master of St. Catherine's Hall, Cambridge, was an eminent Puritan divine and the author of numerous popular devotional books.

Coffin, Mr. Tappan, father and Son, Mr. Payson of Rowley, (though muffled) Mr. Hale their Minister, Cousin Dummer and family, Mr. Bennet, Bradstreet. About a mile or more to the Burying place. Bro^r Moodey led his Mother, Sam, his Sister Mary; then Dorothy and Mehetabel went together (Sarah was so overpowered with Grief that she went to Town and was not at the Funeral.) I led Sister Gerrish; Bro^r, Sister Short, [*blank*] Sister Northend. Aunt Northend was there. Bro^r Tappan, Sister Sewall and her son John; Jacob and Jno Tappan and many cousins: Capt. Boynton.

Our dear sister Mehetabel is the first buryed in this new Burying place, a Barly-earish, pure Sand, just behind the Meetinghouse. Bro^r went home immediately. I went back to the House, lodg'd there all night with Bro^r Moodey. Gave Wheelers wife a piece of 8/8 to buy her a p^r Shoes. Gave cousin Lydia a piece of 8/8. *Augt.* 12. pray'd with them and sung the 146 Psalm. Went to Jno Smith's and took the Acknowledgment of the Deed for the Land of the Meeting-house and Burying place. Rid with Mr. Woodman and Smith to Andover, which is a good In-land Town, and of a good Prospect. Some warned us not to goe to the ordinary, because Mr. Peters was dangerously sick of the Bloody Flux: So went to Mr. Woodmans Daughters, and there din'd on Pork and Beans: Afterward had Fowls rosted and dress'd very well. Right conducts me to Wooburn through the Land of Nod.[18] This is the first time I have seen it. Got late to Fowl's at Wooburn: Sick there, which made me uneasy. *Augt.* 13. Visit Mr. Fox, view the Hop-yards, come home, very hot. Met Mr. Converse, the Father, and discours'd him under a Shady Tree. Wont give his Grand-children till after his death for fear of giving offence. Express'd his Grief that Govr Dudley put men in place that were not good. Call'd at Mr. Woodbridges and drank a Glass of very good Beer. Told him he had got so pleasant a situation he must not re-

---

[18] A full account of the Land of Nod, mentioned several times in the diary between this date and 1727, is given in the *History of Woburn* (1868) by the diarist's descendant, Rev. Samuel Sewall, on pages 540–543. The tract consisted of three thousand acres in Wilmington, given up by Woburn in exchange for land received from Charlestown in 1650. Charlestown granted it to a dozen of her prominent citizens. Francis Willoughby bought enough shares to own eleven hundred acres, and Lawrence Hammond, who married his widow, sold them in 1683 to John Hull, whence Sewall gained the ownership. In 1704 Charlestown claimed the land and contested Sewall's right: the case was tried at Cambridge before a special court 18 September 1705, and again, on appeal before the Superior Court at Cambridge 29 July 1706. On both occasions the decision was in Sewall's favor.

move till he went to heaven.[19] Got home in Lecture-time. After Lecture Council sits. Doe somthing about Judges of Probat. Adjourn. *Augt. 14.* Nominate Col. Townsend for Inferior Court, Suffolke; Col. Hathorne for Superiour, Council advise because new: said would always do so. Adj: till Satterday. *Note.* I said Nom[*ination of*] Hathorne pleas'd me. I gave my voice for him in '92., when this Court was first erected: And County of Essex had thought themselves postpon'd because no Judge of the Court out of their County. Govʳ said that was one Consideration made him name him.

Satterday, Augt 15. p.m. Govʳ brings home Sam., then takes me into the Calash to the Townhouse. Col. Hathorne and Townsend chosen: Govʳ delivers him his Commission, then me and Majʳ Walley. Said would never insert himself any way to influence any proceeding before; which has many times done with great Vehemency; exhorting us to doe Justice. Addington, Hathorne, Sewall, Walley sent for Mr. Elisha Cooke junʳ: constituted him our Clerk, and gave him the Oaths. So now the Superior Court and Inferior Court Suffolk are both open'd this day; which is a considerable celebration of my son Joseph's Birth-day. The Lord cause his face to shine on us!

See June, 7. 1700.

Augt 19. 1702. I give Mr. Joseph Prout, the Town Clerk, the names of my Son and Mrs. Rebekah Dudley to enter their Purpose of Marriage.

Augt 20. Williams publishes them. Mr. Leverett is Sworn after Lecture Judge of the Superior Court.

Augt 21. I gave Madam Cooke a Ring, cost 19s of Cous. Dummer, in Remembrance of my dear Sister Moodey, whom Mr. Cooke visited in May last. Madam Cooke said had got rid of Mr. Cooke. I answer'd, we should much want his Caution, Discretion, and Constancy.[20] Was very thankfull for the present I made her Husband in the Ring. Walter Negro has his Thigh cut off; viz. his Legg above the knee.

Satterday, 7ʳ 5. I set out for Dedham about 3. p.m. to shorten

[19] Benjamin Woodbridge of Medford had been settled over churches in Connecticut, Rhode Island, Maine, and New Hampshire; he remained at Medford until his death 15 January 1709/10.

[20] Elisha Cooke had been a member of the Council which committed Joseph Dudley to prison when Andros was overthrown in 1689. As soon as Dudley became governor he turned Cooke out of his judicial offices and regularly negatived his elections to the Council until 1715. *Sibley.*

my Bristol Journey. Got thither just about Sun-set. Lodg'd at Fishers. 7^r 7th About ¼ after 7. m. Mr. Leverett, Capt Saunders, and I set out (Amos Gates waits on me); set forward. Got to Rehoboth when the Sun was ¾ of an hour high. Lodg'd at the Bear. Rose about 2. past midnight, were on Horseback by 5 because of the Likelihood of Rain. Had a very comfortable journey. Got to our Quarters at Osburns before 8 *mane*. Govr was gon over to Narraganset. All the Justices there: Mr. Isaac Addington, the Chief Justice, said had been no court open'd in the Queens Reign: so his commission was read, then mine, then Walleys, then Hathorn's then Leverett's. Court Treated Govr, Lt Govr, Gentlemen, Council &c. at Osburn's: cost us 15s apiece. Horses and Servants were paid for by the Governours Steward.

7^r 9. Col. Byfield Treats at Osburn's.

Septr 10. Court were of Opinion that Adam's Freedom could not be Tryed by Mr. Saffins complaint, and Adam being kept from the court by the Small Pocks, No proceedings at all could be had thereupon.

Mr. Mackentash, who bought Col. Byfields Farm at the Mount, makes a noble Treat at Major Church's which is his hired house. Got to Rehoboth by dark; Mr. Leverett and I Lodged at Mr. Greenwood's; Col. Hathorn and Sam. at Mr. Smith's.

7^r 11th Went to Billinges in the Cart-way; Had a very good Dinner, Venison &c. Got home in good time. Capt. Williams with his Red-Coats met us between Dedham and the Turning to Fowl-Meadow. Capt Belchar and sundry Boston Gentlemen met us at Dedham. *Note.* Wednesday, at Osburn's, about Break-a-day, I heard one riding as I lay awake. (Mrs. Sparhawk having miscarried, I lodg'd there.) Thought I, I fear there may be some bad News from Boston. The man knock'd, and when he could make any hear, he ask'd if Capt.——were there: I took it he said me. They answer'd yes. He said must come away presently: for his daughter was very bad. Then I said in my self, I must undertake a sorrowfull Journey, as from Salem to Boston, upon the advice of my Still-born son: But God dismiss'd me from the burden of that sorrowfull Surprise, having laid it on Capt Brown of Swansey. We saw the Funeral as went over the Ferry on Thorsday.

7^r 13. Lords-Day, Mr. Bradstreet baptiseth Simon, the Jew, at Charlestown, a young man whom he was Instrumental to convert.[21]

Septr 15. Mr. Nehemiah Walter marries Mr. Saml Sewall and

[21] The entry in the record-book of the First Church of Charlestown reads: "Mr Simon, (quondam Judeus) Barns." *N.E.H.G.R.* xxix, 291.

Mrs. Rebekah Dudley, in the Dining Room Chamber about 8 aclock.[22]
Mr. Willard concluded with prayer, Sung the last part of the 103
Psalm. Mr. Tho. Dudley reading and setting of it out of my Turkey-
Leather Psalm book. Present Govr, Lady, family (all save Mr. Paul,
who was call'd away just then with the news of Capt. Larimore's
prises, Brothers Letter of it the Govr read to us). I and my family,
all save Betty and Judith. Mr. Willard and wife, Mr. Lynde and
wife, Mr. Jno White, Mrs. Mary Hubbard. Got home about 11
aclock.

   Thorsday, Octr 1. 1702. The Govr and Council agree that Thors-
day Octr 22. be a Fast-Day. Governour moved that it might be Fri-
day, saying, Let us be English-men. I spake against making any
distinction in the Days of the week; Desired the same Day of the
Week might be for Fasts and Thanksgiving. Boston and Ipswich
Lecture Led us to Thorsday. Our Brethren at Connecticut had
Wednesday; which we applauded. Governour, it seems, told the
Secretary, He himself would draw up the Order, which he did at
Cousin Dummers by Candle-Light. Some of the Council were there,
but the Govr did not ask their voice. I suggested to Maj^r Genl that
the Drought might be mention'd; Mr. Winthrop spake, but the
Govr refused: I think at our house where the Govr Dined with Mr.
Increase Mather, and Mr. Tim^o Woodbridge; the Govr said was a
better Harvest than had been these Twenty years.

   Octr 6. 1702. Rode with the Govr to Cambridge, saw his field on
the Neck, and Hicks &c. building a large sluice to the Damm. Drove
a Pin. Din'd with Mr. Foxcroft; only us three at Table. Mr. Brattle
came to us and smoked a pipe. As came home, call'd at Mrs. Clark's,
and bespake a Bed for my self during the sitting of the Genl Court,
in case I came not home. She granted it. As came home saw Bastian
and the Negro digging the Drain. Brought home my Daughter Hirst
in the Governour's Chariot, Mr. Hirst went to Salem.

   Tuesday, 8^r 13. Went with the Govr to Hogg Island, son and
daughter Sewall, Mrs. Anne, Mrs. Mary Dudley there, Tho. Dudley,
Capt. Southack, Mr. Paul Dudley, Mr. Tho. Richards, Col. Townsend, Mr. Brattle, Col. Povey the Lieut Govr, Cous. Jer. Dummer
had a good Treat there. I was sorry Mr. Addington and Mr. Pemberton, and Mr. Roberts were not there, and therefore Returning
Thanks closed thus; Bring us to thy Entertainment in Heaven,
where not one of the Company shall be wanting. Son Hirst got to
the House just as were coming away, Gave him a good Plate to

[22] The wedding of Samuel Sewall Jr., 24, and Rebekah Dudley, 21, took place
at the home of her father, Governor Dudley, in Roxbury.

Winnisimmet, where he with Col. Paige and Chris. Taylor eat it.

8^r 14th I carry my Daughter Hirst in the Hackney Coach (Hannah and Mary in Company) to the Salutation, ferry over, and her Husband carryes her to Salem. *Cambridge Court, 8^r 15, 1702.* Mr. Secretary, Mr. Cooke, El^m Hutchinson and I ride in my coach to Roxbury in Lecture Time, Goe with the Govr about 2 p.m. Dine; into the Colledge yard. Goe up into Library, one Deputy is sworn. Govr make a speech to the Council and Assembly about his visiting the Eastern parts, building Pemmaquid Fort, settling Salaries for Govr, Judges &c., building the Govr a House. Came home in the Coach as went out. Young Peleg Sanford, Major Walley's Prentice, was buried this day at Boston. Mr. Cotton Mather preached the Lecture there.

Monday, Octr 26. 1702. Waited on the Govr to Wooburn, dined there: From thence to Billericay, Visited languishing Mr. Saml Whiting, I gave him 2 Balls of Chockalett and a pound Figgs, which very kindly accepted. Saw the Company in Arms led by Capt. Tomson. Went to Chelmsford, by that time got there twas almost dark. Saw Capt. Bowers and his Company; Gave a Volley and Huzza's. Sup'd at Mr. Clark's; I and Col. Pierce in his study. Some went on to Dunstable by Moonshine. *Octr 27.* Went to Dunstable in the Rain, Din'd and lodg'd at Col. Tyng's. Saw and drunk of Merrimack. No Indians come in. *Octr 28.* Went to Groton, saw Capt. Prescot and his company in Arms. (Govr had sent to them from Dunstable that would visit them). Lancaster is about 12 Miles Southward from Groton. Concord is 16 Miles ¾ and Ten-Rod from Groton. Got thither about 2. Horses and Men almost tired by our very hard riding. Dine at Capt. Prescot's. Lodge at Mr. Estabrooks with Col. Foxcroft. Their Foot–Company, and Troop, in Arms, Seem'd to be numerous and well appointed.

Octr 29. Breakfast at Capt. Minott's, Set out for Cambridge. In Company Col. Pierce, Thomas, Partrigge, Foxcroft, Capt. Cutler, son Sewall, young Mr. Tyng. At Mr. Hancocks Mr. Secretary, Leverett met us. Mr. Dyer, Col. Byfield; at Russel's Mr. Dudley. There the Calash met the Govr and weary Major Brenton rid in it with the Govr to the Town: Col. Hobbey rid his Horse. Dined with the Govr at Mr. Leveretts, Madam Leverett the Grandmother. Went home with Col. Hutchinson, Walley, Foster. Col. Foster invited us to drink at his house. Found all well, and David Sinclar[23] rocking Judith; he came to our house after I was gon my Journey.

---

[23] David Sinclair (Sinkler) was a servant in the Sewall home, living in the garret, and is mentioned continually in the diary from this date to 9 November 1717,

Novr 2. 1702. John Adams, a very good man, and John Drury, a desirable young man, dye of the small pocks.

Anthony Checkley dyed last week of the same disease.[24]

Novr 3. 1702. Capt. Tim° Prout died last night, aged more than 80 years.

Mr. Chief Justice Addington opens the Court at Boston. Mr. Wadsworth prays. Mr. Sheriff Dyer officiats with his white Wand. Sits on the Bench for want of a Seat. Col. Hutchinson, Hobby, Mr. Wadsworth dine with us. Mr. Palmer dines with us of's own accord, and no other J[*ustice of the*] peace except Mr. Attorney.

Novr 9. 1702. Go to Salem with Cousin Jane. Dine at Lt Lewes's, where meet Bro^r Sewall, Mr. Dudley comes in also: Ride in company with them to Salem. Lodge at Son Hirst's.

Novr 10. Mr. Leverett comes from Cambridge; open the Court in the Meetinghouse, because the Townhouse is very near a house that has the Small Pocks; so that people are afraid to goe there; and Sharp is not willing to let us have his chamber. Sat in the Deacon's seat, Col. Hathorne on my Right Hand, and Mr. Leverett on my Left. After the Reading of the Queen's Proclamation, I spake to the Grand-Jury, having written it down beforehand in my Daughters chamber.

Novr 13. 1702. Visit Mr. Higginson now in his 87th year. Dine at son Hirst's; Mr. Dudley, and cousin Elsa. Hirst there. Set forward in our way home; viz. Mr. Leverett and Dudley; visit Mr. Kitchen by the way, who makes us very welcom. Rain takes us before get to the Sluice. I had no Boots, and the Southerly wind much disturbed my Cloak: so I lodg'd at Lewes's: Mr. Leverett and Dudley stood on.

Novr 14. 1702. Rid to Winnisimmet and so home, very pleasant day. Find all well. *Laus Deo.*

Novr 30. Rid to Salem to visit my Daughter Hirst, who was brought to bed of a dead child Novr 28.

From Lewis's in company of Mr. Lyde. Got thither about 2 hours by Sun. Daughter very glad to see me. *xr.* 1. My Daughter being threatened with the head-ach, I send Chapman to Cambridge to Dr. Oliver for a Plaister: He follow'd the Dr. to Boston, and brought word of Mrs. Mathers death.[25] Laid on a Plaister; Daughter grows bet-

---

when Sewall recorded his death. On 18 March 1713/4 he married Mary Stedman, a member of the First Church.

[24] The M.H.S. editors incorrectly identified this Anthony Checkley as the attorney-general of the same name who died 18 October 1708, *q.v.*

[25] Abigail Phillips, the first wife of Cotton Mather, died this day; Mather's account of her last hours in his *Diary* (1, 447–449) is very sincere and moving.

ter: but then again had an ill turn; yet grew fine and well agen by
Satterday and cheerfully dismiss'd me. Had a very comfortable Journey home. Son Hirst brought me going to the Butts. At Lewis's fell
in with Maj^r Epes, Major Wainright and Mr. Fitch, going to Ipswich. Maj^r Wainwright tells me of the death of Mr. Brakenbury.

xr. [*December*] 8. 1702. p.m. writt to Mr. R^d Henchman clause of
my Speech to the Grand-jury, Novr 10. at Salem, referring to the
Lord's-Day. Epitaph of my Grand-Daughter. Sence of Rev. 14. 13.
Write *vid. Lib. Cop. Phænom.* Enclos'd the Gazett that had the
Queens Proclamation against Profaneness.

xr. 8. Mr. Robt Gibbs dies, one of our Select men, a very good man
and much Lamented; died suddenly of the Small Pocks. His death,
and the death of Jno Adams, the Master, Isaac Loring, and Paybody,
is a great stroke to our church and congregation. The Lord vouchsafe
to dwell with us, and Not break up Housekeeping among us! *Xr.* 9.
Mr. Gibbs buryed.

I first heard of Mr. Calamy's History.[26]

xr. 16. I went out early with David to carry two of Mr. Mathers
History[27] to my Bro^r to Charlestown: Heard the church [*King's
Chapel*] Bell ring for Capt. Crofts. He dyed last night.[28]

xr. 19. Is buried in the New burying place in Capt. Hamilton's

[26] The *Abridgement of Mr.* [*Richard*] *Baxter's History of his Life and Times* by
Edmund Calamy, D.D. (1671–1732), third of the name, was first published in
May 1702. It was a statement and defence of the case for Nonconformity, with
sketches of the ministers ejected under the Act of Uniformity of 1662, and was
an influential book. A second edition was published in 1713 in two volumes:
Sewall records the presentation of copies to Governor Shute (14 December 1717)
and Rev. Benjamin Colman (8 March 1717/8).
[27] This was Cotton Mather's famous folio, *Magnalia Christi Americana: or, the
Ecclesiastical History of New-England* (London, 1702), which still has its readers today. Mather first saw a copy 29 October (*Diary* I, 445) and set apart the
following day for solemn thanksgiving. On that day a series of domestic afflictions began, and he never mentioned the book again in his diary. The writing
and publishing history of the book, and an analysis of its style by Kenneth Ballard Murdock, are given in T. J. Holmes, *Cotton Mather . . . Bibliography*, II,
573–596.
[28] Crofts may have been a sea-captain, or a captain, R.N. It was in his pinnace
that Sewall, with a delegation from the Council, sailed out into Boston Harbor
to meet Governor Dudley 11 June 1702. His burial in Captain Hamilton's tomb
is significant. Captain Thomas Hamilton, whose death Sewall recorded 9 May
1687, was one of the six sons of Sir George Hamilton, and grandson of the first
Earl of Abercorn and the eleventh Earl of Ormonde; his sister was the famous
beauty, Elizabeth, Comtesse de Grammont. The family were Papists. Hamilton's
escutcheon was the first to be put up in King's Chapel. H. W. Foote, *Annals of
King's Chapel* I, 94; D.N.B. xxiv, 135, 177.

Tomb. Corps was first had into the church and a Funeral Sermon preach'd. For Debauchery and Irreligion he was one of the vilest Men that has set foot in Boston. Tis said he refused to have any Minister call'd to pray with him during his Sickness, which was above a fortnight.

xr. 23. I go to Roxbury, dine with my Daughter Sewall, Mr. Dudley &c in their Chamber, where their Stove is.

Sixth-day, Decr 25. Govr and Lt Govr partake of the Lords Supper; the undersheriff Hawksworth's child was baptised.

Decr 24. Govr din'd at our house, but went not to Lecture: it was very cold: Decr 17. din'd at Col. Hobbies, but went not to Lecture; was at both places at least in part of Lecture time.

xr. 26. Son Sewall comes to Town, dines with us. Grows ill, and we keep him all night.

xr. 25. Jonathan Stoddard 7 years and 8 months old: Subael Dummer 10 years and 8 months old, were buried.

Decr 30. 1702. I was weigh'd in Col. Byfield's Scales: weight One Hundred One Half One Quarter wanting 3 pounds, i.e. 193 pounds Net. Col. Byfield weighed Sixty three pounds more than I: had only my close coat on. The Lord add, or take away from this our corporeal weight, so as shall be most advantagious for our Spiritual Growth. [*In margin*] July 31. 1721 I weighed 228 £ *per* cous. Saml Sewall's Scales.

1703

CHARLESTOWN COURT / CELEBRATION OF THE QUEEN'S BIRTHDAY /
MODERATOR OF TOWN MEETING / SEWALL SETTLES BOUNDS OF HIS
FARM AT BOGGISTOW / COURT AT IPSWICH / ELECTIONS / SAMUEL
JUNIOR'S HOUSE RAISED AT MUDDY RIVER / JOSEPH EXAMINED AND
ADMITTED TO COLLEGE / SEWALL AND GOVERNOR DUDLEY ACQUIRE
A GRANDSON / JOSEPH INSTALLED IN HIS COLLEGE ROOM / FRENCH
CAPTURE NEW PROVIDENCE ISLAND / DEATH AND BURIAL OF HULL
SEWALL

Friday, Jan 8. 1702/3 Between 5. and 6. m. Mr. Edward Turfrey
dyes of the Small Pocks; was dying all night in a manner, having
strong Agonies. He was a person of great Abilities. His death is a
great Loss to the Town and Province: but more especially to Mr.
Addington, to whom Mr. Turfrey was extraordinarily Serviceable, having liv'd with him above Ten years. If real Worth and Serviceableness and Youth wont give a discharge in this warfare, what
shall? He is universally Lamented.

Lords-day, Jan 17. 1702/3 Lt Govr calls a Council, about 5 in the
even. Shews us his Intelligence from Eastham of 3 Sloops and a
Whale bote or 2, Taken at Cape Cod by a French Sloop last Friday.
Order Capt. Southack to take up a Sloop and endeavour to come
up with them. Send away an Express to the Govr. *Jan* 18. Last night
Capt. Hunt's Son went to bed well, and next morn not rising at his
usual hour, his Mistress sent to see what was the matter, and he was
found stark dead. Just now about Ebenezer Bird, a young man of
Dorchester, is kill'd by a fall from a Horse. *Jan* 24. 1702/3 Mr. Simon Willard's Twins, Samuel and Abigail, were baptised: and Samuel Valentine, Mr. Lynde's Grandson, and Richard [*blank*]. Very cold
Day.

Jan 26. 1702/3 Mr. Secretary, Major Walley, and Sewall, went to
Charlestown to hold Court. Had good going over the Ferry, notwith-
standing the cold wether we have had. Met Mr. Leverett there. Col.
Hathorn is not well and stays at home. Chief Justice prays at Open-

ing of the Court; Mr. Bradstreet not being well. Mr. Stoddard's Son dyed last night.

Jany 27. 1702/3 Mr. Tim° Woodbridge Prays at opening of the Court at Charlestown: but dines not with us. *Jan^y* 28. 1702/3 The Chief Justice prays at the opening of the Court. Daughter Hirst comes to Charlestown.

Jany 29. Joseph goes with the Hakney coach and brings his Sister Hirst to Boston. Mr. Secretary and I visit the Govr and congratulate his safe Return.

Feb^r 1. I visit my sick Brother at Salem, find him very ill. Monday Night worse.

Feb^r 3. Had a good night, and I return home. *Note,* I carried the News to Salem that was brought by Andrew Wilson from Oporto, Eight weeks, of the extraordinary success of our Fleet against the Flota in the River of Vigo; which we first heard of in part by way of Cork.[1] Read it to Bro^r. Mr. [*blank*] Burchsted, a German Doct^r, administers to my Brother. Jonathan gives me this Account of Brothers children.

Salem, Feb^r 3. 1702/3. The children of Major Stephen Sewall are, Margaret, Samuel, Susanna, Jonathan, Jane, Mehetabel, Mitchel, Henry and Stephen.

Feb^r 5th 1702/3 Col. Elisha Hutchinson, Col. Penn Townsend, Capt. Andrew Belcher, and Samuel Sewall rid to Roxbury in the Hackney coach; Capt. Jeremiah Dummer, Mr. Edward Bromfield on horseback: Went on purpose to speak to the Governour against having Illuminations, especially in the Town house; That so the profanation of the Sabbath might be prevented. I said twould be most for the Honor of God; and that would be most for the Honor and Safety of Queen Anne. Governour said twould be hard for him to forbid it, considering how good the Queen was, what successes God had given her. I answered, It could not be introduced into the Town-house without his Excellency's Order, for under his Excellency the Government of the Town was (partly) committed to us. Govr answer'd not a word. Others urged our Law, the Grief of Good People, his best Friends. And I think all was said between us, that could be said. Got well home about 9 at night, and had a very comfortable Journey, and sufficient Light Notwithstanding the Fogg, and absence of the very New Moon.

---

[1] English and Dutch forces under the Duke of Ormonde and an English fleet under Admiral Sir George Rooke had captured a flotilla of Spanish galleons laden with great treasure in Vigo Bay, 22 October 1702.

Feb^r 6. between 8 and 9. m. The Bells begin to Ring, to celebrate Queen Anne's Birth-Day, being the last of the Week.

Col. John Pynchon died Jany 17. 1702/3, about Sun-Rise, as Mr. Holyoke tells me Sabbath-Day. Ebenezer Franklin of the South Church, a male-Infant of 16 months old, was drown'd in a Tub of Suds, Feb^r 5. 1702/3.²

Feb^r 11th 1702/3. The Govr under his hand remits the Fines of several sentenced to pay 5^s apiece for drinking at Mrs. Monk's on Satterday night last about 9 aclock. Had warn'd Mrs. Monk an hour before. Said Monk also remitted her 25^s, and the writing given to the Sheriff to Notifie Col. Townsend and Mr. Bromfield.

Feb^r 12. 1702/3. Carry Daughter Hirst to Salem in Mr. Austin's Calash. Visit Bro^r, Col. Hathorne. Bro^r Hirst and sister and daughter sup with us. Saw not Mr. Noyes, but writ to him.

Feb^r 13. Return home very comfortably, notwithstanding much of the way was bad. Had like to have overset two or 3 times, but God upheld me. When came home, ask'd the reason of the Gates being open, and am told Mr. Josiah Willard had the Small Pocks at Cambridge; our coach went to fetch him to Town: but he fainted and could not come.

Tuesday, Feb. 16. 1702/3 2. p.m. Town-Meeting at Boston to chuse Representatives. Mr. Colman pray'd. Chose S. Sewall Moderator, Voters 459. Saml Legg Esqr. 451. Capt. Saml Checkley 446. Mr. Tho. Oakes, 440. Capt. Ephraim Savage 435. This was the most unanimous Election that I remember to have seen in Boston, and the most Voters.

Febr. 22. Mrs. Willard and several of her children had like to have been cast away coming from Cambridge by Water, wind was so very high; put ashore at last on Muddy-River Marsh: Got to the Gov^rs by that time twas dark. This morning as I was praying alone, I was much affected to think how concern'd and inquisitive I was in my Journeying about my Way; whether I was in the right or no; and yet not so constantly and effectually inquisitive about my Way to Heaven, although I was equally hastening to my Journey's End; whether in the right or wrong way. May He who is the Way, the Truth, and the Life, bring me into and always keep me in the right Way!

Lords-Day, Febr. 28. 1702/3 Mr. Jabez Fox dies of the Small Pox in the forenoon.

Lords-Day, March. 7. 1702/3 Nurse Randal is taken with an Ague in her Brest, which much indisposes her: Whereupon my wife begins

² Ebenezer, born 20 September 1701, was an elder brother of Benjamin Franklin.

to wean Judith though it be a few days before we intended. The wether is grown cold.

March, 16. 1702/3 Though all things look horribly winterly by reason of a great storm of Snow, hardly yet over, and much on the Ground: yet the Robbins cheerfully utter their Notes this morn. So should we patiently and cheerfully sing the Praises of God, and hope in his Mercys, though Storm'd by the last efforts of Antichrist.

March, 20th. A Message is sent in to desire the House might attend with an Answer of the Gov^{rs} Speech; which the Speaker, Maj^r Converse, Read. Then a Message sent to desire it might be printed, which the Govr readily assented to. Only afterward desired to read it first.

March 22. Judith is very well weaned, and by a late addition can now shew eight Teeth. Little Jane, Bastian's daughter, died last night 2 hours after midnight. God is pleased to dispense himself variously. Our little daughter gave us very little Exercise after 3 or 4 nights. Then her cousin Mary Moodey could receive her without any noise.

March, 22. Mr. Banister and I Lotted our Fence on Cotton-Hill: He took E, which was prick'd with a pin on a Label of paper for East-End; and W. for West end was left in my hand for me. He chose to put it to Lot. We saw Pits sail up and fires laden with Salt.

March, 27. 1703. Have not yet given Sermons to Lothrop, Perce, Thomas, Thacher, Appleton, Hammond.

March, 29. Set out for Plimouth with Major Walley, and Mr. Leverett; Get thither a little before night. The souldiers gave us a Volley, and those on board Huzzas, at our entrance into Town; kept at Rickets.

Ap. 1. went into Meetinghouse. *Note.* March *ult.* [31]. Mr. Russel preach'd the Lecture.

Ap. 2. Came home, dined at Cushings. I stay'd and Lodg'd at Mr. Torrey's. He told me of Bridgewater Troubles as to Mr. Brett. *Ap.* 3. came home alone, went with Joseph Hunt, and viewed part of the 300 Acres. Found all well at home. Was surprised to find a Letter giving account of the Death of the Rever^d Mr. Israel Chauncy of a Fever and Convulsions at Stratford. March, 14. 1702/3 8 or 9 m. Had not rec^d my Letter. But am now thank'd for it by his son Charles.

April, 12. 1703. I set out with my son S[amuel] and Daniel Allen; meet with Sherman at Spring's, proceed to Sawen's, there bait, thence to Capt. Mosses, where we dine, thence to Kibbee's, look upon the Line next Mr. Lynde, and assert my Right; Thomas Holbrook, the Father, and Capt. Moss offering to take their Oaths to confirm my Bounds.

Tuesday Apr. 13. Mr. Sherman lays out my Farm of 150 Acres, beginning at Mr. Lynde's and extending to Winthrop's Pond. Tho. Holbrook, sent Moss and Joseph Twitchel with us approving what was done, helping to carry the Chain and lay Stones for Bound-Marks.[3]

Wednesday, Apr. 14. Renew'd the Bounds of the Farm Moses Adams lives on. Tho. Holbrook, Sergeant Moss, and Sam¹ Moss with us, also Capt Moss, Sawen, Deacon Larned &c.

Thorsday Apr. 15. I heard Mr. Sherman had run a Line within mine at Kibbee's; I got Deacon Moss, Tho. Holbrook, Ebenez Leland to go with me: Fairbank was also there. Went to my Bounds, asserted them, in the presence of Mr. Lynde's Tenants whom I sent for, then ordered Kibbee to pull up the Stakes. Told Mr. Lynde's Tenants what my Bounds were, and that within them was my Land; forwarn'd them of coming there to set any Stakes, or cut any Wood. This hinder'd my coming home one day. Sup'd at Cous. Gookin's with Pickerill.

Friday, Apr. 16. My son and I come home: Visit Mr. Hobart, who is glad to see us, Dine there, and then come with him by Tho. Stedman's; where is a privat Meeting. Then ride to Bairstow's and gave Lion 2 Reals, he is stoning the Cellar; saith he began the day before. It seems my daughter Sewall had been there a little before. Got home about 4 aclock, found all well, only Judith had fallen this day and hurt her forhead. *Laus Deo.*

Town-Meeting to chuse Representatives, *April,* 27. 1703. 2 p. m. Voters about 244. Capt. Legg had 242. Checkly, 240. Oakes, 238. Savage, 232.

Meeting was much less; but Voters rather more unanimous than last time, Feb. 16. Mrs. Ann and Kate Dudley dined here to day.

Tuesday, May, 11ᵗʰ set out for Newbury by Charlestown, with Sam Robins. Din'd at Perkins's, Beverly: Got to Newbury about 1 h ½ by sun; Lodg'd at Sister Gerrishes.

May, 12. To Portsmouth with Mr. Leverett.

May. 13. To Kittery; after our getting thither it Rain'd sorely.

May, 14ᵗʰ To Newbury, lodg'd at Broʳ Toppans. 15ᵗʰ at sister Gerrishes. 16. Heard Mr. Tappan preach. 17. Visited Mr. Tappan, Broʳ Shortt: when there was a great and sore Tempest of Thunder, Rain, Hail. When over, ridd to Ipswich, lodg'd at Mr. Rogers.

---

[3] The farm was in Boggistow, now Holliston. John Hull owned this farm, which was divided among Sewall's children. In 1728 the Sewalls gave eleven acres of land for the use of the first minister settled there. Abner Morse, *A Genealogical Register . . . of Sherborn and Holliston* (1856), 325, 326.

18th Held Court, Mr. Rogers prayed. Mr. Hubbard, Col. Appleton, and Rogers dined with us.

19. About an hour before sun-set rode to Salem with Col. Hathorne, Cook, Lynde —— 20. Visited Bro^r Hirst sick of the Gout: came homeward with Cousins Sam. and Margaret. Fain to put in at Hart's and Shelter our selves from a vehement Tempest of Wind, Rain, Hail, Thunder. Got hom about 5 p.m. Found all well through the wonderfull Goodness of God. This day Mr. Stoddard comes to Town, being to preach the Election Sermon. *May, 21.* Companies are warned

to attend on their Election Day. *Note.* May, 20. Barth. Green's New Frame being cover'd but not enclosed, was blown down.

Election-Day, May, 26, 1703.

Chosen

Wait Winthrop	P. Townsend
J. Russell.	J. Higginson
Neg[*ative*] Tho. Oakes	A. Belcher
Neg. E. Cooke	E. Bromfield
J. Hathorne	J. Thacher
E[*lisha*] Hutchinson	J. Walley
S. Sewall	J. Saffin, Neg.
I. Addington	J. Bradford, Neg.
W. Brown	Eᵐ Hutchinson
J. Ph[*illips*]	J. Hammond
J. Corwin	B. Brown
J. Foster	J. Lynde
Neg. P. Sergeant	Samˡ Partridge
D. Pierce	S. Hayman

Not finished till about 9 or 10 at night.

May 27. Govʳ sends in for the Deputies; in a speech shows his Resentment of their Election, One of the Massachusetts and three of Plimouth being changed: Saith he will expunge Five; viz. Elisha Cooke, Peter Sergeant, Tho. Oakes, John Saffin, John Bradford. Some poor; one Superannuated, Some might have served the Queen better than they did.

May 28. Some Papers being sent to the Deputies, they decline Receiving them or entering on other Business till the Council be fill'd. Send in a Bill that are ready to compleat the Election: consented. Capt. Hayman sworn, Chosen, Capt. Samuel Legg, Mr. Samˡ Appleton, Col. Ephraim Hunt, Mr. Nathanˡ Pain, Mr. Isaac Winslow. Governour signs his Approbation: Capt. Legg is sent for in and sworn.

Mr. Samˡ Shrimpton, who dyed May 25. is now buried May. 28. By reason of the great Rain, Col. Phillips, Capt. Hayman, and I went not out of the Council Chamber, at Noon: but din'd together on Bread and Cheese from Monk's.

May 31. Col. Hunt comes to Town and is sworn of the Council.

June, 1. 1703. Town-meeting is held in the old Meetinghouse because of the Genˡ Assembly, 2. p.m. Voters 206. Elizur Holyoke 154: by which was chosen a Representative for Boston. Jnᵒ Love Constable, only one vote otherwise. *Note.* Col. Hobby had 45. votes for a Representative. Mr. Cooke invited many of the Council to drink with him. When came found a Treat of Salmon, Neat's Tongues, Lamb &c. 'Twas near Ten before got home. Mr. Addington, Legg, Russel, Phillips, Hayman, Lynde, Byfield not there, only Mr. Corwin of Salem. *June, 8.* Mr. Pain is sworn in the Afternoon, This day there was much agitation about Nominating a Justice for the Super Court, Council pleaded, till there was a Vacancy they could not do it. If any place was vacant it was that of the Chief Justice, and were ready to speak to that. Gov would have a Justice Nam'd and consented to in the first place; else said he should lose one of the Court. Nothing was done. Mr. Taylor chosen Treasurer. Court adjourned to the last of June 9 *mane*.

Adam is again imprison'd to be Tryed at Suffolk Sessions. Trial order'd by the Gen¹ Assembly.

> Superanuated Squier, wigg'd and powder'd with pretence,
> Much beguiles the just Assembly by his lying Impudence.
> None being by, his bold ⁴ Attorneys push it on with might and main
> By which means poor simple Adam sinks to slavery again.

June, 9. 1703. Gov and L Gov set out for Ipswich in order to goe and meet the Indian sachems.

June, 11ᵗʰ between 12 and 1. Mr. Bromfield is struck down by the Boom of a Sloop swinging upon the Dock; which took his Left shoulder Blade. The Collar Bone on that side is dislocated or broken. The Concussion causes great pain in his back, is fain to sit in a great Chair not being able at present to ly down; between 7 and 8, Even.

Friday, June, 18. 1703. My sons House was Raised at Muddy-River;⁵ The day very comfortable because dry, cloudy, windy, cool. I send for Mr. Wigglesworth and his Wife from Deacon Barnard's in the Coach; to discourse with my Wife about her and Judith's Maladies. After they were sent back, being late in the Afternoon, I went alone in the Hackney-Coach to Roxbury, took Mr. Walter with me. By that Time got there, had just done their Work, and were going to Dinner in the new House. Mr. Walter crav'd a Blessing, Return'd Thanks. Many were there from Muddy-River, Dedham, Roxbury. I drove a Pin be-

---

⁴ In the manuscript Sewall gives an alternate reading here: *bold* is written above *sworn*. The lines refer to John Saffin's lawsuit to bring Adam, a Negro, back into slavery; see A. C. Goodell's article in *C.S.M.* I, 85–112.

⁵ On 21 November 1702 the General Court passed Private Act [No. 14], An Act to Enable Samuel Sewall Esq and Hannah his wife, to Settle Certain Lands at Muddy River in the County of Suffolke upon Samuel Sewall their Eldest Son (*Acts and Resolves* VI, 43–44). This tract, containing about three hundred acres, originally belonged to John Hull.

fore Dinner. After Dinner sung the 127th Psal. and 8th v. 28th St. David's Tune, I set and read the Psalm. Brought home Madame Dudley and my Daughter.

Thorsday June, 24. I am kept from Mr. C. Mather's Lecture by my swoln face. Mr. Secretary visits me. *June, 25.* Mr. P. Dudley visits me. Madam Eyre invites me to her Meeting, by her Daughter; but my indisposition detains me at home. Yet I grow much better.

June 27. Goe to the publick Assembly and take no harm. *Laus Deo.*

June 28. 1703. I have my son Joseph to Cambridge in Austin's Calash, where he is examined by Mr. Jonathan Remington in presence of the President and Mr. Flynt. He Answer'd well to Mr. Remingtons Critical Examination. Mr. Willard gave him for his Theme. *Omnis in Ascanio chari stat cura Parentis;* [Virgil. Æn. i, 646] And advised him and 3 others (Wigglesworth, Tuft, Russel) to be studious, saying,

> *Qui cupit optatam cursu pertingere metam*
> *Multa tulit fecitque puer, sudavit et alsit.*
> [Horace, *Ep. ad Pis.* 412, 413.]

Second-day of the Week July 5th 1703. I had my son to Cambridge again in Austin's Calash. Paid Andrew Bordman his Cautionary Three pounds, in order to my Son Joseph's being Admitted. Went to Mr. Flynt's Chamber, where Col. Wainright's Son and others were upon Examination. When that was doing, and over, Mr. Willard call'd for Joseph's Theme. Read it, gave it to Mr. Flynt, Then in Mr. Flynt's Study, The President and Fellows sign'd his Laws; President said, your Son is now one of us, and he is wellcom. I thanked him; and took Leave. Coming home I order'd Mr. Sheriff [6] to take up a Scurvy post out of the middle of the High way, that had been a Nusance for many years. Gave his Son a shilling for his pains. Got home well. *Laus Deo.* Was pretty much Rain at Charlestown; yet we went almost quite dry, being but a small Sprinkling where we were.

Commencement day July, 7th 1703. Mr. Secretary, Major Walley, Major Brenton and I went by Charlestown to the hether edge of Maldon, and so met the Govr in his Return homeward from Casco-Bay. *Note:* in the afternoon Mr. Wells of Almsbury, is made a Master of Art. Mr. Belcher of Newbury Testified his Education under Mr. Andros at Ipswich, that he was a good Latin and Greek Scholar.[7] Came to Charlestown in company with Mr. Thomson and Mr. Webster. Mr. T. tells me his Unkle at Virginia is dead.

[6] Samuel Gookin, sheriff of Middlesex from 1702 to 1715.
[7] The Rev. Thomas Wells leads as the first on the now lengthened roll of those whom Harvard College has in honor adopted among her alumni, without having

July, 8. p.m. Mr. Winslow is sworn and takes his place at the Board. Bombazeen [*an Indian Sachem*] comes to Town as an Express with Rumors of 15. Frenchmen landed near Pemaquid, and of a Frenchman of War.

July 10. From New-York we hear of a ship arrived there June 29; that came out with a great Fleet from Plimouth May, 2ᵈ in which were five ships bound for New-England.

July 12 Bombazeen and his companion before the Council with Serjᵗ Bean.

Monday, July, 19. 1703 my daughter Mrs. Rebecka Sewall is brought to Bed of a son [*Hull Sewall*], about six-a-clock in the Afternoon. My wife and daughter Hirst were there, Madam Dudlcy, Hubbard, Roberts &c. Mrs. Baker Midwife. Mr. Winchcomb first told the Govᵣ of it, at the Council Table, and then me. Stephen brought the News to Town. I ride home with the Govᵣ and send the Hackney-Coach: See my daughter and Grandson: Bring home my wife, Madam Roberts, daughter Hirst. *July, 22.* Governour, A Gentleman sent from New-York,⁸ Mr. Mackentosh, Mr. Dudley, Mr. Belchar, Dedham, Mr. Hirst dine at our House.

July, 23. Deputies after many days Toil, have at last this day come off, and let fall that clause in the Act about restraining the power of the Govᵣ and Council as to incidental Charges, so as they might not exceed Thirty pounds. Mr. Secretary obtain'd leave of the Govᵣ to make this Minute of Council; viz. Whereas yesterday was appointed for chusing of Officers, and was adjourned to this day, the Secretary alleged that through decay of his health, he was unable to sustain the place of Chief-Justice any longer, pray'd to be dismiss'd and offered his Commission at the Board; whereupon the Govᵣ said he would not expect any further service from him at the present, and that he with the Council would Endeavour to fill the Chair so soon as conveniently they might. This the substance.⁹

---

passed through her training. (M.H.S.EDS.) Thomas Wells of Amesbury, John James of Derby, Connecticut, and Thomas Bridge, governor of the Bermudas and minister of the First Church in Boston, are listed by Shipton (*Sibley* v, 7–25) as Masters of Arts who did not attend Harvard College; "their degrees were not honorary because there is no evidence that they were conferred *honoris causa* . . . They were simply degrees conferred by the Governing Boards on middle-aged clergyman who for one reason or another had not obtained a college education, yet were well educated." Thomas Andrews, schoolmaster of Ipswich, had been Wells's teacher; Samuel Belcher of Newbury (Harvard 1659) gave testimony.
⁸ Probably Abraham Gouverneur, clerk of the Court of Chancery in New York province, and speaker of the Assembly 1701–1702.
⁹ Although Secretary Isaac Addington thus obtained leave of absence from the

Mr. Addington much startled at the words *at present* and urg'd to have them left out: but the Governour did not yield to it. This was done in open Council, in the forenoon.

July, 24. 1703. Joseph takes leave of his Master and Scholars in a short Oration.

Bristol Business is Non-concurr'd by the Deputies.

Governour's note to me to instruct a Meeting of the Judges next Monday is in my Court Book.

Augt. 2. 1703. It is said the Colours must be spread at the Castle every Lords Day in honour of it:

Yesterday was first practiced. If a ship come in on the Lord's day, Colours must be taken down. I am afraid the Lord's Day will fare none the better for this new pretended honor.

Monday, Augt 2. Thomas, the Governour's Coachman, having offended him, He sends him aboard Capt Southacks in order to make him a Sentinel under Major March at Casco fort. I mov'd the Govr to Try him a little longer: but would not; said He might send any man a Souldier.

Ab^t 5 p.m. My Wife, Madam Willard, Daughters Hannah and Eliza. visit Daughter Sewall at Roxbury. *Wednesday, Augt 4.* I carried Mary to Mr. Wigglesworth's and left her there; to see if he could help her against her Sickness and Infirmity.

Augt. 6. I visited Mary as I promis'd her. Mr. Wigglesworth thinks her distemper is of a Convulsive nature.

Augt 5. Mr. Thomas Bridge preaches his first Lecture-Sermon from Hab. 3. 2.

Augt 7. 1703. News comes from N. York that my Lord Cornbury has rec'd his commissions, and that the Militia of Connecticut and the Jersies is granted him.

From the Eastward, Fear of the French and Indians, some being seen.

Augt 10. 1703. I went to Roxbury and saw my daughter who is still in very great pain. Went and saw the Drean. Govr Dudley tells me that Mr. Usher has got Partridge's place; that all Actions Tried here must be sent over to England; an account of them. Will have a Sessions in September. This day, Augt 10—is a Corporation-Meeting at Cambridge; chuse Mr. Josiah Willard a Tutor: chuse Mr. Tho. and

---

Superior Court, no changes were made until 19 February 1707/8, when Wait Still Winthrop was made chief justice, and the following day when Jonathan Corwin was appointed justice in place of John Leverett, who became president of the college. Sewall was acting chief justice until Winthrop was appointed. *C.S.M.* iii, 76.

Wm Brattle into the Corporation, in stead of Mr. Allen and Mr. Walter, who have abdicated as they reckon.[10]

Augt 11. News comes of the Onset of the Enemy.

I went to Cambridge Augt 11. to make sure a study for Joseph in Mr. Remington's Chamber: came home with Mr. Torrey, call'd at the Gov^rs, where a Master that came by water from Black-point, gave account of the Fires kindled by the Indians in several places; brought a little youth that narrowly escaped the enemies hands.

Augt 12. at night, News comes from Wells that have buried 15. durst not go to bury their uttermost [outermost]: Lost as they fear 60. Enemy numerous.

This morn. the Lt Govr set out for Portsmouth, Capt. Tuthill goes to the Castle.

Augt 13 Council is call'd to read the sad Letter from Capt. Willard and Wheelwright. Capt. Southack is sent away with a chaplain and chirurgeon.

Augt 9. I read the Transaction of the Govr with the Indians, at the Coffee house.[11]

Second-day of the week, Augt 16, 1703. In the Afternoon I had Joseph in a Calash from Charlestown to Cambridge, carried only his little Trunk with us with a few Books and Linen; Went into Hall and heard Mr. Willard expound the 123 [Psalm]. 'Tis the first exercise of this year, and the first time of Joseph's going to prayer in the Hall.

Augt 23. 1703. I went to Cambridge to see Joseph settled in his study, help'd to open his Chest. Joseph was at home the Sabbath, and went up on foot by Charlestown. This day several very unusual Circles were seen about the sun. Mr. Leverett first told me of them, but I saw them not.

Septr 3. Mr. Banister's eldest daughter is buried. She died very suddenly of convulsions.—Sept. 4. Mrs. Emm Lynde is buried. Bearers, Maj^r Genl Winthrop, Mr. Russel, Col. Hutchinson, Sewall, Capt. Belchar, Col. Savage.[12]

---

[10] After studying the records of the Harvard Corporation in connection with this entry, Josiah Quincy came to the conclusion that it was Nehemiah Walter and Cotton Mather who "abdicated." James Allen continued to attend meetings until 1707. Hist. of Harvard University (1860), I, 150–151.

[11] We omit here a long abstract by Sewall of a memorandum by Governor Dudley on his negotiations with the Indians at Casco Bay in June. Samuel Penhallow, a participant, wrote of this conference in The History of the Wars of New England with the Eastern Indians, or a Narrative of their continued Perfidy and Cruelty . . . (Boston, 1726; reprinted, Cincinnati, 1859. pp. 16–18).

[12] Emma (Anderson) Brakenbury Lynde, the second wife of Joseph Lynde of Charlestown.

Septr 6. 1703. Artil. Training, I Train'd in the Forenoon, As I was going, Mr. Oakes met me and ask'd if I had not heard the News? He said French King; he had his Neck broken by a fall from his Horse, as he was viewing an Army Rais'd to goe against those of the Cevennes. One Bodwin brings the Report, who comes from New Castle, and had it at Sea from Commodore Taylor.

Tho. Oakes had a Tin Granado shell broke in his Hand, which has shattered his hand miserably, his two last fingers are already cut off: This was in the Afternoon, as came from Council, was told of it.

Septr 9. Genl Court is prorogued to Wednesday, Octr 27, 1703, 9 *mane.* Great Rain. Govr went not to the Lecture. *Sept^r* 11th 1703. Col. Hathorn and I set out for Wrentham, lodge at Lt Wear's. *Sept.* 12. Hear Mr. Man. Dine with him. 7^r 13 See Wullamanuppack pond, out of which Charles River runs.[13] Dine at Rehoboth, to Bristow. 7^r 16. return to Rehoboth, sup there and ride in the night to Wood-cock's. Breakfast at Billinges. Bait at Dedham, got home by four p.m. Go to Major Wallies to their Meeting.

7^r 19. Hear of the Taking of [*New*] Providence by the French; surpris'd it in the night July 20.[14] 7^r 20. Wadsworth arrives from Dublin 7 weeks: Brings no News of the French King's death, so that conclude he is alive. I, my wife, Joseph, Mary, visit son and daughter at Muddy-River. I bring Joseph going in his way to Cambridge from Gates's into the Highway. *Tuesday,* 7^r 28. very cold, and snow to cover the ground. 7^r 29th The Snow is now three or four inches deep, and a very cold Norwest wind: a sad face of Winter, to see the Houses and Ground so cover'd with snow, and to see so much Ice.

7^r 25. The Beams and Joyce of the old Hall Floor are laid.

7^r 28. Keats comes to Ground pinning.

8^r 13. 1703 Capt. Rich'd Sprague is buried. Mr. Russell, Capt. Hayman, Capt. Belchar, Mr. Leverett, Capt. Cary, Capt. Fowl Bearers: is buried in Mr. Morton's Tomb. I was there. Most of the Scholars, Joseph for one: My Gloves were too little, I gave them him. Govr there.

Novr 26[15] Harrison the Controller, and Mr. Wm Pain are examined

---

[13] Wrentham was first known by the Indian name of Wollomapaugh.

[14] "New Providence was again recolonized by the British, in 1686, and continued in their hands till 1703, when a formidable force of French and Spanish effected a landing, carried off the Negroes, destroyed Nassau, and drove into the woods the inhabitants, the most of whom, on the invaders having departed, retired to Carolina." Bryan Edwards, *The History of the British Colonies in the West Indies,* 5th ed., IV, 219–220, as quoted by the M.H.S.EDS.

[15] At this point Sewall began Vol. III of his manuscript diary. On the fly-leaf is an entry for 24 January 1703/4, which we have inserted at that place. Sewall

before the Govr and Council by Mr. Russell's Motion. When mention was made of putting them to their Oath, Harrison said he was ready to swear, but then it must be by laying his hand on the Bible: Govr said, So he ought, and order'd Mr. Secretary to fetch the Bible. Mr. Pain also slip'd on his hand. Mr. Harrison first look'd into it to see that 'twas the Bible. When had sworn, seem'd to applaud himself, and said he would have this forwarded and upheld. When Questions were asked him, he answer'd, By that Booke it is True.[16]

Sabbath, Novr 28. A very sore storm of snow, which makes Assemblys very thin. Not one Woman in Roxbury Meeting.

Decr 11. Poor little Hull Sewall dies in Mr. Phips's house at Muddy-River about 6. in the evening, of Convulsions. About 8. at night the Govr sends us word of it. *Decr 14th* Corps is brought to Town in the Governours Slay. *Decr 15.* is born to our Tomb, and set upon a Box that his great Grandfathers Bones now put into it at Williams's desire, some being wash'd out. On the Box is made with Nails, 1683. Bearers were Mr. Nathan^l Oliver and David Stoddard. Gov^rs Lady and my wife rode in the Coach. Son and daughter followed the little Corps in Mourning: then Grandfathers, Joseph and Hannah, Mr. Hirst and his wife. Several of the Council here, and Mr. Cotton Mather, Mr. Nehemiah Walter. Provided new oak Plank for the entrance of the Tomb. Madam Leverett and Usher there. Gave no Gloves.

Decr 23. Dr. Mather marries Mr. Thomas Hutchinson and Mrs. Sarah Foster.[17] A very great Wedding. Mr. Secretary and I not bidden, nor Mr. Bromfield. Mr. Hirst and his wife were invited; but Mr. Hirst was at Portsmouth, and my daughter being very big with child, excus'd her going in Want of her Husband's company. I knew not she was invited till the time was Past.

Decr 23. Mr. Brisco, now my son's Tenant, comes to the Council-Chamber when I was left there almost alone, and desired me to Marrie his Daughter, which I did at his house. Sung the 90th Psalm

---

listed on the verso of the fly-leaf the funerals at which he had been a bearer, beginning in January 1606/7. With two exceptions, this information is recorded in the text; the occasions he failed to mention have been added in footnotes.
[16] Nathaniel Carey, a waiter under James Russell, Commissioner of the Impost, had seized some rum from Michael Shaller of Boston, a distiller, for non-payment of excise. Wishing to keep it safely, he deposited it at the Custom House, by leave of Mr. Ralph Harrison, comptroller, and Mr. William Payne, deputy-collector. But when he went for it these latter claimed it as a customs prize, and refused to deliver it. Massachusetts Archives, LXII, f.446.
[17] They were the parents of Governor Thomas Hutchinson.

from the 12ᵗʰ v. to the end, with earnest desires that this Match might prove better than the former.[18]

Decʳ 30. Col. Hutchinson makes a very great Entertainment: Mr. Bromfield and wife are now invited: Mr. Secretary and I pass'd by, and I do not know who beside.

Decʳ 26. *Sabbath*; very sore vehement Storm of Snow; exceeding high Tide, which did much hurt in Cellars and lower Rooms, and carried many Stacks of Hay quite away. It seems Roxbury Meeting was held at Mr. Walter's Dwelling-house. The Christmas keepers had a very pleasant day, Govʳ and Mr. Dudley at Church, and Mr. Dudley made a pretty large Entertainment after.

Decʳ 20. Five men that were getting home wood at Saco, are sur-pris'd by the enemy, three after found slain. Seven others that were at a distance, escaped to Wells: from whence the News came to Town Decʳ 23.

[18] The record in the town book gives the names of the principals as William Palfree and Abigail Briscow.

1704

SEWALL TURNS HIS CASH OVER TO HIS WIFE / INDIAN TROUBLES /
DEATH OF MAJOR WILLIAM BRADFORD AND OF DEANE WINTHROP /
COURT AT PLYMOUTH / PROPHETICAL DISCUSSIONS WITH NICHOLAS
NOYES / "BOSTON NEWS-LETTER" BEGINS PUBLICATION / TRIP TO
IPSWICH, NEWBURY, AND SALEM / CAPTURE AND EXECUTION OF
QUELCH'S PIRATE CREW / COMMENCEMENT OF 1704 / SUNDAY FIRE /
COURT AT BRISTOL

Jany 1. 1703/4 I carried 2 Duz. Mr. Willard's Books about swearing, to Mr. Phillips; Duz. to Buttolp; Duz. to Eliott; Duz to Boon.[1]

Jany 5. Meeting at Mrs. Stevens; I pray there. Lindsey arrives at
Marblehead this day; came from Isle Wight 29th Jno Balston in her.

Jany 7th Col. Hutchinson's case is put to the Jury of which Mr.
Hirst Foreman. *Jan^y* 8. They bring in a conditional verdict, If Madam
Warren had power to alienat before Division &c. Court would not
accept of it; but said that was it they were to Try: and sent them
out again: Then they brought in for Col. Hutchinson, costs. Col.
Hutchinson said upon the Bench, He would not be Try'd by Infer.
or Sup'or Court; He would be Try'd by the Jury; they were his Judges.

Jany 14th 1703/4 Got an Overseers Meeting at Col Foste[r] [*manuscript imperfect*] and pass my Account but could not get through with
it; met with so[*me*] gross mistakes or such as fear'd were so; and had
not time. Col. Foster offers me to carry all I have done, into Leger
parcells.

Jany 16. A storm of snow; but not so vehement as those in Nov^r
and Dec. In the Afternoon Dr. Jer. Dummer preaches from Luke 13,
ult. Mr. Pemberton baptizes Mr. Daniel Oliver's son Daniel. My wife
not abroad. The last Lecture and this Lord's Day Major Walley appears in his Wigg, having cut off his own Hair. *Jan^y* 19. reckon'd with
the Tenants of the Saw-mill at Braintry, and took their Bonds for
the Arrears, and cancell'd the Leases. In the morning walk'd with

---

[1] Samuel Willard's sermon, *The Fear of an Oath. Or, Some Cautions about
Swearing, If we would approve our selves Truly Godly*, was preached at the Thursday Lecture, 30 January 1700/1, and printed in Boston in 1701.

Major Walley, Capt. Tim° Clark, Mr. Calef, constable Franklin, to visit disorderly poor; Met at my house. Capt Clark took up his Wigg: I said would have him consider that one place; The Bricks are fallen &c. But here men *cut down* the sycamores [*cf. Isaiah ix,* 10]. He seem'd startled.

*Second-Day; Jan*ʸ 24. 1703/4 I paid Capt. Belchar £8–15–0. Took 24ˢ in my pocket, and gave my Wife the rest of my cash £4.3–8, and tell her she shall now keep the Cash; if I want I will borrow of her. She has a better faculty than I at managing Affairs: I will assist her; and will endeavour to live upon my Salary; will see what it will doe. The Lord give his Blessing.

*Wednesday Jan*ʸ 19. 1703/4 Four Men kill'd at Casco-Bay belonging to Capt. Gallop; go out of the Boat; Bennet the Master out of the Sloop; Indians had their canoes, and lay there in wait.

Janʸ 24. express brings the News.

Ice would not suffer him to go to the Fort; so lay by Hog-Island.

*Jan*ʸ 31. Second day of the week, about four hours before day, my Daughter Hirst was delivered of a Living lively Daughter. Her mother went to her after the forenoon exercise Janʸ 30. Mother Hirst came the evening before. We have an Answer of Peace to our many Prayers. *Laus Deo.* Mrs. Wakefield was Midwife. Madam Usher, Pemberton, Hubbard, Welsteed, Nurse Johnson assisted. Nurse is from Salem.

*Jan*ʸ 31. George Pierce brings the News, of a Girl being kill'd at Nichawannuck [*Berwick, Maine*]; 30 Indians assaulted a Garrison there; were received bravely by the English, one of them kill'd, and the rest by Capt. Brown with a small party of men 10 or 12, put to flight, sundry of them wounded; left many of their own Accoutrements, for haste, and carried nothing away of ours. This was done last Friday.

Febr. 1. 1703/4 Third of the week, I went to Dorchester Lecture, and heard Mr. Danforth preach from those words, All is vanity. Din'd with Madam Taylor and Mr. Trott. Before Lecture, I rid into the Burying place, and read Mr. Stoughton's Epitaph, which is very great.[2]

Febr. 3. 1703/4 Mr. Neh. Hobart dines with us in the chamber. Has not been in Town of many weeks before. I Lent him Forbes on the Rev. Gave him 4 Quires paper and box wafers. Told him I was like to have some Bickerings with Mr. Noyes;[3] and he should be Judge

[2] The inscription on Governor William Stoughton's monument in the Dorchester cemetery is transcribed in *Sibley* I, 205–206.

[3] Patrick Forbes of Corse (1564–1635), Bishop of Aberdeen, published *An Exqvisite Commentarie Vpon The Revelation Of Saint Iohn* (319 pages) in 1613 and *An Learned Commentarie Vpon the Revelation Of Saint Iohn* (426 pages) in 1614. For Sewall's bickerings with the corpulent Nicholas Noyes of Salem, see the entry of 17 April.

of the Controversy. I set up this Problem, that Christ set his Right Foot on the New-World; his Left, on the Old. Rev. 10. Pray'd him to assign otherwise if he saw convenient.

Febr. 4ᵗʰ 1703/4 I paid Sarah Mountfort her Legacy with the Three and Twenty pieces of Gold. Mr. Secretary took eight pieces, which 1 ounce and 12ᵈ weight, and gave £8–11–3. Sarah Mountfort had Fifteen pieces, which weighed 16–8–9 Three ounces, 2ᵈ, weight, and 12 Grains by Cousin Dummers Scales £25–0–0. Mr. Secretary took the Acquittance seal'd and Deliver'd in presence of her Brother Wadsworth, and Tom Maccarty.

Lord's-Day, February the 6ᵗʰ 1703/4 I went to Mr. Colman's that I might see my little Grand-daughter baptised; Besides me there were Mr. Brattle, Mr. Clark and Capt. Anth. Checkley in the Fore-Seat. Mr. Colman read the 15ᵗʰ and 16. Psalms, and the last chapter of the first Epistle of Peter. Text was Mat. 26. 38. Went on with the Discourse had begun in the morning for the Lord's Supper. Pray'd excellently at Baptisme, for the Child, Mother, all. Child is call'd Mary.⁴ My [daughter] would have it so for the sake of Mrs. Mary Hirst, her Husband's [moth]er, who was present, and my little daughter Mary. Nurse brought the Child, and Mr. Grove Hirst the father held it up. Though the Child had cry'd before, did not cry at Mr. Colman's pouring on the Water. Daughter reckons herself very ill.

Febr. 7. Nurse Hawkins, who watch'd with her, tells me my daughter had a very good night. *Laus Deo.*

Febr. 5. Seventh-day of the week; I fasted and pray'd to God that Satan might not be commissioned any longer to buffet me and my wife; for my self and family in the advancing year: and Province &c. for Daughter Hirst, and little Mary to be dedicated to Him the next day.

Lᵗ Tristram Coffin dyed Febr. 4ᵗʰ 1703/4.⁵ Joseph Frazon, the Jew, dyes at Mr. Major's, Mr. Joyliff's old house; Febr. 5ᵗʰ Satterday, is carried in Simson's coach to Bristow; from thence by Water to Newport, where there is a Jews-burying place.⁶

Febr. 8ᵗʰ a Garrison-house is surpris'd at Haverhill by 6 or 7 Indians.

Febr. 18. 19. 20. My wife lodges with my daughter Hirst to comfort her. *Febr. 20.* Major William Bradford dies in the 80ᵗʰ year of his

---

⁴ Sewall married this granddaughter to Captain William Pepperrell 21 February 1722/3, but he did not live to see her acquire the title of Lady Pepperrell.
⁵ See our first note for 22 May 1704.
⁶ At this time Newport was the seat of a flourishing mercantile community of Portuguese Jews engaged in commerce with the West Indies and Europe.

Age: He was a Right New-England Christian.⁷ Mrs. Lewis dies at Boston. Isaac Goose junʳ is baptised this day. *Febr.* 22. A great funeral for Mrs. Lewis.

Febr. 25. I went to Charlestown Lecture; heard Mr. Bradstreet preach from 1 Cor. 7. 31.; made a good Sermon. As return'd in the Ferry-boat, I was told Capt. Stephens had done nothing. The Lord pity us.

Febr. 24ᵗʰ 1703/4 This day the new Parishoners meet in the house built for their Minister, and call the Precinct Byfield, as Broʳ Moody tells me, March 4ᵗʰ 1703/4 before his going home.

March, 5. The dismal News of the Slaughter made at Deerfield ⁸ is certainly and generally known, Mr. Secretary came to me in the morning, and told me of it: I told Mr. Willard; by which means our Congregation was made a Bochim. [*Judges, ii.* 1–5.] Tis to be observ'd that the great slaughters have been on the Third day of the week; our Court day. This was Febr. 29ᵗʰ 1703/4 My Tenant Kibbee was arrested this day.

March, 16. 1703/4 Mr. Dean Winthrop, of Pulling Point, dies upon his Birth-day, just about the Breaking of it. He was Taken at eight aclock the evening before, as he sat in his chair, sunk first, being set up, he vomited, complain'd of his head, which were almost his last

⁷ Major William Bradford was the son of William Bradford of the *Mayflower* company, who was Governor of New Plymouth Colony for over thirty years and author of the great Pilgrim record, *Of Plimoth Plantation.* Major Bradford's son, Major John Bradford of Kingston (1652–1736), at some date not now known, placed this manuscript in Sewall's hands. In 1728 the Rev. Thomas Prince, in search of materials for his *Chronological History,* visited Major John Bradford, who lent him several manuscript volumes written by his grandfather the Governor, and others, and told him to get the Plimoth volume from Sewall. Prince apparently retained these volumes in his New England Library, kept in the tower of Old South Church. Lost for many years, the Bradford history turned up in the Bishop of London's library at Fulham Palace in mid-nineteenth century, and was first printed by the Massachusetts Historical Society in 1856. The manuscript was returned by the Diocese of London and formally turned over to the Commonwealth of Massachusetts in May 1897; it is now lodged in the State Library. 1 *M.H.S.Proc.* xix, 64–67, 106–122.

⁸ The Deerfield Massacre occurred on the night of 29 February 1703/4, when a force of 50 French soldiers and 200 Indians attacked the 300 sleeping inhabitants of this frontier town. Fifty were killed, 137 escaped, and 111 were carried off as prisoners. Rev. John Williams (Harvard 1683) was a captive in Canada until 1706; after his release he returned to Boston where he wrote *The Redeemed Captive Returning to Zion* (1707). His wife Eunice, the daughter of Rev. Eleazer Mather of Northampton and sister of Eliakim Mather, who had lived with the Sewalls, was slain. Their daughter Eunice, ten at the time of the massacre, married an Indian and resisted all entreaties to return to Massachusetts (see Sewall's entries of 26 March and 26 June 1713). *D.A.B., Dict. Amer. Hist.*

words. Hardly spake anything after his being in bed. 81 years old. He is the last of Govr Winthrop's children—*statione novissimus exit*.[9] *March,* 20. is buried at Pulling Point by his son and Three Daughters. Bearers Russel, Cooke; Hutchinson, Sewall; Townsend, Paige. From the House of Hasey. Scutcheons on the Pall. I help'd to lower the Corps into the Grave. Madam Paige went in her Coach. Maj^r Genl and Capt. Adam Winthrop had Scarvs, and led the widow. Very pleasant day; Went by Winnisimmet.

March, 24, 1703/4 William Daws, Mason, dyes about 2 p.m. A good old man, full of days, is got well to the end of his weary Race. Arthur Mason's Negro dyes this day, being run over by his own cart on Tuesday. Is a great Loss, being faithfull and in his full strength.

March, 25, 1704. Col. Hathorne and I travel to Braintry, lodge at Cousin Fisk's. *March,* 26. Hear Mr. Fisk preach Forenoon and Afternoon: *Note.* One Sheffield,[10] a very good aged Christian, of about 90 years old, was there, who, as was expected, was never like to have come abroad more. Was accordingly given Thanks for. George Allen waits on me.

March, 27th Bait at Mr. Cushing's. He shews us Accord Pond,[11] hardly ¼ of a mile out of the Rode. Dine at Barkers in company of Major Eels, his son, Mr. Stoddard, Dr. Samsone and others. Sheriff Warren meets us there; before we get away, Major Walley and Leverett come in. We get to Plim° ½ hour before Sun-set.

March [*manuscript torn; probably the text read:* we hold] the Court.

March, 29th Went into the Meetingh[*ouse*] in the [*torn*] Adjourn'd *sine die* before Noon. Din'd and got to Cushings about sunset. In the evening Mr. Cushing desired me to pray, which did, and sang three staves of the 137 Psal. omitting Edom. Mr. Cushing told us, Mr. Danforth us'd to sing. I shew'd Mr. Leverett Accord Pond as came along.

March, 30. Call'd and visited Mr. Torrey. Call'd at the Governours, He told us the particulars of the dreadfull Storm in England in Nov^r.[12] Came home about 4 p.m: found all well. *Laus Deo.*

[9] *Diffugiunt stellæ: quarum agmina cogit*
   Lucifer, et cœli statione novissimus exit.
                        Ovid, *Met.* ii, 114.
[10] Edmund Sheffield, baptized at Sudbury, Suffolk, England, in 1612, was admitted freeman at Roxbury in 1644; he died at Braintree 13 October 1705. *N.E.H.G.R.* LXXVII, 192.
[11] Accord Pond, at the angle of Abington, Scituate, and Hingham, was named as early as 1640.
[12] This was called the most terrible storm that had been known in England. Daniel Defoe compiled an interesting little book about it: *The Storm: Or, A*

April, 1. 1704. Visited my valetudinarious son at Brooklin; gave Baker a shilling to drive a Nail for me in the great Stairs. Call'd at the Gov^{rs} as I came home to condole the Loss of Mr. Samuel Dudley at Suratt, Febr. 22. 1702/3: was taken with the small Pocks Febr. 16th, of which he died the 22th, the day Madam Willard had like to have been cast away and her family, coming from Cambridge by Water. I told the Govr I hoped this young Gentleman might have been a Support to his family; for countenance was one of the Goodliest I had known. Said to Mr. William Dudley that to get more Acquaintance with, and Conformity to Christ, as his Elder Brother, was the best and only way to Repair such a Loss. Read Brothers Letter to the Govr about a Scout-Shallop: He said Southack and Gallop were hastening. The News of Mr. Saml Dudley's death was inclosed to Col. Foxcroft by Mr. Shepard, Govr of the East-India Company: Letter dated Decr 3. 1703. Col. Foxcroft deliver'd it to the Govr the evening following, Thorsday, March 30. 1704, 2 or 3 hours after Major Walley and I took leave of his Excellency.

April, 2. 1704. Ship arrives from England Seven weeks passage; came out with the Fleet that had the King of Spain[13] on board to carry to Portugal. Brings Prints of the November Storm, and the December Mercury.

April, 3. Artil. Company chuses Mr. Henry Gibbs of Watertown to preach their Sermon; chuse Capt. Checkley and me to join Comiss. Officers to acquaint him with it, and desire him to undertake it.

April, 5th Capt. John Ballentine, Lt Tho Savage and Ens. Tho Fitch, Sewal and Checkly, set out at 2 p.m. round for Watertown: Find Mr. Gibbs at home, Acquaint him with our Message, press him earnestly: but can get no Answer, He will give an Answer the 13th after Lecture. I invited him to dine with me. Had comfortable going and returning: Call'd at Brooklin as came home. Baited at Remington's. I used Dr. Witsius's[14] Title of's Oration *De Theologo Modesto*; told him the more Modesty we saw the more vehement we should be in our Assaults.

Apr. 6 & 7th very cold North-east Stormy Wether, and Tuesday

Collection of the most Remarkable Casualties and Disasters Which happen'd in the late Dreadful Tempest, both by Sea and Land (London, 1704).

[13] The War of the Spanish Succession was going on, precipitated by the death of the childless Carlos II. Carlos had bequeathed his dominions to the grandson of Louis XIV, Philip of Anjou, who reigned as Philip V from 1700 to 1746. William III of England and Leopold of Austria had formed the Grand Alliance and were attempting to place on the throne Leopold's son, Archduke Charles; he is the King of Spain whom Sewall mentions.

[14] Hermann Witsius (1636–1708), Dutch theologian.

was the Catechising: so that we took the only day could be had to go in this week.

April, 10. 1704. The Seven and Thirty French privateers are brought to Town, who were put a-Shore at Marshfield last Friday in the vehemency of the Storm. *Feria quarta, Apr. 12.* In the morning I saw and heard three Swallows playing over my head. I think I never observ'd them so soon in the year before. Rowse came in from London, 7 weeks passage, Apr. 10. *Feria Sexta, Ap. 14.* p.m. Tho. Wallis dieth. *Feria septima, Apr. 15. 1704.* Mr. Nathan¹ Oliver dieth between 3 and 4 in the morning. He was born 20 days before me. Joseph comes to see us. *Feria Secunda, April, 17th. 1704,* I go to Salem to see my Broᵣ Hirst; Speak with Mr. Noyes, who conceives that the Witnesses were slain at the conclusion of the Peace of Ryswick, 1697. Passing away of the 2ᵈ Wo. at the conclusion of the Peace of Carlowitz with the Turk [1699]. Resurrection of the Witnesses by the Convulsions following the death of Charles 2ᵈ K[ing] of Spain; The 1260 days Expire, and then the Witnesses Rise; namely the 1260 Days of the Ten-horn'd Beast, his power to make war. Antichrist's Reign begins at the Time of the great Whore's mounting the Beast, the 10 horned beast, viz. Anno 1073. Hildebrand papa [*Pope Gregory VII*]. At the death of Valentinian, the Ten-horn'd Beast set up; viz. anno, 458. Taken from Mr. Noyes's mouth at Broᵣ Sewall's.¹⁵

Apr. 18ᵗʰ Go home in company of Major Brown, Corwin, Higginson, Lynde, Gerrish to the parting way, where turn'd off to Mr. Wigglesworth [*of Malden*], where I din'd: then home by Charlestown: Went to the Funeral of Mr. Nathan¹ Oliver: Bearers, Sewall, Walley; Legg, Dummer; Cooper, [*Je*]ffries. Govᵣ was there.

April, 24. 1704. I went to Cambridge to see some Books on the Revelation, and there met with Mr. Pignet ¹⁶: went into Hall and heard Mr. Willard expound Rom. 4. 9, 10, 11 and pray. I gave Mr. Willard the first News-Letter that ever was carried over the River.¹⁷

---

¹⁵ The M.H.S. editors have a charming footnote for this entry: "The 'bickerings' which Judge Sewall, according to his expectations, had with the Rev. Nicholas Noyes, of Salem [Harvard 1667], on these prophetical mysteries, concern such profound and perplexing matters that the professional attainments of the Editors do not qualify them to attempt any arbitration in the case."

¹⁶ This mysterious name could not be found anywhere in local annals by the M.H.S. editors. We suspect that Sewall was referring to an author, but our bibliographical searchings have not revealed him.

¹⁷ *The Boston News-Letter*, the first regularly published newspaper in America, appeared 24 April 1704, and continued to be published until the evacuation of Boston by the British troops in March 1776. Its first publisher was John Campbell, bookseller and postmaster of Boston; Nicholas Boone was associate pub-

He shew'd it the Fellows. I came home in company with Mr. Adams.

April, 25. My daughter Hannah and I carefully removed all Eben^r Mountfort's Linnen &c out of his crazy, unfaithfull Trunk, and laid them up orderly in the new Chest I bought of Bro^r Nichols for that purpose. Col. Perce died the 22 Ap. in the Afternoon. Son and daughter Sewall lodg'd here last night.

Lord's-Day, Apr. 23. There is great Firing at the Town, Ships, Castle upon account of its being the Coronation-day, which gives offence to many; See the Lord's-day so profan'd. Down Sabbath, Up St George.

Apr, 27, 1704. Little Judith is carried on Horseback, Jane Green attending her, unto the house of Mr. Robert Avery of Dedham, for to be healed of her Rupture. Had Mrs. Wigglesworth's advice. In the morning, not thinking of her departure, I first got her to say after me, Create in me a clean heart, O God; and renew a right spirit within me. It was near sun-set, when they went away, which made us uneasy: But Mrs. Avery was in a readiness with Horses and Company; and the spring advancing apace made us consent. I intended 4. p.m. to be the latest for their setting out.

May, 13. I visit little Judith; find her well: visit Mr. Belchar.

May, 15th Set out for Ipswich with Major Walley; Mr. Leverett falls in at Lewis's; go by Salem: from thence Col. Hathorne goes with us, Sheriff Gedny waits on us: got thither in season. Lodge at Mr. Rogers'. When came away gave Mrs. Martha a Turkey-Leather Psalm-book.

May, 17. Made a shift to get to Rowley, Lodg'd at Bro^r Northend's, who came to Ipswich and invited me.

May, 18. heard Mr. Payson and Hale; No Meeting at Byfield, had not timely notice.

May, 19. ride to Newbury; Dine at Sister Gerrishes; See Cousin Joseph's wife, give her Mr. Cole's Sermons.[18] Knew not of the Clause

---

lisher. Bartholomew Green, John Allen, and again Bartholomew Green, were, successively, its printers. It was issued weekly, on Monday. Sewall kept a bound file of the paper, in which he made marginal notes in ink. Two volumes of his file are extant. The New-York Historical Society copy runs from the first issue to that of 19 April 1708, and contains an index of four pages in Sewall's hand. The Boston Athenaeum copy runs from 19 February 1710/11 to 17 October 1715; both volumes lack certain issues, but include various broadsides bound up for preservation. 2 *M.H.S. Proc.* VI, 171–174; 3 *Proc.* I, 204–209.

[18] Probably Thomas Cole, Principal of St. Mary Hall, Oxford, a nonconformist who held office from 1656 until ejected by the King's Commissioners in 1660; later he was a Congregationalist minister in London. He published several sermons. *Calamy.*

about Perriwigs till I got to Rowley. I read the Discourse of Adoption to my Aunt Northend. Lodge at Bro^r Tapping's. *May, 21*. Goe and hear Mr. Belcher; Dine there. After dinner the aged Ordway comes to see me, complains bitterly of his cousin John Emery's carriage to his wife, which makes her leave him and go to her Sister Bayly.[19]

May, 22. visit Cousin Joshua Pierce, the widow Pierce, widow Coffin.[20] Went with Bro^r Moodey to his house, dine there, went to Perkins's in Beverly, lodge there: because of the extream heat, I travel'd from Ipswich thither in the night. *May, 23*, went early to Salem, convers'd with Mr. Noyes, told him of the Quaker Meeting at Sam. Sawyers, a week ago, profaneness of the young Hoags, professing that hæresy. Visited Bro^r Hirst still confin'd by the Gout. Came home with daughter Sewall, she rides single, Sam. Sewall *de Stephano*,[21] waits on her. Refresh at Lewis's, where Mr. Paul Dudley is in egre pursuit of the Pirats.[22] He had sent one to Boston; and see

---

[19] Probably James Ordway of Newbury, who was born in 1620. His wife, Ann Emery, had died in 1687. Joshua Coffin, *Hist. of Newbury* (1845), 312.

[20] Judith (Greenleaf) Somerby Coffin was the widow of Lieut. Tristram Coffin Jr. of Newbury, who died 4 February 1703/4. Sewall recorded her death in December 1705. They were the first of seven generations of Coffins to occupy the house Sewall visited. It is still standing, a short distance from the house of Sewall's father, on the High Road, and is now restored and maintained by the Society for the Preservation of New England Antiquities. *Savage*; and Nina Fletcher Little in *Antiques*, LXXVII, 482–485.

[21] Sewall often uses this Latin shortcut; here he refers to Samuel Sewall (1689–1729), son of his brother Stephen.

[22] Here begins the exciting tale of Captain John Quelch and his pirate crew. In the summer of 1703 the *Charles*, a newly built brigantine of some eighty tons burden, had been fitted up as a privateer by Sir Charles Hobby, Colonel Nicholas Paige, William Clarke, Benjamin Gallop, and John Colman, Boston merchants, and commissioned by Governor Dudley to prey on French shipping off Acadia and Newfoundland. While riding at anchor at Marblehead, Captain Daniel Plowman, the commander, was taken sick, and informed the ship's owners that he was unable to take her to sea. Plowman had conveyed his suspicions of the crew, but before the owners were able to take any effectual measures, John Quelch, the lieutenant-commander, had come aboard, conferred with the crew, taken command, and sailed the ship off to the southward. Captain Plowman was thrown overboard, but whether alive or dead is not recorded. In November 1703 the *Charles* was off the coast of Brazil, and during the next three months Quelch made nine captures of Portuguese vessels, securing over a thousand pounds of gold and silver, and firearms, ammunition, merchandise, provisions, and rum. Portugal was then an ally of Britain, and whether Quelch knew it or not, a treaty of amity had been signed in Lisbon in May 1703 declaring piratical ships of whatever nation the common enemies of the Portuguese, the English, and the Dutch. The *Boston News-Letter* of 15–22 May 1704 reported the arrival of Cap-

ing me call'd him back again; At such a sudden I knew not what to
doe: but charg'd Tom. Cox and one Jarvis with him, and order'd
them to deliver him to Mr. Secretary Addington. For my daughter's
sake I went by Charlestown, and parted with her where Cambridge
way turns off. George Allen and I got home about Sun-set. *Laus
Deo.* Mr. Bridge and Mr. Bridgham welcom'd me by the New Burying place, met them there. *May, 27ᵗʰ* Mr. Secretary and Capt.
Belcher, Mr. Eᵐ Hutchinson and Palmer, Mr. Bromfield and I ride
to Cambridge to meet the Govʳ. Staid till about 7, then suppos'd
would not come till Monday, and so came home. But the Govʳ came
that night. I knew not of it till 'twas too late to visit his Excellency
on Monday morn. Went to Council, and met with the Govʳ there.
May, 29ᵗʰ Govʳ orders another Proclamation to be issued out, respecting the Pirats.²³ Several bring in Gold; Capt. Tuttle brings three par-
cels; two given him by Wᵐ Clark *de Johane;* one by Capt. Quelch.
May, 31, 1704. Mr. Addington, Walley and Sewall Give the Depts
the Oaths; but one Councellor at Roxbury, *viz.* Capt. Belcher. Mr.
Jonathan Russell preaches. Deputies send in a Resolve that none is
to be accounted chosen who has not the major part of the Voters:
Election finished about eight: Govʳ and Lieut. Govʳ went away long
before.

June 1. Govʳ signs the Allowance of all but Mr. Sergeant and Cook;
them He does not allow.²⁴

June 2. Debated in Council whether or no should not fill up the
Council: Most seem'd for it. Some against it, as Col. Townsend, Foster, Hutchinson.

Wednesday, June 7ᵗʰ. 1704. Col. Nathan¹ Byfield, Mr. Pa[*ul Dudley*]
and my self have rec'd an Order from the Govʳ to search for and seize

tain Quelch at Marblehead "in the Brigantine that Capt. *Plowman* went out in";
two of the owners immediately filed an information with the Secretary of the
Province and the Attorney-General, Paul Dudley. Sewall, returning from Newbury, was plunged into the affair at Lewis's tavern at Lynn. From this point we
shall let Sewall and his contemporaries tell the story. Documentation for the
episode is abundant. A sketch of Quelch is to be found in the *D.A.B.* Abner C.
Goodell Jr. has an exhaustive account in the *Acts and Resolves . . . of Massachusetts Bay* viii (1895), 386–398, which is summarized in *C.S.M.* iii, 71–77.
G. F. Dow and J. H. Edmonds have a chapter on Quelch in *The Pirates of the
New England Coast* (1923), 99–115.
²³ This proclamation appeared in the *Boston News-Letter,* 5 June 1704. The
previous one, dated 24 May, issued by Lieutenant Governor Thomas Povey, was
separately printed by Bartholomew Green. *Massachusetts Broadsides,* 270.
²⁴ On the 13th Simeon Stoddard and Samuel Hayman were chosen as councillors
in place of Peter Sergeant and Elisha Cooke.

Pirats and their Treasure, and to hold a court of Enquiry for this end
at Marblehead; because Capt. Quelch in the Charles Galley arrived
there: we set forward this day for Salem, having James Noyes and
Joseph Gerrish to wait on us. We got to Salem about 8 aclock There
Sam. Wakefield, the Water–Baily, inform'd Col. Byfield of a Rumor
there was that Capt. Larrimore was now with the Larrimore Gally
at Cape-Anne; and that two of Quelch's company designed to go off
in her. Upon this we made out a Warrant to the said Wakefield to
goe and see into this matter and seize the Men if true. Dispatch'd
him about midnight.

Thursday, June 8. We went to Marblehead in the Rain, and held
our Court at Capt. Brown's by the Fire–side; took Major Sewall with
us, who return'd to Salem the same night.

Friday, June, 9th about 6. m. An Express from Cape-Anne, gives an
Account of 9. or 11. Pirats, double arm'd, seen in a Lone-house there.
This Express found us a-bed. We rose immediatcly, Sent for Col.
Legg, and directed him to send warrants to the Northward Companies within his Regiment; to send such parties as they could raise,
to Cape-Anne upon this Extraordinary occasion. And writt to Col.
Wainright to do the Like in his Regiment, intimating that we were
moving thither our selves to be Witness of their forwardness of Her
Majesties Service. Sent this by James Noyes to shew it to Capt. Fisk
of Wenham, as he went along. Col. Byfield and I rode to Salem;
there met Dr. Gatchman, took his Affidavit for some better foundation for our Actions. Sent him post to the Govr. Bro^r got a shallop,
the Trial, and his Pinace, and about a score of his Comp^a to go by
water. Mr. Dudley went by water from Marblehead with Col. Legg.
Col. Byfield and I proceeded with Sheriff Gedney and Capt. Turner
and part of his Troop by Land: call'd on Lt Brisco at Beverly; that
Troop resolv'd to go by Jabacko [*Chebacco*]. Manchester Company
was mustering upon the top of a Rock; shook hands with Mr. Webster. When drew nigh the Town of Glocester a Letter from Mr.
Dudley and Legg met us, to acquaint us that Larramore Sail'd in the
morning and took in the Pirats at the head of the Cape. Messenger
seem'd to discourage our going forward. However, we sent back the
Sheriff to post their Letter to the Govr, and as many of Salem
Troops as would go back, persuading them to return. Mr. Dudley
had sent to stay Ipswich Regiment and direct their Return. When
came to Capt. Davis's, waited Brother's arrival with his Shallop
Trial, and Pinace: When they were come and had Din'd, Resolv'd
to send after Larramore. Abbot was first pitch'd on as Captain. But

matters went on heavily, 'twas difficult to get Men. Capt. Herrick pleaded earnesly his Troopers might be excus'd. At last Brother offer'd to goe himself: then Capt. Turner offer'd to goe, Lieut Brisco, and many good Men; so that quickly made up Fourty two; though we knew not the exact number till came home, the hurry was so great, and vessel so small for 43. Men gave us three very handsom cheers; Row'd out of the Harbour after sun-set, for want of wind. Mr. Dudley return'd to Salem with Beverly Troop. Col. Byfield and I lodg'd at Cape-Ann all night; Mr. White pray'd very well for the Expedition Evening and morning; as Mr. Chiever had done at Marblehead, whom we sent for to pray with us before we set out for Glocester. We rose early, got to Salem quickly after Nine. Din'd with Sister, who was very thoughtfull what would become of her Husband. The Wickedness and despair of the company they pursued, their Great Guns and other war-like Preparations, were a terror to her and to most of the Town; concluded they would not be Taken without Blood. Comforted our selves and them as well as we could. Call'd at Lewis's. Col. Byfield went to Cambridge; Mr. Dudley and I to Boston, Joseph Gerrish waiting on us. *June. 12th* Joseph Gerrish comes to my Bed-Chamber-door and Tells of Brother's good success. He dispatched Chapman in the night to the Gov[r] He came to the Isles Sholes about 7. m. June 10, kept his men rank'd with their Arms on both sides the shallop in covert; only the four Fishermen were in view: as drew near saw the Boat goe ashoar with six Hands, which was a singular good Providence of God. Wormwall and three of the Pirats were of the six. When were so near that were descryd, Larramores Men began to run to and fro and pull off the Aprons from the Guns, draw out the Tomkins [*tampions*], Brother shew'd his men. Ask'd Larramore to come aboard. He said he could not, his Boat was gon ashoar. Bro[r] told him he would come to him: immediately man'd the Pinnace, and did it as soon almost as said it, He, Capt. Turner, Abbot step'd aboard. Brisco attempted; but one swore no more armed Men should come there. Bro[r] got the Capt ashore to discourse him, got him there to sign two orders; one to send the L[t] and one of the Pirats ashore; the other for Abbot to command the Galley till they return'd; and so quickly finish'd his business thorowly without striking a stroke, or firing a Gun. See the News-Letter.[25] Twas all order'd and Tim'd and effected by the Singular all-powerfull gracious Providence of God.

[25] We print in full the accounts in the *Boston News-Letter* to which Sewall refers us. The first is from issue No. 9, "From Monday June 12 to Monday June 19. 1704."

GOD Save the QUEEN.

Marblehead, June 9. The Honourable *Samuel Sewall, Nathaniel Byfield,* and *Paul Dudley* Esqrs. came to this place yesterday, in obedience to His Excellency the Governour, his Order for the more effectual discovering and Seizing the Pirates lately belonging to the Briganteen *Charles, John Quelch* Commander, with their Treasure. They made *Salem* in their way, where *Samuel Wakefield* the Water-Baily informed them of a Rumor that two of *Quelches's* Company were lurking at Cape *Anne,* waiting for a Passage off the Coast: The Commissioners made out a Warrant to *Wakefield* to Search for them, and dispatched him away on *Wednesday* night. And having gain'd intelligence this Morning, that a certain number of them well Armed, were at Cape *Anne* designing to go off in the *Larrimore* Galley, then at Anchor in that Harbour. They immediately sent Men from the several adjacent Towns by Land & Water, to prevent their escape, and went thither themselves, to give necessary orders upon the place.

Glocester, upon Cape *Anne, June* 9. The Commissioners for Seizing the Pirates and their Treasure, arrived here this day, were advised that the *Larrimore* Galley Sail'd in the Morning Eastward; and that a Boat was seen to go off from the head of the Cape, near Snake Island, full of men, supposed to be the Pirates. The Commissioners seeing the Government mock'd by Capt. *Larrimore* and his Officers, resolved to send after them. Major *Stephen Sewall* who attended with a Fishing Shallop, the Fort Pinnace, offered to go in pursuit of them, and Capt. *John Turner,* Mr. *Robert Brisco,* Capt. *Knight,* and several other good men Voluntarily accompanied him, to the Number of 42 men, who Rowed out of the Harbour after Sun-sett, being little Wind.

Salem, June 11. This Afternoon, Major *Sewall* brought in to this Port, the *Larrimore* Galley, and Seven Pirates, viz. *Erasmus Peterson, Charles James, John Carter, John Pitman, Francis King, Charles King, John King,* whom he with his Company Surprized and Seized at the Isles of Sholes the 10*th* Instant, *viz.,* four of them on Board the *Larrimore* Galley, and three on Shoar on *Starr* Island, being assisted by *John Hinckes* and *Thomas Phipps* Esqrs. Two of Her Majesties Justices of New-Hampshire, who were happily there, together with the Justices, and the Captain of the place. He also Seized 45 Ounces and Seven Penny weight of Gold of the said Pirates.

Capt. *Thomas Larrimore, Joseph Wells* Lieutenant, and *Daniel Wormmall* Master, and the said Pirates are Secured in our Goal.

Glocester, June 12. Yesterday Major *Sewall* passed by this place with the *Larrimore* Galley, and Shallop *Trial,* standing for Salem, and having little wind, set our men ashore on the Eastern Point, giving of them notice that *William Jones,* and *Peter Roach,* two of the Pirates had mistook their way, and were still upon the Cape, with strict charge to search for them, which our Towns People performed very industriously. Being strangers and destitute of all Succours, they surrendered themselves this Afternoon, and were sent to Salem Prison.

Boston, June 17. On the 13. Instant, Major *Sewall* attended with a strong guard brought to Town the above mentioned Pirates, and Gold he had Seized, and gave His Excellency a full Account of his Procedure in Seizing them. The

June, 27ᵗʰ feria tertia, Madam Richards dies about 3 hours after midnight. Heard not of it till at Mr. Stoddard's noble Treat in the evening. Mr. Secretary invited the Govʳ, Lᵗ Govʳ, several of the Council to Dinner at North's, the Stone-house. I there. In the morn-

---

Prisoners were committed to Goal in order to a Tryal, and the Gold delivered to the Treasurer and Committee appointed to receive the same. The Service of Major *Sewall* and Company was very well Accepted and Rewarded by the Governour.

His Excellency was pleased on the 13 Current to open the High Court of Admiralty for Trying Capt. *John Quelch* late Commander of the Brigantine *Charles* and Company for Piracy, who were brought to the Barr, and the Articles exhibited against them read. They all pleaded *Not Guilty*, excepting three *Viz. Matthew Pimer, John Clifford* and *James Parrot*, who were reserved for Evidences, and are in Her Majesties Mercy. The Prisoners moved for Council, and His Excellency assigned them Mr. *James Meinzes.* The Court was adjourned to the 16*th.* When met again, Capt. *Quelch* preferr'd a Petition to His Excellency and Honourable Court, craving longer Time, which was granted Monday Morning at Nine of the Clock, when said Court is to Sit again in order to their Tryal.

The trial is reported in the *News-Letter* of 19–26 June:
Boston, June 24. On Monday last, The 19. Currant, The High Court of Admiralty Sat again, when the Tryal of *John Quelch* late Commander of the Briganteen *Charles,* and Company for Piracy and Murder, Committed by them upon Her Majesties *Allies* the Subjects of the King of *Portugal,* was brought forward, and the said *Quelch* was brought to the Bar, being charged with Nine several Articles of Piracy and Murder whereupon he had been Arraigned and Pleaded, *Not Guilty:* The Queen's Attorney opened the case, and the Court proceeded to the Examination of the Evidences for Her Majesty. And the Council for the Prisoner, and the Prisoner himself being fairly heard, The Court was cleared, and after Advisement, the Prisoner was again brought to the Bar; & the Judgment of the Court declared. That he was guilty of the Felony, Piracy and Murder, laid in said Articles: Accordingly Sentence of Death was pronounced against him.

The next day being Tuesday, *John Lambert, Charles James, John Miller* and *Christopher Scudamore,* were brought to the Bar, who pleaded Not Guilty: And were severally tryed as Quelch was, and found guilty and Sentenced to Dy in like manner.

Then was brought to the Bar, *William Whiting,* and *John Templeton* being Arraigned, They pleaded *Not Guilty,* and the Witnesses proving no matter of Fact upon them, said *Whiting* being Sick all the Voyage, & not active, and *Templeton* a Servant about 14 years of Age, and not charged with any action, were acquited by the Court, paying Prison Fees. Next 15. more being brought to the Bar and Arraign'd, Viz. *Will. Wilde, Benj. Perkins, James Austin, Nich. Richardson, Rich. Lawrance, John Pitman, Will. Jones, Erasmus Peterson, John King, Francis King, Charles King, Peter Roach, John Dorothy, Denis Carter* and *John Carter,* who severally pleaded Guilty, and threw themselves on the Queen's Mercy. And Sentence of Death was past upon them, in like manner as those abovenamed. 'Tis said some of them will be Executed the next Fryday, and the whole proceeding be put out in Print.

ing I heard Mr. Cotton Mather, Pray, preach, Catechise excellently the Condemned Prisoners in the chamber of the prison.

June, 29. Madam Richards buried, in her Husbands Tomb at the North-burying place. Bearers, Russel, Cook; Hutchinson Elisha, Sewall; Sergeant, Foster. Scarfs and Rings, Scutcheons on the Coffin.[26]

Feria Sexta, Junij, 30, 1704. As the Governour sat at the Council-Table twas told him, Madam Paige[27] was dead; He clap'd his hands, and quickly went out, and return'd not to the Chamber again; but ordered Mr. Secretary to prorogue the Court till the 16th of August, which Mr. Secretary did by going into the House of Deputies. After Dinner, about 3. p.m. I went to see the Execution. By the way (cous. Ephr. Savage with me) James Hawkins certifies us of Madam Paiges death; he was to make a Tomb. Many were the people that saw upon Broughton's Hill. But when I came to see how the River was cover'd with People, I was amazed: Some say there were 100 Boats. 150 Boats and Canoes, saith Cousin Moody of York. He told them. Mr. Cotton Mather came with Capt Quelch and six others for Execution from the Prison to Scarlet's Wharf, and from thence in the Boat to the place of Execution about the midway between Hudson's point and Broughton's Warehouse. Mr. Bridge was there also. When the scaffold was hoisted to a due height, the seven Malefactors went up; Mr. Mather pray'd for them standing upon the Boat. Ropes were all fasten'd to the Gallows (save King, who was Repriev'd). When the Scaffold was let sink, there was such a Screech of the Women that my wife heard it sitting in our Entry next the Orchard, and was much surprised at it; yet the wind was sou-west. Our house is a full mile from the place.[28]

[26] Madam Richards was Anne, daughter of Governor John Winthrop Jr. of Connecticut. She was the widow of John Richards, sometime treasurer of Harvard, Speaker of the House, and Assistant. L. S. Mayo, *Winthrop Family* (1948), 57. The *Heraldic Journal* (1,117) gives a description of Richards's arms impaling Winthrop.

[27] Again we refer our readers to E. S. Morgan's article, A Boston Heiress and Her Husbands: A True Story, in *C.S.M.* xxxiv, 499–513. Anna Paige was Governor Dudley's niece, the daughter of Benjamin Keayne and Sarah Dudley. She was successively the wife of Edward Lane and Colonel Nicholas Paige.

[28] The execution took place on the Boston side of the Charles River flats. On the 22d of June at the Boston Lecture Cotton Mather had preached a sermon in the presence of the condemned pirates: it was called *Faithful Warnings to prevent Fearful Judgments. Uttered in a brief Discourse, Occasioned, by a Tragical Spectacle, in a Number of Miserables Under a Sentence of Death for Piracy* (Boston, 1704; T. J. Holmes, *Cotton Mather . . . Bibliography* 1, 363–366.) Three days after the the execution the *Boston News-Letter* published the following account:

July, 1, 1704. *Feria Septima.* News is brought from New-york of Trade to be had with the American Spaniards. This comes in seasonably upon Quelches Spightfull admonition yesterday. Melyen told me of it on the Lords Day.

July, 2ᵈ Lords Day, Madam Paige is buried from her own house, where Mrs. Perry is Tenant, between 6 and 7. p.m. Bearers Lᵗ Govʳ Povey, Usher; Sewall, Addington; Col. Phillips, Foxcroft. Rings and Scarves. The Tomb was near Messengers. The Govʳ, his Lady and family there. *Note.* By my Order, the diggers of Mᵐ Paiges Tomb dugg a Grave for Lambert, where he was laid in the Old burying place Friday night about midnight near some of his Relations: Body was given to his Widow. Son and others made Suit to me.

July, 3, *Feria Secunda,* I read the three first sheets of the Trial of the Pirats. *July,* 4. Send David to Cambridge with Joseph's cloths. *July 5. Feria quarta.* [*Commencement Day*] Last night very refreshing Thunder shower. Rains this morning. Goe to Cambridge with Mr. Tho. Brattle in Stedman's Calash. Spent the forenoon in the Meetinghouse. Waited on the Govʳ from Dinner Time till the last Question: Then follow'd the Govr in. Mr. Gibbs[29] was holding the last Question. Dr. Dummer rose up and in very fluent good Latin ask'd Leave, and made an opposition; and then took Leave again with Commendation of the Respondent. Came home with Col. Townsend.

Mr. Dudley[30] made a good Oration in the morning. mention'd

On Friday was carried to the Place of Execution seven Pirates to be Executed, *viz;* Capt. *John Quelch, John Lambert, Christopher Scudamore, John Miller, Erasmus Peterson, Peter Roach* and *Francis King:* all of which were Executed, excepting the last named, who had a Reprieve from his Excellency. And notwithstanding all the great labour and pains taken by the Reverend Ministers of the Town of Boston ever since they were first Seized and brought to Town, both before and since their Trial and Condemnation, to instruct, admonish, preach and pray for them: yet as they led a wicked and vitious life, so to appearance they dyed very obdurately and impenitently, hardened in their sin.

His Excellency intends to send an Express to *England,* with an Account of the whole matter to her Majesty.

29 No Gibbs was listed on the program. C. K. Shipton suggests that someone from the audience gave a challenge which no one in the Master's class felt ready to meet, and that Tutor Gibbs (A.B. 1685) stepped into the breach. Jeremiah Dummer (A.B. 1699) was fresh from Europe with his Utrecht Ph.D.

30 William Dudley (A.B. 1704) was the son of Governor Joseph Dudley. Sewall had urged him to greater piety on 1 April, and in both entries called him "Mr." —a title normally reserved for masters of arts—presumably because of his family's rank. It was the custom at that time to honor Harvard's benefactors by mentioning them at commencement: Ralph Sprague of Charlestown had died in 1703, bequeathing the college £300 Massachusetts currency. Colonel Daniel

Benefactors, Harvardus, Stoughtonus, Spragus, Decease of Col. Pierce. Captivity of Mr. Williams. Judges as at the first, Councellors as at the Beginning [*Isaiah i, 26.*]

July, 10ᵗʰ 1704. Went to Benj Child beyond the Pond, to bespeak his driving my wife to Brooklin to morrow. As came home visited my old friend Mr. Bailey, who has been confin'd some Moneths by the Stone. He was very glad to see me. Mr. Stoughton's Executors have made offers to him for compliance, which he has taken up with. Rid over the Neck with my Brother.

July, 11ᵗʰ 1704. Son and daughter Hirst, Joseph and Mary, rode with me in the coach to Brooklin, and there dined at my Son's with the Governour, his Lady, Mr. Paul Dudley and wife, Mr. Neh. Walter and wife, Dr. Dummer, Mrs. Anne Dudley, Mrs. Mary Dudley, Mr. Flint and others. Call'd in as went to Hartford. Sung a Psalm.

July, 12. feria quarta, went to Dedham in company of Mr. Gray, and David Jeffries; find Judith well, carried her a little Basket and some Cakes. Mr. Belcher preach'd from Lam. 3. Why doth living man complain. Din'd at Mr. Avery's with Judith. Harvest begun.

July, 13. 1704. Thin Lecture at Boston by reason of the Heat. In the afternoon Jenkyns arrives, 9 weeks from England; brings News of the Arrival of all our Fleet there.

July, 16. Lords-day morn, Miles arrives, who came out with Jenkins.

July, 21, 1704. Mr. Thomas Weld, who proceeded Master of Arts this Commencement, July 5ᵗʰ, died this day at his unkle Wilson's at Braintry. *July, 22, Feria septima,* is buried from his unkle Weld's at Roxbury. Mr. Bromfield and I were there, rode with Madam Bromfield in the Calash. Mr. Walter prayed in the Orchard. Mr. Bromfield and I follow'd the Relations; then Mr. Danforth and Mr. Walter. Mr. Bailey is very bad and in his chamber; as Mr. Bromfield told me, who went to see him. Govʳ is gon to Dedham. It begins to be known that the Bills of Credit are counterfeited, the Twenty-Shilling Bill.

July, 24, 1704. Mrs. Zachary, the Quaker's wife, who died in childbed, is brought in a black Walnut Coffin to the South-end of the Town, carried down the 7-Star Lane, [*now Summer Street*] and then

---

Peirce of Newbury had died 4 April 1704. Rev. John Williams had been carried off by the Indians in the attack on Deerfield in February; William Dudley was one of the party who went to Canada in 1706 to effect his release. Shipton adds (*Sibley* v, 244n) that a piece of the red gown which Dudley wore at this commencement is hanging on the wall of the Harvard Club of Boston.

into Bishop's Lane [*now Hawley Street*], and buried in the inner Corner of Mr. Brightman's Pasture and Orchard. It seems one spake much at the Grave. Proclamation is issued out against the Forgers of the Bills &c.[31]

July, 25, 1704. Major Walley and I rid together in Heton's Calash to Cambridge Court: there met Col. Hathorne and Mr. Leverett. Major Walley and I came home together. Old Bell rung 9 as we got to the Ferry. Gave Heton 6 shillings. Between 10 and 11 by that time we got home. The Forgers are discover'd.

Mr. Barnard of Andover married Lydia Goff last week and din'd with us.[32]

July, 31, 1704. Capt. Ephr. Savage, Mr. Antram and I ride to Dedham, Dine there with Capt. Barber, I visit Judith. From Dedham to Medfield. There I meet Mr. Gookin, his wife and Son. Have Mr. Gookin for our Pilot to his house. Call at Capt. Mors's about an hour in night; and he tells us of the Indians assaulting Lancaster. This was very heavy News to us now in a Fronteer Town; yet we went on, lodg'd at cousin Gookin's, and were kept safe. Tuesday and Wednesday did our business, and came home on Thorsday.

Augt 25ᵗʰ feria Sexta, Mr. Richard Wilkins being blind and help-less, goes to Milton to live and dye there with his daughter Thacher.[33] Mr. Gray and others ride after the coach. He call'd and took leave as he went along: I and my wife went to him as he sat in the Coach.

Augᵗ [27] at the South Church, Mr. Tho. Bridge pray'd, Mr. Pemberton preach'd: just as had done his Sermon and stood up to pray, a Cry of Fire was made, by which means the Assembly was broken up, but it pleas'd God the Fire was wonderfully Quench'd. The wind was Southwardly, so that if it had proceeded from the Tavern Ancor, probably the old Meeting House and Townhouse must have been consumed and a great part of the Town beside. Ministers express'd great Thankfullness in the Afternoon for this Deliverance. Dr. Incr. Mather pray'd, Mr. Willard preach'd and then pray'd. Mr. Thacher and Mr. Danforth sup'd with us.

Augt. 29. rode to Roxbury Lecture. Visited Mr. Bayley. Mr. Walter preach'd from [*Psalm*] 119–71. It is good for me that I have been

---

[31] Governor Dudley's proclamation against a counterfeit twenty-shilling note, issued this day, was printed in the *Boston News-Letter,* 31 July 1704.

[32] Lydia was the third wife of Thomas Barnard (Harvard 1679), minister of Andover.

[33] This was Richard Wilkins, the bookseller, who died the 10th of December. His daughter Susanna was the wife of Sewall's classmate, Rev. Peter Thacher of Milton.

Afflicted: Kept from sin, made more fruitfull, shew me wherefore Thou contendest with me. Waited on Madam Dudley home, presented her with Mr. Fowl's Books for Govr and self. Saw my Daughter there. Son was getting in Hay.

Feria septima, Septr 9. 1704. Col. Hathorne and I set out for Bridgewater, Sam. Moodey waits on me. Bait at Braintry. A Taunton man, Mason, overtakes us and becomes a very good Pilot to us through the wilderness. Dine late at Waldo's upon the edge of Bridgewater. Got to Howard's about a quarter of an hour before Sun-set. *Septr 10.* Mr. Keith administred Baptisme and the Lords supper, whereby my Missing the Administration of it at home, was supplyed.

Septr 11 Rode to Taunton; from thence Capt. Lennard and Mr. King accompanied us through very bad way. Dined at Luther's. I was threaten'd with my sore Throat: but I went to Bed early at Mr. Sparhawk's, pin'd my Stocking about my Neck, drunk a porringer of Sage Tea, upon which I sweat very kindly. The pain of my Throat was the more painfull to me, for fear of my being rendred unable to goe to Court next morning; and then the Court must have fallen, for was only Major Walley with us. *Septr 12.* I was so well recover'd as to go to the Court, not losing any time. *Septr 13.* grew very well. *Septr 14.* Adjourn'd the Court *sine die.* Dined at Col. Byfield's with the Justices at Pappasquash.[34] From thence the Gentlemen accompanyed us to the Ferry: Lodg'd at Mr. Smith's at Rehoboth. *Septr 15.* Baited at Slack's; Dined at Billenges. At Dedham met the Commissioners going to New-York, Col. Townsend, Mr. Leverett: Gave Mr. Leverett my Letter to Mr. Williams: In it was a Letter of Credit for some Money not exceeding Ten Ounces. Visited my Dear little Judith. Got home about Sunset or a little after. *Laus Deo.*

Monday, 7r. 11th Mr. Robert Hawkins dies in the Afternoon. 7r. the 12th buried; Hill, Williams, Checkley, Belknap, Cole, Emory, Bearers. Great Funeral.

Septr 12th Mrs. Tuthill falls through a Trap Door into the cellar, breaks her right Thigh just above the knee, so that the bones pierce through the skin.

Septr 19. Mrs. Tuthill dies.

Thorsday, 7^r 14th. Mr. William Hubbard, of Ipswich, goes to the Lecture, after to Col. Appletons: Goes home, sups, and dyes. that night.[35]

---

[34] The seat of Colonel Nathaniel Byfield was on the Pappasquash peninsula, now a part of Bristol, Rhode Island.

[35] Hubbard was the last survivor of Harvard's first graduating class (1642); he

Thorsday, 7ʳ 21. 1704. Mrs. Mary Tuthill, widow, buried; Govʳ, Lᵗ
Govʳ, Capt. Smith at the Funeral. Bearers, Elisha Hutchinson,
Sewall; Addington, Eᵐ Hutchinson; Legg, Belchar. Laid in a brick
Grave of the South Burying place, southwest corner of it. Mr. Neh.
Hubbard dined with us this day.

Wednesday, Octobʳ 4. 1704. Went to Dedham Lecture in company with Mr. Danˡ Oliver. Mr. N. Hobart fell in with us two miles
before we got to Town. Visited Judith. Text, Wisdom is the principal thing. Grace is Glory in the Bud; Glory is Grace full-blown.
Din'd with Mr. Belchar. Got home about 7 at night.

Octobʳ 12. Mr. Cotton Mather prays for the College and other
schools. Mr. Ezek. Lewis marries the widow [*Abigail*] Kilcup, Octobʳ
12.

Octobʳ 13. Deacon Dyer of Weymouth, Mr. Torrey's Right Hand,
is to be buried to-day. Dy'd with a Fall from's Horse.

Octobʳ 14ᵗʰ 1704. visited Col. Savage. He has kept house 7 weeks.
Mr. Wigglesworth came to Town the 9ᵗʰ Instᵗ and administers to
him. I pray'd God to bless his sickness to him; and his Physick for
his Restauration. He seem'd refresh'd with my company.

Octʳ 24. Went to Roxbury Lecture. Mr. Walter, from Mat. 6. 1.
Shew'd we should have a care of Wrong Ends in doing Duties.
Led my daughter Sewall home. Then visited Mr. Walter; told Mr.
Mather of Alcasar, Dan. 12. 7; and scattering power of the Holy peo-
ple; not to be understood of the Jews, as he had set it in his Pro-
blema Theologicum.

Novʳ 13. set out for Salem with Major Walley; Lodg'd at Lewis's,
being taken with a Storm of Rain.

Novʳ 26. Major Davis dies of a Flux about 6. in the evening after
the Sabbath. I knew not that was sick till about 24 hours before. [*In
margin:* Great Snow.]

Novʳ 30 Major Davis buried; Bearers, Elisha Hutchinson esqr:
Sewall, Addington, Foster, Jeffries, Joseph Parson. Mr. Torrey lodg'd
here last night, and went home this day, Novʳ 30.

Decʳ 1. Went to Charlestown Lecture. After Lecture discoursed
with Capt. Chamberlain, Phillips, and Mr. Austin, all of the Committee could meet with, to persuade them not to go on with their
Action against me. [*In margin:* Nod.]

Decʳ 2. Visited my son and Daughter at Brooklin.

Decʳ 7ᵗʰ Mr. Clark of Chelmsford dies of a Fever; was taken very

had been minister at Ipswich since 1656. His *General History of New England*
(to 1680) was first published as 2 *M.H.S. Colls.* V–VI in 1815. D.A.B.

suddenly the Friday before, after he had been at a Funeral; buried the 11th.[36]

Decr 10th Mr. Richard Wilkins dies at Milton; is brought in the coach to Boston, Decr 12; buried Decr 13 in the upper end of the South-burying place. I went to the Burying as I came from Charlestown Court. Son Samuel there. Several of the Council and Ministers, Mr. Chiever, Williams, Gloves [*to*] Bearers.

Decr 25. Monday, a Storm of Snow, yet many Sleds come to Town, with Wood, Hoops, Coal &c as is usual.

Decr 30. Satterday, Daughter Sewall of Brooklin is brought to Bed of a Daughter, Rebeka. 31. is baptised.

[36] Thomas Clark (Harvard 1670), minister of Chelmsford, had been a chaplain in King Philip's War and was present at the Great Swamp Fight in 1675. *Weis.*

1705

Monday, Jany 1. 1704/5 Col. Hobbey's Negro comes about 8 or 9 *mane* and sends in by David to have leave to give me a Levit [*trumpet-blast*] and wish me a merry new year. I admitted it: gave him 3 Reals. Sounded very well.

Jany 2. Madam Leverett dies; was taken with an Apoplexy last Thorsday, 2 or 3 Hours after her coming from Lecture. Mrs. Mason dies also this night.[1]

Jany 3 Tedman, the Brazier, opens his Shop and dies. Emons, the shoemaker, dies; is older than Benj Emons, his Brother.

Jany 5th I dine at Mr. Paul Dudley's with the Govr, Lt Govr, Capt. Sam. Appleton, Mr. Colman, Mr. White, Mr. Antho. Stoddard.

Jany 6. Begins to be some heat between the Govr and the Deputies. At last the Govr sends in Mr. Secretary, Mr. E^m Hutchinson and Mr. Stoddard, to prorogue the Assembly to the 21. Febr. at 10. m. At first the Deputies seem'd to be against Prorogation; afterward sent in Capt. Checkly to say, That by reason of the thinness of their House, Shortness and Coldness of the days, inclined to a Prorogation. Speaker intimated their Desire of a Fast.

Monday, January, 8. I went to the Funeral of Mrs. Johanna Mason. She was a vertuous, pious woman, in the 70th year of her Age. Then

---

[1] Sarah (Sedgwick) Leverett was the second wife of Governor John Leverett, who had died in 1679. Joanna (Parker) Mason was the wife of Arthur Mason, baker and constable of Boston. Sewall just missed Mason's funeral 6 March 1707/8 because of the pressure of business. *Savage.*

went to the Council-Chamber, and from thence with the Governour to the Funeral of Madam Sarah Leverett; Bearers, Govr Dudley, W Winthrop; Elisha Hutchinson, S. Sewall; Peter Sergeant, E^m Hutchinson. Had very warm discourse with the Govr about Philip Morse, after came from the Tomb, at Mr. Cook's.

Thorsday, Jany 11th The Govr and his Lady essaying to come from Charlestown to Boston in their Slay, 4 Horses, two Troopers riding before them, First the Troopers fell into the water, and then the Govr making a stand, his four Horses fell in, and the Two Horses behind were drown'd, the Slay pressing them down. They were pull'd up upon the Ice, and there lay dead, a sad Spectacle. Many came from Charlestown with Boards, planks, Ropes &c. and sav'd the other Horses. Tis a wonderful Mercy That the Govr, his Lady, Driver, Postilion, Troopers escaped all safe.

January, 19. 1704/5 The Govr coming to Town, the way being difficult by Banks of Snow, his Slay was turn'd upon one side against the Fence next Cambridge, and all in it thrown out, Governour's Wigg thrown off, his head had some hurt; and my Son's Elbow. The Horses went away with the foundation and left the Superstructure of the Slay and the Riders behind.

Jany 26. Mr. Hirst and I went to Brooklin to see my Little Grand Daughter, Rebeka Sewall: He and I were on Horseback; in Simson's slay were Madam Willard, daughter Hirst, Hannah, and Mrs. Betty Hirst. Had some difficulty in going because of some deep descents between Banks of Snow. But went and came very well. Blessed be God. Din'd there. Before we came away, we sung the 113th Psalm. W[*indsor*]. While we were gon, Mr. Edw. Gouge was buried; Mr. E^m Hutchinson call'd at our House to take me with him to the Funeral. The poor Man Liv'd Undesired, and died Unlamented.[2]

January, 29. I buy the two Folios of Mr. Flavell's work for £3.10–0 and gave them to Mr. Foster for his helping me in my Accounts last winter, to send to the Corporation [*for Propagating the Gospel*].

[2] Edward Gouge was a linen-draper, the son of Thomas Gouge, M.A. and Fellow of King's College, Cambridge, an eminent nonconformist divine and philanthropist. John Dunton wrote (1686): "He is the owner of a deal of wit; his brain is a quiver of smart jests. He pretends to live a bachelor, but is no enemy to a pretty woman." The town records list Edward Gouge as the father of a son born to Martha Staples, 25 April 1689. In 1692 he was warden of King's Chapel, and by May 1693 he was married. He was a tenant in Sewall's Cotton Hill house (*see ante* 4 September 1700). Evidently Gouge was unfortunate in his business; administration was granted on his estate 6 March 1704/5 and on 11 June 1708 his widow Frances paid 4s in the pound to his creditors. H. W. Foote, *Annals of King's Chapel* I (1882), 113–114; *Calamy*; 2 M.H.S.Proc. II, 323.

Jany 30. Major Walley and I ride to the Ferry in Simson's Slay, and at Charlestown, with Mr. Leverett, hold the Super^r Court. At Sommers's I mention Justus Heurnius; Mr. Leverett told me he would bring me if in the Library; I promised to Lend him Judge Hales's Origination of Mankind. *Jan^y* 31. We interchange those two Books; which is the first time I ever saw Amiable Heurnius: I first found him quoted by Alsted in his Treatise *De Mille Annis*.[3] *Febr. 6*. Tuesday, Many go to the Council Chamber and there drink Healths on account of its being the Queen's Birth-Day. Maxwell did not call me, and I even staid at home, and went and heard Mr. Willard's Catechising Lecture. It seems the Govr order'd the Inferiour Court to be Adjourn'd upon the Account of it. Cousin Jer. Dummer, Philosophiæ Dr.,[4] going out of the Townhouse about 8 at night, fell by reason of the Ice, hit his left Temple against a piece of Brick-batt, Cut a great Gash at which much blood Issued: He was so stun'd as to ly as dead when Mr. John Winthrop took him up. I dont remember that I knew the Govr was in Town till next day.

Feb^r 11th Mr. Pemberton preaches of the undoubted Interest children have in the Covenant, and baptiseth his son Ebenezer, who was born Febr. 6th Mrs. Hannah Savage, Mr. Phillip's daughter, is taken into the Church, though next Sabbath be the usual Season. It seems she desired it, as being likely then to be detain'd at home by child-birth.

Tuesday, Feb^r 13th Last night I had a very sad Dream that held me a great while. As I remember, I was condemn'd and to be executed. Before I went out I read Dr. Arrowsmith's Prayer p. 274[5] —— which was a comfort to me. A Council was warn'd to meet at Noon.

[3] The books mentioned were Justus Heurnius, *De Legatione Evangelica apud Indos capessanda admonitio* (Leyden, 1618); Sir Matthew Hale, *The Primitive Origination of Mankind, Considered and Examined, According to the Light of Nature* (London, 1677); and Johann Heinrich Alsted, *De Mille Annis Apocalypticis* (London, 1630).

[4] Jeremiah Dummer (Harvard 1699), second-cousin of Sewall, called by President Mather the best scholar of his time in Harvard College, had taken a Ph.D. at Utrecht in 1703, the first American to possess this degree. Sewall was careful to call him by his proper title, but he was dubious about it, writing 10 October 1704: "And as to your Title of Dr. of Philosophy; seeing the very ancient and illustrious Universities of England, Scotland, and Ireland know nothing of it; I am of Opinion it would be best for you not to value your self upon it, as to take place any otherwise than as if you had only taken the Degree of Master." *L.B.* 1, 302.

[5] John Arrowsmith, D.D., Master of Trinity College and Regius Professor of Divinity in Cambridge University under Cromwell, was the author of several theological works.

I was there one of the first: Governour came in and quickly put Capt. Lawson's Petition into my hand; and upon my speaking somthing to it, He fell to a vehement chiding about Philip Morse's business, and then with great Loudness and passion spake to the affair of Capt. Lason's; several times said He would dy if ever any such thing was done in England except in case of Felony or Treason, or the like. I objected against that ridiculous part of the Petition of his being forc'd by Mr. Clark or me to retire into the neighbouring Province; as being a great Reproach to the whole Governm^t. No body appeared, I expected my Accuser face to face. Govr mov'd that a day might be set for a Hearing: but the Council being but 7, besides my self, declared they did not understand what was contain'd in the Petition belong'd to them to deal in, i. e. settling a Maintenance. Govr said, then it must be left to another time.

Feb^r 14. I got a copy: Mr. Secretary told me he had no Money paid for entring of it. *Feb^r* 14. Mrs. Odlin buried; I went to the Funeral.

Feb^r 17. Richardson tells me that the Charlestown Gent have sued me again.[6] Here is Wave upon Wave. The Good Lord be With me when so many, almost all, are against me. Hern tells me the Petition was first in Mr. Dudleys hand, and Mr. Secretary tells me 'tis Weavers writing. When I ask'd Hern who drew it, He answer'd all, i. e. Dudley, Newton, Valentine and he. Newton denys it; but I perceive will stand Neuter. *Febr. 23.* Jer. Dummer, Dr. Philosoph., went with me to Col. Lynde's at Charlestown: I pleaded first to the Jurisdiction of the Court; then to the writ, that it could not ly, because I was in Possession. [*In margin:* Land of Nod.] Went to Lecture. Din'd at Col. Lyndes with Mrs. Everton, Major Davison.

Febr. 24. Singing of Birds is come.

March, 2. Deputies present the Govr with Two Hundred pounds. Towards night the Govr called upon the Council to consider George Lason's Petition; If he might have a Protection, he was ready to come. [*In margin:* Great Dispute.] Council excepted against their meddling with settling estates of Maintenance; knew not that it was his Petition. Spoke pretty much to it.[7]

6 This is the suit over the Land of Nod, which was tried 18 September 1705. See our note for 12 August 1702.

7 The M.H.S. Editors were unable to find any particulars of Lason's case in the surviving records. George Lason, mariner, and once termed "late commander of the Baron Frigate," had several suits about this time for money alleged to be due him. Martha Lason, his wife, represented to the Superior Court, 10 May 1706, that her husband had gone to England, and that he entrusted all his property to

March, 3. Govr said he would now take their vote whether they would hear Lason: Twas carried in the Negative, not one that I observ'd, speaking for it. I read a Clause out of Dalton[8] shewing when an officer might break open a House. Mention'd the Act of Parliam^t about cutting Poles where the Fine is but Ten shillings; yet a suspected person's house might be entred. In presence of 2 Justices Peers house might be broken up and yet peer must not be attach'd or imprison'd. Because the Govr had said, Must be Treason or Felony. And upbraided me, because had broken up the house, and then taken his parol till morning. Should have sent him to Prison with 20 Halberts. No Law for a man to live with his wife. I said Govr [*Thomas*] Dudley's saying was, A bargain's a Bargain and must be made Good; If we look'd to the Form of Marriage should find twas a great deal Lason had promis'd. Govr seem'd to reject it with disdain, and ask'd Col. Hutchinson when he lay with his wife? Col. Hutchinson answer'd, The Question should not have been when he lay with his wife; but when he lay with another woman. I said, The people were ready to pull down Lason's house, high time for the Government to interpose. Mr. Henchman had not complain'd of the Watch for knocking him up the other night. Lason's house was on fire, and he was not aware of it; high time for the Government to awaken him. Last night mention'd the Queen's Proclamation, and Governours to do to the utmost to suppress Immorality and profaneness: None had yet shew'd me any Law I had broken. Govr mention'd Dalton.

March, 4. Lord's-Day. A great deal of snow falls after a great deal of Rain the night before.

March, 9. Govr sails for Piscataqua in a Briganteen belonging to Capt. Belchar and Mr. Pepperil.

March, 13. I go to Charlestown Court. Col. Phillips tells me his wife could not sleep for thinking of the Danger the Govr was in by reason of the vehement storm on Satterday night.

March, 14. go to Charlestown Court: take David with me to carry my Books.

March, 15. between 10 and 11. m. I rec. Brother's Letter giving an

---

David Josse of Boston, who was to pay her six shillings per week for her subsistence. She could not collect this allowance, and so prayed for relief, which was granted.

[8] Michael Dalton of Lincoln's Inn first published *The Countrey Iustice* in 1618; at least eight revisions had been printed before 1700. It is probably this book that Sewall used, rather than Dalton's less popular *Officium Vicecomitum. The Office and Authority of Sherifs*, of which the *British Museum Catalogue* records editions in 1623 and 1700 and an abridgement in 1628.

account of the extraordinary danger the Govr had been in, and their wonderfull Deliverance that was at Glocester, and were going to fetch him to Salem.

March, 17. Mr. E^m Hutchinson carrys me in his chariot to meet the Govr; was got home and at Dinner: After Dinner were call'd in: Told the Govr I did congratulat His Excellency and the Province upon the great Salvation God had wrought for him.[9] Went and visited Mr. Bayly who was very glad to see us.

Satterday, March, 24. 1704/5. Between 1 and 2 p. m. I set out with Sam. Robinson for Weymouth. Call at Cousin Quinsey's and carry Shepard of the Virgins,[10] and take Dalton away with me to Weymouth, where I made use of it in convicting Ichabod Holbrook for Drunkenness, whom I saw drunk as rode into Town the 24th, and convicted and sentenced him at Capt. Frenches. *March 26, 1705.* Lodg'd at Mr. Torrey's, He was full of grief by reason of the dangerous illness of Mrs. Torrey's eldest daughter, the wife of his Nephew Torrey.

Lord's Day, March 25, 1705. p. m. Mr. Torrey after sermon baptised two children, pray'd that God would fit us by this Ordinance for the Other. Administred the Lord's Supper, did not pray after his delivering the wine, but only sung a Psalm. When came home said he was never so weary before; could neither speak or stand any longer. Col. Hunt was in the seat with me.

March, 26. set out for Barker's, a souldier from Deerfield accompanied us with his Fusee.[11] At Barkers the Sheriff met us, and Major Walley and Mr. Leverett came up: So went cheerfully along, and got to the sheriff's House in good season, where were entertain'd.

March, 28. I got up betime and begun my Birth-day in the [*Plymouth*] Meetinghouse. Finished the Court this day.

March 29. Thorsday, came homeward, Din'd at Cushing's: Call'd at Mr. Torrey's, Took my Dalton. Mr. Leverett and I visit Madam

---

[9] "The governor, in the month of March this year, returning by water from his other government of New-Hampshire, before the brigantine in which he had taken his passage came up with Cape Ann, was surprized with as violent a storm as had been known and of as long continuance. There being advice brought to Boston of his sailing from Portsmouth and no further intelligence of him, it was generally apprehended that the vessel must have foundered. At length came news of his arrival in the harbour of Glocester, having been four days at anchor on the back of the cape, expecting every hour to perish. In a proclamation for public thanksgiving, a few days after, notice is taken of his wonderful preservation from shipwreck." Hutchinson, *Hist.* (1936), II, 110–111n.

[10] *The Parable of the Ten Virgins Opened and Applied*, by Thomas Shepard (1605–1649), minister of the church at Cambridge.

[11] Sewall was leaving Weymouth for Plymouth. The Deerfield soldier was carrying a flintlock musket.

Shepard. Got home in good season, and found all well; never had a more comfortable Journy.

March, 30. Went to the Funeral of young Mr. Allen, Mr. Daniel Allens son, a very hopefull youth, Mr. Georges Apprentice. Govr and his Lady there. Bearers Willard, David Stoddard; Bronsdon, Colman; Banister, Foxcroft. Mr. Willard's Meeting was diverted by it, to a Moneth hence. After Funeral, call'd at Mr. Clark's; I congratulated her Recovery. Mr. Winthrop and Madam Eyre and many more there.

Lord's Day, April, 1. My daughter Hirst is join'd to Mr. Colman's Church. The good Lord Accept her in giving up her Name to his Son.

April, 12, 1705. Thanksgiving Day. The Night was so cold that was a very great Frost, thick Ice, and the street frozen like winter. Remain'd frozen at Noon in the shady places of the street. Mr. Melyen had a great Tub of water frozen so hard, that it bore two men standing upon it in his sight.

April, 17. Council; Capt. Tuthill's Allowance of 80.£ would not pass: so Govr would pass none of the Quarter-Roll for the Castle.

April, 18. 1705. Govr sets out for Piscataway, his Lady in the Calash with him. Brother met his Excellency at Lindsey's. Got to Town that night and lodg'd at son Hirst's.

April, 18. 1705. Sam. Robinson planted 8 Trees at Elm pasture, one white-oake. Three Trees at Phippenys; Elm, White oak, Ash; one Elm at Morey's pasture.

Monday, April, 23. Sam. Robinson sets four Poplars in the Foreyard, to shade the windows from the Western sun in Summer. Remov'd the little Peach-Tree. As were setting the Trees, heard and saw several Swallows; which are the first I remember to have seen this year. Widow Holland visits us. Guns fired about Noon: Flags, and Ships Colours flying.

April, 26. 1705. Mr. Paul Dudley buries his little son Thomas: He was taken with a swelling in's Groin and stoppage of his Water. On the coffin was nail'd a little Plate of Lead with this Inscription

Thomas Dudley.
Pauli Dudlœi Armigeri et Luciœ uxoris Filius primogenitus, Nepos Josephi Dudlœi Gubernatoris Novœ Angliœ. Natus est 13. Aprilis 1705. Obijt 25. ejusdem.

Only Mr. Addington and I of the Council were at the Funeral. Mr. Colman, Mr. Woodward, Mr. Williams Ministers. Mr. Brattle, Mr. S. Lynde Justices.

April, 28. Went to the Funeral of Sarah Bennet, her Maiden Name was Harris: Mr. Perry her uncle. Then to the Funeral of Capt. Bozoon Allen's wife, Mr. Balston's Daughter. A pretty many Graves are open'd: The Lord grant that I may be cloathed upon, and so ready to be uncloath'd.

Friday, May. 4, 1705. I visited my Son and daughter at Brooklin; Little Grand-daughter. Came home in the Rain.

May, 8. Went to Roxbury Lecture: visited Mr. Bayly; join'd with Mr. Torrey in praying for him in his Chamber. His Sister Doggett of Marshfield there. Col. Allen died last Satterday night. Persons kill'd and carried away at York and Spruce Crick last Friday. New-found-Land; Many of the people kill'd and captivated there.

May, 30, 1705. Election. Mr. Secretary, Sewall and Walley Gave the Representatives the Oaths, &c. 64. Councillors 26. Winthrop, 82. Russell, 84. Hathorne, 71. Elisha Hutchinson, 79. Sewall, 83. Addington, 77. Brown, 86. Phillips, 84. Corwin, 78. Foster, 81. Hayman, 42. Townsend, 80. Higginson, 80. Belcher, 74. Legg, 70. Hunt, 53. Bromfield, 69. Stoddard, 56. Plimouth; Walley, 54. Thacher, 81. Winslow, 75. Pain, 80. Main; Hutchinson, 66. Hammond, 71. B. Brown, 71. Zag [*Sagadahoc*]; Lynde 53. Within the Province, Partridge 62, Samuel Appleton, 63. Debate about the Governour's Authority to Approve or refuse the Speaker, made it late; so that twas past Eleven at night before the Election was finished. I advised the Govr again and again to intermit the Debate, and considering the war, to let the election go on with a *Salvo Jure*, as to his Authority respecting the Speaker; Gave my Opinion, that in the clause of the Governour's Negative, General Court or Assembly, was no more than if it had been said Genl Court: and that the House of Representatives was no where in the Charter, call'd Assembly. Govr urg'd the Council to give their votes whether He had Authority to refuse the Speaker or no. Council pray'd it might be defer'd: But at last the Govr prevail'd: And all were in the Negative except Higginson, Thacher, Lynde; 3 or four: and Higginson seem'd not to own his afterward. I said it was a point of great moment, and desired longer time; at present inclin'd to the Negative. Several sent in to the Deputies, I was almost forc'd in with them to persuade the Dept^s to an Accommodation. First, Govr told them He refus'd and directed them immediately to choose another. After an hour or more; Dept^s sent a written vote asserting their Authority by Law and persisting, and shewing were ready to go on with the Election.[12] After this Message, sent to desire this Debate

[12] Hutchinson, and other writers, mention this ill-advised attempt of Dudley's to disallow the election of a speaker by the House of Representatives. Hutchinson

might be laid aside at present, and that might go on with the Election. Govr assented and wish'd us well with our work. Now twas Candle-Lighting: for went into Meetinghouse about 12. Mr. Easterbrooks made a very good Sermon. Twas four, or past, before went from the Anchor to the Townhouse.

May, 31. 1705. Govr, Major Brown, Sewall, Higginson, dine at Mr. Willard's with the Ministers. Brown, Sewall, Lynde go to Thank Mr. Easterbrooks for his Sermon and desire a Copy: He Thanks the Govr and Council for their Acceptance of his mean Labours and shews his unwillingness to be in print. When return'd found this paper on the Board:

GENTLEMEN,—I am very well satisfied of her Maj^s just Right and Prerogative to Allow, or disallow the Speaker of the Assembly of this Province, as well as the Council; being all elected by the Assembly. Therefore have proceeded as I have done, and as far as I can at present in that matter. But I have that just sense of the pressing Affairs of the War, that demand a very sudden Dispatch of this session, that will not consist with long Debates of any thing: And therefore shall not delay the Affairs necessary for the Security of the Province; which I desire may be first attended, Saving to Her most sacred Majesty Her just Rights as abovesaid, at all times.

This was communicated to the Council and Assembly May, 31, 1705.

per J. DUDLEY.[13]

Note. Body was written by a scribe; Signing was the Governour's own Hand-writing.

In the forenoon pretty near Noon, Deputies sent in the Election by Major Converse, Capt. Checkly, Savage, Major Brown, Gardener. Govr gave us a very hearty wellcom to the Board, Sign'd the Bill, and 23. Took the Oaths before went to Dinner at Mr. Willard's.

Lord's Day, June, 10. 1705. The Learned and pious Mr. Michael Wigglesworth dies at Malden about 9. m. Had been sick about 10. days of a Fever; 73 years and 8 moneths old. He was the Author of the Poem entituled The Day of Doom, which has been so often printed: and was very useful as a Physician.[14]

(*Hist.,* 1936, II, 114) writes: "The prejudices against him [Dudley] were great. The people, in general, looked upon him as an enemy, even to the privileges of the new charter." M.H.S. EDS.

[13] The original is in Massachusetts Archives, CVIII, f.30.

[14] Michael Wigglesworth (Harvard 1651) had been pastor of the church at Malden and physician for nearly fifty years, though a constant sufferer from ill-health. D.A.B.

July, 2. 1705. Lt Col. Thomas Savage dies about 6. p. m.

July, 4. Commencement Day. I go by Water, with Neighbour Deming, Green, Judd. Sail'd pleasantly till came about the Capt^s Island,[15] then the wind and Tide being against us, we went ashore and got over the Marsh to the Upland; and so into the Rode and comfortably to Town. Gave Gershom Rawlins a 20^s Bill. Capt. Courtemanch was there and din'd in the Hall.[16] In the morn. Holyoke began that part of his oration relating to Mr. Wigglesworth with, *Maldonatus Orthodoxus.* Mr. Hutchinson in his valedictory Oration Saluted the Justices of the Superiour Court, and Councillors.[17] Came home in a Calash with Col. Hutchinson and Mr. Penhallow: In the Boat with Mr. C. Mather, Mr. Bridge.

July, 5. Mr. Sol. Stoddard preaches the Lecture. Col. Savage buried about 7. p. m. Companies in Arms: Bearers, Sewall, Foster; Walley, Lt Co^l Lynde; Townsend, Belchar. The Street very much fill'd with People all along.

July, 16. 1705. Mr. Barnabas Lothrop, of Barnstable, visits me, with whom had much pleasant Discourse. I gave him Mr. Cotton Mather's sermon of the Lords Day, and Letter to Govr Ashurst about the Indians, Mother Hull's Epitaph.[18]

July, 17. 1705. I go a fishing in Capt. Bonners[19] Boat, Joseph, Edw. Oakes and Capt. Hill with us; went out at Pulling Point, between the Graves and Nahant, Catch'd but 3 Cod. I was sick and vomited; As came back went to the Castle. Neither Lt Govr nor Capt. Tuthill there; yet view'd the Works: Went to Governour's Island; home.

July, 18. The Deptford arrives.

---

[15] Captain's Island is to be seen on Pelham's map of Boston and vicinity and is mentioned by Paige in his *History of Cambridge,* p. 13; it was in the westerly bend of the Charles River; below the Colleges, at the end of Magazine Street. M.H.S. EDS.

[16] Tilly de Repentigny, Sieur de Courtemanche, had come from Quebec to arrange an exchange of prisoners. *C.S.M.* XXVI, 217.

[17] William Hutchinson (A.B. 1702), son of Eliakim, was taking his master's degree.

[18] Barnabas Lothrop (1635–1715) was an Assistant in the New Plymouth government, and after the union of the colonies, Judge of the Court of Common Pleas and Judge of Probate in Barnstable County. The Mather titles he received were *The Day which the Lord hath made. A Discourse concerning the Institution and Observation of the Lords-Day* (Boston, 1703; Holmes 81) and A *Letter; About the Present State of Christianity, among the Christianized Indians of New-England. Written, to the Honourable, Sir William Ashurst* . . . (Boston, 1705; Holmes 193). Sewall's epitaph in verse on his mother-in-law was printed in 1695.

[19] The M.H.S. editors surmised that this was Captain John Bonner, the father of the better-known Captain John Bonner (born in 1693), who drew the famous Bonner map of Boston (1722).

July, 19. Govr had a New Commission read relating to Pirats, and Queens Pleasure read for pardoning the surviving Pirats; and they in prison were sent for, and their Pardon declared in open Court, Chains knock'd off; but must go into Queens service.

18. I visited the widow Hannah Glover, who is blind, is just as old as Mrs. Rock to a few days. Father and Mother Eliot married here.

July, 25. I went to Reading, and heard Mr. Pierpont preach.

July, 27. I, my wife, Mary, Judith and Jane go to Brooklin. Govr and Mr. White came to us there. *July*, 29. *Rimes appulit.*

July, 31. Went to Cambridge to keep Court.

Augt 1. Lodg'd at Mr. Brattles.

Augt 2. Court is finish'd. I visit Cousin Fessenden, and dying Deacon Hasting.[20] *Augt.* 7. Joseph goes to Cambridge. *Augt.* 8. I and Mr. E^m Hutchinson go to Noddles Island, visit Madam Shrimpton. Ride in the Calash to Mr. Goodwin's: return to Madam Shrimpton. Sup, Come home. *Augt.* 10. I visit poor Mr. Baily, sick of the stone. Mr. Walter pray'd with him. Shew'd me his new House which he goes into next week. Cousin Moodey of York comes to us.

Augt. 15. I carry Mrs. Willard to Watertown Lecture and hear Mr. Gibbs preach excellently from John, 9. 4.—While it is Day—Din'd at Mr. Gibb's. When came away were going to see Mrs. Sherman, and the Calash fell backward and we both tumbled down; and twas long ere could fit it again: so came directly home. *Laus Deo.*

Augt. 16. Mr. Walter preach'd the Lecture at Boston in his Bro^r Mather's stead. *Augt.* 17th Cous. Moodey goes away, I give him some folio of Calvin's Exposition. Gave him a pair new Slippers.

Augt. 20. Went to Roxbury to wait on the Govr at his going away to Connecticutt, din'd there; went to Jamaica; Took Leave; went to Brooklin, to Cambridge, To North Farms [*Lexington*] with Mr. Bordman and spoke with Mr. David Fisk about Land of Nod: Came home late.

Augt. 22. Eliezer Moodey comes to us. *Augt.* 23. Judith is once thrown into the dirt above the stone–bridge; and the same day run over by a Horse; yet through God's Goodness receives little hurt. Mr. Sam. Melyen and his wife dine with us. I give him about 4. L. day, and 4. Baptistes.[21]

---

[20] Walter Hastings, tanner, selectman, and deacon of the Cambridge church, died August fifth.

[21] These were sermons of Cotton Mather: *The Day which the LORD hath made* (Boston, 1703; Holmes 81), and *Baptistes. Or, A Conference About the Subject and Manner of Baptism* (Boston, 1705; Holmes 25).

Augt. 24. I gave Mr. Rich'd Henchman Cooper's Dictionary,[22] cost 15ˢ, and Calvin on the Psalms cost 10ˢ, with these verses;

Mitto tibi Psaltem CHRISTUM et sua
Regna canentem;
Non erit ingratum dulce Poema tibi.
Musicus hic lapides cithara sapiente trahebat;
Et trahit: hinc Solymæ moenia celsa Novæ.

Little Sam Green is buried; Bearers Sam. Gerrish, Mr. Eliott's Prentice, Mr. Campbell's Prentice, Sam. Smith. I, Hannah, Mary, Jane, at the Funeral.

Augt. 24. 1705. Mr. Samuel Myles comes with his Broʳ before me; I bid him, Sam., sit down: but he quickly fell upon Nichols [*the constable*], the complainant against his Broʳ, and said by his Looks one might see the Gallows groan'd for him; I check'd him, and said it did not become a Minister so to speak. The constable ask'd me what weight the Money must be, 15. or 17. I answered there was no Money but 17ᵈ wᵗ: but if Capt. Myles offer'd Bills of Credit he must take them. Mr. Samˡ Myles told me he complain'd of Nichols, but withall told me he was not ready to pursue it.[23]

Augt. 27. I sent Mr. Walter, Calvin on Hoseah by young Everden. Gave Mr. Pemberton Mr. Cotton on Ecclesiastes, and the Vials,[24] having their double. He told me the evening before, He had little or nothing of Mr. Cotton.

Seventh-day; Septʳ 8. 1705. Mrs. Mary Lake was buried at the North; Bearers, Sam. Sewall, Jnᵒ Foster; Eliakim Hutchinson, Sam. Checkley; John Ballentine, John Coney; Mr. John Cotton and his wife, Mrs. Lake's daughter, principal mourners: They got not to Town till the day after their Mother's death. Enock Greenlef dyed this day about 11 oclock.

Septʳ 10. 2ᵈ *day*. This morning I made this verse.

---

22 Thomas Cooper's *Thesaurus Linguæ Romanæ et Britannicæ* (1565), known as Cooper's Dictionary, so delighted Elizabeth I that its author received numerous preferments, including the bishoprics of Lincoln and Winchester, but his life was made miserable by a profligate wife (*D.N.B.*) Richard Henchman was master of the North Writing School; he and Sewall were in the habit of exchanging copies of their verses. A longer version of the composition in this entry, and an extensive note on Henchman are printed in *Letter-Books*, i, 314.

23 Samuel Myles (Harvard 1684 and M.A. Oxon.) was rector of King's Chapel 1689–1728. His brother was John Myles of Swanzey, a sea-captain.

24 These were the writings of John Cotton of Boston: *A Briefe Exposition With Practicall Observations Upon The Whole Book Of Ecclesiastes* (London, 1654) and *The Powring Out Of The Seven Vials* (London, 1642).

Oceani fluctus ANNA moderante superbos,
Euphrates cedit; Roma Relicta cadit.[25]

Faxit Deus! (See 8ʳ 15.)

[*In margin: ut majestas tua palam appareat atque ejus sensu per-*
culssa elementa cedant ac obtemperent. Calvin, Isa. 63. ult.]

Septʳ 10. In the Afternoon I went to speak to Mr. Allen that the
Lord's Supper might be celebrated once in four weeks, as it was in
Mr. Cotton's Time and Mr. Wilson's: He was just come out of his
house with Elder Bridgham, Elder Copp, Deacon Marion and Deacon Hubbard: I pray'd them to go back again, and open'd my mind
to them. All save Mr. Hubbard plainly remember'd how it was in
Mr. Wilson's days; and the Alteration upon the coming in of Mr.
Davenport, upon his desire because he had it so at Newhaven: and
seem'd inclinable enough to alter it. Then I went to Mr. Cooke, both
he and Madam Cooke remember'd the change, and seem'd not displeas'd with my proposal. I discours'd with Mr. Pemberton, and told
him it would be a Honor to Christ, and a great Privilege and Honor
to Boston, to have the Lord's Supper administred in it every Lords
Day: we having nothing to do with moneths now; Their Respect now
ceases with the Mosaical Pedagogy. [*Gal. iii. 24.*] It seems odd, not
to have this Sacrament administred but upon the first day of each
Moneth; and the rest of the Sabbaths always stand by.

Third-day 7ʳ 11ᵗʰ 1705. The Deputies send in their Answer to the
Governour's speech dated this day, which begins, May it please your
Excellency, and doth not end with, Sent up for Concurrence.[26]

This day 7ʳ 11ᵗʰ *mane*, Her Majesties Letter of the Third of May
1705. from Sᵗ James's, is read at the Board, wherein a new seal is order'd, and the old one to be defac'd: John Dixwell, the Goldsmith,
being sent for, cut it in two in the middle, with a Chisel.[27]

In the evening I met with Mr. Cotton Mather's Letter which begins thus; Sir, your Distich entertains me. Both the Poetry and the
prophecy of the *Vates*, is very entertaining. I hope it begins to be a
History &c. He had rather read CHRISTO, which I heartily agree;

[25] Sewall sent a letter to Cotton Mather the same day with a copy of his verse
(L.B. I, 313–314). On the 11th he received a reply suggesting that CHRISTO be
substituted for ANNA. On the 23d of October he recorded his new version in
English.

[26] Apparently the document printed by Hutchinson (*Hist.*, 1936, II, 112–113).
M.H.S. EDS.

[27] Dixwell was the son of the regicide John Dixwell, M.P., who fled first to Germany, then to New Haven, where he lived to the age of 82 under the name of
James Davids. *Savage.*

which besides Wars, takes in Storms and Tempests which Christ makes great use of in Governing the World; and in this He only is Moderator.

Friday, 7ʳ 14. I go to Newton, and hear Mr. Hobart. He has a Lecture once in Eight Weeks. Text was Levit. 26. 11. Doct[*rine*] Obedience unto God, is the way to have the continuance of his Tabernacle; and to avoid the abhorrency of his soul.

Tuesday, 7ʳ 18. 1705. I went to Cambridge Court, where Col. Hutchinson, Tyng, Foster, Higginson, by a special Commission, sat Judges of the cause between Charlestown and me [*in margin:* Land of Nod]; Jury brought in for me Costs of Court: Court order'd judgment to be entred: Charlestown Committee Appeal'd. Mr. Dudley was my Attorney; Hern and Valentine for Charlestown. The chief plea they made was to the Jurisdiction of the Court..

Septʳ 20ᵗʰ Mary has a very sick turn, complains much of the palpitation of the Heart.

Septʳ 22. Set forward on my Journey towards Bristol, with Col. Hathorn. Got to Wrentham an hour before Sunset. Kept the Sabbath there.

Septʳ 24. To the Ship at Rehoboth, where din'd. Mr. Newman piloted me to George Bairsto's, where saw him, his wife, sister Gates. From thence Mr. Newman led us the next way through the Neck. Then Mr. Pain accompanied us to Bristol. At Mr. Sparhawk's met with Col. Byfield, his wife, Col. Taylor and wife, Madam Lyde and her children. Major Walley and Leverctt came late next day; which made us almost lose the Forenoon. *Thorsday* din'd with Mr. Mackentash, Lᵗ Govʳ there, who came up with Mr. Lyde. Col. Hathorne desired excuse, and went homeward.

Friday [Sept. 28] broke up the Court and got to Rehoboth. Lodge at Smith's, I got cold, and ventured not with the Company next morning being Rainy. But set out with Samˡ Robinson about 11. m. when wether broke up. Dined at Slack's: Got comfortably to Medfield, lodg'd at Mr. Baxters, thô he not at home. Heard Mr. Jnº Veasy of Braintrey.

Octobʳ 1. Got home pretty early, about 12 or 1. (Mrs. Fyfield and her daughter were at Medfield.) Drove a Pin in the Ministers House which I found Raising; bolted on the Raisers out of Bishop's Lane before I was aware. Found my Family better than I left them. *Laus Deo.* My horse fell with me this Journey, broke my crooper: but I had no harm. Found Joseph at home, who on Satterday was a Bearer to Mr. Banisters' child with Mr. Foster's Stoddard. Heard of the childs death at Slack's.

Octr 15. Three men are carried away from Lancaster from Mr. Sawyers Sawmill [*by Indians*]. This day I made this Distich;

> *Roma inhonesta jacet.*²⁸ *Sanctæ gaudete puellæ*
> *Vindicis et vivi Vivitis Urbe DEI.*²⁹

Gave them and two more to Mr. Phips at Charlestown Octr 16. Hear the bad news from Lancaster. Neighbour Deming's House is Raised. Rainy day.

Octob^r 17. very Rainy day.

Octob^r 18. Dark and Rainy day.

Octob^r 21. Several of the Fleet came in from Barbados. About Noon between Meetings, were several Claps of Thunder, and Hail and Rain.

Feria tertia, Octob^r 23. 1705. My Daughter Hirst is Deliver'd of a Son, a little before Sun-rise. I staid there till about 12 at night, then Mr. Hirst importun'd me to come home. I prevail'd with my wife and Mary to go to Bed (wife not well to go to her daughter.) Hannah and I sat up to be in a readiness if any Messenger should come. But the first we heard was this good News of a Son. *Laus Deo.* As I sat up towards morning, I turn'd my Distich thus

> CHRIST governing the mighty waves of the tempestuous Main:
> Euphrates turns, and leaves old Rome to court Recruits in vain.

At last I fix'd upon beginning, While CHRIST Commands—that, according to our use, carrying more of the likeness of a Military Phrase: as our Governour is Commander in Chief.

Seventh-day 8^r 27th These verses are printed off upon the side of the Almanack. This day we hear that James Blin is cast away. It seems the Castle is ordered to be call'd *Fort William*; and the Governour went down yesterday, and caus'd the inscription to be set up,³⁰ a pretty many Guns fired. 8^r 27. as I was writing to my Brother, I ask'd the Govr; told me 'twas so, and directed me to tell my Bro^r that when he writt his account of Stores, he should style Salem Fort *Fort-Anne*. My wife went in the coach to see her daughter; 6th day,

---

²⁸ Here Sewall placed an asterisk and wrote in the margin: "*Mortua Moecha senex*; &c. Written 8^r 21. 1715. on occasion of the French King's death on the Lord's Day Augt. 21. 1715. Some say, he stunk alive."

²⁹ Sewall sent a revised version of these lines to Governor Gurdon Saltonstall in a letter, 16 July 1722 (*L.B.* II, 139).

³⁰ The inscription is printed in N. B. Shurtleff, A *Topographical and Historical Description of Boston* (1891), 492–493. "The new fort [Shurtleff says], constructed chiefly of brick, was built in a very substantial manner by Colonel William Wolfgang Romer, an engineer of much ability."

which is the first time since she Lay in, her Cold is so hard upon her.

Octob^r 28. Little Samuel Hirst is Baptised by Mr. Colman; tis a very Rainy day.

Novemb^r This Distich finished

> *Desine Belshazzar Templo Omnipotentis abuti:*
> *Proxima fatalis nox sine fine tua est.*

Afterward this English

> Sound! Sound! the Jubilean Trumpet sound;
> Spread the Glad Tidings, Give the Word all round.

Novr 6th Super. Court. *Nov^r* 9th Tho. Odell Sentenc'd to pay a Fine of £300; suffer a years Imprisonment. Rochester, a Negro, sentenced to dye for firing Madam Savages Dwelling House in the night.

Novr 10. Ambrose Daws buried. Gilam and Mason arrive at Cape-Anne.

Novr 11th Hear of their Arrival, of Col. Hobbey being Knighted.[31]

Novr 12th New Commission for the Indian Affairs comes to hand. Brooklin is pass'd to be a Township by the Council. I go to Salem with Major Walley's Man. At Lewis's overtake Mr. Dudley, and have his company to Salem.

Novr 14. After the Court adjourned *sine die*, visited Rever^d Mr. Higginson, Madam Bradstreet, Bro^r Hirst. *Nov^r* 15. Had a very pleasant fair day to come home in. Baited at Sprague's. Visited Mr. Usher. He not at home, his wife entertain'd us. Found Mr. Willard at our house: He pray'd excellently with us. Have had a very comfortable Journey out and home.

Novr 21. Capt. Vech and Mr. Wm Dudley come to Town from Cannada; came from thence last Friday was five weeks. Govr would not let them come till the Fleet sail'd for France.[32]

Novr 24th Snow falls and covers the Ground. Has been very cold wether this week.

The College at Quebec was burnt the third time when they were there; that set a small chapel at a distance, on fire; the chapel fired a

---

[31] Hutchinson writes of Sir Charles Hobby that he "had been knighted, as some said, for fortitude and resolution at the time of the earthquake on Jamaica, others for the further consideration of £800 sterling." *Hist.*, 1936, II, 114.

[32] Samuel Vetch had been sent to Quebec with others by Governor Dudley to negotiate a truce and arrange for an exchange of prisoners. William Dudley (Harvard 1704) was the governor's son. Through the next decade Vetch reappears frequently in the diary; for the full story of his activities, see G. M. Waller, *Samuel Vetch: Colonial Enterpriser* (1960).

high Cross with a Crucifix on it, so that it bowed and fell down. [*Judges v. 27.*]

Novr 25. Mrs. Allen dies, 28, buried. 29. Snow. This day hear of Capt. Samuel Clark's death very suddenly at Sea, about 3 weeks ago: Sail'd from St. Thomas 2 or 3 days before. Was a good man, liv'd in our house more than Ten years, left one Son. The Lord fit me for my change. *Dec^r* 1. made this Distich on the burning of the Quebeck Cross:

> *Crux atrox tandem flammam sentire jubetur:*
> *Ipsa Salus fallax igne probata perit.*

> The bawdy bloudy Cross, at length
> Was forc'd to taste the flame:
> The cheating Saviour, to the fire
> Savoury food became.

Decr 1. Deputies send in a Bill against fornication, or Marriage of White men with Negros or Indians; with extraordinary penalties; directing the Secretary to draw a Bill accordingly. If it be pass'd, I fear twill be an Oppression provoking to God, and that which will promote Murders and other Abominations. I have got the Indians out of the Bill, and some mitigation for them [*the Negroes*] left in it, and the clause about their Masters not denying their Marriage.[33]

Decr 7. Went to Brooklin, set out about Noon, saw the Govr at his Fence, who invited me in to Dinner, stood with his Son Wm But I fear'd should lose visiting Mr. Bayley, and so pass'd on. [*in margin:* Carters affront Governor]. After Dinner met the Govr upon the Plain near Sol. Phips's; told me of what happened on the Road,[34]

[33] Sewall refers to Chapter 10 of the Province Laws of 1705–6, An Act for the Better Preventing of a Spurious and Mixt Issue, passed 5 December 1705. By this act fornication between whites and Negroes or mulattoes was forbidden, and the colored offender was to be sold out of the province. Marriage was forbidden between them. Sewall's benevolent clause is the fifth section: "And no master shall unreasonably deny marriage to his negro with one of the same nation, any law, usage, or custom to the contrary notwithstanding." *Acts and Resolves* I, 578–579.

[34] The affair of Governor Dudley and the carters makes a long footnote, but the M.H.S. editors made no apology for its length, nor do we; it is necessary in order to understand Sewall's entries. Moreover, the trivial occasion of the dispute only brings out more fully the almost insane rage of Dudley, and presents a lively picture of colonial life.

The offending farmers belonged to well-known and respectable families. Thomas Trowbridge (1677–1725) of Newton was the father of Edmund Trowbridge (Harvard 1728), chief justice of the Superior Court and one of the ablest lawyers in Massachusetts prior to the Revolution, and of Lydia (Trowbridge) Dana, mother of another chief justice, Francis Dana (Harvard 1762). John Winchester Jr. (1644–1718) lived in Brookline, and was the first representative of the town. Both were reputable citizens, and the judges evidently felt that justice was on the side of the defendants. Dudley was probably aware of his unpopularity, and evidently took a morbid view of a presumed insult. The evidence seems to show that no offence was meant, but that a casual accident in a public road was rendered a serious matter solely by the position of one of the parties.

The following affidavits in the case were printed by the M.H.S. editors from originals then in the possession of Henry Gardner Denny of Boston (Harvard 1852):

ROXBURY 23 Janu: 1705.

REVERED AND DEAR SIR,—That you may not be imposed upon I have covered to you my memorial to the Judges referring to the ingures offered mee upon the road, which I desire you will communicate to the ministers of your circle whose good opinion I Desire to mayntain, and have not in this matter by any means forfeited.

I am Sir Your humble servant

J. DUDLEY.

The Governour informs the Queen's Justices of her majestys Superior Court that on friday, the seventh of December last past, he took his Journey from Roxbury towards newhampshire and the Province of mayn for her majestys immediate service there: and for the ease of the Guards had directed them to attend him the next morning at Rumney house, and had not proceeded above a mile from home before he mett two Carts in the Road loaden with wood, of which the Carters were, as he is since informed, Winchester and Trobridge.

The Charet wherein the Governour was, had three sitters and three servants depending, with trunks and portmantles for the journey, drawn by four horses one very unruly, and was attended only at that instant by Mr. William Dudley, the Governours son.

When the Governour saw the carts approaching, he directed his son to bid them give him the way, having a Difficult drift, with four horses and a tender Charet so heavy loaden, not fit to break the way. Who accordingly did Ride up and told them the Govr. was there, and they must give way: immediately upon it, the second Charter came up to the first, to his assistance, leaving his own cart, and one of them says aloud, he would not goe out of the way for the Governour: whereupon the Govr. came out of the Charet and told Winchester he must give way to the Charet. Winchester answered boldly, without any other words, "I am as good flesh and blood as you; I will not give way; you may goe out of the way:" and came towards the Governour.

Whereupon the Governour drew his sword, to secure himself and command the Road, and went forward; yet without either saying or intending to hurt the carters, or once pointing or passing at them; but justly supposing they would obey and give him the way: and again commanded them to give way. Winchester answered that he was a Christian and would not give way: and as the Governour came towards him, he advanced and at len[g]th layd hold on the Govr. and broke the sword in his hand.

Very soon after came a justice of peace, and sent the Carters to prison.

The Justices are further informed that during this talk with the carters, the

Govr. demanded their names, which they would not say, Trobridg particularly saying he was well known, nor did they once in the Gov^{rs}. hearing or sight pull of their hatts or say they would go out of the way, or any word to excuse the matter, but absolutely stood upon it, as above is sayd; and once, being two of them, one on each side of the fore-horse, laboured and put forward to drive upon and over the Governour.

And this is averred upon the honour of the Governour.

J. DUDLEY.

I, Thomas Trowbridg of Newtown, being upon the seventh day of December 1705 upon the Road leading to Boston, driving my team, my cart being laden with cordwood, as I passed through the town of Roxbury, in the lane between the dwelling house of Ebenezer Davis and the widow Pierponts, in the which lane are two plaine cart paths which meet in one at the descent of an hill: I being with my cart in the path on the west side of the lane, I seeing the Governors coach where the paths meet in one, I drave leisurly, that so the coach might take that path one the east side of the lane, which was the best, but when I came near where the paths met, I made a stop, thinking they would pass by me in the other path. And the Governors son, viz. Mr. William Dudley, came rideing up and bid me clear the way. I told him I could not conveniently doe it, adding that it was easier for the coach to take the other path then for me to turn out of that: then did he strike my horse, and presently alighting his horse, drew his sword, and told me he would stab one of my horses. I stept betwixt him and my horses, and told him he should not, if I could help it: he told me he would run me through the body, and made severall pases at me with his sword, which I fended off with my stick. Then came up John Winchester, of Muddyriver *alias* Brookline, who was behind me with his loaden Cart, who gives the following account.

I, John Winchester, being upon the road in the lane above written, on the year and day above said, hereing Mr. William Dudley give out threatening words that he would stab Trowbridge his horse, and run Trowbridge himself through the body if he did not turn out of the way, I left my cart and came up and laid down my whip by Trowbridge his team. I asked Mr. W^m. Dudley why he was so rash; he replyed "this dog wont turn out of the way for the Governour." Then I passed to the Governour with my hat under my arm, hopeing to moderate the matter, saying "may it pleas your Exelency, it is very easie for you to take into this path, and not come upon us:" he answered, "Sirrah, you rouge or rascall, I will have that way." I then told his Exelency if he would but have patience a minute or two, I would clear that way for him. I, turning about and seeing Trowbridge his horses twisting about, ran to stop them to prevent damage; the Governour followed me with his drawn sword, and said "run the dogs through," and with his naked sword stabed me in the back. I faceing about, he struck me on the head with his sword, giveing me there a bloody wound. I then expecting to be killed dead on the spot, to prevent his Exelency from such a bloody act in the heat of his passion, I catcht hold on his sword, and it broke; but yet continueing in his furious rage he struck me divers blows with the hilt and peice of the sword remaining in his hand, wounding me on the hands therewith: in this transaction I called to the standers by to take notice that what I did was in defence of my life. Then the Governor said "you lie, you dog; you lie, you divell," repeating the same words divers times. Then said I, "such words dont become a christian;" his Exelency replyed "a

being in a great passion; threaten'd to send those that affronted him
to England. As I went back, Jn° Bartlet, the middlemost Carter,
shew'd me the Ground where the three carts stood, which was a
difficult place to turn; and the Govr had a fair way to have gone by
them if he had pleas'd. Upon the Meetinghouse hill met Mr. P. Dudley: I ask'd him how he got the men along, he said he walk'd them
along. Upon Satterday just at night Mr. Trowbridge and Winchester
came to speak to me that their sons might be released out of Prison.
It being so late, I refer'd them to second-day Morning Decr 10. to
meet at the Secretary's office. Major Walley and I met there and Mr.
Attorney, who desired Mr. Leverett might be sent for, being so near;
and writt a Letter accordingly in our Names, which was given to Mr.
White. Mr. Leverett came not till 3^d day xr. 11th Then in the Afternoon, we agreed to grant a Habeas Corpus, and I sign'd it, but Mr.
Cook being at Charlestown-Court twas not seal'd till Wednesday
morning. The writt commanded them to be brought to the Court-
Chamber in Boston on Friday morn, 9. aclock. Twas put off till then
that might have Mr. Leverett's company, whose business allow'd him
not to be here sooner: And that Mr. Attorney [*Paul Dudley*] who

---

christian, you dog, a christian you divell, I was a christian before you were born."
I told him twas very hard that we who were true subjects and had bene allways
ready to serve him in any thing, should be so run upon; then his Exelency took up
my cart whip and struck me divers blows: then said I "what flesh and blood can
bear this:" his Exelency said "why dont you run away, you Dog, you Divell, why
dont you run away."

I Thomas Trowbridge, further declare that I seeing and hearing the forementioned words and actions, between his Exelency and said Winchester, and seeing
Mr. William Dudley make a pass at Winchesters body, with his naked sword. I
with my arm turned him aside, and he recovering himself, he stabed me in my
hip; then the Governer struck me divers blows with the hilt of his sword; then
takeing Winchesters driveing stick and with the great end there of struck me
severall blows as he had done to Winchester afore. Winchester told his Exelency
he had bene a true subject to him, and served him and had honoured him, and
now he would taked his life away for nothing. The Governer replyed "you lie, you
dog, you know that I intended you no harm." When we spake of tarrying no
longer but of driveing along our teams, his Exelency said "no, you shall goe to
Goale, you Dogs;" when twas askt what should become of our teams his Exelency
said, "let them sink into the bottom of the earth."

JOHN WINCHESTER, jun^r
THOMAS TROWBRIDGE.

The sequel to the matter seems to be given in the following extract from the
court records: At a session of the Superior Court, 5 November 1706, present
Sewall, Hathorne, Walley, and Leverett, both Winchester and Trowbridge
"being bound by recognizance to this court" were "discharged by solemn Proclamation."

was attending Charlestown-Court, might have opportunity to be present.

Sixth-day, xr. 14. Mr. Leverett came, and Mr. Sheriff order'd the Prisoners to be brought: Mr. Attorney spoke against them: They had no counsil, could procure none. Justices withdrew into the Counsil Chamber, and agreed to Bail to the Super^r Court, 300£ Prisoners and 3 Sureties each 100£. Examin'd the first and put it in writing. And I sent Mr. Cook to Mr. Secretary to desire his Assistance, or presence, which he declin'd. Some would have had five Hundred pounds and more sureties. I urg'd the words of the Act, that saith regard is to be had to the quality of the person; These men were not worth so much. At last came to Three Hundred pound. I propounded Two Hundred, and Two sureties. Thomas Trowbridge 300.£ James Trowbridge 100. Abraham Jackson 100. and Capt. Oliver Noyes 100. John Winchester 300£, John Winchester the Father 100£, Josiah Winchester, unkle, 100. Mr. John White £100. I could hardly be brought to their being bound to their Good Behaviour, because there was no Oath to justify the charge laid in the Mittimus; and the Prisoners pleaded their Innocence. No Complaint in writing. A little after Two aclock all was finish'd. I am glad that I have been instrumental to Open the Prison to these two young men, that they might repair to their wives and children and Occasions; and that might have Liberty to assemble with God's People on the Lord's Day. I writt earnestly to Col. Hathorne to desire him, an experienced Traveller, to help us to steer between Scylla and Charibdis: I mentiond it in Court.

xr. 16. Mr. Willard sung 72 PS. from the 4th v. two Staves—Poor of the People.—While we were deliberating in the Council-Chamber, P. Dudley writt a Letter, that would not Bail them yet; that would be an error on the right hand; he would write to his father Mompesson,[35]

---

[35] Paul Dudley's reference to "his father Mompesson" was found to be inexplicable, genealogically, by the M.H.S. editors. Feelings between the Dudleys and Roger Mompesson were distinctly sour. Mompesson had come to America (from Magdalen Hall, Oxford, and Lincoln's Inn) with a commission dated 1 April 1703 as Judge of the Admiralty with jurisdiction from Pennsylvania to Nova Scotia. When he undertook to fulfil his duties in Rhode Island he learned that his commission had been superseded in New England by one granted to Colonel Nathaniel Byfield through the influence of Joseph Dudley. (Mompesson complained to the Earl of Nottingham, Secretary of State, 4 July 1704: "If my commission were continued for that place, I doubt how far I, or any man living, could pretend to be serviceable to the Crown or Church of England under the command or influence of Coll. Dudley . . . or how there could be any due prosecution whilst his son [Paul] is Attorny or Advocate Genl there." *N.Y. Col. Docs.* IV, 1116). Nevertheless Mompesson's talents were by no means wasted: for several years he held at the same time the office of chief justice and council member in

Mr. Secretary was not Settled in his opinion. Not one Gentleman present but thought they would not be Bail'd. Mr. Leverett shew'd me the Letter, writt an Answer and copied it on Mr. Dudley's. In publick I offer'd Coke's pleas of the Crown to be read, especially as to that clause of High Treason for killing the Chancellor &c. He declined having it read. I had the Statute Book there, Coke pleas Crown, and Reading on the Statutes, stuck to 31. Car. 2ᵈ, that Commands all to be Bail'd that are not Committed for Felony or Treason.

Tuesday, Decʳ 18. Great Rain, which hinders my going to Roxbury-Lecture. This day Mr. Colman's sloop arrives; came from Plimᵒ Octobʳ 25ᵗʰ Brings news of a kind of Certainty that Sir Charles Hobby is to be our Governour.

Decʳ 21. Cousin Noyes brings the News of Mrs. Coffin's death the 15ᵗʰ instᵗ, to be buried the 19ᵗʰ Went away suddenly and easily. [*In margin:*] Mrs. [*Tristram*] Coffin. M[*ortuus*] E[*st*]. A very good Woman at Newbury Dead.

Decʳ 22. Very great snow.

xr. 24ᵗʰ I could not persuade Mr. Campbell to print my addition to the Quebeck Article, last [*News*] Letter: but now he does it:

> *Gallica Crux æquam flammam sentire coacta est:*
> *Ista salus fallax, igne probata perit.*
> *Idolum nihil est, restat de stipite longo*
> *Nescio quid cineris, quem capit urna brevis.*

As soon as Mr. Green's daughter brought me a proof, I deled the Title, *In Obitum Crucis*; though I my self had put it in: because the English introduction seem'd to suffice.

I sent a Letter to Mr. Henchman, desiring we might pray that God would make the proud French Helper of the Antichristian Faction to stoop as Low as Quebeck Cross. Visited Mrs. Maccarty, sick Mr. Tho. Downs, and the solitary widow of Mr. Samˡ Clark. Were very thankfull to me; especially Mr. Downs.

Writ to Govʳ Winthrop [*of Connecticut*], advising the Recᵗ of the Bond; enclos'd Letters of the day, Athenian Oracle, Selling Joseph.

Tuesday, Decʳ 25. Very cold Day but Serene Morning, Sleds, Slays, and Horses pass as usually, and shops open. I just went into Town and visited Mr. Secretary, whose Indisposition has increased so much by a pain in his Back or side, that he has kept House from Satterday. Then went to Mr. Treasurers and Rec'd Bills of Credit for my Coun-

---

Pennsylvania, New Jersey, and New York, as well as admiralty judge therein, a unique record in our colonial history. E. A. Jones, *Amer. Members of the Inns of Court* (1924), 159–160; *N.Y. Hist. Soc. Colls.* 1947, 130–142.

cils Attendance. I think the Govr was not in Town to-day; though tis said his Excellency came to Roxbury the night before. Capt. Belchar buried a Negro this day; his Coachman, a very good Servant. He was a Bearer to Cousin Savages Hagar. The Governour came not home till Tuesday, a very cold day; some think the coldest has been these many years, by the Vapor taken notice of at Nantasket. *Decr 27.* Govr warns a Council; reads the Letter that orders a Thanks-giving here: I mention'd the Thanksgiving in October had in general mention'd the same thing: but the Govr would not hear of any thing but appointing a Day in obedience to the Queen. Before went out of the Council-Chamber—Capt. Belchar invited me to his Thanksgiving on account of his Son's preservation.

Sixth-day, Decr 28. Mr. Pemberton prays excellently, and Mr. Willard Preaches from Ps. 66. 20. very excellently. Spake to me to set the Tune; I intended Windsor, and fell into High-Dutch, and then essaying to set another Tune, went into a Key much too high. So I pray'd Mr. White to set it; which he did well, Litchf. Tune. The Lord humble me and Instruct me, that I should be occasion of any Interruption in the Worship of God. Had a very good Dinner at three Tables. Had the Meeting; and few else except Relations in Town, and me. The Lord accept his Thank-offering.

1706

THE TROWBRIDGE-WINCHESTER-DUDLEY FRACAS CONTINUED /
JONATHAN BELCHER MARRIES AND MAKES A GREAT ENTRANCE INTO
TOWN / DEATH OF MRS. PETER SERGEANT, THE FORMER LADY PHIPS /
NEIGHBOR DEMING'S IMPROPER REQUEST / PLYMOUTH COURT TRIP /
ST. GEORGE'S DAY CELEBRATED / JOURNEY TO IPSWICH AND
NEWBURY / STORMY SESSION OF THE GENERAL COURT / LAND OF
NOD CASE / SEWALL ABSENTS HIMSELF FROM GENERAL COURT /
CONTRIBUTION TO NEW CAMBRIDGE MEETING-HOUSE / TRIP TO
MARTHA'S VINEYARD, BRISTOL, AND NARRAGANSETT / DINNER AT THE
GOVERNOR'S

Jany 9. [1705/6] Guns are fired at Boston upon the supposal of Mr.
Belchar's being married at Portsmouth yesterday: very cold wether.[1]

Jany 10.. I corrected David for his extravagant staying out, and for
his playing when his Mistress sent him of Errands.

Jany 11th I visited languishing Mr. Bayley, carried him two pounds
of Currants, which he accepted very kindly. Is in a very pious humble
frame in submitting to the afflicting hand of God.

This day I met Mr. Leverett in the street at Boston, who told me,
he had by the Governour's direction, written to Col. Hathorne to
come to Town. I ask'd him, whether as a Councillor, or Judge; he said
both; the Governor had drawn up a Declaration relating to Winchester and Trowbridge: I enquired whether it might not as well be
let alone till the Trial: It seems Mr. Leverett's Letter went by the
Post.

I call'd at the Governour's, only his Lady at home. Slander. It
seems some have reported that I should say I saw Quarts of blood
that run out of Trowbridges-Horses. I answered, I had never seen, nor

---

[1] Jonathan Belcher (Harvard 1699), son of the wealthy merchant, Captain Andrew
Belcher, had just returned from a two-year visit to England, Germany, and Holland. He was married on the 8th, his birthday, to Mary Partridge, daughter of
William Partridge, sometime lieutenant-governor of New Hampshire. They made
a triumphal entry into Boston on the 23d.

thought, nor reported any such thing. *Seventh-day, Jany 12th 1705/6.* A Council is call'd to meet at eleven aclock. Govr call'd Maxwell, bid him go to Major Walley, and tell him the Govr and Council were sitting, and would have him there also. Maxwell answer'd that Major Walley was sick. Twas said also that Mr. Bromfield was sick. Mr. Leverett was call'd in, and bid to sit down. The Governour's Declaration was read as to the fray xr. 7th with Winchester and Trowbridge, Carters. The Govr said he did not know whether he should live to the time of the Court; bid Mr. Secretary keep it for the Court. Govr mention'd the Story of the blood, I said before the Council, as had said before. Govr said some Minister, mentioning Mr. Allen, had reported that he swore; whereas he said he was as free from Cursing and Swearing vainly, as any there. Made a Ridicule of Winchester's Complaint about Mr. Dudley's striking him last Monday. I mention'd Mr. Taylor's striking, which was inconvenient for a Justice of Peace. The Govr Answer'd, he did well. Brought that as an Argument for himself, his drawing his sword; A Justice of Peace might punish several offences against the Laws upon view. After dinner I went and told Mr. Willard what was Reported of himself and me. He said he knew nothing of it. Col. Hutchinson was not at Council. I laid down this as a position, That of all men, twas most inconvenient for a Justice of Peace to be a Striker. [*Titus, 1, 7.*]

Jany 12. Capt. Belchar appears at Council in his new Wigg: Said he needed more than his own Hair for his Journey to Portsmouth; and other provision was not suitable for a Wedding. *Jany 13th* appears at Meeting in his Wigg. He had a good Head of Hair, though twas grown a little thin.

Jany 18. Sister Stephen Sewall, Son Hirst and his wife, dine with us; Major Walley droops with his Cold and Cough: He was not abroad on the Lord's Day, nor Lecture-day; wears plaisters or Poultices to his right side to ease the intolerable pain his Coughing causes him.

Lord's Day, Jany 20th My Dame Mary Phipps, (Lady Sergeant, *alias* Phypps,) dies about Sun-Rise[2]; Maj^r Genl tells me She was Dying from Satterday Noon. Has Bled excessively at the Nose. Mr. Sergeant was at Meeting in the Afternoon. Mr. Butchers son Alwin taken into Church and a woman; Mr. Ezek. Lewis dismiss'd from Westfield, and enter'd into Covenant with them.[3]

[2] On 9 October 1701 Sewall had recorded the marriage of Lady Phips, the widow of Sir William Phips, to Peter Sergeant, Esq., of Boston, merchant and councillor.
[3] Alwin Butcher, son of Robert, and Abiah Flagg, woman, became members of the South Church. Ezekiel Lewis (Harvard 1695) transferred his membership

Major Walley not at Meeting.

Jany 20. Mrs. Jane Pembrook dies in the afternoon, was taken on Wednesday. Her Husband is at Connecticut.

Tuesday, Jany 22. Mrs. Jane Pembrook buried in the New Burying place. Saw no Minister there but Mr. Colman and Mr. Dallie [*the French minister*]. I and Mr. E^m Hutchinson went together; Capt. Legg was there.

Wednesday, Jany 23. Storm of snow, for which reason the funeral of my Lady is put off to Friday.

Jany 23. Mr. Jonathan Belcher and his Bride dine at Lt Govr Usher's, come to Town about 6. aclock: About 20 Horsmen, Three Coaches and many Slays. Joseph came from College to visit us, and gave us notice of their coming before hand.

Jany 24th. Comfortable day: Mr. Willard not abroad in the Forenoon by reason of pain; but preaches excellently in the afternoon. Mr. Broadhurst of Albany,[4] Mr. Hirst and family, cousin Saml and Jonathan Sewall, dine with us &c.

Jany 25th Friday, My Lady Phipps is laid in Mr. Sergeant's Tomb in the New Burying place. Bearers, Mr. Winthrop, Cook; Elisha Hutchinson, Addington; Foster, Belcher. Govr and Lt Govr there. Mr. Russel and I go together. I had a Ring. Mr. Corwin and B. Brown there from Salem. Mr. Holman married Cousin Ann Quinsey a week ago.

Jany 26. I visit Mr. Sergeant, who takes my visit very kindly, tells me, my Lady would have been 59 years old next March, and that he was two Moneths older. It seems Mr. Chiever buried his daughter Abigail, about an hour before my Lady was entombed.

Jany 29th 1705/6. Col. Hathorn, Leverett, and S. hold the Court at Charlestown; storm began by Noon; yet I got home at night with difficulty. *Jan^y* 30. Extraordinary Storm; yet at Noon I rode to Jn° Russel's with very great difficulty by reason of the Snow and Hail beating on my forehead and Eyes hindering my sight, and the extravagant Banks of Snow the Streets were fill'd with. Waited 3 hours or more, and at last the Charlestown Boat coming over, I went in that very comfortably; got thither a little before four. Lodg'd at Capt. Hayman's with Mr. Leverett.

Jany 31. Got not home till six at night, by reason of much Ice in the River; fain to Land at the Salutation [*Tavern*], having got below the Ice on Charlestown side.

---

from Westfield, where he had been teaching. *Hist. Cat. of the Old South Church* (1883), 324–325.

[4] Jonathan Broadhurst had been sheriff of Albany County from 1700 to 1702.

Feb. 11. Mr. Jnᵒ Marion, the Father, buried; Bearers, Mr. Cook, Col. Townsend; Elder Bridgham, Copp; Deacon Tay, Hubbard. Great Funeral. I think Mr. Chiever was not there.

Feb. 27. My Neighbour Deming came to me, and ask'd of me the Agreement between himself and Joanna Tiler; I told him I was to keep it for them both and could not deliver it; he said he was going to Cambridge to ask Mr. Leverett's Advice, he would bring it safe again. When he still urged and insisted, I told him I would not have him lose his time, I would not deliver it; I would give him a copy if he pleas'd. He said he was in haste and could not stay the writing of it. I said, You would not take it well that I should deliver it to Tiler; no more could I deliver it to him. He said some what sourly, I am sorry you have not more Charity for him. And going away, murmuring said, passing out of the Stove-Room into the Kitchen, I have desired a Copy, offered Money and am Deny'd: I was then more mov'd than before, and said with some earnestness, Will you speak false to my face? He went away, and came not again, but his son came, and I gave him a Copy of the Agreement, written with my own hand. I thank God, I heartily desired and endeavoured a good Agreement between him and his Neighbour as to the Bounds of their Land: although he be thus out of Tune, upon my denying to grant his Unjust Petition.

Satterday, March 2. I visit my son and daughter at Brooklin and little Rebecka: Visited Mr. Bayley as I came home. Most of the way over the Neck is good Summer Travelling.

March, 4ᵗʰ Cousin Dummer and I take Bond of Mr. Rust 30£, to prosecute his Sons Master, Jnᵒ Staniford, for misusing and Evil entreating his Servant; Left Robert Rust with his father in the mean time. The invincible fear of the Mother, who came from Ipswich on purpose, and the high hand wherewith Staniford carried it, did in a manner force it. Mr. Jnᵒ Colman said, If his Servant should answer so, he would trample him under his feet; afterward mention'd that Scripture, Obey in all things. Staniford said scoffingly before us: The Boy would do well with good Correction; words were directed to the Mother.

Wednesday, March, 6. Council of Churches held at Mr. Willard's. They advise that after a Moneth, Mr. Joseph Morse cease to preach at Watertown farms. Adjourn'd to the First of May. Sharp Thunder the night following. Mr. Gookin, Capt. Morse and Deacon Larned dine with us. Cousin Noyes lodges here, and tells of many Sheep being drown'd by the overflowing of Merrimack River. At the breaking up of the River, which was furious by the Flood in Febr. The Ice jam'd and made a great Damm, and so caus'd the River to Rise so much and suddenly.

March, 6. 1705/6. At night, a great Ship, of 370 Tuns, building at Salem, runs off her blocking in the night and pitches ahead 16 foot. Her Deck not bolted off, falls in; and opens at the Bows; so that twill cost a great deal to bring her Right agen; and Capt. Dows thinks she will be Hundreds of pounds the worse.

March 13th Mr. Torrey comes to Town; on Thorsday even, Mr. Wadsworth came to visit him. Mr. Torrey told him of his Elder Rogers's Carriage towards him; and crav'd his pardon for chusing him; acknowledged his fault and plainly seem'd to renounce that office.

March, 16. A Storm of Snow.

Friday, March, 22. Michael Gill arrives from Lisbon, came out 11th Febr. By him have News from London of the 1. of Jany This day Mr. Jer. Cushing dyes at Scituat. Jno Turner dies there suddenly p. m.— the same day: He has the Character of a Drunkard, and Striker of his Wife.

March, 23. Set out for Weymouth with Sam Robbison, stop'd at Gibbs's to shelter our selves from a Gust of Wind and Rain. Twas dusk before got to Mr. Torrey's. I ask'd Mr. Torrey about laying the hand on the Bible in swearing: He said he was against it, and would suffer anything but death rather than do it.

March, 24. Mr. Torrey preach'd out of Amos, 8. 11.

Four children baptised in the Afternoon.

March, 25, 1706. Din'd at Barkers; surpris'd the Sheriff and his Men at the Flat-house: Got to Plymouth about 1½ by Sun.

March, 26. Major Walley and Leverett come from Barker's.

March, 27th I walk in the Meetinghouse. Set out homeward, lodg'd at Cushing's. *Note.* I pray'd not with my Servant, being weary. Seeing no Chamber-pot call'd for one; A little before day I us'd it in the Bed, and the bottom came out, and all the water run upon me. I was amaz'd, not knowing the bottom was out till I felt it in the Bed. The Trouble and Disgrace of it did afflict me. As soon as it was Light, I calld up my man and he made a fire and warm'd me a clean Shirt and I put it on, and was comfortable.[5] How unexpectedly a man may be expos'd! There's no security but in God, who is to be sought by Prayer.

March, 28, mihi natalis, got home about ½ hour after 12, dine with my wife and children.

Apr. 1. 1706. Col. Townsend, Mr. Bromfield, Burroughs and I went in the Hackny Coach and visited Mr. Thacher, din'd with him

[5] This passage, beginning with the word Seeing, was omitted by the M.H.S. editors.

and Mrs. Thacher. Mrs. Niles is there to ly in; but saw her not. Got home well. *Laus Deo.*

Apr. 4, 1706. Last night I dream'd I saw a vast number of French coming towards us, for multitude and Huddle like a great Flock of Sheep. It put me into a great Consternation, and made me think of Hiding in some Thicket. The Impression remain'd upon me after my Waking. GOD defend!

Friday, Ap. 5. I went and visited Mr. Baily whose paroxisms are return'd to once every hour. Carried him two pounds of Currants which he accepted with wonderful kindness. When left him, went forward for Brooklin, and going up the Meetinghouse Hill fell in with the Governour's Coach with two Horses: in it were his Excellency and Lady, Madam Paul Dudley, and Madam Thomas Dudley. I follow'd the Coach mostly, especially at Mittimus Hill,[6] and observed, that the Coachman of his own accord took the Road next Boston, which was refus'd Decemb^r 7, and nothing to incline to it but the goodness of the way. Took it also returning. Mrs. Kate Dudley, little Allen, and Capt. Gillam's little Maiden daughter rode in a Calash. Capt. Thomas Dudley rode on horseback.

Tuesday, Apr. 9. Mr. Danl Oliver and I ride to Milton, and there meet with Mr. Leverett, and as Spectators and Auditors were present at Deacon Swifts when Mr. Leverett discours'd the Punkapog intruders. Dined at the said Swift's with Mr. Thacher. Seth Dwight waited on us.

Ap. 8. Monday, poor little Sam Hirst went through the Valley of the Shadow of Death through the oppression of Flegm.

Ap. 9. Wife takes Physick, has a comfortable night after it. *Laus Deo.* Brother visits us.

Ap. 14. Capt. Belchar is kept at home by the Gout. *Ap. 15.* Abraham Hill arrives; makes us believe the Virginia Fleet is arriv'd.

Ap. 16. I first hear and see the swallows: They are now frequent. Mr. Banister says they were seen by him 2 or 3 days ago. Mrs. Gates lodg'd here last night. At night the Aer being clear, the Eclipse of the Moon was very much Gaz'd upon.

Tuesday, Apr. 23. Govr. comes to Town guarded by the Troops with their Swords drawn; dines at the [*Green*] Dragon, from thence proceeds to the Townhouse, Illuminations at night. Capt. Pelham tells me several wore crosses in their Hats; which makes me resolve to stay at home; (though Maxwell was at my House and spake to me to be

[6] "The elevation beyond the Dudley estate has, from time immemorial, been known as 'Meeting-House Hill.'" F. S. Drake, *The Town of Roxbury* (1878), 265. The M.H.S. editors could not explain why Sewall called it Mittimus Hill.

at the Council-Chamber at 4. p.m.) Because to drinking Healths, now the Keeping of a Day to fictitious St. George, is plainly set on foot. It seems Capt. Dudley's Men wore Crosses. Somebody had fasten'd a cross to a Dog's head; Capt. Dudley's Boatswain seeing him, struck the Dog, and then went into the shop, next where the Dog was, and struck down a Carpenter, one Davis, as he was at work not thinking anything: Boatswain and the other with him were fined 10ˢ each for breach of the peace, by Jer. Dummer Esqr: pretty much blood was shed by means of this blody Cross, and the poor Dog a sufferer.

Thomas Hazard came in from Narragansett about the time should have gon to the Townhouse, said he came on purpose to speak with me; so 'twas inconvenient to Leave him.

Midweek; Apr. 24. Privat Meeting at our House; Read out of Mr. Caryl [7] on those Words, The Lord gives, and the Lord Takes, Blessed —preface my Reading with saying, I will read now what read in course to my family because of the great and multiplied Losses. Cousin Savage and Capt. Hill pray'd, had a pretty full and comfortable Meeting notwithstanding the much Rain and Dirt. Sung 1 part and last v. of 48ᵗʰ Ps. 119.

7ᵗʰ day, Apr. 27ᵗʰ Joseph visits us, it seems he had a Tooth pull'd out by Madam Oliver's Maid, on Mid-week night.

Lords-Day, April, 28. Brief is Read. Bowditch Arrives.

Monday, Apr. 29. Cousin Gookin, his wife and son Richard lodge here.

Tuesday, Apr. 30. I carry Capt. Belchar my Letter to Mr. Bellamy, and he sends me the Comons votes. *Note,* Lords Resolution is dated Decʳ 6. Comons conferr'd with them about it the 7ᵗʰ Agree to it Satterday xr. 8. Address upon it agreed to by the Comons xr. 14ᵗʰ [8]

---

[7] Joseph Caryl (1602–1673), M.A. (Oxon.), nonconformist preacher, chaplain to Oliver Cromwell in Scotland, and member of the Westminster Assembly, published between the years 1644 and 1666 *An Exposition . . . of the Book of Job* in twelve fat octavos which ran to nearly 9000 pages. Fortunately for our New York readers, a complete set is available in the McAlpin Collection at Union Theological Seminary.

[8] Here Sewall copied into the diary what seems to be an extract from the *London Gazette:*

Mercurii [Wednesday]. 19. *die.* Xr's 1705. The Bill for the better Security of Her Majs person and Government, and of the Succession to the Crown of England in the protestant Line, was read a second Time. And Charles Cæsar Esqr, upon the Debate of the said Bill, standing up in his place, saying the Words following (which were directed by the House to be set down in writing at the Table)

There is a noble Lord, without whose Advice the Queen does nothing, who in the late Reign was known to keep a constant Correspondence with the Court at St Germans.

May, 1. *1706*. Eclipse of the Sun, not seen by reason of the cloudy wether.

May, 2^d Mr. Penn Townsend jun^r dies about 10 m. May, 3. is buried; Bearers Mr. Nathan^l Williams, Major Adam Winthrop, Capt. Oliver Noyes, Capt. Jno Ballentine jun^r, Mr. Habijah Savage, Mr. Elisha Cooke; all scholars.[9]

May, 2^d, *1706*. Capt. Stukely arrives from Barbados in the Deptford, 3 weeks passage; was not suffer'd to bring the Fleet with him, neither can they go for Salt; but are embargod at Barbados. Tis much fear'd that Nevis is Taken.

May, 4th Mr. Brattle and I send the School and College Deeds by Mr. N. Niles to be Recorded. Niles tells me that Monotocott [*Braintree*] Meetinghouse is Raised; he came that way, and saw it.

Mid-week, May, 15th *1706*. Went to Brooklin, visited my Daughter and little Grand-daughter. Visited Mr. Bayley. *May*, 16. Capt. Benj^a Gillam buried about 7. p. m. *May*, 20. Set out for Ipswich with Major Walley by Winnisimmet; Rid in the Rain from Lewis' to Salem; staid there, and assisted at the Funeral of Mrs. Lindal, Capt. Corwin's only daughter, a vertuous Gentlewoman. Was buried in the Tomb in a Pasture: Bro^r was one of the Bearers.

May, 21. Set out early for Ipswich; got thither seasonably. Twas late ere Mr. Leverett came. Sarah Pilsbury, Try'd for murdering her young Child, was Acquitted. *May*, 23. Mr. Fitch preaches the Lecture: Companys in Arms, Govr to view them; much fatigued by the Wet.

May, 24th Set out for Newbury with Major Davison: visit Mr. Payson, and deliver him my wives present; I hope he is recovering. Dine at Sister Northend's; Bro^r Northend brings us going as far as Capt. Hale's. At Sister Gerrishes dismiss Major Davison: visit Bro^r and Sister Tappan, Cousin Swett, cousins Jno, Henry, and Saml Sewall. Lodge at Sister Gerrishes.

May 25th Saw the sheep shearing, visited Cousin Rolf.

May, 26th Mr. Tappan preaches. Deacon Cutting Noyes Catechises in the Afternoon. In the evening visit Mr. Tappan.

May, 27th Col. Noyes invites me to his Training Dinner: Mr. Tappan, Brown, Hale and my self are guarded from the Green to the Tavern, Bro^r Moodey and a part of the Troop with a Trumpet ac-

---

Resolved, That the said words are highly dishonorable to Her Majestys person and Government.

Resolved that the said Charles Cæsar Esqr. be for his said offence committed prisoner to the Tower during the pleasure of this House.

[9] The bearers had all been at college with Townsend, who was graduated in 1693.

company me to the Ferry. Sam. Moody waits on me. Get to Brother's
in the night after nine aclock. Mr. Noyes had left his Verses for Mr.
Bayley, which I carried with me next morning. Rested at Lewis' during the Rain.

Got home well, *Laus Deo.*

May, 29. Election-day, Winthrop 83. Russel, 80. (Cooke 50) Ha-
thorn 68. Elisha Hutchinson, 80. Sewall, 83. Addington 74. Brown 76.
Phillips 80. Corwin 75. Foster 75. Townsend, 78. Higginson, 69.
Belcher, 80. Bromfield 55. Legg, 65. S. Appleton, 47. Partridge, 58.
Thacher 79. Pain, 79. Winslow, 86. Cushing, 47. E^m Hutchinson, 75.
(Hammond 62.) Plaisted, 46. Leverett, 42. Walley, 37. Jn° Appleton,
34.

June, 6. In stead of the Negativ'd were chosen B. Brown, 55. Ephr.
Hunt, 42.[10]

Mr. James Taylor, Treasurer; James Russel esqr Commiss^r of the
Customs.

This Court Mr. Lillie Prefer'd a Petition about his Reals not accepted by the Super. Court to go by Tale, which was Untrue in one
Material Article as to matter of fact, and the Justices much reflected
on. Mr. Paul Dudley was Attorney for Mr. Lillie. I pray'd the Petition might be dismiss'd, or those Reflections abated: the Govr brake
forth into a passionate Harangue respecting the Roxbury Carters. He
might be run through, trampled on, &c no care taken of him. Finally,
at another time it was agreed that there should be a Hearing, only
Mr. Lillie should first come into Council, make some Acknowledgement, withdraw that Petition, and file another. The Govr was very
hot and hard upon me at this time, insomuch that I was provok'd
to say, It was a Hardship upon me that the Governour's Son was
Mr. Lillie's Attorney. At which the Govr Storm'd very much. Some
days after Mr. Lillie came into Council. The Govr presently said,
Sir, shall I speak for you, or will you speak for your self, and so
fell a speaking —— at last Mr. Lillie said with a low voice, I have
prefer'd a Petition which I understand is not so satisfactory; I did
not intend to reflect upon the Judges, and desire that petition may be
withdrawn, and this filed in the room of it. Withdrew, Govr ask'd it
might be so, and that the first petition might be Cass and Null. Secretary whisper'd the Govr that the Petition had been read twice in
Council, whereupon the Govr took the pen and obliterated the Minute of its having been read on the head of the Petition. And then
after the Hearing before the whole Court, when the Deputies were

10 Elisha Cooke and Joseph Hammond were the two negatived; Sewall put their
names in parentheses.

Returned, the Govr bundled up the papers and sent them in to the House of Deputies, without asking the Council whether they would first go upon them, with whom the Petition was entered. After many days, the Deputies return'd the papers agen by Mr. Blagrove, expressing their desire that the Council would first act upon them, seeing the Petition was entred with the Secretary.

Some time after, the Govr sent in the Papers again, and then the Deputies voted upon them and sent it in, but before any thing was done in Council, the Court was prorogu'd to the 7th of August, &c., &c. Major Walley sick, staid at home two Sabbaths. came out agen July 27th

July, 28. 1706. Col. Hathorne comes to Town, Dines and lodges at our House.

July, 29. Col. Hathorne, Major Walley, Sewall, ride to Cambridge in the Hackney Coach. Mr. Sheriff, his son, and the Steward of the College met us at Brooklin, drank a Glass of good Beer at my son's, and pass'd on. My case [*In margin:* Land of Nod] was call'd in the Afternoon and committed to the jury. I would have come home but then Major Walley also would come; which made me stay and send the Coach to Town empty. Lodg'd at Mr. Brattles. *July*, 30. College Hall at Cambridge, The Jury brought in for me Costs of Courts.[11] Charlestown Gentlemen and their Attorneys said not a Word that I could hear. Col. Hathorne with Mr. Valentine, Charlest. Attorney, examined my Bill of cost and so did the Clerk, and afterward Col. Hathorne shew'd it to Maj^r Walley and Leverett, and then Allow'd it, subscribing his Name.

Augt 7.. Genl Court meets. *Augt* 10, 1706. A Conference is held in the Council-Chamber, at the desire of the Deputies. Mr. Speaker, The House is doubtfull whether they have not proceeded too hastily in calling that a Misdemeanour, which the Law calls Treason; and are doubtfull whether this Court can proceed to Try the Prisoners. Mr. Jewet, Committee that were appointed to prepare for the Trials, were doubtfull and unsatisfied that they had called the crime of the Prisoners a Misdemeanour: If any wrong steps had been taken, tis fit they should be retriev'd. Mr. Blagrove, If that which the Prisoners are charg'd with, be made Treason by the Law of England; this Court must not make Laws repugnant to the Law of England.

The Governour answer'd, He had not seen the Papers, and could not say that what they had done was Treason. After this the Deputies sent in the Papers. And about Augt 13. Govr put it to vote in the Council, whether the prisoners should be Tried by the Genl Court

[11] See our note of 12 August 1702.

according to the order of last sessions: There were 17. at the Board Nine Yeas, and Eight Nos. Secretary was in the Negative as well as I.

Friday Augt. 16. Capt. Vetch was brought to his Trial in the Afternoon, in the Court Chamber.[12] *Note.* I came home on Wednesday morn, and went not again till the Gov[r] and Council sent for me by Mr. Winchcomb Friday morn. I went though I had a cold; spake that a suit of Cloaths might be made here for Mr. Williams.[13] Depts would have had Mr. John Eliot, and Cousin Dummer M. A.[14] to have assisted Mr. Attorney: Gov[r] did not consent: they insisted so long that the Forenoon was spent, and I fairly got home. *Augt. 17.* I am told Mr. Borland and Lawson are brought to their Trial. Mr. Borland pleads that he was a Factor in the management of this Affair.

Note. Gov[r] would have had the Judges manage the Conference, I declin'd it because was against the procedure. And so declin'd joining with the Judges to prepare for it because I was against it. Col. Hathorne was at Salem with his sick Son; so that only Majr Walley, and Mr. Leverett were active in the matter. And Mr. Leverett said at the Board that he did not interpret that Clause in the Charter of imposing Fines &c. as if it did impour the Gen[l] Court to Try delinquents.

Feria secunda, August 19th 1706. Went and visited my son and daughter at Brooklin, and Dined there: Went to Cambridge; Gave Mr. Bordman, Town-Clerk, Seven pounds in two Bills of Credit to help build the New-Meetinghouse; fourty shillings of it upon Consideration of my ancient Tenant, the widow Margaret Gates, and her family, going there to the publick worship of God. Gave him also Ten Shillings for Mrs. Corlett, widow. Visited Joseph, Mr. Flint, congratulated Mr. Whiting upon his being chosen a Fellow. Went into Hall and heard Mr. Willard expound excellently from 1 Cor. 7. 15, 16. It was dark by that time I got to Roxbury, yet I visited Mr.

---

[12] While Samuel Vetch was in Canada on his mission to exchange prisoners, he improved the opportunity to trade profitably with the French and Indians in Acadia, to whom he furnished arms and ammunition. He was tried for this with five others by the General Court in 1706 and fined. *D.A.B.*

[13] John Williams (Harvard 1683), minister of Deerfield, was being held as a captive by the French and Indians in Canada for ransom. He was taken in the burning of Deerfield, 29 February 1703/4, and carried to Montreal. He returned to Boston 25 October 1706, and Sewall records that he preached the Lecture there 5 December.

[14] Sewall now demotes Jeremiah Dummer from *Philosophiæ Dr.* to M.A. (see our note of 6 February 1704/5); perhaps he had learned that the Continental Ph.D. degree always carried with it the M.A. as well (*Philosophiæ Doctor et Liberalium Artium Magister*). Dummer's diploma was copied into the Harvard College records. *C.S.M.* xv, 307–308.

Bayley, and gave him the Fourty shillings Mr. John Eliot sent him
as a Gratuity: He was very thankful for the Present, and very glad to
see me. I told him, coming in the night, I had brought a small Illumination with me. Rid home; twas past Nine by that time I got there.
Found all well; *Laus Deo.*

   Augt. 26. 1706. feria secunda. About 2 p. m. Mr. Bromfield and I
set out for Martha's Vinyard;[15] got well to Cushing's about Day-light
shutting in. 27, to Morey's. 28, To Sandwich, 29, to Lecture at Pom-
pesprisset;[16] In the way thither, a small stump overset the Calash, and
Mr. Bromfield was much hurt, which made our Journey afterwards
uncomfortable. 30. rested: saw the Harbour, Burying-place, Mill-pond.
31. Went to Succanesset but could not get over.

   Sept[r] 1. Mr. Danforth preach'd there. Lodg'd at Mr. Lothrop's.

   Sept[r] 2. embarked for the Vinyard: but by stormy rough wether
were forc'd back again to Woods's Hole. Lodg'd at B. Skiff's, he
shew'd me the Bay, and Mr. Weeks's Harbour. *Sept*[r] 3. Went to the
Vinyard with a fair wind, and from Homes's Hole to Tisbury and I
to Chilmark, to Mr. Allen's. *Sept*[r] 4. to Gayhead, Mr. Danforth, I,
Mr. Tho. Mayhew, Major Basset. *Sept*[r] 5. Din'd at Mr. Mayhew's:
went to Homes's Hole to wait for a Passage to Rode-Island, or Bristol.
There lay windbound. *Sept*[r] 8. Mr. Danforth and I go to Tisbury
Meeting, Mr. Josia Torrey preach'd forenoon: Mr. Danforth after
Noon. Return'd to Chases to Mr. Bromfield. *Sept*[r] 9. *Monday*, embark'd with a scant wind; put in to Tarpoling Cove: Mr. Bromfield
not yielding to go to Cushnet. There spake with Darby who shew'd
us the prisoners Fines: Spake with Mr. Weeks.

   Sept[r] 10. Gave the Squaw that has lost her feet, Ten pounds of
Wool. When the Tide serv'd, sail'd for Cushnet, had a good passage; lodg'd at Capt. Pope's; he not at home: borrowed six pounds
of Mrs. Pope; were well entertain'd there. *Sept*[r] 11. *Wednesday*, Five
Indians carried Mr. Bromfield in a chair from Spooner's, to Assowamset, and so to Taunton. Twas near midnight by that time we got
there, where by L[t] Leonard, whom we accidentally met late at night,

---

[15] The Commissioners for Indian Affairs in July 1706 ordered Sewall, Edward
Bromfield, and Samuel Danforth, minister of Taunton, to go to Martha's Vineyard
and inquire into the state of the Indians inhabiting the Gay Head Neck. W. Kellaway, *The New England Company* (1961), 219.

[16] Pompæsprisset (Pampaspecitt, Pampaspised, Pumspisset) was near the Herring
Ponds in the present town of Plymouth. Sewall was, before this, at Sandwich, and
later at Succanesset or Falmouth. Next he went to Martha's Vineyard, stopped at
Holmes's Hole (Vineyard Haven) in Tisbury, tarried at Tarpaulin Cove on the
island of Naushon, and thence went to Acushnet. En route to Taunton he stopped
at Assowamset, now Lakeville in Middleboro township.

we were inform'd the Bristol Court was not held for want of Justices;
and that Maj^r Walley and Mr. Leverett adjourn'd *de die in diem*; Jury-
men murmur'd. This put me upon new Straits: but I resolv'd to go
to Bristol, and so did, next day, *Septr 12. Thorsday*, Capt. Hodges's
son waiting on me: got thither about 2. Saved the Afternoon. Mr.
Blagrove is cast, Asks a Chancery in writing; Major Walley and Leverett will be no means suffer it: I earnestly press'd for it.[17] 13, 14.
Court held, and then adjourn'd *sine die*. But twas so late, there was no
getting out of Town.

Septr 15. Lord's Day, Mr. Sparhawk preaches forenoon; Mr. Sever
in the Afternoon. Sup at Mr. Pain's.

Septr 16. By Mr. Niles's Importunity, I set out with him for Narraganset. Din'd at Bright's: while Dinner was getting ready I read in
Ben Johnson, a Folio:

> Wake, our Mirth begins to dye:
> Quicken it with Tunes and Wine.
> Raise your Notes; you'r out; fie, fie,
> This drowsiness is an ill sign.
> > We banish him the Quire of Gods
> > That droops agen:
> > Then all are men
> For here's not one but nods.
> > > > Fol. 13.

Sejanus
———— great and high
The [world] knows only 2, thats Rome and I,
My Roof receives me not, 'tis Aer I tread
And at each step I feel my advanced head
Knock out a Star in Heaven ————
> > > f. 144.

Howere the Age she lives in doth endure
The vices that she breeds above their Cure.
> > > 211.

I went to wait on Govr Cranston: but found him not at home.
Ferried over, got to Narraganset shoar a little before sunset. Twas in
the night before we got to our Lodging about 5. miles off the Ferry.
Tuesday and Wednesday spent in settling Bounds between Niles and

---

[17] See *Province Laws* I, 373 (Sect. 4). Compare *Province Laws* I, 285, 356. M.H.S.
EDS.

Hazard; and the widow Wilson; at last all were agreed. I was fain to forgo some Acres of Land to bring Niles and Hazard to Peace and fix a convenient Line between them.

Thorsday 7^r 19. Forenoon I got Mr. Mumford, the Surveyor, to goe with us, and we found out and renew'd the Bounds of an 80 Acre Lot, just by Place's. Place went with us and assisted. After Dinner, went to Point Judith, was pleased to see the good Grass and Wood, there is upon the Neck. Just as we came there the Triton's Prise Pass'd by, all her sails abroad, fresh Gale, S. S. W., standing for New-port. (News Letter, 7^r 30.—8^r 4.) Woman of the house sick; House miserably out of Repair. Twas night by that time we got home. *Friday, Septr 20.* go into the Quakers Meeting-house, about 35. long 30 wide, on Hazard's Ground that was mine. Acknowledge a Deed to Knowls, of Eight Acres, reserving one Acre at the Corner for a Meetinghouse. Bait at Capt. Eldridges. From thence to the Fulling-mill at the head of Coêset [*Coweset*] Cove, and there dine; a civil woman, but sorrowfull, dress'd our dinner. From thence Niles brings me to Turpins at Providence, and there Bait: From thence over Blackston's River,[18] and there I send him back, and travail alone to Freeman's, where I meet with Piriam, the under-Sheriff, and Capt. Watts, whose company was helpfull to me.

Satterday, Septr 21. Baited at Devotion's, who was very glad to see me. Din'd at Billinges; by Piriam and him was inform'd of Mr. Bromfields being well at home. Baited at Dedham. Was Trim'd at Roxbury; my Barber told me the awfull News of the Murder of Mr. Simeon Stoddard, in England, which much saddened me.[19] Got home a little before Sunset: found all well, *Laus Deo.*

Septr 25. Mr. Bromfield and I took the Hackney Coach to wait on the Govr: met his Excellency on this side the Gate; went out of the

---

[18] It is well known that the first settlers of Boston in 1630 found a solitary gentleman already in residence there, Rev. William Blaxton, M.A. (Cantab.), who was comfortably established with his library in a house near the present Louisburg Square. Disliking the Puritan atmosphere, Blaxton sold his rights and moved about 1634 to Study Hill, as he called it, north of Providence, where he built a house near a river which acquired his name. *Savage* and *D.A.B.* (*s.v.* Blackstone).

[19] Simeon Stoddard Jr. was the son of Simeon and Mary Stoddard; he was born 20 October 1682 and joined the South Church in 1701. A funeral sermon was preached by his pastor, Samuel Willard: *The Just Man's Prerogative. A Sermon Preached Privately, Sept. 27. 1706. On a Solemn Occasion; For the Consolation of a Sorrowful Family, Mourning over the Immature Death, of a Pious Son, viz. Mr. Simeon Stoddard, who was found Barbarously Murdered, in Chelsea-Fields near London, May 14. 1706.* (Boston, 1706). The sermon contains no information about Stoddard, or the circumstances of his death.

Coach and Complemented him, and then went on and visited Mr. Bailey.[20]

Thorsday 8ʳ 17. Son and daughter Sewall and their little Rebeca, son Hirst and his family, dine with us: all here but Joseph. He keeps his Thanksgiving at Cambridge.

Friday, 8ʳ 18. I visit Mr. Baily: as I enter, he saith, I am even gon, even gon! said he had a Fever; the night before and that day had subdued his Nature. In his Paroxism said, Cutting, Cutting, Cutting all to pieces: My Head, my Head; could not bear the Boys chopping without door.

Tuesday, 8ʳ 22. I go to Roxbury Lecture, Mr. Cotton Mather preach'd from 1 Jnº 5. 13. Concerning Assurance, with much affecting Solidity and Fervor. Went to see Mr. Baily, whose Mouth and Tongue were so furr'd, he could hardly speak at first: said he had been a long time in a storm at the Harbours Mouth, hôp'd he should not be swallow'd on Quicksands, or split on Rocks. God had not yet forsaken him, and he hop'd He never would. Said, Here I Wait!

Wednesday, 8ʳ 23. Court meets; but the Govʳ has signified his pleasure that nothing be done till he come from Piscataqua: Adjourn till 3 p. m. after Lecture tomorrow. After Dinner I go and take the Acknowledgment of Mr. Nathanˡ Henchman and Anna his wife to a Deed to their Brother, the schoolmaster: She was lying on the Bed sick of a Fever; yet very sensible and set her hand to the Receipt.

Thorsday, 8ʳ 24. Mr. Wadsworth appears at Lecture in his Perri-wigg. Mr. Chiever is griev'd at it. Court meets, read Mr. Secretary's Letter to Mr. Constantine Phips; adjourn to Ten in the morn. This day I am told of Mr. Torrey's kinswoman, Betty Symmes, being brought to Bed of a Bastard in his house last Monday night.[21] I visit Mr. Chiever.

Novʳ 7ᵗʰ 1706. I invited the Govʳ, Col. Tyng, Mr. Sol. Stoddard, Simeon, Mr. Pemberton, Capt. Belchar, Mr. Bromfield, Capt. South-ack. I suppos'd Mr. Stoddard had preach'd the Lecture. Mr. Cotton Mather preach'd. He did not pray for the Super. Court, or Judges

---

[20] Between 29 May and the first entry for 24 December 1706, Sewall wrote his diary only on the recto pages of his book. There is a gap from 25 September to 17 October. The entry for 7 November, the first entry for 8 November, and the entry for Lord's-Day, 10 November, which we print in their chronological places, were apparently later additions by Sewall, and are written on the opposite verso page.
[21] The Rev. Samuel Torrey of Weymouth had married Mary, widow of Captain William Symmes of Charlestown, in 1695. The Symmes had seven children including a daughter Elizabeth, who would have been about forty at this time. T. B. Wyman, *Genealogies and Estates of Charlestown* (1879) II, 930.

in his first prayer, that I took notice of: but in his last, mention'd the Gen¹ Court, and any Administrations of Justice. I invited him to dine by Mr. Cooke; He said he was engag'd.

Nov 8. There is a Hearing of Roxbury, Spring Street, about another Meeting-house, and of Billericay proprietors and Farmers. Deputies Treat the Gov at Homes's.

Feria Sexta, Nov 8, 1706. I visited Mr. Bayley; find his sister Cheyny with him. He was very low at first; but after awhile revived and Spake freely; has been very ill this Moneth; especially last Satterday and Sabbath day night. Desired his service to Bro, Sister, Mr. Noyes, with much Thanks for his verses which had been a great Comfort to him: To Mr. Higginson, Mrs. Higginson. I gave him 2 five shilling Bills of Credit to buy a Cord of Wood, which he accepted with great thankfulness. I told him it was a time of great expense; he was in prison, and Mrs. Bayley, in Fetters. Upon my coming in, Mrs. Bayley went to Sol. Phip's wife, who was hurt by a fall out of her Calash. I staid with him about 2 hours or more, went from home at 3 and return'd past seven.

Lords-Day, Nov 10. Andrew Belchar, Nicholas Bows, Debora Green, and Sarah [*blank*] are baptised by Mr. Willard.

Tingitur Andreas, Nicolaus, Debora, Sarah.

This morning Tom Child, the Painter, died.

> Tom Child had often painted Death,
> But never to the Life, before:
> Doing it now, he's out of Breath;
> He paints it once, and paints no more.[22]

[22] Thomas Child was an apprentice to a member of the London Company of Painter-Stainers from 1671 to 1679, when he was admitted to the Company. He was in Boston by 14 April 1688, when he married Katherine Marsters, spinster. In 1689 he painted the window frames of the new King's Chapel (H. W. Foote, *Annals* I, 90). When Colonel Samuel Shrimpton was buried 14 February 1697/8, Sewall noted: "Mourning Coach also and Horses in Mourning: Scutcheon on their sides and Deaths heads on their foreheads." In that month Child billed the Shrimpton estate for a hatchment and badges. On 30 October 1702 the Boston Selectmen ordered him to do the following work about "the Latten Schoolmasters [i.e. Ezekiel Cheever's] House viz᳐ finish the gate & prime the fence, finish the Outside work of the House And to prime the Inside worke of the same" (Minutes 1, 63). A few weeks before his death the Province paid him 30*l* for priming and painting twenty carriages for the new cannon at Castle William. The will of Thomas Child, painter-stainer, was dated 14 January 1702/3 and proved 13 November 1706 (Suffolk Wills XVI, 200 and N.S. VI, 240; Case 3002). He appointed his wife Katherine executrix, and mentioned his mother, Alice Martin, "now living in Fryer Lane in Thames Street, London," and his "brother-in-law, John Martin, now in Boston." To this probate information the M.H.S. editors

Novr 11th 1706. Went to Salem with Mr. Dudley. Novr 14th Return'd with Mr. Leverett, Mr. Dudley. Had very comfortable Journey out and home.

Novr 15th Midnight, Mrs. Pemberton is brought to Bed of a dead daughter. Her Life was almost despair'd of, her Bleeding was so much, and Pains so few.

Novr 27. Mr. John Hubbard comes in and tells me Mr. Bayley is very sick, and much chang'd as he thinks; is desirous of seeing me.

Novr 28, 1706. Visited Mr. Bayley after Dinner; went in the Coach. I mention'd Heaven being the Christian's Home: Mr. Bayley said, I long to be at home; why tarry thy chariot wheels? Told me twas the last time she should see me.

Decr 3. I went with Col. Townsend, and Mr. E^m Hutchinson, and visited Capt. Legg: He is in a low and languishing Condition. Then went and talk'd thowrowly with Mr. Cotton Mather about selling Henchman's House; He seem'd to be satisfied; tells me Mr. Williams is to preach the Lecture. Yesterday Mrs. Walker of the Neck was buried, I follow'd for one; I saw none else of the Council there. Mrs. Hannah Oliver is to be buried tomorrow.

Decr 4, 1706. I was at the Burial of Mrs. Hannah Oliver.

Decr 5th Mr. John Williams Preach'd the Lecture.

Decr 6. I went to Mr. Sergeant's and heard Mr. Pemberton preach from Ps. 4. 6.

Decr 7. 1706. The Genl Court is prorogued to Wednesday the 12th of February, at 10. mane. I invited the Govr to dine at Holms's. There were the Govr, Col. Townsend, Bromfield, Leverett, Williams, Capt. Wells, Shelden, Hook, Sewall.

Midweek, Decr 11th I visited Mr. Bayley, find Mr. Walter with him; I moved that seeing Mr. Walter and I seldom met there together, Mr. Walter might go to prayer; which he did excellently; that Mr. Bayley and we our selves might be prepared to dye. Mr. Bayley is

---

added: "Sewall's lines evidently imply that he was a portrait-painter; and here may be the long sought-for artist who preceded Peter Pelham." The implication has not been as obvious to art-historians, who have been perplexed for years by Sewall's quatrain. As might have been expected, a portrait signed "Th Child" turned up in due season (allegedly a portrait of Sir William Phips), but the signature failed to meet scientific tests, and the provenance was clouded. The respected William Sawitzky interpreted Sewall's lines to mean that Child was a painter of hatchments on coffins rather than a limner of the living. F. W. Coburn, Thomas Child, Limner, Amer. Mag. of Art, June 1930, xxi, 326–328; Virgil Barker, American Painting (1950, 1960), 16–20; G. C. Groce and D. H. Wallace, N. Y. Hist. Soc. Dict. of Artists in America (1957), 124.

now, the night before last, taken with Pleuretick Pains, which go beyond those of the stone; New Pains: Cryes out, My Head! my Head! what shall I doe? Seems now to long, and pray for a Dismission. At parting I gave his Sister Cheyny a Ten-Shilling Bill for him, to help to buy some Necessaries; I could not help them to watch. Mr. Bayley said he thought he should dye of a Consumption of the Lungs; by's Cough he found they were touch'd. When he mention'd the pain in his side: I said, twas sad for a Man to be circumvented with his Enemies: He answered pretty readily, He hôp'd there were more with him than against him. He desired me to write to his Brother Joseph to come and see him. *Dec^r* 13. I gave my Letter to J. Bayley to Mr. Simkins, who said he had one to send it by. *Note.* By reason of the Storm yesterday, the council met not; Govr was not in Town: but writt a Letter to the Secretary that the Council was adjourn'd to Friday; [*In margin:* See Jan. 1, 1713/14.] I told the Secretary, the Council that met not, could not be adjourn'd; yet, Govr nominated Mr. Plaisted to be a Justice of peace in Yorkshire, and drove it throw, though he be a Dweller in Hampshire; and has a Brother Ichabod Plaisted, that is of the Council.

This day Mr. Melyen dies.[23] Ætat. 67. Mrs. Mary Pemberton is very low, dangerously ill.

Decr 14th Joseph comes to see us, brings word that Wyth, the Mason, dyed yesterday at Cambridge. Goodman Swan is in a fair way to be Receiv'd into the Church again; was cast out in Mr. Oakes's time, in a very solemn manner, in my sight and Hearing.[24]

Decr 18. 1706. Bastian Lops the Elm by my Lord's Stable;[25] cuts off a cord of good wood. Mr. Sergeant came up Rawson's Lane as we were doing of it. *Dec^r* 19. *mane,* Maxwell comes in the Governour's name to invite me to Dine at Roxbury with his Excellency at one aclock tomorrow. Mr. C. Mather preaches the Lecture in Mr. Bridges Turn, from Gal. 3. 27 —— have put on Christ. Preach'd with Allusion to Apparel; one head was that Apparel was for Distinction.

[23] Jacob Melyen, whose daughter Abigail, then Mrs. William Tilley, later became Sewall's second wife.

[24] John Swan, a farmer in Menotomy, was excommunicated from the Cambridge church in 1684. He made his peace with the church more than twenty years later and was restored 22 December 1706. His death occurred 5 June 1708 at the age of 87. L. R. Paige, *Hist. of Cambridge* (1877), 667.

[25] While Lord Bellomont was in Boston he resided in the house of Peter Sergeant, afterwards the Province House. The stable the governor used was rented from Sewall (2 M.H.S. *Proc.* II, 129–130). Rawson's Lane is now Bromfield Street. The following day Sergeant, who had been a widower since January, took a third wife, Mehitable (Minot) Cooper.

Mr. Walter dines with us, and leaves with me £13.10.9. Roxbury Money. Mr. Sergeant marries Mrs. Mehetabel Cooper.

Decr 20, feria sexta, very Rainy day; Mr. Winthrop, Russel, Elisha Hutchinson, E^m Hutchinson, Mr. Foster, Sewall, Townsend, Walley, Bromfield, Belchar Dine at the Governour's, Mr. Secretary. Go in Coaches. After Dinner I visit Mr. Bayley; Is in great Extremity, Paroxisms return in about ½ hour; seem'd to desire death; and yet once I took notice that he breath'd after some space and recovery of strength before went hence: leave all to God's unerring Providence. He told me he heard Sister Shortt was dangerously sick: heard of by Jon^a Emmery. Came home to the Meeting at Mr. Bromfield's, Mr. Williams of Deerfield preach'd: very Rainy, and dirty under foot. When came home, or a little after, had a Letter brought me of the Death of Sister Shortt the 18th Inst. which was very surprising to me. Half are now dead. The Lord fit me for my Departure. *Decr 21.* Not having other Mourning, I look'd out a pair of Mourning Gloves. An hour or 2 after, Mr. Sergeant, sent me and my wife Gloves; mine are so little I cânt wear them. Mr. Cooper's Son brought them, I gave him Dr. Mather's Treatise of Tithes.[26] [*In margin:* Mr. Peter Serg^t See Jany 20. 1705/6.]

Decr 23. I visit Mr. Sergeant and his Bride; had Ale and Wine. Mr. Cook, Col. Hutchinson, Mr. Colman, Adams, Capt. Hill, Mr. Dering were there. After came in Mr. Bromfield, and Cousin Dummer.

Decr 24. Feria Tertia. My wife and I execute a Lease to Mr. Seth Dwight, for 21. years, of the House he dwells in. Mr. Eliezer Moodey writt the Leases; and hè and David Sinclar were Witnesses: Twas transacted in our Bedchamber.

Feria tertia, Decr 24. 1706. I went to Brooklin, and visited my son and Daughter Sewall and little Rebekah; Paid my son 30^s in full, and he is to send me 15. Fountains, which are paid for in the mention'd Sum. He has been ill, and is not very well now. Mr. Read, with whom he has been, tells him he is Melancholy. Din'd on Salt Fish and a Spar-Rib.[27]

Visited Mr. Bayley as I came home; he has a very sore Mouth. He

---

[26] A *Discourse Concerning the Maintenance Due to those That Preach the Gospel: In Which, That Question Whether Tithes Are by the Divine Law the Ministers Due, Is Considered, And the Negative Proved.* By I. Mather, D.D. (Boston, 1706; Holmes 36).

[27] The *O.E.D.* cites Sewall's sentence in its definition of *spare-rib*. In Kent, an earlier form, *ribspare*, was used, taken directly from Middle Low German; the M.H.S. editors found this word used in 1697 in Cambridge, Massachusetts (B. Cutter, *Hist. of the Cutter Family*, 1871, 325).

tells me he has left off observing the distance of his Fits, is tired and done. I gave him a Banbury cake, of which he eat pretty well, complaining of his Mouth.

Mid-week. Decr 25. Shops open, carts come to Town with Wood, Fagots, Hay, and Horses with Provisions, as usually. I bought me a great Tooth'd Comb at Dwight's; 6^s.

Feria septima, Decr 28, 1706. A large fair Rainbow is seen in the Morning in the Norwest. Madam Walley call'd her Husband into the Shop to see it. The Govr being indispos'd with the Gout, call'd a Council to meet at Roxbury; and by that means I gain'd an Opportunity to see my friend Bayley once again: He is now brought very low by his Stone, Fever, Sore Tongue and Mouth; could hardly speak a word to me. But he said, sit down. His wife ask'd him if he knew me? He answer'd, with some quickness, He should be distracted, if he should not know me. He Thank'd me when I came away. I said Christ would change his vile body, and make it like his glorious body. And when the Coach–man call'd, saying the Company staid for me, I took leave, telling him God would abide with him; Those that Christ loves, he loves to the end. He bow'd with his head. His wife and sister weep over him. He call'd for Mouth-Water once while I was there, and then for his little pot to void it into: I suppos'd it was to enable him to speak. Though he doth not eat at present; yet I left the Banbury cake I carried for him, with his wife: And when came away, call'd her into next chamber, and gave her two Five-Shilling Bills: She very modestly and kindly accepted them and said I had done too much already: I told her No, if the state of my family would have born it, I ought to have watch'd with Mr. Bayley, as much as that came to. I left her weeping. Mark the perfect Man &c. When return'd to the Governour's, I found the other Coaches gon; the sun down some time. Major Walley, Col. Townsend, Mr. Bromfield and I came home well together in the Hackney Coach; though the ways are very deep by reason of the long, strong southerly wind and Thaw. Serene day. Wind W.

Decr 31. 1706. Madam Dudley, and Mrs. Anne Dudley visit my wife just a little before night, and inform of our Son's illness, which they were told off at midnight: Will send us word if he grow worse.

Mr. Salter makes us a little Chimney in my Chimney, make a Fire in it to try it.

1707

DEATH OF REV. JAMES BAYLEY / FRACAS OVER MR. DWIGHT'S
CELLAR / PLYMOUTH COURT / PORT-ROYAL EXPEDITION /
REV. SAMUEL TORREY'S DEATH / COURT TRIP TO IPSWICH AND
NEWBURY / BURGLARY AT SEWALL'S HOUSE / SEWALL ATTENDS
JOSEPH'S GRADUATION / MILE-STONES SET UP / BRISTOL COURT /
SEWALL PRESENT AT PRESIDENT WILLARD'S DEATH / JOHN LEVERETT
CHOSEN PRESIDENT OF HARVARD / NATHANIEL HIGGINSON PETITIONS
GOVERNOR DUDLEY'S REMOVAL / COURT JOURNEY TO SALEM /
GOVERNOR DUDLEY'S TROUBLES / SEWALL WITHDRAWS HIS VOTE ON
THE HIGGINSON PETITION

Midweek, Jany 9th. [1706/7]. visited Mr. Bayley. He is very low,
and the skin of his Hip now broken, and raw, which is very painfull
to him. He said I long to be gon, yet with Submission to God's holy
will: What I writ to him out of Mr. Caryl was a cordial to him. Met
Sam, who came to see us.

Feria Sexta, Jany 10th Capt. Legg buried.[1] Bearers, Govr, Mr. Winthrop; Mr. Cooke, Addington; Col. Byfield, Capt. Belchar. Councillors had Gloves, and many others.

Tuesday, Jany 14th Govr calls a Council, Propounds Mr. Danforth,
Dorchester, and Mr. Belchar of Newbury to Preach the Election
Sermon; Mr. Samuel Belchar is agreed on, Mr. Danforth having
preach'd before.

Midweek, Jany 15th A great Storm of Snow; yet Danl Bayley breaks
through, and brings us a Load of Walnut Wood. I had transcribed
some choice sentences out of Calvin's Exposit. Mat. 4. 1, 2, 3, 4. and
sent them by Daniel; Letter was just seal'd before he came, written
and dated today. The Storm prevail'd so, that not one of our Meeting
ventured to come to our House where it was to be. Mrs. Deming, and
her daughter-in-Law, and Mrs. Salter came over; waited till six-a-

---

[1] Captain Samuel Legg, mariner, left a widow, Deliverance Legg, who lived until
1724. When Sewall visited the captain 3 December 1706 he wrote in the margin
of his diary: "was born July, 1642." The M.H.S. editors incorrectly attached this
note to Sewall's preceding remarks about James Bayley.

clock, and then sung the 2 last Staves of the 16. Ps. Eat some Bread and drank. Gave Mr. Deming one of Mr. Higginson's Election Sermons; Daughter-in-Law, Greek Churches: Mrs. Salter, Greek Churches.[2]

Friday, Jany 17. Mr. Tho. Bridge visits me. In Discourse I gave him my opinion that the Witnesses were not slain. Gave him one of Mr. Higginson's Election Sermons.

Satterday, Jany 18. Going down in the morning, I find David sick: tells me had been sick and vomited in the night: We have the Stove-room-Chamber fitted for him, and place him there; send for Mr. Oakes. Lords-day at even, Mrs. Plimly comes to nurse him.

Saturday morn, Jany 18th James Robinson, the Baker, coming from Roxbury, tells me Mr. Bayley dyed the last night 2 hours after midnight; one in Roxbury-street bid him tell me so.[3]

Jany 20. Mr. Prentice gives me notice that the Funeral was to be on Friday, not before, because Mr. Bayley's Bro^r at Newbury, was to order it. Gave me notice to be a Bearer, Mr. Bayley had appointed it.

Friday, Jany 24. 1706/7. I and Mr. John Clark, Mr. Francis Burroughs, and Mr. John Bolt rode together in Simson's Slay to the Funeral of Mr. Bayley. Were there at One: Went about 3. Bearers Sewall, Bond; Fisk, Walter; Clark, Noyes. Govr was there; intended Mr. Thacher, but the wether was bad over head, and underfoot by reason of the snow in the Night, and Hail and Rain now, and he was not there. Saw not Mr. Denison there. Mr. John Hubbard, Mr. Daniel Oliver, and Mr. Justice Lynde was there; Mr. Bowls. His Brethren Isaac Bayley, and Joshua Bayly followed the Herse. The Widow and her daughter Prentice rode in a slay. The wether being bad, I took Leave at the Grave, our slay being just at hand went into it, and got home by Four; *Laus Deo.* I did condole and congratulat the Relations upon our parting with our Friend, and his being gon

---

[2] John Higginson's election sermon, *The Cause of God and his People in New-England*, was delivered before the General Court 27 May 1663 and printed in Cambridge the same year. *American Tears upon the Ruines of the Greek Churches* was written by Cotton Mather, but published anonymously. Sewall had asked him to write the book, and he paid for printing it; it was printed in Boston "by B. Green & J. Allen, for & Sold by Samuel Sewall Junior. 1701." T. J. Holmes, *Cotton Mather . . . Bibliography* I, 35–39.

[3] James Bayley (Harvard 1669) was two years older than Sewall, and they had been schoolmates in Newbury. For many months prior to his death Sewall visited him often, bringing him gifts of food and money. Bayley was the first minister of Salem Village, now Danvers, but left in 1680 after an acrimonious church row which smouldered for a decade and contributed to the witchcraft episode. He was afterward settled harmoniously over the church at Killingworth, Connecticut, but spent his later years as a physician at Roxbury. *Sibley.*

to Rest after a weary Race. Mr. Walter gave a very good Character of Mr. Bayley. He was with him the evening before he dyed, and pray'd with him: He answer'd pertinently, by Yes and No: thought he should dy that night, of which was not afraid. Mr. Walter pray'd before we went to the Grave.

Jany 26th I dream'd last night that I was chosen Lord Maior of London; which much perplex'd me: a strange absurd Dream!

Febr. 9th Lord's Day; The latter part of the Night, and this morn, we had great Lightening, and Thunder, Rain and Hail.

Febr. 10. A pleasant, Serene, sun-shiny Day; sweet singing of Birds.

Febr. 16, at night, Mr. Thacher of Milton is taken very sick. *Febr. 20*, Sister Hirst, Sister Sewall of Salem, Mr. Flint, Son and daughter Hirst, dine with us after Lecture. *Febr. 25.* Mr. Colman, Sister Hirst, Sewall, Mr. Elisha Coke jun^r and wife, I and Mary dine at Son Hirst's. After that I visit the widow Eliott, who dwells with her daughter Davis.

26th A Fast is kept at Milton.

27th Dr. Mather was not at Lecture. Mr. Cotton Mather preached, Sung 10–14th 27th Ps. Mr. Dwight is much troubled about digging his Cellar; I get Mr. Cook and Capt. Clark to go to him after Lecture, and view the work and speak to Mr. Gibbins; they seem'd to be offended at Mr. Dwight's smart Replyes to Mr. Gibbins and his wife; and spake a little coldly, and told me it were best to agree. I went again near night, and Dwight told me, Mrs. Gibbins intended next day to make another Gate-way, and hinder'd the workmen from digging home at that corner: whereupon I order'd the Men to digg it down, which they quickly did, at which Gibbins storm'd and ask'd me why I did not bid him pull down his House, if I did, they would do it. And Mrs. Gibbins spake many opprobrious words: But the men went on vigorously. *Febr. 28.* Gibbins orders Mr. Bernard's men to cutt another Gate-way, and with the Boards cut out nail'd up her own former Gate-way: then laid a Board, a door, over from the Cutt Gate-way over the Corner of the Cellar and pass that way, and the Negro said, This is our passage-way. I said little to it, but went in, and talk'd with Mr. Gibbins, his wife and son; and were ready to put it to Men to determin what should be; Mr. Dwight came in: and said he would not agree to put it to Men: I told Mr. Gibbins I would speak to him, and come again after Dinner. I went accordingly, and when I return'd found they had been Pumping Tubs of Water, and throwing them into my new-dug Cellar, to soften the Work-men's Corns, as they said, so that the men were forc'd to leave off working.

Several Tubs of water were thrown in while I sat in the House: I only call'd to Mrs. Gibbins and told her I saw she could not wait till I came. Durham came and dug through the Stone-wall into this little new Cellar, and I think that quell'd our antagonists: for our Cellar being a little higher than theirs, all the water would have run upon themselves. And after, the Select-Men, several of them viewing it, countenanc'd my Tenant; Mr. Secretary also look'd in upon us: and the workmen went on peaceably.

Friday, March, 7. 1707. Several Ministers prayed at the desire of the Court; began a little after Ten; Mr. Willard, Wadsworth, Bridge, Colman, Pemberton, C. Mather, Dr. I. Mather. Prayers were made with great Pertinency and Variety; I hope God will hear. Several pray'd that God would speedily, by some Providence, or one way other, let us know what might doe as to going against Port-Royal. Gave Thanks for the News of the 18. Indians kill'd, and one Taken last Tuesday; which heard of just after the Appointment of this Day. Sung the two first staves of the 20th Psalm, York Tune, which I set, Mr. Willard used my Psalm-Booke. Left off about ½ hour past Two. Council gave the Govr and Ministers a Dinner at Homes's.

Feria Septima, Martij 8° 1707. *Anno Regni Annæ Reginæ Angliæ &c. Sexto.*

> *Nobilibus, causas quid præfers Angle latentes?*
> *ANNÆ principiam, Cæsaris annus habet.*

> 'Till ANNÆ's Equal Reign begun,
> We ne'r could well begin the year:
> But now the Controversy's done;
> The Eigth of March can have no peer.

This day is rainy and dark, and the Govr came not to Town. Deputies sent in for going to Port-Royal to take it; if what was necessary in order to it might be provided March, 8th. Having got Mr. Joseph Marion to write the verses fair, I gave them to Mr. Winthrop, in the Governour's absence, saying, I cânt drink the Queen's Health, *parvum parva decent*[4] —— Accept of a small essay for the honor of my Soveraign.

In the Afternoon Mr. Williams visits us, tells me he goes to Dearfield 14 nt hence, next Tuesday. I gave him a copy of the foremention'd verses. He tells me Quebeck Seminary was burnt the 20th of 7r 1705. our Style, Library burnt. His Narrative is now in the

[4] Horace, *Epistles,* I, vii, 44.

Press.[5] *Feria tertia, March*, 18th Mr. Pemberton removes into the Churches House. *March 20.* I visit him, and wish him and her joy. *March, 21.* I give him a 20s Bill to help towards his House-warming, which he accepts kindly. Joseph comes to Town. *March, 20. feria quinta*, Mrs. Gibbs's Warehouse was burnt down in Lecture time. Meeting was disturb'd just as was coming to the particulars of Fighting against our Enemies and praying against them. After Mr. Colman had sat awhile, the people were quiet, and went on again.

March, 21. The Governour, Capt. Sam[l] Appleton, Mr. Jn[o] Williams, Mr. William Williams, dine with us in the new Hall.

Feria secunda, March, 24th I set out in the storm with Sam Robinson, got to Barker's about 5, and there lodg'd, and dry'd my Coat, Hat, Gloves.

Feria tertia, March 25, 1707. Went to Plimouth, got thither about 10. m. Major Walley and Mr. Leverett came in after six; so that could only Adjourn the Court. *March, 26.* Mr. Josiah Torrey preaches the Lecture. *March, 27.* I go into the Meetinghouse. Hannah Parker is found guilty of Adultery. I spake with two of the Middlebury Men at Mr. Little's about Mr. Palmer, who is impos'd upon them as their Minister.[6] Gave Mr. Little a pound of Chockalat. *March, 28. 1707.* Baited at Bairsto's; Din'd at Cushing's: Then I left the Company and went to Hingham; visited Mr. Cobb, Mr. Norton, cousin Hobart: Got to Mr. Torrey's just before sunset; He was very glad to see me. Read 17th Rev. Pray'd excellently. Pray'd excellently in the Morn. Visit Cousin Hunt, Quinsey; Got home about One and Dine there. Am well notwithstanding my journeying in the Rain, and find mine well; *Laus Deo! March, 29.* Mrs. Tucker, Mrs. Lothrop's Sister, is found dead in her apartment. *March, 30.* My wife goes out in the Afternoon. *March 31. feria secunda*, I visit my Son, and dine with him; He is all alone. Visited Mr. Gibbs, presented him with a pound

---

[5] *The Redeemed Captive, Returning to Zion. A Faithful History of Remarkable Occurrences, in the Captivity and Deliverance of Mr. John Williams; Minister of the Gospel, in Deerfield* . . . (Boston, 1707). Williams (Harvard 1683) is commemorated in the *D.A.B.* and *Sibley.*

[6] Thomas Palmer, who did not receive a Harvard education, had been ordained over the church at Middleborough 2 May 1702. The Plymouth Church records give a report of a church council at Middleborough in November 1706 at which complaints were heard of Palmer's "Intemperance and Exexsive drinking." He was advised to make a "peaceful and Orderly secession" and the church was advised to dismiss him. Palmer and some of the church members were dissatisfied with the decision, and he stayed on. A second council 11 June 1707 repeated the recommendation, and he was dismissed 2 June 1708. *C.S.M.* xxii, 203 and *Weis.*

of Chockalett, and 3 of Cousin Moodey's sermons;[7] gave one to Mrs.
Bond, who came in while I was there. Visit Joseph; He pronounc'd
his valedictory Oration March 28ᵗʰ Heard Mr. Willard Expound from
1 Cor. 13. 8, 9, 10. Came home by the Ferry. Shall be Language in
Heaven; but no need to Learn Languages as now; which is a fruit of
the Curse, since the Confusion. Mr. Metcalf comes in late, and I
ask him to lodge here; which he accepts: is going to Falmouth, where
he preach'd last winter.

April, 5. Eclipse of the Moon: is seen in a serene Aer, Moon is of
a Ruddy Colour when Eclipsed. *April, 7.* Mr. Sparhawk is again
chosen to preach the Artillery Sermon. *April, 8.* I go to Cambridge
and carry Joseph a small piece of Plate to present his Tutor with,
Bottom mark'd, March, 5, 1706/7 which was the day his Tutor took
Leave of them; price 39ˢ 2ᵈ View'd his Chamber in the President's
House, which I like. Came home and went to the Funeral of little
Mary Bastian. Isaac Marion walk'd with me.

Midweek Apr. 9. I waited on Col. Hutchinson, Checkley, and
others of the Committee, as far as the last house of Roxbury; came
home by Mr. Wells's. Din'd at Mr. Brewer's, about 3 p.m. It was a
Frost, and Ice of half an inch, or inch thick in the morn. Cold wind
that I was fain to wear my Hood. I got well home about Sun-set;
David stood at the Gate to take the Horse, and told me the amazing
News of Mr. Willard's dangerous Sickness. He was taken at Dinner
in his Study, so that he quickly grew delirious. Some think he took
cold at the Funeral of Mr. Myles's child, the evening before. This
day Mr. Noyes preached his Lecture from Heb. 11ᵗʰ 32. 33. 34, encouraging the Expedition to Port-Royal. *April, 10, 1707.* Mr. Bridge
preaches our Lecture, from Psal. 149. 9. Encouraging the Expedition.

Feria Sexta Apr. 11ᵗʰ I see a Swallow or two. 'Tis Capt. Belchar's
Meeting; Mr. Pemberton and he come to propose to me, the be-
ginning at 3. aclock, and inviting the Ministers to spend the Time in
Prayer. Mr. Pemberton, Colman, Wadsworth, Mather, Bridge. Dr.
Mather pray'd Excellently, Copiously. Dr. Mather, speaking of the
Port-Royal Affair, call'd it the uncertain Expedition; Pray'd God not
to carry his people hence, except He prosper'd them.

Apr. 12, feria septima, I see three Swallows together. Mr. Willard
grows more compôs'd. Lydia [*wife of*] William Lowder, a young
woman of 16 years, is deliver'd of a daughter, and dyes this morning;
I think in the room where her Mother Balston dyed, and as suddenly.

---

[7] Two editions were published this year in Boston of Samuel Moody's sermon,
*The Vain Youth summoned to Appear before Christ's Bar. Or, an Essay to Block
Up the Sinful Wayes of Young People* . . .

Friday, April, 18. 1707. Just before Sun-set there is a Small piece of a Rainbow in the South-east and by south: I saw it out of our Chamber-window. Mr. Fisk tells me he saw it.

Monday, Apr. 21. Mr. Bromfield and I set out about 9. *mane*, to visit Mr. [*Samuel*] Torrey. Twas hot, and when were got to Braintrey, Mr. Bromfield grows weary, and chose to call at Cousin Fisk's, which we did; He is gon to Weymouth. This was about 11. m. Cousin Fisk would have us Dine; and while we were at Table, Mr. Fisk came in and told us Mr. Torrey was gon to Rest, dyed about Eleven aclock.[8] So our journey was sadly determined. It seems the Souldiers go to Hull this day from Weymouth, there to imbark in the Port-Royal Expedition; Mr. Fisk pray'd with them. The Death of Mr. Torrey, a Laborious, Faithfull Divine, Excellent in Prayer, is a sad epocha for the Commencement of this Expedition.

Coming home, I turn'd off at Roxbury, and went to Brooklin; found my son and daughter gon to Boston. Look'd upon his Sheep and Lambs, and came home. Met Mr. Roberts on the Neck going to the Governour, I told him of Mr. Torrey's Death as had told the Gov^{rs} Maid before. His Excellency was gon to his Farm towards Dedham; and his Lady to Boston with my Son, but came not to our House.

Feria quarta, Apr. 23. 1707. Capt Nathl Williams and I ride to Weymouth, to the Funeral of Mr. Torrey: When were at Braintrey, the Guns went off; overtook Mr. Danforth, got to Cous. Hunt's about one, Din'd there at Two; went to the House of Mourning: Saml Sewall, Zech Whitman; Peter Thacher, John Norton: John Danforth, Joseph Belchar, Bearers. Had a Table spread, which could not leave without offense. Mr. Whitman pray'd before the Funeral. Mr. Fisk craved a Blessing, Mr. Thacher Return'd Thanks. Mr. Fisk led the widow. Grave was caved in, Mr. Thacher and I let down the Head, Mr. Hugh Adams also put to his Hand under ours. Stood a pretty while before any appeared to fill the Grave, some words and enquiry was made about it: At length two Hoes came, and then a Spade. Set out to come home at ½ hour after Six: Baited at Miller's, Got home a little before Ten, before the Moon went down; *Laus Deo.* Besides Relations, I saw none at the Funeral from Boston, save S. S., P. Dudley, esqr. Capt. Williams, Seth Dwight.

May, 12. 1707. Mrs. Lydia Scottow buried; Bearers, Sewall, Addington; Hill, Williams; Ballentine, Coney. *May, 13.* Mr. Danl Oliver, Capt. Tho. Fitch and I ride to Natick, and hear Mr. Gookin preach and pray to the Indians there: Din'd at Capt. Fuller's as came back:

---

[8] Torrey had been minister of Weymouth since 1656.

got home well. *Laus Deo. May,* 15. Govr moves in Council that Mr. Willard might be spared, because of his late sickness, and continued weakness; and that Mr. Will Brattle, and Mr. Flint might regulat the Commencement: Govr said, Sundry had spoken to him about it. Major Walley, Capt. Belchar, Mr. Bromfield and I were desired to go and speak to Mr. Willard.

May, 16. Mr. Bromfield and I wait on Mr. Willard: I took a fit opportunity to enquire when he would go to Cambridge; and He said next week, without any hesitancy: so reckon'd we were not to enquire any further. We went to Mr. Pemberton first, and his opinion was, we should not express our desires, or the desires of any other, of Mr. Willard's immediat giving over College-work, except he himself inclin'd to it.

May, 16. visit Madam Coke, Mr. C. Mather, Mr. Gibbs, who came to this Town this day sennight to see if the change of Aer would mend him.

May, 19. Went with Robinson to Salem: got thither late by reason of Robinson's late coming from Cambridge, and Madam Leverett's illness. Neither Col. Hathorn nor the Sheriff did accompany me; went with Mr. Attorney Dudley to Ipswich, got thither a little before Nine aclock. Mr. Harris came to meet us, but heard we came not till next day, and went back. *May,* 20th Court rises about 7. Visit the widow Appleton. *May,* 21. Looks like a storm; but breaks up; I ride to Rowley, dine at Bro^r Northend's. Essay to visit H. Sewall, who was gon from home. Bro^r and Sister Northend go to the Causey, and then return. Visit the poor Orphan Shortts, hear Jane and Mehetabel read; gave them Five Shillings. Went to sister Gerrishes; to Mr. Brown, but he was not at home, saw Cous. Noyes, Mr. Woodbridge.

May, 22. *Thorsday,* Mr. Coffin Trims me, reckon with Mr. Brown and take fourty shillings of him in full. Went to Cous. Pierce, and there eat sturgeon with Mr. Pike, Abr. Adams, Cousin Jno Tappin's wife. Went to Bro^r Tappin's, visited Cousin Sweet, they have a lovely Son. To Jno Sewall, saw his new House where he now dwells; saw the Ashes of the old House. Bro^r Tappin tells me of the death of Col. Saltonstall on Wednesday after Lecture. Went to Joshua Bayley, discours'd him about his Brothers debt, staid a long time there, then went to Byfield across the Woods. Bro^r Tappin left me. I desired him that if heard Col. Saltonstall was to be buried on Friday he should send an Express to me of it. *Friday,* 23. Bro^r Moodey and I see Mr. Hale, on Horseback, drink a Glass of Cider; look on Sister Mehetabel's Grave; ride to Topsfield, visit Mr. Capen who is very glad to see

me.[9] Went to Phillip's, dined there. Parted with B. Moodey at the
Fulling-mill. Baited at Lewis's. Got over Charlestown Ferry about
8. *Note*, as came down Winter Hill saw a Rainbow, was so much
Rain as to oblige me to put on my Riding Coat, but it prov'd very
little Rain.

Midweek, May 28, 1707. Mr. Samuel Belcher preached, from Mat.
6. 10. Thy Kingdom come. Shew'd it was the duty of all to promote
the Kingdom of Christ. At Dinner Mr. Belcher crav'd a Blessing, Mr.
Jn° Danforth return'd Thanks. Sir John Davie[10] dined with the Govr.
In the morn, Mr. Secretary, major Walley and I gave the Deputies
the Oaths, 66. and after, five more were sworn in the Council-Chamber, which made 71, and Councillors 24. (95 votes).

1 Wait Winthrop	88	17 Saml Partridge	53
2 James Russell	90	3^d Stroak	
3 Jn° Hathorn	60	18 Peter Sergeant	45
4 Elisha Hutchinson	91	Plimouth	
5 S. Sewall	92	John Thacher	53
6 Isaac Addington	92	Isaac Winslow˙	84
7 Wm Brown	82	Nathan^l Pain	81
8 Jn° Phillips	75	John Cushing	80
9 Jon^a Corwin	75		
10 Jn° Foster	79	Main	
11 Penn Townsend	90	Eliakim Hutchinson	69
12 John Appleton	61	Benj^a Brown	72
13 John Higginson	78	Ichabod Plaisted	59
14 Andrew Belcher	78		
15 Edw. Bromfield	82	Zagadahock	
16 Saml Appleton	53	Joseph Lynde	54
2^d Stroak		[Leverett 30]	

[9] The house of Parson Capen (Joseph Capen, Harvard 1677), raised 8 June 1683,
is still standing and is open to the public. Professor Hugh Morrison calls it "perhaps the most perfect of New England Colonial houses." *Early American Archi-
tecture* (1952), 57.

[10] John Davie (Harvard 1681) was the son of Humphrey Davie of London,
Boston, and Hartford, whose father was created a baronet in 1641. John Davie
was a farmer and town clerk in Groton, Connecticut; he succeeded to the baron-
etcy in 1707. Sewall had written to Samuel Shepard, 26 May 1707: "Some of
the best News we have is, that Mr. Davie of New-London is come to be a Knight
and Baronet, which Honor is supported with an estate of 4 or five Thousands
per annum." (*L.B.* I, 348). Sir John and his lady (Elizabeth Richards) removed
to England shortly, and he became high sheriff of Devon; he died in 1727. *Sibley*.

At Large		Ephraim Hunt	47
Simeon Stoddard	44	[Walley 18]	
2ᵈ Stroak		[Leverett 12]	

Lord's Day, June, 15ᵗʰ I felt my self dull and heavy and Listless as to Spiritual Good; Carnal, Lifeless; I sigh'd to God, that he would quicken me.

June. 16. My House was broken open in two places, and about Twenty pounds worth of Plate stolen away, and some Linen; My Spoon, and Knife, and Neckcloth was taken: I said, Is not this an Answer of Prayer? Jane came up, and gave us the Alarm betime in the morn. I was helped to submit to Christ's stroke, and say, Wellcome CHRIST!

June, 19ᵗʰ The measuring Bason is found with Margaret Barton just carrying of it to Sea, to Hingham; said she had it of James Hews, he gave it her to sell for him. Mr. Secretary sent her to Prison.

June, 21. Billy Cowell's shop is entered by the Chimney, and a considerable quantity of Plate stolen. I give him a Warrant to the Constable, they find James Hews hid in the Hay in Cabal's Barn, on the Back side of the Common; while they was seising of him under the Hay, he strip'd off his Pocket, which was quickly after found, and Cowell's silver in it. At night I read out of Caryl on Job, 5. 2. The humble submission to the *stroke* of God, turns into a *Kiss*—which I thank God, I have in this Instance experienced. *Laus Deo.*

July, 1. A Rainbow is seen just before night, which comforts us against our Distresses as to the affairs of the Expedition, and the Unquietness of the Souldiers at Casco, of which Gideon Lowel brings word, who came thence yesterday.[11]

Midweek, July 2, 1707. Commencement Day is fair and pleasant. Jane and I go betime by Charlestown; set out before 5.; had a very pleasant journey; went from Charlestown in a Calash, Harris. Got Joseph a Table, and Bread, which he wanted before. Went into the Meetinghouse about 11. Mr. Willard pray'd. Mr. Wigglesworth began to dispute; before he had done, the Govʳ came; when the first Question was dispatch'd, the Orator was call'd forth: His Oration was very well accepted; I was concern'd for my son, who was not well, lest he should have fail'd; but God helped him. His Cous. Moodey of York had pray'd earnestly for it the night before; and gave Thanks for it in prayer the night after. My Son held the first Question in the

11 Hutchinson (*Hist.*, 1936 ed., II, 123–124) tells of this abortive expedition against the French. Massachusetts, Rhode Island, and New Hampshire sent a force to attack Port Royal. They sailed 13 May, arrived the 26th, had some skirmishes, and re-embarked 7 June.

Afternoon; *Anima non fit ex Traduce;* by reason of the paucity of the Masters, being but two, Russell, and Mighill; for Mr. Dudley was in the Fleet bound for Port-Royal. Had opportunity to pronounce his Thesis. My Son was the first that had a Degree given him in the New Meetinghouse. The Desks were adorned with green curtains, which it seems, were Wainwrights. I could not hear one Word while the Degrees were giving.[12] My wife durst not go out of Boston. Got home in good season, Jane and I by Charlestown again; Daughters in the Coach. Mr. Russel, Mr. Winthrop, Sewall, Major Walley, Col. Lynde, Mr. Eliakim Hutchinson, Mr. Bromfield, Mr. Stoddard, were there in the morn. Mr. Secretary and Capt. Belcher were there p. m. Mr. Willard made an excellent Prayer at Conclusion. Ladies there, Governours Lady, Madam Shrimpton, Madam Usher, Madam Walley, Madam Bromfield, Madam Stoddard &c. Mr. Whiting, Bilerica, Mr. Belcher, Newbury. Mr. Easterbrooks not there.

July, 3. Feria sexta Mr. Stoddard preached excellently from Mica, 1. 5 What is the Trangression of Jacob? is it not Samaria? and what are the high places of Judah? are they not Jerusalem? Said he could see no reason why a papist might not *cross himself* Ten times a day, as well as Minister cross a child once. Spake *plainly* in Several Articles again Superstition. Spake against excess in Commencem't entertainments. Gov⁰ call'd at night with Mr. Stoddard and told me I should cause them to conclude.

July, 4. 1707. I printed

Feria Sexta; Quintilis quarto, 1707.

CLAUDITE *jam rivos, Pueri; sat prata biberunt.* [*Virg. Ecl. iii,* 111]

Gave to several Scholars, and order'd one or two to be nail'd upon the Out-Doors. Brought home my Son, Plate, Clôths in Stedmand's Calash, 4ˢ. Gave his Son a piece of eight and bid him take the overplus to himself. Did it in remembrance of his Father's hard Journey to Martha's Vinyard. In the Ferryboat, heard the sad News from Spain, by Grant and the Loss of English ships.[13] Got home before 9.

Laus Deo. This day I visited Mrs. Corlet who seems dying: Mrs. Wigglesworth, who has the Jaundice; Madam Oliver who is not well.

---

[12] Here is evidence of Sewall's deafness. On 30 July 1706 at his trial in the Land of Nod case in the College Hall he was unable to hear the plaintiffs or their attorneys.

[13] At the Battle of Almanza, 25 April 1707, the Allies (our side), under Henri de Massue de Ruvigny, second Marquis de Ruvigny and Earl of Galway, were defeated by the Duke of Berwick (James Fitzjames, natural son of James II), Maréchal de France, through the cowardice of the Portuguese. *D.N.B.*

Note. Mr. Veazy of Braintry died the day after the Commencement, a young hopefull Minister.[14]

July, 5th Go to Col. Hutchinson's to wait on him, Mr. Leverett and others to the Water side. Go off at Scarlet's Wharf. Gave three cheers, they 3. one from us. After Col. Townsend went off alone; did the like by him. The Lord prosper them.

Feria tertia, July, 8. 1707. I bring Mr. Solomon Stoddard going as far as Watertown Mill; and there staid at Churches till the Rain was over; then took Leave. Mr. Sampson Stoddard and I dined there. In returning call'd upon Capt. Tho. Oliver, and drunk of his Spring in his Orchard. Look'd upon N. Sparhawk's Family: Call'd at my Son's at Brooklin; from thence Mr. Stoddard went to Cambridge, and I home. *Note.* In the morn, going down Roxbury Meetinghouse Hill, my Horse stumbled, fell on his Knees and there struggled awhile, broke his Crouper: I kept on and had no harm, not so much as a strain, *Laus Deo.*

I gave Mr. Stoddard for Madam Stoddard two half pounds of Chockalat, instead of Commencement Cake; and a Thesis.

Feria secunda, July, 14th 1707. Mr. Antram and I, having Benj. Smith and David to wait on us, Measured with his Wheel from the Town-House Two Miles, and drove down Stakes at each Mile's end, in order to placing Stone-posts in convenient time. From the Town-House to the Oak and Walnut, is a Mile wanting 21½ Rods.[15] Got home again about Eight aclock.

July, 23. 1707. Midweek, visited Madam Leverett; her son, Thomas Berry, is afflicted with a sore under his left Arm ready to break: all else are well.[16]

July, 29. 1707. *Feria tertia,* Major Walley and I walk to the Ferry. From Charlestown, Heaton carries us in his Calash, the Sheriff, Under-Sheriff, Mr. Bordman, Capt. Henry Phillips accompanying us. Finish'd the Court. Visited Madam Leverett, visited Mrs. Corlett, look'd upon her Grand-daughter Minott. Left a copy of Mr. Noyes's verses on Mr. Bayley;[17] two Banbury Cakes, and a piece of eight, with

[14] John Veazie (Harvard 1700) had preached occasionally, and Sewall had heard him in September 1705, but he had not been settled in a pastorate.

[15] Dr. Samuel Abbott Green has a paper on Old Mile-stones leading from Boston in *M.H.S.Proc.* XLII, 87–111.

[16] Margaret, the daughter of President John Rogers of Harvard, had married first, Captain Thomas Berry of Boston. She was now the wife of Tutor John Leverett, who became President of the College in October. Thomas Berry (Harvard 1712), her son, was a boy of thirteen. *Sibley.*

[17] Nicholas Noyes of Salem had put the manuscript in Sewall's hands in May 1706. The poem, "May 28th, 1706./To my Worthy Friend,/Mr. James Bayley,/

Mrs. Champney; Gave her a piece on Commencem't day; both for her Mother.

Feria quinta, Augt 7th 1707. Peter Weare set up the Stone Post to shew a Mile from the Town-House ends: Silence Allen, Mr. Gibbons's Son, Mr. Thrasher, [*blank*] Salter, Wm Wheelers [*blank*] Simpson and a Carter assisted, made a Plumb-Line of his Whip. Being Lecture-Day, I sent David with Mr. Weare to shew him where the second should be set; were only two little Boys beside.

Monday, Augt 11. 1707. Mr. Willard goes to Cambridge to Expound, but finds few scholars come together; and moreover was himself taken ill there, which oblig'd him to come from thence before Prayer-Time.

Tuesday, Augt 12. between 6 and 7. I visited Mr. Willard to see how his Journey and Labour at the College had agreed with him; and he surpris'd me with the above-account; told me of a great pain in's head, and sickness at his stomach; and that he believ'd he was near his end. I mention'd the business of the College. He desired me to do his Message by word of Mouth; which I did, Thorsday following, to the Govr and Council.

Quickly after I left Mr. Willard, he felt very sick, and had three sore Convulsion Fits to our great sorrow and amazement.

Thorsday, Augt 14th When the Govr enquired after Mr. Willard, I acquainted the Govr and council that Mr. Willard was not capable of doing the College work, another year; He Thank'd them for their Acceptance of his service and Reward. Govr and Council order'd Mr. Winthrop and Brown to visit the Rev^d Mr. Willard, and Thank him for his good service the six years past. Sent down for Concurrence, and Depts to name persons to join in the Thanks and Condolence. Depts concur and nominat the Rever^d Mr. Nehemiah Hobart to officiat in the mean time till Octr next. This the Govr and Council did not accept, and so nothing was done.

Satterday, 7^r 6. 1707. Col. Hathorn and I go to Wrentham, Lodge at Wear's.

7^r 7th Sat down at the Lord's Table with Wrentham Church.

7^r 8th Went to Rehoboth, din'd at Mr. Smith's, invited Mr. Greenwood, who came and din'd with us; told us that Mr. Goodhue was sick of a Fever at his house: went to Bristol by the Bridge; at Carpenter's heard of the French Privateer in Marthas Vinyard Sound, and Rode-Islanders gon after him. Lodg at the ordinary with Capt.

Living (if Living) in Roxbury," was printed as a broadside. 2 *M.H.S.Proc.* VI, 172–173.

Lennard, Mr. Sparhawk's Indian Boy being sick of a Fever. 7ʳ 9ᵗʰ at Dinner had the good News brought of the French privateer being Taken. Mr. Leverett came from Billinges just as were going to Dinner. 7ʳ 10ᵗʰ Midweek, sentenced a woman that whip'd a Man, to be whip'd; said a woman that had lost her Modesty, was like Salt that had lost its savor; good for nothing but to be cast to the Dunghill: 7 or 8 join'd together, call'd the Man out of his Bed, guilefully praying him to shew them the way; then by the help of a Negro youth, tore off his Cloaths and whip'd him with Rods; to chastise him for carrying it harshly to his wife. Got out of Town to Rehoboth.

7ʳ 11ᵗʰ *feria quinta*, rid home very well. *Laus Deo*. Col. Hathorn and Mr. Leverett turn'd off to Cambridge from Jamaica.

7ʳ 12 Mehetabel Thurston tells me Mr. [*Samuel*] Willard was taken very sick. I hop'd it might go off, and went to Dinner; when I came there, Mr. Pemberton was at Prayer, near concluding, a pretty many in the Chamber. After Prayer, many went out, I staid and sat down: and in a few minutes saw my dear Pastor Expire: it was a little after Two, just about two hours from his being taken. It was very surprising: The Doctors were in another room Consulting what to doe. He administered the Lord's Supper, and Baptiz'd a child last Lord's Day: Did it with suitable voice, Affection, Fluency. Did not preach: 7ʳ 11ᵗʰ went to Lecture and heard Mr. Pierpont. At even seem'd much better than had been lately. Tis thought cutting his finger, might bring on this tumultious passion that carried him away. There was a dolefull cry in the house.[18] *Feria secunda*, 7ʳ 15ᵗʰ Mr. Willard is laid by his Tutor in my Tomb, till a new one can be made. Bearers, Dr. Mather, Mr. Allen; Mr. Tho. Bridge, Mr. C. Mather; Mr. Wadsworth, Mr. Colman. Fellows and students of the College went before. Mr. Pemberton Led Madam Willard. Govʳ and his Lady had Rings: Bearers Scarvs and Rings. The Lady Davie, and Lady Hobbie were there. Son Sewall led his Sister [*Madam*] Paul Dudley; he being gon to Plimouth–Court. Very Comfortable Day.

Octobʳ 1. 1707. *Feria quarta*, I went to Brooklin, and chose some Apple-trees from which my Son is to send me Apples: Din'd with my Son and Daughter and little Grand-daughter; went to Amos Gates's; Went into the Cedar-Swamp Meadow. Govʳ makes a Treat to day for

[18] The eminent Samuel Willard (Harvard 1659) had been minister of the South Church since 1678 and the administrative head of Harvard, with the title of vice-president, since 1701. He was a voluminous writer. At his death he left the manuscripts of a series of expository lectures on the Shorter Catechism, delivered over a period of thirty years, which were edited by Joseph Sewall and Thomas Prince and published in 1726 as *A Compleat Body of Divinity*. It was the largest book printed in the colonies, a folio of a thousand pages. *D.A.B.*, *Sibley*.

Govr Winthrop, Major Genl Winthrop and Madam Eyre. Col. Paige, Madam Usher, Mr. Paul Dudley and wife. [*In margin:* 8^r 1. 1707. The five stone posts are set up in our Front.]

Feria quinta, Octr 2. Fast at the South church. Mr. Wadsworth prays, Mr. Pemberton preaches: Mr. Bridge prays and gives the Blessing. Capt. Atwood, Bernard, Gooding, Atkins go home with me at Noon. I give each of them one of Mr. W[*illiam*] Williams's Sermons.[19] p. m. Mr. Cotton Mather Prays, Dr. Mather Preaches, prays, gives the Blessing. Was a great Assembly.

Octr 3. had a Meeting of the Church and Congregation: But very thin, Several came not because Mr. Pemberton said Gentlemen of the church and Congregation; affirmed they were not Gentlemen and therefore they were not warned to come. Mr. Pemberton prayed, upon debate appointed this day sennight for the meeting.

Feria quinta, Octob^r 2. 1707. John Sewall, Sam. Moodey, and Abrah. Tappin brought home Hannah Sewall, Mary Sewall, and Jane Tappin from Newbury. Tis a fortnight since they went. Had a good passage thither by water. *Laus Deo.*[20]

Feria sexta, Octob^r 24th 1707. Capt. David Mason, Holberton, Seers and Winter arrive from London in Boston Harbour: Began to be in great fear about them lest they were Taken; because they might have been expected before the Mast-Ships. Thanks were given on this account at Mr. Willard's Meeting, which was kept at his widows House this Afternoon; began between 1 and 2. Mr. Wadsworth, Colman pray'd, Mr. Pemberton preach'd and pray'd excellently.

Tuesday, Octr 28. 1707. The Fellows of Harvard College meet, and chuse Mr. Leverett President: He had eight votes, Dr. Increase Mather three, Mr. Cotton Mather, one, and Mr. Brattle of Cambridge, one. Mr. White did not vote, and Mr. Gibbs came when voting was over.[21]

[19] *The Danger of Not Reforming Known Evils Or, The Inexcusableness of a Knowing People Refusing to be Reformed.* As it was set forth on a Day of Publick Fasting, April 16, 1707. at Hatfield (Boston, 1707).

[20] It should be recorded here that Sewall wrote a letter 7 October 1707 to Thomas Buckingham, minister of Saybrook, to accompany a gift of the five volumes of Matthew Poole's *Synopsis Criticorum* "for the use of your Collegiat School." He desires the "Acceptance of this Token of my being a Well-wisher to the Prosperity of your College; though possibly it may import the less increase of our own." The Collegiate School of Connecticut, founded in 1701, was being conducted at Saybrook at this time. Later moved to New Haven, it took the name of its building, Yale College, in 1718. The books given by Sewall are no longer in the Yale library. *L.B.* 1, 354.

[21] John Leverett (Harvard 1680) was the first layman to be president of an American college. From 1685 to 1700 Tutors Leverett and William Brattle had

Thorsday, Octr 30. The Man of War, and Physick arrive from Lisbon, bring News that the siege of Tholoun [*Toulon*] was Raised.

Octr 31. Mr. John Jekyl was sworn Collector, and Mr. Thomas Newton Controller: The Governour call'd for the Bible for them to swear on.

Novr 1. just about Noon the Govr produces the Petition sign'd by Mr. Higginson and others for his Removal: And urges the Council to vote an Abhorrence of it. I pray'd that it might be consider'd of till Monday, which the Governour would not hear of, but order'd Mr. Secretary to draw up a Vote: which with some alteration was pass'd. Said He had no Gall. After coming from Council I read the Book printed against the Governour in London. I had not seen it before.[22]

---

done most of the governing and teaching at Harvard in the absence of President Mather. Because of his liberalism and his kindly feelings toward the Church of England, Leverett fell afoul of the Mathers, was accused of subversive teaching, and was dropped in 1700. Meanwhile he had studied law and had been elected Representative. In 1702 his friend Governor Dudley appointed him judge of the Superior Court and probate judge for Middlesex. He was elected to the Council in 1706. In 1713 he was made a Fellow of the Royal Society.

"The election of Leverett was insupportably grievous to Increase Mather and his son. They had anticipated, that the choice would have fallen upon one or the other of them . . . Their indignation was excited against Dudley, who, as they thought, had buoyed up their hopes until he had arranged measures to insure their defeat." (Josiah Quincy, *Hist. of Harvard University*, 1860, I, 201). See our note for 23 January 1707/8.

Leverett and his friends knew well that the Mathers would bring all their influence to bear to prevent the General Court from accepting Leverett's election and voting him a salary. His friends drafted an address to the governor testifying to Leverett's character and competence, circulated it among the ministers of the province, and obtained thirty-nine signatures. The Mathers "promptly wheeled their batteries into action" as expected. On 11 November 1707, the Council, after the addresses of the Harvard Corporation and the ministers had been read, voted that the election of Leverett be accepted. The House non-concurred and talked of another president *pro tempore*, as Sewall recorded 28 November. Morison writes that Dudley, "whose education, begun on the parental farm and continued at Harvard, had been perfected in the House of Commons, thought up an ingenious horse-trade. If the lower House would concur in the election of Leverett and vote him a suitable salary, Governor and Council would agree to discard the 'Temporary Settlement,' forget about the Charter of 1700, and declare the Charter of 1650 in force again! Such a concession on the part of Her Majesty's Governor, a tacit recognition of the old Bay Colony principle that the General Court had a right to charter a college without permission from the Crown, carried the House off its feet." (*H.C.S.C.* II, 555). Sewall recorded the concurrence of the Deputies 5 December. The next day the concurrent resolve was signed and the government of Harvard was resumed under the Charter of 1650, still in effect at the present day.

[22] See 21 November.

Novr 8th Mr. Coffin of Nantucket is appointed by the Govr and Council to have an oversight of the Indians there. I had mention'd Capt. Gardener, whom Capt. Belchar withstood about a week ago. Govr mention'd Gifts as piety. Mr. Benja. Brown said Capt. Gardener was prefer'd before Mr. Coffin for Piety: then the Govr said no more. I now mov'd that both might be appointed; Capt. Belcher said; then let there be three. I said Capt. Gardener was already appointed to receive what was sent from the Commissioners. The Govr said it was all the better; they would be a Check upon each other.

Novr 7. Mr. James Allen stood up, and said I was a Party, and therefore ought not to be a Judge in the Cause of Govr Bellingham's Will. I had got of that Land in a wrong way; which I resented; for no Land on this side the water is mentioned except for Life, and my Fragment on the Hill is not mention'd at all.[23]

Novr 10th I received a Letter from Bro^r, who says Doct^r Toppan[24] fell off Mr. Titcomb's Wharf last Tuesday, was found by it on Wednesday morn: buried Thorsday in the Rain.

Feria Secunda Novr 10. 1707. I set out for Salem with Capt. Bennet; at Lewis's overtook Mr. Dudley, Valentine, Hern; from thence went together, had a very good Journey; got to Salem so early as to anticipat the sheriff; the wind being fair, went by Winnisimet.

Novr 13. Adjourn a little before night *sine die*. Visit Mr. Higginson the aged Minister; He can well and sensibly speak to us still, call'd me by my name; Mr. Leverett he did not hit of. Said he was sorry that his son should petition against the Govr. Speaking of the Union he repeated very well a verse of K. James.

Jam cuncti gens una sumus; sic simus in ævum.

His wife very decrepit and in pain; glad to see me. Visit Madam Bradstreet, Bro^r Hirst.

Novr 14. very good wether; Mr. Noyes Breakfasts, prays with us: at taking Leave, I gave him a 20^s Bill in a paper writ on *Scalpellum* —— and verses on Mr. Goodhue. Had a very good Journey home by Charlestown, Mr. Leverett in company till parting.

Novr 15. Maj^r.Genl sends my wife and me a pair of Gloves on ac-

---

[23] The will of Governor Richard Bellingham had been set aside by the General Court, 6 September 1676, but any title from his only son should have been without flaw. Sewall had bought a back lot on Cotton Hill 11 October 1697 from Elizabeth, the wife of Samuel Bellingham, son of the governor. Samuel (Harvard 1642) spent much of his life in London, and had sent his wife to New England to manage his affairs. *Sibley;* 5 *M.H.S.Colls.* vi, 197–198, 6 *M.H.S.Colls.* v. 147–148; *L.B.* i, 100n–104n.

[24] Dr. Peter Toppan of Newbury.

count of his wedding the 13th. Novr 17 I and others visit Mr. Winthrop, and his Bride.[25] See 7r 19, 1707 in my Justices Book.

Novr 18. Daughter Sewall is brought to Bed of a Son at Brooklin between 5 and 6. *mane.* Danford told me of it; I gave him a shilling.

Novr 20. 1707. The Deputies not having voted as the Council did Novr 1., a Conference is agreed on: Col. Hathorne, Col. Hutchinson, Mr. Secretary Addington, Mr. Commissary Belchar are appointed to be Managers: others may speak as they see occasion.

Govr made a long speech beginning from his father, who laid out one Thousand pounds in the first adventure, was Governour.—— He himself the first Magistrat born in New England. Managers all spake in their order: Mr. Blagrove spake on the part of the Deputies; said twas before the Queen and Council, not fit for us to intermeddle; Mention'd some Trade, as Nails, Pots, Sithes. Govr deny'd the quantity of Nails.

The Govr took an opportunity to say, he heard some whisper'd as if the Council were not all of a mind: He with courage said that all the Council were of the same mind as to every word of the vote. This gall'd me; yet I knew not how to contradict him before the Houses.

Novr 21. Depts vote again as to the Councils vote, and tis carried in the Negative. Conference about Vetch and Borland trading with French &c. Draw up a vote themselves shorter than ours, and vote it and send it in. Upon this, some began to be hot to send for the Book wherein the Affidavits are, and Mr. M's Letter; and to burn it:[26]

[25] Wait Still Winthrop, the major-general and chief-justice, married secondly, 13 November 1707, Katherine, daughter of Thomas Brattle and widow of John Eyre.

[26] A hundred pages of the second volume of the M.H.S. edition of this diary were devoted to type-facsimiles of three pamphlets in the warfare between the Mathers and Dudley. The one Sewall refers to is *A Memorial Of the Present Deplorable State of New-England, With the many Disadvantages it lyes under, by the Male-Administration of their Present Governour, Joseph Dudley, Esq. And his Son Paul, &c* . . . It was put together by Cotton Mather, probably brought to London by John Calley, William Partridge, or Thomas Newton, placed in the hands of Sir Henry Ashurst for finishing touches, and printed there in 1707 by Benjamin Harris. "The text consists mainly of letters and affidavits with comment upon them, showing the alleged perfidy, chicanery, and corruption of Governor Joseph Dudley. The governor is accused of encouraging trade in munitions with the French and Indians, particularly through his son William Dudley and Captain Samuel Vetch, thus enabling the enemy to continue their devastating raids . . ." T. J. Holmes, *Cotton Mather . . . Bibliography* II, 666; Holmes's analysis of the pamphlet covers pp. 664–672.

The second pamphlet, *A Modest Enquiry into the Grounds and Occasions of a Late Pamphlet, intituled, A Memorial of the Present Deplorable State of New-*

others were for deliberation. *Note*. At the Conference the Govr had the Extract of many of Mr. C[*otton*] M[*ather's*] Letters read, of a later Date than that in the printed Book and Observator, giving him a high character. See Decr 12. Novr 22. In the morn, I went to Mr. Borland, and enquired of him whether the Govr knew of their Trade with the French. He said he order'd Capt. Vetch to acquaint him. I enquired whether he did it or no: Mr. Borland said, he did not hear him acquaint the Govr with it. By this I gather'd that Capt. Calley's Affidavit was true; and that the Govr did connive at their Trading with the French, which has open'd a Tragical scene that I know not when we shall see the close of it.

Went to the burying of Mrs. Busby the widow.

Novr 23. Mr. Pemberton preaches more fully and vehemently against being cover'd in Sermon Time. *p. m.* Simeon Stoddard, the Son of A. Stoddard, is baptised.[27] David Stoddard and others taken into Church.

Before family prayer, went to the burying of Capt. Thomas Dudley's Daughter: Sir Wainwright, and Capt. Southack's son Bearers. Govr was at the Funeral. About the middle of this Novr I dried up the Issue in my Left Arm; trusting to that of my Legg only.

Novr 23. 1707. My Son Samuel has his Son Samuel Baptised by Mr. Walter at Roxbury: Col. Partridge, who was present, inform'd me of it, Novr 24th

Novr 25. 1707. The Govr read Mr. Cotton Mather's Letter to Sir

---

England, was written by Joseph Dudley and printed in London in 1707. "The charges of the Mathers are taken up in detail and either ridiculed or answered one by one . . . The whole reply is more temperate in tone and convincing in reason than the attack of the Mathers . . . The Board of Trade believed Dudley's defence . . . and the Privy Council . . . heard both sides and dismissed the charges as 'frivolous.' " Everett Kimball, *The Public Life of Joseph Dudley* (1911), 188–189.

The Mathers retorted in a third pamphlet, *The Deplorable State of New-England, By Reason of a Covetous and Treacherous Governour, and Pusillanimous Counsellors* . . . (London, 1708); this was not a rejoinder to Dudley's pamphlet, but was occasioned by the forcibly-obtained votes of the Council and Representatives exculpating Dudley from the charges made in the Petition to the Queen signed by Nathaniel Higginson and others. Sewall's withdrawal of his vote for the "Blanching Business" (or whitewash), which we print, is given in full. See T. J. Holmes, *op. cit.*, I, 240–263. Higginson's petition is printed in Hutchinson's *History* (1936 ed.) II, 118n–119n.

27 This was the unfortunate Simeon Stoddard (Harvard 1726) who was ruled *non compos mentis* by the probate court in 1751; his father was Anthony Stoddard (Harvard 1697), the Boston merchant.

Charles Hobby[28] in Council, the Copey being sign'd by Mr. Povey, and animadverted on several paragraphs; When the Govr came to the *horrid Reign of Bribery*: His Excellency said, None but a Judge or Juror could be Brib'd, the Governour could not be bribed, sons of Belial brôt him no Gifts. Mov'd that Col. Hutchinson, Mr. Secretary, Col. Townsend and Mr. Cushin go to Mr. Cotton Mather with the Copy of his Letter to Sir Charles Hobby, and his Letters to the Govr, and speak to him about them: this was agreed to. I shew'd some backwardness to it, fearing what the Issue might be; and hinting whether it might not be better for the Govr to go to him himself: That seem'd to be Christ's Rule, except the Govr would deal with him in a Civil way.

Novr 25. 1707. p. m. The Govr mov'd that Mr. Newton might be sent for; which was done; and the Govr minded him of the Confession he had made for signing the Petition against him; and Mr. Newton renew'd his acknowledgment of his misdoing, in some measure, and excus'd it by saying that he was surpris'd by being told that the Govr had written against his being Collector. When he was gon, the Govr order'd the Secretary to make a Minute of it, which was done. When this was over, I desired the Governour's patience to speak a word: I said I had been concern'd about the Vote pass'd Novr 1. "At the Conference his Excellency was pleas'd to say, that every one of the Council remain'd steady to their vote, and every word of it: This Skrewing the Strings of your Lute to that height, has broken one of them; and I find my self under a Necessity of withdrawing my Vote; and I doe withdraw it, and desire the Secretary may be directed to enter it in the Minutes of the Council." And then I delivered my Reasons for it, written and sign'd with my own Hand; which were read. The Govr directed that it should be kept privat: but I think Col. Lynde went away before that Charge was given. The Govr often says that if any body would deal plainly with him, he would kiss them; but I rec'd many a Bite, many a hard Word from him. He said I valued Mr. Higginson's *Reputation* more than his *Life*. When Mr. Newton was call'd in, Govr told him that the Court at N-Hampshire had voted an Abhorrence of the Petition; and the Council and Representatives here had voted it a scandalous and wicked Accusation. Just after our uncomfortable Discourse was over, and to help terminat it, a Master comes in from Virginia, who brings News that both Tholoun and Marseilles are Taken. *Note*, before I Withdrew my Vote: The Govr took occasion to speak thus; "To

[28] This letter, dated at Boston, 2 October 1706, was printed by Dudley in his pamphlet, *A Modest Enquiry* (London, 1707), 10–13, above.

The Reasons of my withdrawing my Vote from what was Pass'd in Council, upon *Saturday*, November the First, relating to an Address offered to Her Majesty, Sign'd *Nath. Higginson,* &c.

I. BECAUSE my Motion for leaving the Consideration of it till the *Monday* following, was not admitted ; and it was Enter'd upon, and Pass'd about Noon, in a very short time ; being a matter of great Concernment to our Liege Lady Queen ANNE ; to the PROVINCE ; to his Excellency our Governour ; and to the Council, and Representatives.

II. The Governour's Personal Interest was much in it ; and therefore, I humbly conceive, the Vote ought to have been debated, and framed by the Members of the Council apart by themselves, in the absence of the Governour.

III. The Words [*Firmly believe*] and [*always Apparent*] were never pleasing to me. And now I do not firmly believe that the Governour did no way allow Mr. *Borland* and Capt. *Vetch*, their Trading Voyage to Her Majesties Enemies the *French* :

Qui non vetat peccare, cum possit, jubet.

Not that I suspect, the Governour design'd to hurt the Province : but to gratify grateful Merchants. And I readily and thankfully acknowledge the Governour's Orders for the Defence of the Frontiers, to be truly Excellent ; both respecting the Suitableness of the Orders themselves, and the Quickness of their Dispatch. And I Bless GOD for the Success that has attended them.

IV. I have been acquainted with Mr. *Nathanael Higginson* these forty years ; and I cannot judge the Offering this Address to Her Majesty to be, in Him, A Scandalous and Wicked Accusation ; unless I knew his Inducements. And I fear, this Censure may be of ill Consequence to the Province in time to come, by discouraging Persons of Worth, and Interest to Venture in Appearing for them ; tho' the Necessity should be never so great.

Samuel Sewall.

Boston N. E. Printed *December*, 10. 1707.

say the best, The House of Deputies is out of Humour, though after all their search, all is as white as Chalk, as clear as the Driven snow; yet—

Nov 26. Mr. Secretary reports the Discourse with Mr. Cotton Mather favourably; It seems they stay'd there more than two Hours; and Dr. Mather was present. Mr. Mather neither denys, nor owns the Letter: Think his Letters to the Gov, and that to Sir Charles Hobbey, not so inconsistent as they are represented. By Candle-Light before they went, It was debated whether Mr. Mather should be sent for before the Council; or whether the Gentlemen should go to him. Then I that had been backward to meddle in it before, plainly declar'd my mind that twas best for the Gentlemen to go to him; and so twas carried when put to the Vote. Mr. Secretary is well pleas'd that he went.

The Council invited the Gov to Dinner to day; I drank to his Excellency, and presented my Duty to him. Col. Townsend drank to me. At Dinner Col. Hutchinson invited us to drink a Glass of Wine at Mr. Eliakim Hutchinson's by his order. We went some of us. And between 7. and 8. His son William and his Bride came; and Mr. Phips and his Bride; they were married privatly last Thorsday morn: and now both weddings are kept together.[29] Had Musick, Cake and Cheese to eat there, and bring away. They had a hard Journey from Rehoboth to Billenges yesterday in the Rain. Mr. Hutchinson told us the Bride was gon ill to Bed. Gov Winthrop had a very bad night.

This day the Gov appoints Wednesday Dec 3. for Nominating Officers; says He has only a Justice of Peace or two on Essex side.

In the evening by Candle-Light I fell asleep in the Council-Chamber: and when I waked was surprised to see the Gov gone.

Col. Townsend ask'd me to withdraw my Paper, and put it in my Pocket, pleasantly: I answered pleasantly, I could as easily put him in my Pocket.

Friday, Nov 28. 1707. The Gov puts forward to have the vote of July 9. 1706. of the Representatives, the vote of the Council of Nov 1., the vote of the Representatives Nov 21., Printed, to prevent spreading false Reports: I said I could not vote to it because I had withdrawn my vote. The Gov said, I pray God judge between me and you! Col. Townsend told me I was a Temporiser; I hôp'd Mr. Higginson would be Gov, and endeavour'd to procure his favor.

---

[29] The weddings celebrated by Colonel Elisha Hutchinson's party were those of the children of his cousin Eliakim. William Hutchinson (Harvard 1702) had married Elizabeth Brinley, and Elizabeth Hutchinson had married Spencer Phips (Harvard 1703) the 20th of November. *Sibley.*

Prayer. Lord, do not depart from me, but pardon my sin; and fly to me in a way of favourable Protection! Capt. Phips brings in Mr. Leverett Non-Concurr'd. Moves from the House that a suitable person be thought of to take care of the College till May Sessions. Col. Townsend tells me that my purpose to withdraw my Vote was known a week ago; Mr. Oaks mention'd it in the House; He was my Counsellor. Whereas he really knew nothing of it; and now tells me, he never mention'd my Name.

Decr 1. Our children visited their Sister at Brooklin.

Decr 4. Mr. C. Mather preaches a very good Funeral sermon. Govr [*Fitz John*] Winthrop is buried from the Council Chamber, Foot-Companies in Arms, and Two Troops. Armor carried, a Led Horse. Bearers, Govr, Mr. Russell; Mr. Cooke, Major Brown; Col. Hutchinson, Sewall; Mr. Secretary, Mr. Sergeant. Father, Son, and Grandson ly together in one Tomb in the old burying place. Was a vast concurse of People.

Decr 5. Dine at Holm's. I suppos'd the Council had Treated the Govr, But the Govr would pay. A Message is sent in to the Deputies about the College; whereupon they withdraw their Non-concurrence; rase out (Non) and turn it to Concur'd; And vote Mr. Leverett a Salary of One Hundred and Fifty pounds per annum out of the publick Treasury.

Decr 6. Some desire that it may be put in the Bill that Mr. Leverett Lay down all his Civil offices; as Judge of Probat, and Judge of the Superiour Court. And entirely to attend that service, was inserted, and Mr. Secretary carried it in to the Deputies, and took their Consent. Govr has Two Hundred pounds given him. Col. Jn° Appleton, Hunt and I are sent in to speak to the Deputies about their denying any Reward to the commissioners to Port-Royal; Told them, denying all Remuneration was in a manner to make them Criminals: Twas a burden God in his providence had laid on us, and to go about thus to shake it off, would be to his Dishonor. Spake also in behalf of Salem Fort and Marblehead. Upon this a Resolve was sent in to leave the consideration of it to another Sessions, being now a very thin House. Deputies had sent in a long Roll of Grievances to be Reform'd, as their Advice: Govr would have had the Council advis'd the contrary in the whole: I opposed it, as inconvenient to vote against all together: and it was staid. And yet when the Deputies were come in, the Govr took the paper and spoke to it; said he could not go according to it without having the Frontiers defenceless; said the Council were unanimously against it. Court is prorogued to the fourth of February.

Decr 10. Married [*Jonathan*] Hayward and Susanna Mills.

Feria quinta, Decr 11th 1707. Thanks-giving-day, very serene, moderate, comfortable Wether. Mr. Pemberton preaches forenoon and afternoon. Yesterday I was told of a vast number of Pigeons in the Woods this Moneth. Capt. Mills at his Sister's Wedding says he saw an incredible Number at Woodstock last Friday.

Madam Usher, son and daughter Hirst and their family, Cousin Sam and Jonathan Sewall, Bro^r Wheeler and his wife, M[*ash?*] & her daughter, dine with us. *Feria sexta, Dec^r* 12. 1707. Just before the Funeral of Mrs. Eliot, I went to Mr. Borland, told him he had been at my House and I was not at home, so I now call'd at his. He seem'd to express some Concern that the Govr was troubled; and said they gave the Govr nothing. I told him what my discourse with him was the 22^d Novr He owns the substance of it now; and is confirm'd in it because he saw it in Capt. Vetches Petition at home. I desired to see the Petition but he declin'd it.

Bearers to Mrs. Eliot, widow of D[*eacon*] Jacob Eliot: Sewall, Bromfield; Hill, Williams; Checkly, Mr. John Hubbard. Was buried from her daughter Davis's. At the Return to the house, I said to Mr. Holyoke, it was a happiness that our Condolance for the departure of our friend, was join'd with Congratulation for her being gon to her Rest and Reward. At parting with the Bearers, I told them we were often concern'd in Funerals; it would be well for us to pray one for another that God would prepare us for our own Dissolution.

Joseph return'd to Cambridge before the Funeral, last mention'd.

Feria septima, Decr 13. 1707. I enquir'd of Mr. Jn° Winthrop whether he had seen his Sister Sewall; he said not since her Lying in; I told him I would not impose upon him; but if he pleas'd, we might go together (he told me must go to Roxbury with the Coach and back again); we rid together, call'd at Roxbury and took in Madam Paul Dudley, and Mrs. Anne. Found my daughter and her little Samuel well; his Father has a Cold. Little Rebekah well. When return'd, went in again to the Governour's, his Lady only now at home. Madam Paul Dudley came home with us; had a comfortable Journey. *Laus Deo.*

Feria Secunda, Decr 15. 1707. The Governour calls a Council, Reads a Letter of Mr. Bridger complaining of Trees cut contrary to Charter and of a great Mast ship'd: Now it seems Mr. Collins deals for Masts by the Royal Authority, though his Powers are not shewn here: The Govr press'd for a Proclamation as is emitted this day; I express'd my self unready to vote for it; because twas only Mr. Bridger's naked complaint, Without any Affidavit to justify it. He had been

here above a 12 moneth; and to set forth a proclamation now, would
be but to serve a Turn. Ichabod Plaisted esqr. is of the Council, and,
dwelling in those parts, might inform the Board. I mov'd that Mr.
Mico might be sent for, who transacts for Mr. Collins: but the Govr
would not hear of it. I feared lest this proclamation should prejudice rather than forward the Queens Interest, and therefore was
against setting it forth. The Govr was displeas'd, and said twas due
to a Tinker, much more to Mr. Bridger.

Feria tertia, Decr 16. 1707. Mr. John Winthrop marries Mrs. Anne
Dudley. Roxbury Lecture-Day.

Feria quinta, Decr 18. Mr. Bridge appoints the 15th Psalm to be
sung: and takes Job. 15. 34. for his Text; especially that clause,—Fire
shall consume the tabernacles of Bribery: From which he preach'd
an excellent sermon. Mr. Pemberton's Cold suffer'd him not to be
abroad; Dr. Mather not at Lecture. Governour, and Maj^r Genl Winthrop were there, notwithstanding the Wedding.

Feria sexta, Decr 19. 1707. Went to the Meeting at Mr. Bromfield's. Mr. Nathl Williams preach'd from 1 Cor. 7. 29. The Time is
short. Mr. Stoddard tells me the Govr has the Gout, and bespeaks
my Company to visit him to morrow. Sent a Letter to .my Bro^r to
day by Mr. B. Marston.

Feria septima, Decr 20. Mr. Bromfield, Mr. Stoddard and I ride
together in Mr. Briggs's Hackney Coach and visit the Govr, who
keeps his Chamber; was taken ill on Thorsday. Wish his Excellency
Joy of his Son and Daughter Winthrop; gave the Bride Mr. Willard's, Blessed Man. Mr. Paul Dudley came home with us and fill'd
up the Coach.

Receive a Letter from my Bro^r, who says, the generality of thoughtfull people there approve of my Mount Etna Eruption: That's his
expression. Hopes to see us in 10 days. Mary is taken ill.

Decr 30. Joseph goes home. Brother comes to Town.

1708

INSTALLMENT OF PRESIDENT LEVERETT / SEWALL GIVES A NIGHT'S
LODGING TO AN INDIAN PREACHER / SOCIAL VISIT TO CAMBRIDGE /
OMITS CELEBRATION OF THE QUEEN'S BIRTHDAY / PRIVATE FAST-DAY /
SEWALL BERATED BY A CREDITOR AND CUT BY MR. HENCHMAN /
RUNS LINES ON MILTON PROPERTY / ELECTION / SEWALL MISSES
COMMENCEMENT BY REASON OF JOSEPH'S ILLNESS / DEBAUCHERIES
AT THE EXCHANGE TAVERN / CAMBRIDGE COURT IN COLLEGE
HALL / LAST DAYS AND DEATH OF EZEKIEL CHEEVER / INDIAN ATTACK
ON HAVERHILL / THE SEWALL MARE MISBEHAVES IN DANA'S BROOK /
COURT TRIP TO BRISTOL / FAMILY DINNER FOR JOSEPH / VISIT TO
SALEM / DEATH OF A GRANDSON

Jany 2. [1707/8] Bro^r goes home in very cold windy wether, lyes at
Lewes's, then home 3. *Jany 8.* 1707/8. The Govr appoints a Council
to meet at Cambridge the 14th Inst for the Installment of Mr. Leverett: warns the Ministers of the Six Towns[1] mention'd to be overseers
of the College.

Midweek, Jany 14. 1707/8. Went to Cambridge in Mr. Briggs's
Coach, with Col. Townsend, Mr. Bromfield, and Mr. Stoddard. Mr.
E^m Hutchinson went in his own Charet, taking Mr. Wadsworth with
him. Capt. Belchar carried Mr. Secretary in his Calash. Mr. Pemberton carried his Bro^r in his Slay over the Ice; Mr. Mico carried Mr.
Treasurer Brattle. Mr. Colman there. Maj^r Genl Winthrop, Col.
Elisha Hutchinson, Mr. Foster, Mr. Sergeant, Dr. Mather, Mr. Cotton Mather, Mr. Bridge, Mr. Allen were not there. The day was
very pleasant; Col. Phillips, Mr. Russel in his black cap, Col. Lynde
met us from Charlestown; Mr. Bradstreet, Angier, there, Mr. Woodbridge of Meadford, Mr. Neh. Hobart. In the Library the Governour
found a Meeting of the Overseers of the College according to the

---

[1] The first Board of Overseers which governed the college beginning in 1637
consisted of six magistrates, and the teaching elders of the six towns (*sex vicinis
oppidis*) of Cambridge, Watertown, Charlestown, Boston, Roxbury, and Dorchester.

old Charter of 1650, and reduced the Number to seven;[2] viz. Mr. Leverett President, Mr. Neh. Hobart, Mr. Wm Brattle, Mr. Ebenezer Pemberton, Mr. Henry Flint, Mr. Jonathan Remington, Fellows; Mr. Tho. Brattle, Treasurer. The Govr prepar'd a Latin Speech for Installment of the President. Then took the President by the hand and led him down into the Hall; The Books of the College Records, Charter, Seal and Keys were laid upon a Table running parallel with that next the Entry. The Govr sat with his back against a Noble Fire; Mr. Russel on his Left Hand innermost, I on his Right Hand; President sat on the other side of the Table over against him. Mr. Neh. Hobart was called, and made an excellent Prayer; Then Joseph Sewall made a Latin Oration. Then the Govr read his Speech and (as he told me) mov'd the Books in token of their Delivery. The President made a short Latin Speech, importing the difficulties discouraging, and yet that he did Accept: Govr spake further, assuring him of the Assistance of the Overseers. Then Mr. Edward Holyoke made a Latin Oration, standing where Joseph did at a Desk on the Table next the Entry at the inside of it, facing the Govr. Mr. Danforth of Dorchester pray'd. Mr. Paul Dudley read part of the 132 ps. in Tate and Bradey's version, Windsor Tune, clôs'd with the Hymn to the Trinity. Had a very good Dinner upon 3 or 4 Tables: Mr. Wadsworth crav'd a Blessing, Mr. Angier Return'd Thanks. Got home very well. *Laus Deo.*

Jany 15th 1707/8. Mr. Bridge preaches; (Govr not at Lecture.) He speaks against Levillism, Buying and Selling Men. Council after Lecture: Col. Redknap had a Muster-Roll offer'd which the Council Refus'd. It seems he had Thirty pounds allow'd him at his embarking. This day Mr. Belchar brings me Squash-Seeds from Dedham.

Jany 16. 1707/8. Snow. I had a hard fall coming from daughter Hirst's, yet through the goodness of God, had little or no hurt. Tis very slippery under the Snow.

Jany 22. 1707/8. Mrs. Winthrop, *vid.* of Mr. Dean Winthrop, I suppose, dines with us after Lecture. Govr was at Lecture.

Jany 23. I go to the Funeral of Anne Needham, who died in Childbed: her former Husband was Lawson: her first, Airs, to whom I mar-

---

[2] Morison points out (*H.C.S.C.* II, 555) that the Representatives did not realize until it was too late that the restoration of the Charter of 1650 reduced the Corporation to seven (the president, the treasurer, and five fellows); this enabled Dudley to select from the large *de facto* Corporation that elected Leverett the five fellows most acceptable to him and the president. The Board of Overseers had not met since 1692. Sewall's "Overseers" do not correspond to the present body; for the changes over the years, see *Harvard University Quinquennial Catalogue* (1930), 13–17.

ried her Novr 5. 1690. At first I walk'd next the women with Mr. Wentworth: when had gon a little way Mr. Cotton Mather came up and went with me. Funeral was from Conney's Lane, to the new Burying-place. There Mr. Mather ask'd me to go with him to Madam Usher's, where we staid till past six. Speaking of death, I said twas a Happiness to be so Conform'd to Christ, And it was a pleasure to take part with God in executing a righteous Sentence upon one's self, to applaud his Justice——Mr. Mather said that was high-flying; he would have such High-flyers be at his Funeral. Had been mentioning Mr. Dod's Will. As went thence told me of his Letter to the Govr of the 20th Ins^t and Lent me the Copy; intends to send another to Mr. Paul Dudley. Dr. Mather it seems has also sent a Letter to the Govr.[3] I wait with Concern to see what the issue of this plain home-dealing will be! I desir'd Mr. Mather to promote Col. Thomas's being brought into the Superior Court, if there was opportunity: the 12th Feb^r is appointed for a Nomination.[4]

Jany 30. 1707/8 John Neesnummin [*Indian preacher*] comes to me with Mr. R. Cotton's Letters; I shew him to Dr. Mather. Bespeak a Lodging for him at Matthias Smith's: but after they sent me word they could not doe it. So I was fain to lodg him in my Study.[5] *Jany 31 p. m.* I send him on his way towards Natick, with a Letter to John Trowbridge to take him in if there should be occasion. About half an hour by sun I went to the Funeral of my neighbour Sam Engs: I went first with Mr. Meers, and then with Mr. Pemberton, who talk'd to me very warmly about Mr. Cotton Mather's Letter to the Govr, seem'd to resent it, and expect the Govr should animad-

---

[3] Following the induction of Leverett, the Mathers could not contain themselves any longer, and on 20 January 1707/8, in the character of his spiritual advisers, they each wrote letters to Dudley so full of abuse and virulence that they have to be read to be believed (the letters are printed, with Dudley's reply, in 1 *M.H.S.Colls.* III, 126–137). They accuse the governor of covetousness, lying, hypocrisy, treachery, bribery, Sabbath-breaking, robbery, and murder. Dudley wrote a dignified and restrained reply, calling the attack "an open breach upon all the laws of decency, honour, justice and christianity" and desiring them to "let fifty or sixty good ministers, your equals in the province, have a share in the government of the college, and advise thereabouts as well as yourselves." Though they were both Overseers, the Mathers shunned the college meetings thereafter.

[4] Colonel Nathaniel Thomas had to wait until 4 June 1712 for his appointment to the court.

[5] The M.H.S. editors have an extensive note on the "strong antipathy felt by all those of English blood here, at that time, against coming into any close relations with the Indians on terms of social equality" and remark that Sewall, "in his gentle kindness of spirit and his humanity of righteousness, proved himself far in advance of his contemporaries in his sympathies with negroes and Indians."

Increase Mather

Cotton Mather

vert upon him. See Feb. 6. Said if he were as the Gov[r] he would humble him though it cost him his head; Speaking with great vehemency just as I parted with him at his Gate. The Lord appear for the Help of his people.

Second-day, Feb[r] 2. Council for passing Muster-Rolls. Somebody said, I think Capt. Belchar, That no man was admitted to be a Captain without giving the D. of Marlborough, or his Dutchess five hundred Guinys: the Gov[r] took it up, and said, What is that! Speaking in a favourable, diminutive way. And said that there had not been any admitted these thousand years but in a way like that; mentioning his own experience in the Isle of Wight.[6] His Excellency seems hereby to justify himself against those who charge him with Bribery. Gov[r] seem'd backward to grant, or say he would not grant the Chaplains &c, Unless Col. Hutchinson &c, had wages allow'd them.

Febr. 3. Went to the Funeral of Capt. Timothy Stephens of Roxbury. Mr. Walter pray'd, and tells me was a very good Christian, usefull Man, had great Assurance of the Love of God to him before he died; though he had much darkness before. Gov[r] and all his family there. Capt. Belchar, Mr. Bromfield, Mr. Stoddard and I there.

Feb[r] 4. Mr. Townsend, Bromfield, Stoddard, I, went and visited Mr. Leverett the President: I wish'd Madam Leverett Joy of the new Employment of her Husband. First din'd at Capt. Parker's. Visited Col. Foxcroft, who is abed with the Gout. When had paid our Reckoning at Capt. Parkers, rode to my sons chamber, sat awhile by his fire, Mr. Flint came to us. From thence came home slowly, which made us late. At Col. Foxcroft's was Col. Byfield, Taylor, Mr. Brattle, Cambridge. At coming from the President's Col. Townsend said he hop'd he should hear of his being in the Hall every day. He expounded the first of Matthew yesterday; Moderated the Bachelours Dispute to day. But we hear as if he intends to go into Hall but on some certain days.

Febr. 5. Mr. Colman preaches the Lecture in Mr. Wadsworth's Turn, from Gal. 5. 25. If we live in the Spirit, let we also Walk in the Spirit. Spake of Envy and Revenge as the Complexion and Con-

[6] Dudley was made deputy-governor of the Isle of Wight by Lord Cutts on his third visit to England in 1693, and held the office for over nine years. He was a member of the House of Commons for the borough of Newton in that Island. "Cutts also obtained for Dudley a commission, probably through some irregular means; and thereafter Dudley was known as Colonel Dudley." Everett Kimball, *The Public Life of Joseph Dudley* (1911), 69.

demnation of the Devil; Spake of other walking: it blôted our sermons, blôted our Prayers, blôted our Admonitions and Exhortations.
It might justly put us upon asking our selves whether we did live in
the Spirit, whether we were ever truly regenerated, or no. 'Tis reckon'd he lash'd Dr. Mather and Mr. Cotton Mather and Mr. Bridge
for what they have written, preach'd and pray'd about the present
Contest with the Govr. I heard not of it before, but yesterday Col.
Townsend told me of Dr. Mather's Prayer Jany 25, Wherein he
made mention of One in Twenty-Eight being faithfull; which makes
many look on me with an evil eye: supposing Dr. Mather ment my
withdrawing my vote of the first of Nov^r. *Feb^r* 6. Queen's Birthday,
I could not find in my heart to go to the Town-House; because
hardly anything is professedly there done but drinking Healths. And
Mr. Maxwell left his Message with David; I saw him not. And I
was entangled that I could not conveniently go. I had written to
Mr. Borland earnestly desiring to see the Copy of Capt. Vetches
Petition: and he sent me word he would wait on me this day; which
did in a manner bind me at home, lest I should be out of the Way.
He came and told me with an air of Displeasure, that I had made a
bad use of what he had told me. Afterward I ask'd upon what head
he intended I had made a bad use: He said little, but talk'd of making a Flame. I had said in my Letter, I hôp'd he should not have
cause to complain that I had made a bad use of his lending me the
Petition till morning, or a less while, if he pleas'd. Thus my neighbour Borland can take an oath which is made use of to hide the
Truth, and cause men to believe a Lye; but he, with unjust reflec-
tion, refuses to shew a Copy of a Petition for clearing the Truth of
a controverted matter of Fact: though the petition be publickly
lying before the Queen and Council, and any one may have a Copy
for their Money. I said little to him; but gave him the last of Mr. W^m
Williams' Sermons. Master Chiever his coming to me last Satterday
Jany 31. on purpose to tell me, he blessed God that I had stood up
for the Truth; is more Comfort to me, than Mr. Borland's unhand-
someness is discomfort. But, above all, I hope I have a good
Conscience, and a good GOD to bear me out.

Second-day, Feb^r 9. 1707/8. Mr. D. Oliver, Capt. Keeling, Constable Loring and my self walk'd in the 7th Comp^a to inspect Disorders. Found this to our Comfort, that the widow Harman's daughter Ames is gon to her Husband at Marshfield, which was a gravamen
for many years, I used constantly to visit them and expostulat with
them. I carried ½ Duz. Catechises in my Pocket, and gave them to
such as could read, Orphans several of them; Harman, Hannah

Dinsdal, Tho. Watson, Jn° Phips, Hallowell, Odel. That might not
fail of meeting again, Din'd at Hobins's; gave the Constable his
Dinner, so it cost us 2ˢ apiece. Had a very comfortable day overhead.

The Appointment of a Judge for the Super. Court being to be made
upon next Fifth day, Febr. 12, I pray'd God to Accept me in keeping
a privat day of Prayer with Fasting for That and other Important
Matters: I kept it upon the Third day *Febr.* 10. 1707/8 in the upper
Chamber at the North-East end of the House, fastening the Shutters
next the Street.⁷ —— Perfect what is lacking in my Faith, and in the
faith of my dear Yokefellow. Convert my children; especially Samuel
and Hannah; Provide Rest and Settlement for Hanah: Recover
Mary, Save Judith, Elisabeth and Joseph: Requite the Labour of
Love of my Kinswoman Jane Tappin, Give her health, find out Rest
for her. Make David a man after thy own heart, Let Susan live and
be baptised with the H[oly]G[host], and with fire. Relations. Steer the
Government in this difficult time, when the Governour and many
others are at so much Variance: Direct, incline, overrule on the
Council-day fifth-day, Febr. 12. as to the special Work of it in filling
the Super. Court with Justices; or any other thing of like nature; as
Plim° infer Court. Bless the Company for propagation of the Gospel,
especiall Govʳ Ashurst &c. Revive the Business of Religion at Natick,
and accept and bless John Neesnummin who went thither last week
for that end. Mr. Rawson at Nantucket. Bless the South Church in
preserving and spiriting our Pastor; in directing unto suitable Supply, and making the Church unanimous: Save the Town, College;
Province from Invasion of Enemies, open, Secret, and from false
Brethren: Defend the Purity of Worship. Save Connecticut, bless
their New Governour: Save the Reformation under N. York Gov-
ernmᵗ. Reform all the European Plantations in America; Spanish,
Portuguese, English, French, Dutch; Save this New World, that
where Sin hath abounded, Grace may Superabound; that CHRIST
who is stronger, would bind the strong man and spoil his house; and
order the Word to be given, Babylon is fallen. —— Save our Queen,
lengthen out her Life and Reign. Save France, make the Proud
helper stoop [*Job. ix.* 13], Save all Europe; Save Asia, Africa, Europe
and America. These were genˡ heads of my Meditation and prayer;
and through the bounteous Grace of GOD, I had a very Comfortable
day of it. The reading of Mr. Tho Horton's Sermon upon a Monethly
Fast, before the House of Lords xr. 30. 1646. was a great furtherance
of me, which was happily put into my hand by Major Walley the

⁷ Probably the most full and minute existing record of a private fast-day as kept
by the devout of that time.

latter end of last Moneth.[8] I rec'd a Letter from Mr. Rawson at Nantucket about 2 p. m.

Feb^r 12. 1707/8. Mr. Bridge preaches from Hebr. 12. 17. In his Explication and Exhortation put a great Emphasis upon *Afterward,* to stir up all presently to embrace Christ, Instanc'd in the Misery of Judas returning his 30 pieces. The Govr was at Lecture.

The Business of the Council was not attended because the Stormy Wether had prevented the Justices coming, so that had but about 13. None but from Boston and Charlestown. Adjournment is made to next Thorsday, and persons to be Notified.

I went to the Govr at Major Winthrop's after Lecture and told him I could be glad Mr. Higginson might be brought into the Superior Court. Advis'd that Mr. [*Isaac*] Winslow might be brought into the infer. Court at Plim° and Mr. [*Joseph*] Otis left out; Col [*Nathaniel*] Tho[*mas's*] son-in-Law. Told him of the fraudilent Deed complain'd of by Mr. Tomson of Middleborough; and that the said Otis's hand was to the fraudulent Deed as a Witness, has now a part of what was granted by it: and probably was the Adviser in the whole matter. Told the Govr I intended to waite on his Excellency on Wednesday: but was hindered by the Storm. *Note.* The Govr us'd to Tell the Councillors how acceptable 'twould be to him to be discours'd in privat about such matters.

Febr. 13. 1707/8. Though I walk in the midst of trouble, thou wilt revive me; thou shalt stretch forth thy hand against the wrath of my enemies, and thy right hand shall save me. 138. 7. I read the 137, 138 Psalms in course this morn, and have noted this for Memory.

Feria Septima,[9] *March,* 6. 1707/8. Having the Company's Account [*for Propagating the Gospel*] written out; I went to Col. Foster to pray him to be present to examin it; went to the Maj^r Genl to acquaint him that I design'd a Meeting at my house which he consented to: Then I went to Maxwell to order him to warn the Commissioners; which he immediatly took in hand. Then going up the prison-Lane I met Mr. Sergeant, who told me of Mr. Arthur Mason's Funeral,[10] which I knew nothing of before; neither did I suspect it;

---

[8] *Sinne's Discovery And Revenge. As it was Delivered in a Sermon to the Right Honorable House of Peers in the Abbey Church at Westminster on Wednsday, December 30. 1646. being the Day of the Monethly Publick Fast.* By Thomas Horton, B.D. . . . (London, 1646).

[9] For a while Sewall numbers the week-days in Latin.

[10] Mason was a baker who lived in School Street and belonged to the South Church. His daughter Mary was the wife of Sewall's classmate, Rev. John Norton of Hingham. Another daughter, Joanna, a beauty celebrated by John Dunton as "the very Flower of Boston," married first Robert Breck, then Michael Perry.

thinking it would be defer'd till next week for sake of Mr. Norton and his wife. But now I could not go back for fear of losing my opportunity of finishing and sending my Accounts. As soon as ever had Sign'd, left other important Business; and went all away to go to the Funeral; but when we came to the Schoolhouse Lane end, we saw and heard the Funeral was gon; and so came back. I even despair'd of finishing my Account the Ships threatn'd to sail so soon; and I was taken up so much with my Inventory. But by the Kindness of God, I got well through it, made two fair Copies of the Original, and had them Subscrib'd by the Commissioners attesting their examination and Allowance of them. Not one error discern'd. *Laus Deo Adjutori*.

Midweek, March, 10, 1707/8. The privat Meeting was at Mr. Cole's, where Mrs. Noyes was, I read a Sermon of Mr. Willard's. I went away a little before her but she overtook me near the New Meetinghouse; I saw the Glimpse of her Light and call'd to her; spake a few words and parted; feeling in my self a peculiar displeasure that our way lay no further together.

March 12. She was at the Meeting of Majʳ Genˡ Winthrop, where Mr. Adams preached. Presently after her getting home, she was seised with the Palsie, which took away her Speech. I heard of it at Scarlet's Wharf, March 13, as I was taking Leave of Mr. Jonathan Belcher, and Mr. Sam. Banister going aboard the Fleet ready to sail. *Midweek, March*, 17, 1707/8. my Country man, Mr. Josiah Byles,[11] dyed very suddenly. *Feria quinta, March* 18ᵗʰ the Fleet sails, though the Skie cover'd with Clouds.

Feria sexta [*March* 19] Reginald Odell dies suddenly. Heard of it at Mr. Byles Funeral. About Candle-lighting, the day sennight after her being taken, my old cordial Christian dear friend, Mrs. Sarah Noyes, Expires.[12] I saw her on Wednesday, she knew me, and ask'd how Madam Sewall did. She was Laborious, Constant at Privat Meeting, Lecture, Lords-Day. I am much afflicted for the Loss of her. Capt. Brattle tells me that a vertuous young Woman at Marblehead died in 4 or 5 Minutes after taken.

Feria secunda, March, 22, 1707/8. Mr. Zechariah Symmes, pastor of the church of Christ at Bradford, died in the morning. He was born at Charlestown, January 9. 1637. He was a Worthy Gentleman,

---

11 Byles had come, like Sewall, from Hampshire, England. He was from Winchester and was a saddler. Rev. Mather Byles was his son.

12 Sarah, daughter of Peter Oliver, widow of John Noyes, and mother of Dr. Oliver Noyes (Harvard 1695), had been a member of the South Church since 1670.

Scholar, Divine. *Feria quinta, March,* 25, 1708. Intending to set out for Plimouth the 27th I went to the Major Gen¹ˢ and to Mrs. Sergeant's to Receive their Bills if they pleas'd to pay them: found neither at home, and so went not in. Coming back, in the prison-Lane I met Mr. Sergeant. He ask'd me where I had been, I told him at his house: He said, What for, Money? I said Yes. At which he was angry, and said I was very hasty, I knew very little of that nature. He would enquire how others paid me &c. I told him I was going out of Town, this was the day,[13] and I thought it convenient to offer the Bills; he said he should not break; and at last call'd out aloud, he should not break before I came back again! I know no reason for this Anger; the Lord sanctify it to me, and help me to seek more his Grace and favour. This day was very stormy with Rain, and then with Snow; a pretty deal of Thunder. Majʳ Cutler was with me in the morning.

March, 27. 1708. Rode with Mr. Nehm. Hobart to Hingham, visited Madam Shepard by the way at Cousin Holman's, visited Mr. Fisk: visited Mr. Norton, who invited Mr. Hobart to preach next day. Lodg'd at Cousin Hobart's.

March, 28. See the Sermons in one of my Cover'd Almanacks. Din'd at Mr. Norton's. *March* 29. by 6. m. Gam¹ Rogers, the son, who had been sent Express in the night, came to my Lodging with an Adjournment of the Court to the 20th of April. This as desired, I forwarded to Plimouth by Cous. David Hobart, who accompanied his Brother Mr. N. Hobart. I agreed with Major Thaxter to run the Line of my 300. Acres of Land at Braintrey just by Milton. Din'd with Cousin Quinsey, and engag'd him to meet me at Milton next Monday: Spake to Mr. Swift to assist me. Call'd at the Governour's; came home well. *Laus Deo.*

April, 1. Great Rain with Thunder. Mr. Wadsworth preaches: Work out your own Salvation with Fear.

Feria Sexta, April, 2. Last night I dream'd that I had my daughter Hirst in a little Closet to pray with her; and of a sudden she was gon, I could not tell how; although the Closet was so small, and not Cumber'd with Chairs or Shelves. I was much affected with it when I waked.

Feria septima, Apr. 3. I went to Cous. Dumer's to see his News-Letter: while I was there Mr. Nath¹ Henchman came in with his Flaxen Wigg; I wish'd him Joy, i. e. of his Wedding. I could not

---

[13] Up to 1752, when England adopted the Gregorian calendar, 25 March was the first day of the year.

observe that he said a Word to me; and generally he turn'd his back upon me, when none were in the room but he and I. This is the Second time I have spoken to him, in vain, as to any Answer from him. First was upon the death of his Wife, I cross'd the way near our house, and ask'd him how he did: He only shew'd his Teeth.

Feria secunda, Apr. 5. Great Rain, whereby I am prevented meeting Major Thaxter at Milton to run a Line, as I intended.

Feria secunda, Apr. 12, 1708. I went and met Major Thaxter at Miller's at Milton to run the Lines of the 300. Acres bought of Mr. Stoughton; Cousin Quinsey, Mr. Swift, Miller, White, Hunt, assisted us. Mr. William Rawson, having Land adjoining, was with us all day; Billing a considerable while. Capt. Culliver and others perambulating for Braintrey and Milton, went with us from B. to C. which was measured, whereby the place we set out from was ascertain'd to be the North Corner, of which there was some doubt before: At C. the old white Oak mark with H., we drank a Bottle of Madera together, read the Queens Speech to the first Parliament of great Britain,[14] and so took leave of the perambulators. Major Thaxter, Cous. Quinsey, and White went quite through the Swamp, marking Trees: southward of the Swamp is a small Chestnut White-Oak; a little after that the Line brushes by a Ledge of Rocks, touches them. At D. the Oak upon the Rock is cut down injuriously, there it lyes and no use made of it: by the Stump grows up a fine little Chestnut Oak, which was prun'd; twas double and one is cut away to make the other grow the better. In the Line from D to A found several Trees mark'd with H. At A. we enlarg'd the Heap of Stones upon the Rock and from thence, as all along, run by Compass and the anciently marked Trees to C., where we begun; which prov'd all the Work to be Right: There we made a large heap of Stones upon the Stump of a Tree burnt down.

Paid to Major Thaxter	£0—8–0
To White 3ˢ Hunt for formerly, and now 3ˢ	0—6–0
To Miller for entertainment and Help	0–15–0
To the Widow Gray for my Horse	0—5–0
	£1–14–0

To Cousin Quinsey, Mr. Swift, and Mr. Lawson I am oblig'd.

[14] The union of England and Scotland under the name of Great Britain went into effect 1 May 1707, and the first Parliament of Great Britain met 23 October 1707.

It is a Mercy that our work succeeded so well. Got home before eight, and found all well. *Laus Deo.*

Apr. 11, 12, 13. Swallows proclame the Spring.

Feria Sexta, Apr. 16. I visit my daughter Hirst, and finding her alone in her Chamber, pray with her. Afterward by Maj^r Genl Winthrop's direction I carry her a vial of Spirits of Lavender. And of my self I join with it a pound of Figs, that food and Physick might go together. Leave her with Mrs. Hubbard.

Apr. 17. 1708. Col. Hathorne, Mr. Corwin and I set out for Scituate. Lodg'd at Job Randall's. *Apr. 18.* Heard Mr. James Gardener of Marshfield.

Apr. 19. To Plimouth, stay at Mr. Bradford's till Mr. Attorney Cook came up. There the sheriff meets us. Lodge at Rickard's. *Apr. 22.* Return'd.

May, 4. Daughter Hirst Deliver'd of a Daughter. *May, 7.* Boston: Upon the Special Verdict, between Wats and Allen, Sewall, Hathorne, Corwin for Watts; Walley for Allen.

Feria secunda, May, 17, 1708. Major Walley and I set out with a Coach and 4 Horses from Charlestown; Dine at Lewis's; bait at Phillips's, Wenham, got to Mr. Rogers's before Sun-set.

Major Walley had a Fit or 2 of his Cholick, and yet by God's Goodness, came away about 3 p. m. *May 21,* got comfortably to Salem. Lodg'd at Brother's.

May, 22. set out about Eight m. Baited at Lewis's: Din'd at Cambridge, call'd at Brooklin, lighted at the Governour's. Got home well about 6. *Laus Deo.*

Midweek, May, 26. 1708. Mr. Secretary, Sewall, Eliakim Hutchinson administer the Oaths to the Representatives: 72 at first, and 2 more. 74 in all. Mr. Jno. Norton preaches a Flattering Sermon as to the Governour. Dine at the Exchange. Number of Councillors 25. Together, 99. Election.

Wait Winthrop	95	[*John*] Foster	95
James Russell	95	John Apleton	85
Elisha Cook	57	[*John*] Higginson	91
Jn° Hathorn	93	Peter Sergeant	82
Elisha Hutchins[*on*]	81	Saml Partridge	69
S. Sewall	98	2^d voting	
I. Addington	94	Ephraim Hunt ·	61
W. Brown	71	Nathan^l Norden	52
J. Phillips	86	3^d vote	
J. Corwin	89	Andrew Belchar	54.

Plimouth		Zagadahock	
Nathan¹ Pain	88	Joseph Lynde	65
Isaac Winslow	86		
Jnº Cushing	74	At Large	
Jnº Otis	65	1 Vote None chosen.	
		2 Vote	
Main[e]		Edʷ Bromfield	64
Eᵐ Hutchinson	85	3ᵈ vote Sam. Appleton	41
Ichabod Plaisted	86	which brought him in; the voters being	
John Wheelright	45	now less in number.	

For Col. Townsend had 42. in the first voting for the Massachusets. Finished about ¼ past Ten.

May, 27. I was with a Committee in the morn at Mr. Eᵐ Hutchinson's, appointed the 10. of May; and so by God's good providence absent when Mr. Corwin and Cushing were order'd to Thank Mr. Norton for his sermon and desire a Copy. About 6. p.m. The Govʳ bid the Secretary swear the Council: About 20. were sworn; Then the Deputies were sent for in, and the Govʳ made a speech. When court was adjourn'd I enquired of Mr. Secretary what the Govʳ had done with the Election; and he inform'd me that He had Negativ'd Mr. Cooke and Mr. Pain, which was never done in this secret way before that I remember: but used to be done openly in Council.

May, 27. Mr. Joseph Noyes lodg'd at our House; I gave him the Broad Side of Boston streets,¹⁵ which came out this week: to shew him that he was in Newbury Street. He pray'd with us very well. Is in the 71 year of's Age.

May, 31. The Govʳ call'd a Council in the Morning, and had Capt. Chandler's Letter from Woodstock concerning Nenemeno, an Indian that went away ten years ago; He said the Govʳ has a Crooked heart, he has taken away our Land, and now would send us to Salt Water. He first enquired after Ninequabben, who it seems was sent to sea upon Wages with his own Consent, and Taken. Govʳ and Mr. Secretary writ what was convenient.

In the afternoon the Govʳ went home indispos'd. Council pass'd an Act for altering the Style.¹⁶

Deputies sent in Capt. Savage, Capt. Hutchinson, Mr. Patch, with a Motion for a Committee of both Houses to prepare a draught of

¹⁵ *The Names of the Streets, Lanes & Alleys, Within the Town of Boston in New England.* Boston: Printed by Bartholomew Green . . . 1708.
¹⁶ This was to notice the union of England and Scotland (*Province Laws* II, 622). See also Sewall's entry of 12 July.

an Address to Her Majesty; on several heads; viz. To Apologize for neglecting to Address so long, &c.

This day, May, 31, Mr. Crease removes to his own new shop next Mr. Sergeant's: Nothing now to be seen in his former empty place. Cousin Fisk must get a new Tenant.

About the 23 or 24th of June, Mr. Bromfield Rec'd a Letter without a name, putting him upon enquiring after Debaucheries at North's, the Exchange Tavern, and that he should ask my Advice. At last, June, 28. he got in writing what North's Wife and Maid had to complain of. I went to Mr. Sim. Stoddard's; he put it into my hand, and I read it first, being surpris'd to find my self unaccountably abused in it: I told Mr. Bromfield, I should not meddle in it, I must not be a Judge in my own Cause. At last when the matter was heard before Mr. Bromfield, Townsend, Dummer, by Mr. Banister's procurement, sundry Gentlemen were present, Capt. Tho. Hutchinson, Capt. Edw Winslow, and others, at Mr. Bromfield's; They gave Mrs. North and her Maid their Oaths, fin'd Mr. Tho. Banister junr 20s for Lying; 5s Curse, 10s Breach of the peace for throwing the pots and Scale-box at the maid, and bound him to his good behaviour till October sessions.[17] At the latter end of the Court, I think about the first of July, the Dept's sent in for the Govr £200.; for Mr. Treasurer £225: at which the Govr was very angry, and said he would pass none of them, they would starve together. Sent for Mr. Taylor, Govr told him his Salary would not be pass'd, enquir'd whether he were ready to serve.

July, 2. Capt. Joseph Shelden dyes by reason of the great Heat.

July, 3, is buried at the publick charge, £21.6.1. Corps was set in the Depts Room. In the afternoon I and Mr. Commissary and one more were sent in with a Message to shew the Indignity of the Treasurer being above the Govr, and carried in both the Bills, and left them. In the way of argument I mention'd the vastness of the Govrs Authority; we could not lift up hand or foot or step over a straw; at which the house was mightily heated and said, They were slaves; I explain'd my self, that nothing could be pass'd but what the Govr Sign'd.

Tuesday, July, 6. The Treasurer is sworn; the Depts return the Bills without any alteration. The Govr orders the Secretary who draws up a vote to shew that the Council, having done all in their power to

17 Thomas Banister (Harvard 1700) had been a highly troublesome undergraduate. In 1712 he flouted the good people of Connecticut and was indicted for journeying on the Sabbath. Sewall had to break up a drinking party he was having on the Queen's Birthday, 6 February 1713/4. *Sibley.*

increase the Gov^{rs} Salary: but by reason of the length of the Sessions were necessitated to break. It was a Surprise to me. I said, I could not tell what Benefit it would be of. But when it was driven, I got it alter'd in the beginning, to, having used the proper Means. Court is prorogued to the first of September.

July, 7. I go to Cambridge by Water with Mr. Tappan in Capt. Bonner; had a pleasant passage, wind and Tide for us. Boston Troop waited on the Govr, and Cambridge Troop, Capt. Goff, met his Excellency. Exercise was well entered before he came. Then the orator was call'd.

At Dinner I was surpris'd, being told my Son was ill and desired to speak with me. I went to him in a Garret in the old College, got Mr. Addington to us.[18] After, Mr. Cooke came; cheer'd my son and staid with him; they left us. *Note.* Heard not a jot of the Singing in the Hall. I got a Calash, and brought my son home by Charlestown: so I saw nothing of the Afternoon Exercise, Disputes, Presidents Oration, Degrees. The Lord prepare me for Disappointments, Disgraces, Imprisonments.

July, 8. Mr. Pemberton comes with Mr. Stoddard into the Pulpit. Mr. Stoddard preaches a good Sermon against building on the Sand. Col. Foxcroft is made Judge of Probats in the room of Mr. Leverett.

Feria secunda, July, 12, 1708. Mr. Sol. Stoddard returns home. In the Afternoon the Govr holds a Council, and reads Two Letters from Whitc-Hall, dated May, 1707, ordering the Union to be published in the most solemn manner; and the Govr accordingly appointed Thorsday, the 22th Inst^t, for it. In the former part of the Letter, the Govr is order'd to write to the Lords an Account of Things here and persons; sign'd Stamford, Dartmouth, Herbert, Ph. Meadows, J. Poultney.

May, 3. The Queen gives an Instruction, that in absence of the Govr and Dep^t Govr, the eldest Councillor shall execute the Powers of the Governour. In passing the Muster-Rolls, It appeared that Capt. Turfrey was allow'd for wages at Saco when absent so as could not be answer'd: Govr said must be allow'd except would pull his Teeth out: Pleaded how many dead Souldiers, Military officers, were allow'd. I pleaded against that Lying way; and pleaded the poverty of the Country.

Maj^r Genl Winthrop came home from N. London July, 10. and was sworn and took his place at the Board this day *July 12. 1708.* He pleaded that what the Queen now orders, was so before: But I cant

18 Isaac Addington, Sewall's colleague on the bench, had been trained as a surgeon.

understand the Charter in that manner. I believe we practis'd right.

July, 24, 1708. Mrs. Anna Fisk dy's a little before Sun-set.[19]

July, 27. is buried at Braintrey in her Husband's Tomb. Govr and his Lady there. Bearers Mr. Peter Thacher, and Mr. Peter Thacher of Weymouth; Mr. B. Tomson, Mr. Belcher; Mr. Danforth of Dorchester, Mr. Flint. By reason of Cambridge Court I was not there. The wether was vehemently hot, My Coach was there. I rode to Cambridge with the Maj^r Genl in his Coach. Finish'd the Court; being but one civil Action; viz. Ephraim Savage against Major Swain. Savage Cast in his Review. Court held in the College Hall. Adjourned *sine die*. Visited Mr. President's Sick Anne;[20] twas almost dark, and then staid so long at the Gov^{rs} that twas about 11. at night before got home; Madam Winthrop staid at the Gov^{rs} and came home with her Husband as went thither. Govr carried her to the Funeral.

Monday, Augt 9. 1708. I went to Brooklin, and Din'd there with my Son and Daughter; Saw little Sam well. Then went to the Funeral of Mrs. Wigglesworth.[21] The Govr met me at my Sons Gate and carried me in his Chariot to Cambridge, in his way to Col. Paiges, and so to Ipswich. Bearers of Mrs. Wigglesworth, The President and Mr. Hobart; Mr. Thacher, Mr. Danforth Dorch^r; Mr. Brattle, Mr. Walter. Only Col. Phillips and I of the Council were there: Mr. Speaker was there.

Feria tertia, Augt 10. Mr. [Moses] Fiske dies about Noon at Braintree.

Feria quinta, Augt 12. I rode with Cous. Savage to Mr. Fisk's Funeral. Lighted at Cous. Quinsey's, whether came Mr. Wadsworth, Mr. Colman, and Mr. George. There we din'd. Bearers Mr. Whitman, Mr. Thacher; Mr. Danforth of Dorchester, Mr. Belchar; Mr. Wadsworth, Mr. Thacher of Milton. There was little Thunder and Rain; but near and at Boston, much Rain, Thunder; at Dorchester a Barn was burnt by the Lightening. Got home well about 8 a'clock, found all well; *Laus Deo*.

Feria sexta, Augt. 13. Mrs. Mary Stoddard dies; The hot Wether occasion'd her being open'd, and two great Stones were taken out of her Bladder. She was a vertuous Gentlewoman, and one of the most

19 Mrs. Fiske was the wife of Rev. Moses Fiske of Braintree (Harvard 1662), who survived her less than three weeks. She was the daughter of Rev. Thomas Shepard of Charlestown (Harvard 1653) and her first husband was Daniel Quincy. *Sibley*.

20 The Leveretts had a daughter Anne, who was born 5 July and died 30 July 1708.

21 Sybil (Sparhawk) Avery was the third wife of Rev. Michael (*Day of Doom*) Wigglesworth of Malden, who had died in 1705. *Sibley*.

kind Friends I and my wife had. *Augt 17th Feria Tertia.* Mrs. Stoddard is buried; being the day of Genl Council, they accompanied the Govr to the House of Mourning: Bearers, Sewall, Addington; Foster, Sergeant; Walley, Townsend. Was buried in a Tomb in the New-Burying place.

Feria quarta, Augt. 18. Yesterday the Govr committed Mr. Holyoke's Almanack[22] to me; and looking it over this morning, I blotted against Feb^r 14th *Valentine;* March, 25. *Annunciation of the B. Virgin;* Apr. 24, *Easter;* Septr 29. *Michaelmas;* Decr 25. *Christmas;* and no more. (K. C. mart) [*King Charles, Martyr, Jan.* 30] was lined out, before I saw it; I touched it not.

Feria quinta Augt 12. Mr. Chiever is abroad and hears Mr. Cotton Mather preach; This is the last of his going abroad: Was taken very sick, like to die with a Flux. *Augt 13.* I go to see him; went in with his Son Thomas, and Mr. Lewis. His Son spake to him, and he knew him not: I spake to him, and he bid me speak again: Then he said, now I know you, and speaking cheerily mention'd my Name. I ask'd his Blessing for me and my family; He said I was Bless'd, and it could not be Revers'd. Yet at my going away He pray'd for a Blessing for me.

Feria quinta, Augt 19. I visited Mr. Chiever again, just before Lecture; Thank'd him for his Kindness to me and mine; desired his prayers for me, my family, Boston, Salem, the Province. He rec'd me with abundance of Affection, taking me by the Hand several times. He said, The Afflictions of God's people, God by them did as a Goldsmith, Knock, knock, knock; knock, knock, knock, to finish the plate: It was to perfect them not to punish them. I went and told Mr. Pemberton, who preach'd.

Feria sexta, Augt 20. I visited Mr. Chiever, who was now grown much weaker, and his Speech very low. He call'd, Daughter! When his daughter Russel came, He ask'd if the family were compôs'd: They apprehended He was uneasy because there had not been Prayer that morn; and solicited me to Pray; I was loth, and advis'd them to send for Mr. Williams,[23] as most natural, homogeneous: They declin'd it, and I went to Prayer. After, I told him The last Enemy was Death; and God had made that a friend too: He put his hand out of the Bed, and held it up, to signify his assent. Observing, he suck'd a piece of an Orange, put it orderly into his mouth, and chew'd it, and then took out the core. After dinner I carried a few of the best Figs I could get, and a dish Marmalet. I spake not to him now.

[22] Edward Holyoke (Harvard 1705) became president of the college in 1737.
[23] Nathaniel Williams (Harvard 1693) was Cheever's assistant.

Feria septima, Augt 21. Mr. Edward Oakes tells me Mr. Chiever died this last night.[24]

Note. He was born January, 25. 1614. Came over to N–E. 1637. to Boston: To New-Haven 1638. Married in the Fall and began to teach School; which Work he was constant in till now. First, at New-Haven, then at Ipswich; then at Charlestown; then at Boston, whether he came 1670. So that he has Labour'd in that Calling Skillfully, diligently, constantly, Religiously, Seventy years. A rare Instance of Piety, Health, Strength, Serviceableness. The Wellfare of the Province was much upon his Spirit. He abominated Perriwigs.

Augt 23. 1708. Mr. Chiever was buried from the School-house. The Govr, Councillors, Ministers, Justices, Gentlemen there. Mr. Williams made a handsom Latin Oration in his Honour. Elder Bridgham, Copp, Jackson, Dyer, Griggs, Hubbard &c. Bearers. After the Funeral, Elder Bridgham, Mr. Jackson, Hubbard, Dyer, Tim. Wadsworth, Ed^w Procter, Griggs and two more came to me, and earnestly solicited me to speak to a place of Scripture at their private Quarter-Meeting in the room of Mr. Chiever. I said, 'twas a great Surprise to me; pleaded my inability for want of memory, Invention: Said, doubted not of my ability; would pray for me. I pleaded the Unsuitableness, because I was not of that Meeting. They almost took a denial. But said one would come to me next night. Time is near, Lords-day Sennight. Argued much because thereby a Contribution for poor Widows would be forwarded.

Augt 23. *mane*, at Council, A Petition for building a Quaker Meeting house with Wood, pass'd by the Selectmen and Justices of the Town; was now offer'd to the Govr and Council: I oppos'd it; said I would not have a hand in setting up their Devil Worship. I pleaded that Mr. Dudley had been at great Charge to Slate his House Roof and Sides; Govr listen'd to that, and said, we always enquired of the Neighbourhood to gain their Consent: so Mr. Dudley should be spoken with.

Augt 23. 2. *p. m.* Go to Cous. Dummer's, where Mr. Wadsworth, Mr. Cotton Mather pray'd excellently: then Mr. Bridge and Dr. Mather pray'd 'for Cous. Jer. Dummer going to England. Sung the 121 Ps. I set York Tune. Went from thence to the Funeral. Mr. Allen and Mr. Pemberton did not pray. Few there; their little Room not full.

Augt 26. Mr. Henry Flint, in the way from Lecture came to me

[24] Ezekiel Cheever, Londoner educated at Christ's Hospital and Emmanuel College, was New England's most famous schoolmaster; his *Accidence, a Short Introduction to the Latin Tongue,* was used there for two centuries. D.A.B.

and mention'd my Letter, and would have discoursed about it in the Street: I prevail'd with him to come and dine with me, and after that I and he discours'd alone.

He argued that saying *Saint* Luke was an indifferent thing; and twas commonly used; and therefore, he might use it. Mr. Brattle used it. I argued that 'twas not Scriptural; that twas absurd and partial to *saint* Matthew &c. and Not to say *Saint* Moses, *Saint* Samuel &c. And if we said *Saint* we must goe thorough, and keep the Holy-days appointed for them, and turn'd to the Order in the Common-Prayer Book.

Aug[t] 27. Mrs. Sarah Taylor, wife of Col. William Taylor, died last night. Col. Byfield gave her to him in Marriage. March, 2. 1698/9. He has now only one Child living; viz. Mrs. Lyde who has Children.

Feria Septima, Aug[t] *28. 1708.* Mrs. Taylor is buried in Mr. Stoughton's Tomb: Bearers, Col. Foxcroft, Mr. Palmer; Mr. Newton, Mr. Mico; Mr. Pain, Mr. Harris. Col. Byfield there and Mr. Lyde with three Children. Mr. Leverett and wife; Mr. Brattle and wife; Mr. Angier and wife. Mr. Sergeant and Col. Hutchinson were there with their wives as Relations. Gov[r] and his Lady, Maj[r] Gen[l] Winthrop and his Lady, Mr. Secretary, Sewall, Mr. E[m] Hutchinson, Belchar, Mr. Bromfield there; and many others. There was no Prayer at the House; and at the Grave Mr. Myles Read Common-Prayer; which I reckon an Indignity and affront done to Mr. Stoughton and his Friends: There appears much Ingratitude and Baseness in it because twas Mr. Danforth's Parish, and Mr. Danforth's wife is Cousin German to Col. Taylor: and Col. Byfield and his deceased daughter dissenters as I suppose. I was much surpris'd and grieved at it, and went not into the burying place. Maj[r] Gen[l] said, Mr. Stoughton heard them not. Mr. Leverett went not in. He spake to me about his Letter, desiring a Copy of his Memorial. I answered, I knew not who brought the Letter; I writt out a Copy; but he neither came for it himself, nor sent any body. He ask'd not for it now: but said he intended to lay it before the Company. The Gov[r] seem'd to haste into the burying place, when Mr. Miles's voice was heard. Coming home Mr. Belchar told me that the widow Park, a very good woman, in her 94th year, was buried last Thorsday, at Roxbury.

Lords-day, Aug[t] *29. 1708.* about 4 p. m. An Express brings the News, the dolefull News, of the Surprise of Haverhill by 150. French and Indians. Mr. Rolf and his wife and family slain.[25] About Break

---

[25] Benjamin Rolfe (Harvard 1684), minister of Haverhill, his wife, and a young child were brutally slain by Indians. Two small daughters were concealed by a servant, and survived. *Sibley*.

of Day, Those Words run much in my mind, I will smite the Shepherd, and the Sheep shall be scattered: What a dreadfull Scattering
is here of poor Havarill Flock, upon the very day they used to have
their solemn Assemblies. Capt. [*Simon*] Wainright is slain.

Augt 31. *Feria tertia*, I ride with Joseph, and visit Mr. Hobart. I
drove through Dana's Brook to let the Mare drink, and she lay down
in it; so that Joseph and I were fain to jump into the Water up to
the ankles; and then had much adoe to get her out. Din'd with Mr.
Hobart, Mrs. Hobart, Mrs. Jackson, Mr. Hobart's Daughter.[26] Got
home with difficulty: but our Wellcome there at Newton made
amends for all. This day, Augt. 31. Mr. Rolf, his Wife and Child,
and Capt. Wainwright were buried in one Grave, Several Ministers
were there [*Haverhill*].

Septr 1. Went to the burial of Mr. Simson's only daughter, 2 years
and a few days old. *Sept^r* 2. Mr. Colman preach'd from Numb. 14.
19. pardon—the iniquity of this people.—Mr. Colman said he would
not declare what our iniquities were; but propos'd that a Synod
Might be call'd to do it. At 3, p. m. the Council meets, from thence
they goe to the Funeral of Mrs. Lyde, Col. Byfield's eldest daughter.
Remembering what I had met with at her Sister's Buriel at Dorchester last Satterday, I slipt from the Company up to my daughter's, and
so went home, and avoided the Funeral. The office for Burial is a
Lying, very bad office; makes no difference between the precious and
the vile. Jer. XV. 19. They ought to return to us, and not we go to
them by sinfull Compliances. Mrs. Lyde was in the Thirtieth, and
Mrs. Taylor in the 26th year of her Age: born in January and February.

7^r 3. I went to the Funeral of Mrs. Whetcomb's Grand-daughter;
who is also Grand daughter to Col. Townsend. I used to go to the
same Room for the Sound of Mr. Brattle's Organs.

7^r 5. Mr. Pemberton preaches, and administers the Lords Supper.
7^r 6. I Train under Capt. Fitch, and by that means dine with Maj^r
Turner at North's. He was, I think, the only Guest. Mr. N. Williams
pray'd in the field in the morn; and Mr. Allen at his own Gate, p. m.
As were Shooting at the Mark, the Rain oblig'd us to put on our
Cloaks. Went to Capt. Lieut. Ballentines; made an excellent Volley
at Lodging the Colours, Mad^am Ballentine rec'd them in at window.
Mr. Hirst brings word that Mr. La Bloom has set up another Window on the partition-wall behind him and me, that stands half on

26 The Sewalls visited Rev. Nehemiah Hobart and his family at Newton. The
M.H.S. editors were unable to locate Dana's Brook, but state that it must have
been in Cambridge, Brighton, or Newton.

my Ground. 7ʳ 7ᵗʰ I view it, and advise about it; all say tis unjust. 7ʳ 8ᵗʰ Last night we were alarm'd by Fire between 2 and 3. in the night. I look'd out at our South-east Window, and fear'd that our Warehouse was a-fire: But it proves a smith's shop, Hubbard's by Mr. Dafforn's, and a Boat-builders Shed: 'Tis thought a Hundred pounds Damage is done. Blessed be GOD it stop'd there. Mr. Pemberton's Maid saw the Light of the Fire reflecting from a Black Cloud, and came crying to him under Consternation; supposing the last Conflagration had begun.

7ʳ 8 or 7ᵗʰ I order Mr. Hirst to speak to Mr. Labloom to take away his Window. 7ʳ 9ᵗʰ I meet the Workman by Mr. Pemberton's Gate, and forewarn him from making of it; and warn him off the Ground, and threaten to take away his scaffolding if he proceed. I speak to Mr. Pemberton that a Day of Prayer may be kept respecting his Health. I was mov'd last night at Mr. Josiah Franklin's[27] at our Meeting, where I read the Eleventh Sermon on the Barren Fig-Tree.

Tis the first time of Meeting at his House since he join'd.

7ʳ 9. Mr. C. Mather Preaches from 2 Tim. 3. 15. In the end of his sermon gives a great Encomium of his Master Cheever.[28] Mr. Hirst goes to Salem to-day.

Satterday, 7ʳ 11ᵗʰ Mr. Corwin and I set out for Wrentham. David waited on me. Visited Mr. Belchar who is Recovering. At Meadfield, Capt. Wear's son met with us in his way from Sherburn, and accompanied us to Wrentham, which was a great comfort to us; got thither before sun-set.

7ʳ 12. Heard Mr. Mann preach excellently. Mr. Corwin is much Taken with him. At Noon are told of Mr. B. Ruggles's death.

7ʳ 13. Capt. Weare accompanied us; At Rehoboth I visited Capt. Peck, who was very glad to see me; so much of the flesh and bone of his upper Jaw is eaten away with the Canker, that he has much adoe to speak so as to be understood; the want of the upper part of his Mouth disables him from making articulat Sounds. Din'd at Smith's; where Mr. Greenwood was, but could not stay, because of Sick he had to visit. Before got out of the Green, Mr. Cooke overtook us. Lodge at the Ordinary.

7ʳ 14ᵗʰ Mr. Corwin, Dudley and I visited Col. Byfield and Lady in a way of Condolance on account of the Death of their Daughters.

---

27 Josiah was the father of Benjamin Franklin, then a boy under three years of age, who never managed to get mentioned by Sewall in the diary.
28 Mather published his funeral sermon and eulogy, *Corderius Americanus* (Boston, 1708; Holmes 75), anonymously. The title-page states that it was "By one that was once a Scholar to him."

Major Walley came not to Town till past One; By that time had din'd, being a little hindred by Col. Byfield's employing the Sheriff to send Express of the Privateer, was four p. m. before the Court was open'd, which the people murmur at. This Express brought News of Major Brenton's Death; in a Hospital, it seems, at Campeche, where he was a Captive. Col. Byfield, Mr. Sparhawk, Mr. Fisk dine with us.

7^r 15th Mr. Sparhawk, Mr. Church, the Councillour, Capt. Fyfield dine with us. Court holds so late, that we lodge at Bristol.

7^r 16. The Sheriff and Capt. Davis bring us going to the Ferry.

Dine at Rehoboth; Bait at Devotion's: get to Billinges a pretty while after Sun-set, where we lodge; viz. Walley, Corwin, Sewall, Dudley.

7^r 17. Friday, bait at Dedham, get home about One, and dine with my wife and family, all well. *Laus Deo*.

7^r 18. Visit Cous. Dummer's wife, who lyes speechless, was taken last Wednesday night; which we heard of at Billenges.

7^r 19. Mary Winthrop is baptised, her Father held her up: She bears the name of his Mother, who dyed in June, 1690. The child was born yesterday. Madam Dudley was hastening to the Travel as we came home; and was at our Meeting this afternoon, and Mr. Paul Dudley.

Feria secunda, Septr 27. 1708. I went to the Funeral of Mr. John Wainwright, son of Col. Francis Wainwright; He was a Senior Sophister, in the 18th year of his Age.[29] What cause of humble Thankfullness have I, who liv'd 7. years of my Life at the College; had Leave to come away; and have liv'd 34. years since that! The Corps was set in the College Hall. Gentlewomen in the Library: Bearers, Major Epes, Mr. Holyoke &c. Twas in a manner dark before got out of the burying place; yet I got home very well in a Calash with the Wainwright that is prentice with Mr. Harris. *Laus Deo*.

Septr 28. A very pretty Boy of 4 years old, Son of Saml Rand, grandson of Wm Pain, was flourishing at Training this day; fell into a scurvy open Privy before night; of which loathsom Entertainment he died in a day or two.

Septr 30. Mr. Pemberton preaches the Lecture. Council for Appointm^t of a Judge for Bristol. The Govr gets 2000£ past for Capt. Belchar. Nominats Col. Church: I said there was a better: Govr said he could not name him: He went from house to house to get Mr. Blagrove chosen Deputy; that was the reason. The Govr made a mo-

[29] There were two John Wainwrights, cousins, in the Class of 1709.

tion that the Gen[l] Court might be prorogued further, past the time of the Superiour Court's sitting: See News Letter, Oct. 25, 1705. Some objected the wether would grow cold. Then the Gov[r] mov'd that Boston Superiour Court might be adjourn'd to the last Tuesday of Nov[r], and Salem Court, to the first of Dec[r]. Said he could not miss the Judges in the Gen[l] Court: So at the Governours Importunity the Council advis'd to it. Maj[r] Gen[l] is indispos'd and keeps his Chamber, I wait upon him with the order the same Evening: He puts me in mind of the Trial of Mr. Borland: and that Capt. Vetch is expected with my L[ord] Lovelace: so that now I suppose I see throw the Governour's Dissimulation. Major Gen[l] seems to decline signing a Writt for Adjournment because he shall be absent at Connecticut during the time of the Court's Sitting.

Tuesday, Oct[r] 5. Went to Dorchester Lecture. This day Cousin Elizabeth Noyes is buried at Newbury, died of a Fever yesterday; is under 26 years of Age.[30] Has left 3 sons and a daughter.

Oct[r] 7th Mr. Cotton Mather preaches from Job, 37. 14. on occasion of the victory which heard of the 5th Inst.[31] Sister Hirst, Mrs. Betty Hirst, Mr. Thacher, Mr. Clap dine with us.

8[r] 8th Went to Newtown Lecture, din'd at Mr. Hubbard's; then Walked with him; Mrs. Jackson went on foot. In sermon-time Gov[r] and his Lady, Cap[t] Belchar and his, Mr. Pemberton, Mr. Colman and theirs, came in. Mr. Hobart preached excellently, from Luke, 17. 10.—Say, we are Unprofitable Servants.—113th psalm sung, Y[ork metre] then 122 L. to delay the Sermon; the speaker having conferr'd with Mr. Hobart just as was going to begin. I got home before Eight, about an hour before the Coaches; I think twas before 7.

Feria Sexta, Octob[r] 15, 1708. In the Afternoon I visited Capt. Nathan[l] Green, who is near 80. years old. Has been a Prisoner in his house almost two years by reason of Sickness. He was refresh'd with my Company. He is a Suffolk man. His Mother brought him over about 9. years old: serv'd his Time with old Mr. Graften of Salem; has been married one and Fifty years.

Oct[r] 15. Mr. Hirst, Sister Sewall, and daughter Susan; my Daughter Hannah, and Cous. Betty Hirst go to Cambridge to see Joseph.

Octob[r] 18th Mr. Bromfield, Stoddard, Sewall, Joseph, ride in the Coach to Dorchester, to the Funeral of Elder Samuel Clap, who is much lamented. He was the first man born in Dorchester, 74 years

---

[30] Elizabeth Toppan Noyes, Mrs. Cutting Noyes Jr. of Newbury, was Sewall's niece. She was born 20 December 1680. *Savage.*

[31] Probably the victory of Marlborough and Eugene, prince of Savoy, at Oudenarde, 11 July 1708. Mather's sermon was not printed.

old. Saw Mrs. Wing by the way; she lies in a very sad distracted condition.

Octob^r 20. Capt. Anthony Chcckley buried in a Tomb in the New Burying place. Bearers, Winthrop, Cook; Elisha Hutchinson, Sewall; Addington, Lynde of Charlestown.[32]

Octob^r 22. Feria sexta, I mentioned in full Council the Adjournment of the Super. Court to the last of November; That when twas advis'd by the Govr and Council Septr 30. I was not aware that the Trials of Mr. Borland were to be brought on by order of Her Majesty; that May-Court was pass'd over already, and I doubted the Conveniency of adjourning the Court to a further day: especially because the Super. Court of Boston did not use to be adjourn'd by reason of the Genl Court's Sitting.

The Govr seem'd earnest that we should Adjourn; Several of the Council back'd the Govr and no body Spake for holding the Court at the usual Time. Col. Hutchinson and Foster particularly, spake that the former Advice might stand. So that we saw if we held the ˙Court, we must in a manner do it *Vi et Armis.* And the Govr said plainly, that if we would not Adjourn the Super. Court, He would Adjourn the Genl Court. And it was considered, that the Governour was ordered by the Queen to bring forward the Trial of Mr. Borland; and if any thing should fail, the Governour would lay the blame upon the Justices of the Super. Court, for not observing his Advice in adjourning the Court: and Mr. Attorney being his Son, He had advantage in his hand to cast that blame upon us. So all, but Major Walley, agreed to adjourn the Court. He was not present at our Consultation. I advis'd Mr. John Clark of this a day or two before; to see if the Deputies would move. I mov'd that the Deputies might be advis'd; it concern'd them; that the Genl Court might give order about it; or at least the Deputies might signify their Liking of it. The Govr utterly refused.

Octr 22. Mr. Saml Phillips's daughter of about 7 years old, is buried: Six Bearers. Mr. Sergeant and I walk'd together to the Funeral.

Octob^r 23. We adjourn the Super. Court: Chief Justice and I sign for Salem Court, and send it by Mr. Epes to be sign'd by Col. Hathorne, and Mr. Corwine; they were slipt away. Chief Justice, Sewall,

[32] Captain Anthony Checkley, Boston merchant, was attorney-general during the inter-charter period from June 1689, and was appointed under the province charter 28 October 1692, serving until Paul Dudley, the governor's son, became Queen's Attorney 6 July 1702 (2 *M.H.S.Proc.* x, 289). The M.H.S. editors killed off Checkley in a 1702 footnote, but Sewall sat in church with him 6 February 1703/4.

Walley sign for Boston Court; and about 3. p. m. I give the Warrant
to Mr. Sheriff; and send an Advertisement to Mr. Campbell.

Wednesday, 8ʳ 27, 1708. My wife is taken very sick as she was last
April; taken with Shaking and intolerable pain in her Brest. Majʳ
Genˡ visits her and she takes some of his powder; but is cast up so
soon, that it works little. Great Rain. Dr. Noyes visits and administers: on Friday grows better, *Laus Deo.*

Monday, Novʳ 1. Govʳˢ best Horse dyes in his Pasture at Roxbury
as goe to Dedham. Bouroughs, a worsted-comber, was at Mr. Col-
mans' Meeting on the L. day p. m., went homeward towards Roxbury
in the night; got beyond the Salt-ponds, and fell down a-cross the
Cart path in the Mud, and there perished; was found dead on Monday morn, Novʳ 1. And thô the Coroner did his Office in the Morning; yet the Corps lay as a sad spectacle, gazed on till late in the
Afternoon.

Govʳ calls and smokes a pipe with my wife at night 9ʳ 1.

Novʳ 4. Mr. Cotton Mather preaches from Jnᵒ 20. 19. Govʳ not in
Town. In the Evening Col. Checkly, Lᵗ Colˡ Winthrop, and Major
Savage came to me, and acquainted me that the Guards for the
Prison would be dismiss'd to morrow; the Govʳ sent them to tell me
so. Now I objected to the Bill about Odell, that no mention was
made in it of any Person at the Castle to receive him, and that might
be oblig'd to have him forth-coming when the Court should demand
him.

Friday, Novʳ 5. At the Conference this day about weighing Hay,
Measuring Boards, Searching Turpentine, &c. As the Majʳ Genˡ had
desired, the Govʳ mentioned Odell's business before the whole Court;
and the chief Justice said nothing could be done upon that Act, it
did not direct the Justices what to do. I said I could not have a hand
in sending a man to that place where a Habeas Corpus could not
demand him. Deputies seem'd to incline to laying the Bill aside, and
having him kept in the prison where he is; it should be made more
strong. The Govʳ plainly said before that the Justices might not send
him thither; nor send for him thence: and he had them words added
in the Margin—(in order to his being sent)—for fear it should be
interpreted that the Justices sent him by the sheriff: The Govʳ would
give his order, without which it could not be. Chief Justice said at
the Conference, The man would be put out of the Law; which he
and I had discoursed of before.

Novʳ 15. 16. Our Malt-House by the Mill-Crick is Raised.

Second-day, Novʳ 15. 1708. Mr. Attorney Genˡ enquired whether
Odel might not have the Liberty of the yard upon Bail. I answer'd,

I suppos'd the Law was made only in favour of Debtors, not Criminals. And calling for the Law-Book, it plainly appear'd so to be by the preamble, and body of the Law, and Mr. Davenport also observ'd the Law was now Expired. It is to me amazing, that Mr. Attorney should speak of Bailing such a man as Odel, who is in a manner *Hostis Humani Generis! Quid non mortalia pectora cogis Auri sacra fames?*[33] Me thinks now I see the reason why the Govr desired to have Odel at the Castle of his own sending thither; and so as a Habeas Corpus might not affect him there.

    Novr 20. 1708. Sent by Aspinwall of Brooklin, Three Bushels of Salt; one for Madam Oliver, one for Mr. Brattle, one for the President. Writt to Col. Higginson about the Salt sold him, expecting an Answer by Monday. Gave Madam Brown one of the Verses on Mr. Clap, for her self, another for Mr. Benj. Brown.

    Novr 19. Visited Madam Saffin, and rec'd of her 20^s, towards Tiverton Meetinghouse.

    Novr 19. A Ship wherein Mr. Bromfield is much concern'd is taken by a Sloop from Port-Royal, as she was Turning out of the Cape-Harbour. Had not notice of it till Tuesday about 10. m: Order'd Capt. Southack to go out after them in a sloop that outsail'd the other.

    Novr 24. Joseph comes to Town. 25. Mr. Pemberton preaches excellently. Dine in my wives Chamber at the great Oval Table; Sat down, My wife, Mrs. Betty Hirst, Hannah, Elisa H., Mary, Mr. Hirst, Capt. Nathl Niles, Joseph, Sam and Jonathan Sewall, my self; Eleven in all. Novr 26. is so windy, and Cold, that Joseph goes not home till 27. with Sir Oakes. I give Sir Oakes 20^s Cash to buy some Necessaries, his father is so far off.[34]

    Novr 28. Mrs. Anne Winthrop is propounded, in order to be rec'd into the Church.

    Novr 30. Feria tertia, Last night Sir Charles Hobbey comes home

[33] The warrant now preserved in Massachusetts Archives, LXXI, f.474, is "to commit to Castle William, Thomas Odell, now a prisoner in the Gaol under a sentence to twelve months' imprisonment, and to pay a fine of £300, for being concerned, with others, in counterfeiting and uttering false bills of credit on this Province." It seemed, also, that he had once broken prison and escaped, and was charged with since committing various thefts, and "being a very dangerous person." It was suggested "that some ill-minded persons were contriving again to work his escape." Hence he was to be sent to Castle William, "there to be straitly confined until he perform the above sentence," etc. The quotation is from Virgil, *Aeneid*, iii, 56. M.H.S.EDS.

[34] Sir Oakes (Josiah Oakes, Harvard 1708), close friend of Joseph Sewall, was the son of Dr. Thomas Oakes and Martha, his wife, the woman Sewall sharply rebuked in his letter of 10 September 1696.

to his own house about eleven at night; Came from Portsmouth about the 7ᵗʰ of Octoberʳ. Lisle not Taken; Sir William Ashurst and Mr. Higginson are well. Came out with the Queen of Portugal; and my Lord Lovelace for New York. I call'd upon Sir Charles in the mornin and bad him Wellcom.

Decʳ 5. 1708. Mr. Nathanael Gookin preaches in the forenoon; I think every time he mention'd *James,* twas with prefixing *Saint:* about 4 or 5 times that I took notice of. I suppose he did it to confront me, and to assert his own Liberty. Probably, he had seen the Letter I writt to Mr. Flint.³⁵ Spake also of Reverence in G[*od's*] Worship; he may partly intend being Cover'd in Sermon-Time: It had better becom'd a person of some Age and Authority to have intermeddled in things of such a nature. *Quædam Confidentia non est virtus, at audacia.*

Decʳ 6. Major Genˡ and I set out for Salem; had a good passage over Winnisimmet Ferry, and Comfortable Journey: yet setting out late, got not thither till about 6. in the evening.

Decʳ 7ᵗʰ Hold the Court. *Note.* Mr. Benjamin Brown dyes just about three aclock p. m.,³⁶ Mr. Noyes being call'd to him, Major Genˡ Winthrop and I followed, and heard him pray with him, as he lay groaning. In the evening were invited to see his Will open'd, and hear it read; which we did at his house.

Wednesday, Decʳ 8. The Court is adjourned *sine die.* Were fain to use Candles before we got out of Pratt's Chamber. *Note.* This evening Mr. Noyes pray'd last, and spake last, with the aged and excellent Divine, Mr. John Higginson.

Feria quinta, Decʳ 9. Snowy stormy Wether. The Majʳ Genˡ comes to Brothers, and tells me hc would not take his Journey that Wether, so I also agree to stay. As we were at Dinner at my Brother's Paul Doliver calls Mr. Noyes, saying his Grandfather slept so they could not Wake him. Mr. Noyes answer'd, He would come as soon as he had dined; (We din'd late) He and I went together: but before we got thither, the good man was got to a blessed State of Rest.³⁷ He

---

³⁵ Sewall had heard a sermon by Tutor Flynt 22 August; the next day he wrote to tell him how distasteful to him was Flynt's employment of the titles *Saint* Luke, *Saint* James, etc.—terms "disused in New England." *L.B.* 1, 370–371, and p. 601 *ante.*

³⁶ Benjamin Browne was a wealthy and charitable Salem merchant and councillor. His sister Mary was the first wife of Major General Wait Still Winthrop. J. D. Phillips, *Salem in the Eighteenth Century* (1937), 33, 66–67.

³⁷ John Higginson had been minister of Salem since 1660; he was 93. His daughter Anna, who married William Dolliver, was accused of witchcraft and imprisoned in 1692, but was one of the many who were not brought to trial (T. W

expired 2 or 3 Minutes before we got into the room. *Note.* A good Christian Woman of Salem, 92 years old, died the same day Mr. Higginson did. I had sent home David in the morning with Mr. Dudley, and Cook; and now I began to resolve to stay the Funerals. I consider'd I had order'd my Brother to be sure to send me Word of Mr. Higginson's Death; and now I my self was one of the first Witnesses of it. Col. John Higginson is at Boston, to whom an Express is sent.

Feria sexta, Decr 10. a very Cold day, and the snow fiercely driven with the Wind. Maj^r Genl calls at my Brother's, and tells me he was going home; he thought his Children would hardly come else: I told him he might write to Mr. Sergeant, and he would bring them. When I saw he would needs go, I told him his Courage exceeded mine as much as the title of a major Genl did that of a Captain. He had a very hard difficult Journey, and told some he met, he would not have undertaken it for £100. if he had known it had been so bad.

Feria Septima, Decr 11th Bro^r Hirst invites me to Dinner, there dine also Mr. Noyes, Mr. Woolcot, and my Brother. Sister Hirst, and Cousin Betty sat down. Bro^r Hirst kept in the warm end of the House by the fire, being sick of the Gout. *Note.* This day my dear Grandson, Samuel Sewall, was taken sick at Brooklin.

Lord's day, Decr 12. Mr. Noyes preaches in the forenoon from a Text he formerly had taken—He that sets his hand to the plough and looks back.—Spake considerably of Mr. Higginson especially; and of Mr. Brown. Mr. George Corwin preaches in the Afternoon from Rev. 14. 13. Blessed are the dead.—Mr. Noyes put him upon giving the Blessing. I dined at my Brother's.

Feria Secunda, Decr 13th Had Fish for dinner at Brother's; which was put by the 7th day. I call'd for Honey, and Mr. Noyes and all, seem'd to approve of it. Mr. Benjamin Brown is buried; Tho. Bernard came in the morning from his Master, Major Brown jun^r, and invited me to be a Bearer. Bearers, Hathorne, Sewall; Corwin, Jn° Appleton; Col. Higginson, Maj^r Stephen Sewall. The Ministers present had Scarvs. Was laid in his father's Tomb at the Burying Point. Mr. John Winthrop told me of my Grandson's illness.

Feria tertia, Decr 14. The Appletons, Mr. Rogers, and Mr. Fitch dine at my Brother's. In the afternoon, the aged and Excellent Divine Mr. John Higginson is laid in Govr Bradstreet's Tomb: Bearers, Mr.

Higginson, *Descendants of the Rev. Francis Higginson,* 1910, 11). It was in character for Nicholas Noyes, Higginson's corpulent bachelor colleague, to permit no interruption of his meal.

Chiever, Mr. Noyes; Mr. Shepherd, Mr. Gerrish; Mr. Blowers, Mr. Green. Are all of that Association, and wear their own Hair. Was laid in the Tomb a little before Sunset, had a very Serene, and very Cold Aer; And yet the Ipswich Gentlemen went home, having lodg'd in Salem the night before. Mr. Shepherd lodges with me.

Feria quarta, Decr 15. I take leave of my Brother; gave Margaret 10ˢ, Susan, 5ˢ, Jane, 3ˢ, Mehetabel, 1ˢ, Mitchell, 1ˢ, Henry, 1ˢ, Stephen, 1ˢ, Nurse, 3ˢ, Scipio, 2ˢ 6ᵈ. I and Mr. Corwin rode in Mr. Kitchen's slay to the Butts; the Curtains defended us from the most Sharp, and Opposite Wind. At the Butts took our Horses and got comfortably to Lewis's, where Capt. Norden fell in with us; a good fat tender Goose was ready rosted. Capt. Norden, Mr. Jno. Winthrop and his Sister, Col. Taylor, Mr. Lichmore there. *Note.* I crav'd a Blessing, and return'd Thanks, not thinking of Mr. Corwin till had begun to return Thanks, then I *saw* him, and it almost confounded me—I crav'd his pardon, and paid his Club, saying I had defrauded the Company.³⁸ I intended to go by Cambridge; but by the way I was told the Ferry was passable; and so I alter'd my mind, and went with Capt. Norden, and Mr. Bayly to Charlestown: the Boat was ready, and had as comfortable a passage over, as if it had been September; entred my own House about an hour before Sun-Set, found all well, *Laus Deo.* Privat-Meeting at our House. The Condition of my Granson was commended to GOD. Capt. Hill return'd Thanks for my safe Return home.

Decr 16. very Cold and Lecture day, that I could not tell how to travail over the Neck so soon after my former Journey. *Dec^r* 17. Court sits and only 3 Justices, which hindered my going to Brooklin. And Alas! Alas! seventh-day *Dec^r* 18, News is brought that the poor Child is Dead about an hour by sun *mane.*³⁹ Alas! that I should fail seeing him alive! Now I went too late, save to weep with my Children, and kiss, and mourn over my dear Grandson. My son desired me to pray with his family; which I did. Madam Dudley, the Gov^{rs} Lady, Mrs. Katharin, and Mrs. Mary came in while I was there; and brought my little Rebekah with them. Call'd at the Governour's as came home. Seem to agree to bury the child next fourth day. I mention'd its being best to bury at Roxbury, for my son to keep to his own parish. Govr said I might put the Child in his father's Grave if

³⁸ Although George Curwin (Harvard 1701) was not yet an ordained clergyman, he was a preacher, and headed for that profession; normally he would have been called upon to say grace.
³⁹ Samuel Sewall III had lived exactly a year. His parents were Samuel Jr., and Rebeckah, daughter of Governor Dudley.

I pleas'd. Got home well in my slay, had much adoe to avoid Slews. *Laus Deo.*

My son perceiving the Governour's aversion to have the child buried at Roxbury, writes to me of it. I go to the Governour's on Tuesday, and speak about Bearers, He leaves it to me; so does my son; as I come home I speake for Sir Ruggles, Tim° Ruggles, son of Martha Woodbridge, my ancient acquaintance and Townswoman; and Col. Checkley's son for the other. *Wednesday, Decr 22, 1708.* My dear Grandson, Saml Sewall, is buried; Son and daughter went first: then Govr and I; then Madam Dudley led by Paul Dudley esqr; Then Joseph and Hannah; Then Mr. Wm Dudley and daughter Hirst—Major Genl and his Lady here with their Coach—Mr. Bromfield, Stoddard &c. Gave Mr. Walter a Lutestring scarf, Bearers, Capt. Noyes, Mrs. Bayley, scarves. *Decr 30.* Daughter Hirst is much oppress'd with a Fear of Death; desires to speak with me: I go to her presently after Lecture, and discourse with her, and she seems better compos'd.

xr. 31. Feria sexta, Committee meets for incorporating the Town.[40] Mr. Bridgham was absent, being taken sick that day.

[40] There were numerous attempts to incorporate Boston, beginning in 1650, but none met with success until 1822. *C.S.M.* x, 352–356.

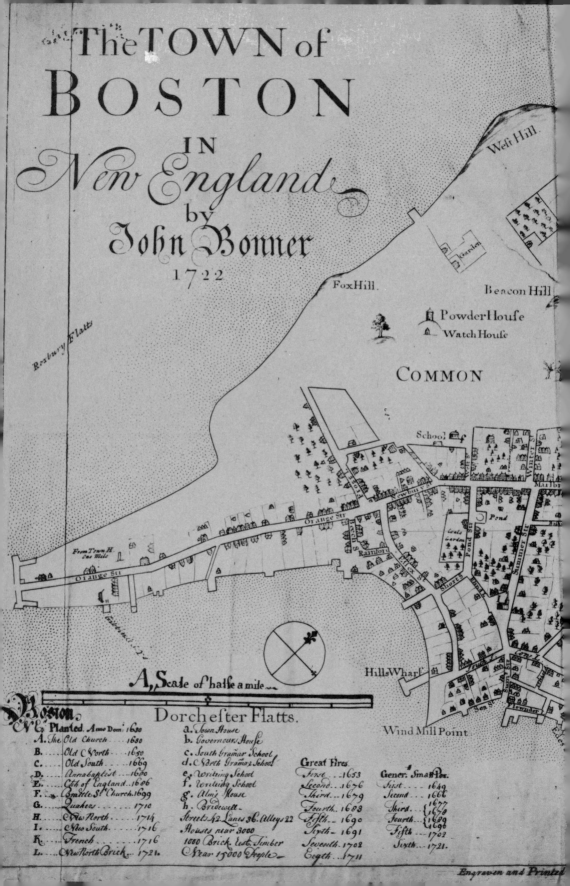

The TOWN of BOSTON
IN
New England
by
John Bonner
1722

West Hill

Garden

Fox Hill.

Beacon Hill

Powder House

Watch House

Roxbury Flatts

COMMON

School

Winter Str

Marlb.

From Town H. one Mile

Newbury Str

Pond

Frogs

Orange Str

Rainford

Cole garden

Pond Str

Summer Str

From Town H. one Mile

Orange Str

Shorts

Hills Wharf

Sea Str

Fowder

Eales

A Scale of halfe a mile

Wind Mill Point

Boston N.E. **Planted** Anno Dom: 1630 — **Dorchester Flatts.**

A. The Old Church 1630	a. Town House		
B. Old C North 1650	b. Governours House		
C. Old South 1669	c. South Gramar School	**Great Fires**	**Gener. Small Pox.**
D. Annabaptist 1680	d. C North Gramar School	First 1653	First 1649
E. Cth of England 1686	e. Writing School	Second 1676	Second 1666
F. Bruttle St Church 1699	f. Writing School	Third 1679	Third 1677
G. Quakers 1710	g. Alms House	Fourth 1683	Fourth 1689
H. New North 1714	h. Bridewell	Fifth 1690	Fifth 1702
I. New South 1716	Streets 42 Lanes 36 Alleys 22	Sixth 1691	Sixth 1721.
K. French 1716	Houses near 3000	Seventh 1702	
L. New North Brick 1721.	1000 Brick rest Timber	Eigth 1711	
	Near 15000 People		

Engraven and Printed